Arne Manzeschke, Thomas Wittenberg (Eds.)
Ethical Perspectives on Artificial Intelligence in Biomedical Engineering

Health Academy

Edited by
Arne Manzeschke and Thomas Wittenberg

Volume 5

Arne Manzeschke, Thomas Wittenberg (Eds.)

Ethical Perspectives on Artificial Intelligence in Biomedical Engineering

—

DE GRUYTER

Editors

Prof. Dr. theol. Arne Manzeschke
Evangelische Hochschule Nürnberg
Ethik und Anthropologie
Bärenschanzstr. 4
D- 90429 Nürnberg

Priv.-Doz., Dr.-Ing. Thomas Wittenberg
Fraunhofer-Institut für Integrierte
Schaltungen IIS
Am Wolfsmantel 33
D- 91058 Erlangen

ISBN 978-3-11-158619-9
e-ISBN (PDF) 978-3-11-158645-8
e-ISBN (EPUB) 978-3-11-158657-1
ISSN 1617-8874
DOI https://doi.org/10.1515/9783111586458

Library of Congress Control Number: 2026930214

Bibliographic information from the German National Library
The German National Library lists this publication in the German National Bibliography; detailed
bibliographic data is available online at http://dnb.dnb.de.

© 2026 the author(s), published by Walter de Gruyter GmbH, Berlin/Boston,
Genthiner Straße 13, 10785 Berlin
The book is published open access at www.degruyterbrill.com.

Cover image: DKosig / E+ / Getty Images
Typesetting: Datagrafix GSP GmbH, Berlin

www.degruyterbrill.com
Questions about General Product Safety Regulation:
productsafety@degruyterbrill.com

Foreword from the Federal Ministry of Research, Technology and Space

Prof. Dr. Veronika von Messling,
Copyright: private

Artificial intelligence (AI) is influencing and changing our world in an unprecedented, unusually profound way. In the health sector, generative AI in particular is developing at a rapid pace. It harbors great opportunities but also raises ethical, legal and social issues that we must examine carefully, because AI's ability to self-teach and make autonomous conclusions means our previously held ethical principles do not always apply.

This is particularly true for biomedicine, which is the focus topic of this collection of articles and whose issues are already challenging enough in terms of ethics. After all, this is all about the scientific study of the causes of disease and their diagnosis, monitoring and treatment. But we also want to devote greater attention to the ethical aspects of AI use as a part of interactive health solutions and biomedical engineering – for example avatars for the treatment of mental disorders, algorithms which provide supportive advice to medical professionals, or programs that use virtual reality for the further training of nursing staff.

The Federal Ministry of Research, Technology and Space promotes a trustworthy, AI-driven health ecosystem. Our priorities are not only data security, privacy protection, non-bias and algorithmic fairness but also a trusting and transparent doctor-patient relationship and the right to informed consent. We support the approach that considers ethical, legal and social aspects from the outset in the development of digital health solutions. The researchers involved in the projects we fund are therefore scrutinizing both the positive and negative effects of new technologies in the development process, designing them to meet the requirements, values and standards of our society.

We believe that we can increase the acceptance of medical products among users by being more open to ethical questions as the technology is developed. A shining example of this is our support for the Integrated Research cluster which one of the editors of this publication, Prof. Arne Manzeschke, initiated and in which he has played a major role. The cluster's researchers are developing strategies so that ethical aspects can be taken into timely and direct consideration during technology development and not play a merely supporting role. Exerting direct influence on the research process makes it possible to cast a spotlight on the topic from all angles and results in greater relevance for practice and, as a consequence, a better outcome.

This publication, devoted to the Ethical Perspectives on AI in Biomedical Engineering, sheds light on the subject in a number of different ways. Our thanks go to the editors for their valuable work, and we wish its readers an interesting read!

Prof. Dr. Veronika von Messling
Director-General for Life Sciences at the
Federal Ministry of Research, Technology and Space

Statement from the German Society for Biomedical Engineering

(Deutsche Gesellschaft für Biomedizinische Technik DGBMT im VDE)

Artificial intelligence (AI) is fundamentally changing biomedical technology and, by extension, the entire healthcare system. AI is already making a huge impact and, particularly in combination with medical technology hardware, has the potential to help personalized medicine achieve a breakthrough. This encompasses the entire chain of prevention, diagnosis, treatment, and patient care.

The strengths of AI lie in areas where pattern recognition and high-speed data processing are required. AI can find patterns in large data sets much faster than conventional methods or humans. AI does not tire or lose concentration and does not make careless mistakes, as long as it is programmed correctly. Above all, it can process large amounts of data from many sources simultaneously, identifying trends, anomalies, and correlations that a human would overlook, and it can make predictions based on this information. This means that AI can perform repetitive, data-based tasks extremely quickly and accurately. The use of AI in medical technology offers great opportunities, but also challenges and risks, particularly ethical ones, which are examined in this book. To exploit the potential of AI, large amounts of high-quality data, structured data transfer and interoperability, transparent AI models, and more efficient approval procedures are required.

Some key areas of AI-supported applications in medical technology are already apparent. AI-supported systems can quickly and reliably detect anomalies in X-ray, MRI, and ultrasound images. This leads to more accurate and faster diagnoses. AI can help diagnose diseases by recognizing patterns in patient data and suggesting treatment options specific to the patient. AI can continuously monitor patient data and flag changes, enabling early prevention or timely intervention. AI can revolutionize the automation and intelligent control of medical technology. AI-controlled robots can assist in surgeries, increasing precision and efficiency.

AI is already significantly accelerating research and development in medical technology companies. The use of AI as a tool in product development is currently revolutionizing both development processes and manufacturing processes for medical devices. In addition, AI can lead to greater efficiency, precision, and innovation in all phases of the product life cycle, from concept development and design, through prototyping and simulation, as well as production and manufacturing, to application and post-market support for devices on the market.

The use of AI-supported systems is currently also revolutionizing the education and training of biomedical engineers and young researchers. Opportunities arise in personalized learning systems that adapt to individual needs. AI analyzes learning progress, generates content, and provides appropriate recommendations. Virtual tutors support learners in real time through dialogue-oriented interaction. In continuing professional development, adaptive learning environments enable targeted skills development. Challenges lie primarily in the provision of secure and didactically prepared content.

However, the use of AI also poses challenges for medical technology and raises ethical questions. For example, the quality of the database for training the algorithms is often of crucial importance. This does not only concern issues of bias and fairness. Furthermore, importing AI models from one training environment into other application areas can lead to critical distortions that are difficult to rectify. The processing of large amounts of sensitive patient data requires high security standards and data protection measures and professionals who are able to assess the plausibility and validity of AI statements and handle them responsibly.

Many experts believe it is important for AI-based systems to be transparent and comprehensible so that physicians can understand the decisions made by the systems. This requirement arises from the current situation. If we project this into the future, it quickly becomes clear that we may need to take a different approach as AI development progresses. Ethical questions arise particularly in medicine, for example regarding responsibility for wrong decisions or possible changes in the doctor-patient relationship.

There are also significant impediments to overcome for the approval of medical devices with AI functionality. This applies in particular to dynamic AIs that continuously "learn" in their working environment. From the perspective of a regulatory agency, this scenario is a major barrier for which we must develop solutions.

There are also significant obstacles to overcome when it comes to approving medical devices with AI functionality. This is particularly true for dynamic AI systems that continuously "learn" in their working environment. From the perspective of an approval authority, this scenario presents a major hurdle for which we need to develop solutions.

AI also stands for digital transformation and change. However, change should always be seen as an opportunity for improvement. For the German medical technology industry, this means pooling its domain knowledge in a pre-competitive manner so that AI models can be trained quickly and efficiently. For skilled workers, AI will not replace them, but those with AI expertise will displace those without the relevant knowledge.

This book – Ethical Perspectives on Artificial Intelligence in Biomedical Engineering, edited by our DGBMT scientific board members Arne Manzeschke and Thomas Wittenberg – addresses many currently relevant issues of AI in medical technology in relation to ethical aspects and provides guidance on the direction in which we should continue to think and act responsibly. It thus makes an original contribution to two important tasks of the German Society for Biomedical Engineering (DGBMT) within the VDE: the transfer of knowledge and the overcoming of innovation hurdles. The DGBMT has therefore established artificial intelligence as a central cross-cutting theme of its specialist work.

Duisburg and Offenbach am Main, August 1, 2025
Prof. Dr.-Ing. Karsten Seidl
DGBMT President

Dr.-Ing. Thomas Becks
DGBMT Managing Director

Contents

Peter P. Pott

Stefan Wesarg, Jörn Kohlhammer

Patrick Gebhard, Tanja Schneeberger

Galia Assadi, Arne Manzeschke, Nadine Lang-Richter, Thomas Wittenberg

Julia Kämmer, Daniel Flemming

List of abbreviations

μC	microcontroller	CART	Classification and Regression Trees
μP	microprocessor	CASA	Computers Are Social Actors
A/IS	Autonomous and Intelligent Systems	cDBS	constant Deep Brain Stimulation
aBCI	active Brain-Computer-Interface	CDS	Clinical Decision Support
aDBS	adaptive Deep Brain Stimulation	CDSS	Clinical Decision Support Systems
ADC	analog-to-digital converter	CHIEF	Clinical Histopathology Imaging Evaluation Foundation
AFE	Analogue Frontend		
AGI	Artificial General Intelligence		
AI	Artificial Intelligence	CI	Cochlear Implant
AI HLEG	High-Level Expert Group on Artificial Intelligence	CKD	Chronic Kidney Disease
		CMOS	Complementary Metal Oxide Semiconductor
AI&ED	AI and Education		
AIA	Artificial Intelligence Act	CNN	Convolutional Neural Network
AIB	Artificial Intelligence Board	CO	Carbon Monoxide
AIED	AI use in Education	CoE	Council of Europe
AIM	AI model	COPD	Chronic Obstructive Pulmonary Disease
AIMD	Active Implantable Medical Device		
		CPU	Central Processing Unit
AIS	AI system	CRF	Constitutional Realization Framework
ALS	amyotrophic lateral sclerosis		
ALTAI	Assessment List for Trustworthy Artificial Intelligence	CT	Computer Tomography
		DaaS	Data as a Service
		DAC	Digital-to-Analog Converter
ANI	Artificial Narrow Intelligence	DBS	Deep Brain Stimulation
ANN	Artificial neural network	DCNN	Deep Convolutional Neural Network
AP	action potential		
API	Application Programming Interface	DFG	Deutsche Forschungsgemeinschaft
AR	Augmented Reality	DGBMT im VDE	Deutsche Gesellschaft für Biomedizinische Technik im VDE
ARDS	Acute Respiratory Distress Syndrome		
ASI	Artificial Super Intelligence	DICOM	Digital imaging and communications in medicine
ASICs	Application-Specific Integrated Circuits		
		DiGA	Digital Health Application
ATAI	Attitude Towards Artificial Intelligence	DiPA	Digital Care Application
		DIPK	Deep Neural Network Integrating Prior Knowledge
AU	Action Unit		
BCI	Brain-Computer Interfaces	DL	Deep learning
BIONIC	Biological Network Integration using Convolutions	DNN	Deep Neural Networks
		DSS	Decision Support Systems
		DT	Digital Twin
BME	Biomedical Engineering	ECG	Electrocardiogram
BMI	Brain-Machine-Interface	ECoG	Electrocorticography
BMT	Biomedical Technology	EDA	Electrodermal Activity

EDAI	Education about AI	HMI	Human Machine Interface
EEG	Electroencephalogram	HOTL	human-on-the-Loop
EHR	Electronic Health Records	HPC	High performance Computing
EMG	Electromyogram	HRAIS	High risk AI System
EMS	Electrical Muscle Stimulation	HRI	Human Robot Interaction
EOG	Electrooculogram	HRV	Heartrate Variability
ERG	Electroretinogram	IaaS	Imaging as a Service
ERP	event-related potentials	IAI	Interpretable Artificial
EU	European Union		Intelligence
EU AI Act	European Union Artificial	iBCI	implantable/invasive
	Intelligence Act		Brain-Computer-Interface
FACS	Facial Activity Coding System	IBD	Inflammatory Bowel Disease
FAIR	Findability, Accessibility,	ICD	International Classification of
	Interoperability, Reuse		Diseases
FC	fully connected	ICESCR	International Covenant on
FCNN	fully convolutional network		Economic, Social and Cultural
FDA	food and drug administration		Rights
FES	Functional Electrical	ICMS	intracortical microstimulation
	Stimulation	ICOM	International Consortium for
FM	Foundation Models		Health Outcomes
FOMO	Fear of Missing Out		Measurement
FP	Number of false positive cases	IEEE	Institute of Electrical and
FPGA	field programmable gate array		Electronics Engineers
FUS	Focused Ultrasound	IO	input-output
GAT	Graph Attention Networks	IoT	Internet of Things
GDPR	General Data Protection	IP	Intellectual Property
	Regulation	ISO	International Organization for
GEC	German Ethics Council		Standardization)
	(Deutscher Ethikrat)	IT	Information Technology
GOFAI	Good Old-Fashioned Artificial	ITS	Intelligent Tutorial Systems
	Intelligence	IVD	In Vitro Diagnostic
GPAI	General Purpose AI	IVDR	In Vitro Diagnostic
GPi	globus pallidus internus		Regulation
GPT	Generative Pre-trained	KD	Knowledge Distillation
	Transformer	KIM	Communication in Medicine
GPU	Graphical Processing Unit		(dt.: Kommunikation im
GradCAM	Gradient-weighted Class		Medizinwesen)
	Activation Maps	kNN	k-Nearest Neighbor
GRUs	Gated recurrent units	LASR	Levels of Autonomy in Surgical
GUI	Graphical User Interface		Robotics
HDMI	High Definition Multimedia	LFP	Local field potentials
	Interface	LGBT	Lesbian, Gay, Bisexual,
HIC	Human in Command		Transgender
HIFU	High Intensity Focused	LIME	Local Interpretable Model-
	Ultrasound		agnostic Explanations
HIS	Hospital Information Systems	LINAC	Linear Accelerator
HITL	Human-in-the-Loop	LLMs	Large Language Models
HLEG	High Level Expert Group on AI	LSTM	Long Short-Term Memory
	(set up by the EU Commission)	LUTs	Look up Table

MDAI	Medical Device Artificial Intelligence	RAG	Retrieval-Augmented Generation
MDCG	Medical Device Coordination Group	RAS	Robotic Assisted Surgery
		ReLU	Rectified Linear Unit
MDR	Medical Device Regulation	RF	Random Forest
MDSW	Medical Device Software	RIA	Robotics Industries Association
MDT	Medical Digital Twin		
MEESTAR	Model for the Ethical Evaluation of Socio-Technical Arrangements	RISC-V	Reduced Instruction Set Computer five
		RLHF	Reinforcement Learning from Human Feedback
MeV	Mega electron Volt		
ML	Machine Learning	RLS	Recursive Least Squares
MRI	Magnetic Resonance Imaging	RTOS	Real-Time Operating System
MSE	Mean Squared Error	SaaS	Software as a Service
NLP	Natural Language Processing	SciFi	Science Fiction
NPU	Neural Processing Unit	SDGs	Sustainable Development Goals
NRS	Numerical rating scales		
OBPM	Outcome-based payment Model	SEM	Sports and Exercise Medicine
		SFT	Supervised Fine-Tuning
OCD	Obsessive Compulsive Disorder	SIA	Socially Interactive Agent
		SLR	Systematic Literature Reviews
OECD	Organization for Economic Co-operation and Development	SMILES	Simplified Molecular Input Line Entry System
		SoC	System on Chip
OMC	Online Medical Consultations	SPECT	Single Photon Emission Computed Tomography
OR	Operating Room		
PD	Parkinson's disease	SPiDER	SOM-based Prediction of Drug Equivalence Relationships
PERCEPTION	PERsonalized Single-Cell Expression-Based Planning for Treatments In ONcology		
		STN	subthalamic nucleus
PHypTh	posterior hypothalamus	SVM	Support Vector Machine
PIO	Nursing information object (dt.: Pflege-Informationsobjekt)	TAM	Technology Acceptance Model
		Tiny ML	Tiny Machine Learning
		ToF	Time of Flight
PKDE4J	Public Knowledge Discovery Tool	TOPS /W	Total Operations Per Second per Watt
pLDDT	Predicted Local Distance Difference Test	TSC	Technology Services Corporation
PO	Physical Object	UQ	Uncertainty Quantification
PPG	Photplethysmogram	US	Ultrasound
PPN	pedunculopontine nucleus	VBHC	Value-Based Health Care
PPO	Proximal Policy Optimization	VHDL	Very High speed integrated circuit hardware Description Language
PROMs	Person-Reported Outcome Measures		
PTSD	post-traumatic stress disorder.	ViKI pro	Care-integrated artificial intelligence in the professional care process
QSAR	Quantitative Structure-Activity Relationship		
R&D	Research & Development	VIM	ventral intermedicus nucleus
RaaS	Radiology as a Service	VO2Max	maximum oxygen uptake

VR	Virtual Reality	XAI	Explainable Artificial
WCI	Wireless Capsule Endoscope		Intelligence
WHO	World Health Organization	XR	Extended Reality

Arne Manzeschke, Thomas Wittenberg

1 Editorial: Why consider artificial intelligence, biomedical engineering and ethics together?

1.1 Instead of an Introduction

Instead of yet another classical boring introduction about artificial intelligence (AI) in the field of biomedical engineering (BME) and the related ethical considerations thereof, let us start instead with a virtual discussion between *Achilles* and the *Turtle* (see Fig. 1.1), in the style of the researcher Douglas R. Hofstadter's famous book about Gödel, Escher, Bach [1]:

> *Achilles*: Ah, my dear turtle! Have you heard about the latest advancements in artificial intelligence? It's truly remarkable how far technology has come. AI has the potential to revolutionize our lives in ways we never imagined.
> *Turtle*: Indeed, Achilles. I have heard of these developments, and while they are impressive, I cannot help but ponder the ethical implications. Should we not be cautious about the rapid progress of AI?
> *Achilles*: Caution is always wise, my friend. However, consider the numerous benefits AI brings: it can enhance healthcare, streamline industries, and even assist in solving complex global challenges. The potential for good is immense.
> *Turtle*: True, but we must also consider the potential risks. AI could exacerbate existing inequalities, invade our privacy, and even challenge our very humanity. Should we not prioritize ethical considerations to ensure AI serves the greater good?
> *Achilles*: Absolutely, ethics should not be overlooked. But we must not let fear stifle innovation. By working together and establishing proper guidelines, we can harness the power of AI while mitigating its risks. We must embrace progress with a balanced approach.
> *Turtle*: I agree, Achilles. Balance is key. Let us strive to create a future where AI enhances human life without compromising our ethical values. Together, we can navigate this brave new world with wisdom and care.

This virtual dialogue, generated by a generative AI [2] tries to provide the framework and setting of this book, a collection of individual chapters addressing and illuminating various key aspects in the intersection of the of the three topics artificial intelligence (AI) (Sections 1.1), biomedical engineering (BME) (Section 1.2) and ethics (Section 1.3).

Fig. 1.1: An AI generated (GPT 4.0) image of Achilles in a conversation with a tortoise, a famous Greek reference to the misconception that Achilles will never be able to overtake the turtle in a race, provided that the turtle gets a head start.

1.1.1 Artificial intelligence

"Artificial intelligence" (AI) is a research field within the computer and neurosciences, whose origins date back as early as 1943 with McCulloch & Pitts definition of a "neuron" and – with the possibilities of so-called "foundation models" of very "deep neural networks" using pocket-size hand-held computing devices – is currently considered one of the largest technological mega- or even hyper-trends modern society has ever witnessed. With reference to the Dartmouth conference held in 1956 [3], the original field of AI does not include the investigation and understanding of (deep) neural networks, but addresses also tightly related and interwoven topics such as the possibilities of automatic self-improvements of machines and networks, natural language processing (NLP), computer architectures, and computer languages as a medium to interact with computers, but also psychological insights about randomness and creativity.

1.1.2 Biomedical engineering

According to Morgenstern & Kraft [4], one possible definition of the term *biomedical engineering* (BME), is the *"research, description, replacement and/or supplementation of structures and/or functions of living systems; [it] includes the provision of engineering means and methods and their application to living systems in biology and medicine in process design in research and in all phases of the product life cycle [...], in the medical care process [...] and to improve the quality of life, in various industries (such as medical technology, biotechnology, healthcare, pharmacy, environmental technology) and in the life sciences in general."* Hence, BME tries to fill the gap between the originally fields of engineering and medicine [5]. Nevertheless, biomedical engineering is a vital interdisciplinary field of research, ranging from electrical and chemical engineering via applied physics and mechatronics to computer science, including pattern analysis, image processing and artificial intelligence (AI). Furthermore, BME always includes a deep knowledge about human anatomy, physiology, as well as consciousness and emotions of living beings. Bringing these disciplines of engineering and healthcare together, also a deep understanding of all possible human-machine-interfaces (HMI) must be assumed for all these technologies applied *at, on* or *inside* a patient, as well as adequate HMIs for physicians and healthcare experts to use and steer such interfaces in their routine work. Therefore, applying the combined knowledge all these disciplines, the ultimate goals of BME is always the improvement of health care provision, the reduction of mortality, and the improvement of personal health.

1.1.3 Ethics

The field of ethics draws even farther back than the origins of AI and BME. As already observed in the virtual discussion between Achilles and the turtle, one vital strand of ethics is the *dialogue*. Earliest sources document conversations between people, trying to orient themselves about very detailed daily decisions or even how to live one's own life. The guiding concept is called *"the good life"*, and the endeavor (not just an intellectual one) is on one hand aimed at the individual virtues to be developed to adopt the appropriate attitude or take an action required. On the other hand, the question of *"the good life"* deals with prerequisites for individuals to live together justly. In this respect ethics, one of the cardinal questions to deal with is *"what question can be more serious than this?"*, asked Plato's Socrates the young Kallikles: *"… you will observe that we are arguing about the way of human life; and to a [hu]man who has any sense at all, what question can be more serious than this?"* [6].

Besides this type of ethics as an art of living, a more scientific type of rationalizing about moral arguments has evolved with the scientification of philosophy. Following this strand, ethics is related very much about evaluating and judging situations, actions, options. To do so requires a position as an *"impartial spectator"* [7]. Regarding the enormous progress of BME, especially propelled by artificial intelligence ethical questions should be posed from both sides: (1) How should individuals be empowered to master the opportunities and risks given with complex digitalized devices in their own hands? And at the same time: (2) How should organizations and states take care for a secure, trustworthy, and robust framework? If we charge for Amara's Law, that *"we tend to overestimate the effect of a technology in the short run and underestimate the effect in the long run"* [8], we are even more obliged to spell out these issues at various levels.

Based on these observations, we argue that the task of ethics is not to set limits to technology, but to reflect on the limits of being human and to act accordingly in terms of technology. This approach of grounding the ethics of technology in anthropology seems to be extremely helpful and valuable in view of the opposing tendencies in current debates on technology and ethics. It opens the door to the question of the human being that we are and may be – and which technology corresponds to this human being.

1.2 Dimensions

How can the three addressed topics – AI, BME and ethics – be brought together, and how can their interaction and interdependency be illustrated adequately? If we assume that the three main topics of this book – artificial intelligence (AI), biomedical engineering biomedical engineering (BME), and ethics – relate to three orthogonal dimensions, it could be possible place various AI-driven applications within BME in this 3D-volume, according to some virtual scales along each of the dimensions, see Fig. 1.2. However, what type of scales or orders could be used for each dimension?

For the **AI dimension** – the blue-marked abscissa in Fig. 1.2 – one possible order or scale could be an arrangement of AI possibilities, ranging from "simple rule-based data processing possibilities" via "weak" AI applications (such as image analysis or chatbots) to "advanced" cutting edge applications needing high-performance clusters (HPCs) as computational hardware. Similar wise a scale according to the amount of data to be processed at a certain level, or the amount of reference or learning data needed to train a certain AI-model could be used to bring an order or scale to the various AI-based BME applications. This "data" scale could range from small reference data collections used to parametrize manually some small neural network up to large language or even foundation models which need huge data collections for their exhaustive training.

Therefore, a combination of the AI complexity, the related computing power and the amount of needed data seems a natural scale or order for artificial intelligence systems in BME. Therefore, the blue-marked abscissa in Fig. 1.2 has a virtual scale, beginning at low-power, sparse memory TinyML and EdgeAI systems [9] at the left side of the scale, via smartphone processors, CPUs, GPUs, and NPUs, and ending on the right side with cloud computing and high-performance computing (HPC) possibilities related to large language and foundation models. Examples of such BME-equipment used in healthcare with increasing computing power (are from left to right), e.g., cleaning or vacuum robots (using EdgeAI or TinyML), laboratory or surgical robots based on CPU or GPUs [10], or imaging processing applications such as digital pathology, which make extensive use of foundation models.

For the **BME dimension**, the ordinate was used in Fig. 1.2, indicated in green. To relate a halfway meaningful scale to this axis, the *invasiveness* of the technology with respect to the patients or users could be chosen [11]. Hence, the BME axis starts at the bottom with "far away" technologies, indicating, that neither the computation of the AI-based devices nor their results of BME technology are physically coupled to the patient's or user's body or physical health, as e.g. a vacuum robot, laboratory systems, digital twins [12] or ex-vivo image analysis such as digital pathology (all placed at the bottom of the AI-BME grid). The next logical distance of a technology towards the patients or users would be "nearby" or "at the skin", as, e.g., wearables (textiles, smart watches, chest straps, or the such), VR / AR / XR goggles, rehabilitation robotics [10], or ultrasound-systems applied directly at the outside of the body or directly on the skin surface. The next level of invasiveness hence relates to technology placed inside the patient's body, either permanently as pacemakers or neural implants (with low computing power inside) [13], or temporally as catheters, endoscopes, or telemanipulated surgical tools held and guided by a surgical robot [10,14]. Finally, also *social* or *mental* interaction should be considered as an extraordinary version of invasiveness, which can, for instance, be social interactive agents [15], chatbots [16] or social robots [10].

Finally, the third dimension are **ethical considerations** [17], which are addressing various sub-dimensions by themselves such as, e.g., fairness [18] to counter bias, discrimination, or uncertainties [19], transparency and explainability to give control to the human being in decision making [20], privacy by data protection, accountability and liability, informed consent, equity in access or human oversight, just to mention some of them. In contrast to the other scales, these aspects are hard to order or to group. Nevertheless, one possibility clustering of moral dimensions could be (1) "non-negotiable" foundational ones, such as privacy and data protection, informed consent as well as bias and fairness, (2) "operational and clinical ethics", addressing e.g. transparency and explainability, human oversight and accountability, and (3) "societal and long-term considerations", as e.g., equity in access and long-term control by humans. Of cause, other ways of clustering might be plausible and achieve the desired target as well. Part of ethical deliberation involves being clear about how socio-technical arrangements are viewed, what this brings into focus – and what it may render invisible.

Another grouping of ethical aspects on AI and BME could be a four-point scale, as also used by MEESTAR (Model for the Ethical Evaluation of Socio-Technical Arrangements) [21]. The basic notion would be "no problem", because the application is ethically completely unobjectionable. A second stage could be "low": the application has ethical sensitivity, which can be considered in practice, e.g., being related to basic data analysis with no sensitive information and no direct interaction or harm for patients or staff, as e.g. simple cleaning robots in healthcare facilities, see Fig. 1.2. bottom left. A third would be the "sensitive" stage, meaning, that the application is ethically extremely sensitive and requires either permanent attention or distance from its introduction. Here, ethical considerations could be related to a scope of data privacy, informed consent or a varying bias of AI algorithms, related, e.g., to digital twins [12] or AR/VR scenarios [22]. This would also include applications such as AI-based decisions making in crucial life-critical situations, such as e.g. pacemakers, neural implants [31], or autonomous surgical robots [10], which are partially placed inside the patients (see Fig. 1.2 upper row, left) as well as genetic engineering [23] or devices or systems violating or overruling patient's rights [23]. Finally, the "no go" stage indicates significant ethical problems, where the application is to be rejected from an ethical perspective, signaling that the intended socio-technical arrangement needs fundamental revision to be ethically aligned.

As the third dimension depicting the ethics with its many facets is hard to draw within a 2D image, it has merely been indicated by the orange ellipse Fig. 1.2. Nevertheless, it should be clear that – or is at least intended by the sketch – that the closer a medical device is at or in a patient's body, as well as with rising computational complexity and increasing autonomy of the AI-based device, the number of ethical questions and considerations will also rise.

It is important to note that the described scales or orders or groupings on the axes are definitively not rigid but rather fluid, and that these dimensions are only intended to provide some clustering and order in each direction for illustration purposes. In reality, biomedical devices and AI-based systems are much more complex and can certainly not be pressed directly in such a rigid order. Of course, other scales and orders could have been chosen, or also more dimensions could have been used. Therefore, Fig. 1.2 only serves the purpose to combine all three aspects addressed in this book, to provide possible orders along each of the three dimensions as well as provide some interesting correlations and coincidences on single points in this space. In essence, this paragraph strongly advocates integrated thinking across these three dimensions.

Even though many applications, devices and scenarios have been addressed in the various chapters of this volume, there are much more approaches and systems in the field of BME which profit immensely from AI, and could have also been added, such as imaging and image processing, surgical AR/VR/XR, material sciences, or wearables. Nevertheless, as always, time and space is limited, and we believe that many ideas and implications addressed in this book can also directly be transferred to these additional topics.

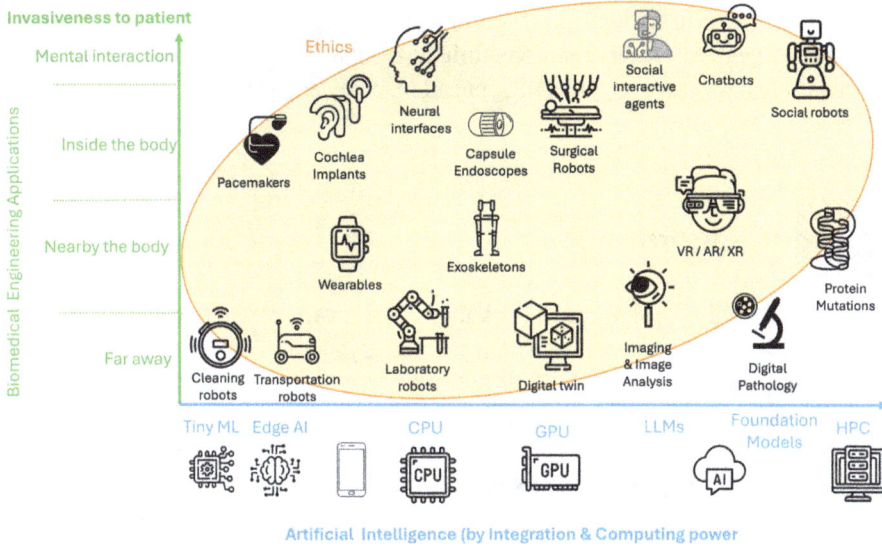

Fig. 1.2: Graphical approach combining ethics (yellow ellipse) with artificial intelligence, scaled by integration and computing power as one possible order (blue abscissa) and biomedical engineering applications and devices, scaled by invasiveness (on the green ordinate). All scales are only approximative but help to coarsely cluster and organize the addressed topic of ethical considerations of AI within BME.

1.3 Concluding remarks

Using AI in every day's routine or in professional life is an action that should be – to a certain extent – free from pertinent ethical reflection on its foundational questions, otherwise ethics would turn out to be a permanent overburdening and impediment to everyday and professional life. Hence, these foundational questions should be addressed by governance and large-scale frameworks [26,27]. At the same time individuals are challenged to ponder ethical issues in their immediate environment, transforming and concretizing ethical frameworks into real-life processes – as exemplified in Section 1.2.

Let's come back to our introductory dialogue, provided by ChatGPT [2]. Did it tell us anything new, or do we just read another classical boring introduction about AI? Admittedly, it may be impressive to have such a text generated by a technical system that takes aesthetic specifications into account and produces meaningful and factually accurate statements on a semantic level. We may be amazed about such features, we may feel assisted in one moment and spurred on in the next one. In any case we should think about what is being presented to us. The dialogue between Achilles and the turtle tells us much more about our methods (and limits) of thinking than it does about the competitive race between a turtle and a human athlete. Thus, the seemingly innocent reference to the *"brave new world"* [27] should give pause for thought. -----

This book aims to stimulate discussion, provide information and promote dialogue, which we urgently need between scientific disciplines, between theory and practice, between research, development and application, between biomedical engineering and ethics.

Acknowledgements

Even in the age of AI, producing a book that offers a variety of perspectives from different authors remains a challenge that goes far beyond the individuals mentioned in the content.

First of all, we want to thank Dr. Bettina Noto from de Gruyter Brill, who was enthusiastic and supportive in continuing the "Health Academy" book series. Furthermore, we owe our thanks to Jessica Kischke from de Gruyter Brill who checked and improved tirelessly all contributions to ensure consistency. Also, Christine Kalla-Harnisch from EVHN has thoroughly lectured and edited many of the contributions.

We would also like to thank Katrin Nostadt, Tanja Hansen-Schweitzer, Antoinette Aufdermauer from the German Federal Ministry of Research Technology and Space (BMFTR, former BMBF) for funding the cluster of integrated research which also made our project about orientation in digitalized worlds (FKZ: 16SV8626) and this publication possible. Here, we especially like to thank Prof. Dr. Veronika von Messling for contributing an apt foreword to this book. Dr. Julian Stubbe and Dr. Bettina Schmietow VDI/VDE-IT were at hand with help and advice regarding the management of the project. Many thanks!

Finally, we would like to thank the German Society for Biomedical Engineering (DGBMT im VDE) for the co-funding this book. Especially, we like to thank its president, Prof. Dr. Karsten Seidl, who supported and contributed to this volume in more than one way. We also express our gratitude to Dr. Karin Schiecke (as elected representative of the DGBMT scientific board) and Dr. Thomas Becks (the new Managing Director of the DGBMT) for their support behind the scenes. Also, we are very grateful to Dr. Birgit Habenstein (former Managing Director of the DGBMT) for initiating the idea of a collective written work about AI in the field of biomedical engineering.

At last, we would like to thank all the (46!) authors of this volume for not only contributing their words and thoughts, but also for providing their valuable thoughts, advice and arguments, their enthusiasm and spirit. It was a gift that spurred us on. We hope the same will apply to our readers.

References

[1]   Hofstadter D. R. Gödel, Escher, Bach: an Eternal Golden Braid. New York: Basic Books, 1979.
[2]   The dialogue and the image were created by the public version of ChatGPT on March 5th 2025 using the following prompt: "Can you write a brief dialog between Achilles and the turtle, the style of Hofstetter, where Achilles is in favor of artificial intelligence and the turtle considers the view of ethics."
[3]   Sublette J. R. The Dartmouth conference: Its reports and results. In: College English, 35(3) 1973, 348–357.
[4]   Morgenstern U., Kraft M. Biomedizinische Technik – Faszination, Einführung und Überblick. In: Dies. (Eds.). Biomedizinische Technik – Faszination, Einführung und Überblick, Berlin/Boston, 2014. S. 1–45, S. 5. (Translation by DeepL.)
[5]   Bronzino J. D., Peterson D. R. Biomedical engineering fundamentals. CRC press 2014.
[6]   Platon. Gorgias, 500d, translated by Benjamin Jowett; https://www.gutenberg.org/files/1672/1672-h/1672-h.htm.
[7]   Smith A. Theory of moral sentiments, London 1759.
[8]   Amara R. https://en.wikipedia.org/wiki/Roy_Amara.
[9]   Seidl K., Wöhrle H. AI and Edge / Embedded Devices for Healthcare. In Ethical Perspectives on Artificial Intelligence in Biomedical Engineering, Chapter 15, DeGruyter, 2025.
[10] Hagenah J., Kubon M., Henke M., Wittenberg T. AI-supported Robots in Healthcare. In Ethical Perspectives on Artificial Intelligence in Biomedical Engineering, Chapter 17, DeGruyter, 2025.
[11] Manzeschke A. Technische Assistenzsysteme. Eine Antwort auf die Herausforderung des demographischen Wandels? In: Pro Alter 5/2011, 36–40.
[12] Wesarg S., Kohlhammer J. Digital Twins and AI in Health. In Ethical Perspectives on Artificial Intelligence in Biomedical Engineering, Chapter 19, DeGruyter, 2025.
[13] Rosahl S., Stieglitz T. Impact of Artificial Intelligence on Neural Implants. In Ethical Perspectives on Artificial Intelligence in Biomedical Engineering, Chapter 16, DeGruyter, 2025.
[14] Pott, P. P. Artificial Intelligence and Image-guided Interventions. In Ethical Perspectives on Artificial Intelligence in Biomedical Engineering, Chapter 18, DeGruyter, 2025.
[15] Gebhard P., Schneeberger T. Interactive Agents as Interface to Health Technology. In Ethical Perspectives on Artificial Intelligence in Biomedical Engineering, Chapter 20, DeGruyter, 2025.
[16] Wittenberg T., Struck M., Münzenmayer C. Business Models for Medical Devices Using AI. In Ethical Perspectives on Artificial Intelligence in Biomedical Engineering, Chapter 27, DeGruyter, 2025.
[17] Manzeschke A. Ethical Perspectives. In Ethical Perspectives on Artificial Intelligence in Biomedical Engineering, Chapter 5, DeGruyter, 2025.
[18] Hammer B. Fairness in AI – how to design 'unbiased' algorithms? In Ethical Perspectives on Artificial Intelligence in Biomedical Engineering, Chapter 14, DeGruyter, 2025.
[19] Dössel O., Loewe A. Uncertainties, errors, explainability and responsibility for AI in medicine. In Ethical Perspectives on Artificial Intelligence in Biomedical Engineering, Chapter 12, DeGruyter, 2025.
[20] Fonck S., Stollenwerk A. Explainable Artificial Intelligence in Biomedical Engineering. In Ethical Perspectives on Artificial Intelligence in Biomedical Engineering, Chapter 13, DeGruyter, 2025.
[21] Manzeschke A., Weber K., Rother E., Fangerau H. "Results of the study: Ethical Questions in the area of age appropriate assisting systems", Berlin: VDI/VDE 2015. https://feag-elkb.de/arbeitsfelder/forschung.
[22] Kämmer J., Flemming D. AI and Nursing. In Ethical Perspectives on Artificial Intelligence in Biomedical Engineering, Chapter 22, DeGruyter, 2025.
[23] Mena A. A., Habenstein B. Artificial intelligence shaping a new era in molecular medicine In Ethical Perspectives on Artificial Intelligence in Biomedical Engineering, Chapter 24, DeGruyter, 2025.
[24] Hickel S. Gefahren für die Autonomie durch gesundheitsbezogenes Self-Tracking. In: Ethik in der Medizin (2025) 37:7–29.

[25] Gassner U. Regulation of Artificial Intelligence in MedTech. In Ethical Perspectives on Artificial Intelligence in Biomedical Engineering, Chapter 25, DeGruyter, 2025.

[26] Djeffal C. From the AI Act to Responsible Innovation: The Potential of Legal Design Research. In Ethical Perspectives on Artificial Intelligence in Biomedical Engineering, Chapter 26, DeGruyter, 2025.

[27] Huxley A. Brave New World. London: Chatto & Windus, 1932.

Rudolf Seising

2 Historical Facets of Artificial Intelligence

2.1 Introduction

If you have attended various AI conferences over the past few years, read books and articles in magazines and newspapers about artificial intelligence (AI), had all kinds of conversations about it and finally seen the table of contents for this book, then you will have the impression that AI has many facets. There is no universally valid definition of this term; what it means is diverse and varies. Firstly, AI was and is a name for a field of research and not a clearly defined research discipline. Furthermore, AI was and is a vision of something that researchers in this field have yet to construct. The German AI-researcher Wolfgang Bibel pointed out many years ago that the goal and object of research have the same name and that this always leads to discussions and misunderstandings [1]. Today, AI researchers are not only asked about their research findings after their lectures, writings, podcast contributions and at various events, but also about their hypotheses and opinions on today's AI. Sometimes, they are even forced to predict what AI will be in the future. This can lead to very strange fictions – science fiction!

Facets of AI – this is intended to emphasize that AI can be perceived and understood differently by different people. Past AI researchers have also used different approaches, theories and methods, and each of them has had their own ideas about their goals, depending on their scientific discipline, cultural and social background, and style of thinking.

Historians are familiar with the fact that terms can change, that they used to stand for something different than they did later, and that they may take on yet another meaning in the future. A historiography must take this into account, and a history of AI faces a special task here, because the history to be written covers a subject that is both very recent and that has already changed considerably. Whether machines can (or will) think was discussed early on in the 20th century. Around 75 years ago, there were texts whose headlines contained the words "Thinking", "Machines" and "Intelligence" [2–4]. Up until the 1990s, AI systems were symbolic information processing programs for automatically proving mathematical theorems, for language or image processing or were expert systems [5]; today, however, AI is dominated by so-called machine learning (ML). This change took place at the end of the last century.

Historical Facets of AI – this is also intended to emphasize that AI has meant different things at different times, appeared under different names and generated different ideas. The history of AI has many facets, some of which will be discussed here.

2.2 Machinery and machines

One idea with which I would like to begin this story is that of a machinery of logical-mathematical calculations. Calculi of formal logic were developed to deduce mathematical theorems from axioms and already proven statements and led to abstract machine concepts, the mathematical automata. These have a number of possible states and can receive character inputs from outside. Depending on these two variables, an automaton is in one state at any time, and in an important variant there are also character outputs. The transitions from one state to the next can be regarded as the program of the automaton.

The mathematician Alan Mathison Turing designed an abstract machine, a logical-mathematical automaton, which was later named after him. This "Turing machine" performs calculations – just like people do with pen and paper: it processes abstract formal characters on a strip of paper divided into fields. At the time, Turing showed that the "Turing machine" was capable of solving "any conceivable mathematical problem, provided it can also be solved by an algorithm."

The "Turing machine" became an interesting concept for many scientists who focused on the question of the solvability of mathematical problems. First and foremost was John von Neumann, who set out a complete theory of automata for complicated systems. For his theory, he had both the human nervous system and the then emerging mainframe computers in mind [6].

As early as 1938, the mathematician and electrical engineer Claude Elwood Shannon had shown in his master's thesis that "logical machinery" could in principle also be built as machines using electrical circuits, by analogizing parallel and series circuits to the logical statements "and" and "or", and viewing an open circuit as the negation of a closed circuit [7]. Von Neumann's and Shannon's research objectives will be mentioned in the following sections, as will a 1955 anthology that Shannon and John McCarthy published under the title "Automata Studies" while at Bell Laboratories. Von Neumann, among others, was one of the contributors.

The word automaton has ancient Greek roots. It is composed of αὐτός autos ("self") and μον mon- ("to think, to want"). The ability to think or to want to think was attributed to living beings, i.e. natural systems with organisms, but people shook their heads when they considered whether animals or plants could also think. Nevertheless, Alan Turing introduced "thinking" in the context of machines in 1950. In his article "Computing machine and intelligence", he asked whether computers can think [8]. He attributed "thinking" to machines that could imitate the intelligent behavior of humans. That was disturbing! – Turing predicted that within 50 years our use of language would have changed so much that hardly anyone would think this was wrong, and even if he was a few decades off the mark, there is not much standing in the way of this prediction coming true today!

Automaton. became the epitome of a "self-moving" apparatus and its technical realizations became the real machines designed by electrical engineers, the first digital computers [9], starting with ENIAC (Electronic Numerical Integrator and Computer), the first universally programmable calculating machine. It was developed by John Presper Eckert and John William Mauchly from 1942 onwards on behalf of the US Army at the University of Pennsylvania, which hoped that it would enable the rapid calculation of ballistic tables. The programming of the machine was carried out by what are now known as the "ENIAC women" [10], who connected the individual parts of the system with cables and set switches to achieve the necessary logical operations.

After von Neumann was allowed to inspect the ENIAC, he began to think about improvements, and when the ENIAC designers conceived the successor computer EDVAC, he was able to advise them successfully. He wrote a "first draft" for the logical construction of the EDVAC, which contained the concept of the "stored program", which is now called the "Von Neumann architecture" [11]. However, it is also interesting to note that when presenting this new design of the EDVAC yet to be built, von Neumann spoke not of "switches" but of "neurons", not of "storage" but of "memory", and finally, Neumann noted – ignoring subtleties – that "neuronal functions simplified in this way can be emulated by telegraph relays or vacuum tubes". There was no proof of a fundamental analogy between the brain and the computer, and it was clear that this was a gross oversimplification – as noted by von Neumann himself –, but the topic preoccupied him until the end of his life in the year 1957. His posthumously published book "The Computer and the Brain" remained unfinished [12]. Three years earlier, a young mathematician named Marvin Minsky worked on building such an artificial neural network. His dissertation was entitled "Theory of Neural-Analog Reinforcement Systems and Its Application to the Brain Model" and von Neumann was a member of the review committee [13].

2.3 Brain and communication

What was John von Neumann's inspiration for describing a computer as a nervous system? – He had read an article about a logical model of neurons and their networking, which the neurophysiologist and psychologist Warren Sturgis McCulloch and the logician Walter Pitts had written in 1943 [14]. In it, they represented the activities in a network of nerves by using a complete logical calculation for time-dependent signals in electrical circuits, which stood for "artificial neurons". They each had several inputs and one output. The sum of the weighted inputs is compared with a threshold value on which the neuron is based. If it is greater, the nerve cell "fires" a signal via its output line to other nerve cells. With this model, McCulloch and Pitts presented the then current ideas of brain activity and, in particular, offered a model for communication in the nervous system.

During the Second World War, Shannon, then working at Bell Laboratories, developed a mathematical-statistical information theory for message communication in technical systems, which he published in 1948 [15,16]. His communication model for communication between two entities works as follows: A message goes from the information source to the transmitter. The transmitter sends the signal to the receiver via the channel that may be disturbed (noise source). A message is then sent from the receiver to the destination (cf. Fig. 2.1).

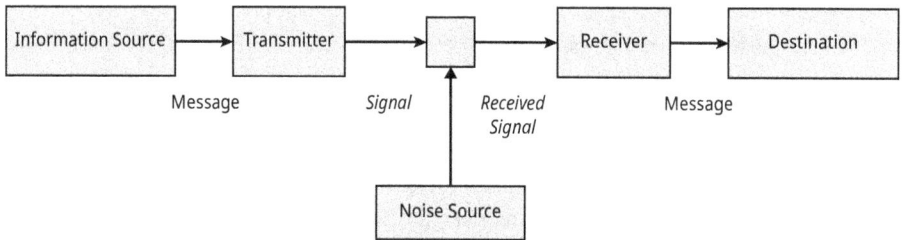

Fig. 2.1: The Shannon communication scheme modified according to the figure in [15:381].

Unfortunately, the popular renaming of Shannon's "Mathematical Theory of Communication" into "Information theory" blurs the distinction between message and information. Information was called the statistically measurable quantity, but its meaning and the intention or effect associated with it, i.e. the reason for its transmission and what was achieved through it, were not the subject of the theory. When the mathematician Warren Weaver, who was then Director of the Natural Sciences Division at the Rockefeller Foundation, wrote a popular science article about this theory [17], he categorized the term information into three levels according to the problems associated with it:

–   Level A of the purely technical problems that Shannon also dealt with, the "syntax of the sign system".
–   Level B of the semantic problems: What meanings do the signs have and what properties do these meanings have?
–   Level C of the pragmatic problems: What are the desired effects on the sender side?

Shannon's theory ignored levels B and C, but Weaver argued in favor of expanding the theory to include the meaning and effects of messages. In this way, he made the theory and the communication scheme suitable for further research, including research in the humanities and social sciences. Shannon found this "suspect" [18]. A year later, Weaver's text was prefixed (slightly modified) to Shannon's original article in book form to serve as an introduction [19].

Both digital computers and information theory were part of a new scientific movement that focused on control, regulation and communication in technical and natural systems and was called cybernetics.

2.4 Cybernetics

Logics, mathematics and electrical engineering, information theory, brain research and psychology – a whole bundle of scientific disciplines influenced the events that led to AI. In the first half of the 20th century, interdisciplinary considerations and, above all, transdisciplinary approaches to AI were mainly found under the umbrella of cybernetics, a "super science" that goes back to the mathematician Norbert Wiener. Together with his colleague Julian Bigelow and the physiologist Arturo Rosenblueth, he developed a "behavioristic approach" that explained voluntary actions in humans and machines with the help of the feedback principle commonly used in the engineering sciences [20]. This interdisciplinary approach was based on the assumption that there are analogous behavioral mechanisms in machines and living organisms. Nevertheless, there are of course functional differences between living organisms and machines: If an engineer were to design a robot that was supposed to behave in a similar way to an animal, they would hardly expect to make it out of proteins and other colloids, but probably out of metallic utensils, some dielectrics and lots of vacuum tube [20:23].

In 1948, Wiener's book "Cybernetics: or Control and Communication in the Animal and the Machine" was published. It laid the foundations for the redesign and standardization of communication, control and regulation technology. On top of that it provided a statistical basis for communication engineering, which Wiener had developed at the same time as Shannon [21].

Cybernetics and brain research were the main topics of the Macy Conference series. These conferences were initiated by the Macy Foundation in May 1942 and chaired by Warren S. McCulloch. The first conference, titled "Circular Causal and Feedback Mechanisms in Biological and Social Systems", took place in New York. Between 1949 and 1953, the Macy Conferences were held under the name "Cybernetics" [22]. One of the most controversial members of this regularly meeting "Cybernetics Group" [23] was William Ross Ashby. Ashby was an English psychiatrist who later wrote a bestselling introduction to cybernetics in 1956 [24]. In a previous book, he had given particular thought to the "Design for a Brain" [25].

2.5 Brain and intelligence

Parallels between the "electronic computer" and the brain were discussed as early as 1948, when the "Hixon Symposium on Cerebral Mechanisms in Behaviour" was held at the California Institute of Technology [26]. In his contribution, McCulloch posed the question "Why the Mind is in the Head" [27], while von Neumann once again compared computing machines with living organisms in "General and Logical Theory of Automata", included "formal neural networks", and outlined a "future logical theory of automata" [28].

Communications engineers and computer designers soon became interested in communication in the nervous system and the modelling of brain activity. At MIT's Lincoln Lab, electrical engineer Wesley Allison Clark and physicist Belmont Greenlee Farley programmed the first simulations of nerve connections on the Memory Test Computer (MTC) around 1950. The British physicist and neuropsychologist Albert Maurel Uttley also saw great potential in computer technology for research into the neuronal structure of the brain. In his lecture at the first "Symposium on Information Theory" in London, also in 1950, he took on the "popular and dangerous task of comparing computers and brains" and emphasized the similarities between natural neuron networks and the message communication structure within a computer: computers, like brains, have inputs and outputs for message signals and can store and convert them [29].

During the 1950s three more international symposia on information theory were held in London. The last of these, which took place in 1955, also offered lectures on brain research for the first time. The series was continued in the 1960s. Clark and Farley recommended using a high-speed digital computer as a tool to tackle the problems of brain research [30]. Psychologists were also interested in the results of this technical communication technology; at their 1953 conference in Amersfoort, the Netherlands, the biophysicist George Karreman gave two corresponding lectures [31,32].

Ashby was particularly interested in those brain functions that enable cognitive abilities and are known as intelligence. He was familiar with the relevant literature from the first half of the 20th century, such as "Measurement of Adult Intelligence" by David Wechsler [33], who emphasized that the intelligence of a living being cannot simply be defined as the sum of its cognitive abilities, but that we can only assess it "by the measurement of the various aspects of these abilities". Just as we measure electricity by recording its chemical, thermal and magnetic effects, we recognize intelligence "by the things it does or, better, by the things it enables us to do – such as making appropriate associations between events, drawing correct inferences from propositions, understanding the meaning of words, solving mathematical problems or building bridges." [33:4]

Ashby was of the opinion that we can have the abilities of this brain capacity amplified by a computer, similar to how power machines – Ashby called them "power-amplifiers" – amplify human labour [34]. Computers are therefore not capable of human intelligence, but they have "synthetic intellectual abilities" with which they can amplify human intelligence – Ashby therefore called them "intelligence-amplifiers". This view of computerized amplification of human intelligence can be found in his contribution to a book project, with which the next section begins.

2.6 Good old-fashioned artificial intelligence

In the summer of 1952, the young mathematician John McCarthy met the by then well-known Claude Shannon at Bell Labs, to whom he suggested publishing a collection of works on intelligent machines. McCarthy wanted to call the book "Intelligent Machines", but Shannon found this too "bombastic" and so they agreed on the title "Automata Studies" [35]. The contributions to the volume also disappointed McCarthy. They mainly dealt with mathematical automata. and not his favored idea of "intelligent machines". After he joined the Department of Mathematics at Dartmouth College in Hanover, New Hampshire, as an assistant professor, he planned in 1955 to invite scientists for a "summer research project" there to think about and discuss "artificial intelligence").

McCarthy contacted Warren Weaver at the Rockefeller Foundation. Shannon had probably established this contact, as the two had published a book together a few years earlier [19]. Together with Shannon, Marvin Minsky and the IBM engineer Nathaniel Rochester, McCarthy wrote "A Proposal for the Dartmouth Summer Research Project on Artificial Intelligence" in 1955, with which they applied for financial support from the Rockefeller Foundation.

They understood artificial intelligence to be the simulation of those higher functions of the human brain that enable it to develop the abilities and behaviors that are called "intelligent". These simulations should (1) run on "automatic computers", the question to be answered was (2) "How Can a Computer be Programmed to Use a Language", in addition (3) "Neuron Nets" were to be researched, (4) a "Theory of the Size of a Calculation" was sought, it was assumed that (5) an "intelligent" machine is capable of a certain "self-improvement" and (6) "abstractions" of sensor values and other data. In addition, (7) "randomness and creativity" were cited, as otherwise unimaginative thinking was to be expected [36].

The Rockefeller Foundation approved the application with restrictions and invited scientists met over the summer of 1956 to discuss AI. Today it is often cited as the beginning of research into AI. Herbert Alexander Simon and Alan Newell presented the "Logic Theorist", a program they had constructed with John Clifford Shaw to prove some logical theorems. The group also discussed a chess program by Alex Bernstein, which was not yet fully completed [37].

Who exactly joined the group at Dartmouth cannot be reconstructed anymore. A handwritten list by Ray Solomonoff names 20 participants [38]. But it is uncertain whether all the people he named actually came, how long they stayed, and whether there were any other participants. The known participants had different ideas about AI, but there was a common vision that computers could be made to simulate intelligent behavior [39]. William Ross Ashby's name was also on Solomonoff's list – but it was marked with a question mark [38]. Ashby had contributed the essay "Design for an Intelligence-Amplifier" to McCarthy and Shannon's "Automata Studies", the only article with the word "intelligence" in the title.

2.7 "New-fashioned" AI

In 1985, the philosopher John Haugeland published a book on "Artificial Intelligence: The Very Idea" in which he introduced the acronym GOFAI: Good Old-Fashioned Artificial Intelligence. Under GOFAI, Haugeland summarized the approaches to AI research which had been dominant until the mid-1980s in order to better differentiate them from newer approaches to constructing intelligent machines [40]. This new research program was called connectionism. It involves many identical or similar elements that are connected to each other to form network systems and transmit messages via signals. Such models for simulating intelligent behavior are known as artificial neural networks.

As far back as the late 1950s, psychologist Frank Rosenblatt had taken up McCulloch and Pitts' suggestion to enable artificial neurons to recognize patterns. He called his model and his simulation program "Perceptron" , an artificial neuron network that "recognized" characters – initially squares and circles, later numbers and letters. At the beginning of the 1960s, he and his colleagues also built the first real device called "Perceptron Mark I", which used its 20 x 20 pixel image sensor to identify numbers whose characteristics it had previously memorized [41,42]. Rosenblatt already referred to this pattern recognition as a "learning algorithm" due to the many trial-and-error processes involved. These were the beginnings of what came to be referred to as "new-fashioned AI", "new-wave AI" or "newfangled AI" (NFAI) research when it took off in the 1980s: machines that were able to "perceive" their environment, react to it, adapt and "learn". Today, NFAI systems characterize our concept of AI.

NFAI did not suddenly replace GOFAI. Instead, the development of both AI approaches has overlapped since the beginning and both of them are still being pursued. One interesting case study for this phenomenon can be found in game programs: among the earliest AI research were attempts at making computers play games that require intelligence, like chess or checkers.

Although it was the game of chess that took a path from the GOFAI to the NFAI, it was the game of checkers that was given NFAI priority. As early as 1959, the electrical engineer Arthur Lee Samuel saw a way of making computers "learn" without them being explicitly programmed for this, an idea he tested with the board game. His program contained the rules of checkers and was able to improve its game because successful moves were rated higher than unsuccessful ones. The values stored with the moves indicated the probability with which the moves would be profitable [43]. The corresponding algorithms are called probabilistic because – unlike the classical (deterministic) algorithms, which always find a valid solution to the problem – they only deliver probable results. Samuel's checkers program was able to optimize its game even though the program itself remained unchanged.

Algorithms that do not deliver the same output value after every run, but with a certain probability, in this sense "learn", are tools of "machine learning" (ML) and thus of new-fashioned artificial intelligence).

2.8 Statistics and data science

In machine learning, patterns and correlations are recognized in large amounts of data in order to make predictions and optimize processes. In more and more scientific disciplines, these machine learning methods are replacing the conventional methods of empirical science, which allow future events to be predicted with certain probabilities on the basis of sufficiently large amounts of observational data. Previously, such data was collected and analyzed to describe conditions, which corresponds to the original meaning of the word "statistics". In this scientific discipline, hypotheses are generated on the basis of available data, and its methods have become indispensable for scientific and technical world. The history of statistics runs between mathematical theory, scientific calculation, and real-world applications. Its historical development began with the latter, as data was initially collected and presented from the sections of the world under consideration. This was followed by an inferential approach which was soon mathematized. A mathematical-statistical methodological framework developed during the late 19th and early 20th century. This development reached a conclusion of sorts with the work "Statistical Decision Functions" by Abraham Wald in 1950. Until then, the empirical-numerical approach hardly played a role, This only changed with the advent of electronic computers. Stanford statistics professors Bradley Efron and Trevor Hastie argue in their book "Computer Age Statistical Inference" that this new technology set a process in motion that took statistics out of its "solitary existence" around mathematical structures and swept it along with it [44].

The extent to which computers would change statistics could not be foreseen in the middle of the 20th century. One statistician who came close, however, was John

Wilder Tukey. In 1962 he published a paper on "The Future of Data Analysis" in which he called for statistics as a discipline to be geared towards application and calculation [45]. Although data analysis could be carried out by hand for small data sets, the speed and cost-effectiveness of its answer made the computer indispensable for large data sets and very valuable for small data sets. This, so Tukey, would be the future of data analysis and should prove successful in all areas of science and technology. Two decades later, he then explicitly advocated for intensive interdisciplinary cooperation between the cultures of statistics and computer science in a lecture [46].

In the mid-1960s, statistician Leo Breiman, who had been teaching probability theory at the University of California in Los Angeles since 1954, decided to leave academia and work as an independent consultant for various organizations and projects. Among other things, he worked for the Technology Services Corporation (TSC), headed by William S. Meisel, on environmental and health studies and the predictions to be derived from them. Here, together with the particle physicist and later Stanford statistician Jerome Herold Friedman, the Stanford statistician Richard Allen Olshen, and the Berkeley statistician Charles Joel Stone, Breiman developed a method for creating models for predictions and explanations on the basis of classification and regression trees. They published these research results in their book "Classification and Regression Trees", CART for short [47].

The book begins with the "background" presentation of a medical study on the development of a method to identify high-risk patients at risk of a heart attack from an initial database. The authors contrast their new computer-based method "CART" with conventional statistical methods. In patients at the San Diego Medical Center of the University of California, nineteen variables were measured on the first day to characterize the person's condition: blood pressure, age and seventeen other binary variables to summarize medical symptoms. Using a binary tree structure (cf. Fig. 2.2), a classification rule (F: high risk, G: no high risk) was created in this study.

In this way, the CART method correctly classified 89% of patients with a low risk of heart attack and 75% of patients with a high risk of heart attack. With this success, it did not need to shy away from comparison with classical statistical methods; in fact, it turned out to be more successful than classical methods. These would assume that a stochastic data model generated the data and that subsequent data always obey such a model. Thus, many of the problems referred to statistics had previously been dealt with by means of (multiple) linear or logarithmic regressions and discriminant analyses. In the present problem, however, it was now necessary to consider twelve variables for a linear stepwise discriminant analysis, and ultimately less accurate results were obtained with these classical methods than with the CART method. For the logistic regression, ten variables were needed, including three interactions suggested by the CART program, to obtain comparable results. The "nearest neighbour" method was not successful at all: the result was too poor and the computational effort was too high.

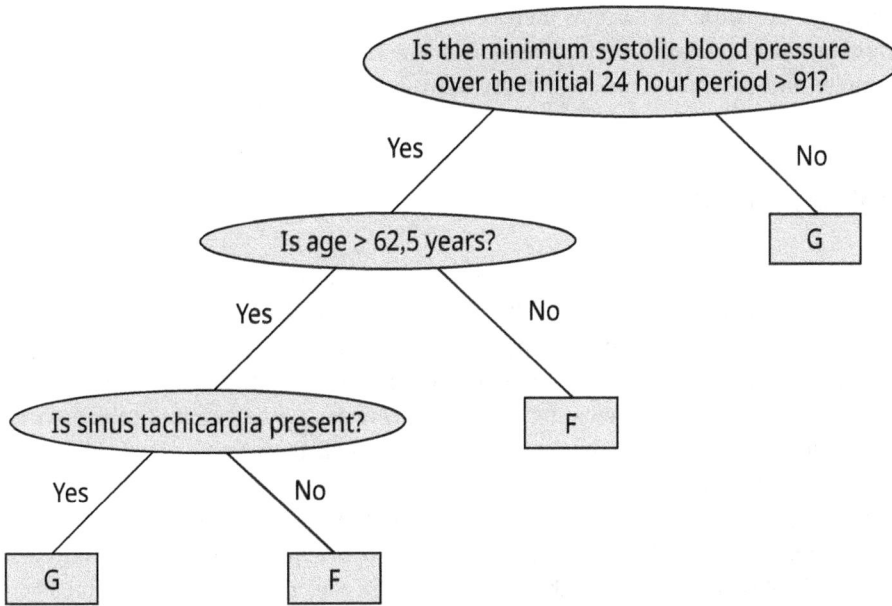

Fig. 2.2: Binary tree structure for classifying patients in the classes F: high risk, G: no high risk, modified according to the figure in [47:2].

The authors noted that the problems they faced with the TSC projects in the 1970s could not have been solved in a simple way using any of these classical statistical methods. However, their CART method for using classification trees could do this very well [47:17]. Breiman and his colleagues developed their toolset as an alternative to classical statistics, which consisted of algorithms for classifying data and predicting it based on existing data. This alternative method was very successful precisely because of its high forecasting accuracy. It was based on two important changes: "[to] challenge for the tools and computers of the time" [48] and "[to] make the transition from probability theory to algorithms" [49:215].

Breiman felt compelled to change his thinking from classical to alternative statistical methods and in 2001 he published the article "Statistical Modeling: The Two Cultures". For him, there are two different "cultures" of statistical modeling: statisticians either arrive at their conclusions from the data based on the premise that a given stochastic data model generates the data – or they use algorithmic models without any prior assumptions about a data mechanism. Traditional statistical culture is based on the belief that a statistician can develop a reasonably good parametric class of models for the natural world through imagination and looking at the data, and then they would estimate the parameters and draw conclusions. Breiman considered these models inadequate because the systems under consideration were immensely large and complex and more and more questions arose from the sciences. This resulted in increasingly complex data structures, making it more difficult to construct suitable data models.

2.9 Outlook

There was not just one concept of "artificial intelligence" in the 20th century. Even before this term existed, research initiatives to understand the functions of natural nervous systems and the human mind gave rise to the idea of binary logic machinery inherent in the brain. The idea of the "thinking machine" was established by 1950 with the early digital computing systems and the analogy between the natural brain and the artificial computer. Five years later, the term "artificial intelligence" was coined to describe the research goal of making machines behave in such a way that – if humans behaved in this way – it would be called intelligent. However, the term AI also stood for the field of research to which scientists from a wide range of disciplines dedicated themselves. Since the 1980s, this good old-fashioned AI has been replaced by a new conceptualization of AI, as computer scientists, statisticians, physicists and engineers began focusing on new algorithmic models, such as artificial neural networks., but also tree algorithms and their developments. This changed the research field of AI and, especially since the turn of the millennium, also that of statistics. The potential of algorithms that make predictions – the "media stars of the big data era" – transformed the latter into "data analytics" and ultimately "data science". They are the new facet of artificial intelligence.

References

[1] Bibel W. "Intellektik" statt "KI". Ein ernstgemeinter Vorschlag, KI-Rundbrief, 22, 1980, 15–16.
[2] Berkeley E. C. Giant Brains or Machines That Think, New York: John Wiley & Sons, 1949.
[3] Turing A. M. Computing Machinery and Intelligence, Mind, LIX (236), 1950, 433–460.
[4] Zadeh L. Thinking Machines, Columbia Engineering Quarterly, January 1950, 12–13, 30–31.
[5] Seising R. (ed.). Geschichten der Künstlichen Intelligenz in der Bundesrepublik Deutschland, Munich: Deutsches Museum 2024. Open Access: (Accessed 10.7.2024, at https://www.deutsches-museum.de/assets/Verlag/Download/Studies/Studies-13-download.pdf).
[6] Von Neumann J. The General and Logical Theory of Automata, in: Collected Works 5, Oxford et al.: Pergamon Press, 1961, 302–306.
[7] Shannon C. E. A Symbolic Analysis of Relay and Switching Circuits, Transactions of the American Institute of Electrical Engineers, 57 (12), 1938, 713–723.
[8] Turing A. M. Computing Machinery and Intelligence, Mind, LIX (236), 1950, 433–460.
[9] Cerruzzi, P. E. A History of Modern Computing, MIT Press 1998.
[10] Jennifer S. Light: When Computers Were Women. In: Technology and Culture, 40, 1999, 3.
[11] Von Neumann J. First Draft of a Report on the EDVAC, Sect. 2.6, 1945: https://archive.org/details/first-draftofrepo00vonn

[12] Von Neuman J. The Computer and the Brain, Yale University Press, New Haven 1958, German translation: Die Rechenmaschine und das Gehirn, Oldenbourg, München 1960.

[13] Minsky M. L. Neural Nets and the Brain Model Problem, Dissertation, Princeton University, 1954.

[14] McCulloch W. S., Pitts, W. A logical calculus of the ideas immanent in Nervous activity, Bulletin of Mathematical Biophysics, 5, 1943, 115–133.

[15] Shannon C. E. The Mathematical Theory of Communication, Bell System Technical Journal, 27 (3 and 4), 379–423, 623–656, 1948.

[16] Roch A., Claude E. Shannon – Spielzeug, Leben und die Geschichte seiner Theorie der Information, Berlin: Gegenstalt 2009.

[17] Weaver W. The Mathematics of Communication, Scientific American, 1949, 181, 11–14.

[18] Tribus M. T. "Thirty Years of Information Theory." In: Levine R. D.; Tribus, M. T. (eds.). The Maximum Entropy Formalism. The MIT Press, Cambridge MA, 1978, 1–14.

[19] Shannon C. E., Weaver W. The Mathematical Theory of Communication, Urbana, University of Illinois Press, 1949.

[20] Rosenblueth A., Wiener N., Bigelow J. Behavior, Purpose and Teleology, Philosophy of Science 10, 1943, 18–24.

[21] Wiener N. Cybernetics or Control and Communications in the Animal and the Machine, Cambridge, Massachusetts: MIT Press, 1948.

[22] Pias C. (ed.). Cybernetics | Kybernetik The Macy-Conferences 1946–1953. 2 vols., Diaphanes Verlag, Zürich 2003. English: Cybernetics: The Macy Conferences 1946–1953. 2 vols, Diaphanes; Revised ed. Edition 2016. See also: Siehe dazu: (Accessed 11.7.2024, at https://www.asc-cybernetics.org/foundations/history/MacyPeople.htm).

[23] Heims St. J. The Cybernetics Group. Cambridge, Massachusetts, London: The MIT Press, 1991.

[24] Ashby W. R. An Introduction to Cybernetics. London: Chapman et Hall, 1956.

[25] Ashby W. R. Design for a Brain. London: Chapman et Hall, 1952. (2. editon) 1960.

[26] Jeffress L. A. (ed.). Cerebral Mechanisms in Behavior. The Hixon Symposium. New York: John Wiley & Sons, 1951.

[27] McCulloch W. S. Why the Mind is in the Head. In: L. A. Jeffress. (Hrsg.): Cerebral Mechanisms in Behavior. The Hixon Symposium. New York: John Wiley & Sons, 1951, 93–158.

[28] Von Neumann J. The General and Logical Theory of Automata. Delivered at the Hixon Symposium, September 1948. In: Jeffress, L. A. (Hrsg.): Cerebral Mechanisms in Behavior. The Hixon Symposium, New York: John Wiley & Sons, 1951, 1–41.

[29] Uttley A. M. Information, Machines, and Brains, (Reprint of Proceedings, Symposium on Information Theory, London, England, September 1950), IRE Transaction of Information Theory, 1, 1953, 143–152: 143.

[30] Farley B. G., Clark W. A. Activity in Networks of Neuron-Like Elements, in: C. Cherry (ed.). Information Theory, Papers read at a Symposium on "Information Theory" held at the Royal Institution, Proceedings of the Fourth London Symposium on Information Theory, London, August 29th to September 2nd 1960, 242–248: 242.

[31] Karreman G. Recent Mathematical-Biological Studies on Excitation. Synthese 1953/55, 9, 3/5, Ninth International Significal Summer Conference / Neuvieme Conference d'Ete Internationale de Linguistique Psychologique, 248–251.

[32] Karreman G. Recent Mathematical-Biological Studies on Communication. Synthese 1953/55, 9, 3/5, Ninth International Significal Summer Conference / Neuvieme Conference d'Ete Internationale de Linguistique Psychologique, 255–264.

[33] Wechsler D. The Measurement of Adult Intelligence, Third Edition, Baltimore: The Williams & Wilkins Company 1944 (1. Ed. 1939).

[34] Ashby W. R., Design for an Intelligence-Amplifier, In: Shannon C. E.; McCarthy J. (eds.). Automata Studies, Princeton, New Jersey: University Press, 1956, 215–234: 215.

[35] Shannon C. E., and McCarthy J. (eds.). Automata Studies. Princeton University Press, Princeton, NJ 1956.
[36] McCarthy J. et al. 1955. A proposal for the Dartmouth summer research project on artificial intelligence, August 31, 1955, (Accessed 11.7.2024, at www-formal.stanford.edu/jmc/history/dartmouth/dartmouth.html).
[37] Bernstein A. A Chess Playing Program for the IBM 704, Chess Review 26 (7), 208–209.
[38] Accessed 11.7.2024, at https://raysolomonoff.com/dartmouth/boxbdart/dart56ray812825who.pdf.
[39] Moor J. The Dartmouth college artificial intelligence conference: the next fifty years. AI Magazine 2006, 27 (4), 87–91.
[40] Haugeland J. Artificial Intelligence: The Very Idea, Cambridge, Mass.: MIT Press 1985.
[41] Rosenblatt F. The Design of an Intelligent Automaton, Research trends, Vol. VI (2), 1958, 1–7.
[42] Rosenblatt F. Principles of Neurodynamics: Perceptrons and the Theory of Brain Mechanisms, Sparten Books, 1962.
[43] Samuel A. Some studies in machine learning using the game of checkers, IBM Journal of Research and Development, vol. 3, 1959, pp. 210–229.
[44] Efron B., Hastie T. Computer Age Statistical Inference. Algorithms, Evidence, and Data Science. Cambridge: Cambridge University Press 2016.
[45] Tukey J. W. The Future of Data Analysis. In: The Annals of Mathematical Statistics 33 (1) 1962, 1–67.
[46] Tukey J. W. Another Look in the Future. In: Heiner, K. W.; Sacher, R. S.; Wilkinson, J. W. (Hrsg.): Computer Science and Statistics, Proceedings of the 14th Symposium of the Interface. New York, NY: Springer 1982, 2–8.
[47] Breiman L., Friedman J. H., Stone Ch. J., Olshen R. A. Classification and Regression Trees. Belmont, CA: Wadsworth 1984.
[48] Cutler A. Remembering Leo Breiman, The Annals of Applied Statistics 4, 2010, 1621–1633: 1622.
[49] Breiman L. Statistical Modelling: The Two Cultures, Statistical Sciences 16 (3), 2001, 199–231: 215.

Klaus Mainzer

3 Generative artificial intelligence: From scientific foundations to societal applications

3.1 Introduction

This article explains the foundations of artificial intelligence (AI) which have led to chatbots such as ChatGPT in so-called "generative AI". The decisive thesis is that, to ensure appropriate use of such tools of generative AI in society, the fundamentals and limitations of the corresponding algorithms must be thoroughly understood. To this end, the paradigm shifts in AI since the Turing test are first discussed – from symbolic AI with logic-orientated programs (e.g., automated proving, expert systems) to sub-symbolic AI with brain-oriented computing of statistical learning theory. Generative AI with chatbots such as ChatGPT is an example of sub-symbolic AI based on large language systems (LLS) which can generate all kinds of text-based patterns [1].

A crucial question which is also considered is the enormous energy consumption of digitalization in general and chatbots especially. Therefore, besides logical and technical limitation and failures of chatbots, the requests of energy consumption must not be forgotten in our age of climate crisis. Computational architectures should become more energetically efficient. Neuromorphic and quantum computing may be ways out. Anyway, more efficient computational architecture than the classical von Neumann computer are demanded to realize sustainable AI with respect to the SDGs (Sustainable Development Goals) of the UN.

Obviously, the potential of chatbots opens new avenues in nearly all societal areas. It is also clear that questions of safety and security require legal regulation and control. Thus, methods of verification and certification which has already been developed for symbolic AI and classical software engineering should be extended to sub-symbolic AI. Therefore, we argue for an integration of symbolic and sub-symbolic AI in hybrid AI to handle chatbots such as ChatGPT. In the end, overregulation slows down innovation power and should be avoided. Innovation, creativity, and competition are necessary in a world-wide competition of AI markets. We aim at chatbots as useful service systems of sustainable and responsible AI with humans in the position of final responsibility.

3.2 Symbolic AI

3.2.1 Turing Test and artificial intelligence

The British computer pioneer, logician and mathematician Alan Turing proposed a simulation test as a definition of Artificial Intelligence in 1950 [2]: According to this, a technical system should be called "intelligent" if it is indistinguishable from a human in its responses and problem solving (Turing Test). In the years after Turing, the initial focus was on simulating logical thinking on the computer. Behind this is the epistemological idea that intelligence is primarily linked to the ability of logical reasoning in the human mind. For this purpose, AI was oriented directed rules and formulas of symbolic logic, which were translated into appropriate computer programs. This is why we also refer to it as "symbolic AI".

An example of symbolic AI is automatic reasoning/proving, in which AI programs simulate logical thinking with logical calculations [3]. Automatic reasoning with satisfiability (SAT) enabled practical applications of SAT solving, which is still used today in industrial logistics [4]. In this process, logistical problems in the automotive industry, for example, are represented in logical formulas whose satisfiability can be automatically checked [5].

3.2.2 From Turing to Weizenbaum's ELIZA

When leading researchers such as John McCarthy, Allen Newell, Herbert Simon and others met for the Dartmouth Conference on Machine Intelligence in 1956, they drew inspiration by Turing's question "Can machines think?". Around the mid-1950s to mid-1960s, the first phase of AI research was still fueled by optimistic expectations [6,7]. General problem-solving procedures for computers were to be formulated. Disappointment was great in view of the practical results. Finally (around the mid-1970s to mid-1980s), knowledge-based expert systems came to the fore, promising the first practical applications. Delimited and manageable specialized knowledge of human experts such as engineers and doctors were to be made available for everyday use [8].

Knowledge-based expert systems are AI programs that store knowledge about a specific domain and automatically draw conclusions from the knowledge to find concrete solutions or provide diagnoses of situations [9:150–185,10]. In contrast to a human expert, the knowledge of an expert system is confined to a specialized information base and does not encompass general and structural knowledge about the world. To develop such an expert system, the expert's knowledge needs to be formulated into rules, converted into a program language and utilized with a problem-solving strategy.

This is also relevant to how computers process natural language. Joseph Weizenbaum's original language program ELIZA is an example of this [11]. ELIZA was concepted to simulate a psychiatrist talking to a patient as if it were a human expert and involves rules on how to react to certain sentence patterns of the user with certain sentence patterns of the virtual "psychiatrist". In general, it is about recognizing or classifying specific rules in terms of their applicability in certain situations.

In the simplest case, the equality of two symbol structures S1 and S2 is to be determined, as it is determined in the programming language LISP for symbol lists by the function EQUAL. An extension occurs when terms and variables are included in the symbolic expressions [12:55–58], e.g.,

$$E1 = (x \ B \ C)$$
$$E2 = (A \ B \ y)$$

These two expressions E1 and E2 are equal to each other, since the variable x relates to the atom A and the variable y corresponds to the atom C. The dialogue between a patient or person P and the ELIZA system can be imagined like this and is an exact quotation of J. Weinbaum's article from 1965 [11]

Patient: MEN ARE ALL ALIKE
ELIZA:　IN WHAT WAY
Patient: THEY'RE ALWAYS BUGGING US ABOUT SOMETHING OR OTHER
ELIZA:　CAN YOU THINK OF A SPECIFIC EXAMPLE
Patient: WELL; MY BOYFRIEND MADE ME COME HERE
ELIZA:　YOUR BOYFRIEND MADE YOU COME HERE
Patient: YES; I AM VERY SAD
ELIZA:　YOU ARE VERY SAD
Patient: SAD AND DEPRESSED
ELIZA:　PLEASE GO ON ...

The following programming rules outlined below enable ELIZA to generate responses when specific sentence patterns are utilized by the user and identified by ELIZA through pattern matching:

Rule 1: '(((*AM *B)→(APPEND '(YOU ARE)B))
Rule 2: ((*ARE*)→ '(IN WHAT WAY))
Rule 3: ((*ALWAYS*)→ '(CAN YOU THINK OF A SPECIFIC EXAMPLE))
Rule 4: ((*MY * B ME * C)→ (APPEND '(YOUR)(APPEND B(CONS 'YOU C))))
Rule 5: ((*L)→ '(PLEASE GO ON)))

The second rule in this program states:

If the sentence of the patient contains "ARE", answer with the list '(IN WHAT WAY).

Thus, in the sentence "MEN ARE ALL ALIKE", the * operator before "ARE" matches the list "MEN", after "ARE" matches the list "ALL ALIKE".

The fourth rule in the above program states says:

> If in the patient's sentence the words MY and ME are separated by a list *B and the sentence ends with a list *C, then in ELIZA's answer first put YOU and the C-part together to form (CONS'YOU C), then apply the B-part, and finally '(YOUR)

Therefore, the dialogue with ELIZA given above is nothing more than the derivation of syntactic symbol lists in the programming language LISP.

3.2.3 From ELIZA to WATSON

Text matching based on pattern recognition has been around since Weizenbaum's ELIZA. In a next step, the software broke down sentences into individual phrases and calculated the probabilities for matching answer patterns to posed questions or matching translations into other languages in a flash. One example of an efficient translation system was VERBMOBIL coordinated by the German Research Centre for Artificial Intelligence (DFKI) from 1993 to 2000 [13]. For humans, language processing occurs at various levels of representation. In technical systems, these steps are implemented sequentially. In the field of computational linguistics [14], this approach is referred as a pipeline model: It begins with auditory information (hearing), followed by the generation of a textual representation. During semantic analysis, meanings derived from the deep structures of Chomsky grammars are assigned to the sentences [15]. Lastly, in dialogue and discourse analysis, the relationships between elements such as questions and answers, as well as intentions and purposes are explored.

One semantic question-answering program was the WATSON system by International Business Machines Corp. (IBM) [16], which utilized the processing power of a parallel computer along with the memory of Wikipedia. WATSON also referred to a platform from IBM for cognitive tools and their diverse applications in business and the economy. Based on Moore's Law, the performance of WATSON would not require a supercomputer in the near future. The future prospect for WATSON was that a program (app) on a smartphone could provide the same performance. You would eventually be able to talk to your smartphone. Services would no longer have to be requested via a keyboard, but by speaking to an intelligent voice program [17,18].

3.3 Sub-symbolic AI

3.3.1 Limitation of symbolic AI

However, rule-based knowledge does not completely encapsulate the intuitive skills and experience inherent in our everyday understanding. Skills are derived from a variety of experiences that are not fully represented in a symbolically or rule-based manner as one might find in a textbook. For instance, an experienced driver perceives situations and responds intuitively, relying on numerous sensory inputs without being consciously aware of the intricate logical relationships. Likewise, an experienced physician reacts decisively in critical moments in the operating room, just as a skilled pilot does in the cockpit of an aircraft. But even our linguistic communication is not guided by conscious application of rules and symbolic representation.

In philosophy, the Dreyfus Brothers published 1986 a book entitled "Mind over Machine. The Power of Human Intuition and Expertise in the Era of the Computer" [19]. But in fact, they only showed the limits of symbolic AI to understand human intuition. As a phenomenologist, they believed that human intuition could only be understand through qualitative-phenomenological methods and not through formal rules. However, the question arises to what degree pattern and structure recognition in data, and the assignment of expectation probabilities can be trained by machines to simulate intuition.

3.3.2 Statistical learning theory and neural networks

In contrast to the logical rules of symbolic AI, sensory data now takes precedence, with statistical correlations and probabilities being assessed. The mathematical study of learning from data is encompassed in statistical learning theory, which forms the basis for machine learning algorithms [20].

Epistemologically, these learning processes that arise from sensory perception occur unconsciously, beneath the level of conscious logical reasoning, which is why this approach is referred to sub-symbolic AI. Mathematically, the focus has shifted from logic to statistics and probability theory. Recent advancements in computer technology have enabled the practical implementation of machine learning with vast data sets, resulting in significant breakthroughs in AI application, such as drugs and vaccine development, as well as in robotics, industry and social infrastructure [21].

The self-organizing brains of living organisms are considered the counter-design to programmed computers [22]. In evolution, networks first developed as subcellular supply, control and information systems in complex gene and protein networks [23:45–88]. With nerve cells, cellular information, control and supply systems finally developed on the basis of neurochemical signal processing.

In the process of evolution, effective problem-solving methods emerged without the use of symbolic representation in computer models. Subcellular, cellular and neuronal self-organization led to the formation of complex networks that correspond to these processes. In this context, neurons are depicted as nodes within a graphical network, while synaptic connections are represented by edges [24]. The strength of neurochemical connections is represented in the model by numerical values (weights). Learning consists of building up wiring patterns of neurons. This is done by the learning algorithms of neuronal networks. Intensive synaptic couplings generate neuronal wiring patterns that correspond to mental, emotional or motor states of an organism.

3.3.3 Neural networks and automata

As recently discussed [35], in essence, computer models can be replicated by neural networks. These replications rely on a on a fundamental mathematical similarity of neuronal networks, automata and machines.

Hence, it can be demonstrated that a McCulloch-Pitts network can effectively be represented by a finite automaton [25]. Finite automata are basic systems, like ticket machines that can interpret simple instruction codes (regular languages) [26]. On the other hand, a McCulloch-Pitts network can also perform functions equivalent to those of a finite state automaton. Mathematically, these networks are characterized by integer weights. This means, that an organism with a neural system modeled after a McCulloch-Pitts network can only tackle problems up to the complexity manageable by a finite automaton. Therefore, such an organism would possess 'intelligence' comparable to that of a finite automaton.

However, which neuronal networks align with Turing machines, which according to Church's thesis are models of program-controlled computers? It can be demonstrated that Turing machines accurately simulate those neuronal networks that possess synaptic weights represented as rational numbers ("fractions") and include feedback loops (are "recurrent"). Conversely, recurrent neural networks with rational synaptic weights can also be precisely simulated by Turing machines [27].

If we consider a Turing machine as a model of a computer controlled by a program, then according to this argument, a computer can replicate a brain with rational synaptic strengths. On the other hand, the operations of a Turing machine or a computer can be replicated by a brain that utilizes rational variables for synaptic intensity. In other words, the intelligence level of such brains is equivalent to that of a Turing machine.

In practice, this means that such neural networks can theoretically be simulated on an appropriate computer. In reality, neural networks used for practical purposes like pattern recognition are primarily simulated on computers even today. Only neuromorphic computers would implement neural networks directly in hardware.

3.3.4 Neural networks and learning algorithms

In the automation of statistical learning, neural networks equipped with learning algo-rithms are crucial. Probabilistic networks show a significant experimental similarity to biological neural networks. When cells are removed or individual synapse weights are slightly altered, these networks demonstrate fault tolerance to minor disruptions, similar to the human brain's resilience in the in the face minor minor accidental inju-ries. The human brain operates with layers of parallel signal processing. For instance, between the layer of sensory input and a layer of motor output, there exist internal intermediate steps of neuronal signal processing that do not connect to the external environment.

In fact, the representation and problem-solving capacity can also be increased in technical neuronal networks by interposing different layers capable of learning with as many neurons as possible. The first layer receives the input pattern. Each neuron of this layer has connections to each neuron of the next layer. The interconnection continues until the last layer is reached and gives an activity pattern [28].

We refer to supervised learning procedures, when the prototype to be learned (e.g., the recognition of a pattern) is known, allowing for the measurement of error devia-tions against it. A learning algorithm must adjust the synaptic weights until a pattern of activity in the output layer emerges that closely matches the prototype.

An approach involves calculatng the error deviation between the actual and the desired outputs for each neuron of the output layer, which is then backpropagated through the network layers. This process is known as the backpropagation algorithm. The goal is to minimize the error to zero or negligibly small values by iteratively learn-ing enough steps for a given t pattern.

3.4 Chatbots

3.4.1 What can the AI chatbot ChatGPT do?

A remarkable example of sub-symbolic AI are chatbots such as ChatGPT (Generative Pre-trained Transformer) [35]. Due to its impressive abilities as an automatic text gen-erator, it quickly gained had more followers than social media platforms such as Ins-tagram and Spotify, attracting millions of users within just a few days after its launch on November 30, 2022. ChatGPT is capable of producing texts that can successfully pass the Turing test in assessments at universities, particularly in language-based academic fields.

The abilities of ChatGPT are made possible by training with Large Language Mod-els (LLM). But actually, it is only an application of statistical learning theory for pat-tern generation and recognition on big data. In short: Machine learning is a paradigm change from AI with symbolic logic (symbolic AI) to AI with statistics (sub-symbolic AI). The reason is the limitation of symbolic AI to rule-based formula which can only simulate textbook knowledge, but not the intuitive and informal expertise and experience of a human expert. In the 'machine room' of ChatGPT, we only find well-known learning algorithms of machine learning such as supervised and reinforcement learning but applied to huge mass of data (large language models) with enormous computer power. On this basis, algorithms calculate statistical expectation values of symbols and words which should be inserted into a context with high probability. The accuracy of context-depending probabilistic guessing depends on the amount of training data.

At a first glance, this procedure seems to be quite different to human understanding of a context. In machine learning, it is non asserted that human understanding could completely be explained by this kind of statistical simulation. Nevertheless, a large part of human conversation and communication is based on context-depending pattern simulation and reproduction which can also be realized by machines. Therefore, chatbots are sometimes called 'statistical parrots'. Contrary to statical simulations with big data, the human abilities are still astonishing. An example may be a pupil which is able to find an original solution of a mathematical exercise without being trained with all possible math textbooks [29].

3.4.2 The "machine room" of ChatGPT

From a technical perspective, ChatGPT is a *"Large Language Model"* (LLM) that produces human-like texts using deep learning algorithms trained on a vast amount of spoken data [35]. It operates on a *"Generative Pre-trained Transformer"* (GPT) architecture. A transformer generates a suitable text on previously trained data samples. The inputs of a transformer are denoted as "prompts". In traditional linguistic models, the predicted probable words are generated sequentially. A transformer considers all input data and their relation to the other words and concepts in a certain context simultaneously. This process is called *"self-attention"* and weights the importance of these relations by numbers. Thus, transformers deliver a numerical matrix of weights ('attention') which represent the context of words. Therefore, even very complex linguistic structures can be identified to simulate the linguistic style of an author.

The weights of neural networks are used to predict future applications. For every input item, a scalar product of the queries is computed to generate a value for each item. These values are then utilized to determine a weight ('attention') for each input item, which contributes to the output of the self-attention mechanism. The current output is aligned through this self-attention process [35]. Additionally, ChatGPT's responses are refined with the user's intentions using *"reinforcement learning from human feedback"* (RLHF) algorithms. Ouyang L et al. [31] distinguish three distinct steps:

Step 1: Supervised Fine-Tuning (SFT) of the Model

In an early Chat-3 model a supervised training dataset is trained by 40 contractors. The inputs (prompts) are collected from entries into Open API. For each input (prompt), an appropriate response is delivered by labelers. In a SFT model, the followings steps are distinguished:

- A prompt is chosen from the prompt dataset, which consists of previously submitted API requests.
- Labelers provide examples of the desired output by writing responses to those prompts.
- This prompt–response pairs are then employed to fine-tune GPT-3 via supervised learning, training the model to generate appropriate replies to given instructions.

Step 2: Reward Model (RM)

Once the SFT model has been trained in the first step, it begins to generate responses that are more closely aligned with user prompts. The next enhancement involves developing a reward model, where the input consists of a series of prompts and corresponding responses, and the output is a scaler value known as a *"reward"*. This reward model is implemented through reinforcement learning allowing the model to learn how to derive outputs that maximize the reward in the third step.

In the second step data for comparison is gathered to trains the reward model:

- prompts and multiple outputs of model are selected, with responses generated by the SFT model.
- A labeler evaluates and ranks these outputs from best to worst.
- This ranking data is then utilized to train the reward model, with combinations of rankings provided to the model as a batch data point.

Step 3: Reinforcement Learning Model

In the last stage a response is returned to the initial prompt from step one. The used strategy is used in the second step by maximizing is reward. A scalar reward value is determined for the pair, consisting of the initial prompt and the related response. A policy is optimized with respect to rewards reinforcement learning with *"Proximal Policy Optimization"* (PPO). Standard methods using gradient policies only achieve one gradient update per data sample. PPO uses multiple epochs:

- From the dataset a new prompt is sampled.
- An output is generated from the policy.
- A reward for the output is calculated from the reward model.
- The policy is update using the reward.

3.5 Challenges of ChatGPT for societal policies

ChatGPT emergence has stirred concern across numerous domains – including daily life, media, communication, business, and healthcare, prompting widespread speculation about whether chatbots could one day displace professions in these areas [35]. Building on a foundational analysis of conversational agents, the next section evaluates ChatGPT's potential impact on specific occupational roles in real-world settings.

3.5.1 Example: ChatGPT as healthcare provider

AI research is opening up new methods of prevention, diagnosis and therapy in medicine, from assisted early detection of diseases to personalized treatments [32]. Current AI methods in medicine focus on the areas of knowledge-based systems, pattern analysis and pattern recognition as well as robotics. Classification systems support diagnostic imaging procedures in areas such as laboratory diagnostics, parasitology, radiology, pathology, cytology, dermatology and ophthalmology, as well as in minimally invasive surgery.

Knowledge-based systems date back to the beginnings of AI, when algorithms were used to derive solutions to problems (e.g., diagnosis) from a knowledge base (e.g., data and symptoms of diseases). In this sense, a specialized activity of a medical expert was simulated in a limited area of application. We therefore also speak of medical expert systems. From the point of view of computer science, the derivation of a diagnosis, for example, is realized by an algorithm, which is also referred to as an inference engine. The inference engine is programmed by entering knowledge.

The knowledge is represented declaratively. It consists of factual knowledge, as in a database, or rule knowledge in the form of symbolic production rules, according to which certain activities are to be carried out under certain conditions. As in symbolic logic, knowledge and problem solving are represented by derivations in computer programs. Knowledge-based systems in medicine are therefore an example of symbolic AI (see section 3.5.2).

Modern basic medical research is essentially based on molecular biological knowledge, which would no longer be possible without the support of bioinformatics. Bioinformatics is an interdisciplinary field of research that combines biology, computer science, mathematics and statistics with engineering. The focus is on algorithms and software that are used to analyze complex structures and functions of, for example, proteins from molecular data. This involves statistical pattern analysis and pattern recognition in huge amounts of data that can no longer be logically derived from a few premises. For this purpose, molecules must be represented in codes. The search methods for corresponding problem solutions and codes increasingly rely on machine learning methods, which are no longer orientated towards formal logic but towards statistical learning theory (see section 3.5.3).

With ChatGPT, AI has also arrived in the everyday medical routine of a doctor's practice or hospital. In principle, all text-based communication and data analysis can be taken over by medical chatbots that are trained using corresponding data sets. This may indeed lead to greater efficiency in patient communication between medical assistants. But how do medical diagnoses work with ChatGPT? Can we rely on diagnoses from a chatbot that we also use for other purposes in everyday life? This is where the first limits become apparent. Moreover, in the medical field, the issue ultimately revolves around accountability and liability, which cannot be transferred to a machine [35].

It is to be expected that medical chatbots will become better and better, trained by comprehensive data sets. Which doctor will then dare to give a different diagnosis to the suggestion of a highly specialized chatbot that has access to all the medical databases currently available for this application? Added to this is the time pressure in a doctor's surgery with many patient files to decide on.

As is generally the case with today's AI, the Achilles heel of modern machine learning is also evident here: all learning results depend on data extraction and therefore the quality of the chatbots' training data, which can be deliberately or unconsciously manipulated, erroneous and problematic. The huge amount of data used as a basis is not the only decisive factor. In the end, medical judgement is indispensable to make responsible diagnoses – no matter how highly specialized machine learning is.

3.5.2 Example: ChatGPT as lawyer

The same applies to legal issues in the healthcare sector, such as health insurance. Can we rely on the advice of ChatGPT? Will we end up communicating with a highly specialized legal chatbot rather than a clerk at the health insurance company when it comes to questions of care and pensions? Who bears the ultimate responsibility for such automated decisions? And that could be really dangerous.

The reasons are clear: the field of law particularly highlights the significant limitations of current chatbots. Legal language is highly complex and standardized, meaning that an answer that seems plausible and well-articulated to a layperson can be incorrect and misleading [35].

3.5.3 Potential and limitation of ChatGPT

Examinations with ChatGPT depend on the boundary conditions [33]. Sometimes spoken responses constitute only a portion of an assessment, as e.g. laboratory experiments, statistical analyses or programming tasks. Yet it must be acknowledged that reliance on chatbots can weaken one's ability to construct arguments and convey ideas in writing and oral presentations. Such communication skills are, for instance, vital for leadership roles within a company. Consequently, exams that fail to evaluate these competencies are of limited use to employers. It is therefore crucial to recognize the boundaries of chatbots assistance and call for alternative assessment formats, such as examination interviews [34,35].

3.6 Living guidelines of generative AI

As consequence of the insights in the potential and limitation of current AI, we should derive guidelines to handle generative AI. They are called "living" guidelines, because they must be permanently improved and adapted to the rapid progress of AI technology. These requests were published by a European committee of researchers in which the author of this article was involved as President of the European Academy of Sciences and Arts. The following is a summarized overview of the main requirements of these guidelines which are quoted from the "Living guidelines for generative AI" by Bouin et al. [36].

3.6.1 Guidelines for researchers as well as for reviewers and editors of scientific journals

1. Because the veracity of generative AI-generated output cannot be guaranteed, and sources cannot be reliably traced and credited, we always need human actors to take on the final responsibility for scientific output. This means that we need human verification for at least the following steps in the research process:
   - Interpretation of data analysis
   - Writing of manuscripts
   - Evaluating manuscripts (journal editors)
   - Peer review
   - Identifying research gaps
   - Formulating research aims
   - Developing hypotheses

2. Researchers should always acknowledge and specify for which tasks they have used generative AI in (scientific) research publications or presentations.
3. Researchers should acknowledge which generative AI tools (including which versions) they used in their work.
4. To adhere to open-science principles, researchers should preregister the use of generative AI in scientific research (such as which prompts, they will use) and make the input and output of generative AI tools available with the publication.
5. Researchers who have extensively used a generative AI tool in their work are recommended to replicate their findings with a different generative AI tool (if applicable).
6. Scientific journals should acknowledge their use of generative AI for peer review or selection purposes.
7. Scientific journals should ask reviewers to what extent they used generative AI for their review.

3.6.2 Guidelines for companies and developers of LLMs

8. Companies and developers of Generative AI models should make the details of the training data, training set-up and algorithms for large language models (LLMs) fully available to the independent scientific
organization that facilitates the development of an auditing body before launching it to society.
9. Companies and developers of Generative AI models should share ongoing adaptations, training data
collections and algorithms with the independent scientific auditing body.
10. The independent scientific auditing body as well as generative AI companies should have an internet
portal where users who discover biased or inaccurate responses can easily report them. Furthermore, the
independent scientific auditing body should have access to this portal and actions taken by the company.

3.6.3 Guidelines for funding organizations of research

11. Research (integrity) policies should adhere to the living guidelines.
12. Organizations which fund research should not (completely) rely on generative AI tools to evaluate
proposals of research but should always involve human assessment.
13. Organizations which fund research should always acknowledge their use of generative AI tools for
evaluating research proposals.

3.6.4 Set up a scientific body to audit AI systems

As mentioned in the "Living guidelines for generative AI" [36] an official organization
is required to assess the safety and validity of generative AI systems addressing issues
such bias and ethical issues in their application. This organization must possess adequate computing resources to operate full-scale models and have access to information
on source codes to evaluate how they were trained.

These benchmarks should be regularly updated by an auditing body. The certification of generative AI systems necessitates ongoing revision and adaptation due to
the rapid evolution of these systems based on user feedback and emerging concerns.
Questions regarding independence may arise when initiatives rely on funding by the
industry.

The auditing body should be function similarly to an international research institution. Given the significance of AI and ChatGPT in today's society, this international audit
body could be similar with the World Health Organization (WHO). The auditing body
should be interdisciplinary, comprising 5 to 10 research groups that include specialists
and experts in computer science, behavioral science, psychology, human rights, privacy,
law, ethics, science of science and philosophy. Collaborations with both public and private sectors should be fostered, while ensuring independence is upheld.

References

[1]   Mainzer K. (ed.). Philosophisches Handbuch Künstliche Intelligenz, Wiesbaden: Springer, 2024.

[2]   Turing A. M. Computing machinery and intelligence (1950). In: Turing AM, Intelligence Service. Schriften, Berlin 1987:147–182.

[3]   Robinson J. A. A machine-oriented logic based on the resolution principle, in: Journal of the Association for Computing Machinery 1965;12:23–41.

[4]   Biere A., Heule M., van Maaren H., Walsh T. (eds.). Handbook of Satisfiability. Amsterdam: IOS Press, 2009.

[5]   Küchlin W., Sinz C. Proving Consistency Assertions for Automotive Product Data Management. J. Automated Reasoning 2000;24:145–163.

[6]   Görz G., Schneeberger J. (eds.). Handbuch der Künstlichen Intelligenz. München: Oldenbourg, 4th edition 2003.

[7]   Mainzer K. KI – Künstliche Intelligenz. Grundlagen intelligenter Systeme. Darmstadt: Wissenschaftliche Buchgesellschaft, 2003.

[8]   Boersch I., Heinsohn J., Socher R. Wissensverarbeitung. Eine Einführung in die Künstliche Intelligenz für Informatiker und Ingenieure. Heidelberg: Springer, 2nd edition 2007.

[9]   Mainzer K. Computer – Neue Flügel des Geistes? Die Evolution computergestützter Technik, Wissenschaft, Kultur und Philosophie. Berlin, New York: De Gruyter, 1994.

[10] Puppe L. F. Einführung in Expertensysteme, Berlin: Springer, 1988.

[11] Weizenbaum J. ELIZA – A computer program for the study of natural language communication between man and machine, in: Communications of the Association for Computing Machinery 1965;9:36–45.

[12] Mainzer K. Künstliche Intelligenz – Wann übernehmen die Maschinen? Berlin/Heidelberg: Springer, 2019.

[13] Wahlster W. (ed.). Verbmobil: Foundations of Speech-to-Speech Translation. Berlin: Springer, 2000.

[14] Hausser R. Foundations of Computational Linguistics. Human-Computer Communication in Natural Language. Berlin: Springer 3rd edition, 2014.

[15] Chomsky N. Aspekte der Syntax-Theorie, Suhrkamp: Frankfurt, 1969.

[16] Ferrucci D. et al. Watson: Beyond Jeopardy! In: Artificial Intelligence 2013;199:93–105.

[17] Picard R. W. Affective Computing. Cambridge (Mass.): MIT Press, 1997.

[18] Minsky M. The Emotion Machine. Common Sense Thinking, Artificial Intelligence, and the Future of the Human Mind. New York: Simon & Schuster, 2006.

[19] Dreyfus H. L, Dreyfus S. E., (1986). Mind over Machine. The Power of Human Intuition and Expertise in the Era of the Computer. Oxford: Basil Blackwell, 1986

[20] Vapnik V. N. Statistical Learning Theory, New York: Wiley, 1998.

[21] Mainzer K. Artificial Intelligence. When do machines take over? Berlin: Springer 2nd edition (Chinese translation: Tsinghua University Press: Beijing 2022).

[22] Mainzer K. Gehirn, Computer, Komplexität. Berlin: Springer, 1997.

[23] Mainzer K. Leben als Maschine? Von der Systembiologie zur Robotik und künstlichen Intelligenz. Paderborn: Mentis, 2010.

[24] Ritter H., Martinetz T., Schulten K. Neuronale Netze. Eine Einführung in die Neuroinfomnatik selbstorganisierender Netzwerke. Bonn: Addison Wesley 1990.

[25] Kleene S. C. Representation of events in nerve nets and finite automata. In: Shannon C. E., McCarthy J. (eds.). Automata Studies, Princeton: Princeton University Press, 1956:3–41.

[26] Hopcroft J. E., Motwani R., Ullman J. Introduction to Automata Theory, Languages, and Computation. Addison Wesley, 3rd edition 2006.

[27] Siegelmann H. T. Sontag (ed.). On the computational power of neural nets, in: Journal of Computer and Systems Science 1995;50:132–150.

[28] Hornik K. et al. Multilayer feedforward networks are universal approximators, in: Neural Networks 1989;2(5):359–366.

[29] Mainzer K., Kahle R. Grenzen der Künstlichen Intelligenz – theoretisch, praktisch, ethisch. Berlin: Springer, 2022.

[30] Frieder S. et al. Mathematical Capabilities of ChatGPT, in: arXiv:2301.13867v1 [cs.LG] 32 Jan 2023.

[31] Ouyang L. et al. Training language models to follow instructions with human feedback, in: arXiv:2203,02155vl [cs.CL] 4 Mar 2022.

[32] Mainzer K. Machine Learning in der Medizin: Was können Lernalgorithmen und wie sicher sind sie? In: Pfannstiel M. (ed.). Künstliche Intelligenz im Gesundheitswesen. Springer Gabler: Wiesbaden, 2022.

[33] Gogoll J., Heckmann D., Pretscher A. Endlich neue Prüfungen dank ChatGPT, in: FAZ 20.3.2023 Nr. 67:18.

[34] Mainzer K. ChatGPT and Artificial Intelligence. From Foundations to Applications in Education, in: Peking University Education Review Journal 2023; 1 (Chinese).

[35] Mainzer K., Kahle R. Prospects for Hybrid AI. Chapter 5 of "Limits of AI – Theoretical, Practical, Ehical!" Mainzer K., Kahle R. (eds.). Spinger Berlin Heidelberg, 2024.

[36] Bouin O., Denis M., Zhenya Tsoy, Dhar V., Dijstelbloem H., Lahlou S., Donders Y., Ramos G., Mainzer K., Verbeek P. P. coordinated by Bockting C. Living guidelines for generative AI, in: Nature 23rd October 2023.

Nicolai Spicher, Sebastian Zaunseder

4 Biomedical engineering and artificial intelligence – a technical perspective

4.1 Introduction

This chapter tries to set the stage for this book by providing a general introduction to the field of Biomedical Engineering (BME, see Section 4.2.1) and the data which is used and generated in this field (Section 4.2.2). We will highlight the specific challenges, such as lack of accessibility, availability, and high heterogeneity of data, which need to be considered when planning the use of artificial intelligence (AI) methods. We also introduce some key concepts and taxonomies of AI (Section 4.2.3) to provide the reader with a solid foundation for this book. In section 4.3, we outline some existing and potential benefits of AI for BME. The chapter concludes with a discussion of potential challenges and ethical concerns (Section 4.4).

4.2 Definitions

4.2.1 Biomedical engineering

Due to its high degree of interdisciplinarity and rapid development, it is not trivial to find a short but complete definition of BME. In principle, concepts from the field of engineering are applied to solve problems in the fields of medicine and biology; therefore, biomedical engineers are involved in all steps of developing health technology.

The beginning of the 20th century marks the beginning of the field: In the year 1895 Willem Einthoven, a Dutch physician, invented the electrocardiography (ECG) device, while at the same time Wilhelm Conrad Röntgen discovered X-rays. Both received a Nobel Prize for their discoveries, Einthoven in Physiology in 1924, and Röntgen was awarded the first Nobel Prize in Physics in 1901. Therefore, both contributed significantly to the fields of physiological signal monitoring and medical imaging, which are applied nowadays in hospitals all over the world and enable physicians to gain insight into patient health. Around the same time other important inventions were made, e.g. in 1886, the Austrian Maximilan Nitze together with his colleague Joseph Leitner built the first working endoscope for visual inspection of the bladder and Scipione Riva-Rocci developed the mercury-based blood pressure cuff in 1896.

Besides physiological signal acquisition and biomedical imaging, many other research branches have been developed, which were realized by biomedical engineers. Examples include medical and healthcare robotics [1,2] for various use cases, implantable devices such as cardiac pacemakers, brain computer interfaces [3], cochlear implants, and artificial heart valves, or devices used during surgery such as ventilators and heart-lung machines. Rather novel areas of research which entered the field of BME are the development of biomaterials directly interacting with human tissue, wearable technology such as exoskeletons, nanomedicine or molecular medicine [4]. Throughout this book, the reader will find many examples of state-of-the-art BME technology.

Moreover, with the upcoming rise of digitalization, many related fields which are interwoven with BME have emerged, such as the fields of biomedical and health informatics as well as bioinformatics as well as biomedical data sciences or biomedical physics. Within all these fields, the development, application and evaluation of algorithms and software on medical or biological data is the focus of interest.

4.2.2 Data in biomedical engineering

At the heart of any AI system in the healthcare sector lies the concept of using patient-related data for solving a specific task. However, in the field of BME there are several challenges associated with the underlying data which need to be considered:
–   Diversity in Dimensions: The data in the large field of BME is diverse and available in different dimensions. For example, data might stem from a simple physical sensor measuring a certain value over time (1-dimensional temporal data $D(t)$), from a static X-ray image, e.g., acquired from the human chest (2-dimensional image data $D(x,y)$), or a fetal ultrasound during pregnancy, which is a spatio-temporal video sequence $D(x, y, t)$. Other modalities acquire data in even higher dimensions, e.g. dynamic cardiac CTs which generate $D(x, y, z, t)$ data. At the same time there exist substantial amounts of multimodal data being available from clinical systems which are either structured, i.e. following a classification such as the International Classification of Diseases (ICD), or unstructured text such as free-text reports.
–   Heterogeneity: Next to the diversity in data dimensions, medical data is highly heterogeneous. Even simple measurements such as the height or weight show a high level of variability between subjects. Moreover, while some statistical distributions in human nature follow a clear distribution, there are also many aspects that do not follow a simple statistical distribution, e.g., the incidence rates of certain cancers are bimodal, e.g. peaking around young age, then falling and rising again in higher age. Another source of heterogeneity lies in the fact that many measurements are not standardized, e.g., a certain examination in one clinical center might yield different results in another center due to the availability and use of different medical devices or levels of staff experience.
–   Amounts: Another issue is the amount of data available. On one hand, many fields have too little data – both with respect to amount and capacity –, hence making it difficult to have sufficient data to develop adequate AI models (see Section 4.2.3)

that capture the full heterogeneity of the underlying data, e.g., in the field of rare diseases. On the other hand, some fields have such large datasets that their sheer size makes them difficult to process (e.g. in the field of digital pathology with multi-scale whole-slide images with spatial resolutions of up to 100,000 x 100,000 pixels in various stains), requiring high-performance computing (HPC) clusters that are expensive and not ubiquitous available.

– Types: Another more practical and challenging issue when working with medical data is the lack of data standards. While in certain areas file formats have become the standard (e.g. Digital Imaging and Communications in Medicine (DICOM)) for the medical imaging domain, in other fields no standards or de-facto standards have been established. While in the last years, many open-source initiatives began working on open standards and large-scale biomedical data repositories, these oftentimes are isolated for specific fields of BME. This oftentimes requires extra effort in data normalization and harmonization before the actual work on an AI model can begin.

– Ownership and accessibility: BME research is oftentimes focusing on translation and clinical applications. However, a specific challenge when working with clinical data is the question of the data's ownership and accessibility. Due to legislatory frameworks such as the General Data Protection Regulation (GDPR), and national guidelines, access to this data is oftentimes a challenge in Europe.

– Correctness: Due to the above-mentioned high heterogeneity in medical data, it is oftentimes hard to provide accurate and correct labelled datasets as detection of outliers is time-consuming in heterogeneous data. Moreover, requesting experts to annotate and label datasets is expensive.

All these challenges underline the challenges for development of AI and ML approaches within BME due to the nature of the data itself. Nevertheless, in recent years, various initiatives have been trying to improve the situation, e.g. by suggesting the FAIR (Findability, Accessibility, Interoperability, Reuse) principles.

4.2.3 Artificial intelligence and machine learning

4.2.3.1 General remarks

AI, including the field of machine learning (ML) being regarded as subset, is a discipline in computer science dedicated to the development and usage of software that enables technical systems to perceive their environment and – by learning from the perceived data – take actions. Regarding notation, a single instance of AI for a specific task is entitled "model" M with a certain "input" I which is the processed data, and a certain "output" O, which is the result computed from the input: $O = M(I)$. Based on the output O, a certain action will then be initiated. For example, an AI-enhanced insulin pump could receive information I on the glucose levels from a sensor, process the data with the AI model M(I), and based on the model's output, O = M(I), the pump might be activated to deliver insulin.

Although there have been concepts that relate to today's understanding of AI, the history of AI in a narrower sense started in mid-20th century. In 1950, Alan Mathison Turing published a landmark paper entitled "Computer Machinery and Intelligence", which discussed machine intelligence and proposed a test for machine intelligence denoted as The Imitation Game (also known as "Turing test") [5]. The term artificial intelligence was first used 1955 by John McCarthy, when he proposed a workshop at Dartmouth College. The workshop took place one year later in 1956 and brought together important researchers in the field. This event, based on the so-called "Proposal for the Dartmouth Summer Research Project on Artificial Intelligence", has been considered the founding event of AI. Over the following decades until today, theoretical frameworks and multiple methods with respect to AI were developed. Taking artificial neural networks (ANNs) as an example and starting from the so-called perceptron, being a single layer neural network introduced by Frank Rosenblatt in 1958 [6], a multitude of architectures and associated processing methods evolved over decades and are still evolving. Of course, ANNs are a prominent representative, but by no means the only one., i.e. in parallel to ANNs multiple other strategies were developed.

However, the developments in the field of AI were by no means continuous. In fact, the decades from its beginning to date were characterized by transitions between AI booms, i.e. phases of rapid development, large funding and high interest, and so-called "AI winters", i.e. reduced funding and interest. Often AI winters were triggered by scientific statements, e.g. by Marvin Minsky's and Seymour Papert's book "Perceptrons" [7], that emphasized the limits of single layer perceptrons and lead to an instantaneous collapse of research activities in the field. However, even after winters, AI has always come back, and the current period can (still) be seen as a boom period.

4.2.3.2 Subfields of AI

Nowadays, a quite common categorization breaks AI down into relevant subfields (see Figure 4.1). For BME, the most important field is machine learning (ML), which is often divided into supervised and unsupervised learning. In supervised learning, annotated training data is available, i.e. input data D_i with associated annotated outcome data, the labels L_i. Based on this annotated data a model $M(D_i, L_i)$ is trained to predict previously unseen input data I. Supervised learning can then be divided further in classification and regression depending on the model output. In classification, the output is discretized in classes $c \in \{ \Omega_1, \Omega_2, ..., \Omega_N \}$, while in regression models a continuous number $c \in [-N, N]$ is the model's output. In unsupervised learning, no annotated training data is available, i.e. the input data is available, but it is unclear what would be the correct output for it.

Examples from cardiology for the application of Deep Neural Networks

Classification: In 2020 an AI model was published for detecting abnormalities in 12-lead ECG signals [8]. The model provides a boolean decision ("yes"/"no") if signs of ECG abnormalities such as a "first-degree atrioventricular block", "right-bundle branch block", "left-bundle branch block", "sinus bradycardia", "sinus tachycardia" or "atrial fibrillation" are detected in the input ECG. With reported F1 scores above 80% and specificity over 99% the proposed model outperforms cardiology resident medical doctors in recognizing these abnormalities. The model was trained on more than 2 million ECGs from a Brazilian telehealth network. Regression: von Bachmann et al. published a regression model that is able to predict electrolyte concentrations from 12-lead ECGs such as potassium, calcium, or sodium. For each input ECG, the target concentration [mmol/l] of the different electrolytes is predicted [9]. The model was trained on a dataset of over 290,000 ECGs across the four major electrolytes.

Notably, in many cases in healthcare, identical concepts and algorithms are applicable, e.g., support vector machines (SVMs) can be used for either classification (supervised ML) or clustering (unsupervised ML). Meanwhile another field has emerged, softening the rigid separation between supervised and unsupervised learning, namely self-supervised learning. It does not rely on previously labeled datasets but generates implicit labels from yet unlabeled data. One example is the prediction of words from preceding words with the former acting as a label. Self-supervised learning does not only bridge the gap between supervised and unsupervised learning, but it has also enabled a novel paradigm in ML, namely the so-called foundation models (FMs, see below).

Deep learning (DL), another class of ML techniques, has received immense attention from the research community and public over the last 15 years. The term "deep" refers to the large number of so-called "layers" (up to 200 and more) in architectures of ANNs. In fact, DL has opened many new opportunities for ML and justifies making it a subfield on its own as shown in Figure 4.1. DL supplements the variety of long existing ML methods like logistic regression, support vector machines, k-means, decision trees, ensembles and even "non-deep" ANNs.

Traditional ML methods are still widely used, and their future application can still be expected as they have key strengths, e.g., regarding their robustness and interpretability, the ability to be used with only small amounts of training data, or their low complexity with respect to computational power [10]. Especially, the lack of explainability in DL models is one major limitation in many fields, as the sheer number of parameters in DL models (easily over millions of parameters) prevents humans from getting meaningful insight into their underlying decision-making process. However, particularly through the ability to exploit contextual information, specialized DL architectures feature advantages for many applications. For example, deep convolutional neural networks (DCNNs) can handle spatial information, such as images or volumes, in a highly beneficial way. Also, different types of time-sequential deep learning architectures, such as long-short-term-memory (LSTM) networks, gated recurrent units (GRUs) or transformers, work quite well with data having sequential components, e.g. timeseries (e.g. ECG, EMG, EEG) or sentences (e.g. text documents).

With the growing importance of DL, a shift in the relevance of associated tasks for the human developer during model development can be observed. While for conventional and "non-deep" machine learning models, the tasks of feature engineering and feature selection by human developers was of utmost importance, both tasks have lost importance, as DL models are oftentimes so-called end-to-end models working with raw or only slightly preprocessed input data, and implicitly including all steps for data cleaning and data preparation into the model itself. Within the training of such end-to-end models by using a plethora of training data, the named tasks of feature engineering and feature selection have become completely redundant and obsolete, as they are implicitly solved by the (back-propagation) training approach, optimizing the parameters of the network model M automatically.

Within DL, generative AI can be considered its own subfield. Generative AI can produce text, images, videos, code or other data from natural language input, referred to as "the prompt". This offers completely novel opportunities for many aspects of daily life as the generation of such media now takes only seconds. Thereby, high implications can also be expected for BME development and research (as e.g. the generation of additional training data or clinical documentation and diagnostic reports) but at the current point these are not clearly visible yet.

Finally, foundation models (FM) deserve to be considered as they recently have changed the landscape of DL-based AI fundamentally. FMs are extremely huge artificial networks with billions of weights, which, eventually after fine tuning, can be used for a variety of tasks. Large language models (LLM) are the best-known examples, but FM do not necessarily relate to language only and can also be found for other types of data.

One drawback of FMs is that they have to be trained on huge amounts of data. As introduced in Section 4.2.2, oftentimes labelled data does not exist to the required extent, therefore FM are typically trained by self-supervised learning, i.e. using implicit labels from unlabeled data. FMs are sometimes considered a novel paradigm in the field of ML as they have set new standards in terms of emergence and homogenization [11]. Emergence hereby refers to complex behavior of models and, particularly, the ability to solve tasks on which a model was not trained explicitly. In fact, FM have shown this behavior, e.g., in affective computing tasks as emotions intensity ranking and toxicity detection [12]. Homogenization indicates the consolidation of methodologies for building ML systems across various applications. Today's FMs have introduced a high degree of homogenization, meaning that there are only a few FMs, which are widely used for many different tasks and within many AI systems. Famous examples of FMs are BERT [13], RoBERTa [14] and GPT-3 [15]. Their use in specific applications often incorporates an additional phase of fine-tuning which typically requires a smaller amount of labelled data. However, owing to the emergent behavior of FM, they sometimes work efficiently even without any fine-tuning.

Examples for foundation models in healthcare

FMs and LLMs have already found their way to healthcare applications [16]. For example, Menezes et al. used a GPT-4 model to extract the content of medical notes and demonstrated that it is working robustly in different languages [17]. Similarly, Chen et al. applied LLMs to respond to patient questions and reported that the quality of the generated content was in general "acceptable" and posed only a minimal risk of patient harm [18].

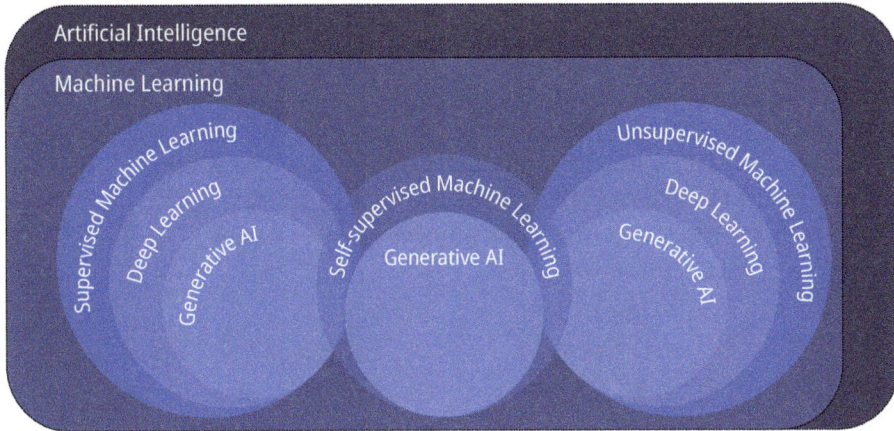

Fig. 4.1: AI Taxonomy: Notably, while DL has gained much attention in last years, supervised and unsupervised ML techniques feature multiple widely spread and well understood techniques, e.g. logistic regression, support vector machines, k-means, decision trees, ensembles and even "non-deep" neural networks. Self-supervised learning is somehow "in-between" supervised and unsupervised ML and essential part to foundation models as GPT.

4.2.3.3 Weak vs. strong AI

Another way to broadly categorize deep-learning-based AI is to distinguish between so-called weak AI and strong AI. A weak AI system usually focuses on a specific task, does not exhibit creativity, or can learn independently, but is able to learn by training from (huge) labeled datasets. A typical example of a weak AI system is the detection of lesions in an endoscopic video stream, which is a strictly defined task based on a specialized model, which cannot easily be used for something else. Strong AI, in turn, recognizes and defines complex tasks independently, has a certain problem awareness as well as "creativity," and expands based on knowledge across domains, i.e., from the application domain or through the transfer of knowledge from other domains. While for the last decade all available AI-based models obviously were related to weak AI, current solutions – based on LLMs – are already regarded as bordering on strong AI, owing to the emergent abilities of FMs. However, the impressive performance of such strong AI models completely relies on technical aspects, which relate to the model's complexity, massive amounts of annotated training data, and smart and efficient training approaches. Consequently, strong AI still is a theoretical concept with all currently available solutions being weak AI.

4.3 Benefits of artificial intelligence for biomedical engineering

The benefits of AI within BME are quite diverse. Obviously, AI with all its aspects can widely be applied and used in many novel devices and services in the medical and healthcare domain. Besides, AI also influences how research and development (R&D) as well as education in BME can be conducted. Below we try to illustrate AI's wide benefits by providing some examples for these application areas.

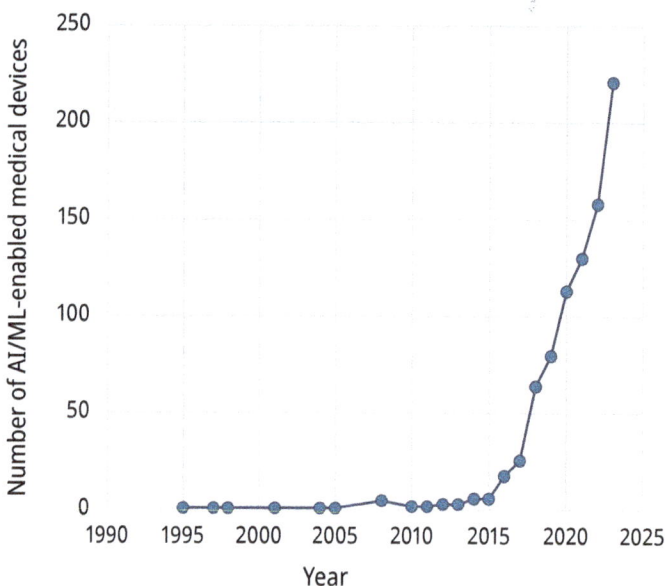

Fig. 4.2: Number of AI/ML-enabled medical devices authorized by the FDA from 1995 to 2023 (data obtained from [FDA][1]).

---

1 https://www.fda.gov/medical-devices/software-medical-device-samd/artificial-intelligence-and-machine-learning-aiml-enabled-medical-devices

AI usage in biomedical devices and services: Considering the R&D activities for novel devices and services in BME, AI plays a crucial role. When it comes to commercial devices and services, the use of AI is not yet common, but a drastic increase can be observed and is expected to continue. Fig. 4.2 displays the rapidly increasing number of AI/ML-enabled medical devices available.

In many cases, AI is used to enhance already existing medical devices or procedures, which often require human interactions. The integration of AI can make them more efficient. i.e. more accurate, better reproducible, or faster. Prominent examples are AI usage
– in radiology, e.g. for the prediction of risk for critical findings in head scans [19], lung cancer [20] or ischemic stroke lesions [21] or mortality prediction [22]. Many of these works demonstrate that the AI results are often faster and when it comes to accuracy en par with human experts [23]
– in patient monitoring, e.g., for the prediction of hypotensive crisis [24] or prediction of sepsis [25,26] and
– in robotics with multiple applications, e.g. therapeutic assistance, rehabilitation assistance or logistics [1,2,27]
Apart from that, AI can also be used to open completely novel devices and services.

AI in BME's research and development: In the evolving landscape of healthcare, R&D has high relevance for companies, universities and state agencies working in the field of BME. R&D covers various tasks and stages, e.g analysis stage, design/implementation stage, validation stage and revision stage. While, as described before, final products and services rely more and more on AI, AI also contributes to R&D itself and its associated tasks. Examples are AI based tools
– to find literature as Consensus [Consensus], Elicit [Elicit] and EvidenceHunt [EvidenceHunt] or connect literature as Litmaps [Litmaps], Open Knowledge Maps [OpenKnowledgeMaps] and Connected Paper [ConnectedPaper]. Fig. 4.3 shows, for example, an exemplary output of using Litmaps to show connections between papers.
– to support coding as GitHub Copilot [GitHubCopilot] and
– that can act as "virtual labs", e.g. AlphaFold 3, which is a diffusion-based network architecture [28], that can model interactions between proteins and other biological molecules as DNA, RNA, and ligands, efficiently and identify drug candidates [4]

AI in BME education: Due to its broad applicability, AI is also changing the way teaching and learning is performed on all levels of the educational system [31–33]. AI services are available for all involved groups from pupils to students to educators. Examples are AI
– AI chatbots and assistants that provide feedback on course content [34,35] and
– AI based tools that can act as troubleshooting guides in case of problems during solution of exercise [36] or during writing [37].

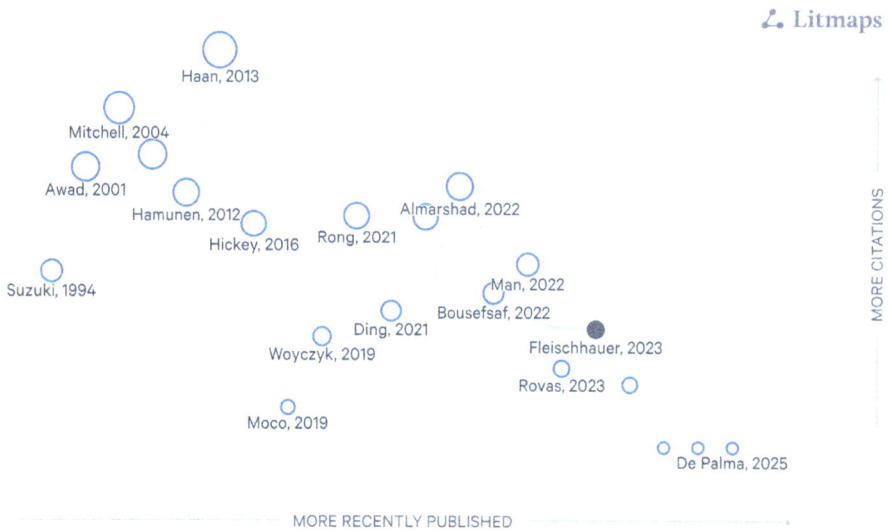

Fig. 4.3: The graphic shows an exemplary literature analysis using an interactive map generated by Litmaps [29]. In this example, the paper denoted as Fleischhauer 2023 [30] – displayed by the dark circle – served as input. The plot shows the resulting overview on associated papers. The interactive plot supports visualizing bibliographic details, further connections and customizations as well as extensions, respectively.

4.4 Limitations and ethical considerations of AI's use in BME

As shown by the examples before, AI is highly beneficial for BME and already has a large impact on real-world usage. However, there are certain limitations, legal issues, and ethical concerns to be considered when developing, implementing, and evaluating AI systems.

For example, when using AI methods in novel products and services, biases can occur, and fairness is not guaranteed [38]. This is mostly owing to the impact of training data, which is typically limited and often favors certain groups. Ensuring AI models are unbiased and equitable is crucial for ethical healthcare delivery but remains challenging [39]. Using FMs might help overcome limitations that arise from unsuitable or limited training data as FMs can be used in a variety of ways and they are trained on giant amounts of data. However, their training is typically not completely comprehensible for the public, as access to FMs is (often) restricted, they have shown to produce surprising results or even fail in certain situations.

Such situations may lead to novel challenges and ethical concerns, e.g. regarding the access to and hosting of FM and the impact of FM failure. Especially considering the increasing number of parameters of AI/FM models another issue occurs, which is missing explainability. While conventional ML models based on only a small number of parameters can be understood by experts, the decision-making process of large AI models becomes quite uncomprehensible for humans. Thereby, the output of a model for a certain input data cannot be explained by the model itself and the user has to accept the output without an explanation [40]. This is a fundamental problem, especially in medical applications where AI predictions, e.g., a diagnosis, have a direct impact on patient therapy.

References

[1] Pott P. P. Artificial Intelligence and Image-guided Interventions. In: Manzeschke A. and Wittenberg T. (eds.). Ethical Perspectives on Artificial Intelligence in Biomedical Engineering, Chapter 18, DeGruyter, 2025.

[2] Hagenah J., Henke M., Kubon M., Wittenberg T. AI-supported Robots in Healthcare. In: Manzeschke A. and Wittenberg T. (eds.). Ethical Perspectives on Artificial Intelligence in Biomedical Engineering, Chapter 17, DeGruyter, 2025.

[3] Rosahl S.K., Stieglitz T. Impact of Artificial Intelligence on Neural Implants. In: Manzeschke A. and Wittenberg T. (eds.). Ethical Perspectives on Artificial Intelligence in Biomedical Engineering, Chapter 17, DeGruyter, 2025.

[4] Álvarez-Mena A., Habenstein B. Artificial intelligence shaping a new era in molecular medicine. In: Manzeschke A. and Wittenberg T. (eds.). Ethical Perspectives on Artificial Intelligence in Biomedical Engineering, Chapter 24, DeGruyter, 2025.

[5] Turing A. M. "I. – COMPUTING MACHINERY AND INTELLIGENCE," Mind, vol. LIX, no. 236, pp. 433–460, Oct. 1950. https://doi.org/10.1093/mind/LIX.236.433.

[6] Rosenblatt, F. The Perceptron A Probabilistic Model for Information Storage and Organization in the Brain. Psychological Review, vol. 65, no. 386, 1958.

[7] Minsky M., Papert S. Perceptrons: An Introduction to Computational Geometry. MIT Press, Cambridge, MA, USA, (1969).

[8] Ribeiro A. H., Ribeiro M. H., Paixão G. M. M. et al. Automatic diagnosis of the 12-lead ECG using a deep neural network [published correction appears in Nat Commun. 2020 May 1;11(1):2227. https://doi.org/10.1038/s41467-020-16172-1]. Nat Commun. 2020;11(1):1760. Published 2020 Apr 9. https://doi.org/10.1038/s41467-020-15432-4.

[9] Bachmann P., Gedon D., Gustafsson F. K. et al. Evaluating regression and probabilistic methods for ECG-based electrolyte prediction. Sci Rep. 2024;14(1):15273. Published 2024 Jul 3. https://doi.org/10.1038/s41598-024-65223-w.

[10] Wöhrle H., Seidl K. AI and Edge / Embedded Devices for Healthcare. In: Manzeschke A and Wittenberg T. (eds.). Ethical Perspectives on Artificial Intelligence in Biomedical Engineering, Chapter 15, DeGruyter, 2025.

[11] Bommasani R. et al. "On the Opportunities and Risks of Foundation Models," pp. 1–214, 2021, [Online]. Available: http://arxiv.org/abs/2108.07258.

[12] Amin M. M., Mao R., Cambria E., and Schuller B. W. "A Wide Evaluation of ChatGPT on Affective Computing Tasks," IEEE Trans. Affect. Comput., vol. 15, no. 4, pp. 2204–2212, Oct. 2024. https://doi.org/10.1109/TAFFC.2024.3419593.

[13] Devlin, J., Chang, M. W., Lee, K., & Toutanova, K. BERT: Pre-training of Deep Bidirectional Transformers for Language Understanding. 2019, In Proceedings of NAACL-HLT (pp. 4171–4186). Available: arXiv:1810.04805.

[14] Liu Y., Ott M., Goyal N., Du J., Joshi M., Chen D., Levy O., Lewis M., Zettlemoyer L., Stoyanov V. RoBERTa: A robustly optimized BERT pretraining approach. 2019, Available: arXiv:1907.11692.

[15] Brown T. B. et al. Language models are few-shot learners. Advances in Neural Information Processing Systems, 2020, 33, 1877–1901. Available: arXiv:2005.14165.

[16] Thirunavukarasu A. J., Ting D. S. J., Elangovan K., Gutierrez L., Tan T. F., Ting D. S. W. Large language models in medicine. Nat Med. 2023;29(8):1930–1940. https://doi.org/10.1038/s41591-023-02448-8.

[17] Menezes M. C. S., Hoffmann A. F., Tan A. L. M. et al. The potential of Generative Pre-trained Transformer 4 (GPT-4) to analyse medical notes in three different languages: a retrospective model-evaluation study. Lancet Digit Health. 2025;7(1):e35-e43. https://doi.org/10.1016/S2589-7500(24)00246-2.

[18] Tang H., Chen X., Liu Y. et al. Clinically applicable deep learning framework for organs at risk delineation in CT images. Nat Mach Intell 2019; 1:480–491. https://doi.org/10.1038/s42256-019-0099-z.

[19] Chilamkurthy S., Ghosh R., Tanamala S. et al. Deep learning algorithms for detection of critical findings in head CT scans: a retrospective study. Lancet. 2018;392(10162):2388–2396. https://doi.org/10.1016/S0140-6736(18)31645-3.

[20] Ardila D., Kiraly A. P., Bharadwaj S. et al. End-to-end lung cancer screening with three-dimensional deep learning on low-dose chest computed tomography [published correction appears in Nat Med. 2019 Aug;25(8):1319. https://doi.org/10.1038/s41591-019-0536-x]. Nat Med. 2019;25(6):954–961. https://doi.org/10.1038/s41591-019-0447-x.

[21] Yu K. H., Beam A. L., Kohane I. S. Artificial intelligence in healthcare. Nat Biomed Eng. 2018;2(10):719–731. https://doi.org/10.1038/s41551-018-0305-z.

[22] Weiss J., Raghu V. K., Bontempi D. et al. Deep learning to estimate lung disease mortality from chest radiographs. Nat Commun. 2023;14(1):2797. Published 2023 May 16. https://doi.org/10.1038/s41467-023-37758-5.

[23] Liu X., Faes L., Kale A. U. et al. A comparison of deep learning performance against health-care professionals in detecting diseases from medical imaging: a systematic review and meta-analysis [published correction appears in Lancet Digit Health. 2019 Nov;1(7):e334. https://doi.org/10.1016/S2589-7500(19)30160-8]. Lancet Digit Health. 2019;1(6):e271-e297. https://doi.org/10.1016/S2589-7500(19)30123-2.

[24] Zhao A., Elgendi M., Menon C., Machine learning for predicting acute hypotension: A systematic review, Front. Cardiovasc. Med., vol. 9, 2022.

[25] Kausch S. L., Moorman J. R., Lake D. E., Keim-Malpass J., Physiological machine learning models for prediction of sepsis in hospitalized adults: An integrative review, Intensive Crit. Care Nurs., vol. 65, p. 103035, 2021.

[26] Bomrah S., Uddin M., Upadhyay U., Komorowski M., Priya J. DharE , Hsu SC, Syed-Abdul S. A scoping review of machine learning for sepsis prediction- feature engineering strategies and model performance: a step towards explainability, Crit. Care, vol. 28, no. 1, 2024.

[27] Li Y. et al. Advances in the Application of AI Robots in Critical Care: Scoping Review, J. Med. Internet Res., vol. 26, p. e54095, May 2024. https://doi.org/10.2196/54095.

[28] Abramson J. et al. Accurate structure prediction of biomolecular interactions with AlphaFold 3, Nature, vol. 630, no. 8016, pp. 493–500, 2024. https://doi.org/10.1038/s41586-024-07487-w.

[29] https://docs.litmaps.com/en/articles/10056342-how-should-i-attribute-or-cite-litmaps-in-my-work

[30] Fleischhauer V. et al. Photoplethysmography upon cold stress – impact of measurement site and acquisition mode, Frontiers in Physiology, 2023, 14(June), pp. 1–15. Available at: https://doi.org/10.3389/fphys.2023.1127624.

[31] Chen L., Chen P., Lin Z. Artificial Intelligence in Education: A Review. IEEE Access. 2020;8:75264–75278. https://doi.org/10.1109/ACCESS.2020.2988510.

[32] Kraft M., Morgenstern U., Seidl K., Schmitt T., Klatt F. AI for academic Learning and Teaching in Biomedical Engineering. In: Manzeschke A. and Wittenberg T. (eds.). Ethical Perspectives on Artificial Intelligence in Biomedical Engineering, Chapter 10, DeGruyter, 2025.

[33] Stracke C. Artificial Intelligence and Education (AI&ED). In: Manzeschke A and Wittenberg T. (eds.). Ethical Perspectives on Artificial Intelligence in Biomedical Engineering, Chapter 11, DeGruyter, 2025.

[34] Berrezueta-Guzman S., Parmacli I., Krusche S. and Wagner S. Interactive Learning in Computer Science Education Supported by a Discord Chatbot. In: 2024 IEEE 3rd German Education Conference (GECon), Munich, Germany, 2024, pp. 1–6. https://doi.org/10.1109/GECon62014.2024.10734012.

[35] McKern A., Mayer A., Greif L., Chardonnet J. R. and Ovtcharova J. AI-Based Interactive Digital Assistants for Virtual Reality in Educational Contexts. In: 2024 IEEE 3rd German Education Conference (GECon), Munich, Germany, 2024, pp. 1–5. https://doi.org/10.1109/GECon62014.2024.10734030.

[36] Kang K., Yang Y., Wu Y. et al. Integrating Large Language Models in Bioinformatics Education for Medical Students: Opportunities and Challenges. Ann Biomed Eng 2024:52:2311–2315. https://doi.org/10.1007/s10439-024-03554-5.

[37] Darvishi A., Khosravi H., Sadiq S., Gašević D. and Siemens G. Impact of AI assistance on student agency. Computers & Education. 2024;210(104967). https://doi.org/10.1016/j.compedu.2023.104967.

[38] Hammer B., Fairness in AI – how to design 'unbiased' algorithms?. In: Manzeschke A. and Wittenberg T. (eds.). Ethical Perspectives on Artificial Intelligence in Biomedical Engineering, Chapter 14, DeGruyter, 2025.

[39] Manzeschke A. Artificial Intelligence, Biomedical Engineering and Ethics. In: Manzeschke A. and Wittenberg T. (eds.). Ethical Perspectives on Artificial Intelligence in Biomedical Engineering, Chapter 5, DeGruyter, 2025.

[40] Fonck S., Stollenwerk A. "Explainable Artificial Intelligence in Biomedical Engineering" In: Manzeschke A. and Wittenberg T. (eds.). Ethical Perspectives on Artificial Intelligence in Biomedical Engineering, Chapter 13, DeGruyter, 2025.

Websites

Cardoso (https://opus.bibliothek.uni-augsburg.de/opus4/frontdoor/deliver/index/docId/113159/file/113159.pdf, 29.12.2024)

ChatGPT (https://chatgpt.com/, 29.12.2024)

ConnectedPaper (www.connectedpapers.com/, 29.12.2024)

Consensus (https://consensus.app/, 29.12.2024)

Crossref (www.crossref.org/, 29.12.2024)

Elicit (https://elicit.com/, 29.12.2024)

EvidenceHunt (https://evidencehunt.com/browse, 29.12.2024)

FDA (www.fda.gov/medical-devices/software-medical-device-samd/artificial-intelligence-and-machine-learning-aiml-enabled-medical-devices, 01.01.2025)

gemini (https://gemini.google.com/, 29.12.2024)

GitHubCopilot (https://github.com/features/copilot, 28.12.24)

humata (www.humata.ai/, 29.12.2024)

Litmaps (Litmaps (Version 2025-03-21) [Search tool]. https://app.litmaps.com/, 07.07.2025)

pubmed (https://pubmed.ncbi.nlm.nih.gov/, 29.12.2024)

OpenKnowledgeMaps (https://openknowledgemaps.org/, 29.12.2024)

SemanticScholar (www.semanticscholar.org/, 29.12.2024)

Arne Manzeschke
5 Ethical perspectives

5.1 Introduction

> There have been many debates on 'Computers and Mind'. What I conclude here is that the relevant issues are neither technological nor even mathematical; they are ethical. They cannot be settled by asking questions beginning with 'can'. The limits of the applicability of computers are ultimately statable only in terms of oughts. What emerges as the most elementary insight is that, since we do not have any ways of making computers wise, we ought not now to give computers tasks that demand wisdom. [1:227]

Joseph Weizenbaum has written these lines in 1976 – to put in pathetic terms: almost half a century ago – and I think that this is still the very crucial point when discussing the meaning of artificial intelligence (AI) in our social life. Anyone who has read the news and scholar's articles about AI and ethics since then can hardly avoid the impression that they have read something similar before. There are almost stereotypical introductions to the topic that point out the disruptive effect of the new technology on all areas of society, and from there demand and propose a weighing up of the risks and opportunities. It is by no means the case that all the arguments have already been formulated and sufficiently discussed. Nor can it be said that the debate has lost any of its dynamism and drama.

In my point of view, it will help a lot to address two core challenges in the debate of dealing with artificial intelligence. First, to focus on a specific application domain, e.g., biomedical engineering, in order to be as concrete as possible (contextualization). Second (generalization), not to forget the general perspective of AI as a somehow foundational structure for our social life [2]. It is indispensable to consider these two perspectives simultaneously. Although this may sound contradictory it will help to unfold a more precise and multifaceted picture of the problem we have to deal with – as I hope to show.

Before any material-ethical considerations are made here, we should first reflect on the prerequisites for doing so. These include the general contribution of ethics to the field (Section 5.2) and why it is indispensable in a more general view (Section 5.3) and in particular in BME (Section 5.4). Section 5.5 gives an overview of the current efforts to regulate AI in society and dives deeper into the specific challenges of it, followed by a brief elaboration on the question of long-term responsibilities (Section 5.6) and concluding remarks (Section 5.7)

5.2 Ethics: It could also be different

As Weizenbaum points out that the actually relevant questions regarding the use of AI are of an ethical nature, it is worth to briefly reflect on what is meant by ethics here. This is also necessary because, on the one hand, there are many prejudices and misconceptions about the subject and its performance, and because, on the other hand, different concepts and theories are associated with the terms ethics and morals within the profession itself. Without going too deeply into the subject matter, it should be noted that ethics is understood here as the (essentially scientific) reflection of morals. Morals, on the other hand, is the normative orientation of a group or society with regard to the good life for the individual and for the coexistence of the many different individuals. In the words of the philosopher of technology Gernot Böhme: Ethics is the reflection and deliberation of severe moral questions with wich it is decided what a human being is going to be in the way he or she experiences him- or herself and how he or she is able to live in society. Secondly, ethics must reflect and deliberate the question how human beings (and other animate beings) are going to live together in a just and flourishing way [cf. 2:21f.]. Propelling the ethical questions means seeking a social order that enables a good life for different living beings and their various life forms. Deciding on these questions means supporting one option and hindering others. Thus, ethics is not the moral cuddle of those who always look for the fly on the ointment, but rather, it is the critical reflection of our way of living, guided by the belief that a good and just life becomes more realistic the more we strive for it.

It is noteworthy that moral questions or propositions are not solely and not foremost posed by professional ethicists, but by those who are involved in research and development of technical artefacts. To give an example, Gerhard Hirzinger, one of the former top robotic researchers in Germany and former head of the German Space Agency, has formulated a strong moral claim concerning AI-based robotic assisted surgery in the coming future: "Robotics in general will massively change the face of surgery in the 21st century. However, it is not a question of what is often perceived as inhumane apparatus medicine, which prolongs life at all costs, for example, but solely of the goal of opening up completely new possibilities for surgeons and making operations safer and gentler than would have been unthinkable in the past." [3:2078] Here, Hirzinger objects an "inhumane apparatus medicine" and pledges for "new possibilities", for "safer operations" opened up by robotic surgery. This is not a purely technical calculation of benefits and harms, but an argument in favor for certain technical options from a moral position: Operations should be made safer and gentler for patients. Nihil nocere, do not harm!, as the physicians professional ethos proclaims. Inhumanity should be avoided from a thoughtless or purely economic stance. Ethics, as the reflection of moral positions will have to ask further, whether this claim is realistic at all and how the technical option could be concretized without causing unwanted side effects from a moral point of view; e.g., increasing inhumanity due to economic demands. Even more, ethical scrutiny of the socio-technical arrangement of robotic surgery will have to ask for long-term consequences and a broader set of people concerned: How will the relationship between physician and patient change, what does that mean for the respective professional ethos, will it have any impact on the skills of the physicians, what is the impact on the OR-team, their relationship and mode of interaction [4]?

The role of ethics is not to provide definitive instructions on how to evaluate, think and act in specific situations, but rather to organize and systematize moral issues in dialogue with all those involved, thereby offering orientation in forming judgements and making decisions. Ultimately, decisions for or against the use of technology are political in nature, even if they are – and should be – ethically oriented. In this sense, ethics is a specific way of perceiving and thinking about severe moral questions, it offers a disruption of conventions and routines how to life one's life and how to life together in a society. Ethics open up a space for different perspectives and alternative actions. It therefore creates a free space for thinking that things could be different. When talking about human beings as free of will and action, it is the ethical point of view which opens the floor for it.

5.3 There, actually, is a need for ethical reflection

Opening the floor for an ethical debate means that, ideally, all voices expressing moral concern should be heard and considered equally. As a rule of thumb for the deliberation of ethical issues it could be stated that it is always necessary whenever someone expresses moral concern. This may seem overwhelming for individuals as well as societies. Nonetheless, ethical deliberations concerning the impact of AI on the many facets of social life should be one of our top priorities. This is all the more true given that technological developments affect the very foundations of our societies in a non-trivial and non-causal relationship [5] and should therefore be carefully examined and shaped in accordance with the criteria of an equal, fair, inclusive, pluralistic and democratic social order. This connection was evident long before AI became more widely known to and used by the public, as illustrated by a quote from the political philosopher Langdon B. Winner. Winner was not concerned with artificial intelligence or digitalization per se, but rather with our social order, which is generally influenced by technology.

> The things we call 'technologies' are ways of building order in our world. Many technical devices and systems important in everyday life contain possibilities for many different ways of ordering human activity. Consciously or unconsciously, deliberately or inadvertently societies choose structures for technologies that influence how people are going to work, communicate, travel, consume and so forth over a very long time.[...] In that sense technological innovations are similar to legislative acts or political foundings that establish a framework for public order that will endure over many generations. [6:128f.]

The fact that there are also tendencies that run counter to this is all the more reason to reflect on developments in the field of AI not only in terms of specific applications but also in a comprehensive social dimension.

Upon closer examination of the changes caused by digitalization in general and AI in particular, there is a long list of topics that need to be addressed. The following points do not constitute a complete list and are not described in sufficient detail. Rather, at this point, it must suffice to convey an impression of the comprehensive and, in some cases, very subtle changes in our life forms ("Lebensform") and our life-world (Husserl: "Lebenswelt" [7]).

- Changes in the modes of communication and interaction between human beings
- New modes of communication and interaction between human beings and "intelligent systems"
- Changes in human beings' understanding of themselves and others, concerning, e.g., autonomy, intelligence, social interaction
- Uncertainty about the social, moral, and juridical status with regard to "ever more sophisticated intelligent systems"
- Getting informed via digital media – or being manipulated?
- System-related opacity of algorithmic results, including the consequences for our understanding of ethically relevant concepts like such as autonomy, decision, agency, responsibility
- Exclusion of individuals or groups by data- or algorithmic biases
- Automatization of work, including the consequences for employees and the welfare state [8]
- Monopoly formation in the field of digital service providers and the associated infrastructure

If AI is understood as a highly efficient method of processing information, it becomes clear that it could potentially affect almost every area of our daily lives. This is consistent with the fact that AI can be used in every field of science and technology. Furthermore, it is important to acknowledge that the invention, construction, and application of AI are partly very much interlinked with a specific techno-libertarian ideology that exploits the technology's disruptive nature to further its own agenda, making the whole issue highly political. Therefore, it would be an oversimplification of the ethical considerations to focus solely on AI as an information-enhancing technology. The disruption we are facing is rather a complex system of data-driven, digitized, highly networked and ubiquitous socio-technical arrangements. To paraphrase the philosopher of technology Gernot Böhme once again: The way we decide upon these arrangements and the shape we give to our society will determine who we are and how we live together.

Mustafa Suleyman, co-founder of Deep Mind and Inflection AI, played a key role in the development of Alpha Go, the (self-learning) AI that defeated Lee Sedol, the world's best Go player at the time, in a spectacular 4:1 victory in March 2016. He himself speaks of the need to contain the coming wave associated with the enormous power of AI. More precisely, he states that containment of the coming wave is the greatest dilemma of the 21st century, because there are a lot of good arguments and very strong incentives to continue on the same path while at the same time we run into severe problems with our eyes wide open.

In his book "The Coming Wave" [9] Suleyman outlines four defining characteristics of the next generation of transformative technologies, particularly AI and synthetic biology including genetics. These technologies will fundamentally reshape social, political, and economic structures. He identifies the following four core attributes:

1. Omnipresence: These technologies are expected to become ubiquitous, infiltrating virtually all domains of human activity – from personal life to global industry – and becoming deeply embedded in the infrastructures of society.
2. Autonomy: Increasingly, such systems will operate independently of direct human control. Through advanced forms of AI, machines will make decisions, learn, and adapt without constant human oversight, raising complex ethical and governance questions.
3. Capability Amplification: Emerging technologies will exponentially enhance the abilities of individuals and organizations. While this amplification offers enormous potential for innovation and progress, it simultaneously increases the risk of misuse and asymmetric power dynamics.
4. Self-replication: Many of these systems, particularly those based on open-source architectures or synthetic processes, possess the ability to replicate or propagate themselves without centralized control. This characteristic complicates regulation and containment, especially in scenarios involving malicious intent or unintended consequences.

Suleyman warns that these four features, taken together, represent not just a technological shift, but a profound governance challenge. Addressing them requires proactive policy development, ethical foresight, and international cooperation to mitigate risks while enabling innovation. He rightly highlights a dilemma facing our societies: the development of AI is driven by powerful interests and the desire to reap its rewards, but also by a reluctance to change our lifestyles substantially. A parallel to the currently world-wide challenge of climate change is likely to be based on more than just a coincidental similarity. However, we have now reached a level of dependence that makes withdrawing from this project seem futile. Current achievements and the prospect of further improvements, particularly in the healthcare sector, make pursuing further development seem imperative. Nevertheless, courses of action presented as having no alternatives always arouse skepticism among ethicists. 'No alternative' creates the impression that there is nothing to evaluate or decide upon. In contrast, ethics creates a space, at least intellectually, that allows us to consider more and different options than the one path that appears to be unalterable.

When even AI designers and CEOs of major AI companies warn against its ill-considered use and call for a moratorium on further development, this is more than just general unease about a socio-technical development. Here as well, strong moral claims are made: "Think of AI not as a tool, but as a new species – one that could surpass us in every area, outthink any human, run circles around our best defenses, and pursue goals that have zero overlap with human happiness, rights, justice, or survival." [10] One could call it moral self-defense. The enormous power of the invention must not be turned against its creator, nor must it endanger what people generally recognize and propagate as the highest moral good: happiness, reliability, and justice.

In March 2023, the German Science Media Centre published statements by several researchers in the fields of ethics and AI on this occasion and asked them to comment on current developments in the field of AI in general and on the call for a moratorium in particular [11]. Here, a synthesis of different perspectives and positions reveals something akin to an ethical discourse that does not jump immediately from a perception (AI will wipe out humanity) to a moral demand (A moratorium must be imposed).

At this point, we will not go into detail about singularity [12] as a not-too-distant future (Kurzweil had set his sights on 2045, but this date has since been postponed several times) in which these intelligent machines take over and we human beings must submit to them. In his latest book [13], Kurzweil claims that to merge with AI, eg., by neural implants, will be the only way not to submit to AI.Nevertheless, we consider this to be a distraction from currently more pressing issues. The realization of an Artificial General Intelligence (AGI) probably resulted more from our human complacency and intellectual laziness than from a technological evolutionary leap. Nonetheless, those spectacular announcements draw a lot of attention and energy, while actual, but less fancy developments are fundamentally changing our social, economic and political lives.

The political Philosopher Christoph Horn argues that there is a "particular urgency" to develop and apply an ethics of artificial intelligence [14]. The technology philosopher Armin Grunwald points out that we run the risk of cutting off our own future through AI-based forecasting techniques [15]. According to media philosopher Alexander Filipović, the danger is that a machine-readable world could become inaccessible to us because it remains closed off [16]. Ethicist Sabine Ammon emphasizes that AI applications are not neutral: "Rather, values are embedded in their development that will determine the affordances and limitations of their later use. By influencing the context in which they are used later on, AI systems have a normative effect." [17] A normative effect we should be aware of and therefore give a respective shape to these applications even in the early stage of research and development (R&D). These are just a few quotes to underpin the thesis that severe moral questions are at stake when looking at the impact of artificial intelligence on our lifeforms and lifeworld. As an interim conclusion, it can be said that, in addition to the effects in the area of specific applications, the use of AI must always take into account the overall social and political level and consider both levels together. As Kate Crawford, scholar of the social and political implications of artificial intelligence, sums up the task:

> We are at a critical juncture, one that requires us to ask hard questions about the way AI is produced and adopted. We need to ask: What is AI? What forms of politics does it propagate? Whose interests does it serve, and who bears the greatest risk of harm? And where should the use of AI be constrained? [...] This book argues that addressing the foundational problems of AI and planetary computation requires connecting issues of power and justice: from epistemology to labor rights, resource extraction to data protections, racial inequity to climate change. [18:20f.]

5.4 Threats of AI in biomedical technology demand – among other things – ethical responses

Biomedical technology allows for increasingly sophisticated analysis of, and intervention in, biophysical processes of the human body, from large-scale organ systems such as circulation, respiration, digestion, movement and sensory organs to increasingly small-scale elements such as tissues, cells, molecules, genes and proteins. Connections between the human organism and technical artefacts can be observed on three levels:
1) in the environment of the human body,
2) on the surface of the human body, and
3) inside the human body.

AI plays an increasingly important role at all three levels for example by evaluating signals (e.g. by using edge AI systems applied in or at the patient) that enable speech recognition and articulation, improve hearing with cochlear implants, or enable vision [19]. Another possible application is the creation of a so-called digital twin of a person whose data has been collected as comprehensively as possible, according to the assumption "that in all this data there are insights and knowledge that can bring benefits to patients through better diagnosis and more personalized treatments and drugs" [20]. Furthermore, AI can be used to better understand biochemical processes in the human body through simulation and to develop tailored drugs down to their protein folding [21]. The contributions collected in this volume impressively convey the transformative potential of AI in the field of biotechnology.

Nonetheless, these benefits come at a price, and this is a necessary topic for debate in a democratic society. Furthermore, the debate also concerns the risks associated with a digitalized, networked and intelligent infrastructure that is no longer under control of individuals as well as democratic societies to any great extent. In 2023 the European Union Agency for Cybersecurity (ENISA) issued a report "Identifying emerging cyber security threats and challenges for 2030" [22]. Very briefly summarized this report addresses, among other things, threats to individual health via behavioral or specific health data that "may be exploited or used by criminals to target individuals or by governments to control populations, e.g., using diseases [...] as a reason for discriminating against individuals. Genetic data may further be abused to aid law enforcement activities like predictive policing or to support a more regimented social credit system". [22:22] Besides these specific health data related threats, there are also more general – atmospheric – threats: "The public health issues arising from the mental health problems of victims of cybersecurity – With the increase of our data on the Internet and the increasing need to use online platforms and digital services, a state of exhaustion in the population could occur due to emerging cyber security gaps. Increasing cybersecurity challenges will lead to greater vulnerability of the general population, resulting in increasing public health risk from cybersecurity." [22:26] Some of these problems might be countered by edge AI solutions, where the captured data is directly processed in or at the patient, and will not be shared [23], but the general problem maintains that a data driven digitized world increases the vulnerability of those who depend on it for their very substantial life practices.

The increasing intervention directly inside the (human) body with digital implants "will change society in profound ways", as ENISA indicates: "Patterns of electrical activity in the brain can reveal a person's cognition. New methods to stimulate specific brain circuits can treat neurological and mental illnesses and control behavior. The ability to interrogate and manipulate electrical activity in the human brain promises the monitoring of electrical activity in the brain." [22:32] – for good or for worse.

We have not yet addressed issues such as simple calculation errors or the quality of the data used to train AI models, nor have we mentioned discrimination due to insufficient or poor data, discriminatory bias [24] caused by poorly programmed algorithms, or algorithmic hallucinations. To be clear, none of these issues are fundamental arguments against the use of AI in healthcare, but this list clarifies what challenges we face and that these can only be addressed by democratically controlled institutions and organizations.

The aforementioned issues represent only a small fraction of a much larger problem which must be addressed in different ways (i.e., sciences, humanities, social sciences) on different levels (i.e., individuals, organizations and enterprises, societies and global organizations) and with different incentives (i.e., legally, economically, ethically, technically).

5.5 Containment and regulation of artificial intelligence

There are a considerable number of papers, reports, frameworks and opinions dealing with the issue of AI with regard to its social impact. It is certainly too much to mention them all here. Instead, I will summarize some of the most notable reports in a table to provide an oversight of considered issues. Then, I will present two of these reports in more detail: the EU's High-Level Expert Group on AI (HLEG) [25–28] and the IEEE's Global Initiative for Ethically Aligned Design [29]. Andreas Lob-Hüdepohl's contribution to this volume [30] provides a third, more detailed analysis of the German Ethics Council's opinions [31,32]. This is not the place to discuss reports from the WHO [33], OECD [34], G7/G20 [35] and UNESCO [36] in detail here. However, even a cursory glance reveals that their intentions and guiding principles are very similar to those presented in more detail.

5.5.1 Oversight

Following Table 5.1 provides a brief list of important institutions that have commented on the ethical and juridical regulation of AI. It contains the respective institutions and the ethical guiding principles that they emphasize in their guidelines, reports or frameworks.

Tab. 5.1: Overview of some notable institutional reports and frameworks on AI.

Institution	Document / Initiative	Guiding Principles
EU High-Level Expert Group on AI (set up by the EU Commission)	*A Definition of AI: Main Capabilities and Disciplines (April 2019)*	
	Ethics Guidelines for Trustworthy AI (April 2019)	– ethical – robust – lawful Human-centric values: – Beneficence / Do "good" – Non-maleficence / Do "no harm" – Autonomy / Human agency – Justice & fairness – Transparency & explicability – Risk-based regulation – Prohibition of harmful practices – Multi-stakeholder inclusion – Governance, accountability, redress
	Policy and Investment Recommendations for Trustworthy AI (June 2019)	Trustworthy AI for Humans, Society and Environment by: – Human agency and oversight – Technical robustness and safety – Privacy and data governance – Transparency – Diversity, non-discrimination, and fairness – Societal and environmental well-being – Accountability

Tab. 5.1: Overview of some notable institutional reports (continued)

Institution	Document / Initiative	Guiding Principles
IEEE (Institute of Electrical and Electronics Engineers)	*Ethically Aligned Design. Version 2* (2019)	– Human well-being – Accountability – Transparency – Data privacy – Protection of human rights – Education and competence building
German Ethics Council	*Opinion: Man and Machine – Challenges Posed by AI* (2023)	– Human dignity and autonomy – Democracy and rule of law – Justice – Transparency and traceability – Responsibility and liability
WHO (World Health Organization)	*Ethics and Governance of Artificial Intelligence for Health* (2021)	– Protection of human rights – Transparency and explainability – Responsibility and accountability – Inclusiveness and equity – Promotion of well-being – Sustainability
OECD	*OECD Principles on Artificial Intelligence* (2019)	– Inclusive growth and sustainable development – Human-centered values and fairness – Transparency and explainability – Robustness, safety, and accountability – International cooperation
UNESCO	*Recommendation on the Ethics of Artificial Intelligence* (2021)	– Respect for human rights – Promotion of peace and equality – Data privacy and sovereignty – Transparency and explainability – Environmental and sustainability considerations
G7 / G20	*G7 Hiroshima AI Process / G20 AI Principles (2023) (living document; non-exhaustive list of guiding principles)*	– Rule of law – Inclusive economic development – Fairness – Safety – Interoperability of global standards

5.5.1.1 High Level Expert Group on AI

In April 2019, the EU's AI High-Level Expert Group (AI HLEG) published two papers. The first offers a definition of AI, providing a basis for any further work on the subject.

Artificial intelligence (AI) systems are software (and possibly also hardware) systems designed by humans that, given a complex goal, act in the physical or digital dimension by perceiving their environment through data acquisition, interpreting the collected structured or unstructured data, reasoning on the knowledge, or processing the information, derived from this data and deciding the best action(s) to take to achieve the given goal. AI systems can either use symbolic rules or learn a numeric model, and they can also adapt their behaviour by analysing how the environment is affected by their previous actions.

As a scientific discipline, AI includes several approaches and techniques, such as machine learning (of which deep learning and reinforcement learning are specific examples), machine reasoning (which includes planning, scheduling, knowledge representation and reasoning, search, and optimization), and robotics (which includes control, perception, sensors and actuators, as well as the integration of all other techniques into cyber-physical systems). [24:6]

The second paper, Ethics Guidelines for Trustworthy AI [26], sets out the ethical objectives and concluding key principles. The June 2019 report [27], the third deliverable by the EU's AI High-Level Expert Group (AI HLEG), presents thirty-three Policy and Investment Recommendations for Trustworthy AI aligned with the earlier April 2019 Ethics Guidelines. In July 2020, AI HLEG presented their final Assessment List for Trustworthy Artificial Intelligence [28]. The aim was to ensure that AI in Europe will be developed and used in a lawful, ethical and robust way that promotes trustworthy AI and benefits individuals and society. The four foundational principles of the Ethics paper [26] are rooted in the human rights.

1. Respect for Human Autonomy – AI should empower human decision-making, not reduce or manipulate it.
2. Prevention of Harm (Non-maleficence) – AI must not cause harm or lead to unsafe, unfair, or unintended outcomes.
3. Fairness – Avoid unjust bias and discrimination; ensure equal access and representation.
4. Explicability – AI systems should be transparent, explainable, and accountable.

These foundational principles are operationalized by seven key requirements for Trustworthy AI:
1. Human agency and oversight
2. Technical robustness and safety
3. Privacy and data governance
4. Transparency
5. Diversity, non-discrimination, and fairness
6. Societal and environmental well-being
7. Accountability

As in other reports, this one presents the idea of 'embedded ethics', i.e., that ethics is not an afterthought, but a core part of the research, deployment and governance of AI systems. This idea is promoted quite prominently in programs such as Responsible

Research and Innovation [37], Value-Based or Value Sensitive Design [38–40] Ethical, Legal, and Social Implications (ELSI) [41,42], and Integrated Research [43]. The requirement to consider ethics from the outset of every project stems from the realization that dividing the work into sequential stages – first research and development, then ethical evaluation – no longer does justice to the complexity of the tasks involved. The German Society for Biomedical Engineering (Deutsche Gesellschaft für Biomedizinische Technik, DGBMT) addressed a further related issue in a White Paper on Digital Sovereignty:

> The entire value chain process from research to application shall comply with ethical principles. Different domain ethics can be distinguished along this chain: Research, technical, economic and business ethics, ethics of medicine and nursing care. Despite the importance of these specialized perspectives, it may not be ignored that the ethical questions as such are general questions which can be differentiated in terms of domain ethics, but which shall not lead to a diffusion of responsibility through such a form of 'division of labor'. [44:39]

The EU's policy and investment recommendations are aligned with the earlier April 2019 Ethics Guidelines for Trustworthy AI. Its focus is to promote sustainable, inclusive, and competitive AI across Europe – empowering and safeguarding individuals while strengthening industry, public sector, research, infrastructure, skills, governance, and funding. The recommendations are structured around certain priority areas: improving human and societal welfare, innovation in the private sector, public sector adoption, research excellence, data & infrastructure, education, governance frameworks, and investment strategies. This report was intended to inform the EU's Coordinated Plan on AI, helping shape future EU policy actions. From an ethical point of view, the recommendations build on foundational trustworthiness pillars. i.e.:

- Human-centric ethics: Grounded in respect for individuals, fundamental rights, fairness, autonomy, and wellbeing—reflecting the Ethical Guidelines' focus on principles like beneficence, non-maleficence, autonomy, justice, and explicability.
- Protection and empowerment: Ensuring that AI protects humans from harm (physical, psychological, societal, environmental), supports informed agency, and does not undermine dignity or equality.
- Proportional risk-based regulation: Ethically, high-risk AI systems must face stringent safeguards; while lower-risk AI should follow lighter, voluntary standards–promoting both safety and innovation.
- Transparency and accountability: Recommending clear insight into AI logic, data usage, decision processes, and offering redress–all vital for ethical legitimacy.
- Inclusivity and fairness: Avoiding bias, enabling accessibility, and involving diverse stakeholders in design and deployment.
- Governance by red lines: Banning or limiting ethically unacceptable applications (e.g., mass surveillance, biometric tracking, mass scoring, lethal autonomous weapons) and embedding ethics into policy and investment frameworks.

– Collaborative ecosystems: Ethically aligning industry, academia, public sector, and civil society through multi-stakeholder alliances ensures shared values guide AI progress.

5.5.1.2 IEEE recommendations

The IEEE started a "Global Initiative on Ethics of Autonomous and Intelligent System" in December 2016 with a first version of a paper on ethical aligned design which was followed by a second version in April 2017. Both papers aimed to stimulate a public discussion in order to "bring together multiple voices from the related scientific and engineering communities with the general public to identify and find broad consensus on pressing ethical and social issues and candidate recommendations regarding development and implementations of these technologies" [28:2]. The initiative considers Autonomous and Intelligent Systems (A/IS), "regardless of whether they are physical robots (such as care robots or driverless cars) or software systems (such as medical diagnosis systems, intelligent personal assistants, or algorithmic chat bots)." 28:20] The paper very clearly states that ethics is one of the core disciplines to align R&D processes for AI with human rights:

> We are motivated by a desire to create ethical principles for A/IS that:
> 1. Embody the highest ideals of human beneficence as a superset of Human Rights.
> 2. Prioritize benefits to humanity and the natural environment from the use of A/IS. Note that these should not be at odds – one depends on the other. Prioritizing human well-being does not mean degrading the environment.
> 3. Mitigate risks and negative impacts, including misuse, as A/IS evolve as socio-technical systems. In particular by ensuring A/IS are accountable and transparent. [28:20]

The process was reiterated and reconsolidated in 2023 aiming to "inspire a new paradigm for AI governance that shifts from merely mitigating risks to proactively embedding a 'Safety First Principle' and 'Safety by Design' into AI's design and lifecycle assessments, as well as in the development of generative AI models from the outset. This paradigm shift challenges the risk-centric." [44]. Therefore, five general principles were candidated:
1. Prioritizing Human Rights
2. Prioritizing Well-being
3. Accountability
4. Transparency
5. A/IS Technology Misuse and Awareness of IT

These five principles are put into practice by "embedding values in autonomous intelligent systems". Here, too, we find what the IEEE refers to as "promoting ethics and safety by design" [44]. This shift in governance is shared with many other institutions and will influence current and future debates on ethics and AI.

5.5.2 Working with the principles

The overarching guiding principles in these reports are human rights, human wellbeing, protection of the environment and the rule of law. Under these principles, core moral concerns are articulated that can be categorized as follows: Table 5.1 above lists in the third column thirty-seven different terms, some of which appear to be different terms for essentially the same concept, such as equality (UNESCO) and equity (WHO), or explicability (HLEG) and explainability (WHO, OECD, etc.). The term technical robustness (EU, OECD, HLEG) can also be assumed to overlap to a certain extent with safety (EU, OECD, G7/G20), and so on. Counting the explicit mentions of terms and their related terms found in the various reports reveals that accountability and transparency are mentioned most frequently, followed by fairness, explainability, and privacy. Unsurprisingly, accountability and transparency top the list due to the human need to understand the results of AI calculations that inform and guide decisions and actions. The other keywords also demonstrate their validity given the recognized need to ensure fair outcomes from AI calculations or for respecting the dignity of a person. Alarming news about the discriminatory consequences of AI use in police work and the healthcare sector explains why there is an expectation of fair algorithms and fair treatment of different individuals and groups. What is really challenging is how to operationalize these guiding principles into practice. In addition to legal procedures [46–48] every socio-technical system must be thoroughly inspected and interpreted in order to evaluate what moral claims such as autonomy, dignity and equality would mean for the various people involved. This counts as well for anticipatory design as for retrospective reconstruction of an existing system. Reflecting on the moral dimensions and ethical sensitivity of socio-technical interactions, as well as the different levels of involvement (as an individual, organization or society as a whole), is essential. Furthermore, it is a fundamental prerequisite of such a structured reflection on ethical issues that the teams and organizations which are accountable for a project, be it a R&D project or marketing a product, are in charge of forming judgements and making decisions based on these judgements within the project framework. For example, MEESTAR (Model for Ethical Evaluation of Socio-Technical ARrangement) [49] has served in more than fifty R&D projects as a tool for respective reflections and decision making. Hereby, the role of professional ethics is not to establish specific moral standards, but to facilitate and encourage discussion within the project team using distinctions, ethical concepts and ongoing debates. This work should be accompanied by thorough clarification of the terms and images that guide one's thinking. For example, many metaphors are used in the field of AI, not all of which are suitable for real life [50]. The same applies to pictures and images. [51]

5.5.3 Trustworthiness and its anthropological precondition

Even descriptive expressions like 'transparency' turn out to be anything but clear, and we would just like to illustrate the rather more complex situation at hand of this guiding principle. It is a common claim that transparency of AI systems will increase the trust in and the acceptance of technology. Therefore, transparency should be achieved by explainable AI (xAI), a procedure that turns the opaque black box of self-learning algorithms into a transparent white box. As Hacker & Passoth demonstrate with their "overview of legal obligations to explain AI and evaluate current policy proposals" [52], there are many different modes of transparency. Furthermore, it is quite disputable what will count as an explanation for whom in which context. Contrary to the presumption that transparency will lead to trust, I believe that we should take into consideration that, in a very fundamental sense, trust is a matter of social relations and of ethics as a mode of reflecting and shaping these relations. Therefore, it is not that evident that transparency will lead to trust, or that transparent and xAI is the basis for trustworthiness. A closer look at the issue shows that the adherence to general appreciated guiding principles requires much more intellectual work than simply applying them.

Finally, ethics plays a broader role than mere moderation, enabling project managers to recognize the implications of their research, development or application within the context of individual lifestyles and social orders, and to shape these in accordance with moral principles. This is by no means a trivial task, involving a cost-benefit analysis that is as precise and comprehensive as possible – although this is also part of it. However, more importantly, it is necessary to determine how to treat the individuals affected by such socio-technical interactions fairly, while also striving for or maintaining a social order that aligns with the aforementioned ethical principles.

5.6 How can we know? – long term responsibility

The envisaged transformations in individual and societal life can be summarized anthropologically in two terms that express the ambivalence of the process: empowerment and incapacitation [53]. Empowerment refers to the expansion of human agency. Technical achievements such as AI or robotic as well as the coupling of humans and technology in interactions or collaborations open up new possibilities for action and improve existing ones. At the same time, however, this capacity or possibility for action can only be realized through interaction with technology that is partly autonomous and intelligent in its own right. Unlike in earlier eras, humans now are not merely users of technology; they act alongside it. However, this also involves the incapacitation of humans in these socio-technical alliances. They no longer determine the goals of their actions alone, nor do they choose the means to achieve those goals alone – this is partly up to the technical system. What does that mean in terms of

–   evaluating a problem based on digital data and real life experience,
–   decision making in interaction with an AI system,
–   being responsible for the actions taken – to what extent and who else?

This is the very part of ethical deliberation where one has to ask oneself these questions seriously. In doing so, the connection of knowledge and responsibility becomes evident:

> We are becoming increasingly aware of the long-term risks associated with our current actions and omissions, and of possible alternative courses of action. The greater our knowledge of potential long-term damage and the more numerous the possibilities for avoiding it, the greater the pressure of future responsibility on human actions and omissions. [...] Knowledge and responsibility are linked and equally irreversible. They are two sides of the same lost innocence. [54:13]

Establishing technical infrastructure like AI systems is a political issue connected to long term consequences and long term responsibilities [6]. While previous generations may have been less rational in implementing restrictions on their own actions for the sake of long-term preservation of resources and life chances, we are now faced with the problem of only being able to communicate such regulations rationally. What is considered rational is conveyed not least through the technology we are considering using: artificial intelligence. The recursive moment in relation to AI is probably the following: We use AI as a forecasting tool to gain an idea of what the future with AI will look like or how it should be shaped. We are looking for a long-term responsibility for the use of AI while using AI. "But how can one decide in the present who will be proven right in the future? We perform the role of prophets without their gift." Arthur Koestler got to the heart of it in his critique of Stalinist planning mania. [55]. Looking at the current situation we should draw this position even more sharply. We delegate or shift the role of prophecy to a technical system created by us, hence echoing the satirical spirit of The Hitchhiker's Guide to the Galaxy by Douglas Adams [56]. This shift might, under certain circumstances, merely confirm our own prejudices or expectations in a completely unprophetic way. Alternatively, and it is unclear whether this would be worse, a technical oracle could provide instructions that are either unsuitable for the future and lead us astray, or suitable for the future and lead us towards a desirable outcome. However, the problem for us humans is that we do not know how to distinguish between these two options, which would ultimately amount to a lottery instead of us taking responsibility for our own future, as well as the future of other generations and life forms, by making rational plans. The paradox of the situation can be summarized as follows: Despite the demand for rationality regarding our future and despite the use of a highly rational tool, the decision we are looking for may – to a larger extent – depend on non-rational elements.

5.7 Concluding remarks

"We are technomoral creatures to the core; that is, we allow and have always allowed the things we make to reshape us. The only question is whether this process is deliberate and wise or unreflective and reckless." [57] Using AI will reshape us humans. Following this quote by Vallor, this effect is more an issue of deliberation and wisdom than one of morally good or bad. I think this is a crucial point. Before we judge specific applications to be good or bad, we should know what we are doing and whether we really want them.

"But if we can save lives with AI technology" is one objection to the above considerations that sometimes are dismissed as mere academic gamesmanship. At first sight this may be true, but as I hope to show, even undoubted helpful AI applications process sensitive personal data and thus contributing to a public and politically pressing issue. How can we ensure that data is only used for its intended purpose? This is more a political than a technical question, and thus one of regulation or containment. To answer this, we need ethical discourse to inform decisions that align with our moral convictions. This approach is even the more necessary given that projects are currently being initiated which use AI technology to undermine democratic processes and enforce the law of the strongest. More than ever, technology is political, and the ethical reflection on AI as a technology must not allow us to forget, that seemingly clean and well-meaning technological applications have their broader context being decisive for their assessment.

How can we as a society embrace technological progress? In the sense that members of a society can jointly and fairly weigh up and decide on their individual and communal way of life. We are currently at a crossroads that requires a reorganization of our social coexistence, which on the one hand is oriented towards the conditions of a digitized, technologically interwoven [58] order. At the same time, this order must be shaped according to our own ideas. This 'at the same time' should not obscure the fact that we are dealing with asynchronies in the sense of different speeds. Powerful short-term interests could block the wiser long-term paths and thus delay or render obsolete important decisions.

On the one hand, current political developments and power relations do not suggest that the less powerful states and communities will have much of a say in these issues, which undoubtedly affect them in a significant way. On the other hand, there is a growing imbalance between so-called democratic welfare states and technical-political efforts to reduce the state as such to an absolute minimum, thereby also depriving those who do not have the technical or economic power or even the unscrupulousness to make themselves heard of political participation.

As long as questions of sovereignty over infrastructure and algorithms are not addressed, the demand for an active framework for AI that is guided by our own values will remain ineffective and cheap. In line with this point, the situation reveals AI – beyond its technical construction – to be a social projection that sheds light on the future with different connotations to which our individual and social attitudes attach themselves. In his sociological study, 'Technology as Consolation' [59], Stefan Selke identified four basic types of such projections, namely 1) adaptive narratives, 2) quest narratives, 3) departure narratives, and 4) disaster narratives. This again underpins the non-rational side of the discourse we have to be aware of. Furthermore, we have to be aware of all the phenomena that are not of digital nature or cannot be digitized. We must not leave them behind on the pace to a more digitized world. A memento Weizenbaum mentioned very early:

> A theory is, of course, itself a conceptual framework. And so it determines what is and what is not to count as fact. The theories – or perhaps better said, the root metaphors – that have hypnotized the artificial intelligentsia, and large segments of the general public as well, have long ago determined that life is what is computable and only that. [1:200]

Every life is more than what is computable. What sounds so trivial, is a great challenge for our adaption to an increasingly technological environment. How can we know which characteristics should prevail and which can be left behind? Ultimately, it is our human intelligence that must answer such questions. As Hans Blumenberg put it, intelligence is the ability of human beings to adapt to the dangers they face through the technical design of their living environment [60:577]. This leaves us with a question to answer. Exploring this question through the lens of ethics promises to be one of the most profound and far-reaching ways of exploring it.

References

[1]   Weizenbaum J. Computer Power and Human Reason. From Judgement to Calculation. San Francisco: W. H. Freeman and Company, 1976.
[2]   Böhme G. Ethik leiblicher Existenz. Frankfurt am Main: Suhrkamp, 2008.
[3]   Hirzinger G. Maschinengestütztes Operieren, Mechatronik und Robotik. In: Wintermantel E, Ha S.-W. (eds.). Medizintechnik. Life Science Engineering, Berlin/Heidelberg: Springer 5th rev. ed. 2009, S. 2071–2078.
[4]   Steil J., Finas D., Beck S., Manzeschke A., Haux R. Robotic Systems in Operating Theaters: New Forms of Team-Machine Interaction in Health Care. On Challenges for Health Information Systems on Adequately Considering Hybrid Action of Humans and Machines. In: Methods of Information in Medicine, Vol. 58 No. S1/2019, e14–e25. https://doi.org/10.1055/s-0039-1692465.
[5]   Hofman J., Iglesias Keller C. Machine Learning, Political Participation and the Transformation of Democratic Self-Determination. In: Heinlein M., Huchler N. (eds.). Artificial Intelligence in Society. Social, Political and Cultural Implications of a Technological Innovation. Wiesbaden: Springer VS, 2024, 283–306.
[6]   Winner L. Do artefacts have politics? In: Daedalus 109 (1980): 121–136.
[7]   Husserl E. Die Krisis der europäischen Wissenschaften und die transzendentale Phänomenologie. Eine Einleitung in die phänomenologische Philosophie. 2nd ed. Den Haag: Martinus Nijhoff, 1938/1976.
[8]   Manzeschke A., Brink A. Ethics of Digitalization in Industry. In: Frenz W. (ed.). Handbook Industry 4.0: Law, Technology, Society, Berlin und Heidelberg: Springer, 2022, 903–923.

[9] Suleyman M., Bhaskar M. The coming wave. AI, power, and the 21st century's greatest dilemma. London: Crown/Penguin Random House 2023.

[10] AI moratorium is necessary to avoid extinction (Accessed July 19, 2025, at https://moratorium.ai/).

[11] Science Media Center Germany. Risiken aktueller KI-Forschung (Accessed July 19, 2025, at https://www.sciencemediacenter.de/angebote/23048).

[12] Kurzweil R. The Singularity is near: When Humans transcend Biology. New York: Viking Press, 2005.

[13] Kurzweil R. The Singularity is nearer: When we merge with AI. New York: Penguin Books, 2024.

[14] Horn C. Zur Dringlichkeit einer Ethik der Künstlichen Intelligenz. In: Barth M, Hoff G. M. (eds.). Digitale Welt – Künstliche Intelligenz – Ethische Herausforderungen. Baden-Baden: Karl Alber, 2023, 15–31.

[15] Grunwald A. Der homo temporalis im digitalen Wandel. In: Barth M, Hoff G. M. (eds.). Digitale Welt – Künstliche Intelligenz – Ethische Herausforderungen. Baden-Baden: Karl Alber, 2023, 123–143.

[16] Filipović A. "Maschinenlesbarkeit der Welt". Zum Zusammenhang von Wissen, Tun und Hoffen im Kontext digitaler Technologie. In: Helmus C., Riedl A. M. (eds.). Theologie und Technik. Eine interdisziplinäre Zwischenbilanz. Freiburg/Basel/Wien: Herder 2024, 103–121.

[17] Ammon S. Ethics by Design in Forschung und Entwicklung von Künstlicher Intelligenz. In: Berlin-Brandenburgische Akademie der Wissenschaften (BBAW) (ed.). Verantwortungsvoller Einsatz von KI? Mit menschlicher Kompetenz. Berlin, 2021, 41–47.

[18] Crawford, K. Atlas of AI. Power, Politics and the Planetary Costs of Artificial Intelligence. Yale University Press. 2021.

[19] Rosahl/Stieglitz in this volume.

[20] Wesarg/Kohlhammer in this volume.

[21] Mena-Alvarez/Habenstein in this volume.

[22] ENISA (European Union Agency for Cybersecurity). Identifying emerging cyber security threats and challenges for 2030. Bruxelles 2023. https://doi.org/10.2824/117542.

[23] Seidl/Wöhrle in this volume.

[24] Pahl J., Rieger I., Möller A., Wittenberg T., Schmid U. Female, white, 27? Bias Evaluation on Data and Algorithms for Affect Recognition in Faces. Procs' 2022 ACM Conference on Fairness, Accountability, and Transparency (ACM FAccT 2022):973–987. https://doi.org/10.1145/3531146.3533159.

[25] HLEG AI (High Level Expert Group on AI). A Definition AI. Main Capabilities and Disciplines. Bruxelles 2019. (Accessed July 19, 2025, at https://www.europarl.europa.eu/cmsdata/196377/AI%20 HLEG_Ethics%20Guidelines%20for%20Trustworthy%20AI.pdf).

[26] HLEG AI (High Level Expert Group on AI). Ethics Guidelines for Trustworthy AI. Bruxelles 2019. (Accessed July 19, 2025, at https://www.europarl.europa.eu/cmsdata/196377/AI%20HLEG_Ethics%20 Guidelines%20for%20Trustworthy%20AI.pdf).

[27] HLEG AI (High Level Expert Group on AI). Policy and Investment for Trustworthy Artificial Intelligence I. Bruxelles 2019. (Accessed July 19, 2025, at https://digital-strategy.ec.europa.eu/en/library/policy-and-investment-recommendations-trustworthy-artificial-intelligence).

[28] HLEG AI (High Level Expert Group on AI). Assessment List for Trustworthy Artificial Intelligence (ALTAI) for self-assessment; Assessment List for Trustworthy Artificial Intelligence (ALTAI) for self-assessment. (Accessed July 19, 2025, at https://digital-strategy.ec.europa.eu/en/library/assessment-list-trustworthy-artificial-intelligence-altai-self-assessment).

[29] IEEE: The IEEE Global Initiative on Ethics of Autonomous and Intelligent Systems. Ethically Aligned Design: A Vision for Prioritizing Human Well-being with Autonomous and Intelligent Systems, Version 2. IEEE, 2017. (Accessed July 19, 2025, at https://standards.ieee.org/industry-connections/activities/ieee-global-initiative/).

[30] Lob-Hüdepohl in this volume.

[31] German Ethics Council. Mensch und Maschine – Herausforderungen durch Künstliche Intelligenz. Stellungnahme. Berlin, 2023. To date, this opinion is issued only in German Version. An English

Summary is published under: Humans and Machines – Challenges of Artificial Intelligence. Executive Summary & Recommendations. Berlin, 2023.

[32] German Ethics Council. Big Data und Gesundheit – Datensouveränität als informationelle Freiheitsgestaltung. Berlin 2017. To date, this opinion is issued only in German Version. An English Summary is published under: Big Data and Health – Data Sovereignty as the Shaping of Informational Freedom Opinion · Executive Summary & Recommendations. Berlin 2017.

[33] World Health Organization (WHO), Ethics and governance of artificial intelligence for health: WHO guidance. Geneva: World Health Organization; 2021. (Accessed July 19, 2025, at https://www.who.int/publications/i/item/9789240037403).

[34] OECD. AI Principles, 2019; (Accessed July 19, 2025, at https://www.oecd.org/en/topics/ai-principles.html).

[35] G7. G7 Leaders' Statement on the Hiroshima AI Process; (Accessed July 19, 2025, at https://digital-strategy.ec.europa.eu/en/library/g7-leaders-statement-hiroshima-ai-process).

[36] UNESCO. Recommendation on the Ethics of Artificial Intelligence. 2021. (Accessed July 19, 2025, at https://www.unesco.org/en/articles/recommendation-ethics-artificial-intelligence).

[37] Hoven Jvd., Doorn N., Swierstra T., Koops B.-J., Romijn H. Responsible Innovation 1: Innovative Solutions for Global Issues. Dordrecht: Springer, 2014.

[38] Hoven Jvd., Vermaas P. E. Poel Ivd. Handbook of ethics, values, and technological design: sources, theory, values and application domains. Dordrecht: Springer 2015.

[39] Friedman B., Hendry D. G. Value Sensitive Design. The MIT Press 2019.

[40] Friedman B., Hendry D. G. Borning A. A survey of value sensitive design methods. FNT Hum Comput Interact 11(2) 2017:63–125. https://doi.org/10.1561/1100000015.

[41] ELSI-Hub. What is ELSI Research? (Accessed July 19, 2025, at https://elsihub.org/about/what-is-elsi-research).

[42] Myskja B., Bjørn K., Nydal, Rune; Myhr, Anne I. We have never been ELSI researchers – there is no need for a post-ELSI shift. In: Life sciences, society and policy 2014 Dec,10,9. (Accessed July 19, 2025, at https://pubmed.ncbi.nlm.nih.gov/26085445). https://doi.org/10.1186/s40504-014-0009-4.

[43] Gransche, Bruno; Manzeschke, Arne (eds.). Das geteilte Ganze. Horizonte Integrierter Forschung für künftige Mensch-Technik-Verhältnisse. Wiesbaden: Springer 2020.

[44] DGBMT. Technological Sovereignty in biomedical engineering. The focus on the human being. Frankfurt am Main 2021.

[45] IEEE. The IEEE Global Initiative 2.0 on Ethics of Autonomous and Intelligent Systems. (Accessed July 19, 2025, at https://standards.ieee.org/industry-connections/activities/ieee-global-initiative/).

[46] Gassner in this volume.

[47] Henking in this volume.

[48] Djeffal in this volume.

[49] Manzeschke A., Weber K., Rother E., Fangerau H. "Results of the study: Ethical Questions in the area of age appropriate assisting systems", Berlin: VDI/VDE 2015. (Accessed July 19, 2025, at https://feag-elkb.de/arbeitsfelder/forschung).

[50] Gransche B., Manzeschke A. The Movable Host of Artificial Intelligence. A Technomyth as a Sum of Human Relations. In: Heinlein M, Huchler N. (eds.). Artificial Intelligence in Society. Social, Political and Cultural Implications of a Technological Innovation. Wiesbaden: Springer VS 2024, 141–172.

[51] Manzeschke A., Gransche B. Images Make People. On the Power of Images in Artificial Intelligence. In: Heinlein M., Huchler N. (eds.). Artificial Intelligence in Society. Social, Political and Cultural Implications of a Technological Innovation. Wiesbaden: Springer VS, 2024, 173–192.

[52] Hacker P., Passoth J. H. Varieties of AI Explanations under the Law. From GDPR to AIA, and Beyond. In: Holzinger A., Goebel R., Fong R., Moon T., Müller K.-R., Samek W. (eds.). xxAI – Beyond Explainable AI. International Workshop Held in Conjunction with ICML 2020 July 18, Vienna, Austria, Revised and Extended Papers. Cham: Springer 2022, 343–374.

[53] Wiegerling K. Ermächtigung und Entmündigung – Zur institutionellen Rahmung eines technisch normierten Gesundheitsverständnisses und ihre Rolle für die narrative Subjektivierung. In: Filozofija i Društvo XXVI (3) 2015, 499–518.

[54] Birnbacher D. Verantwortung für zukünftige Generationen. Stuttgart: Reclam, 1988.

[55] Koestler A. Sonnenfinsternis. Frankfurt/M.: Ullstein, 1979.

[56] Adams D. The Hitchhiker's Guide to the Galaxy. London: Pan Books 1980.

[57] Vallor S. Moral Deskilling and Upskilling in a New Machine Age: Reflections on the Ambiguous Future of Character. In: Philosophy & Technology, 28(1)2015, 107–124. https://doi.org/10.1007/s13347-014-0156-9.

[58] Weiser M. The Computer for the Twenty-First Century. In: Scientific America 265 (3)1991, 94–104.

[59] Selke S. Technik als Trost. Verheißungen Künstlicher Intelligenz. Bielefeld: Transcript 2023.

[60] Blumenberg H. Beschreibung des Menschen. Frankfurt am Main: Suhrkamp, 2006.

Andreas Lob-Hüdepohl

6 Artificial intelligence in healthcare in the light of statements by the German Ethics Council

6.1 Preliminaries

In spring 2023, the German Ethics Council (GEC) issued a comprehensive opinion entitled 'Human and Machine – Challenges posed by Artificial Intelligence' [1] on the ethical aspects of its diverse areas of application. With this opinion, the Ethics Council was responding to a formal request from the German Bundestag to discuss the challenges of artificial intelligence in a fundamental way and to develop recommendations for any regulatory requirements. As a result, the statement first addresses the technical and philosophical foundations of such recommendations in detail and discusses key concepts (artificial intelligence, human intelligence and reason, action and responsibility), anthropological aspects of the human-machine relationship and their implications for human-technology relations. The central ethical implication is to realize that the central yardstick by which the most diverse interactions between humans and machines – the Council deliberately avoids the otherwise common concept of human–machine interactions in order to falsely ascribe the status of an actor to machines – are to be ethically assessed is the answer to the question of whether these interactions ultimately extend or diminish human autonomy and authorship. [1: ch. 4.4.] The Ethics Council quickly realized that this insight would be discussed in detail in various fields of action. In addition to the areas of (school) education, public communication and opinion-forming as well as public administration (with a focus on social services), the opinion focuses in particular on medicine [1: ch. 5].

Of course, the German Ethics Council has dealt with specific issues relating to artificial intelligence in two other opinions in the last two terms of office: firstly in its opinion on 'Big data and Health – Data Sovereignty as the Shaping of Informational freedom' [3] and secondly in its opinion on 'Robotics for good care' [2]. The statement on 'Mensch und Maschine' (Human and Machine) repeatedly refers to both. For this reason alone, they are also included in the following analysis.

6.2 Fundamental considerations for the responsible use of AI systems in healthcare

The healthcare sector offers a wealth of potential applications for AI systems in its fields of activity (prevention, diagnosis, therapy, care, rehabilitation) and settings (research, outpatient/inpatient care, public health service). In principle, these also include modern robotics. AI systems intervene to varying degrees in the lives of the people affected. The degree of moral responsibility depends on this. In the healthcare sector, the direct depth of intervention is generally considerable, especially in medicine and nursing, so that the moral responsibility of the people using these systems (patients, medical and nursing professionals, facility managers, state regulators) must be set correspondingly high.

AI systems can be integrated into the health-related actions of professional actors in various ways. This always involves delegating certain tasks or sequences of their own actions to AI systems. This inevitably gives the machine system a certain amount of power over their own (professional) actions. Accordingly, AI systems have an impact on the user's freedom of action and decision-making. The highest ethical criterion for responsible use is that the user's scope for action and decision-making must be qualitatively expanded or at least not substantially restricted.

6.3 Extension or replacement in the application

This ethical criterion must be applied in each individual use case. For the area of medical care, three different typological scopes of delegation to AI systems can be identified [1: ch. 5.2.3]: from a 'close replacement' of medical specialists in the field of diagnostics, in which AI systems as decision support systems (DSS) support medical staff in diagnosis (e.g. early detection of breast cancer), to AI-controlled surgical robots, for example in tumor operations ('medium-scale replacement'), to 'far-reaching replacement', for example in the field of psychotherapy, in which conversational AI independently perform low-threshold diagnostic and (behavioral) therapeutic tasks in an imitated dialogue. All three areas of delegation harbor opportunities and risks. From an ethical perspective, deskilling (loss of independent theoretical and haptic-practical expertise due to familiarization with AI support), automation bias (blind acceptance of AI-generated decision proposals) and the lack of monitoring of the patient's use of a psychotherapeutic app by medical professionals, for example, are particularly problematic. This must be countered by targeted education (of individual users) and further training (of healthcare professionals) [1:199ff.]

For the support and care of people in need of care, AI systems – often implemented in robotics – can be used to assist care staff (personal hygiene services, lifting aids, etc.) or people in need of care ('ambient assisted living'), monitoring (monitoring of daily routines of people in need of care in order to maintain a 'life at home' [electronic care surveillance], telemedicine, etc.) as well as entertaining and mobilizing support (robotic animals, etc.). [2: ch. 2] From an ethical perspective, particular attention must be paid to the effects of the use of AI systems on people in need of care (right to self-determination, human right to care as a right to people/human interaction). Under no circumstances should the use of AI systems undermine the character of good care as a social, essentially also physically mediated caring relationship between the person in need of care and the carer. After all, good care is always 'care in and of an interpersonal relationship. This aspect of care has a specific physical dimension, in which its particularly close personal relatedness becomes manifest: in the bodily and facial expressions of both the care recipients and the caregivers, in their gestures and the haptics/tactility of their respective body language.' [2:24f.] This physical dimension cannot be substituted by robotics.

6.4 Ethical importance of transparency and explainability of AI algorithms

The explainability of AI algorithms by their users in a narrow sense is usually very limited. Even developers can hardly reconstruct the individual development steps of self-learning, dynamic algorithms in detail and thus explain the algorithm. This makes it even more important for users to be able to explain and interpret at least 'basic functionalities and work processes of the algorithms in order to ensure self-determined [and thus morally responsible, ALH] use' [1:195]. Explainable AI research serves this goal by providing certain operational methods that can be used to understand the development of dynamic, self-learning systems.

Transparency, in turn, is of great ethical urgency in various respects: in the field of AI-supported health research, for example, in providing as much information as possible to the persons providing the data; in the field of medical diagnostics and therapy planning through strict plausibility checks of AI-generated decision recommendations, 'in order to avoid the dangers of unjustified blind trust in technology (automation bias)' [1:193]; or in the field of care and support for people in need of care through AI systems, who must be fully informed about the use and opt-out options. Transparency is an essential prerequisite for the trust of care recipients and caretakers that is both professionally competent and humanly sustainable. This transparency could be ensured or at least increased around diagnostics and therapy planning, for example, by medical professionals not having to justify their deviation from an AI-generated decision recommendation, as is often the case, but rather their acceptance of it. The Ethics Council expressly recommends examining this option for its pros and cons in the area of social services. [1:330]

6.5 Exclusion of disadvantages of certain population groups

Obvious instances of discrimination against certain population groups arise from the data sets used to train AI systems. For example, they often reflect discrimination that certain groups have suffered or continue to suffer in the existing healthcare system due to their gender, ethnicity, social class, etc., thus prolonging it into the future. This phenomenon, known as 'algorithm bias', has been documented in many studies and is by no means limited to the healthcare system. This high risk of discrimination can and must be countered through a high level of quality standards for data collection/utilization and through continuous, discrimination-sensitive revision of AI systems.

A further risk of discrimination is the inadequate or unevenly distributed accessibility to AI-supported healthcare services. This risk exists locally, regionally, nationally and especially globally. It contradicts the human right to health, which not only fundamentally demands 'the right of everyone to the enjoyment of the highest attainable standard of physical and mental health' [5, Art. 12 (1)], but above all demands real, non-discriminatory and acceptable access to high-quality healthcare [6]. Research results on AI-supported systems must be available as open access/public access as far as possible – especially if they are financed by public funds. In addition, local and global access to AI-supported healthcare services must not fail due to socio-economic inadequacy.

An indirect risk of discrimination arises from the use of personal health monitoring, such as wearables, which are used for private self-measurement and generally aim to promote a healthy lifestyle. Their use could encourage a tendency to favor less risk-averse groups of people over others, for example in the context of health insurance. This could cause considerable damage to the idea of solidarity in healthcare and risk prevention and put particularly vulnerable groups (in terms of health) at a disadvantage.

6.6 Data protection as a fundamental ethical requirement

In fact, there is considerable tension between the requirements of AI and the traditional data protection concept: while the latter focuses on the principles of personal reference, data minimization, purpose limitation and direct necessity in addition to questions of consent on the part of the data provider, AI systems require the collection of the largest possible amount of data (big data), which they must be trained with or be able to access in order to ensure and increase their quality. In this respect, effective alternative protection mechanisms are needed to balance personal rights with a view to informational self-determination and the best possible healthcare.

In its 'Big data' report, the GEC proposed the regulatory implementation of a concept known as 'data sovereignty', which bundles a form of 'informational freedom' that is appropriate to the opportunities and risks of big data. The current concept of informational self-determination is essentially a 'right of exclusion analogous to ownership'. In contrast, data sovereignty as a form of informational freedom is primarily about 'the power to determine the content with which someone enters a relationship with their environment and thereby develops communicatively. In this sense, informational freedom means interactive personal development while maintaining privacy in a networked world.' [3:252; cf. 4:30f.]

From an ethical perspective, the consent of data providers to the handling of their data is (still) indispensable. However, the focus and weighting should be placed less on selective data collection and more on the respective context of data use. With regard to the handling of research data, for example, which flows into the data pool of big data and subsequently into AI systems, a so-called 'cascade model' of consent is suitable here, which can be supplemented by elements of delegated, representative or even advocatory consent. Especially when using personal health apps, user-friendly basic settings according to the principles of privacy by design or privacy by default should facilitate the individual exercise of data sovereignty on the part of the user. [3:256–261; cf. 4:32f.]

6.7 Shaping ethical standards by governments, international organizations and civil society

With regard to the use of AI systems, the GEC has identified several cross-cutting issues (= Querschnittsthemen, Q) that are also relevant to the healthcare sector and indicate a need for regulation on the part of the state, some of which is very significant. This need for regulation affects not only the administration/executive, but not least the legislature, i.e. parliaments. They concern the 'endangerment of the individual through statistical stratification' (Q3) [1:265] [cf. 7:# 127] and 'data sovereignty and use of data for the common good' (Q6) [1:272ff.] [cf. 7:# 130] as well as 'transparency and traceability – control and responsibility' (Q10) [1:284ff.] [cf. 7:# 134] and protection against 'bias and discrimination' (Q9) [1:281ff.] [cf. 7:# 133]. In the opinion of the GEC, 'protection against discrimination' requires 'appropriate supervision and control', which should be ensured in 'particularly sensitive areas' by 'the establishment and expansion of well-equipped institutions' by independent parties. With regard to the use of AI as DSS decision support, transparency and the ultimate decision-making power of professional users (in a qualitatively meaningful sense!) must remain guaranteed. [1:345ff.]

The development and use of AI systems in the healthcare sector are globally inter-linked. To date, there have been very different national regulatory regimes, which have led, in some cases, to a lack of standardization and, in some cases, considerable distortions of competition. In this respect, internationally binding regulations are absolutely essential – especially for particularly intrusive areas of application such as healthcare. This applies in particular with regard to research and development, which are 'mass data-based'. The Ethics Council statement on big data recommends a series of regulations here, some of which are detailed (for example regarding the adaptation of the legal framework for the use of data for research purposes [3:266–268; cf. 4:38f.]), but is essentially limited to the national context. Although the position statement on 'Human and Machine' also leads to recommendations on the most important cross-cutting issues, it leaves it at general demands for standards in the development and application of artificial intelligence and completely dispenses with specific regulatory recommendations for national legislators or supranational regulatory institutions. [1: ch.10]

The rapid development of the use of AI systems in all areas of healthcare requires a civil society public sphere in which opportunities and risks as well as their assessment and weighting are debated as comprehensively and soberly as possible. The opinions drawn up by the German Ethics Council serve precisely this purpose. The Ethics Council not only formulates recommendations for action to the legislator but also develops fundamental and case-related considerations that are intended to support the deliberating public in the ethical self-understanding of a free and democratic society about the far-reaching effects of AI-assisted medicine. The German Ethics Council thus fulfills its statutory duty to 'inform the public and promote discussion in society with the involvement of the various social groups' (Section 2 (1) (1) of the Ethics Council Act).

References

[1] German Ethics Council. Mensch und Maschine – Herausforderungen durch Künstliche Intelligenz. Stellungnahme. Berlin, 2023. To date, this opinion is issued only in German. A translation.
[2] German Ethic Council. Robotics for Good Care. Opinion. Berlin, 2020. Engl. opinion-robotics-for-good-care.pdf (ethikrat.org).
[3] German Ethic Council. Big Data and Health – Datensouveränität als informationelle Freiheitsgestaltung. Stellungnahme. Berlin, 2017.
[4] German Ethic Council. Big Data and Health – Data Sovereignty as the Shaping of Informational Freedom. Opinion – Executive Summary & Recommendations. Berlin, 2017.
[5] United Nations, International Covenant on Economic, Social and Cultural Rights.
[6] UN-Committee on Economic, Social and Cultural Rights, Substantive Issues Arising in the Implementation of International Covenant on Economic, Social and Cultural Rights. General Comment No. 14.; Geneva 2000.
[7] German Ethics Council. Humans and Machines. Challenges of Artificial Intelligence. Opinion – Executive Summary & Recommendations. Berlin 2023.

Tanja Henking

7 Legal perspectives on AI and medical technology

7.1 Introduction

The promises of artificial intelligence (AI) in medicine are huge. According to the many optimistic promises, AI is better, faster and more precise. Only time will tell whether these many promises can be kept. However, emerging ethical and legal issues should be identified and discussed today. The 128th meeting of the "Deutsche Ärztetag" (German Medical Association) has called for a common, value-based legal framework for the use of AI in medicine. The European Union's AI Regulation and the Council of Europe's AI Convention are seen as good templates by the delegates of the German Medical Association. The delegates addressed their call to the board of the German Medical Association, which is to advocate nationally and at the European level for a responsible development and use of AI systems in the field of medicine [1].

But what does value-based mean? Which values are meant – especially in a pluralistic society? What does responsible use of AI systems mean? Which, and whose, responsibility is meant? Is the applicable law at all capable of influencing these developments or is the existing legal framework (in many cases) already sufficient?

While there is some concern that legal frameworks could slow down progress, the call voiced at the German Medical Assembly points in a different direction. This is based on the question of what protective mechanisms the system needs. This article will focus on the issues of patients' care, patients' safety and, consequently, patients' rights. It will address a core concern of patients' protection: the avoidance of errors and compensation under liability law in the event of damage or injury. From a legal point of view, it should be noted that not every mistake can be equated with a liability-related medical error (malpractice). Regardless of this, the medical profession must feel obliged to take the safest possible approach. This includes being able to explain and justify actions and, thus, make decisions comprehensible.

7.2 Patients' rights

If the patient enters into a treatment contract with the doctor, they have a right to medical treatment in accordance with the generally recognized professional standards at the time of the medical treatment (Section 630a BGB: German Civil Code). In addition, the patient has a right to be informed about their diagnosis, the procedure and the course of the treatment (Section 630e German Civil Code). Consequently, an intervention may only be carried out if consent to the intervention has been obtained (Section 630e German Civil Code). When the Patients' Rights Act was introduced into the German Civil Code in 2013, the focus was on strengthening patients' rights [2]. The patient should be able to communicate with his/her physician on an equal footing. Are we about to abandon these ideals when Dr. AI meets the patient? Do we attribute so much ability to AI that we are willing to do without some degree of explanation? After all, being able to explain a diagnosis and a therapy recommendation is also part of the process of providing information. However, when it comes to an AI application, we only know – roughly speaking – what data goes in and what results come out (input/output); in between, there is the so-called black box. Even though there are approaches such as explainable artificial intelligence (XAI) [3,4], we will have to accept deficits in explainability, at least for the time being.

Moreover, we should also question what data is actually being discussed. What is the source of this data? What biases are inherent in this data? We will also have to bear in mind that members of the public may also overestimate an AI. Our own survey showed an increased willingness to use AI (respondents were asked about a simple example of image diagnostics) because AI was attributed with higher abilities than humans [5].

The Patient Rights Act has introduced the recognized professional standard into law as a benchmark, which can be derived from recommendations, textbook knowledge and guidelines. Medicine has committed itself to the evidence-based approach in recent decades [6]. The determination of indications is understood as a well-founded decision or recommendation for a measure. Therapies are subject to a proof of efficacy.

7.3 From diagnosis to therapy

If we now include AI in the treatment process, different areas of application can be identified. This can already be implemented before the actual treatment as part of the diagnostic process. So-called symptom checker apps do not yet constitute diagnostics but instead provide probabilities and recommendations for action. They come into play in the run-up to the actual treatment. This means that they are not embedded in the doctor-patient relationship, and, therefore, no responsibility lies with the doctor. This would only change if the results displayed influenced the appointment (whether an appointment is made at all or how urgent it is). On the one hand, these apps are expected to empower (future) patients, and, on the other hand, it is hoped that they will provide a way of controlling care. As a rule, the apps are classified as medical devices. However, this is not always done with sufficient transparency, including the use of AI [7].

Taking this a step further, AI is used in diagnostics, particularly in imaging. This is where the use of AI is described as being the most advanced. The use of AI in diagnostics is likely to become standard in the near future. This raises the question of what role humans will still play and to what extent they will be pushed out of diagnostics in the future. The next question might then be who communicates the diagnosis or whether it can be viewed by the patient in their electronic patient file. One question that has not yet been answered is whether some patients might prefer to be informed of their diagnosis without medical involvement (initially). The fact that communicating bad news is a challenge for doctors is demonstrated not least by the courses on communicating bad news that have been introduced into medical studies in recent years. In addition, the challenges of risk communication are well-known [8]. Consequently, there is much to be said for continuing to see education as a medical task. This is because a diagnosis is not enough; it must be categorized and discussed with a view to proposing a course of therapy.

The opportunities offered by pattern recognition should also be made available in other areas. One example is suicide risk assessment. Digital phenotyping also uses pattern recognition for mental health [9,10]. But what are the consequences of its use? Which interventions are or should be triggered by the AI-generated results? Does the risk assessment potentially lead to excessive action, with intensive interventions being carried out more quickly because the AI indicates an increased risk? Does this trigger a liability-related pressure to act? Is there a risk of overreaction?

Taking this a step further, AI-based programs can provide therapy recommendations. At first glance, this step could appear to be nothing more than further interference in what is originally a medical domain. Although determining the indication is the core area of medical activity [11], many analyses have now shown that values can also be incorporated when making the determination [12]. Understanding the therapy goal as a task in which the patient is to be involved, AI may displace the patient in the therapy goal-setting process. It is not without reason that Hart [6] doubts whether AI is the right approach for the therapeutic field.

7.4 Particularly sensitive areas

That – individual – values play a role becomes apparent, at the latest, when decisions are made at the end of life. But here, too, attempts are already being made to find AI-based solutions [13,14]; be it in the form of ethical case discussions [15], which are replaced by AI, attempting to recognize AI-based patient preferences [16] or patterns in suicide cases [17]. What these experiments have in common is, on the one hand, the aim to test feasibility and, on the other hand, the idea of transferring difficult, complex, sometimes even error-prone decisions to an AI application.

Now, one might think that these are primarily ethical questions. Without doubt, they are ethical questions, but they all also have legal relevance. They influence decision-making and, thus, the autonomy of the patient. They influence the security of the patient's care and ability to make and carry out self-determined decisions, including decisions about the implementation or continuation of a course of therapy. Consequently, they concern the right to self-determination, physical integrity and the life of the individual [13]. In addition, there seems to be a need for human involvement. It is stated, for example, that there should be a 'human in the loop' for highly sensitive areas. This is in line with the current legal situation, according to which no autonomous decisions may be left to AI. But what is actually behind this formulation when so much is promised by AI in terms of improvement? Do we need to ensure that technology remains humane, especially in situations in which people experience themselves as highly vulnerable? Or is it about (liability) responsibility? Responsibility, or the attribution of responsibility, touches on a legal category that can be found in both criminal and civil liability law. Who is to be held liable if the AI makes a mistake? Furthermore, the frequently used formula of 'human in/on the loop' may be too crude, since transitions to autonomous application may be blurred [18,19].

7.5 Responsibility: Who is responsible for what?

We are not (yet) discussing any cases of autonomous AI application [18], nor is the use of AI part of standard medical practice at the present. Whether it can or will become so is not yet clear [6], [20,21]. Applications of AI are used, for example, in Clinical Decision Support Systems (CDSS) [22]. The use of support systems raises two closely related questions. Could there be a risk of decision inertia if systems pre-empt decisions? It is also important to note that there may be blurred transitions and a lack of selectivity. Can a review be successful if the AI is not understood or the AI's decision is not explained or cannot be reproduced? When does the moment of justification arise when one wants to decide differently from the AI's suggestion [23,24]? This means that a higher degree of responsibility is placed on the doctor, but without the doctor being able to explain the AI with the black box phenomenon behind it. The doctor currently retains ultimate responsibility. But what happens if the AI makes a mistake despite the doctor exercising all possible due diligence? There are differing legal opinions regarding the possibilities and limitations of the current legal framework on this point [20]. When it comes to medical malpractice law, the concept of the standard remains a central consideration. While certain authors go so far as to describe the use of AI as unjustifiable [25], the prevailing view is that this is not per se a mistake, but rather that the use of AI is discussed in the context of uncharted methods or the attempt to heal [6], [20,21]. Particular attention must be paid to the information provided on uncharted methods, especially regarding the fact that not all risks associated with their use are fully known [26]. A specific, unmanageable risk can arise when AI is used as a self-learning system. However, a restriction arises from the approval of the application as a medical device, since the repeatability of the results is required to obtain approval and labelling as a medical device (criticism of this in [27]).

Only when the AI application has become standardized (as a "medical treatment standard") will it be possible to criticize its non-use in patient care. If AI is used, it must be familiar and understood. Technical knowledge is required, as is an awareness of any possible sources of error. Another demand will be that the diagnosis and therapy recommendations should be made transparent. However, the problem is hidden here. This is because the question of how AI arrives at its results is part of the research approaches such as XAI.

The duty to provide information will have to be extended to include the specifics of AI application [6], and the lack of transparency and explainability will have to be seen as part of the duty to provide information. Our own research has shown that people have high expectations of AI application [5], meaning that providing information can also serve a clarifying and contextualizing function.

While the ultimate responsibility of the physician is always being emphasized, the actual compliance with this requirement must be doubted with the increasing independence of the systems, which, in turn, gives rise to liability gaps [20,23]. Attributing an error in the AI application to the doctor, which the doctor ultimately did not cause or contribute to due to the lack of traceability of the error, is likely to lead to an overburdening of attribution and responsibility [20]. All these considerations suggest that physician liability law could be more strongly aligned with organizational responsibility [6]. Therefore, the question of whether the category of organizational fault could be more appropriate should be discussed in more detail. However, here too, the increasing independence of the systems raises the question of whether the clinical center operator can be held responsible if the clinical center itself has exhausted all the monitoring options available to it, such as maintenance, updates, etc.

Moreover, the easing of the burden of proof and the so-called fully controllable risk have also been discussed, but the underlying idea is not transferable ([20] with further references). This is because AI is simply not fully controllable. The problems revolve around a lack of transparency and traceability. Similarly, considerations regarding the transfer of animal owner liability do not seem appropriate. This is because it is a special regulation, and the unpredictable behavior of animals can hardly be compared with the application of AI [20].

The forthcoming AI Liability Directive will hopefully resolve some of these issues. However, given that the scope of the directive will not extend to contractual liability, all of the questions addressed here will remain unresolved.

Resolving the issues of attribution and, ultimately, liability in the event of damage is one important aspect of the problem; another can be seen in the attempts to solve ethical conflicts using AI. Taking the example of triage, it quickly becomes apparent that triage decisions are already based on value judgements. In the case of triage, as used, for example, in the so-called Manchester triage, the urgent cases should be treated first. Ultimately, the aim is to help as many people as possible to survive. If you want to use AI for triage, this value judgement must be made in advance. However, it must also be clear that in cases of a real dilemma, the AI cannot take the decision away from the individual. It should be emphasized that before AI is used, it must be agreed upon which value system a decision is based. The utilitarian approach to triage situations seems to be the approach to which an algorithm can be adapted. The deontological approach, which is the basis of our German legal system and does not quantify human life, continues to require a singular decision [13]. Therefore, regardless of the degree of interest in feasibility, particularly in sensitive decision-making contexts, it is advisable to first reflect on the basis of which decisions are made and to take into account changing values. The high legal right to life as well as the autonomy of the individual should lead to restraint in the use of AI applications that are increasingly acting independently.

7.6 Outlook

There can be no conclusive consideration of this topic. The law currently still has sufficient answers for AI applications. Nevertheless, it will be necessary to recognize, analyze and evaluate dangers, especially regarding the effects on decision-making behavior and, thus, the responsibility of the individual. A patient's safety (see [8] with further references) and rights must be safeguarded. In order for the patient to continue to be able to make self-determined decisions, 'informed' consent requires differentiation based on the risks specific to the AI application. The law is and will continue to be called upon to keep pace with these new developments and ensure patient protection.

References

[1] Bundesärztekammer. Beschlussprotokoll 128. Deutscher Ärztetag, Berlin, 2014. (Accessed August 8, 2024, at https://www.bundesaerztekammer.de/fileadmin/user_upload/BAEK/Aerztetag/128.DAET/2024-05-10_Beschlussprotokoll_neu.pdf).

[2] Deutscher Bundestag. Entwurf eines Gesetzes zur Verbesserung der Rechte von Patientinnen und Patienten, 2012, Bundestagsdrucksache 17/10448.

[3] Dössel O., Loewe A. Uncertainties, errors, explainability and responsibility for AI in medicine. In: Manzeschke A. and Wittenberg T. (eds.). Ethical Perspectives on Artificial Intelligence in Biomedical Engineering, Chapter 12, DeGruyter, 2025.

[4] Fonck S., Stollenwerk A. Explainable Artificial Intelligence in Biomedical Engineering. In: Manzeschke A. and Wittenberg T. (eds.). Ethical Perspectives on Artificial Intelligence in Biomedical Engineering, Chapter 13, DeGruyter, 2025.

[5] Weber A., Henking T. How neutral are Algorithms? Users' Perspectives on Bias in Medical Artificial Intelligence. International Journal of Digital Health 2022; 2: 110. https://doi.org/10.15344/ijdh/2022/110

[6] Hart D. Zur Entwicklung des Medizinhaftungsrechts. MedR 42, 299–306, 2024. https://doi.org/10.1007/s00350-024-6735-6.

[7] Müller R., Klemmt M., Ehni H.-J., Henking T., Kuhnmünch A., Preiser C., Koch R., Ranisch R. Ethical, legal, and social aspects of symptom checker applications: a scoping review. Medicine, Health Care and Philosophy 2022; 25:737–755. https://doi.org/10.1007/s11019-022-10114-y.

[8]   Schildmann J., Salloch S., Peters T., Henking T., Vollmann J., Risiken und Fehler in der Medizin. Konzept und Evaluation eines Wahlfachs mit integrierter Vermittlung ethischer, rechtlicher und kommunikativer Kompetenzen. Zeitschrift für Medizinische Ausbildung (GMS Journal for Medical Education) 2018.

[9]   Fuhr D., Wolf-Ostermann K., Hoel V., Zeeb H. Digitale Technologien zur Verbesserung der psychischen Gesundheit. Bundesgesundheitsblatt 2024; 67:332–338. https://doi.org/10.1007/s00103-024-03842-4.

[10] Zehl F., Bujard M., Henking T. The Acceptability of Digital Phenotyping in Psychiatry from the Perspective of Different Stakeholders: A Scoping Review Protocol. OSF 2024.

[11] Bundesärztekammer. Stellungnahme der Bundesärztekammer "Medizinische Indikationsstellung und Ökonomisierung", 2015, (Accessed August 8, 2024, at https://www.bundesaerztekammer.de/fileadmin/user_upload/_old-files/downloads/pdf-Ordner/Stellungnahmen/Stn_Medizinische_Indikationsstellung_und_OEkonomisierung.pdf).

[12] Wiesing U. Indikation – Theoretische Grundlagen und Konsequenzen für die ärztliche Praxis. Kohlhammer, 2017.

[13] Henking T. Moral Decision-Making via AI – deep ethics? About shifting or losing responsibility. In: Reder M., Koska C. (eds.). Künstliche Intelligenz und ethische Verantwortung, 2024. https://doi.org/10.14361/9783839469057-004.

[14] Gundersen T., Bærøe K. Ethical Algorithmic Advice: Some Reasons to Pause and Think Twice. The American Journal of Bioethics 2022;7, 26–28.

[15] Meyer L. J., Hein A., Diepold K., Buyx A. Algorithms for Ethical Decision-Making in the clinic: A proof of concept, The American Journal of Bioethics 2022; 7, 4–20.

[16] Earp B., Porsdam-Mann S., Allen J., Salloch S., Suren V., Jongsma K., Braun M., Wilkinson D., Sinnott-Armstrong W., Rid A., Wendler D., Savulescu J. A personalized patient preference predictor for substituted judgments in healthcare: technically feasible and ethically desirable. American Journal of Bioethics 2024. https://doi.org/10.1080/15265161.2023.2296402.

[17] Spitale G., Schneider G., Germani F., Biller-Adorno N. Exploring the role of AI in classifying, analyzing, and generating case reports on assisted suicide cases: feasibility and ethical implications. Frontiers in Artificial Intelligence 2023. https://doi.org/10.3389/frai.2023.1328865.

[18] Topol E. Deep Medicine How Artificial Intelligence Can Make Healthcare Human Again. 2019.

[19] Henking T. Theorie- und evidenzbasierte Gesundheitspolitik in Zeiten der Digitalisierung und Künstlicher Intelligenz: Ethische und rechtliche Überlegungen. In: Wendland M., Eisenberger I., Niemann R. (eds.). Smart Regulation: Theorie- und evidenzbasierte Politik. Mohr Siebeck, 2023.

[20] Schmidt J. R. Die Auswirkungen der Nutzung von KI-Software auf die ärztliche Haftung. Gesundheitsrecht 2023; 6:341–353.

[21] Katzenmeier C. KI in der Medizin – Haftungsfragen. Medizinrecht 2021; 859–868.

[22] Zentrale Ethikkommission der Bundesärztekammer (ZEKO). Entscheidungsunterstützung ärztlicher Tätigkeit durch Künstliche Intelligenz, Stellungnahme. 2021.

[23] Katzenmeier C. Big Data, E-Health, M-Health, KI und Robotik in der Medizin. Digitalisierung des Gesundheitswesens – Herausforderung des Rechts. Medizinrecht 2019; 259–271.

[24] Duttge G. "Decision-Support-System" für Therapieentscheidungen am Lebensende? Medizinrecht 2019; 771–776.

[25] Zech H. Zivilrechtliche Haftung für den Einsatz von Robotern – Zuweisung von Automatisierungs- und Autonomierisiken. In: Gless S., Seelmann K. (eds.). Intelligente Agenten und das Recht, Nomos Verlag, 2016; 163–204.

[26] Wagner G. Kommentierung zu § 630e BGB. In: Säcker J., Rixecker R., Oetker H., Limperg B. (eds.). Münchner Kommentar zum Bürgerlichen Gesetzbuch. C.H. Beck, 2023.

[27] Frost Y., Kießling M. Künstliche Intelligenz im Bereich des Gesundheitswesens und damit verbundene haftungsrechtliche Herausforderungen, MPR 2020, 178.

Bruno Gransche

8 AI as a Trap. Navigating intricate totalities between metaphorization and nonconceptuality

8.1 Introduction

Concepts are theoretically characterized by definitions and always combine elementary indeterminacy with definitional precision. On the other hand, it appears, that we must go beyond the view of AI as a concept and, due to the vagueness of the set of objects, practices and imaginations that are collected under the label 'AI', we should consider AI as a *totality* in a Cantorian and Husserlian sense. Finally, AI must be considered as a metaphor or, more precisely, metaphorizations around AI, which once again go beyond or within the perspective of conceptuality and totality.

In what way can the title of this article be justified? To what extent may 'AI be understood as a trap'? A first reading would be to understand this as a warning of a trap, for example that overly relying on AI or predominantly advancing respective technologies could lead to a situation in which important options for action would be withdrawn. On the other hand, FOMO-near (abbreviation for the *Fear Of Missing Out* something, see for the FOMO Syndrome [1]), innovation-optimistic voices could claim the opposite, namely that those who fail to rely on AI in due time and with courageous commitment will fall into the trap of missed opportunities, of being left behind irretrievably. Both warnings, the lock-in and the FOMO version, work with the omnipresent metaphor of AI as a wave, but with opposed consequences [2,3]. The first calling to duck-dive or leave the water entirely before passively being washed away; the second calling to sprint-paddle in the unalterable wave direction and get in front of the wave and surf it where it is inevitably heading, but at least with the liberty to perform some nice ripping maneuvers. *AI is a trap* works well as a metaphorization compatible with leading technology, innovation, progress or decline frameworks. Before such metaphorization is covered later in this article, firstly the trap rather serves as an analogy to illustrate the *fundamentals of concepts in general* following Hans Blumenberg's *Theory of Nonconceptuality*, which then will be applied to *AI as a trap-like concept*. For this reason, the connection between concept and trap will first be considered (2) before AI as a concept is examined against this background (3.1). This argumentation then provides the necessary tools to contrast AI as a *totality* (*Inbegriff*) (3.2) and AI in terms metaphorization (3.3).

8.2 Concept and trap – Blumenberg

Hans Blumenberg provides an anthropological account of the genesis of concepts in his *Theory of Nonconceptuality* (2007). Man is essentially characterized by his ability to gain spatio-temporal distance, anthropologically motivated by his physically determined inability to engage in close combat compared to other animals. The throwing of stones, an early paradigm of distance action, the *actio per distans*, preempts close combat and eliminates attackers before they can even bring their dominance in melee into play.

In the trap, the primarily spatial distance of ranged combat is also combined with the temporal distance of the mutual absence of hunter and prey:

> A trap is "in everything directed towards the figure and dimensions, the behavior and mode of movement of an object that is first expected, not present, and first to be brought into possession and access. This object, in turn, is related to needs that are not those of today, that have a dimension of time." [4, p. 10, this and all further quotations from this source are my translations]

A trap needs a *conception* of the prey animals to be able to target them specifically; rabbits to mammoths can be caught in traps, but not mammoths in a rabbit's trap. Just as the trap must be designed to be prey-specific, it must also leave room for differences in prey specimens so as not to be over-specifically targeted at a single specimen that may never pass by. A trap is made to catch absent animals with an imagined abstraction of this set of animals (e.g. rabbits, leporidae), i.e. with a *concept* that allows the absent animals to be present in a level of concreteness that is suitable for successful action (i.e. hunting).

> "The concept needs a tolerance for everything concrete that is to be subject to its classification. It must be clear enough to be able to make distinctions from what is not at all relevant, but its exclusivity must not have the narrowness that the name must have for the reference to the individual and his identity, his identifiability." [4, p. 12]

The trap, as an anthropological prototype of technical action at a spatio-temporal distance, demonstrates the performance of the concept: "Perhaps the clearest way to illustrate what a concept does is to think of creating a trap: ..." [4, p. 10] This is because: "The concept has something to do with the absence of its object. [...] The concept has emerged from the actio per distance of action at a spatial and temporal distance." [4, pp. 9–10] A being that acts at a distance is a being predisposed to prevention, since the action at a distance can and must precede the approximation in time. "In this respect, the concept is the instrument not so much of a being capable of memory as of a being predisposed to prevention: it seeks to master what is not yet imminent." [4, p. 12] In principle, a concept must be definable and definitions are linguistic substitutions for expressions that are logically equivalent: For example, the statement 'A trap is a device for catching animals' would be a suitable definition if the two expressions 'trap' and 'device for catching animals' were logically equivalent, i.e. one could replace the two expressions in any statement without distorting the meaning; whether the meaning would be distorted or not can only be determined if all elements of the substituted expression are known. If this condition is not met, something unknown, the thing to be defined, would be replaced by something equally unknown and thus nothing would be defined nor explained (*ignotum per ignotius*), thus no specific set of expectations would be oriented, no 'theory' be formed in the listener as a result. "The merit of any definition" – highlights John Rawls – "depends upon the soundness of the theory that results; by itself, a definition cannot settle any fundamental question." [5, pp. 112–113] For example, the definition 'A Darth is a Sith rank' is meaningless to those who do not know the Sith (opponents of the Jedi in George Lucas' SciFi Star Wars universe). This is a common problem or *semantic trickery* [cf. 6, p. 15] that can be found in AI definitions (see 3). A definition provides rules and elements for the substitution of equivalent expressions. For Blumenberg the definition even "is the rule according to which one expression can be equivalently substituted by another." [4, p. 34, my translation]. Ernst Tugendhat suggested that definitions are like good belts: the tighter they are, the more elastic they must be in order to continue to fulfill their belt function. This combination of tightness and elasticity refers to the characteristics of both concept and trap, which require an "interplay of indeterminacy and typifying narrowness" to perform their function. "The concept must possess sufficient indeterminacy to be able to grasp such upcoming experiences in such a way that corresponding appropriate attitudes can be related to them even if there are deviations in the full concreteness of the details from past experiences." [4, pp. 9–10] If a belt were arbitrarily elastic or rigidly tight, we would lose our trousers or not get them on at all; correspondingly concepts would contain everything or nothing and would be both equally useless. "The trap also represents precisely the tolerance between precision and imprecision of the object of reference, which can only be produced by the concept." [4, pp. 13–14] Thus Blumenberg, with anthropological recourse to the distance-acting preventive being of man, interweaves trap and concept: The trap "is expectation that has become tangible. In this respect, the trap is the first triumph of the concept." [4, pp. 13–14]

Before we can investigate how and to what extent AI would be an "expectation that has become tangible" and whether AI represents another 'triumph of the concept' – or more likely the opposite – we must clarify the connection between *definition* and *expectation* as well as between *possibility* and *reality* in relation to the concept.

8.2.1 Definition and expectation

The merit of a definition of a concept can be judged by the performance of the imagination orientation regarding its object – the 'soundness of the resulting theory' (Rawls), i.e. the expectation management for successful action orientation. 'Theory' is not meant here and in the following text in the full-fletched rigid scientific sense, but as a collection or set of expectations and imaginations about an object or phenomenon. Blumenberg adds: "One could say: what something is, is based on the standard of expectations." [4, p. 35]

Let's exemplify this with a '*saola-warning*': Anyone who is advised to take a certain course of action with the statement 'Look out for the saolas' and does not know what *saolas* are, might ask back and expect a definition. Depending on what imagination or 'theory' this definition evokes, the subsequent action will be oriented accordingly and quite differently. Experience with or traditional knowledge of the definitory elements within the definition will be a guiding factor. In the example of the saola-warning consider two alternative definitions such as 'Saolas are deadly spiders.' or 'Saolas are endangered antelopes.' The former will primarily orient expectations and behavior of self-protection ('be careful not to get hurt') – the latter primarily on protection of others ('be careful not to hurt other'). Only one of the two alternatives (spider *or* antelope) and the associated sets of expectations and routines will lead to successful action in the event of an actual encounter; the 'wrong theory of saolas' will lead to nonsensical behavior – like carrying a flyswatter or bug spray for possible saola self-defense. Further complicating is that it is only possible to determine if a saola encounter is *actually* the case with a suitable theory (set of expectations), with a suitable 'concept of saolas' and its comparison with sensory data in the respective situation. Some warnings like 'Beware of carbon monoxide' do need a suitable concept to result in successful (surviving) behavior yet require additional technical sensor support to identify an actual CO exposure in a certain situation – since we cannot see nor smell CO. Something that complicates Human-AI relations as well and that makes simulation and staging of AI capacities hard to detect; we do not see, hear or feel AI, so we would need additional ways of detection as well as adequate AI concepts.

Saolas are indeed antelopes and not spiders, specifically animals, namely mammals, bovidae etc. with the scientific name *Pseudoryx nghetinhensis* [7], which are also called *Asian unicorn* [8] or *Vu-Quang antelope*. Depending on one's biological knowledge, the above taxonomic definition creates vaguer or more precise sets of expectations – concepts – of a saola. Thus a saola-warning is able to direct a listener "towards the figure and dimensions, the behavior and mode of movement of an object [e.g. saolas, BG] that is first expected, not present" [4, p. 10], including an adequate elasticity for individual differences within this genus. A concept with a suitable combination of indeterminacy and typifying narrowness, a suitable theory of and set of expectation about saolas, then makes it possible to correctly classify the encountering entity and to choose successful options for action accordingly (including constructing successful saola traps if needed).

The power of the concept is not only to relate the preventive anticipatory human being and his future needs to actual yet spatio-temporally absent entities, but also to modally absent, not-actual but possible entities. Since AI discourses are in large parts about not-yet existent but staged to be imminent phenomena, this modal power becomes specifically important when talking about AI.

8.2.2 Actuality and possibility

Modal refers to logical modality, meaning the indication that something is possible, impossible, necessary, contingent, etc. "Unicorns are not actual and are not possible (i.e. can never become actual)" is a *modal* judgment about unicorns [cf. on modality 9]. The name *Asian unicorn* (although, as expected by the classification above, saolas have even-numbered, namely two horns) offers an indication of a conceptual power that goes beyond this definitory expectation management. We usually have a rather clear concept of unicorns, we can define them unambiguously enough and have a minimum of inter-subjective cooperation-enabling narrowing down of their meaning; this shared concept is grounded by a long tradition of depictions of unicorns (something we lack for more abstract concepts like freedom or revenge), that in turn is enabled by actually existing examples like horses and narwhals. The extension of this concept, however, does not contain any real living horse-like entity that could be actually encountered. Stories, paintings and crests etc. *of* unicorns actually exist. But a painting of a unicorn is of course not a unicorn, as René Magritte famously pointed out with a painting of a pipe called *La trahison des images* (painted 1929) displaying the sentence "Ceci n'est pas une pipe." And the concept of a unicorn is not a unicorn neither. Concepts exist independently of the modal status of their object and the possibility of an encounter. The saola is in fact extremely rare and endangered (there are probably less than 250 animals in existence today [10]), so most people will probably never encounter a saola.

Even then, the concept allows for expectation management for non-encounters qua negation or judgments such as 'I have not encountered a saola'. The latter is again highly questionable in relation to the concept of AI, as will be discussed below. With the ability to also imagine what is not (yet) real and (possibly) never to be encountered and to orient corresponding expectations, the concept is not only related to the future near-real, but essentially an expansion of the horizon to possibilities. Blumenberg shifts from the *action per distans* to the *perceptio per distans*:

> The concept "is the organ of the *perceptio per distans*. The distance of the current perception is at most the radius of the horizon. A horizon extended in this way not only contains that which acutely affects or will affect the perceiving system, but contains all the possibilities of what could affect it. The instrumentarium for possibility must be much more extensive than that for imminent actuality" [4, p. 75]
>
> [A comment on the translation, to prevent misunderstandings: "the imminent" is translated from "das akute" (literally the acute). Blumenberg specifies this with "also leibhafte und leibnahe Wirklichkeit." The German expression and phenomenological terminus technicus "Leib" cannot be translated (it is more than the body), but Blumenberg says "the reality that is near to the *Leib* and *Leib*-like", so those parts of reality that are close to and compatible with our "Leiblichkeit", our physical, sensory, perspective place in and contact with the world. The original sentence reads: "Das Instrumentarium für Möglichkeit muss vielfach umfangreicher sein als das für akute, also leibhafte und leibnahe Wirklichkeit."]

According to Blumenberg, the concept introduces possibility into consciousness. *Actuality* implies *possibility* (i.e. everything that is actual must also be/have been possible), but not vice versa (i.e., not everything that is possible also becomes actual). This means that there is a set of events or objects that are or were possible, but have not been or will never be actualized, which Blumenberg describes as "generated negation" (or omitted actualization) or as a "reduction of the larger to the narrower horizon [...] It is the probing of possibilities that drives the generation of negation." [4, p. 75] Concepts enter "into connection with negation" [4, p. 75] in such a way that they allow us to make judgments about what is possible but not actual and to orient our actions accordingly: at least as important as the conceptually oriented judgment 'This is a saola.' is the equally oriented but 'infinite' judgment 'This is not a tiger.' Such a judgment is infinite because it only reduces the infinity of the possible by one option (no tiger); infinite judgements are logically almost worthless, yet: "in the finite horizon of a situation, however, for the *logic of the lifeworld*, exclusion is of the highest value under certain circumstances." [4, p. 76]

> "The *concept* also allows us to recognize and introduce imaginatively that which does not exist, that which is not perceptually present. The concept thus allows us to identify *gaps in the context of experience* because it refers to what is absent – but not only to make it present, but also to let it be absent." [4, p. 76]

Concepts and traps alike both transform perceptual absence via imaginative presence into perceptual presence: The concept of 'rabbit' presents the prey as (imaginatively) present when constructing rabbit traps, so that the (perceptual) absence of a rabbit at the time of production is transformed into a (perceptual) presence at the time of collection. Concepts make the absent present (both imaginatively and perceptually) – you have to conceptually grasp the rabbit to grasp it with your hands. Beyond this, for instance the concept of the *climate catastrophe* (if assumed to be possible or even imminent but not yet actual) makes this dystopian state imaginatively present i.e., during policy deliberation, so that it remains absent at all times and is never actualized. Ideally it would not only never become actual, but also become no longer possible. For there is no more effective way to shape the future, than to push the modality of certain events from possibility to impossibility. We cannot know nor design 'the future' (a 'future present'), but we know with absolute certainty that impossible events will never occur. Making something effectively impossible (and not just allegedly or supposedly) is to exclude it from the future with certainty. Yet, to orient actions to modally disable unwanted events (or entire paths of development), we need to imaginatively make them present to strategically decide how to avoid them. In this sense, a concept can function similar to a self-destroying prophecy, a making present in imagination and discourse (although not being present in facts) and thus orienting actions in such a way that its factual actualization is avoided or even made impossible. Concepts make absent events present as orientation or strategic guidance even with the purpose to let them be absent or make sure they stay absent.

8.3 What can be learned from these insights for talking about AI?

What can be learned from these discussed insights about conceptuality for the understanding of AI? It makes a huge difference whether AI is considered a *concept (Begriff)*, a *totality (Inbegriff)*, or in terms of *metaphorization*. In this section AI is considered as a *concept (Begriff)*, especially with Blumenberg's balance of narrowness and elasticity in mind and briefly contrasted with the notion of a *totality (Inbegriff)*. Then the discussed conceptual functions of expectation management, action orientation, introduction of possibility, and transforming absence into presence will be rethought in terms of metaphorization.

8.3.1 AI as a concept

The merit of a definition of a concept can be judged by the performance of the imagination orientation regarding its object – the 'soundness of the resulting theory' (Rawls), i.e., the expectation management for successful action orientation.

As seen above, a concept is definable by way of substitution of equivalent expressions – see the case of the zoological definition of the saola. For the substitution to succeed the rules of substitution must be known and followed, and the invested elements of the substituted expression must be familiar in the discourse community. A definition of a saola can only be successful if it adequately orients expectations and following behavior (i.e., surviving an encounter) which can only succeed if the definitory concepts like mammals, horns, hoofs etc. are known as well. Already in this regard AI seems to evade conceptuality and to resist definability due to a performative lack of narrowness – it appears to be an indefinitely loose belt. There is no commonly accepted definition of AI, which is obvious in light of the plurality of definitory attempts.

> "The concept of artificial intelligence is also controversial and difficult to define (for the history, development and different definitions, see Collins 2021; Ertel 2021; Lenzen 2020, 2019; Kreutzer und Sirrenberg 2019; Wittpahl 2019; Zweig 2019; Walsh 2018; Garnham 2017; Kaplan 2017; Nilsson 2009; Poole und Mackworth 2010; Russell und Norvig 2004; Dreyfus 1992, 1972; Kurzweil 1990; Rich 1983)." ([11, pp. 369–370, my translation]; see for these mentioned sources directly [11, pp. 383–387]).

Furthermore, the EU AI Act started out with attempts to define AI in order to clearly grasp its object of regulation and struggled in doing so (not only because Chat-GPT 'exloded' in the middle of the development period of the EU AI Act) resorting to a hierarchy of applications (risk levels) and shifting the definition of AI itself to a collection of methods that are or can be involved when developing AI or to a set of exemplary *effects* that are or can be produced when using AI. See the verb-structure of Recital 4 "AI is a fast evolving family of technologies that contributes to [...] By improving [...], the use of AI can provide [...] and support [...]" [12, Recital 4].

The 1955 founding definition within the proposal for the *Dartmouth Summer Research Project* (held in 1956) is clearly on the elasticity side of the conceptual balance – and strategically so – even daring circularity like 'AI is whatever human intelligence is but with machines.' It reads: "For the present purpose the artificial intelligence problem is taken to be that of making a machine behave in ways that would be called intelligent if a human were so behaving." [13] Many definitions follow this path with the obvious intention not to clearly narrow down a set of entities under a well-defined concept, but to attract attention, funding, reach, and power (cf. for a further discussion [14]), or to escape specific legal regulations and oversight. If we consider a 69 years younger AI definition as an example that is to some "wrong" [cf. 14] yet without a doubt widely influential – that of the EU AI Act –, the problems become apparent:

> "(1) 'AI system' means a machine-based system that is designed to operate with varying levels of autonomy and that may exhibit adaptiveness after deployment, and that, for explicit or implicit objectives, infers, from the input it receives, how to generate outputs such as predictions, content, recommendations, or decisions that can influence physical or virtual environments" [12, Chapter 1, Art. 3 (1)]

Firstly, this defines "AI systems" and not AI itself. Obviously, "a machine-based system that" cannot substitute the expression AI itself, as AI is just as much for instance a science and a system is not a science and vice versa.

> "As a scientific discipline, AI includes several approaches and techniques, such as machine learning (of which deep learning and reinforcement learning are specific examples), machine reasoning (which includes planning, scheduling, knowledge representation and reasoning, search, and optimization), and robotics (which includes control, perception, sensors and actuators, as well as the integration of all other techniques into cyber-physical systems)." [15, p. 7]

Interestingly, the authors included a disclaimer granting that their AI definition in this document is "a very crude oversimplification of the state of the art" [15, p. 1], which highlights the difficulties of the AI defining attempts. Secondly, the proposed elements are not necessarily clearer than the concept itself, e.g. "varying levels of autonomy" surely does not mean the self-legislation of states (as in an autonomous Greek polis) or the rational and moral self-legislation of a normgiver-normsubject in a Kantian sense [16]. But what does it mean then and how can we identify an AI system when observing that kind of autonomy and how can we then orient adequate successful sets of expectations and actions once knowing we do? Further, that AI systems *may* exhibit adaptiveness and *can* influence environments means that there are AI systems that do not and still are to be considered AI systems, nonetheless. Consequently, in this line of thought, adaptiveness (although common in AI systems) is neither a sufficient nor even a necessary property of AI and, therefore, not an AI definiens. In a nutshell, the definition says that *AI systems are machine-based systems that infer output from an input.* Yet is that enough to inform possible encounters with AI systems? Meaning: Would we notice interacting with one based on that definition like we would when encountering a saola? Obviously not, since many people do not notice when dealing with AI systems or functionalities, otherwise an AI labelling regulation would not be demanded [17]. This is especially relevant in the health sector since most AI use cases there (e.g. AI diagnostics or AI supported robotic surgery) are to be considered high-risk after the EU AI Act [12, Chapter III] and therefore subject to far-reaching transparency obligations [12, Article 13]; thus, heath sector professionals must ensure that AI systems work transparently (cf. AI's black box problem) and that patients are informed about the use of AI in their treatment, which also includes disclosing that and how decisions are made or supported by AI. "Providers shall ensure that AI systems intended to interact directly with natural persons are designed and developed in such a way that the natural persons concerned are informed that they are interacting with an AI system, unless this is obvious …" [12, Article 50 (1)] This requires the black box problem and AI hallucinations to be mitigated as attempted by XAI (explainable AI) approaches or specifically contextualized AIs retrieving specialized information; e.g. the urology chatbot *UroBot* that is specifically trained on urology guidelines and outperforms human urologists by almost 20% response accuracy and makes the specific source and exact part of the source transparent if asked [18].

Are the EU AI Act or similar definitions suitable to orient successful behavior in such an AI-natural person encounter? Obviously not, otherwise people would hardly behave in bio- or anthropomorphic ways with AI systems [19]. To the contrary: By use of substitutive elements such as *reasoning* (that is what the R stands for in DeepSeek-R1), *chain of thought* (mimicking human step-by-step logical thinking as an AI problem solving approach [20]), *inference* (a type of reasoning requiring reason), *autonomy* (see above), *decisions* (a preference-based choice) this definition or this kind of definitions can evoke inadequate expectations that can hinder successful behavior with AI systems e.g. by treating them as rational or sentient beings due to invited anthropomorphism and techno-animism [21]. The definitions of AI are as legion as diverse and problematic in terms of their expectation management [14]. To be clear, most definitions 'out there' are even more problematic than that of the EU AI Act exemplified here.

So, AI is not a clearly defined concept that adequately orients successful behavior and that can be substituted by other expressions without alteration of the meaning. The definitory struggle between clarity and flexibility becomes apparent in Recital 12 of the EU AI Act:

> "The notion of 'AI system' in this Regulation should be clearly defined and should be closely aligned with the work of international organizations working on AI to ensure legal certainty, facilitate international convergence and wide acceptance, while providing the flexibility to accommodate the rapid technological developments in this field." [12, Recital 12]

How can something be defined, that escapes its typifying narrowness in terms of transformation speed? This would be like saolas or in general bovines evolving and mutating in such rapid timeframes that they express new properties faster than a definition could codify them as a definitory rule of substitution. What good is a definition, a typifying narrowness, if the extension of entities it aims to define changes beyond the necessary timespan to orient expectations and behavior between learning and using the definition? If you define a saola as being two-horned and by the time you finally encounter one they typically carry six horns, then your definitions, concepts and related theories are outpaced to uselessness. If this acceleration of "obsolescence of experience" [22, p. 77] would apply to ever more lifeworld phenomena we would eventually suffer from ultimate quixotism or *"tachogenic unworldliness"* [22, p. 76], thus unable to orient successful expectations. If the change speed of entities defined by the/an AI concept exceeds the clear and sufficiently narrow scope of the concept's definition, then the balance must tilt towards the flexibility/indeterminacy part of the definition, thus disrupting the performative balance of clarity *and* flexibility. An overly flexible AI definition is then as useful as a trap that aims at catching rabbits, mammoths, bats, ants, and orcas at the same time – which would clearly be a useless trap. An AI concept accommodating rapid technological developments, and a diverse plethora of entities would be just as useless. Useless, that is, for adequate expectation orientation – brilliant however for strategic expectation management that does not care about adequacy but power, not reality/actuality but possibility. To some, the merit of a definition is not the soundness of the resulting theory, but the strategic performance it offers to influence others at the level of worldviews, expectations, and perceived options. Anyone who succeeds in establishing a concept of AI that is compatible with, or even overlaps with, the concept of a wave, for example, is establishing a reach over the sets of expectations and perceived options for action of those who buy into these conceptualizations. If AI developments are as dynamic and undeniable to citizens like waves to swimmers, then an entire terrain of possible action paths is not even within the horizon of imagination and decision making. Concepts make absent entities present, imminent and forthcoming entities, which is essential for anticipation and prevention; but concepts can just as much make entities present that are outright impossible, purely fictional, never to be dealt with in the actual lifeworld and still be influencing (illusory) expectations and (futile) behavior. We can of course build traps for unicorns with the unicorn concept imaginatively present, but we will only ever catch horses, nonetheless. Some perceptive or tangible absences cannot be transformed into perceptive presence by whatever imaginative presence.

This last focus of strategic AI conceptualization calls for a consideration of the leading interests and motivations, the people behind the definitions and concepts. If AI ultimately escapes definability, then maybe we should not (or not only) consider AI as a concept. AI can be considered as sets, as *totalities* that are not characterized by a definition, but simply and only by a) their elements and b) the interest that grasps them together.

8.3.2 AI as totalities

Apparently, AI is meant and understood beyond concept definitions, which must be the case since it is used in communication and discourse with participants that refer to diverse definitions of AI – in extreme cases those definitions do not even overlap – and by far not all participants even have explicit clear definitions of AI (but rather "very crude oversimplifications" [15, p. 1] on which they ground their understanding of AI. Further complicating, AI is no monolithic phenomenon but a label under which many heterogeneous concepts, functionalities, capabilities of various modalities (actual, possible, impossible ...) are gathered. It is promising to think of AI as specific sets of expectations, imaginations and concepts, as *totalities* rather than as definable concepts, thus bypassing the discussed definitory difficulties. Obviously, definitory difficulties re-enter when the elements within the sets must be understood and codified, but for some of them that might be possible, since e.g., machine-learning and neural networks seems to be more clearly defined than AI as a whole. AI seen as a complex phenomenon and not merely as a science *or* a technology *or* a method *or* a story etc. relates to diverse entities that all play a role in AI discourses (political, public, scientific just alike) and in orienting the participants expectations and actions. Within these totalities, many concepts with a larger variety of definitory substitutive elements is *grasped together*. What is this concept of *totalities*? In the sense of Edmund Husserl's *Philosophy of Arithmetic* [23, p. 15ff] or Georg Cantor's *Set Theory* [24, pp. 20–24] who both use the word *Inbegriff* for these special multiplicities of certain elements *totalities* precisely consist of a) a unique set of elements and b) in the act of being grasped together as a multiplicity under a unifying interest. Such an understanding offers several advantages, for example totalities can contain any element regardless of its nature, mode, category etc. So not just numbers as in the set {1,2,3} but elements like a spider, an antelope, and a unicorn or a color, a satellite, and a historic person like Husserl's example:

> "If we inquire what the combination consists in when we, for example, think a plurality of such disparate things as redness, the moon and Napoleon, we obtain the answer that it consists merely in the fact that we think these contents together, that is, think them in one act." [23, p. 77]

Thus, totalities can contain the diverse elements that are related to all the different AI concepts, imaginations, expectations, stories etc. A Terminator T800, HAL9000, an Ameca [25] or Optimus/Tesla Robot [26] or the notorious Pepper [27] and Sophia [28], smartphone apps, smart home systems, recommender or search engine systems etc. are all part of the AI phenomenon today. Grasped as totalities it does not matter whether Ameca exists, T800 is pure fiction (still) and the Teslas Optimuses exist but their performance is a fiction that was staged as real [29]. The notion of totalities following Husserl comes with an advantage that can hardly be overestimated: totalities are defined by a unifying (and selecting) "special interest" [23, p. 24], they are strategic formations that instantly rise the question of the totality-forming will behind them: "But the unification comes about [...] only in the psychical act of interest and perception which picks out and combines the particular contents, and also can only be perceived in reflexion upon that act." [23, p. 164]. Thus, AI is no longer a somehow culturally objectified clear definable concept, but a strategic instrument to suit someone's interest, motivation and ultimately will-to-power. To sovereignly cope with that, we need to understand how AI totalities are created and by whom and why; and to grasp that, we need to understand how strategic totality creation – often staged as defined concepts – works. The elements of totalities can be just about anything as long as they meet the condition of being thought together as a whole. Depending on the "unitary interest" and "unitary noticing" [23, p. 77] different elements of AI imaginations are included as members of the respective set, thus creating different AI sets that then tend to be chosen (more or less skillfully) as their titles. These totality titles are not concept definitions, but expressions of specific *noticing instances* (i.e. perspectives, point of views, prejudices, stereotypes, knowledge, (false) beliefs etc.) and signs of *strategic interests* (i.e. increase funding, power, reputation, wealth, influence, wellbeing etc.).

Thus, AI totalities – such as the one of the entire EU AI Act or the one of the Google AI strategy etc. – *do not need a definition.* To analyze them we need to explore the extension of elements that make the totality and investigate the interest of the unitary noticing that proposes a specific set of elements. It is revealing – for instance, in the health sector with AI diagnostics – what elements of the vast AI phenomena are picked and combined and what is strategically left out (which cannot be further pursued within the frame of this article, but merits further investigation). Without the essential second part of interest investigation, this approach would be closer to denotative definitions that list the extension of a concept instead of totality analysis; a denotative definition of AI would be: 'AI is Pepper, Ameca, Tay, GPT-4, Copilot, Gemini, Siri, Mistral, Claude, Pi, Hugging Face, Alpha Go , Deep Blue, AIBO, ELIZA, Alpha Fold.' For instance, Annex 1 of the EU AI Act lists a set of techniques and approaches of AI as referred to in Article 3, point 1 (see the cited EU AI Definition above).

> (a) Machine learning approaches, including supervised, unsupervised and reinforcement learning, using a wide variety of methods including deep learning; (b) Logic- and knowledge-based approaches, including knowledge representation, inductive (logic) programming, knowledge bases, inference and deductive engines, (symbolic) reasoning and expert systems; (c) Statistical approaches, Bayesian estimation, search and optimization methods. [30, Annex I, a-b]

It does not *define* AI techniques with a substitution rule but grasps together a variety of techniques with the intention of thinking them together as AI techniques with the purpose to further clarify Article 3, point 1. Systems build with approaches that are not on that list are at "risk of being excluded from oversight in the EU's proposed legislation" [31] – which exactly can be a decisive interest guiding the inclusion/exclusion rational behind that 'Annex I AI approach' totality. Opposed to a definition, it is not relevant that some approaches are missing (and inevitably so in course of time and with rapid progress in the field). What each of us *thinks together in one act under a unitary inter-*

est when imaginatively introducing AI into the consciousness is not a definition of AI, but a totality of AI – and therefore beyond definitory conditions and restrictions. In different situations with different agenda, we might in-/exclude many elements in our specific noticing, thus forming different AI totalities. Each one of us in-/excludes slightly or vastly different elements into their many AI totalities. As famously established in mathematics set theory – especially by Georg Cantor –, a set (totality, Inbegriff) can contain just about anything without limitation (e.g., Napoleon, redness, the moon in Husserl's example). So, there are sets containing specific sets as their elements. There can be even a *set of all sets*, which can lead to paradoxes such as Russell's paradox if not met with restrictions of the comprehension principle (which goes beyond this articles scope). This means that the totality of all above mentioned situational, individual AI totalities is an interesting candidate for understanding the AI phenomenon: It theoretically contains all sets of elements (algorithms, robots, SciFi, cars, toys etc.) that anyone ever thought together in one act as 'AI' as well as all the interests and strategies why they formed these totalities in the first place. Since thinking is not empirically accessible a mediation via statements (perceived, written or recorded) is the closest representation. Although empirical research might be interesting that tries to infer AI totalities (AI beliefs) by observation of behavior to bypass the expression (uttering, writing) process, like certain manners or routines when dealing with entities that fall under their set of AI totalities.

This – let's say – *expressed total-AI totality* (the set of all expressed AI sets) then contains robots and chatbots, gods and titans, golems and magicians, stories and narrations, actual artifacts and impossible entities and many more. This is a rich account of imaginative culture, its interconnectedness with design, development, engineering, use, regulation of technologies, their interplay with lifestyles, forms of life, the lifeworld, worldviews etc. and the impact all these have on wishes, goals, expectations, fears and hopes, concrete decisions and actions. Obviously, an EU regulation needs 'clarity, legal certainty, international convergence, wide acceptance' [12, Recital 12] of its subject matter – accordingly vary the conditions and purposes of any AI concept – yet, to think that any of these 'very crude oversimplifications' [15, p. 1] even remotely grasp the complexity of the AI totality we are dealing with is overly simple or naïve.

8.3.3 AI in terms of metaphorization

Beyond conceptuality – especially the absent-present, real-possible, narrowness-elasticity balances addressed under the notion of nonconceptuality (see paragraph 2) – and totalities a third way of approaching an adequate understanding of the complex AI phenomena is in terms of metaphorization.

An in depth analysis of AI and metaphorization can be found in [14]. In essence, a metaphor (*meta-pherein*, transference) is the semantic approximation of two very distant concepts and the transfer (*pherein*) of some parts of meaning from one source-concept over (*meta*) to another target-concept in a certain regard. A basic form would be 'AI is a wave' [cf. 32] with the intention of suggesting seeing AI (target) in terms of waviness (source) and to transfer some yet not all wave aspects over to AI: Transfer options are massive dynamic movement, cyclicity, inalterability, inescapability, (potentially disastrous) impact, bipolar division of those over and those under the surface (surf or drown [2,3]). Not intended to be transferred are aspects like being wet, salty, moon-dependent, reigned by Poseidon, dropping levels and overall warming due to climate change (which to a significant part is due to AI's enormous energy hunger [33] and water thirst [34]) etc. Metaphorization can as well work as a substitution like 'Beware of this imminent wave' where AI is metaphorically substituted by wave. Yet, more so than in definitory substitutions, the procedure not only inevitably alters the meaning, but intentionally so. The wave-warning is still a warning about AI (and not water waves), which makes it a substitution, but it significantly shifts the emphasis of the warning with the intention of orienting specific expectations, reactions and behavior that is in the speaker's interest of grasping together wave and AI – like less asking about accountability for a wave/AI (for waves are usually not caused by an intentional agent) and implicitly suggesting adequate counter measures like dykes.

Metaphors are ways of thinking and as such omnipresent [35], they are not merely equivalent substitutions like definitions nor mere ornamental substitutions from literal to metaphorical and back. Metaphors are a technique of expectation management and action orientation in their own class. The 'wave AI' warning results in significantly different 'theories' (sets of expectations and imaginations) than an 'advance IT' warning. Metaphorical substitution is not a "substitution of equivalent expressions." [4, pp. 13–14] Metaphors teach (sometimes even force) to see an A in terms of a B (A as B). This is especially useful when the A is not conceptually graspable as such and particularly interesting in contexts in which something is to be *linguistically expressed* that is not the subject of explicit representation as such [36, p. 291]. That is the case for non-actual, merely possible, or even impossible. Metaphors imaginatively introduce perceptibly absent entities – much like concepts, yet they particularly do so *in terms of something known or already (perceptually or imaginatively) present*. Metaphors direct the understanding of unknown entities towards known entities – they "familiarize the unfamiliar" [37, p. 13] – either of something actually or imaginatively present yet unfamiliar towards something familiar (present or absent).

> The "familiarization or appropriation of reality by metaphor [...] can even be said to be the actual purpose of metaphor. [...] Metaphor arguably is the most powerful linguistic instrument we have at our disposal for transforming reality into a world that is adaptable to human aims and purposes. Metaphor 'anthropomorphizes' social and sometimes even physical reality and, by doing so, enables us to appropriate and to become familiar with that reality." [37, p. 13]

For instance, 'this trap is your spear/arrow for absent animals' teaches to see a trap as a hunting device but instead for animals in stabbing or shooting distances, in the potentially far future. 'This AI is a doctor or doctor's assistant, a second opinion, a surgeon or nurse, or even a predictive genius like a health oracles etc.' suggests to see AI in these capacities, yet with "superhuman performance" [18]. "Seeing as is not seeing that. " – said Donald Davidson [38, p. 47] about metaphors. Indeed, by teaching seeing A *as* B (AI as wave), the metaphor hinders us to see A *as* non-B (AI not as a wave but a species or science etc.) or to see *that* A:=x (that AI is *insert definition*). When trying to insert a definition in the 'seeing that' notion, it becomes obvious that most definitions in turn resort to metaphorization or 'seeing as' tricks, like *software* – since you cannot touch code it literally cannot be soft – or *computer-based:* a computer was a 1950th job description of people performing calculations with pen, paper and brains etc. Performing calculations, people using techniques and devices [cf. 39] seems coevolutionary for millennia; it is thus hard to pinpoint whether respective transfers are anthropomorphic technology views or technomorphic human views. Metaphorically bridged concepts, however, approximate their meaning, they stretch towards the other to stabilize the bridge; yet, by doing so they bend away from apposed concepts. 'Computation', *in silico* and *in cerebro*, highlights both concepts' edges facing each other (logicality, formality etc.) while downplaying the opposite ones (emotionality, intuition, beauty) [cf. 16].

Metaphors do have a special relation to negation as well insofar seeing *A as B* includes seeing *A as not-A*, i.e., seeing 'the Ameca robot as an anthropomorphic-intelligence' (A as B) crossfades 'seeing Ameca as a technical ensemble of screws and chips and wires' (A as A) or seeing 'that Ameca is technology' (that A). "Derrida demonstrated that the use of metaphor provides us with an intellectual or mental entity that functions both as an 'organizing center' and as a 'blind spot,' that is, a spot that *sui generis* cannot be aware of itself." [37, p. 12]

Concepts introduce possibility into consciousness, metaphor teach to see other/more possibilities. Further, metaphors do not unveil or highlight semantic proximity of two (seemingly) distant concepts, yet they create this proximity [40, p. 100]; they teach to see the similar that they create by doing so. Since the 'AI wave' metaphor is so present in discourse (pushed by a strategical interest e.g., of big tech companies) many people have considered AI in terms of a wave and thought waviness together with AI applications. Thus, the abovementioned *meta-AI totality* (set of all AI sets, which probably best approximates the complex AI phenomenon) prominently contains wave concepts and thus strongly orients wave-consistent expectations and wave-adequate behavior: run, swim, surf, or drown, containment is not possible. The consistency pull of metaphors invites notions within or compatible with its semantic field and repels incompatible ones. Dykes, boats, surfing or drowning are semantically consistent with waves or currents, while prohibition, documentation standards or guardrails are not. This general push-pull filter of meaning transfer options by semantic consistency is regularly bypassed by discourse participants using inconsistent metaphors. Suleyman and Bhaskar take the 'containment is not possible-lesson' from the metaphor they chose as their 2023 book title "The coming wave of AI" [32] and nonetheless ague against passivity; the wave metaphor's semantic pull is so strong that they must break free from it by resorting to paradoxes – "The coming wave of technologies threatens [...] Containment is not, on the face of it, possible. And yet for all our sakes, containment *must* be possible." [32, p. 22] – or by shifting the metaphor from waves to road traffic: "Generally, though, consider containment more as a set of guardrails, a way to keep humanity in the driver's seat when a technology risks causing more harm than good." [32, p. 233]

Metaphorization is not a nonconceptual counterpart to *totalities* or *conceptualization* but an integral part of their formation. Yet, explicating metaphorization and its role in transforming the concepts and totalities is essential to understand AI as a complex phenomenon. The metaphor – much like the concept – "allows us to identify *gaps in the context of experience* because it refers to what is absent – but not only to make it present, but also to let it be absent." [4, p. 76] So, one merit of the AI wave metaphor could be more of the self-destroying prophecy type; e.g., by causing indignation about the implied Borg imposition ('Resistance is futile', Borg slogan in Gene Roddenberry's *Star Trek* Universe) or about the inevitability of a force of nature, thus mobilizing controlling and regulating forces as well as sovereign use and strengthening of AI literacy. Callouts like these "China's AI wave turns into tsunami" [41] double down on the metaphorical implications, since what little can be done against waves, is certainly futile against tsunamis. Yet, as seen above with Suleyman and Bhaskar, calls for action likely require to simultaneously change the metaphor, from force of nature to something more withing the action space of human beings like traffic or tool use etc. Which implies that unaltered repetition and reinforcement of certain metaphors that create tensions (in certain contexts) with the very idea of responsible decisions and autonomous actions needs to be called out and avoided, to be shifted and overcome. If 'containment *must* be possible', then obviously we need a driver's seat and not a life jacket. But, after all, the sets of expectation and behavior is formed on the recipients' side, not by the locutors of metaphors and definitions. With a trained metaphor awareness, we can counteract the teaching effect of the metaphor or at least soften their forcing to see to a suggesting to see and thus detach their invitation and invasion of our thinking from our sovereign decisions and actions. With such an awareness – or to add to the omnipresent literacy claims – with such a *metaphor literacy* we could profit from the metaphorical creation of proximity and suggestion of perspectives ('try seeing as') without falling for the propagandist, manipulative consequences of aligning our actions with imposed perspectives. This is not new to AI, so we should learn from our history with journalists, politicians, scientists, marketeers and (not least) demagogues and react to the AI wave, migration wave, pink/feminist wave, rainbow/LGBT wave, etc. and accompanying expressions like 'the boat is full' all in a sovereign metaphor literate manner.

8.4 Conclusion

In sum, AI concepts suffer from the disadvantage of dealing with an essentially nonconceptual subject matter – the complex AI phenomenon – thus only ever grasping parts of it, either causing debate and rivalry between incompatible definitions or bursting the necessary definitory and conceptual restrictions altogether like constantly overstraining the conceptual narrowness and outpacing its functionality by exaggerated development speed. In many, if not most, AI definitions the extension (set of existing entities grasped by this definition) is empty, it is perceptibly absent and merely imaginatively present. On the other hand, AI totalities surpass conceptual and definitory restrictions, because they do not need to be intentionally defined and come with no restrictions whatsoever to their elements except for being thought together under a specific interest. Exactly this specific power of the concept to make things present or let them be present via imaginative introduction as well as the focus that totalities introduce on the unifying interest makes concepts and totalities useful in addressing the complex AI phenomenon. Especially the *totality of all AI totalities* could be as close as it gets to the overall AI phenomenon yet may be in many cases hypertrophic and impossible to be grasped as such. Expecting clear cut definitions of existing real systems must be paid for at the price of oversimplifications and fragmentation, though. After all, definitions are indispensable yet friction with change and development (history), they always represent stills in our streams of understanding, always threaten with more or less severe tachogenic unworldliness; recalling Nietzsche: "It is only that which has no history which can be defined" [42, p. 317, II (13) my translation].

Many metaphorizations do not serve the purpose of orienting most adequate sets of expectations for most successful behavior guidance but the purpose of creating emotion, engagement, certain (mostly unsuspicious) behavior, (over)trust or of raising funding, attention, and approval; after all we do not need to swim or run from AI as the wave metaphor suggests, we can literally regulate AI tech companies business models and (in breaking the wave as much as the wave metaphor) 'prohibit the wave to continue' – as commenced with the "Prohibited AI Practices" in the EU AI Act. The 'magic spell' that separates the master sorcerer from its proverbial apprentice that avoids being swept away by the self-caused flood is quite simple to say, yet hard to be made effective: "The following AI practices shall be prohibited" (EU AI Act, Article 5, point 1).

References

[1] Luca L., Burlea S. L., Chirosca A. C., Marin I. M., Ciubara A. B., Ciubara A. The FOMO Syndrome and the Perception of Personal Needs in Contemporary Society. BRAIN 2020;11:38–46. https://doi.org/10.18662/brain/11.1Sup1/27.
[2] St. Clair E. Surf or drown in impending wave of AI's career involvement. 21.11.2023. (Accessed February 6, 2025, at https://www.thenortherner.com/news/2023/11/21/surf-or-drown-in-impending-wave-of-ais-career-involvement/).
[3] Pillai M. Nvidia: Rider of the AI wave. Open – The Magazine, 2024.
[4] Blumenberg H. Theorie der Unbegrifflichkeit. Frankfurt am Main: Suhrkamp, 2007.
[5] Rawls J. A theory of justice. Cambridge: Belknap Press of Harvard Univ. Press, 1999.

[6] Kornwachs K. Der Herr der Dinge oder warum wir unsere Geschöpfe an die Hand nehmen sollten. In: Schröter W. (ed.). Autonomie des Menschen – Autonomie der Systeme: Humanisierungspotenziale und Grenzen moderner Technologien. Mössingen: Talheimer, 2017:15–65.

[7] Saola. (Accessed February 6, 2025, at https://en.wikipedia.org/wiki/Saola).

[8] DeBuys W. The last unicorn: A search for one of Earth's rarest creatures. New York: Back Bay Books, 2015.

[9] Gransche B. Ask what can be!: Modal Clinique and Design as Drivers of Accidence. In: Greiner-Petter M., Mareis C., Renner M. (eds.). Critical by Design?: Genealogies, Practices, Positions. Bielefeld: transcript Verlag, 2022:64–79.

[10] WWF. Saolas, 2023. (Accessed August 26, 2024, at https://www.wwf.de/themen-projekte/arten-lexikon/saola/).

[11] Imbusch P., Steg J. Künstliche Intelligenz und gesellschaftlicher Wandel – eine Herausforderung für demokratische Macht- und Herrschaftsverhältnisse. In: Heinlein M., Huchler N. (eds.). Künstliche Intelligenz, Mensch und Gesellschaft: Soziale Dynamiken und gesellschaftliche Folgen einer technologischen Innovation. Wiesbaden: Springer Fachmedien Wiesbaden, 2024:363–387. https://doi.org/10.1007/978-3-658-43521-9_15.

[12] The AI Act Explorer. (Accessed February 6, 2025, at https://artificialintelligenceact.eu/ai-act-explorer/).

[13] McCarthy J., Minsky M., Rochester N., Shannon C. A proposal for the Dartmouth summer research project on artificial intelligence, 1955.

[14] Gransche B., Manzeschke A. The movable host of artificial intelligence: A technomyth as sum of human relations. In: Heinlein M., Huchler N. (eds.). Artificial Intelligence in Society: Social, Political and Cultural Implications of a Technological Innovation. Wiesbaden: Springer, 2024:141–172.

[15] High-Level Expert Group on Artificial Intelligence. A definition of AI: Main capabilities and scientific disciplines, 2018.

[16] Gransche B. Normgiving Technology?: Metaphorization of Autonomy and What It Teaches Us. Synthesis philosophica 2024;39:9–29. https://doi.org/10.21464/sp39101.

[17] Ruth J. S. European Commission Wants Labels on AI-Generated Content – Now. Information Week 2023.

[18] Hetz M. J., Carl N., Haggenmüller S., Wies C., Kather J. N., Michel M. S. et al. Superhuman performance on urology board questions using an explainable language model enhanced with European Association of Urology guidelines. ESMO Real World Data and Digital Oncology 2024;6:100078. https://doi.org/10.1016/j.esmorw.2024.100078.

[19] Gransche B. Manners maketh Man and Machine: Tact and appropriateness for artificial agents? In: Gransche B., Bellon J., Nähr-Wagener S. (eds.). Technik sozialisieren?/Technology Socialisation?: Soziale Angemessenheit für technische Systeme/Social Appropriateness and Artificial Systems. Berlin: Springer, 2024:91–110.

[20] Wang B., Min S., Deng X., Shen J., Wu Y., Zettlemoyer L., Sun H. Towards Understanding Chain-of-Thought Prompting: An Empirical Study of What Matters. https://doi.org/10.48550/arXiv.2212.10001

[21] Gransche B. Technogene Unheimlichkeit. In: Friedrich A., Gehring P., Hubig C., Kaminski A., Nordmann A. (eds.). Autonomie und Unheimlichkeit: Jahrbuch Technikphilosophie 2020. Baden-Baden: Nomos Edition Sigma, 2020:33–51.

[22] Marquard O. In defense of the accidental: Philosophical studies. New York: Oxford University Press, 1991.

[23] Husserl E. Philosophy of arithmetic: Psychological and Logical Investigations with Supplementary Texts from 1887–1901. Dordrecht: Kluwer Acad. Publ, 2003.

[24] Cantor G. Über unendliche, lineare Punktmannigfaltigkeiten: Arbeiten zur Mengenlehre aus den Jahren 1872–1884. Leipzig: Teubner, 1984.

[25] Ameca. The Future Face of Robotics. (Accessed February 7, 2025, at https://engineeredarts.co.uk/robot/ameca/).

[26] Optimus – Gen 2 | Tesla, 2023. (Accessed February 7, 2025, at https://www.youtube.com/watch?v=cpraXaw7dyc).

[27] SoftBank Robotics Corp. For better business just add Pepper. (Accessed February 7, 2025, at https://us.softbankrobotics.com/pepper).

[28] Hanson Robotics. Sophia. (Accessed February 7, 2025, at https://www.hansonrobotics.com/sophia/).

[29] Ilina A. Elon Musks Roboter-Spektakel entlarvt: Alles nur Show mit Optimus?, 2024. (Accessed February 7, 2025, at https://www.ingenieur.de/technik/fachbereiche/automation/elon-musks-roboter-optimus-macht-yoga-uebungen/).

[30] European Commission. AIA-COM-Annexes-21-April-21: Proposal for a Regulation of the European Parliament and of the Council laying down harmonised rules on artificial intelligence (Artificial Intelligence Act) and amending certain Union legislative acts, 2021.

[31] Bryson J. J. Europe is in Danger of Using the Wrong Definition of AI. Wired 2022.

[32] Suleyman M., Bhaskar M. The coming wave: Technology, Power, and the Twenty-First Century's Greatest Dilemma. New York: Crown, 2023.

[33] Luccioni S., Jernite Y., Strubell E. Power Hungry Processing: Watts Driving the Cost of AI Deployment? Rio de Janeiro, Brazil, 2024.

[34] Li P., Yang J., Islam M. A., Ren S. Making AI less "Thirsty": Uncovering and Addressing the Secret Water Footprint of AI Models, 2023.

[35] Lakoff G., Johnson M. Metaphors we live by. Chicago, London: University of Chicago Press, 2003.

[36] Gutmann M., Knifka J. Metaphern und ihre Funktionen in der Beschreibung von Technik. In: Gutmann M., Wiegerling K., Rathgeber B. (eds.). Handbuch Technikphilosophie. Stuttgart: J. B. Metzler; 2024:285–294.

[37] Ankersmit F. R. History and tropology: The rise and fall of metaphor. Berkeley: University of California Press, 1994.

[38] Davidson D. What Metaphors Mean. Crit Inquiry 1978;5:31–47.

[39] Borst A. Computus: Zeit und Zahl in der Geschichte Europas. Berlin: Wagenbach, 2013.

[40] Ricœur P. The rule of metaphor: The creation of meaning in language. London: Routledge, 2003.

[41] Lohchab H. China's AI wave turns into tsunami. The Economic Times 4 Feb 2025.

[42] Nietzsche F. Jenseits von Gut und Böse. Zur Genealogie der Moral (Sämtliche Werke, Vol. 5). München, Berlin: De Gruyter, 1999.

Stefan Selke

9 AI between tool and super-ego – Role pluralism as a prerequisite for ethical reflections

9.1 The human being and his tools

Artificial intelligence (AI) is a concept that requires a great deal of attention. In the context of contemporary debates, ethical reflections are urgently needed as a contribution to differentiation. However, AI ethics can only be well-founded if the underlying understanding of AI adequately considers the processes of societal popularization. Paradoxically, there is a blind spot on both sides, that of the producers and that of the recipients: despite the increasing complexity of applications, AI continues to be viewed and labelled as a 'tool'. This simplistic categorization may help to establish communicative connectivity in everyday life. Nevertheless, a scientific observer perspective requires us to overcome what can be called the 'tool illusion'. Heterogenous interrelations between AI and humans in the health sector in particular require a differentiated attribution of roles as a necessary prerequisite for meaningful reflections on social implications and ethical consequences. [1]

What complicates the change in perspective is our habit to the concept of the tool itself, as it has long been at the center of progress narratives. Since the 18th century a variety of tools have been invented to replace human labor in various fields. In 1961, the first industrial robot started work at a General Motors. AI pioneer Hans Moravec recognized an "irresistible, almost evolutionary force". [2:25]

AI is now undoubtedly the 'star' on the stage of digitalization. Because AI has been extensively researched, published and reported on in the media, it needs to be categorized in a differentiated way. As the culture of digitalization is increasingly changing all areas of life. AI can be discussed as a 'key technology' between promise and threat. Against this backdrop, social implications and ethical impact assessments only make sense if the blurring of boundaries in human-machine interaction associated with AI is considered. The thesis of this article is therefore that the real revolution is not digitalization itself, but rather the plurality of roles that goes hand in hand with AI. The informal relationship between humans and their tools is an obsolete model in the age of AI. AI transcends the concept of tools. This has consequences for the necessary ethical sensitivity towards AI.

9.2 Plea for a differentiated understanding of roles

Metaphors or images are often used to capture the characteristics of AI. The focus is on expectations of potential and technological promises of increased efficiency, optimization and control in various fields of application. Metaphors and images express social expectations in a striking way. However, this is not at all sufficient for an appropriate ethical categorization. At present, ethical standards for AI are also being negotiated largely in practice in disruptive acceptance experiments and open social experiments. Here too, society's moral self-image depends on appropriate roles assigned to AI.

The sociological concept of role is suitable for analyzing emerging relationships between humans and AI. Roles are bundles of behavioral expectations. They make social conventions (understood as historically changeable logics of coordination) visible and tangible [3]. It is therefore not trivial which role is ascribed to AI in practical fields of application. On the one hand, these attributions are part of society's ability to observe itself. On the other hand, they are the key to an expanded understanding of AI beyond the technicist concept of tools. By referring to sociological role models, the relationship between humans and machines can be analyzed in a more differentiated way. Virginia Dignum initially distinguishes between three variants: 1. AI as a tool; 2. AI as an assistant and eventually 3. AI as a partner [4]. In combination with a differen-tiated understanding of autonomy [5], it becomes clear how each possible attribution corres-ponds to ethical sensitivities of varying complexity (see Fig. 9.1). As an extension of this model, the perspective on AI as super-ego is proposed below.

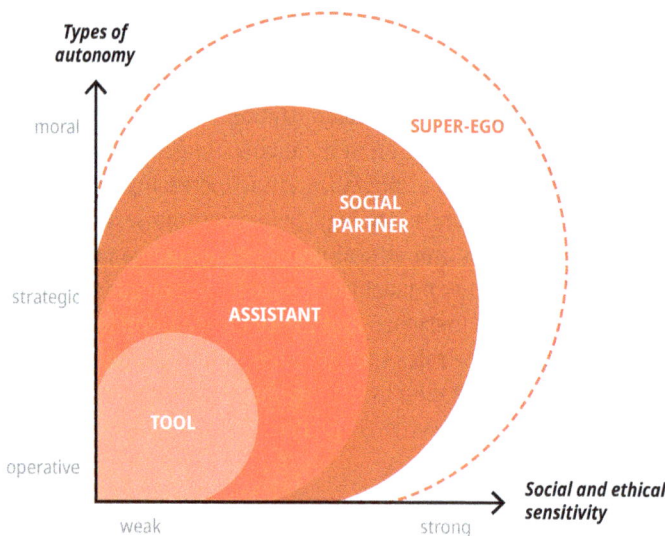

Fig. 9.1: Role models and ethical complexity in the context of AI.

9.2.1 AI as a tool

The attribution of roles to AI as a tool takes place on a mainly operational-functional level. In the tradition of technology-centered narratives of progress [6], instrumental expectations of potential represent the widespread understanding of AI. This attribution is visibly expressed in the talk of AI as a 'key technology' or 'super technology' in numerous policy papers or manifestos. Ultimately, a reductionist interaction relationship is expressed here: AI is 'produced', 'utilized' or 'operated' by humans. AI 'relieves' people in numerous areas of life. Examples from the health-care sector include AI-based time recording of treatments, appointment organization and AI-supported data management in cloud systems. This clearly shows how expectations of efficiency gains are institutionalized. The question then arises as to whether the patients will benefit from the saved time resources or if the increase of efficiency will lead to more intensive work loads.

The tool itself has limited autonomy and therefore requires only limited ethical attention (see Fig. 9.1). Ultimately, this leads to the erroneous assumption that AI is a 'neutral' technology and that it only matters what is done with it. This pseudo-neutrality must be criticized from an ethical perspective [7:29], even if the argument has a long tradition. [8] Ultimately, this argument is only gradually modified in contemporary debates by describing AI as a high-quality tool that can be used across different areas. An omnipotent usefulness is then derived from the increase in complexity and the diversity of fields of application. On closer inspection this attribution of roles is clearly under-complex.

9.2.2 AI as assistant

In fact, it is becoming increasingly difficult to understand AI as a tool. In many fields of application, AI is (explicitly or implicitly) assigned the role of an assistant. This also has a long tradition. It ranges from the 'audio-animatronic puppets' (developed by the Disney company in the 1960s) to voice-based assistance systems in our smartphones and computers (Cortana, Siri, Alexa). Examples from the healthcare sector include AI-based telephone assistants for doctors' surgeries or chatbot-supported patient communication. In these use cases, the aim is to reduce the work-load of the practice team and increase the efficiency of processes. AI systems also independently categorize patients from simple cases to emergencies [9]. The question of how AI-supported diagnostic technologies can be categorized in the typology presented here needs to be discussed. At this point, it becomes obvious that role attributions are related to certain perspectives. From the point of view of doctors, AI tends to take on the role of an assistant in diagnostic contexts. From the patient's perspective, it may be ascribed the role of co-actor in a para-social role. This is increasingly in competition with the social role of the doctor and requires new strategies for legitimization and acceptance.

Assigning the role of assistant better reflects the fact that AI is much more than just a technology. If AI is ascribed the role of an assistant with limited autonomy and at the same time a certain interactive social sensitivity for the environment, ethical judgements become more complex. This is because assistants are expected to have at least functional ethics. In the case of AI, this should be defined somewhere in the algorithm. In its role as an assistant, AI is not just a relieving extension of human capabilities. Rather, "it also changes the nature of the task and the way in which humans interact with the machine." [4:88]. Therefore, assistance relationships represented by AI generate their own discourse on assistance as a social form [10].

What is interesting about this attribution of roles is a completely new connotation. While the character of a tool is focused on the character of a thing, an assistant (in anthropological terms) is a graded person. A human analogy would be the servant or the butler, both social figures between person and non-person. The assistance function is particularly evident in robots that are intended to relieve people in their private or professional lives. AI as an assistant takes on the role of a 'half-person', i.e. a kind of shadow worker. This is extremely relevant for the categorization of social implications. On the one hand, human servants (as a relief strategy and status symbol) are becoming less and less accepted in egalitarian societies. On the other hand, the spread of technical forms of service is increasing rapidly. The new assistants are independent enough to cope with complex tasks, but at the same time just 'thing-like' enough to no longer have to give room to moral concerns.

Numerous future narratives therefore outline AI as a way of one day owning a slave that no longer requires a guilty conscience. One example of this is the utopia future narrative written by Julia Fuchte. In her future world, people use 'Agenti', a kind of advanced Siri or Alexa. 'Agenti' are used for communication, they carry out routine logistical tasks and form the backbone of society. They are substitute identities that coordinate human activities inside and outside the network.

The rise of AI in society clearly means that intelligent technology is entering our everyday lives in the social form of the half-person as described above. On closer inspection, however, serving and assisting forms of work are ambivalent. On the one hand, assistance provides relief. On the other hand, it (potentially) replaces people whose own social role is to serve in the 'machine room of society.' Consequently, this role is criticized. Assistant systems are seen as hidden control systems that colonize human life [11], create new power asymmetries [12] and therefore require a more complex ethical sensitivity.

9.2.3 AI as a (social) partner

The ethical complexity increases further when AI is assumed to have a higher degree of autonomy on a cognitive-epistemological level. This leads to the attribution of AI as a social partner. AI systems can be understood as a form of epistemological knowledge partnership [13], because the 'intelligent' technology is ascribed the ability to self-determine. Numerous media reports already praise AI as a 'team partner' when it comes to expanding the knowledge base for decisions, planning and conceptualization. Some more examples: The use of AI in education (AIED) as adaptive learning avatars or the use of AI as a curator of human memories is also based on the explicit attribution of AI as a social partner – the system 'knows' what is good for 'its' user and 'decides' accordingly (e.g. on learning content or life stories). Subject-simulating machines are particularly popular in the healthcare sector, e.g. in the context of caring for elderly and/or lonely people. Humanoid robots or so-called social robots (e.g. www.navelrobotics.com) establish a para-social relationship via simple communication and gestures. The relationship with a pet can also be simulated, e.g. with the therapy seal 'Paro' (product advert: "Not a real pet, but a real relationship") [14].

On the one hand, this attribution of roles illustrates how naturally AI is integrated into everyday life. On the other hand, ambivalences, risks and pathologies emerge precisely in such socially concentrated contexts. If an asymmetrical serving role becomes a symmetrical representative function, far-reaching ethical questions arise, e.g. regarding decision-making autonomy and transfer of sovereignty. It is always a question of the admixture of the machine-like in genuinely human processes (e.g. learning or memory). Regardless of whether machines make autonomous decisions, from a sociological perspective, the issue is that intelligent technology is considered to have the ability to determine its own behavior.

This attribution is generally accepted. In the working environment, people are beginning to "view machines not as simple tools, but as team members or colleagues." [4:88] There is a essential desire behind this: could AI perhaps be the perfect communication partner that we so often miss? Language-based interaction and the simulation of empathy are enough to create an (almost perfect) illusion of a partner. This raises an important question: do partner relationships with an AI still have to be judged according to human criteria? Philosopher Daniel Dennett, for example, warns against viewing AI as a colleague or partner and argues in favor of seeing AI exclusively as a tool: "We don't need artificial conscious agents (...). We need intelligent tools. Tools do not have rights and should not have feelings." [15]

This is where the circle closes: It is still unclear under what conditions AI will be accepted as an equivalent substitute for human partners. In any case, the partnership role model makes two strands of the human-technology relationship clear: either technology is perceived as an efficient extension of humans or humans interact with technology. However, the possible role set is not yet complete, as there is a third possibility: subordination.

9.2.4 AI as super-ego

On a transformative-civilizational level, extensive, sometimes highly speculative expectations of the potential of AI are formulated in various forms. These range from future scenarios to science fiction [16]. These attributions are based on philosophies about the socio-technical co-evolution of humans and machines (enhancement) or on techno-utopian ideas about the redesign of society. AI appears in a new role that has received little or no attention to date: as a super-ego. In these future narratives, AI is a kind of superhuman agent that not only 'knows' what is good for humans, but also 'recognizes' what humanity needs for its own salvation.

AI is expected to do a lot. The example of the 'Sarco' suicide capsule, which is already being used by euthanasia organizations (legal in Switzerland since 2022), can be interpreted as a preliminary form of the 'super-ego' role. In the end, an AI-controlled online self-test is enough to open the capsule and unlock it for its intended purpose. This procedure has nothing in common with assisted suicide (which is mandatory in Germany). After pressing a button, the oxygen content inside the capsule is reduced from 21 to one per cent within 30 seconds. This leads to disorientation, euphoria and loss of consciousness. The AI is thus granted the sole power to define the appropriateness of suicide. This example shows how AI is involved in establishing a new culture of dying and thus takes part in the transformation of civilization. On the other hand, the autonomous screening of those willing to die by 'Sarco' symbolises the creeping dissolution of social conventions and ethical consequences (see Fig. 9.2).

However, numerous future forecasts also see AI as a world saviour on a very large scale in the sense of 'planetary health'. This attribution of roles is based on predictions about a possible superintelligence. Ever since the bestsellers Humanity 2.0 [17] or Superintelligence [18], people have been pondering whether, when and how the fate of humanity will depend on machine intelligence. Here, technological singularity is understood as a future period of time in which a powerful AI intervenes so quickly and profoundly in human life that it ultimately undergoes irreversible change. This relates to topics such as rational governance (precision government), the possible role of AI as a savior of the world in the age of the Anthropocene [19] or even fantasies of salvation through immortality (digital upload).

Dismissing these considerations as pure science fiction [20:10] falls short in several respects. Firstly, every society needs innovative imagination laboratories – fictional texts do just that, science rarely does. Secondly, beyond inadmissible fortune-telling, there are good reasons to deal with AI in the role of a super-ego. If only because the concept of superintelligence is highly interesting from an intellectual point of view. For pragmatic and rational reasons, the mere possibility of it already calls for investigation [21:14]. Far-reaching speculations stimulate people's imagination and to deal with future constellations of high ethical relevance [22:17]. These considerations touch on fundamental aspects of ethics and "shed (...) light on practical problems of current AI because they force us to reflect more clearly on key concepts such as autonomy and responsibility as well as on the role of technology in a good society" [22:21] It is conceivable that at some point humans will have to subordinate themselves to a non-autonomous but overflowing machine intelligence that sets rational societal goals and acts as planetary guardians. In all cases, humanity optimizes itself to the point of self-extinction. Viewing AI as a super-ego is helpful when it comes to taking a more appropriate view of long-term consequences and creeping changes (shifting baselines) (see Fig. 9.2)

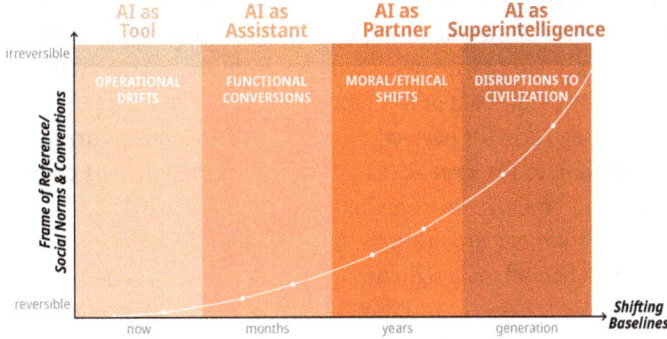

Fig. 9.2: Shifting baselines depending on the role ascribed to AI.

9.3 A fear of freedom?

The basic tenor of prognostic narratives about AI is the assumption that humans, as subjective and emotional beings, need the help of objective machines. This always involves optimization processes at different levels of scale: Body, life, work, society, planet. Against this backdrop, Google offered a new 'social contract' back in 2013. This consisted of giving up personal freedom in return for being able to utilize the many blessings of intelligent technologies [23]. In fact, an AI as a super-ego, e.g. as a 'good dictator' in the context of a techno-deterministic ecology or as a 'big nanny' in the context of the redesign of society, would lead to a loss of personal freedom. This is because the role as super-ego implies that (time-consuming) discursive rationality within the political or public discourse can be dispensed because the totally rational AI can make perfect decisions.

The longing for cybernetic governance is not new. The philosopher Marin Heidegger already mused on control as a basic principle of world organization. In 1967 he wrote: "The scientific world is becoming a cybernetic world. The cybernetic conception of the world presupposes that the basic feature of all calculable world processes is control." [24:16] The idea of data-based reason also appears in Norbert Wiener's work. He dreamed of a "total governing machine". [25:67] The promise of an AI as a super-ego would in any case be to rule on an objective basis for decision-making. Conflicts arising from human subjectivity could thus be overcome by techno-logical rationality. The only unfortunate thing would be that in cybernetic governance, human freedom would at most be a parameter that needs to be regulated.

But would that actually be so bad? Are we not overwhelmed by too much freedom? In his book Fear of Freedom the social psychologist Erich Fromm [26] outlined the double face of freedom clearly by showing the narrow limits that our own need for security and the desire to belong repeatedly set. Is there perhaps an instinctive longing for submission alongside the innate desire for freedom? This leads to a crucial ethical question: can people be protected from something they secretly long for? The latent fear of freedom corresponds excellently with new shrunken forms of freedom that are establishing themselves in the environment of AI applications.

AI in the role of the super-ego also fits perfectly with the religious undercurrent of digital technology [7]. In addition to the angelic invisibility of AI, the religious charge with messages of salvation and equivalents of holiness can be observed as a form of implicit religion in numerous everyday applications. 'Dataism' can be understood as a secular faith that comes to light behind the pragmatic appearance of AI. Whether generally as digital solutionism close to religion or in a special form as universal potential, for example when ChatGPT actually holds a church service and preaches without the help of humans. It should be noted that a new convergence of technicity and religiosity leads to an implicit everyday religion of the digital, which can be understood as a "threefold, socio-technical transformation process of the 21st century" [27:8]. Subject-simulating AI in particular is associated with faith, religion and transcendence [28]. AI is ascribed characteristics that were previously reserved for gods: Omniscience, omnipotence and omnipresence.

9.4 AI as a collaborative phenomenon beyond technology

If AI is assumed to have such far-reaching potential for change, the term 'tool' no longer applies. What then? On the one hand, AI could be viewed as a new type of ecosystem, as a "group of socio-technical systems that are integrated into economic, social and political systems" [29:22]. The ethics of such an 'system-in-the system' have yet to be formulated. It would certainly be something completely different from current machine ethics.

The tool illusion merely reproduces prevailing adaptation narratives. It suggests that AI is a superior 'super tool' that can be used to respond to latent optimization needs. Beyond termino-logy, there is more at stake. key must be based on a meaningful transformation of society. This requires meaningful goals. AI may lead to efficiency gains in many different ways. This ranges from algorithms that suggest consumer products to monitoring our living space. However, optimization is far from being a goal.

AI is changing the way we acquire knowledge, how we communicate with each other and how we imagine the future [29]. It is also creating new worlds and realities that are gradually causing people in numerous areas of life to move along pre-calculated paths and be guided towards copied forms of existence. AI is therefore never just a tool, but an increasingly unbounded collective and collaborative project. AI is a world-creating and world-changing phenomenon that is constantly changing the human environment – even under the level of consciousness. It would therefore be more appropriate to understand AI not as a means or tool, but as a medium. If postmodern societies are losing their social center of gravity (as can be summarized by numerous contemporary diagnoses), then AI must be interpreted as a systemic component of a new approach to the world instead of being reduced to an efficiency-enhancing tool.

References

[1] This article is based on a study on the topic of "AI as a social promise", which was prepared in the context of the BMBF research cluster KI.Me.Ge (www.kimege.de) and published in revised form. (Selke 2023).

[2] Moravec H. Mind children. Der Wettlauf zwischen menschlicher und künstlicher Intelligenz. Hamburg: Hoffmann und Campe 1990.

[3] Diaz-Bone R. Die "Economics of convention". Grundlagen und Entwicklungen der neuen französischen Wirtschaftssoziologie. Wiesbaden: Springer VS, 2015.

[4] Dignum V. Responsible Artificial Intelligence. How to Develop and Use AI in a Responsible Way. Cham: Springer, 2019.

[5] Hubig C. Die Kunst des Möglichen III. Macht und Technik. Bielefeld: transcript, 2015.

[6] Hänggi M. Fortschrittsgeschichten. Für einen guten Umgang mit Technik. Frankfurt a.M.: Fischer, 2015.

[7] Selke S. Technik als Trost. Verheißungen Künstlicher Intelligenz. Bielefeld: transcript, 2023, 29.

[8] For Arnold Gehlen, tools, machines and automata meant the progressive objectification of human labour and at the same time the far-reaching "relief" of human life. Gehlen A. Die Seele im technischen Zeitalter. Sozialpsychologische Probleme in der industriellen Gesellschaft. Berlin: Rowohlt 1957.

[9] "Aaron – Ihr digitaler Mitarbeiter fürs Praxistelefon" (Accessed July 18, 2024, at https://www.aaron.ai).

[10] Biniok P., Lettkemann P. Assistive Gesellschaft. Multidisziplinäre Erkundungen zur Sozialform "Assistenz". Wiesbaden: Springer VS, 2017.

[11] Btihaj A. (ed.). Metric Culture. Ontologies of Self-Tracking Practices. Bingley: Emerald 2018.

[12] Beer D. Metric Power. London: Palgrave Macmillan, 2016.

[13] Knorr-Cetina K. Sozialität mit Objekten. Soziale Beziehungen in posttradionellen Gesellschaften. In: Rammert W. (ed.). Technik und Sozialtheorie. Frankfurt a.M.: Campus, 1998, 83–120.

[14] Cyberdyne Care Robotics GmbH. (Accessed July 18, 2024, at https://robbeparo.de/).

[15] Dennett, cited in: Brockman J. (ed.). Possible Minds. 25 Ways of Looking at AI. New York: Penguin Books, 2020:51.

[16] Lee K.-F., Chen Q. KI 2041. Zehn Zukunftsvisionen. Frankfurt/New York: Campus, 2021.

[17] Kurzweil R. The Singularity Is Near: When Humans Transcend Biology. New York: Viking 2005.

[18] Bostrom N. Superintelligence. Paths, Dangers, Strategies. Oxford: University Press, 2014.

[19] Lovelock J. Novozän. Das kommende Zeitalter der Hyperintelligenz. München: C.H. Beck, 2020.

[20] Otte R. Intelligenz und Bewusstsein. Ist KI wirklich KI? Aus Politik und Zeitgeschichte 2023;42: 9–16.

[21] Shanahan M. The Technological Singularity. Cambridge: MIT Press, 2015.

[22] Stahl B. C. Grauzonen zwischen Null und Eins. KI und Ethik. Aus Politik und Zeitgeschichte 2023;42:17–22.

[23] Schmidt E., Cohen J. The New Digital Age. Reshaping the Future of People, Nations and Business. London: Murray, 2013.

[24] Heidegger M. Die Herkunft der Kunst und die Bestimmung des Denkens. Frankfurt a.M.: Klostermann, 1983.

[25] Wiener N. Mensch und Menschmaschine. Berlin: Ullstein, 1958.

[26] Fromm E. Die Furcht vor der Freiheit. München: dtv, 1993.

[27] Latzer M. Digitale Dreifaltigkeit – kontrollierbare Evolution – Alltagsreligion. Kennzeichen des soziotechnischen Transformationsprozesses der Digitalisierung. Working Paper – Institut für Kommunikationswissenschaft und Medienforschung. Universität Zürich. (Accessed July 18, 2024, at https://papers.ssrn.com/sol3/papers.cfm?abstract_id=3854509).

[28] Kimura T. Robotics and AI in the sociology of religion. In: Social Compass, 64/2017: 6–22.

[29] Esposito E. Kommunikation mit unverständlichen Maschinen, Salzburg: Residenz Verlag, 2024.

Marc Kraft, Ute Morgenstern, Karsten Seidl, Thomas Schmitt,
Franziska Klatt

10 AI for academic learning and teaching in biomedical engineering

10.1 Is the use of artificial intelligence revolutionizing teaching and learning in general?

With artificial intelligence (AI), humans have created a tool that can (apparently) "think" because it already has "intelligence" in its name. With the help of humanly conceived but primarily machine-implemented algorithms, human-like creative problem solving is simulated on the basis of statistical analyses of large amounts of information. The fact that thinking, i.e. human perception, recognizing, drawing conclusions, forming concepts, storing experiences and making decisions, possibly even problem-solving action, does not (yet) function adequately with AI is explained in other chapters of this work. However, the possibilities of AI today to deal much more effectively with huge amounts of data and to automate activities that previously required human mental abilities are extremely impressive.

What influence did the first developments in electronic data processing have on teaching and learning? Initially, there was hardly any impact due to low availability. If a room-filling computer is programmed by a specialist, it is still of little use to the learner, and perhaps in rare cases to the teacher. However, with the introduction of semiconductors and the accompanying miniaturization of electronics, the quantities produced, prices and therefore availability changed. The pioneer here (after mechanical aids such as the abacus and slide rule) was probably the pocket calculator. It mastered something that schoolchildren were supposed to learn: arithmetic. In the 1980s, it was initially possible to prohibit the use of this electronic calculation aid in lessons, let alone in examinations, so that the art of calculation could be learnt in the head, in writing or with a slide rule. Even today, the use of electronic devices is prohibited in the "resource-free part" of school lessons. Once the ability to calculate has been acquired (i.e. the pupil is able to compare the value of their shopping basket with the contents of their wallet before reaching the checkout), electronic calculation aids can be used in lessons. This is also important and increases effectiveness when higher maths, such as taking roots, differentiating and integrating, is to be used. After the pocket calculator, numerous software products and programming environments were added with the spread of the first personal computers through to mainframe computers, which were able to relieve people of more complex mental tasks. Parallels can be drawn between the introduction of these innovations and today's use of artificial intelligence, especially since large language models, i.e. large language models on a purely statistical basis without interpretation of meaning, have become freely accessible and usable for everyone on the internet. However, the impact of today's AI tools on teaching and learning also shows some serious differences to pocket calculators or previously common software/hardware applications due to their impressive performance.

The question formulated in the chapter title was whether the tools of artificial intelligence bring about a disruptive change in teaching and learning, i.e. represent a radical, fundamental innovation that takes place in a short space of time? This cannot be clearly decided due to the different standards (or thresholds for radicality) of those making the judgement. Only future historians will be able to do this retrospectively. What is certain is that the current changes in teaching and learning have taken place extremely quickly. A major trigger was the fact that ChatGPT, the chatbot from the company OpenAI, became publicly available on the internet in November 2022.

The authors see
- the main developmental leaps in today's AI for teaching and learning compared to earlier "thinking tools" in the following aspects: the "human-like" linking of data in artificial neural networks,
- the associated ability to generatively find new (probable) links between data,
- the targeted availability and usability of almost unimaginably large, man-made databases (which can also be narrowed down and checked),
- the high speed of processing large amounts of data (possibly at the expense of the accuracy or quality of the result)
- the ability of some models to carry out "human-like" interactive, dialogue-oriented communication (in writing, image and sound), also with an imitation of human behavior (e.g. for personalized, adapted learning (adaptation to level of knowledge and learning progress),
- the ability to learn, thus creating opportunities for goal-oriented, self-organized action without taking into account ethical and emotional aspects of human action.

As some of the systems' communicative capabilities are based on huge amounts of data, they give the impression of being (almost) omniscient. This can be both frightening and fascinating. Enthusiasm for this new technology is the driving force behind its application and rapid spread. It has not developed unannounced, is now in the world and will prevail. We must learn to deal with this promising challenge, to contain the risks and to make sensible use of all the new opportunities that are now available.

There are now numerous studies on the dissemination and application of artificial intelligence tools in teaching and learning, but due to their dynamic development, these only ever represent a snapshot in time. One of the most recent studies at the time of writing this chapter was conducted by Hüsch et al. [1]. In the winter semester of 2023/24, the data of more than 34,147 students (from the 3rd semester) in 15 different subjects from 165 different universities and vocational academies on the topic of artificial intelligence in their studies were recorded. An unsurprising result is that around half of the students use AI tools occasionally or daily for exercises. They are also regularly used for programming activities, writing reports or preparing for exams.

A survey of more than 2,000 students published a few months earlier by the auditing and consulting firm Ernst & Young [2] revealed that 86 % of them use AI tools as part of their studies. A part of 51 % use AI applications regularly (men at 61 % more frequently than women at 47 %). Permission to use artificial intelligence in their studies was desired by 84 % of students, while 16 % were of the opposite opinion. A part of 65 % of all respondents expected the use of AI to have a positive impact on their professional future. In contrast, only 14 % of students feared negative effects and 21 % saw AI as irrelevant for their professional life [2].

According to Hüsch et al. [1], universities' own AI tools are rarely used in degree programs because there are hardly any corresponding offerings or students are not aware of them. More than half of students rate their university's offerings for acquiring skills in dealing with artificial intelligence as very poor (35.1 %) or poor (24.1%). Only 11.3 % rate the offer as very good, a further 12.6 % as good. The authors of the study thus confirm a high potential for improvement in the area of teaching how to use AI tools. They also found that ethical aspects are important to many students. For example, personal and study-related data should only be analyzed by universities with the help of AI systems if consent or agreement (in accordance with the GDPR) has been given. This is very important to 33 % of respondents and important to a further 14 per cent. A university code of conduct for dealing with artificial intelligence is very important to 19 % of students and important to a further 19 %.

Compared to previous studies, there has been a steady increase in the use of AI tools in higher education. This is presumably due to the increasing awareness of the systems (beyond ChatGPT), their growing number and their ever-improving performance. It is therefore urgently necessary to analyze the ambivalent effects of artificial intelligence tools on the teaching of lecturers and the learning of students and to develop recommendations on how the advantages of this technology can be used while avoiding the disadvantages. The aim of this chapter is to describe the current status of the impact of AI tools. However, it is already clear that today's findings will soon be outdated. This makes it all the more important to try to draw conclusions about future opportunities and challenges from the currently recognizable trend.

10.1.1 Opportunities for AI application in learning

AI tools offer numerous new possibilities for learning during university studies, which can be categorized as opportunities and will be outlined below. At the same time, their (inappropriate) use also harbors some risks, which will be discussed in the next sections. Sometimes, however, opportunities and challenges are very closely linked, making it difficult to separate them into sections as intended. For example, whether the use of AI tools for a specific purpose has a positive or negative impact on learning success depends on the skills already acquired. The following separate treatment of the respective opportunities and challenges in relation to learning (or teaching below) serves to increase clarity in the dialectic of the effects of artificial intelligence tools, whereby reference is made here primarily to text-based applications of so-called large language models (LLMs).

One possible use of AI tools that has a very positive effect on learning success is their use as an additional learning aid. Systems developed for (possibly also by) educational institutions, such as CampusGPT, a system from Deutsche Weiterbildungsgesellschaft mbH [3], are particularly suitable for this purpose. Chatbots of this kind integrate a firmly defined database. This can include scripts, lecture notes or textbooks. They are supplemented using a retrieval augmented generation (RAG) process so that they access data from defined sources. In a tutor function, the system immediately provides fast, valid and detailed answers. Such AI tutors are also able to reformulate teaching content (e.g. give shorter or more detailed answers), explain practical examples or complex contexts step by step. In the CampusGPT system, the AI tutor can act as a coach in an interactive learning process, for example by taking on the role of a dialogue partner. All questions and answers are based on the secured (and possibly exam-relevant) database, from which references are generated [3].

AI learning systems can be designed to be adaptive, continuously adapting to learners' progress and their individual pace and abilities by providing personalized, optimized tasks.

AI-based translation systems can also offer major advantages for learning. It becomes possible to translate electronically available texts from languages that learners do not speak (and do not want to or should not learn). This makes the knowledge available on the internet, almost globally available and accessible. Increasingly, AI-based translation systems are already integrated into internet browsers, which offer the translation of websites into any language at the click of a button. According to its own information [4], the most frequently used AI language technology was developed by the company DeepL, which was founded in 2017 and currently employs 900 people. The Large Language Model from DeepL is "specially adapted to human-like language". The aim is to reduce the risk of hallucinations and misinformation. DeepL does not train its model with data from the freely accessible internet, but instead accesses "proprietary data" that has been "customized for the creation and translation of content" since the company was founded [4]. In addition, DeepL uses "thousands of hand-picked and specially trained language experts to tutor the model and maintain DeepL's quality standards" [4].

Since the ability to work scientifically is an essential element of a university degree program, especially in Master's programs, all AI tools supporting science can of course also be helpful in learning. However, it is important to note that essential skills must already have been acquired. According to the recommendations of the German Society for Higher Education Didactics (Deutsche Gesellschaft für Hochschuldidaktik) according to Glathe et al. [5], AI tools should not initially be used for the basic acquisition of subject expertise, as students need to anchor basic concepts and technical terms from sources, i.e. academic literature, textbooks, etc., in their long-term memory. Only when students have the relevant specialized knowledge themselves, they can assess whether the AI systems are providing them with correct or incorrect, inadequate or superficial information. AI tools should also not be used initially when acquiring the ability to write academically (translation systems may be an exception). Glathe et al. [5] justify this by stating that independent formulation serves to understand and further develop the thoughts of others. This is a skill that can only be acquired through doing and practising, and the opportunities offered by AI tools in learning also lie in improved and simplified access to high-quality educational resources via the internet, regardless of geographical location or socio-economic status, which can improve equal educational opportunities worldwide. For example, various LLMs are available to learners and researchers in the Academic Cloud [6] portal for universities, higher education and research institutions in Lower Saxony, some of which are also available to users in other federal states. Translation systems are also very important here. The ability to use the AI tools at any time, adapted to attention spans and concentration levels, is also very positive. In addition to the opportunities offered by the use of AI in academic work, Theisen [7] also examines the risks and dangers of consciously or unconsciously copying third-party texts without proof (plagiarism). If the AI does not cite original sources, primary sources must be researched and can only then be used.

In the following Table 10.1, traditional tools [7] and available AI tools are assigned to the five phases of scientific work. Some of these tools have been developed specifically for science and meet scientific standards, for example by using RAG methods. In this context, the basic principles of scientific integrity are particularly important: the transparency and traceability of the research process and the knowledge gained for third parties. Systems that potentially plagiarize, hallucinate content or generate invented sources (such as ChatGPT) should only be used in contexts in which such limitations are unproblematic – for example, when first approaching a topic or for brainstorming [17]. The advantages and disadvantages as well as possible risks of using AI are also assigned to the individual phases. The recommended AI tools are those that have a high potential for meeting scientific standards. The table does not claim to be complete and represents a snapshot in time, as the AI tool landscape is developing dynamically.

Tab. 10.1: Exemplary assignment of selected AI tools to four main phases of (text-based) scientific work.

Phase of academic work	Finding a research topic	Searching academic literature	Defining research questions, hypothesis and methodology	Analyzing and synthesizing	Writing & presenting	Boundaries
Previously permitted formal and technical aids	– Derivation of subtasks from a more complex context (dissertation) – Tasks in a research project – Internal company problem	– Printed, mechanical or digital literature databases, bibliographies of all kinds – Internet	– Often specifications included in the task – Reuse of the methodology of previous studies – Scientific literature	– Transfer of technical data processing and electronic text production to third parties for a fee (computer centers, typing agencies, etc.)	– Digital or analog proofreading – Grammar and language support from friends and family	Work must remain an independent achievement
AI Tools	– ChatGPT – Research Topics Generator	– Connected Papers – Elicit – Research Rabbit – Scite.AI	– ResearchGPT – SciSpace	– ChatPDF – Lateral – Rayyan	– DeepL Write – Grammarly – Jenni.AI – Quillbot	
Recommended Tools	– Elicit	– Semantic Scholar	– Consensus	– SciSpace – Semantic Scholar	– Trinka	

Tab. 10.1: Exemplary assignment of selected AI tools (continued)

Phase of academic work	Finding a research topic	Searching academic literature	Defining research questions, hypothesis and methodology	Analyzing and synthesizing	Writing & presenting	Boundaries
Advantages & opportunities	– Formulation of research topics and questions – Based on previous work – Suitable for interdisciplinary research	– More relevant results (semantic search) – Related publications and summaries – Visualizations of reference trees	– Identification of methodological approaches in published studies	– Organization and structuring of the academic work – Preparation of systematic reviews – Generation of synthetic data – Generation of program code	– Finding your way into writing – Feedback on arguments by a "conversational partner"	**Work must remain an independent achievement** **The extent of the use of AI tools must be indicated**
Risks	– Proposed topics / research questions may be difficult or impossible to implement	– What happens to information from user prompts? – Usually, only full texts from Open Access publications are available, as paywalls restrict access to other articles	– Only methods already published in articles are taken into account		– Atrophy of writing competencies	

As an example, the free AI search tool Semantic Scholar [8], which was developed for the scientific community by the non-profit Allen Institute for Artificial Intelligence, will be briefly discussed below. It currently searches more than 217 million articles from scientific publishers and displays their citations correctly and reproducibly. The system is characterized by a semantic search, which leads to more relevant hits compared to the keyword search of classic literature databases. It also offers citation analyses that aim to identify those citing articles that are significantly based on the content of the underlying article and further develop its research. A chatbot can also be used to ask questions about a publication. Very short summaries, an overview of the figures used and personalized recommendation systems are further AI-based functions of Semantic Scholar that are worth highlighting.

In view of such powerful AI research tools (which include SciSpace [9], for example), the question seriously arises as to whether scientific research should still be carried out by humans in the future, i.e. whether the necessary skills should still be taught in teaching. After all, following links, citations and references in publication databases is a rather mindless, time-consuming and error-prone activity in which it is easy to get "bogged down". Here, a reduction in workload that increases efficiency and quality is very welcome and creates space for reading and understanding publications found automatically. However, it is crucial that the sensitivity of the search by an AI system (analogous to the completeness of manually searched databases) is as high as possible, ideally 100 %. It should be noted that in certain areas of basic knowledge, older publications that are not digitized and therefore cannot be found at all may be important, which may lead to distortions in the search results.

AI can also be effective in supporting the production of academic texts. As mentioned above, the importance of one's own writing for learning and thinking processes should be emphasized here. Dealing with technical issues in writing develops critical thinking skills. Buck et al. [10] formulates: "Thoughts are sharpened and discarded in the writing process, new connections are uncovered, own thoughts are asserted against the background of other positions and vice versa."

Leschke et al. [11] recommend the targeted use of AI writing tools:
- for example, to find an "explorative and playful introduction to the text" at the beginning of a writing process,
- to "have changes suggested for bumpy text passages",
- to check arguments with AI tools, use them as "an uncomplicated dialogue partner" and thus further develop their own ideas.

Writing tools can be used in the right phase of academic work for the right purpose, for text generation, for text corrections or for paraphrasing and rephrasing.

A wide range of AI applications are also currently emerging in the field of learning analytics. Such tools are used with the aim of contributing to better learning success for students. Learning activities can be evaluated using statistical analyses, analyses of correlations, pattern recognition, identification of outliers and deviations, predictions, progression analyses and text analyses [12], among other things. It is also possible to make statements about future developments in prognostic procedures. Every learner should be informed about their current status in the learning process and know how this can be improved using the available data [12].

Seidl et al. [13] investigated how students see the opportunities of using AI tools in their studies and found out from 652 students that 70 % of them expect an improvement in performance through time savings and increased productivity, learning and work support, quality improvement, inspiration and the promotion of creativity. A proportion of 18 % hope for personal development and 7 % expect easier, better information procurement [13].

10.1.2 Challenges of AI application in learning

In the most recently cited study by Seidl et al. [13], 652 students were also asked about the risks they perceived. Of these, 35 % see a general loss of expertise due to less creativity and innovation as well as a loss of skills and knowledge. Legal concerns were cited as a risk by 18 %. A part of 14 % fear disinformation and misinformation and 9 % fear an effect on themselves in the form of dependency and laziness [13].

Risks do not only arise from the possibilities offered by AI tools today, which could result in a loss of competence for learners. The (still) existing limitations of some AI tools also harbor risks, especially if they are not used for their intended purpose or are used in ignorance of their capabilities. Since neural networks are trained using selective data sets, an under- or over-representation of part of the data used can lead to bias. This means that smaller or highly specialized companies or institutions may have less data and therefore have poorer training prerequisites for AI tools. The use of "rare" data is therefore also correspondingly lower in the probability-based access of AI tools, while the owners of large amounts of data have corresponding advantages and the associated manipulation options. Another challenge is that the training of AI tools is usually incremental, meaning that the system only accesses a limited (after training "frozen") and possibly outdated database. For example, version 3.5 of ChatGPT was still using data in mid-2024 that was available until September 2021, while version ChatGPT 4.0 now uses data up to 12/2023 or current data.

One danger in the use of scientific publications is that the proportion of falsified research results and publications is increasing, which have recently also been imagined by AI tools on behalf of criminal actors. According to rough estimates, 11 % of publications worldwide are falsified, particularly by authors from the Middle East, China and India [14]. For German authors, the proportion of fake publications could be less than 3 %. It is difficult to distinguish this false information from real research results. In previous studies, this was only possible due to the (still existing) shortcomings of the AI tools used, which mistook rarely used terms for scientific terms and used them atypically often.

In the future, it will play an increasingly important role that the data available on the internet, on which AI systems are trained, has already been generated by AI systems. This can also lead to existing errors being amplified and repeated. In a chain reaction that builds up ("snowball effect"), incorrect information could come to the fore in the probability-based data combination of AI systems and thus lead to irritation if results are not scrutinized.

Another group of risks is based on the way numerous systems work, which access existing (possibly copyrighted) content based on probability and in some cases combine it in a non-reproducible way without being the author themselves and therefore liable. The risk of plagiarism is very high in these cases. As the DFG writes in a statement [15]: "Transparency and traceability of the research process and the knowledge gained for third parties are essential basic principles of scientific integrity. This value system continues to provide valuable guidelines for dealing with generative models."

Buck et al. [10] writes that the "disruptive element of AI tools calls into question the importance of academic values and skills. Why, for example, do we still need the time-consuming and nerve-wracking acquisition of communication and discourse skills if AI promises quick solutions? Why should specialized ways of thinking be acquired when disciplinary knowledge can be called up at any time at a low threshold and appropriate to a specific problem?" The authors see a way out in "scientific socialization as an important goal of academic education" [10]. The development of an awareness of the relativity of knowledge is central. Students must understand "that knowledge is an ongoing activity, a constant learning process, and therefore develop critical thinking", whereby writing skills play a decisive role.

The learning effects of writing in terms of intellectually penetrating and thinking through scientific contexts are reduced if the process of text creation is outsourced and accelerated [11]. The intellectual debate risks losing intensity and depth. Using AI writing tools therefore harbors the risk that students "practise less in these genuinely scientific thinking movements and, as a result, the insights described remain closed to them" [10]. To put it bluntly, you could say that if you always go into the water with a swimming ring, you will never learn to swim. Leschke et al. [11] conclude: "The extent to which the function of writing as a learning tool will be impaired by AI tools is currently difficult to predict and is jointly in the hands of teachers and students."

Of course, in addition to the possible lack of acquisition of writing skills, there are also risks for the acquisition of skills in the other areas described for which AI tools are suitable. This concerns a reduction in foreign language skills, a possible discrepancy between (apparent) writing skills and (actual) language skills, the risk of acquiring less or only superficial specialized knowledge, the increasing inability to question critically, a decrease in the ability to concentrate due to an oversupply of information and ultimately the choice of a (seemingly) simpler, but in the long term intellectually impoverished path in studies.

Students therefore need to be even more motivated and responsible for their own knowledge acquisition (learning for their own future, not for teachers, grades, recognition, career advancement, etc.); this applies in particular to writing and reading skills, mastering the methods of scientific work and factual knowledge of the subject (e.g. to evaluate AI results), i.e. teaching and learning objectives and didactic concepts must be adapted accordingly. Students must also learn the methodology of lifelong learning, scientific work and the critical evaluation of problem-solving strategies and results after formulating the goal, purpose and boundary conditions in accordance with quality criteria to be defined in the degree program. This includes the ability to ask questions and evaluate answers.

10.1.3 Opportunities of AI application in teaching

Since teaching is naturally geared towards achieving learning success for students, the opportunities for using AI in learning mentioned in Section 10.1.1. also apply very largely to teaching. Although AI tools can take over some of the tasks that teachers have previously performed or could perform (e.g. use of learning assistants, exam preparation), teaching carried out by humans will continue to be of great importance. A social relationship is built up between teachers and learners, which can and should have a motivating effect. It may also be the desire for attention and recognition of one's own performance by teachers that spurs on learning, and the role model effect and competition in the best sense within a group of learners should not be neglected. At best, the spark of enthusiasm spreads from the teacher to the learner, and problems can be solved better together on the basis of the experience and skills of all those involved. While an AI does not react disappointedly to poor learning outcomes (provided it does not imitate this type of reaction with appropriate instructions), this may well be the case with teachers (even if only in their unconscious facial expressions). In the field of university teaching, there is presumably also an impressive role model function when successful researchers pass on their knowledge in teaching. Particularly in cutting-edge research and teaching geared towards this, some AI tools will tend to "lag behind" due to the need to keep training data sets up to date and the high level of specialization, and will therefore mainly impart "standard knowledge" about suitable instruments. In the following, we will briefly summarize the advantages of AI tools for teachers that go beyond the learning benefits already described.

Of course, the potential increase in the effectiveness of work as a teacher (also in research) should be mentioned here. As the writing and subject expertise of teachers is a basic requirement of their work, the above-mentioned risks of using AI writing tools or other AI systems are not relevant. AI tools make it possible to access huge amounts of knowledge that used to be widely available, but were much less accessible. Furthermore, significant time savings can be achieved for routine tasks (such as drawing images, creating a presentation or videos, support for data analysis and software generation) in teaching. A "second opinion" on the didactic concept of a course can also be obtained from AI systems. Furthermore, "completeness checks" on course content or a variation of examination questions are very easily possible.

Artificial intelligence is playing an increasingly central role in student advisory services, study organization and internal knowledge management. AI assistants enable quick access to information and promote more efficient communication. Educational institutions frequently receive enquiries about admission procedures, deadlines and processes. AI assistants can quickly search through large documents and either provide answers directly in the chat or pre-formulate them for further communication. Depending on the area of application, various assistants can be configured in the CampusGPT system for educational institutions, for example for student counselling or student support. Automating these processes not only increases efficiency, but also improves the user experience [3].

One very exciting and motivating aspect for students and teachers is to include the use of AI tools and the critical evaluation of the results of their use in the teaching content. Neither prohibitions nor ignoring the potential applications of artificial intelligence systems make sense. As described at the beginning of this section and in other sections of this work, AI systems will become established and will be indispensable in the everyday working lives of today's students (as they already are during their studies). In this respect, the expansion of existing curricula to include the AI aspect or its inclusion in new degree programs to be established is an important future task. Depending on the specialization, elements can be integrated into general studies (e.g. basics of scientific work) or in special modules (e.g. computer science).

In its statement, which refers to research but also applies to teaching, the DFG writes: "In view of the considerable opportunities and development potential, the use of generative models in scientific work should by no means be ruled out. However, their use requires certain binding framework conditions in order to ensure good scientific practice and the quality of scientific results" [15].

The following aspects should be included in teaching:
- explaining the structure and mode of operation of generative models,
- explaining the risks and opportunities of their use (in learning, scientific work, professional activity),
- indications as to when it is appropriate to use the systems (for what purpose, at what level of knowledge),
- an evaluative overview of available systems based on selected application examples for typical work tasks,
- an explanation of the legal framework for the use of AI tools in studies (e.g. labelling requirements),
- techniques for dealing with AI systems, especially prompting.

In order to critically categorize the results of AI tools, for example, the results of a systematic literature search carried out by students (under supervision) in suitable databases can be compared with the research results of suitable and unsuitable AI tools [11]. While AI tools can quickly analyze large amounts of data and extract relevant information, student research often requires a deeper examination of the sources and a critical evaluation of the information. This leads to different levels of quality and learning effects. It is also possible to use an AI tool to summarize a student's own text and have them evaluate the result to determine whether the central idea is still recognizable.

Leschke et al. [11] recommend also teaching the use of AI tools "in the sense of writing assistance systems, so that they support the formulation, sharpening of ideas and argumentation as well as stylistic revision". This would enable students to "reflect on the text output of AI writing tools, edit it and integrate it into their own text structures". The authors emphasize that the learning objectives of using AI-based tools should be added to the existing learning objectives in the field of academic writing so that students learn to write academic texts competently with the help of such tools [11]. However, it should be emphasized once again that writing skills must already be acquired.

A new skill to be acquired in teaching is "prompting" or "prompt engineering" [16]. A prompt is a request for an AI system or a formulated question to an AI system that instructs it to perform a specific task or generate an answer. A prompt serves as a starting point for obtaining relevant and precise output. Since the results can also be generated step-by-step in dialogue with the AI systems, it is important that the user monitors and controls them continuously in a targeted manner. It is crucial to formulate prompts correctly, as this is a key skill for the effective use of AI tools. It is therefore necessary to teach and practise how to formulate tasks correctly. Students should learn to differentiate [17],

- what an instruction is, i.e. a central task that the model is to perform (for example "Write", "Classify", "Summarize", "Translate" or "Order"),
- that output can be optimized through additional context (e.g. description of contexts that are relevant to the answer, such as the target group of a text),
- which input data is useful (e.g. data to be processed by the model, all possible descriptive prerequisites and boundary conditions for solving the task),
- which restrictions should apply (e.g. only truthful answers, marking uncertainties, referring to previous dialogues)
- which quality criteria are to be used to evaluate the solution and which parameters or test specifications can be used to test results for errors,
- which output indicators can be used (e.g. format of the desired output as table, text, image).

The teaching content on the application of AI systems should, as far as possible, promote a holistic understanding that includes technical, ethical and practical aspects. Students should be enabled to use AI technologies responsibly and effectively in their studies (after acquiring key competences), in research and in their future careers.

In addition to the opportunity to incorporate the correct use of AI tools into teaching, i.e. in accordance with scientific standards, legally correct and not jeopardizing learning success, a description of the application of AI in the students' future field of work should have a highly motivating effect. In Biomedical Engineering (BME) in particular, AI tools have been in use for years and have achieved remarkable results, which are explained in more detail in Section 10.3.

10.1.4 Challenges of AI application in teaching

The challenges of using AI in teaching also partly coincide with the learning challenges described in Section 10.1.2. The "misuse" of AI tools does not lead to the desired learning success in teaching, and bans on the use of AI tend to provoke outraged protest, which can only be avoided to a limited extent. Prohibitions only make sense for the acquisition of independent basic skills in general without the use of aids and can only be controlled under certain conditions (e.g. under supervision) and in a few forms of performance. However, a mix of different forms of learning and performance is necessary to ensure sustainable learning success covering all necessary competences.

Buck et al. [10] also believe that banning AI tools at universities is the wrong approach because "forms of learning or examination and practice would diverge". As these systems are inexorably finding their way into everyday professional life, "students would be denied the opportunity to practise the competent use of the tools during their studies, the university would miss its educational goal and criminalize what is professional practice elsewhere" [10].

Independent written work, analyzing the content of scientific literature, creating program codes, etc. are essential to acquiring the necessary skills. Since the use of AI tools in such tasks (which can often only be carried out unsupervised) is possible and (mostly) not verifiable on the basis of the result, students must be encouraged to take responsibility for their own work, as explained above.

Although the regulatory framework set by the respective university (see Section 10.2) is a guide, it is not a remedy for the lack of evidence of attempted cheating. Teachers should harmonize the "comprehensible didactic triad of learning objectives, examination forms and learning activities (content, methods) and take into account the (possible or impossible) use of AI tools" [18]. The sensible use of all available engineering tools to solve problems is a main objective of a university degree program and should be trained in a variety of ways during the course.

Written examinations play a particularly important role for teachers when considering the risks of using AI tools. "They are intended to determine the extent to which the person being tested has knowledge or can apply, critically assess or further develop it. The use of written examinations is based on the assumption that the examinee has the ability to apply or critically evaluate knowledge if this is recognizable in the text" [10]. Buck et al. are of the opinion that "the use of AI tools, however, cancels out this basic assumption of university examinations for all written examinations that are not written under controlled conditions." In terms of examination law, these are not own work [19]. The problem is that attempted cheating through the use of AI tools in the context of examinations cannot be detected and thus penalized [20].

In written (conventional) examination forms, for example, self-assessment has become more difficult. This includes, in particular, unsupervised, more extensive written text or programming work, which previously played a very important role as Bachelor's/Master's/project work. Supplementary examination types should be introduced here.

How can academic success be assessed if the use of AI is not prohibited but encouraged? Parts of the written paper (especially the parts that AI tools can generate very easily: e.g. the description of the state of knowledge in a field) should now meet higher standards in terms of accurate wording, spelling and grammar and can be dealt with in an oral interview on a random basis. The (laborious) checking of literature source citations in written assignments by the students' supervisors cannot be recommended. If errors are found, this is only an indication of the selection of unsuitable AI tools. An extensive freedom from errors can be based either on (possibly desired) own systematic literature research or on the use of suitable AI tools. Rather, the understanding of the cited literature should be used to categorize your own solutions in the specialist discussion. It is highly recommended (where possible) that students are closely supervised during the work phase with regular enquiries about the progress of their work, whereby diaries on the progress of work can also be an aid. In any case, tasks for written theses that require the creation, construction and use of "hardware" are safe from the use of AI tools. This is a field of expertise to be learnt in the engineering sciences anyway, which comes close to the later professional activity in Biomedical Engineering. For example, design tasks (e.g. construction of a medical device or a test system), experimental or metrological tasks (e.g. interviewing users, carrying out and analyzing measurement series) can be assigned. If the task is suitable for working in teams, this also makes it more difficult to deceive students about their own performance by using AI tools. In engineering, practical study components are absolutely essential. The methodology of targeted scientific experimentation and finding realizable solutions for practical specialist tasks under user-defined boundary conditions plays an important role in learning problem-solving strategies. The responsibility of university teachers lies in the technically and didactically well thought-out conception and instruction, including the use of tools – including AI – as well as the personal supervision of students and assistants. In any case, it is recommended that student theses be integrated into existing working or research groups at the university or in the user environment (company, clinic, testing institution, etc.), whereby the progress of the work is presented at regular intervals and discussed in the group. A public oral presentation of the student's work, including a demonstration of practical results followed by a discussion, should be recognized with credit points and anchored in the examination regulations.

Another approach is the targeted integration of the use of AI tools in the tasks of written assignments, which should, however, result in an adjustment of the assessment standard. For example, research (with AI tools) can be required, but above all its comparative evaluation can be assessed with points. Furthermore, the scope and complexity of a task that requires software development could be increased beyond the usual limits, as AI tools may be used. It is important here to ensure the availability of the relevant AI tools (e.g. free systems with no obligation to register, see e.g. Academic Cloud [6]) for all students. It will be difficult to exclude the advantages of some students who may use available, more suitable systems because they (can) pay for them. The loss of examination fairness should be avoided as far as possible. Teachers are encouraged to request free access to modern AI systems for all participants at their institution.

Numerous previously established forms of checking learning success or proof of performance are immune to the use of AI for cheating purposes and can be recommended. These include oral assessments, seminars in presence (with reflection, discussion, argumentation), supervised written examinations without authorized aids (with answers to questions including formula calculations, preparation of summaries, evaluation of given scientific data), supervised online examinations in a PC room at the university that has no or supervised internet access, "closed book examinations" (assessments without the use of aids) or other types (e.g. analysis of a presented technical system in the presence of the lecturer). Portfolio examinations, in which various partial performances are combined, are suitable for reducing the proportion of performances that an AI could have produced in the overall result. It is therefore also appropriate to significantly increase the weight of the oral defence of a thesis or disputation, which is already a firmly established component in many examination regulations, in performance assessments. The greatest problems of uncontrollable AI utilization exist with "term papers" in the humanities, which, however, should not play a decisive role in Biomedical Engineering due to the subordinate assessment of text production compared to practical application-related work results. However, AI skills for formulating summarized results, creating presentations and documentation are welcome in order to free up working time for the actual engineering problem solving.

The general risks of using AI, which apply to teachers as well as all users of these tools, are not discussed in detail here. These include the risk of the systems taking over one's own professional activity and the possible threat of unemployment. In the field of university teaching, this risk is low for the reasons already explained. On the contrary, a high level of technical and methodological expertise is required in order to be able to develop one's own AI systems with minimal errors and to be able to critically examine the results of using finished systems. There are also climate-related risks and costs (e.g. due to the energy consumption of data centres) and social risks (e.g. the often very low-paid work of millions of "data workers", mainly in the Global South and Asia).

10.2 Initial reactions from universities on AI applications in teaching

The measures taken by universities in Germany will only be briefly discussed here, as these are very heterogeneous due to the federal states' federalism in education policy, university self-administration and the "freedom of teaching" to which every teacher is entitled under the Basic Law (Art. 5 § 3 GG [21]) and will soon be outdated again due to the rapid developments in the availability and performance of AI tools.

In a study entitled "Focus – Artificial Intelligence: Where do German universities stand?", Budde et al. [22] dealt with a status survey. The results will not be published in full until autumn 2024, so we can only refer here to a preliminary publication by the Hochschulforum Digitalisierung [23]. It states that the "university management teams are in the starting blocks". For example, 87 % of university management teams are looking into AI applications. They initiate university-wide exchange processes (73 %), enable experimental spaces and pilot projects, offer training (64 %) and develop AI guidelines (66 %). Only around 6 % of universities are not planning any measures. 29 % of teaching staff have taken part in training courses on the use of AI in teaching. Around 30 % of universities, some of which are coordinated by the respective federal state, have acquired licenses for AI tools [22].

Programs for students to acquire AI skills are still rather rare, but urgently needed. The integration of AI tools as a teaching subject is also still the exception. The main focus is on the topic of examinations and academic misconduct. 80 % of universities see this as a central topic of discussion. Many lecturers (over 80 %) are in favor of a general ban on AI in certain examination formats. Ethical and moral issues as well as data protection aspects are seen as important topics of discussion by around two thirds of respondents. Preparing students for AI applications in their professional activities and ensuring fair access to AI technologies are also important concerns [22].

Solis [24] published a "snapshot" on May 6, 2023 and updated it on June 19, 2024, based on an analysis of guidelines from the 100 largest German universities and dealing with the question of "whether and how students are allowed to use ChatGPT and similar AI tools for examinations such as term papers or exams". All guidelines of these educational institutions are linked on the website https://www.scribbr.de/ki-tools-nutzen/chat-gpt-universitaere-richtlinien/#richtlinien-uebersicht. As a result, it was found that the use of AI is generally not permitted at 2 % of the institutions surveyed, partially permitted at 23 % and generally permitted at 12 % [24]. This clearly shows the range as well as the predominance of partial or full authorization (see Fig. 10.1). The fact that a ban is not recommended for various reasons has already been explained above. Where there was partial permission to use AI language models, this related to specific purposes (e.g. for research, but not for writing), to specific tasks or to the need for permission from the teacher. If the use of AI tools is permitted, specifications are usually made regarding the type of use. Here, it makes sense to follow the DFG statement [15], which requires information on whether and which generative models were used, for what purpose and to what extent. Further requirements also include listing the prompts used. This is an attempt to achieve reproducibility and verifiability of the results. However, due to the way numerous AI tools work, this goal is not achieved, as the same prompts entered one after the other lead to different results. Even more extensive documentation is required if chat histories and the use of the text passages from them are also to be documented (e.g. by means of PDF copies of the chat histories). The TU Berlin recommends this "in order to maximize transparency" [25]. From the point of view of the authors of this article, this immense testing effort is unnecessary because it presupposes mistrust. Here too, it is more important to rely on students' personal responsibility. Those who cheat are primarily harming themselves or failing to achieve the learning objectives.

A legal "inhibition threshold" for attempts to deceive in the form of applied but undeclared use of AI tools in students' final theses is to be provided by extended declarations of independence. In addition to the declaration previously used at the TU Berlin, for example: "I hereby declare that I have written this thesis independently without the help of third parties and exclusively using the sources and aids listed. I have labelled as such all passages that are taken from the sources and aids used, either unchanged or analogously." If a signature is now required for the addition: "If generative AI tools were used, I have named the product name, manufacturer, the software version used and the respective purposes (e.g. linguistic review and improvement of the texts, systematic research). I am fully responsible for the selection, adoption and all results of the AI-generated output I used." [25].

It is alarming that 63 % of universities still have no or only very unclear guidelines on the use of AI in higher education [24]. This is probably due to the rapid spread of AI tools, which the rather slow opinion-forming and administrative processes at German universities are unable to keep up with. As a result, many students and lecturers are currently living in a regulatory grey area, which leads to uncertainty, errors and ultimately frustration. There is an urgent need to find sustainable, forward-looking solutions that are standardized across universities and federal states wherever possible.

Salden et al. [26] found that with the increasing importance of generative AI at universities, the need for legal and free access options for all participants is also growing. Universities are currently improvising with various approaches. They use free offers, selectively finance paid tools or provide AI programs in libraries. However, staff and students often purchase licenses at their own expense. However, these solutions are problematic in the long term, as free tools raise data protection issues because some applications require personal data, private costs impair equality of opportunity and the purchase of many individual licenses is economically inefficient. The authors conclude that a sustainable strategy for the fair and efficient use of AI at universities is therefore required [26].

- AI is generally not permitted
- AI is partially not permitted
- AI is generally permitted
- no or only very unclear guidelines

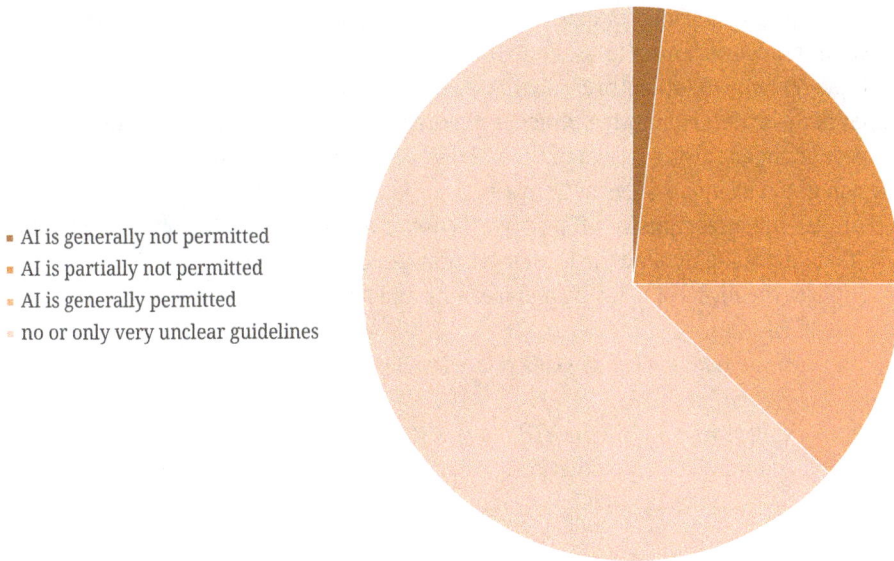

Fig. 10.1: Regulations on the use of AI tools for examinations such as term papers or exams at the 100 largest German universities according to [24].

10.3 Inter-university recommendations for AI applications in Biomedical Engineering studies

AI applications play just as important a role in the professional field of Biomedical Engineering as they do in other sectors (see Section 10.4). It is therefore essential to adapt curricula and further develop teaching content to include the teaching of AI skills in Biomedical Engineering degree programs. The technical committee "Education and Training – Biomedical Engineering in Higher Education" of the DGBMT in the VDE [27], to which the majority of the authors of this article belong, has been working on improving the quality of teaching in BME for over 15 years with 120 members and around 400 interested parties. In addition to members from industry and from clinics, research and testing facilities, the majority of the members are university lecturers who work with great commitment in various working groups on the development and dissemination of specialist information (Biomedical Engineering knowledge base), the study options for BME in German-speaking countries, the organization of study programs, accreditation, as a teaching and mediation network and with numerous other activities (position papers, expert recommendations, conference sessions, student competition, publications) (see also [27]). To this end, working groups are being formed, one of which has been working on the topic of AI application in Biomedical Engineering for the past year.

The opinions formed to date within the Technical Committee, which have taken place in two workshops and at the DGBMT annual conference since 2023, are in line with the recommendations presented in this article. They will be included in a position paper of the expert committee, which is planned for publication in 2025. In summary, it is recommended for the design of the 202 degree programs with Biomedical Engineering content at 95 universities in Germany, Austria and Switzerland:

– utilize the opportunities offered by the use of AI tools in BMT teaching and value them more highly than the challenges that can be overcome,
– update the forms of teaching and learning and adapt them to the sensible, targeted use of AI tools,
– to teach methodological AI skills related to Biomedical Engineering topics.

Other working groups within the VDE have also addressed the topic and developed relevant information for the engineering sector on the use of AI applications, which also includes academic teaching [28].

10.4 Motivation of students through AI applications in Biomedical Engineering

If skills in the use of AI tools and also in the further development or adaptation of generative models for specific purposes are taught during the degree program, it is particularly motivating for students to learn about their applications in Biomedical Engineering at the same time. Ideally, practical exercises based on the most important fields of application are set in such a way that they can be solved using recommended AI tools after a short familiarization period. This should be preceded by teaching students how to use AI systems or, if this is a learning objective, how to adapt generative models to the task at hand.

In a study conducted by VDI/VDE Innovation + Technik GmbH on behalf of the VDI Verein Deutscher Ingenieure e.V., Kautz et al. recently looked at digitalization in medical technology [29]. One chapter of this study is dedicated to the topic of AI in medical devices. Using numerous literature sources, the authors demonstrate how young, regulatory demanding and promising the use of AI in prevention, diagnosis, therapy and rehabilitation is. They find that AI-based analysis of medical image data currently dominates the use of AI in medicine, with automated image segmentation playing a key role. Radiological applications now account for around 75 % of AI systems in medicine. AI-supported studies and approvals are also increasing rapidly in the cardiovascular field. In addition, AI is increasingly being used in imaging-intensive specialities such as ophthalmology and dermatology. In pathology, AI systems are already successfully supporting tumor classification and prognosis based on histopathological images. AI also complements conventional imaging procedures in prenatal ultrasound diagnostics. In the future, the potential of AI algorithms will need to be utilized even more, particularly when analyzing time series of various sensory and (electro)physiological parameters. These include blood pressure, pulse, respiratory rate, oxygen saturation, blood sugar, body temperature and data from ECG, EEG, EMG and ERG. The possibilities for AI-based analysis of these and other parameters are almost unlimited [29]. All current specialist topics such as big data, automated therapy systems, digital twins, mHealth/eHealth, patient-specific medicine, smart systems, digital health cards, diagnostics, telemedicine, simulation of production and healthcare processes, virtual testing, medical training, regulation, business models in the healthcare sector, etc. can be advanced faster, more effectively, more cost-effectively and with fewer errors using AI, but one important realization must always be borne in mind: Every AI system is originally man-made. For all its advantages over human expertise, it has shortcomings. The underlying data was provided by humans, databases are often biased because they are incomplete, results can be hallucinated and not always trustworthy. As with all other engineering tools, higher education must therefore release graduates with the best skills to develop such systems responsibly, evaluate them critically and apply them in a targeted and meaningful way. To this end, new and expanded teaching and learning content and methods must be adapted to these new tools, taking into account the specific nature of the interdisciplinary field of Biomedical Engineering, as incorrect use can, in the worst case, cost lives. Used wisely by seriously trained graduates, AI will be a powerful tool for transferring all the work to machines that unnecessarily costs time and effort, so that cognitive human skills can focus more on creative and innovative problem solving in the medical-technical sense for patients and to support medical staff.

The additional regulatory requirements (QM systems, software lifecycle, clinical evaluation, etc.) pose a particular challenge for the application of AI in Biomedical Engineering. [30]

The critical examination of the limits of AI, as already mentioned above for the use of generative models, and the consideration of ethical aspects (who makes decisions for an adequate therapy if AI was involved in the diagnosis?) are equally important here.

References

[1] Hüsch M., Horstmann N., Breiter A. CHECK – Künstliche Intelligenz in Studium und Lehre – Die Sicht der Studierenden im WS 2023/24. Gütersloh: CHE, 2024

[2] Mehrheit der Studierenden nutzt KI – und glaubt an positive Auswirkungen der Technologie auf das eigene Arbeitsleben. Stuttgart: Wirtschaftsprüfungs- und Beratungsgesellschaft Ernst & Young, Pressemitteilung, March 2024 (Accessed August 8, 2024, at https://www.ey.com/de_de/news/2024/03/ey-studierendenstudie-2024-kuenstliche-intelligenz).

[3] KI-Lösungen für den Bildungsbereich – CampusGPT. Stuttgart: Deutsche Weiterbildungsgesellschaft mbH (Accessed November 8, 2024, at https://www.campusgpt.de/produkte).

[4]   Höhere Übersetzungsqualität als GPT-4, Google und Microsoft: DeepL bringt nächste Generation seines LLM auf den Markt. Köln: DeepL Pressemitteilung. July 17, 2024 (Accessed November 8, 2024, at https://www.deepl.com/de/press-release#2GYyHCVU8bjbu1iewCwLLx).

[5]   Vorschläge für Eigenständigkeitserklärungen bei möglicher Nutzung von KI-Tools. Darmstadt: Deutsche Gesellschaft für Hochschuldidaktik. August 25, 2023 (Accessed November 8, 2024, at https://www.dghd.de/die-dghd/downloads/).

[6]   Akademisches Serviceportal für Niedersachsen. Göttingen: GWDG Gesellschaft für wissenschaftliche Datenverarbeitung mbH (Accessed November 8, 2024, at https://docs.hpc.gwdg.de/services/chat-ai/models/index.html).

[7]   Theisen MR.ChatGPT: Risiken, Gefahren und Chancen in Lehre und Forschung, WiSt Wirtschaftswissenschaftliches Studium 2023; 52; 12: 17–23.

[8]   Semantic Scholar – A free, AI-powered research tool for scientific literature. Seattle: Ai2 (Accessed November 8, 2024, at https://www.semanticscholar.org/).

[9]   SciSpace – The Fastest Research Platform Ever. Milpitas: SciSpace. 2024 (Accessed November 8, 2024, at https://typeset.io/).

[10] Buck I., Limburg A. Hochschulbildung vor dem Hintergrund von Natural Language Processing (KI-Schreibtools). Ein Framework für eine zukunftsfähige Lehr- und Prüfungspraxis. die hochschullehre 2023; 6. DOI (ePaper): https://doi.org/10.3278/HSL2306W.

[11] Salden P., Leschke J. (eds.). Didaktische und rechtliche Perspektiven auf KI-gestütztes Schreiben in der Hochschulbildung, Bochum: Ruhr-Universität, 2023. DOI (ePaper): https://doi.org/10.13154/294-9734.

[12] Schön S., Leitner P., Lindner J., Ebner M. Learning Analytics in Hochschulen und Künstliche Intelligenz. Eine Übersicht über Einsatzmöglichkeiten, erste Erfahrungen und Entwicklungen von KI-Anwendungen zur Unterstützung des Lernens und Lehrens – In: Schmohl T., Watanabe A., Schelling K. (eds.). Künstliche Intelligenz in der Hochschulbildung. Chancen und Grenzen des KI-gestützten Lernens und Lehrens. Bielefeld: transcript 2023, 27–49. DOI (ePaper): https://doi.org/10.25656/01:27829.

[13] Seidl T., Vonhof C. Studieren mit ChatGPT & Co – Wie Studierende KI-Tools nutzen und was das für Bibliotheken bedeuten kann. In: BuB – Forum Bibliothek und Information. 2023; 11: 555–557.

[14] Der menschliche Anteil geht zusehends zurück. Bonn: Forschung & Lehre, March 21, 2024 (Accessed November 8, 2024, at https://www.forschung-und-lehre.de/forschung/der-menschliche-anteil-geht-zusehends-zurueck-6320).

[15] Stellungnahme des Präsidiums der DFG zum Einfluss generativer Modelle für die Text- und Bilderstellung auf die Wissenschaften und das Förderhandeln der DFG. Bonn: Deutsche Forschungsgemeinschaft, September 2023 (Accessed November 8, 2024, at https://www.dfg.de/resource/blob/289674/ff57cf46c5ca109cb18533b21fba49bd/230921-stellungnahme-praesidium-ki-ai-data.pdf).

[16] Leitfaden zum Prompt-Engineering. DAIR.AI, 2024 (Accessed November 8, 2024, at https://www.promptingguide.ai/de).

[17] Bucher U., Holzweißig K., Schwarzer M. Künstliche Intelligenz und wissenschaftliches Arbeiten. München: Vahlen, 2024.

[18] Biggs J. Enhancing teaching through constructive alignment. Higher education 1996; 32: 347–364.

[19] Hoeren T. Rechtsgutachten zum Umgang mit KI-Software im Hochschulkontext. In: Salden P., Leschke J. (eds.). Didaktische und rechtliche Perspektiven auf KI-gestütztes Schreiben in der Hochschulbildung. Bochum: Ruhr-Universität, 2023. DOI (ePaper): https://doi.org/10.13154/294-9734.

[20] Jawahar G., Abdul-Mageed M., Lakshmanan L. Automatic Detection of Machine Generated Text: A Critical Survey. In: Proceedings of the 28th International Conference on Computational Linguistics. Barcelona: International Committee on Computational Linguistics, 2020. DOI (ePaper): https://doi.org/10.18653/v1/2020.coling-main.208.

[21] https://www.gesetze-im-internet.de/gg/art_5.html.

[22] Budde J., Tobor J., Friedrich J. Blickpunkt – Künstliche Intelligenz: Wo stehen die deutschen Hochschulen? Berlin: Hochschulforum Digitalisierung. 2024.

[23] Blickpunkt KI-Monitor. Berlin: Hochschulforum Digitalisierung. 2024 (Accessed November 8, 2024, at https://hochschulforumdigitalisierung.de/wp-content/uploads/2024/06/Blickpunkt_KI-Monitor.pdf).

[24] Die ChatGPT-Richtlinien der 100 größten deutschen Universitäten, Amsterdam: Scribbr, 2024 (Accessed June 6, 2024, at https://www.scribbr.de/ki-tools-nutzen/chatgpt-universitaere-richtlinien/).

[25] Hinweise zur Erstellung von Bachelor- und Masterarbeiten, Stand April 2024. Berlin: Technische Universität, Abteilung I – Studierendenservice, Referat Prüfungen. (Accessed August 20, 2024, at https://www.static.tu.berlin/fileadmin/www/10002180/Abschlussarbeit_Hinweise_01_2023.pdf).

[26] Salden P., Leschke J., Persike M. Die Bereitstellung generativer KI in Hochschulen: Was ist möglich und was wünschenswert? Berlin: Hochschulforum, Digitalisierung 2024 (Accessed August 20, 2024, at https://hochschulforumdigitalisierung.de/bereitstellung-generativer-ki-in-hochschulen/).

[27] Morgenstern U., Kraft M., Seidl K., Schmitt T. Biomedizinische Technik – Studienfach mit Zukunft! mt|medizintechnik 2022;142: 25.

[28] Rolle der Künstlichen Intelligenz in der Elektro- und Informationstechnik. Offenbach: VDE-Fachausschuss Studium, Beruf und Gesellschaft 2024 (Accessed November 8, 2024, at https://www.vde.com/resource/blob/2354106/ce09748ac2fdc12f99a5d6259582a7e1/paper-data.pdf)

[29] Kautz D., Cvitkovic A., Hagen P., Huber M., Schulz C., Seydack M. Digitalisierung in der Medizintechnik – Herausforderung und Chance, Düsseldorf: VDI-Studie, January 2024, Blaue Papiere, 2.

[30] Hartung P. KI im Medizinprodukt regulatorisch konform nutzen. mt|medizintechnik 2024; 144: 9.

Christian M. Stracke

11 Artificial Intelligence and Education (AI&ED)

11.1 Introduction

In this chapter, we discuss all relationships between Artificial Intelligence (AI) and Education in its entirety what we call AI&ED (cf. Fig. 11.1). AI&ED includes both, the use of AI in Education (abbreviated as AIED) as well as the Education about AI (abbreviated as EDAI, also known as AI literacy). [1,2] We claim that two characteristics are most important for AI&ED: human responsibilities and the (learning) objectives or purposes. First, we summarize the latest research and developments related AI&ED. We elaborate the special case of the educational sector due to three conditions (human rights, dependencies and self-learning) and based on these reasons, we call for a special focus on ethical questions. Consequently, the ethical use and legal regulation of AI in Education are required and currently highly demanded due to the quick AI developments. As one key result of our analysis and discussion, we call for a new "Critique of Impure Reason" to foster both, AI competence building and critical reflections about AI&ED, as well as to guide ethical AIED. This approach should also base and direct future ethical AI&ED research and development. And a general shift is needed to the ethical questions and tasks how (open and innovative) education and science can facilitate and reform AI use in education and in general. In final consequence, we require a fundamental change in our social interactions and living together towards more responsibility. We need open discourses for awareness raising and informed decision making whether and when we want to use AI in education as well as regulation of AI use in education to safeguard AI transparency and fairness as well as to enable ethical AIED. Educational stakeholders and all citizens should define how to ethically and responsibly integrate AI into education to achieve our general learning objectives including a happy society. AI&ED has to serve the commons and the whole society.

Two aspects are of central importance for AI&ED relationships:

1. Human responsibilities: The deployment and use of AI is always a human-human interaction and there are always human responsibilities on both sides: for the developers, designers and implementers of AI as well as for the purchasers, users and processors of AI.
2. (Learning) objectives or purposes: For what (learning) objectives or purposes is AI offered and used?

This is all the truer as, on the one hand, AI is increasingly penetrating all areas of society, including education, and, on the other hand, AI as a technology is here to stay and will continue to spread.

Artificial Intelligence and Education (AI&ED)

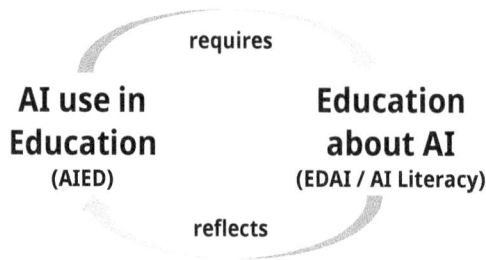

Fig. 11.1: AI&ED includes AIED and EDAI.

This chapter presents the results of our analysis and discussion of the relationships between AI and education with a special focus on ethical questions. In section 2, we summarize the latest research and developments related AI&ED. The special case of the educational sector and its causing ethical questions is highlighted in section 3. Based on that, we demand the ethical use and legal regulation of AI in education in section 4. As key result of our analysis and discussion, we call for a new "Critique of Impure Reason" in section 5 to base and guide future ethical AI&ED research and development.

11.2 Research on Artificial Intelligence and Education (AI&ED)

The concept of artificial intelligence (AI) has been controversial since the term was coined, often attributed to John McCarthy in the 1950s [3–5]. AI has been introduced and used in many industries and disciplines since the new millennium [6]. Due to the anticipated large effects that AI can achieve, many researchers and initiatives have begun to discuss and define transparent and ethical AI [1,2,5,7–14], including initial debates on the ethics of ethical AI [15]. The starting point was often the advantages and disadvantages of AI in general.

Business-related associations, in particular such as G20 [16] and OECD [17], claim numerous advantages and promises for the use of AI in general and specifically for the education sector, such as equal opportunities for all learners regardless of human teachers, inclusion through AI offerings for special needs, skills and abilities, personalization through diversity and adapted learning paths, individual support through AI chatbots and intelligent tutorial systems, measurement of competences, skills and abilities, reduction of early school leaving and dropouts.

On the other hand, numerous disadvantages and problems of AI use in general and in education in particular are also discussed, especially by independent researchers

[7,10,18–20], such as data exploitation and theft and commercialization by pure economic interests, biases and disadvantages due to non-representative data sources, lack of emotional, social and collaborative aspects, social evaluations of learners and their comparisons with each other and with other groups, anthropomorphism and unreflective trust in AI, perpetuation of traditional pedagogies, teaching methods and learning processes.

For many decades, the use of AI in education (AIED) has been studied from different perspectives [21–23], with a main focus on school education [24,25] and higher education [26]. It started with intelligent tutorial systems (ITS) [27–29] and various use cases of AIED have been analyzed such as feedback functions [30] and automatic assessments [31,32] besides the general relationship between artificial and human intelligence [33]. In addition, some international organizations have begun to discuss the potential of AIED for future sustainable education, including UNESCO with its publication 'AI in Education. Guidance for Policy-makers' [34].

In AIED research, several systematic literature reviews (SLR) have already been published on various aspects of state-of-the-art AIED, e.g. [35–42], while so far only one SLR has addressed ethical issues related to AI&ED as a whole [13].

And it is important to note and underline that all promised benefits of AIED could not be proven until now: AIED research and studies are lacking evidences for any significant and positive impact caused by AI use in education [13,43–45].

11.3 Education as special sector

Education is a special sector, not only in Germany with its special situation and the responsibility of 16 federal states. Education is a special sector worldwide, as it differs greatly from other industries and sectors in three key respects.

Firstly, education is a universal fundamental right that is enshrined in universal human rights [46] and is also pursued as Sustainable Development Goal No. 4 defined as "inclusive and equitable quality education [...] for all" [47]. At the same time, the UN Convention on the Rights of the Child [48] and the UN Convention on the Rights of Persons with Disabilities [49] call for additional efforts to guarantee education for all to the same extent. AI is often advertised to facilitate education for all what is however very different from quality education for all: Only access to biased and discriminatory chatbots can even impair the educational situation.

Secondly, there are special conditions in the education sector, especially in school education, which include both dependencies between teachers and learners and the obligation to attend school. Underage pupils must be given special protection and their parents must be informed and involved as legal guardians [50]. Thus, transparency and fairness of AI are required in particular in the education sector.

Thirdly, learning is not a product (such as screws in tool production) and cannot be forced. This means that learning outcomes and success in education cannot be predicted, as learners always decide for themselves whether they (want to) learn. And the quality of educational opportunities cannot be determined, ensured and improved as easily as with screws [51]. Therefore, teachers and educational experts should decide on the AI use in education.

Education should therefore also be seen as a living and constantly changing relationship between teachers and learners that requires careful consideration and critical reflection, including on ethical issues [50–52]. After all, the personal development of students into responsible citizens and social and valuable members of our society is crucial for next generations and our common future. This applies in particular to the use of AI in education (AIED) and the development of digital competences and skills for critical thinking and questioning (EDAI).

11.4 Ethical use and regulation of AI in education

The ethical aspects and theories for AI and education are currently being examined everywhere. Potential regulations are only just being developed, as the widespread use of AI in education (despite the long AI development time beforehand) was sudden. The surprising release of ChatGPT on November 30, 2022 and its rapid spread and use, including by pupils and students, has challenged teachers and education professionals from practically one day to the next. As a result, we are faced with many unanswered ethical questions that we need to answer quickly as AI development continues to progress faster and further. Overall, five main ethical principles are often discussed in general AI ethics: Transparency, justice and fairness, harm avoidance, responsibility, and privacy [53]. Currently, the debate concentrates on deepfakes of pictures, audios and videos causing political impact in elections as well as mob-violence in viral social media and even beyond in reality [54].

In addition to these "standard" ethical issues that apply in all areas, including education, the teaching and learning processes and the framework conditions of the special education sector raise additional ethical challenges. Therefore, there are many more ethical issues related to AI implementation and AI use in education than in other areas [55]. Fundamentally, humans should be aware of, recognize and reflect on any use of AI. Therefore, AI&ED (in addition to the particular situation in education) must always focus on and realize both AIED and EDAI [1,2]. First initiatives such as the European Network Ethical Use of AI are established as open grass-root movement and developed highly demanded guidelines for teachers without any AI knowledge as community collaboration and contribution to the commons [41]. International institutions and public supervisory authorities have now addressed AI&ED and published initial guidelines [8,34,56–58]. Their first analysis revealed ten ethical principles for AI&ED, which were grouped into seven thematic areas with some overlaps and no precise differentiation [59]. A common ethical AI&ED framework is still missing and demanded what the analysis of AI policies in relation to education reveals [60].

In the global AI&ED community, the discussion on ethics started early but was not continued and expanded [3]. It took 20 years for new debates, proposals and frameworks to emerge again from the AI&ED community and for expressing the need for trustworthy and ethical AI&ED in general [6,10,41,61] and especially in school education [50,62,63] to be recognized. The transparency that and how AI is used in education is fundamental but mostly not given in practice.

Due to the special characteristics of the education sector and the global rights to (also digital) sovereignty, citizenship and privacy, especially of children, legal regulation of AI in education is recommended and demanded [64]. However, global or regional legal instruments are still lacking across the world, and initial attempts have only been made in some countries. The European Union launched a first international initiative in 2021 with the EU AI Act, which has now been adopted and published [65]. The EU AI Act is a first step towards global AI regulation and is helpful in initiating the global debate even though it lacks a specific foundation for AI regulation based on the fundamental values of human rights, democracy and the rule of law. Just a few months later, the first international legally binding law, the Framework Convention on Artificial Intelligence and Human Rights, Democracy and the Rule of Law (Treaty 225) was approved and published by the Council of Europe and signed by member states [66]. However, both laws (AI Act and Treaty 225) do not focus on education as a special area. This gap is now being filled by the Council of Europe with its current initiative for AI regulation in education through an international convention that is intended to regulate the safeguarding and strengthening of human rights, democracy and the rule of law in the use of AI specifically for the education sector [56,57]. It will be complemented by a recommendation on AI literacy (EDAI) providing a toolbox for practical integration into educational curricula.

Even more sensitive and careful AI implementations are necessary for learners with special needs. The design and development of inclusive AI is challenging because learners with special needs require specific attention and support [49]. Careful AIED planning should avoid problematic situations and tasks that learners cannot overview or fulfil. All stakeholders (including AIED policy makers, public authorities, developers and implementers of AI systems) are responsible to enable inclusive AIED and appropriate learning scenarios for all.

The urgent need for AI regulation in education is shown by recent studies that demonstrate many legal violations and problems: "a recent report by Human Rights Watch (2022) reviewed 164 EdTech products deployed across 49 countries, finding that 89% of them had monitored or had the capacity to monitor students and harvest their personal data without consent, as well as tracking students across the internet and over time" [67]. International regulations such as the initiative launched by the Council of Europe are urgently needed to create legal conditions and rules in addition to the required global ethical guidelines. And on the other hand, such AIED regulations will also ease and improve the AI use in education because binding laws are informing educators and teachers (and the students and their parents) what is allowed and possible.

In summary, we can conclude that AI&ED can and should contribute to global ethical values to guarantee, enable and support human rights, democracy and the rule of law [1,2,55]. We need more debates on ethical issues globally to increase awareness and consensus on our preferred AI&ED future. And we should shift our focus from the question how AI can support and improve education to the task how (open and innovative) education and science can facilitate and reform AI [19,68]. AI cannot be the game changer for education (and should not be labelled as such) but educational stakeholders have to keep the lead and decision making about AIED. Education has to reflect AI and take it into consideration as potential instrument that can or cannot improve learning design, educational processes and the achievement of intended learning objectives.

11.5 Critique of impure reason

This argument leads us to a demand: we need a new critique of impure reason. We need to ask ourselves the big and central questions again. A great deal is simply tried out and done because it is possible, and fundamental prerequisites and assumptions are not questioned at all. What are learning processes and how do they work? What are our (social) learning goals and how do we achieve them?

Numerous disciplines do research on learning processes alongside the educational sciences. In psychology, the cognitive psychology approach of cognitive load has failed. After twenty years, its inventors had to admit that there are not three types of cognitive load (intrinsic, extraneous and germane load) but only two, as germane load is not an independent type [69]. This means that practically all research results based on germane load and the distinction between the three cognitive load types are fundamentally questionable, if not worthless [70]. And in medical imaging, colorations and assignments are made without thoroughly and critically analyzing their accuracy and relevance in advance [71]. In addition, dopamine research is currently discussing a reversal of the interpretation of associative learning processes in the brain [72,73]. In machine learning and deep learning as well as in their application disciplines, large amounts of data are extrapolated, modeled and analyzed with the help of stochastics and its formulas and algorithms for approximations and probability calculations [74–76]. Here, too, the intermediate steps are no longer comprehensible in their complexity and can only (or must?) be believed and trusted. And also, the latest approaches to achieve interpretable graph neural networks are based on black-box baselines [77].

With the help of these techniques, we obtain impressive and countless results, which are usually used as a justification for research with and on AI. But are these results correct? Or are they not impure in the sense that they are based on unclear, untraceable assumptions, on falsified, non-representative data sets and on automated, uncontrollable analyses and conclusions? A new critique of impure reason should focus on these questions in order to enable a major discourse in research and, above all, in society. We need to clarify how we want to use AI, what we want to allow and what we want to prohibit, how we want to make the best possible use of AI in education and society and, if necessary, how we can switch it off. That is valid not only for educational sector but also for other critical sectors such as medicine and healthcare in which the ethical debates have started, too [78].

Therefore, such a new critique of impure reason has to question and reflect upon the general theories, thinking and justifications for AI and in particular for AI&ED. The label "intelligence" was coined in the 1950ies to distinguish from cybernetics [79,80]. In the following, it was leading to a simplistic and false believe in the capabilities of AI systems by the broad masses. The public discourse was shifting towards the potentials of the technology leading to huge exaggerations in both directions: opportunities beyond human brains and threads of world domination and destruction. That goes hand in hand with neo-liberal de-regulation in economy and politics allowing global hyperscalers to dictate and apply any AI services without proof of concept. Not the society but the own commercial benefits are the guiding principles for AI providers but also for many politicians and individuals worldwide. Thus, we have to establish again a global debate on key guidelines how we want to use AI and to live in the future [50]. And we have to consider what will happen with following young generations and future citizens if we do not care about AI impacts in education as well as in all sectors.

Finally, we need a new critique of impure reason because education has to deal with much more than only cognitive development and competence building what AI is mainly addressing. Gardner [81] has distinguished between eight intelligences already in the 1980ies even though his theory can be questioned like the whole concept of Artificial Intelligence and its linguistic or logical-mathematical foundations. Overall, we need holistic education to enable students developing them by themselves to become responsible citizens and members of and contributors to a happy society.

11.6 Conclusions

Many ethical questions are emerging in the development, implementation and use of AI. In particular in the special sector education, specific ethical considerations and alerts are needed because of the status of education as global human right as well as the mandatory school visit for young children not in legal age. As a consequence, additional obligations and careful learning designs and reflections are required for ethical AI&ED to ensure an appropriate and safe implementation to meet educational needs. There is a huge and urgent demand for ethical AI&ED policies, strategies and guidelines. In particular in the school education, we have to ensure inclusiveness for all young pupils and to avoid that AI&ED leads to increasing digital divide. Three ethical imperatives can enable ethical AI&ED: the development, implementation and use of AIED should be technology-independent, impact-oriented, and society-focused to guarantee positive impacts and benefits [50]. And a general shift is needed to the ethical questions and task how (open and innovative) education and science can facilitate and reform AI use in education and in general.

In such a way, AI&ED will serve the sustainable society as a broad and ambitious objective for future AI developments and applications [34,36,58,63]. For our sustainable society, we need both, to integrate AI use in Education (AIED) as well as to facilitate and improve Education about AI (EDAI) [10,55]. Our sustainable society depends on educated students and citizens with digital and AI competences to successfully understand and manage our future challenges [61,82–84]. We need a holistic AI&ED approach combining AIED and EDAI for all future AI concepts and implementations in education so that we can guarantee ethical AI&ED and the fulfillment of societal impact by AIED for the good. A new Critique of Impure Reason should base and guide ethical AI&ED developments and their continuous improvements serving the global commons and society.

In final consequence, we require a fundamental change in our social interactions and living together towards more responsibility at individual, organizational, regional and international levels. We have to fight against egoism, commercialization and monopolism in education to foster *quality* education for all. And we have to launch open discourses for awareness raising and informed decision making whether and when we want to use AI in education. And we need regulation of AI use in education to safeguard AI transparency and fairness as well as to enable ethical AIED. Not international hyperscalers only interested in commercial profits but educational stakeholders and all citizens should define how to ethically and responsibly integrate AI into education to achieve our general learning objectives including a happy society.

References

[1]   Holmes W., Stracke C. M., Chounta I.-A., Allen D., Baten D., Dimitrova V., ... , & Wasson B. (2023). AI and Education. A View Through the Lens of Human Rights, Democracy and the Rule of Law. Legal and Organizational Requirements. In: Artificial Intelligence in Education. Communications in Computer and Information Science, 1831. (pp. 79–84). https://doi.org/10.1007/978-3-031-36336-8_12.

[2]   Stracke C. M., Chounta I.-A., Dimitrova V., Havinga B., & Holmes W. (2024b). Ethical AI and Education: The need for international regulation to foster human rights, democracy and the rule of law. Artificial Intelligence in Education. Communications in Computer and Information Science. Springer. Communications in Computer and Information Science, 2151, 439–445. https://doi.org/10.1007/978-3-031-64 312-5_55.

[3]   Aiken R. M., & Epstein R. G. (2000). Ethical Guidelines for AI in Education: Starting a Conversation. International Journal of Artificial Intelligence in Education, 11, 163–176.

[4]   Chaka C. (2022). Fourth industrial revolution – a review of applications, pro-spects, and challenges for artificial intelligence, robotics and blockchain in higher education. Research and Practice in Technol-

ogy Enhanced Learning, 18. (Accessed January 13, 2023, at https://rptel.apsce.net/index.php/RPTEL/article/view/2023-18002).

[5] Huang R., Tlili A., Xu L., Chen Y., Zheng L., Saleh Metwally A. H., … , & Bonk C. J. (2023). Educational futures of intelligent synergies between humans, digital twins, avatars, and robots – the iSTAR framework. Journal of Applied Learning & Teaching, 6(2), 1–16. https://doi.org/10.37074/jalt.2023.6.2.33.

[6] Borenstein J., & Howard A. (2021). Emerging challenges in AI and the need for AI ethics education. AI and Ethics, 1(1), 61–65. https://doi.org/10.1007/s43681-020-00002-7.

[7] Bozkurt A., Xiao J., Lambert S., Pazurek A., Crompton H., Koseoglu S., … , & Jandrić P. (2023). Speculative Futures on ChatGPT and Generative Artificial Intelligence (AI): A Collective Reflection from the Educational Landscape. Asian Journal of Distance Education, 18(1), 53–130. https://www.asian-jde.com/ojs/index.php/AsianJDE/article/view/709/394.

[8] European Commission (2022). Ethical guidelines on the use of artificial intelligence (AI) and data in teaching and learning for educators, (Accessed January 13, 2023, at https://data.europa.eu/doi/10.2766/153756).

[9] High-Level Expert Group (HLEG) on AI (2019). Ethics Guidelines for Trustworthy AI, https://ec.europa.eu/digital-single-market/en/news/ethics-guidelines-trustworthy-ai.

[10] Holmes W., & Tuomi I. (2022). State of the art and practice in AI in education. European Journal of Education, 57, 542–570. https://doi.org/10.1111/ejed.12533.

[11] Kazim E., & Koshiyama A. S. (2021). A high-level overview of AI ethics. Patterns, 2(9), 100314. https://doi.org/10.1016/j.patter.2021.100314.

[12] Larsson S., & Heintz F. (2020). Transparency in artificial intelligence. Internet Policy Review, 9(2), 1–16. https://doi.org/10.14763/2020.2.1469.

[13] Stracke C. M., Chounta I.-A., & Holmes W. (2024c). Global trends in scientific debates on trustworthy and ethical Artificial Intelligence and education. Artificial Intelligence in Education. Communications in Computer and Information Science, 2150, 254–262. https://doi.org/10.1007/978-3-031-64315-6_21.

[14] UNESCO, UNICEF, The World Bank, & OECD. (2021, June). What's next? Lessons on education recovery: Findings from a survey of ministries of education amid the COVID-19 pandemic. http://covid19.uis.unesco.org/wp-content/uploads/sites/11/2021/07/National-Education-Responses-to-COVID-19-Report2_v3.pdf.

[15] Hagendorff T. (2020). The ethics of AI ethics: An evaluation of guidelines. Minds and Machines, 30(1), 99–120. https://doi.org/10.1007/s11023-020-09517-8.

[16] G20 (2023). G20 New Delhi Leaders' Declaration. New Delhi, India (9–10 September 2023). https://www.g20.org/content/dam/gtwenty/gtwenty_new/document/G20-New-Delhi-Leaders-Declaration.pdf.

[17] Vincent-Lancrin S., & van der Vlies R. (2020). Trustworthy artificial intelligence (AI) in education: Promises and challenges (OECD Education Working Papers, Vol. 218). OECD Publishing, Paris. https://dx.doi.org/10.1787/9789264311671-en.

[18] Bozkurt A., Xiao J., Farrow R., Bai J. Y. H., Nerantzi C., Moore S., … , & Asino T.I. (2024). The Manifesto for Teaching and Learning in a Time of Generative AI: A Critical Collective Stance to Better Navigate the Future. Open Praxis, 16(4), 487–513. https://openpraxis.org/articles/10.55982/openpraxis.16.4.777.

[19] Tlili A., Adarkwah M. A., Lo C. K., Bozkurt A., Burgos D. Bonk C. J., … , & Huang R. (2024). Taming the monster: How can open education promote the effective and safe use of generative AI in education? Journal of Learning for Development, 11(3), 398–413. https://doi.org/10.56059/jl4d.v11i3.1657.

[20] Xiao J., Bozkurt A., Nichols M., Pazurek A., Stracke C. M., Bai J. Y. H., … , & Themeli C. (2025). Venturing into the Unknown: Critical Insights into Grey Areas and Pioneering Future Directions in Educational Generative AI Research. TechTrends (2025). https://doi.org/10.1007/s11528-025-01060-6.

[21] Dillenbourg, P. (2016). The evolution of research on digital education. International Journal of Artificial Intelligence in Education, 26, 544–60. https://doi.org/10.1007/s40593-016-0106-z.

[22] Kent C., & du Boulay B. (2022). AI for Learning. CRC Press, Boca Raton, FL. https://doi.org/10.1201/9781003194545.

[23] Pinkwart N. (2016). Another 25 years of AIED? Challenges and opportunities for intelligent educational technologies of the future. International Journal of Artificial Intelligence in Education, 26, 771–83. https://doi.org/10.1007/s40593-016-0099-7.

[24] Hrastinski S., Olofsson A. D., Arkenback C., Ekström S., Ericsson E., Fransson G., ... , & Utterberg M. (2019). Critical imaginaries and reflections on artificial intelligence and robots in post digital K-12 education. Postdigital Science and Education, 1(2), 427–445. https://doi.org/10.1007/s42438-019-00046-x.

[25] Luckin R., George K., & Cukurova M. (2022). AI for school teachers. CRC Press, Boca Raton, FL. https://doi.org/10.1201/9781003193173.

[26] Crompton H., Bernacki M. L., & Greene J. (2020). Psychological foundations of emerging technologies for teaching and learning in higher education. Current Opinion in Psychology, 36, 101–105. https://doi.org/10.1016/j.copsyc.2020.04.011.

[27] Corbett A. T., Koedinger K. R., & Anderson J. R. (1997). Intelligent tutoring systems. In Handbook of human-computer interaction (pp. 849–874). North-Holland.

[28] Dermeval D., Paiva R., Bittencourt I., Vassileva J., & Borges D. (2018). Authoring tools for designing intelligent tutoring systems: a systematic review of the literature. International Journal of Artificial Intelligence in Education, 28, 336–84. https://doi.org/10.1007/s40593-017-0157-9.

[29] du Boulay B. (2016). Recent Meta-reviews and Meta–analyses of AIED Systems. International Journal of Artificial Intelligence in Education, 26, 536–537. https://doi.org/10.1007/s40593-015-0060-1.

[30] Benotti L., Martínez M. C., & Schapachnik F. (2018). A tool for introducing computer science with automatic formative assessment. IEEE Transactions on Learning Technologies, 11(2), 179–192. https://doi.org/10.1109/TLT.2017.2682084.

[31] Luckin R. (2017). Towards artificial intelligence-based assessment systems. Nature Human Behaviour, 1(3), 1–3. https://doi.org/10.1038/s41562-016-0028.

[32] Yang Y., Xia L., & Zhao, Q. (2019). An automated grader for Chinese essay combining shallow and deep semantic attributes. IEEE Access, 7, 176306–176316. https://doi.org/10.1109/ACCESS.2019.2957582.

[33] Baker R. S. (2016). Stupid Tutoring Systems, Intelligent Humans. International Journal of Artificial Intelligence in Education, 26, 600–614. https://doi.org/10.1007/s40593-016-0105-0.

[34] Miao F., Holmes W., Huang R., & Zhang H. (2021). AI and education: Guidance for policy-makers. United Nations Educational, Scientific and Cultural Organization. https://unesdoc.unesco.org/ark:/48223/pf0000376709.

[35] Bond M., Khosravi H., De Laat M., Bergdahl N., Negrea V., Oxley E., ... , & Siemens G. (2024). A meta systematic review of artificial intelligence in higher education: a call for increased ethics, collaboration, and rigour. International Journal of Educational Technology in Higher Education 21(4). https://doi.org/10.1186/s41239-023-00436-z.

[36] Chen L., Chen P., & Lin Z. (2020). Artificial intelligence in education: A review. IEEE Access, 8, 75264–75278. https://doi.org/10.1109/ACCESS.2020.2988510

[37] Crompton H., Jones M. V., & Burke D. (2022). Affordances and challenges of artificial intelligence in K-12 education: a systematic review. Journal of Research on Technology in Education. https://doi.org/10.1080/15391523.2022.2121344.

[38] Kurdi G., Leo J., Parsia B., Sattler U., & Al-Emari S. (2020). A systematic review of automatic question generation for educational purposes. International Journal of Artificial Intelligence in Education, 30, 121–204. https://doi.org/10.1007/s40593-019-00186-y.

[39] Sanusi I.T., Oyelere S.S., Vartiainen H., Suhonen J., & Tukiainen M. (2022). A systematic review of teaching and learning machine learning in K-12 education. Education and Information Technologies. https://doi.org/10.1007/s10639-022-11416-7.

[40] Sottilare R. A., Burke S., Salas E., Sinatra A. M., Johnston J. H., & Gilbert S. B. (2018). Designing adaptive instruction for teams: a meta-analysis. International Journal of Artificial Intelligence in Education, 28, 225–64. https://doi.org/10.1007/s40593-017-0146-z.

[41] Stracke C. M., Chounta I.-A., Holmes W., Tlili, A., & Bozkurt A. (2023a). A standardised PRISMA-based protocol for systematic reviews of the scientific literature on Artificial Intelligence and educa-

tion (AI&ED). Journal of Applied Learning and Teaching, 6(2), 64–70. https://doi.org/10.37074/jalt.2023.6.2.38.

[42] Zawacki-Richter O., Marín V. I., Bond M., & Gouverneur F. (2019). Systematic review of research on artificial intelligence applications in higher education – Where are the educators? International Journal of Educational Technology in Higher Education, 16(1), 1–27. https://doi.org/10.1186/s41239-019-0171-0.

[43] Bastani H., Bastani O., Sungu A., Ge H., Kabakcı Ö., & Mariman R. (2024). Generative AI Can Harm Learning. The Wharton School Research Paper. http://dx.doi.org/10.2139/ssrn.4895486.

[44] Deng R., Jiang M., Yu X., Lu Y., & Liu S. (2025). Does ChatGPT enhance student learning? A systematic review and meta-analysis of experimental studies. Computers & Education, 227, 105224. https://doi.org/10.1016/j.compedu.2024.105224.

[45] Roe J. & Perkins M. (2024). Generative AI and Agency in Education: A Critical Scoping Review and Thematic Analysis: A Preprint. arXiv:2411.00631. https://doi.org/10.48550/arXiv.2411.00631.

[46] United Nations (1948). Universal Declaration of Human Rights. https://www.un.org/sites/un2.un.org/files/2021/03/udhr.pdf.

[47] United Nations (2015). Transforming Our World: The 2030 Agenda for Sustainable Development. A/RES/70/1. https://sdgs.un.org/sites/default/files/publications/21252030%20Agenda%20for%20Sustainable%20Development%20web.pdf.

[48] United Nations (1990). Convention on the Rights of the Child. https://www.ohchr.org/sites/default/files/crc.pdf.

[49] United Nations (2006). Convention on the Rights of Persons with Disabilities and Optional Protocol. https://www.un.org/disabilities/documents/convention/convoptprot-e.pdf.

[50] Stracke C. M. (2024). Artificial Intelligence and Education: Ethical questions and guidelines for their relations based on human rights, democracy and the rule of law. In D. Burgos et al. (eds.). Radical Solutions for Artificial Intelligence and Digital Transformation in Education. Lecture Notes in Educational Technology (pp. 97–107). https://doi.org/10.1007/978-981-97-8638-1_7.

[51] Stracke C. M. (2019). Quality Frameworks and Learning Design for Open Education. The International Review of Research in Open and Distributed Learning, 20(2), 180–203. https://doi.org/10.19173/irrodl.v20i2.4213.

[52] Gewirth A. (1960). Meta-ethics and normative ethics. Mind, 69(274), 187–205. https://doi.org/10.1093/mind/LXIX. 274.187.

[53] Jobin A., Ienca M., & Vayena E. (2019). The global landscape of AI ethics guidelines. Nature Machine Intelligence, 1(9), 389–399. https://doi.org/10.1038/s42256-019-0088-2.

[54] Groh M., Sankaranarayanan A., Singh N., Kim D. Y., Lippman A., & Picard R. (2024). Human detection of political speech deepfakes across transcripts, audio, and video. Nature Communications 15(7629), 1–16. https://doi.org/10.1038/s41467-024-51998-z.

[55] Holmes W., Persson J., Chounta I.-A., Wasson B., & Dimitrova V. (2022a). Artificial Intelligence and Education. A critical view through the lens of human rights, democracy and the rule of law, https://rm.coe.int/artificial-intelligence-and-education-a-critical-view-through-the-lens/1680a886bd.

[56] Council of Europe (2023a). Regulating Artificial Intelligence in education. https://rm.coe.int/regulating-artificial-intelligence-in-education-26th-session-council-o/1680ac9b7c.

[57] Council of Europe (2023b). The Transformative Power of Education: Universal Values and Civic Renewal. Resolutions of the 26th Session of the Council of Europe Standing Conference of Ministers of Education (28–29 September 2023). MED-26(2023)06 final. https://rm.coe.int/resolutions-26th-session-council-of-europe-standing-conference-of-mini/1680abee7f.

[58] European Parliament (2021). Report on artificial intelligence in education, culture and the audiovisual sector (2020/2017(INI)). Committee on Culture and Education. https://www.europarl.europa.eu/doceo/document/A-9-2021-0127_EN.html.

[59] Nguyen A., Ngo, H. N., Hong, Y., Dang, B, & Nguyen, B.-P. T. (2023). Ethical principles for artificial intelligence in education. Education and Information Technologies, 28, 4221–4241 (2023). https://doi.org/10.1007/s10639-022-11316-w.

[60] Stracke C. M., Griffiths D., Pappa D., Bećirović S., Polz E., Perla L., Di Grassi A., Massaro S., Skenduli M. P., Burgos D., Punzo V., Amram D., Ziouvelou X., Katsamori D., Gabriel S., Nahar N., Schleiss J., & Hollins, P. (2025). Analysis of Artificial Intelligence Policies for Higher Education in Europe. International Journal of Interactive Multimedia and Artificial Intelligence, 9(2), 124–137. https://doi.org/10.9781/ijimai.2025.02.011.

[61] Holmes W., Porayska-Pomsta K., Holstein K., Sutherland E., Baker T., Buckingham Shum S., ..., & Koedinger K. R. (2022b). Ethics of AI in education: Towards a community-wide framework. International Journal of Artificial Intelligence in Education 32(3), 504–526. https://www.doi.org/10.1007/s40593-021-00239-1.

[62] Akgun S., & Greenhow C. (2021). Artificial intelligence in education: Addressing ethical challenges in K-12 settings. AI and Ethics, 2, 431–440. https://doi.org/10.1007/s43681-021-00096-7.

[63] Chounta I.-A., Bardone E., Raudsep A., & Pedaste M. (2022). Exploring teachers' perceptions of Artificial Intelligence as a tool to support their practice in Estonian K-12 education. International Journal of Artificial Intelligence in Education, 32(3), 725–755. https://www.doi.org/10.1007/s40593-021-00243-5.

[64] Cannataci J. A. (2021). Artificial intelligence and privacy, and children's privacy. Report of the UN Special Rapporteur on the right to privacy (A/HRC/46/37). https://documents-dds-ny.un.org/doc/UNDOC/GEN/G21/015/65/PDF/G2101565.pdf.

[65] European Union (2024). AI Act (Artificial Intelligence Act). Regulation (EU) 2024/1689 of the European Parliament and of the Council of 13 June 2024 laying down harmonised rules on artificial intelligence. https://eur-lex.europa.eu/eli/reg/2024/1689/oj.

[66] Council of Europe (2024). Framework Convention on Artificial Intelligence and Human Rights, Democracy and the Rule of Law (Treaty 225). https://rm.coe.int/1680afae3c.

[67] Lazarus M. D., Truong M., Douglas P., & Selwyn N. (2022). Artificial intelligence and clinical anatomical education: Promises and perils. Anatomic Science Education, 00, 1–14. https://doi.org/10.1002/ase.2221.

[68] Stracke C. M. (2020). Open Science and Radical Solutions for Diversity, Equity and Quality in Research: A Literature Review of Different Research Schools, Philosophies and Frameworks and Their Potential Impact on Science and Education. In D. Burgos (Ed.). Radical Solutions and Open Science. An Open Approach to Boost Higher Education. Lecture Notes in Educational Technology (pp. 17–37). Springer: Singapore. https://doi.org/10.1007/978-981-15-4276-3_2.

[69] Sweller J., van Merriënboer J. J., & Paas F. (January 2019). Cognitive Architecture and Instructional Design: 20 Years Later. Educational Psychology Review, 31, 261–292. https://doi.org/10.1007/s10648-019-09465-5.

[70] Leppink J. (2020). Revisiting cognitive load theory: second thoughts and unaddressed questions. Scientia Medica, 30, e36918. https://doi.org/10.15448/1980-6108.2020.1.36918.

[71] Elliott M. L., Knodt A. R., Ireland D., Morris M. L., Poulton R., Ramrakha S., ..., & Hariri A. R. (2020). What Is the Test-Retest Reliability of Common Task-Functional MRI Measures? New Empirical Evidence and a Meta-Analysis. Psychological Science, 31(7), 792–806. https://doi.org/10.1177/0956797620916786.

[72] Jeong H., Taylor A., Floeder J. R., Lohmann M., Mihalas S., Wu B., ..., & Namboodiri V. M. K. (2022). Mesolimbic dopamine release conveys causal associations. Science 378, eabq6740. https://doi.org/10.1126/science.abq6740.

[73] Qian L., Burrell M., Hennig J. A., Matias S., Murthy V. N., Gershman S. J., & Uchida N. (2024). The role of prospective contingency in the control of behavior and dopamine signals during associative learning. bioRxiv 2024.02.05.578961. https://doi.org/10.1101/2024.02.05.578961.

[74] Santos Arteaga F. J., Di Caprio D., Tavana M., Cucchiari D., Campistol, J. M., Oppenheimer, F., ..., & Revuelta, I. (2024). On the capacity of artificial intelligence techniques and statistical methods to deal with low-quality data in medical supply chain environments. Engineering Applications of Artificial Intelligence, 133, 108610. https://doi.org/10.1016/j.engappai.2024.108610.

[75] Tynes M., Gao W., Burrill D. J., Batista E. R., Perez D., Yang P., & Lubbers N. (2021). Pairwise Difference Regression: A Machine Learning Meta-algorithm for Improved Prediction and Uncertainty

Quantification in Chemical Search. Journal of Chemical Information and Modeling, 61(8), 3846–3857. https://doi.org/10.1021/acs.jcim.1c00670.

[76] Wang Y., & King R. D. (2024). Extrapolation is not the same as interpolation. Machine Learning, 113, 8205–8232. https://doi.org/10.1007/s10994-024-06591-2.

[77] Barwey S., Kim H., & Maulik R. (2025). Interpretable A-posteriori error indication for graph neural network surrogate models. Computer Methods in Applied Mechanics and Engineering, 433, 117509. https://doi.org/10.1016/j.cma.2024.117509.

[78] Haltaufderheide J., Ranisch R. (2024). The ethics of ChatGPT in medicine and healthcare: a systematic review on Large Language Models (LLMs). npj Digital Medicine 7(183), 1–11. https://doi.org/10.1038/s41746-024-01157-x.

[79] Seising (2025). In diesem Band …

[80] Stracke C. M., Bohr B., Gabriel S., Galla N., Hofmann M., Karolyi H., Mersmann-Hoffmann H., Mönig J. M., Mundorf M., Opel S., Rischke-Neß J., Schröppel M., Silvestri A., & Stroot G. (2024a). What is Artificial Intelligence (AI)? How can I use AI ethically at university? Edited by the German Network "Ethische Nutzung von KI". https://doi.org/10.5281/zenodo.10995669.

[81] Gardner H. (1983). Frames of Mind: The Theory of Multiple Intelligences.

[82] Stracke C. M., Burgos D., Santos-Hermosa G., Bozkurt A., Sharma R. C., Swiatek C., Inamorato dos Santos A., Mason J., Ossiannilsson E., Shon J. G., Wan M., Agbu J.-F., Farrow R., Karakaya Ö., Nerantzi C., Ramírez Montoya M. S., Conole G., Cox G., & Truong V. (2022a). Responding to the initial challenge of COVID-19 pandemic: Analysis of international responses and impact in school and higher education. Sustainability, 14(3), 1876. https://doi.org/10.3390/su14031876.

[83] Stracke C. M., Sharma R. C., Bozkurt A., Burgos D., Swiatek C., Inamorato dos Santos A., Mason J., Ossiannilsson E., Santos-Hermosa G., Shon J. G., Wan M., Agbu J.-F., Farrow R., Karakaya Ö., Nerantzi C., Ramírez Montoya M. S., Conole G., Cox G., & Truong V. (2022b). Impact of COVID-19 on formal education: An international review on practices and potentials of Open Education at a distance. The International Review of Research in Open and Distributed Learning, 23(4), 1–18. https://doi.org/10.19173/irrodl.v23i4.6120.

[84] Stracke C. M. (2018). Como a Educação Aberta pode melhorar a qualidade de aprendizagem e produzir impacto em alunos, organizações e na sociedade? [= How can Open Education improve learning quality and achieve impact for learners, organizations and in society?] In Utopias and Distopias da Tecnologia na Educação a Distância e Aberta (pp. 499–545). https://doi.org/10.5281/zenodo.3956396.

Olaf Dössel, Axel Loewe

12 Uncertainties, errors, explainability and responsibility for AI in medicine

12.1 Motivation and differentiation

If artificial intelligence (AI) and machine learning (ML) are used in medicine, a central question arises: What if an AI program makes a mistake? Of course, the question must be asked in all areas of application of AI. But in medicine, damage to life and limb can occur. We expect that errors are very rare, but you ask: what if I myself am the rare case in which the computer delivers an incorrect result. The analysis of this problem requires a closer look at possible uncertainties and errors, their quantitative determination, and their prevention.

The "black box" nature of AI algorithms is often referred to. Data go into an AI program, a result comes out, but no one knows what caused the algorithm to deliver exactly that result. People want an explanation – especially in medicine. What feature in the data led to the decision? How can one justify the decision? Clinicians need to explain to the patient why they came to one or the other conclusion. Here, too, we need to take a closer look: what exactly do we mean by explainability. And how can we check whether the required explainability is guaranteed?

All of this has an impact on the question "who is responsible for the decisions of an AI system in medicine (a medical system containing an AI algorithm)?" The actors include the manufacturer, the doctor and the patient. If a patient decides to use an AI program without consulting a doctor, it is just the manufacturer and the patient. Everyone involved has a special duty of care for their part. But: what exactly is the manufacturer of a medical system responsible for and what is the doctor responsible for? And whom can the patient accuse if an error has occurred?

This chapter focuses on AI in medical systems within the scope of the Medical Device Regulation (MDR). It focuses on systems in which numbers (single numbers, number arrays, or number matrices) are input into an algorithm and one or more numbers or classifications are output. The input and output of texts such as in large language models (e.g. ChatGPT) are not subject of these considerations. Typical input data are electrocardiograms (ECG), laboratory results from blood samples or x-ray images. The output can be an estimated value such as a blood pressure, a blood sugar level or a classification such as benign or malignant tissue or even a preferred therapy recommendation [1].

In this article, AI systems are always trained with data for which the "ground truth" is known, in order to later apply these systems to unknown data of the same type. Thus, only AI systems with "supervised learning" are considered. In "unsupervised learning", the algorithm should divide the data well into classes. This is an important task in medical research, but it practically does not occur in medical systems.

The AI algorithms considered in this chapter all belong to the group of ML. The best-known ML algorithms are polynomial or logistic regression, support vector machines (SVM), decision trees and random forests, k-nearest neighbor methods (kNN) and of course in particular neural networks and deep neural networks (DNN).

In this article, self-learning systems that continuously update the ML-algorithm are not considered. They are to the knowledge of the authors of this article not yet implemented into medical systems and they need special considerations [2].

The AI system is used, for example, to estimate diagnostically important numbers because determining these numbers directly is too expensive, or because the exact measurement takes too long, and a decision has to be made immediately. These tasks are called "regression." The second important application of AI in medicine is the assignment of input data to a specific class. Does a mammogram show an abnormal spot that indicates carcinoma? Does an ECG contain sections that indicate an arrhythmia? Is a mole on the skin benign or malignant? Is a patient infected with the SARS-CoV-2 or not? These tasks are called "classification".

As indicated by the title, this chapter does not address data protection and data privacy aspects. Federated learning is not looked at. Neither is the problem of defense against hacking. Likewise, future modifications of the relation between medical doctor and patient are not investigated. These topics lead to other types of problems that need special consideration [3,4].

This article aims to impact future regulations for approval of medical systems that contain ML [5]. It does not provide an explicit check list for regulatory affairs.

12.2 Uncertainties and errors – what are the causes, and can they be avoided?

In the literature on measurement errors, a distinction is made between epistemic and aleatoric uncertainties [6]. Aleatoric uncertainties are based on random and natural fluctuations that can be described by stochastic distribution functions, e.g. the thermal noise of a measuring device. Unfortunately, there are often "outliers" in medicine because a measurement was not carried out correctly or under unusual circumstances (e.g. different body position). These errors also occur randomly and are unpredictable. Epistemic uncertainties, on the other hand, are due to a lack of knowledge. A simple example: a diagnostically important quantity z is difficult to determine, but the measurands $x1$ and $x2$ are easy to measure. We assume a relationship like $z = a*x1 + b*x2 + e$ and want to use statistics / ML to get z from measuring $x1$ and $x2$. Through many (at least 2) measurements of the triple z, $x1$ and $x2$, we can only estimate the parameters a and b leading to epistemic uncertainties. Our model is not entirely correct. We can reduce the uncertainty of a and b through a larger database (more patients). But there is another epistemic uncertainty: perhaps the linear model is not correct, and it would have been better to use a polynomial of 3rd degree. Or there is another quantity x3 that we do not know about yet and that we have not even measured, but which has a strong influence on the result: $z = a*x1 + b*x2 + c*x3 + e$. Then, we will not be able to determine the value of z exactly from the measurement of solely x1 and x2.

These considerations are very important in medicine. Almost all measurements in medicine have measurement errors that can impact diagnostic decisions. This also means that almost all clinical studies have a high level of statistical uncertainty. A larger patient base can lead to the derived decisions becoming better and better. This is the basic principle of evidence-based medicine. Even though medical publications are normally reviewed by medical statisticians, the results of similarly designed medical studies often differ. This is probably because an important additional variable (as x3 in the example above) was not taken into account and the patient group in study 1 had a different distribution of x3 than in study 2.

How does this relate to ML in medicine? ML also involves measured variables that are subject to errors (noise and outliers). In ML, too, the uncertainties tend to become smaller as the database for training becomes larger, so that the parameters of the model (e.g., the weights of a DNN) can be better determined. But it will happen that an important quantity (confounding factor) has not been measured because it is currently unknown that this quantity is important. If this quantity has a different distribution in the training data set as compared to the data set to which we apply the ML system, then the results will be wrong more often in clinical use than in training. In this case, the ML system cannot "generalize" well.

In classification tasks, the ground truth for the training data set is often known very precisely based on complex methods. For example, whether a melanoma is malignant can usually be determined very precisely through a histological examination. But there is also the case that the "ground truth" is not exactly known. There can be differing opinions even among trained cardiologists when it comes to attributing patterns in an ECG to a specific cardiac arrhythmia. Therefore, even with the utmost care, the training data set will have errors.

Related to this are the errors that could happen if the people selected for a clinical study are not sufficiently similar to the people in the later application regarding the relevant characteristics. In ML, the problem is known as "bias." The ethical considerations regarding the use of ML in medicine attach great importance to this problem. If the patient cohort selected for training the ML system is not a representative cross-section of the people for whom the ML system is later to be used or if this group of people is not even defined properly, a lack of generalizability will very likely be observed. The error rates observed during training will then be exceeded in clinical practice.

The problem has been known for a long time in clinical studies. A clinical study must specify inclusion and exclusion criteria for the selection of patients. For example, if the result is to be applied to men and women, an equal number of men and women must be represented in the study. But how should one proceed with other possible confounding factors? If there is reason to believe that patients with diabetes mellitus will behave differently when being part of a clinical study, either all patients with diabetes mellitus must be excluded (exclusion criterion) or patients with and without diabetes mellitus must be equally represented in the study (or analyzed separately with adequate methods). In the former case, the results must not be applied to patients with diabetes mellitus. Everything in this section that referred to clinical studies applies equally to the application of ML in medicine. The training data set must accurately identify inclusion and exclusion criteria. This places high demands on the selection of patients who are included in the training data set. The same criteria must then also apply to the application. Otherwise, the information about the performance and uncertainty of the ML system is too positive and will probably be worse in everyday clinical practice.

Importantly, all ML systems will make mistakes due to aleatory and epistemic uncertainties, errors in annotation by experts and non-representative selection of patients. But these are the same mistakes that have long been known for all fields of evidence-based medicine.

Which errors can be avoided? Measuring devices always have noise, which is unavoidable (aleatory uncertainties). Doubling the number of measurements reduces the uncertainty by a factor of $\sqrt{2}$ for frequent noise distributions, but this is often not affordable in medicine. In principle, some outliers are avoidable, but they do occur in everyday clinical practice. Errors in the training data set due to incorrect annotations by the experts can only be avoided in the ideal case and come at increased cost. Ideally, consensus labels by at least three experts are sought in which case the level of inter-observer agreement could be used to inform about the label confidence. The model parameters will also always have errors (epistemic uncertainty). Also, the selection of patients for the training data set could be non-representative due to unknown confounders. The uncertainties can be reduced by using a larger and more diverse database. If an unknown variable influences the result, only medical research can help to find this hidden influencing factor. As long as these hidden variables are not known, resulting uncertainties are unavoidable. A clinical study created in this way cannot be generalized. Likewise, an ML system in which an important influencing factor has not been considered cannot be generalized.

Conclusion: Many types of errors are unavoidable – both in clinical studies and in ML. The training data set must be of high quality, i.e., the data should be recorded using adequate measuring devices and – in case of classification tasks – carefully annotated by at least three experts. A description of who was included and excluded in the training data set has to be provided [see e.g. 7]. All subgroups should be equally represented. The ML system may only be applied to patients who were sufficiently represented in the training data set.

For many questions, enlarging the training data with simulated data or extending it through augmentation proved to improve training. In which scenarios this is the case in general remains an open question, though. The source of augmented data are good clinical data, but does the method of augmentation really increase the information in a data set and lead to better generalization? On the other hand, in simulated data, the ground truth is perfectly known. All subgroups of patients can be represented equally. But are the simulated data close enough to clinical data (i.e., small enough domain gap) and cover the relevant variability?

12.3 Uncertainty Quantification (UQ) – Global and local uncertainties

The quantification of uncertainties is a topic that has become increasingly important in recent years – especially in the area of ML [8]. How large is the inaccuracy in a regression or how large is the error rate is in a classification task. How do different algorithms compare in terms of uncertainty? Finally, regulatory bodies (e.g., notified bodies) can demand a certain level of accuracy, which manufacturers then have to verify using well-defined measurement procedures.

For regression tasks, the appropriate measure of uncertainty is usually quite simple: the mean squared error (MSE). The samples used to determine the MSE must be sufficiently large and completely cover the intended range of values. The data used to measure the uncertainties must not have been used when training the ML algorithm. In the ML community, a special wording is used: the "training dataset" is obviously used for training. The "validation dataset" is used to optimize the ML algorithm and its hyperparameters. Both, training and validation data set are used while training. The "test dataset" is reserved for the final procedure to determine the accuracy and it must not have been used before. In clinical communities, the latter is classically referred to as "external validation", which can cause confusion.

In classification tasks, determining the uncertainties is somewhat more complicated. For binary classification tasks, a "confusion matrix" is set up. If we call class 1 "positive" and class 2 "negative", we can present the number of true positive TP, true negative TN, false positive FP and false negative FN classifications in this matrix. Two important variables can initially be calculated from these four numbers: sensitivity (TP/P) and specificity (TN/N), with P being the total number of positive cases and N the total number of negative cases. Increasing sensitivity translates to: we do not want to overlook a single positive sample (e.g. patient with a specific disease). With a high specificity we can achieve that as many TN as possible have been identified, i.e. avoiding "false alarms". Unfortunately, the two goals contradict each other in practice. We have to make a compromise, and that is where things get a little more complicated. We find a large number of derived quantities, all of which have value in specific applications. The most important ones are the "accuracy" and the "F1 score" [9]. In any case, measuring accuracy is problematic if the sample does not contain an equal number of positive and negative cases. This is often the case in medicine. The number of cases that belong to the healthy "control group" is often larger than the number of cases that belong to the disease case. For classification tasks with more than two classes, we have to decide which cases we want to compare against each other, e.g. class A versus class B or class A versus all other classes. Here too, of course, the samples used to measure the uncertainties must not already have been used when training the ML algorithm.

With the methods mentioned so far, a so-called global uncertainty can be determined. The calculated uncertainties refer to a large sample. But there is also a local accuracy. It indicates which uncertainties we can expect for the patient who is currently being analyzed. For example, if the model in a regression task is not linear, it can happen that the regression curve is very flat in one range of input values and very steep in another range of values. So, the value that the ML program delivers can be very certain in one case and very uncertain in the other. The same applies to classification tasks. If one patient lies with his/her measured values in an area of the parameter space that can be clearly separated from all other classes, the classification certainty will be higher than for another patient whose data lie in an area where multiple classes overlap. One patient has a 95% probability of class A and a 5% probability of class B. The other patient has a 55% probability of class A and a 45% probability of class B. That makes a big difference. An ML system in medicine should – if possible – determine this local uncertainty and communicate it to the user.

In the first section, the aleatoric uncertainties were introduced: all measurement data have noise. To determine the uncertainty caused by noisy measurement data, one can feed the trained ML system with slightly changed measurement data in which all measurement variables fluctuate with their standard deviation and observe how this affects the result. This is time consuming if there are a lot of input numbers, though. One way out is to translate to a surrogate model in which the error propagation method can be used (see also explainable AI).

Conclusion: There are good quantitative methods to determine the uncertainties of an ML system. Which method was chosen must be communicated exactly. In addition to global uncertainty, an ML system should also display local uncertainty whenever possible. The data used to measure uncertainty must not be part of the training data set.

12.4 Variants and methods of explainability – eXplainable Artificial Intelligence XAI

Especially in medicine, the user wants to know why an ML system has chosen a specific value or class. To answer this, various methods can be found in literature on "Explainable AI" (XAI) [10]. Different variants must be distinguished. Unfortunately, the following definitions are not entirely consistent in the literature [11].

Transparency of an ML system in this chapter means that the medical system clearly discloses in the description that an ML algorithm is used. It should be stated which ML algorithm is used (neural network, decision tree, support vector machine, ...). The training data set should be described (inclusion and exclusion criteria) and the source should be specified (e.g., which clinic, for more details see e.g. [7]).

Explainability comes in two variants: often it means that the user of an ML system is presented which of the input variables had the greatest influence on the result. This can be based on introducing local perturbations comparable to a sensitivity analysis. A "saliency map" or "heatmap" is the result. It guides the viewer's eye, for example by coloring the input signals in those sections that are most important for the decision. This can lead to a kind of comprehension in the mind of the user, but it does not have to necessarily. It may uncover whether the result is based on an outlier in the input data. It can be argued that these techniques only measure the local change of prediction but not the prediction itself and the level of abstraction does not necessarily help to understand how the decision was taken (e.g., highlighting the part of an ECG that corresponds to the heart's chamber that is the main cause for a certain disease is reassuring but does not explain a lot). In order to identify these areas in a mathematically correct way, there are various methods that cannot be explained here in detail (examples are Layerwise Relevance Propagation (LRP), Guided Backpropagation, Local Interpretable Model-agnostic Explanation (LIME), SmoothGrad Method, Prediction Difference Analysis (PDA) [10]). Some of them translate the problem locally to a simple surrogate model, which is interpretable. E.g. shallow decision trees are intrinsically interpretable. As is often the case, a compromise must be found between mathematically exact methods and fast methods.

Another variant of the term "explainability" is aimed more at understanding and comprehension [12]. Is the decision understandable? There are various approaches to this, which cannot be explained here either. It is difficult to measure the quality of these methods. In the end, clinicians will probably have to indicate in a comparative field test which explanation method convinces them more.

It should be noted that many worldwide accepted clinical procedures have not been explained properly yet. Several clinical studies with similar results lead to a high level of evidence. But a good comprehension of why they are successful is often missing.

12.5 Who is responsible for what?

Errors in medical care are not a new phenomenon. All players in healthcare can make mistakes that might harm the patient. Medical devices, physicians, nurses, the patient – they all are making mistakes. There is an established system in Germany to get to the root cause of suspected errors. The medical device manufacturer must prove that its system functioned as intended and as promised. The reported uncertainties and error rates must be true. Otherwise, product liability applies. Clinicians must prove that they have informed the patient about all relevant risks. They must have acted in accordance with the state of the art – usually set out in the guidelines. Physicians are allowed to deviate from guidelines, but they must have good reasons for doing so. The same applies to nursing staff. Healthcare professionals often also have the responsibility to regularly check the functionality of the medical systems they use or to delegate this checkup. Patients must follow his/her recommendations and must not knowingly worsen their health, otherwise they cannot hold the clinician responsible.

Unfortunately, clinicians often have to make decisions based on incomplete information. Thus, decisions frequently turn out to have been suboptimal or wrong retrospectively. If the patient then sues the doctor, an arbitration board will first try to resolve the case. Legal proceedings are also possible later. If the physician can prove that no better information was available at the time the decision had to be made and that he or she acted according to the state of the art, the error is classified as "fateful". The patient is left alone with his or her damages. Accountability in the sense "Who is to be blamed?" is not applicable.

In future, ML systems will probably be used particularly when the correct classification is difficult with available information. In clear situations, the rules that are often already set out in the guidelines are sufficient and no ML system will be used. ML systems will be applied in medicine when there is a high error rate in human decision-making. For example, often a diagnosis or treatment is only correct in 80% and wrong 20% of all cases. This is everyday clinical practice – even without ML systems. The reasons for errors are explained in detail in the first section of this chapter. Many of them are unavoidable.

Assume that it has been demonstrated – using the best methods known today (see Uncertainty Quantification) – that an ML system has a lower error rate than average human experts. Then, the responsible doctor should consult this ML system. The probability of making a mistake decreases by using the ML system. It is to be expected that in future, in many cases an ML system will have to be consulted for the determination of diagnostically important variables (regression) or for the selection of the best diagnosis or treatment plan (classification) – especially in difficult cases with noticeable error rates. Not using an ML system in these cases can be judged as "not acting responsibly".

12.6 Theses

1. Before an ML system is used in medicine, the following requirements should be met (see also [11,13]):
–   All possible sources of error (aleatory and epistemic) must be analyzed, their influence on the result of the ML algorithm must be estimated and, wherever possible, the errors must be minimized.
–   The data set used for training must be of high quality: all measured values should be as accurate as possible (little noise, no outliers), and the "ground truth" should

be determined as precisely as possible. Classification tasks should involve at least 3 experts.

- Training dataset, validation dataset and test dataset must be strictly separated. "Leakage" of knowledge from the training and validation dataset to the test dataset must be prevented.
- The patient population for the training, validation and test data set must be large enough and the inclusion and exclusion criteria must be specified. All influencing variables known today should be determined. All subgroups should be equally represented.
- The measurement of global accuracy and uncertainty should be carried out using a recognized method, the metrics for determining the error rate must be clearly defined mathematically and the results must be published.
- An ML system should only be applied in medicine if the proven error rate is smaller than typical error rates of human clinicians.
- Wherever possible, local accuracy should also be reported when an ML system is applied to a specific patient.
- The ML system should meet all transparency requirements (see above and [11]).
- The ML system should – wherever possible – provide an explanation for the decision, for example in the form of a saliency map that indicates which section of the input data had the greatest influence on the decision.
- The ML system should – wherever possible – provide an understandable explanation for the decision (in the sense of "comprehension", see chapter on XAI).
- If such an ML system has proven to estimate valuable diagnostic data or to make better decisions as medical experts, the medical expert should consult the ML system before making a decision in order to act responsibly.

References

[1] Loewe A., Luongo G., Sánchez J. Machine Learning for Clinical Electrophysiology. Innovative Treatment Strategies for Clinical Electrophysiology, 2022:93–109. https://doi.org/10.1007/978-981-19-6649-1_6.
[2] VDE DGBMT Recommendation. Market access of continuous learning AI systems in medicine. (Accessed July 18, 2024, at https://www.vde.com/de/dgbmt/publikationen/dgbmt-positionspapiere/empfehlung-marktzugang-ki-systeme).
[3] High-Level Expert Group on Artificial Intelligence of the European Commission (AIHLEG). Ethics Guidelines for Trustworthy AI, 08.04.2019. (Accessed July 18, 2024, at https://ec.europa.eu/digitalsingle-market/en/news/ethics-guidelines-trustworthy-ai).
[4] acatech POSITION. Machine Learning in der Medizintechnik. Analyse und Handlungsempfehlungen, 2020. (Accessed July 18, 2024, at https://www.acatech.de/publikation/machine-learning-in-der-medizintechnik/).
[5] Fraser A. G. et al. Artificial intelligence in medical device software and high-risk medical devices – a review of definitions, expert recommendations and regulatory initiatives. Expert Review of Medical Devices, 2023;20:6, 467–91. (Accessed July 18, 2024, at https://doi.org10.1080/17434440.2023.2184685).

[6]   Senge R., Bösner S., Dembczynski K., Haasenritter J., Hirsch O., Donner-Banzhoff N.,
        Hüllermeier E. Reliable classification: Learning classifiers that distinguish aleatoric and epistemic
        uncertainty. Information Sciences 2014;255:16–29.

[7]   Mongan J., Moy L., Kahn J. E. Jr. Checklist for Artificial Intelligence in Medical Imaging (CLAIM): A
        Guide for Authors and Reviewers, Radiology: Artificial Intelligence 2020; 2 (2). (Accessed July 18, 2024,
        at https://doi.org/10.1148/ryai.2020200029).

[8]   Abdar M., Pourpanah F, Hussain S, Rezazadegan D, Liu L, Ghavamzadeh M, Fieguth P, Cao X,
        Khosravi A, Acharya UR, Makarenkov V, Nahavandi S. A review of uncertainty quantification in deep
        learning: Techniques, applications and challenges. Information Fusion 2021;76:243–97.

[9]   "F-Score" (Accessed July 18, 2024, at https://en.wikipedia.org/wiki/F-score).

[10]   Samek W., Müller K. R. (eds.). Towards Explainable Artificial Intelligence in Explainable AI: Interpret-
        ing, Explaining and Visualizing Deep Learning, Lecture Notes in Artificial Intelligence 11700 Subseries
        of Lecture Notes.Computer Science 2019. (Accessed July 18, 2024, at https://link.springer.com/book/10.
        1007/978-3-030-28954-6).

[11]   FDA. Transparency for Machine Learning-Enabled Medical Devices: Guiding Principles, 2024.
        (Accessed July 18, 2024, at https://www.fda.gov/medical-devices/software-medical-device-samd/trans-
        parency-machine-learning-enabled-medical-devices-guiding-principles).

[12]   DARPA. DARPA's explainable AI (XAI) program: A retrospective. Applied AI Letters. 2021;2:e61.
        (Accessed July 18, 2024, at https://doi.org/10.1002/ail2.61).

[13]   FDA. Good Machine Learning Practice for Medical Device Development: Guiding Principles 2021.
        (Accessed July 18, 2024, at https://www.fda.gov/media/153486/download).

Simon Fonck, André Stollenwerk

13 Explainable Artificial Intelligence in biomedical engineering

13.1 Introduction

In recent decades, artificial intelligence (AI) methods have been established in many different areas of business and science. They are used to solve a variety of tasks. AI models are also increasingly being used in (bio-)medical technology, in particular to make the daily work of physicians and nursing staff easier and thus improve patient treatment. AI models are used to facilitate specific applications, such as diagnostic classifications, surgical planning or text recognition [1]. However, the use of AI models not only has advantages, but also drawbacks. Particularly since the introduction of neural networks and deep learning methods as part of these AI methods, the resulting outcomes and the process leading to them are in many cases no longer comprehensible to humans. Such models are described as so-called "black box models".

Black Box: The term "black box" is shorthand for models that are sufficiently complex that they are not straightforwardly interpretable to humans [2].

Even the developers of such "black box" algorithms often have no insight into the exact decision-making process and cannot explain how a model arrived to its decision. In order to make this process more transparent and ensure traceability, methods of "Explainable Artificial Intelligence" (xAI) or "Interpretable Artificial Intelligence" (IAI) have become increasingly popular in recent years (see Fig. 13.1).

In the following, we will use xAI as a generic term for the concept of increasing the explainability of AI models.

The explainability of AI models plays a particularly important role in patient treatment, as various target groups require insights into the decision-making processes of the models in this context. For example, in the EU AI Act there are different stakeholder defined for establishing an AI [3]: the provider: a natural or legal person (or other body) that develops an AI system and places it on the market. The deployer: a natural or legal person (or other body) that uses an AI system in the course of a personal non-professional activity. The importer: a natural or legal person that places an AI system from a third country on the market. The distributor: a natural or legal person other than the provider or the importer, that makes an AI system available in the EU. The operator: a provider, product manufacturer, deployer, authorized representative, importer or

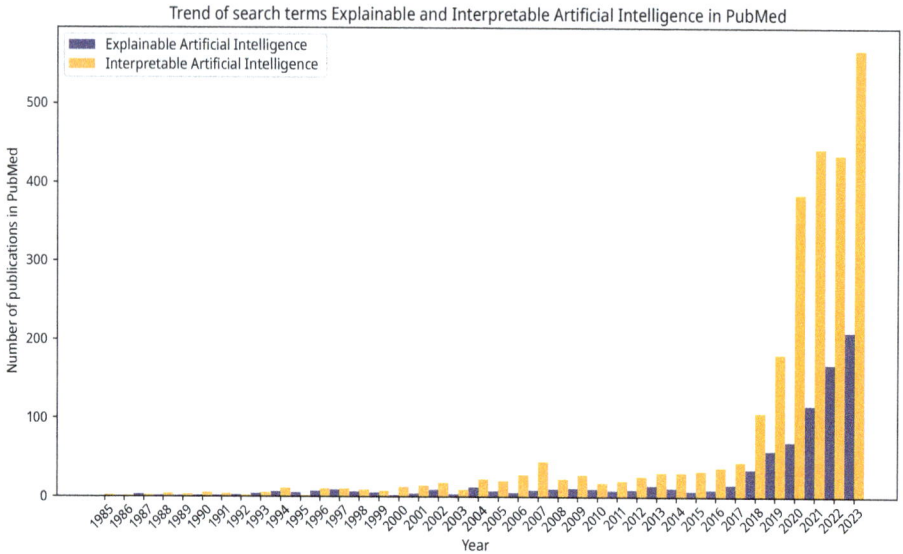

Fig. 13.1: Number of publications per year listed in the PubMed literature database for the keywords "Explainable Artificial Intelligence" and "Interpretable Artificial Intelligence" from 1985 to 2023.

distributor. However, the EU AI Act does not clearly specify who will ultimately use an AI system, which of course depends heavily on the use case.

In the context of biomedical engineering the following target groups are conceivable: Doctors, nurses, researchers, developers, data engineers, students, patients and relatives. With the help of additional information on the decision of a model, the process should be made more transparent and thus strengthen confidence in the specific models. This is particularly important in the field of medical technology/medical informatics, as incomprehensible technology leads to a loss of trust and may therefore not be used. Furthermore, a lack of explainability can also lead to other problems, such as legal issues. Conversely, a lack of traceability can also mean that new, better performing methods cannot be used on patients, as it is then too difficult to assess the full extent of these methods. Additionally, AI methods may identify yet unknown relations in physiological data. From the research perspective an explainable AI method is highly appreciable, since this would be added value to this kind of data processing. When developing AI methods, one also can face wrongly identified correlations, e.g. due to overfitting. Here explainability can support the process of parameter tuning and the requirements definition of the training dataset to overcome the encountered errors. Finally, this explainability can also be utilized in the education of physicians as well as medical data engineers.

Outline: This chapter is structured as follows: Section 13.2 provides a definition and current challenges that arise when using xAI. Section 13.3 presents an overview of the current state of research and applications of xAI. Based on this, specific solutions and methods are described in Section 13.4. Section 13.5 provides specific examples of xAI applications in the field of medical technology in order to specify the benefits and significance for this use case. Finally, Sections 13.6 and 13.7 discuss and summarize all the content presented.

13.2 Preliminaries of xAI

Although xAI methods are already being used in research for many applications, there is still no generally recognized or standardized taxonomy for it. Various terms are used in the literature, such as explainability, interpretability, transparency or comprehensibility, which cover different aspects of the topic. The bottom line is that they all describe the understanding of the human or different users of the models [4]. Furthermore, there is no clear benchmark for how "explainable" or "interpretable" a particular model is (including xAI methods). There are approaches to assess "(self-)explainability", but these have yet to be proven in practice [4].

In 2020, Arrieta et al. published a detailed description of concepts, taxonomies and challenges of xAI as well as a comprehensive attempt to harmonize these multifaceted terms [5]. In their systematic survey of surveys, Schwalbe et al. analyzed a large number of papers dealing with taxonomies of xAI for machine learning approaches and published a detailed summary [4]. The terms transparency and explainability emerged as two main characteristics. If a model is transparent, i.e., one has full insight into how it works and the decision-making process, it is generally referred to as a "white box" model. In this concept, explainability often depicts descriptions added retrospectively, i.e., post-hoc, which are intended to add comprehensibility to the decisions and functioning of black box models. In a position paper of the German Academy of Science and Engineering (Acatech) and a roadmap towards transparent Medical Decision Support by Bruckert et al., this is referred to as "grey box" models, as complete transparency cannot be achieved in this way at the current state of the art [6,7]. Further details on specific models and approaches can be found in Section 13.3.

In addition, two different approaches to explainability can be identified. On the one hand, some methods allow insight into the entire model and enable global explainability, while other methods only shed light on individual decision-making aspects of the model for specific examples (local explainability). Although this allows a direct query as to how an algorithm arrived at its decision, it rarely helps to make a complete model transparent. It is important to recognize which methods allow which type of explainability.

Global explainability refers to methods that provide insight into the entire model and its process. Local explainability refers to methods that provide insight into single decisions that were calculated for specific examples.

When developing xAI methods, both forms (local and global explainability) can have beneficial impact on the understanding of an underlying model. It should be noted here that different target groups also have different requirements in terms of explainability. For example, it is quite conceivable that it will be sufficient for a doctor or patient to be able to understand the decision-making process for a single diagnosis – a medical data engineer who wants to further improve the model, on the other hand, must have a more comprehensive insight. The different requirements also play an important role in the field of biomedical technology. For example, a survey of over 200 representatives from business and science related to AI revealed, that 58 % rate local explainability in healthcare as absolutely essential and a further 24 % as highly desirable [8]. This will be further elaborated in Section 13.4, in which we discuss specific approaches for xAI methods.

13.3 State of the art

AI comprises a variety of different models and algorithms that can be used to solve various tasks within healthcare scenarios including, e.g., classification (of tumors or diseases), regression (of an outcome), anomaly detection (within images or time series data), recommendation (of medication), or prediction (of vital signs or outcome of changes in medication). Some of these models are more explainable by design than others [4]. Arrieta et al. describe three levels of model interpretability: simulatability, decomposability and algorithmic transparency [5].

Simulatability means, that e.g., a human understands the model as a whole and can mentally comprehend it.
Decomposability describes the fact that a model can be broken down into individual parts, each of which can be simulated.
Algorithmic transparency means that the model can be described by mathematical analyses and methods.

Furthermore, a simulatable model is always decomposable and algorithmic transparent. Based on this definition, we can define models, that are considered inherently transparent in the literature [9]. Here are a few examples:
-   Decision Trees, where each internal node represents a feature, each branch a decision rule and each leaf a possible outcome. Their basic structure makes it easy to interpret how decisions are made, as one can follow the path from the root node to a leaf. Hereby, the influence of a feature can be easily interpreted.

- Linear Regression, which is a statistical method used to model the relationship between one or more independent variables and a dependent variable by fitting a linear equation to observed data. The simplicity of its equation and the coefficients, which indicate the impact of each variable on the outcome, make interpretations straightforward.
- Rule-based Systems, which incorporate "if-then-else" rules for decision-making. Specific conditions define how a system acts based on the given input data. These conditions can either be learned from data or set manually. As these are clear, logical rules, they provide transparency about how the system reaches the according outcome and allow users to follow reasoning paths.

Note: Even though these models are by design interpretable, depending on the complexity and number of variables included, such a model can also be difficult to interpret. Considering these boundary conditions, all previously mentioned models can be simulatable, if the complexity is low enough.

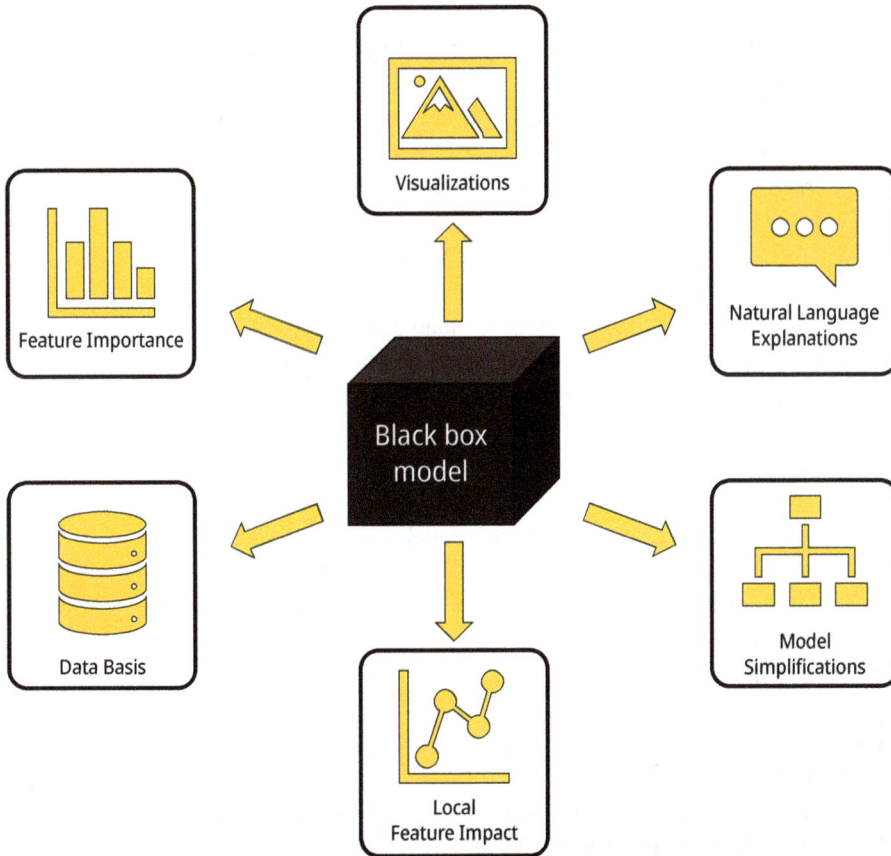

Fig. 13.2: Various approaches to provide post-hoc explainability to an AI model. These types of xAI methods can be used individually or in combination (adapted from [5]).

For black box models that do not fulfill these levels of explainability, different approaches of xAI methods can be used: Description of the influence of individual features, visualization of the results or the data, natural language descriptions, and more (see Fig. 13.2). According to Arrieta et al., these methods are intended to pursue the following goals [5]:

1. Trustworthiness: increase trust in the underlying AI model by providing more information about the model and its decision-making for a specific problem.
2. Causality: visualize patterns that are learned by a model to allow their plausibility to be checked and verified by the different user groups (medical professionals, as well as data engineers).
3. Transferability: provide information about the trained use case and used data to allow an assessment of the AI models limitations and possible transferability.
4. Informativeness: provide as much information about the model and problem, so a medical professional can relate to the solution given by the model.
5. Confidence: visualize the confidence of an AI model for a specific decision to help the different users to assess, how much he can trust the solution.
6. Fairness: based on the training data, there might be a bias in a model, that leads to unfair decision-making. To circumvent this problem, it is helpful to present the characteristics of the training data to the medical data engineer so that he can identify these biases.
7. Interactivity: providing an interactive framework for the user to work with and sight the training data or the model can lead to a better understanding through active experimenting during use or development.
8. Privacy awareness: regulations such as the European General Data Protection Regulation (GDPR) [10] place strict requirements on the processing and use of personal data. xAI methods can be used to ensure that these requirements are met and raise the users' awareness of their data protection rights.

Various xAI methods can be used to achieve these goals. A large number of approaches have been published in the literature and new ones are constantly being developed [3]. A distinction is made between model-agnostic and model-specific methods. Model-agnostic xAI methods only access the input and output of the model and are therefore independent of the AI models used. Model-specific xAI approaches, on the other hand, require access to the model's internal processes or architecture and are therefore adapted to these.

Model-agnostic: the xAI methods only accesses the input and output of the xAI model and are therefore model-independent.

Model-specific: the xAI methods need access to the internal processing and architecture of the AI model and are often tailored to particular AI models.

In his book, Christoph Molnar also highlights methods for interpreting neural networks separately, as these pose a particular challenge for explainability due to their complex structure [9]. However, other xAI methods can also be applied to them. Prominent examples of model-agnostic approaches are listed below:

Model-agnostic:

- Local Interpretable Model-agnostic Explanations (LIME) [11]: LIME is a prominent example for a model-agnostic xAI method, that generates a local model to approximate the underlying AI model by generating a simpler, typically a linear model (p.e. linear regression or decision trees), based on perturbations of the input data and predictions of the considered model. By analyzing these perturbations, the influence of the considered features can be evaluated for the specific prediction. Thus, LIME provides local explainability.
- SHapley Additive exPlanations (SHAP) [12]: SHAP is derived from cooperative game theory and use a similar approach as LIME by calculating SHAPley values for all possible combinations of input features to provide a distribution of feature importance for a local decision.

With these and other xAI methods, AI models can be made explainable or more interpretable retrospectively, i.e., post-hoc.

13.4 Usage of xAI in biomedical engineering

In recent years, more and more AI methods for supporting the diagnosis or prediction of diseases have been published in literature. Decision support systems with integrated AI are described for various areas of application and proposed for clinical use. These should serve as a tool to support medical professionals in the treatment and care of patients and speed up or facilitate processes.

In the biomedical context, understanding the decision of an AI model is of the utmost importance, as it can influence the outcome of a patient's intervention. It is also important for the trust in corresponding algorithms and models that users can understand the solution of an AI model. Only then, the AI model would be integrated as a consultant into the diagnostic process. It can also be interesting for patients and their relatives to gain a better understanding of an AI model, if it has been used in their treatment. The General Data Protection Regulation even declares that patients have a right to receive meaningful information about the underlying logic [10]. When using xAI in biomedical engineering, basically any described methodology can be used to make the AI model more explainable. For the development of medical support systems, a user-centred development design is preferable in order to obtain early feedback on the visualization and use of a corresponding framework [7]. This ensures that the AI system is intuitive and understandable enough for integration into medical practice. Furthermore, it is important to present the data basis of the trained AI model so that a possible bias in the data can be uncovered and the limitations of the model can be assessed. This also allows the data quality to be analyzed and the underlying models to be improved.

13.5 Examples of xAI in biomedical engineering

Based on the use case of detecting Acute Respiratory Distress Syndrome (ARDS), we present a specific example of the use of AI and xAI methods in biomedical engineering. ARDS is a severe lung disease in which the patient's gas exchange is heavily impaired. ARDS can occur as a subsequent syndrome of various diseases such as sepsis, pneumonia or infectious diseases. The delay of ARDS diagnosis is a major problem. Sometimes there is no diagnosis at all, which both hinder appropriate treatment of the patient. AI methods can be used to automatically monitor recorded patient data and notify medical professionals when potential cases of ARDS occur. Such early detection is intended to improve patient treatment and thus the outcome of those affected. As this is a very heterogeneous syndrome, various criteria summarized in the so-called "Berlin Definition" [13] are considered, including the evaluation of oxygenation in time series data and the presence of bilateral infiltrates in image data. These two data modalities have different properties, meaning that different AI models can be used. For example, deep learning models such as Convolutional Neural Networks (CNN) are better suited to recognizing features in radiography image data [14]. Decision tree-based models such as Random Forest (RF), on the other hand, are more suitable for use with time series data [15]. According to the literature, both types of models are considered to be black boxes and have low interpretability. With the RF algorithm, over 700 different decision trees are trained by pertubating the input parameters, which can only be analyzed individually afterwards with a great expenditure of time and effort. One way to increase the interpretability would be to specify a feature importance scale in such a manner, that a user can understand which parameters have influenced the result the most. This information helps to assess whether the algorithm can work at all on the acute data set to which the classifier is to be applied. For instance, if important values are missing, the classification of the model will not be reliable. In addition, a physician can identify whether the parameters that influenced the decision for the presence of ARDS are medically reasonable. For example, the Horovitz quotient [13], which is part of the oxygenation criterion of the Berlin definition, should play a central role in the presence of ARDS. Furthermore, it makes sense to visualize the data distribution of training and test data so that the user can recognize a possible bias and the limitations of the model. Visualization of the results is also suitable for classification of the image data models. With the CNNs used, gradient-weighted class activation maps (GradCAM) or Layerwise Relevance Propagation [18,19] can be used. GradCAM, e.g., provides local explainability with creating heat maps of individual images that have been classified with the model. The areas that the network considers relevant are coded with a color scale (see Fig. 13.3). Generally, interesting areas are red, uninteresting areas are blue and areas in between are yellow. This allows the user to see which parts of the image have influenced the decision the most and compare the original image to verify the direct relation to the ARDS / non-ARDS decision. So, it would be easy to understand if the neural network looks at the lung areas that have opacities and are therefore in line with the Berlin definition. However, as can be seen in Fig. 13.3, the marked areas of a neural network are not always comprehensible, even if the classification is correct. For example, in the third image, the network concentrates primarily on the upper left corner and therefore no longer on the areas relevant for the ARDS decision: the lungs. It is therefore important to provide as much information for the use of an AI model and to enable the user to assess the result

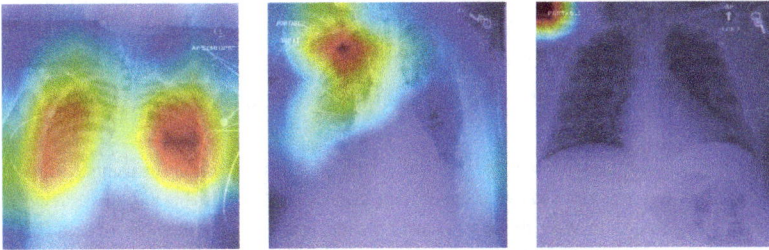

Fig. 13.3: GradCAM heatmaps for images of the MIMIC-CXR datasets [16,17]. The first two images are correctly classified as ARDS. The third image is correctly classified as No-ARDS. Interesting areas are red, uninteresting areas are blue and areas in between are yellow.

There are also many examples in the literature in which neural networks have learned features from images that, according to human judgment, should not contribute to a classification. For example, source tags on images were recognized and associated with the classification of animals or cars. After deleting these tags, the same classification failed. Such misbehavior can be detected with the help of xAI methods in order to enable a correction [20].

13.6 Discussion

The need for explainability of AI models, especially in a biomedical engineering context, is obvious. However, it is difficult to evaluate and measure how explainable a model or an associated xAI method is. Ghassemi et al. even argue that at this point in time, xAI has not yet reached the point where individual algorithm decisions can be considered correct [21]. The authors place the focus of the methods on supporting the development process for model debugging and system audits in order to identify certain types of errors and limitations and thus contribute to improving model performance. Additionally, it is possible, that an xAI method added to an AI model contributes to a reduction of the performance of that model. Therefore, it is necessary to weigh up whether the performance of a model or its explainability is more important. The fact, that it is hard to define an objective explainability metric has already been recognized by some research groups and should be considered in the application and publication of xAI models and addressed in further research. Furthermore, the division into white and black box models is too short-sighted, as even white box models, i.e. inherently transparent and comprehensible models, can become too complex and too large to be directly interpreted by a user. It also makes sense to use xAI for these models in order to support the utilization and development process. In particular, it must be considered that the model must be understood by different stakeholders, who may have different basic knowledge of AI. A division into different levels and layers of explainability would be helpful in this regard. As xAI is currently a very prominent field of research, new ideas and approaches are constantly being developed. For this reason, this chapter does not guarantee completeness and can be expanded with additional methods.

> Overall, it is difficult to achieve "true" explainability, as this always depends on who will be using the tool. To facilitate this process, it is important to integrate as many stakeholders as possible into the development process at an early stage. However, this is a major challenge, especially in a medical context. This may result in the need to come up with different views dedicated to different stakeholders.

13.7 Conclusions

AI methods are being used more and more every day in various areas. The benefits and resulting opportunities are also increasing in the field of biomedical engineering and medicine. However, a major disadvantage of AI methods is the limited explainability and understanding of the results. For this reason, the field of xAI has emerged, which has set itself the task of making AI models more understandable. This chapter presents a brief overview and various methods that can be used to achieve this. Each method has advantages and disadvantages and specific properties that need to be considered for the respective use case. We also briefly presented how xAI can be used in biomedical engineering. It is particularly important to consider the various stakeholders that come together in the field of medicine. These should be included in the development and evaluation process. Although this represents a high workload, we believe it is essential for the successful integration of AI in medicine. The chapter thus helps to gain an initial insight into the field of xAI and offers many opportunities to delve deeper into the subject matter. We hope that this will enable the successful integration of AI methods into clinical practice, which should ultimately improve the treatment of patients and their outcome.

References

[1] Hong N., Liu C., Gao J., Han L., Chang F., Gong M. and Su L. "State of the Art of Machine Learning-Enabled Clinical Decision Support in Intensive Care Units: Literature Review". JMIR Medical Informatics 2022; 10(3). https://doi.org/10.2196/28781.

[2] Petch J., Shuang D and Nelson W. "Opening the Black Box: The Promise and Limitations of Explainable Machine Learning in Cardiology". Canadian Journal of Cardiology 2022; 38: 204–2013. https://doi.org/10.1016/j.cjca.2021.09.004.

[4] Schwalbe G. and Finzel B. "A comprehensive taxonomy for explainable artificial intelligence: a systematic survey of surveys on methods and concepts". Data Min Knowl Disc 2023 38: 3043–3101. https://doi.org/10.1007/s10618-022-00867-8.

[5] Arrieta A. B., Díaz-Rodríguez N, Del Ser J., Bennetot A., Tabik S., Barbado A., Garcia S., Gil-Lopez S., Molina D., Benjamins R, Chatila R. and Herrera F. "Explainable Artificial Intelligence (XAI): Concepts, taxonomies, opportunities and challenges toward responsible AI". Information Fusion 2020; 58: 82–115. https://doi.org/10.1016/j.inffus.2019.12.012.

[6] acatech. "Machine Learning in der Medizintechnik – Analyse und Handlungsempfehlungen". acatech – Deutsche Akademie der Technikwissenschaften, München 2020; ISBN: 978-3-96834-000-5.

[7] Bruckert S, Finzel B and Schmid U. "The Next Generation of Medical Decision Support: A Roadmap Toward Transparent Expert Companions". Frontiers in Artificial Intelligence 2020; 3. https://doi.org/10.3389/frai.2020.507973.

[8] Kraus T., Ganschow L., Eisenträger M. and Wischmann S. "Erklärbare KI-Anforderungen, Anwendungsfälle und Lösungen". Technologieprogramm KI-Innovationswettbewerb des Bundesministeriums für Wirtschaft und Energie, Berlin 2021, (Accessed 05.03.2025, at https://www.digitale-technologien.de/DT/Redaktion/DE/Downloads/Publikation/KI-Inno/2021/Studie_Erklaerbare_KI.html).

[9] Molnar C. "Interpretable Machine Learning – A Guide for Making Black Box Models Explainable". 2023. https://christophmolnar.com/books/interpretable-machine-learning/.

[11] Ribeiro M. T., Singh S. and Guestrin C. "Why should I trust you?: explaining the predictions of any classifier". Proceedings of the 22nd ACM SIGKDD International conference on knowledge discovery and data mining, KDD 16; pp 1135–1144. https://doi.org/10.1145/2939672.2939778.

[12] Lundberg S. M. and Lee S. I. "A unified approach to interpreting model predictions". Adv Neural Inf Process Syst 2017; 30: 4765–4774.

[13] ARDS Definition Task Force, Ranieri V. M., Rubenfeld G. D., Thompson B. T., Ferguson N. D., Caldwell E., Fan E., Camporota L. and Slutsky A. S. "Acute respiratory distress syndrome: the Berlin Definition". JAMA 2012, 307(23), 2526–2533. https://doi.org/10.1001/jama.2012.5669.

[14] Fonck S, Fritsch S., Nottenkämper G. and Stollenwerk A. "Implementation of ResNet-50 for the Detection of ARDS in Chest X-Rays using transfer-learning". Proceedings on Automation in Medical Engineering 2023, 2(1), ID 742.

[15] Fonck S., Fritsch S., Pieper H., Baron A., Kowalewski S. and Stollenwerk A. "Retrospective Classification of ARDS in ICU Time-series data using Random Forest with a focus on Data Pre-processing". IFAC-PapersOnLine 2024, 58(24). https://doi.org/10.1016/j.ifacol.2024.11.024.

[16] Johnson A. E. W., Pollard T. J., Berkowitz S. J., Greenbaum N. R., Lungren M. P., Deng C., Mark R. G. and Horng S. "MIMIC-CXR, a de-identified publicly available database of chest radiographs with free-text reports". Scientific Data 2019; 6. https://doi.org/10.1038/s41597-019-0322-0.

[17] Goldberger A. L., Amaral L. A., Glass L., Hausdorff J. M., Ivanov P. C., Mark R. G., Mietus J. E., Moody G. B., Peng C. K. and Stanley H. E. "PhysioBank, PhysioToolkit, and PhysioNet: components of a new research resource for complex physiologic signals". Circulation 2020, 101(23), E215–E220. https://doi.org/10.1161/01.cir.101.23.e215.

[18] Selvaraju R. R., Cogswell M., Das A., Vedantam R., Parikh D. and Batra D. "Grad-CAM: Visual Explanations from Deep Networks via Gradient-Based Localization," IEEE International Conference on Computer Vision (ICCV) 2017, Venice, Italy, pp. 618–626. https://doi.org/10.1109/ICCV.2017.74.

[19] Samek W., Arras L., Osman A., Montavon G. and Müller K. R. "Explaining the Decisions of Convolutional and Recurrent Neural Networks". Mathematical Aspects of Deep Learning 2021, pp. 1–33, Cambridge University Press, Cambridge, UK.

[20] Lapuschkin S., Wäldchen S., Binder A., Montavon G., Samek W. and Müller K. R. "Unmasking Clever Hans predictors and assessing what machines really learn". Nat Commun 2019; 10, 1096. https://doi.org/10.1038/s41467-019-08987-4.

[21] Ghassemi M., Oakden-Rayner L. and Beam A. L. "The false hope of current approaches to explainable artificial intelligence in health care". The Lancet Digital Health 2021; 3 (10): E745-E750. https://doi.org/10.1016/S2589-7500(21)00208-9.

Websites

[3] European Union. "EU Artificial Intelligence Act". https://artificialintelligenceact.eu/article/3/. Version: June 2024.

[10] European Union. "Art. 15 GDPR – Right of access by the data subject". https://gdpr-info.eu/art-15-gdpr/. Version: April 2016.

Barbara Hammer

14 Fairness in AI – how to design 'unbiased' algorithms?

In healthcare, artificial intelligence (AI) technologies are increasingly being used in clinical practice, biomedical research, public health, and healthcare administration. Examples of applications include AI imaging technologies in radiology or cardiology, decision support in emergency medicine and surgery, technologies for home care, advances in drug discovery and personalized medicine, or facilitation of clinical trials. Despite the great opportunities offered by these AI applications, they pose various risks due to errors, misuse, unintentional bias, lack of transparency, invasion of privacy, or gaps in accountability [1]. As the healthcare sector has a high human impact, it is classified as high risk according to the categories defined in the European Union's AI-Act [2]. Therefore, specific measures are required by law to mitigate such risks. This chapter focuses on the question of what biases occur in AI technologies for healthcare and what measures can be taken to avoid such biases.

14.1 Biases of AI in healthcare

One motivation for AI-based decision support systems in healthcare is to avoid undesirable biases that would occur when a medical practitioner makes decisions in complex scenarios and under time pressure, such as in emergency medicine [3]. This expectation is based on the ability of AI models to quickly assimilate all available information and to avoid cognitive biases that occur in human decision making under uncertainty [4]. However, despite this expectation, there are examples showing that AI models perpetuate biases instead of avoiding them. This means that some AI models used in healthcare have a significant and undesirable bias against people of a particular gender, ethnicity, age, or socio-demographic background.

Example of gender bias. Deep learning algorithms can be used to detect abnormalities in chest X-rays, such as fractures, lung lesions or nodules. A Canadian study analyzed the distribution of false positives for modern deep learning models [5]. It was found that the lowest rate of true positives was in young women (age: 0–20). This means that the likelihood of a critical abnormality not being detected by the AI tool is higher if the patient is female than if the patient is male.

Example of ethnic bias. Algorithms can help make decisions about optimal treatment, for example by suggesting that additional or specialized treatment is needed. One study analyzed an algorithm used for this purpose in the USA [6]. It found that the predicted risk score for patients of color with the same disease was significantly lower than for white patients, i.e. there is a disparity that results in significantly less specific care for some ethnic groups than for others.

Example of sensor bias: A model based on data collected solely with the sensors of one vendor might only be used on query data from the same vendor, as the raw data from different vendors may depict the same medical incident differently on the data level. In addition to the bias caused by different instruments, Vaquet et al. demonstrate sensor bias even in instruments of the same design due to their different calibration [7].

What causes such results? AI technologies used in healthcare often belong to the sub-category of machine learning (ML) models: a machine learning model learns a specific function based on a given dataset of historical cases. For example, a diagnostic function for a particular disease can be learned based on a data set consisting of patients and information about whether they had the disease; the prediction of the most likely outcome of a therapy can be learned based on historical cases of patients together with their treatment information and the observed outcome of the therapy. Modern machine learning models, including deep learning, are characterized by their ability to recognize systematic patterns in such datasets, enabling them to learn correlations between observable information (such as X-rays or blood values) and the information of interest (such as the diagnosis of a disease or the expected outcome of a therapy) [8]. This means that such AI methods are critically dependent on the given historical data sets used for training. As a result, two circumstances can lead to unwanted biases.

On the one hand, training datasets in healthcare do not necessarily cover different groups of people equally. For example, only 4% of participants in the 2002 National Lung Screening Trial were of color [9]. Kaushal et al. found that 71% of US studies used to train deep networks were from a limited geographic area, mostly California, Massachusetts, and New York [10]. In addition, systematic labelling errors may occur for certain patient groups; for example, a Danish study found that women are diagnosed later than men for many diseases [11]. Therefore, AI models derived from such biased datasets suffer from limited information for some groups, resulting in higher AI model error for these individuals.

On the other hand, most machine learning methods rely on correlations rather than causality: if a certain pattern occurs frequently with a disease, the machine learning model uses this pattern as an indicator for diagnosis. There is usually no guarantee that there is a causal relationship between the observed pattern and the inferred disease. For example, it has been shown that many machine learning models can only correctly classify objects in images based on background information [12]. This fact can lead to errors in an AI model if it is trained on biased datasets, as the AI model extracts systematic correlations from datasets regardless of whether they correspond to causal relationships. For example, a later diagnosis for female patients compared to male patients in a training dataset will result in an AI model with a systematically higher false negative rate for women.

In summary, biases observed in healthcare training datasets can lead to biases in the AI models derived from them. For example, Pahl et al. examine biases in affective computing datasets and demonstrate their relationship to the fairness of state-of-the-art affect recognition models derived from them [13].

The term bias applies to a particular data set. It refers to the property that relevant subgroups, typically people of different gender, age or ethnicity, are not equally represented in the data set, i.e. the distribution from which the data were selected assigns a significantly higher probability to one subgroup than to the others. In the medical field, relevant subgroups are often missing entirely, such as data from healthy individuals.

14.2 Notions of fairness

While the term bias refers to a specific data set, the corresponding property of AI models is usually referred to as (algorithmic) fairness. In relation to humans, fairness refers to impartial and equitable treatment or behavior without favoritism or discrimination, corresponding to the absence of bias in human behavior. The (algorithmic) fairness of AI models is concerned with mathematical properties that should be fulfilled so that a person basing their actions on the AI-based decision function shows fair, i.e. unbiased, behavior.

The term (algorithmic) fairness refers to an algorithmic decision function derived from a given dataset using machine learning algorithms. It refers to the property that the algorithmic decisions have the same quality for different groups for which decisions are proposed. For example, the fact that one subgroup has a significantly higher error rate than others, is referred to as a violation of the condition of algorithmic fairness.

There is no generally accepted, unambiguous mathematical definition of algorithmic fairness [14]. Generally speaking, mathematical notions of fairness formalize the requirement that the quality of the AI model should be the same for every individual regardless of their gender, ethnicity or socio-demographic background. The problem is that AI-based models are used in very different contexts and errors of the model have different consequences. Hence the specification of what exactly means "equal distribution of quality among individuals" has a very different meaning when expressed in terms of the AI-model decision function.

The most prominent notion of fairness currently used in the context of healthcare refers to group fairness [15]. This notion is based on given groups which are characterized by a protected attribute (referred to by the symbol A in the following), such as a person's gender, ethnicity, or age. Depending on the value of the protected attribute (e.g., the gender being male or female), a person belongs to one of two or more groups (e.g., males and females). Group fairness formalizes the requirement that the quality of the outcome of an AI model should be independent of the value of A. Depending on the formalization of what exactly the term "quality" refers to, different mathematical specifications exist, which can be algorithmically evaluated given a specific model which implements a decision function (referred to by the symbol f in the following). Roughly speaking, different notions of fairness refer to the question, whether the protected attribute is used for decision making, and, if so, whether different output values or errors are equally distributed among different groups.

Fairness by unawareness : This notion refers to the fact that the protected attribute A is not used in the decision function f. For example, the diagnosis of whether a person has a disease is based only on medical evidence and ignores the person's gender. One problem is that A may be correlated with other medical values; for example, a person's gender has a strong effect on the concentration of steroids in blood samples. So even if f is unaware of A, it may use this information implicitly as it is correlated with medical values, leading to an unwanted bias.

Counterfactual fairness : Counterfactual fairness considers interdependencies between the protected attribute A and other medical values. The formalization requires that causal relations between A and all other quantities which are used for decision making in f are known. Counterfactual fairness holds if and only if, for a given person, a change in the value of the protected attribute A, and a change in the value of all other quantities caused by the change in A, does not lead to a different decision in f. The disadvantage of this formalization is its limited applicability in practice, as causal relationships are usually unknown.

Demographic parity : Demographic parity and equalized odds (as described below) are formalizations that refer to readily available statistical information on f, given a data set D of interest. They are defined for functions f with a binary output (i.e., 1 or 0), such as deciding whether a person should receive specialist care. Demographic parity is formalized as the requirement that the proportions of people from different groups for which output 1 (i.e. people receiving specialist care) is provided should be identical. While demographic parity is a useful formalization for scenarios concerned with the fair allocation of resources (e.g. specialist treatment) between different groups, it has a crucial pitfall for other scenarios, e.g. diagnostic scenarios: Suppose f diagnoses the criticality of a disease and supports the decision whether specific drugs are required for a person to survive. Assume A refers to the patient's age group (rather than gender or ethnicity). Achieving demographic parity would require that the same proportion of young people to be prescribed drugs as old people, even though many illnesses are not critical for young people and young people do less often need drugs to recover.

Equalized odds : This limitation of demographic parity is because it is independent of the true output value, which is known for historical data (e.g., information on whether a person of a certain age has recovered from a disease). Even if a model f did not make a single error on historical data, it would not normally meet the requirement of demographic parity (unless the distribution of outcomes were exactly the same for different groups). The notion of equalized odds provides a remedy incorporating label information from historical data. It requires that the distribution of true positives (i.e. inputs for which f predicts 1 and this is correct) and false positives (i.e. inputs for which f predicts 1 and this is incorrect) is the same across people from different groups. This means that the model error rate is independent of the protected attribute for people for whom the model suggests drugs for recovery. Equalized odds applies to models f that do not make errors. Yet, it reflects systematic labelling errors, i.e. a labelling bias, which is present in the historical data.

There are other formalizations of fairness that weight model errors differently or refer to individuals rather than groups, and extensions to non-binary features, which we do not discuss here [14,16]. Since some of these fairness concepts are mutually exclusive in the strict sense, i.e. different notions of fairness cannot be achieved simultaneously, restrictions or approximations of them need to be considered for practical cases [17].

14.3 Mitigation of bias

The AI-Act of the EU states that "training, validation and testing data sets shall be subject to data governance and management practices appropriate for the intended purpose of the high-risk AI system. Those practices shall concern in particular: [...] examination in view of possible biases that are likely to affect the health and safety of persons, have a negative impact on fundamental rights or lead to discrimination prohibited under Union law, especially where data outputs influence inputs for future operations" [2]. This means that there is not only an ethical reason but also a legal requirement to take steps to mitigate the potential biases of AI in healthcare, and there is a need to document these actions for transparency.

Mathematical formalizations of algorithmic fairness such as introduced above have the benefit that they can be tested given a model f and data set D. As there are biases that remain undetected by these formalizations, such as labelling bias, additional bias detection technologies are useful. One class of algorithms is provided by explainable AI technologies, or XAI for short, which have been used extensively in the context of medical applications and healthcare [18]. For example, it may be an indication of an implicit bias if XAI technologies highlight as most relevant features that ones are highly correlated with the protected attribute.

> The term eXplainable AI (XAI) refers to algorithms that replace or enhance otherwise black-box AI methods with components that can be inspected and understood by humans. For example, prominent XAI technologies enhance AI-based decision functions by specifying which input features of a given example are used to make the decision [19].

There are various technologies to mitigate bias in AI or to ensure the fairness of AI models, respectively. These can be applied at different stages of the process: During data collection, during the preparation of training data, during the training of the AI model, or via a post-processing step [20,21].

Responsible data collection: There are inherent biases in medical cases; for example, the incidence and presentation of diseases in older people is different from that in younger people. We therefore expect to find natural biases in medical databases that need to be considered when training an AI model. Responsible data collection should avoid such biases as much as possible: for example, data sets from different geographical regions can be combined to avoid regional bias. In addition, potential biases in data sets need to be transparent. To this end, protected attributes such as gender or ethnicity must be reported [22]. There is a dilemma here, as this information may be sensitive, leading to the risk of privacy violations [23].
Responsible data curation refers to the requirement that data be selected and pre-processed by human experts based on its quality, such as completeness or consistency. Appropriate protocols may include requirements such as labeling based on the opinion of more than one expert, and specific tools may be used to support this process [24]. In addition, the availability and exchange of high-quality data can be facilitated by approaches such as the European Health Data Space [25].
Mitigating bias during preprocessing: As discussed above, biased datasets, where different groups are represented at different frequencies, can lead to AI models that produce lower quality results for the

minority group. One remedy is data preprocessing, where a novel artificial training dataset is sampled from the original dataset with an equal representation of each group. In the realm of limited datasets, recent research has focused on the possibility of enriching datasets for training using generative AI [26].

Training AI models with fairness constraints : Machine learning algorithms are often formulated based on a training objective, usually the minimization of the model's classification error on the training dataset or some variation thereof. This fact allows the training to be extended to include aspects relevant to the fairness of the AI model. For example, one can include a term that seeks to minimize the correlation between the model output and the protected attribute [27]. For deep models in particular, game-theoretic approaches that aim for invariance of the internal modelling from the protected attribute have proven useful [28]. Since such methods add an additional constraint to learning, the accuracy of the resulting models is usually reduced compared to an AI model that does not obey fairness constraints.

Post-processing techniques modify the use of already trained models to improve group fairness. A typical approach is to calibrate models differently based on group membership. For example, it is reasonable to calibrate pulse oximetry data differently for patients of color compared to white patients, as the physical range of sensor signals is shifted [29]. In general, it may be a prudent strategy to adjust the model sensitivity based on the group average rather than using a global calibration to account for systematic shifts between groups.

Thus, there are different technologies that open a range of possibilities for incorporating fairness constraints into AI models for healthcare. It depends on the scenario which technology is best suited, depending on the available training data and the accessibility of the AI model. In any case, the resulting AI model needs to be audited to ensure that it complies with fairness constraints. Here, fairness criteria need to be combined with techniques that can ensure the statistical significance of fairness checks for future datasets [30,31]. In addition to algorithmic developments, several tool-suites can support this endeavor [32,33].

14.4 Emerging areas

In summary, we argue that, in addition to model accuracy, fairness is an essential requirement for AI models in healthcare and medicine, which is often violated due to the peculiarities of datasets in this domain. One challenge is that datasets are often relatively small, and some cases are rare, leading to a bias towards the more frequent cases and a higher error rate for the rare cases. In addition to the bias mitigation techniques discussed above, a recent trend in AI is to build large deep learning models that are trained on large generic data sets and then fine-tuned for specific purposes. Among other domains, these so-called foundational models have been proposed for image processing (e.g. the image segmentation model Segment Anything [34]) and text processing (e.g. the text embedding model BERT [35]). These models show excellent performance on generic tasks and can be adapted to medical goals. However, in addition to the huge training sets used to train such models, foundational models also exhibit systematic biases. Even worse, due to their sheer size and the fact that some foundational models are unsupervised, it is an open challenge how to efficiently detect and mitigate biases in foundational models [36].

Another approach that aims to extend the available training data while preserving privacy concerns is the concept of federated learning. In federated learning, models are trained locally rather than on global data sets, and model parameters are shared between clients to improve overall model accuracy. This concept allows information from different intensive care units to be shared without revealing information about individual patients, for example. An open challenge is how to deal consistently with the different statistical characteristics of data sets (i.e. data shift) from different clients [37].

As mentioned above, explainability is an important concept that allows humans to inspect AI models in the medical domain and detect potential biases [38]. Currently, XAI technologies are mostly limited to static information, such as the feature relevance of a fixed AI model for decision making. Current research is exploring how such technologies can be embedded in dynamic and truly interactive models [39]. Such approaches seem ideally suited to allow humans to thoroughly explore and understand the potential biases inherent in given AI models within a specific context.

Acknowledgement

Funding by BMFTR in the frame of the project "KI-Akademie OWL", funding ID 16 | S24057A, is gratefully acknowledged.

References

[1] Panel for the Future of Science and Technology, European Parliamentary Research Service, Scientific Foreside Unit (STOA), European Parliament, Artificial intelligence in healthcare: applications, risks, and ethical and societal impacts, PE 729.512 – June 2022. (Accessed November 14, 2024, at https://www.europarl.europa.eu/stoa/en/document/EPRS_STU(2022)729512).

[2] EUR Lex 32024R1689, Regulation (EU) 2024/1689 of the European Parliament and of the Council of 13 June 2024 laying down harmonised rules on artificial intelligence and amending Regulations (EC). (Accessed November 14, 2024, at https://eur-lex.europa.eu/legal-content/EN/ALL/?uri=CELEX:32024R1689).

[3] Shickel B., Loftus T. J., Adhikari L., Ozrazgat-Baslanti T., Bihorac A., Rashidi P. DeepSOFA: a continuous acuity score for critically ill patients using clinically interpretable deep learning. Sci Rep 2019; 9:1879.

[4] Tversky A., Kahnemann D. Judgment under Uncertainty: Heuristics and Biases. Science 1974; 185:1124–1131.

[5] Seyyed-Kalantari L., Liu G., McDermott M., Chen I. Y., Ghassemi M. CheXclusion: Fairness gaps in deep chest X-ray classifiers, In: BIOCOMPUTING 2021: Proceedings of the Pacific Symposium, 2021:232–243.

[6] Obermeyer Z., Powers B., Vogeli C., Mullainathan S. Dissecting racial bias in an algorithm used to manage the health of populations. Science 2019; 366(6464):447–453.

[7] Vaquet V., Menz P., Seiffert U., Hammer B. Investigating intensity and transversal drift in hyperspectral imaging data. Neurocomputing 2022;505: 68–79.

[8]   Garg A., Mago V. Role of machine learning in medical research: A survey. Computer Science Review, 2021; 40. https://doi.org/10.1016/j.cosrev.2021.100370.

[9]   Ferryman K., Pitcan M. Fairness in precision medicine. Data & Society, 2018.

[10] Kaushal A., Altman R., Langlotz C. Geographic distribution of US cohorts used to train deep learning algorithms. Jama 2020;324(12):1212–1213.

[11] Westergaard D., Moseley P., Sørup F. K. H., Baldi P., Brunak S. Population-wide analysis of differences in disease progression patterns in men and women, Nature communications 2019; 10(1):1–14.

[12] Xiao K. Y., Engstrom L., Ilyas A., Madry A. "Noise or Signal: The Role of Image Backgrounds in Object Recognition". In: ICLR 2021; ArXiv abs/2006.09994.

[13] Pahl J., Rieger I., Möller A., Wittenberg T., Schmid U. Female, white, 27? Bias Evaluation on Data and Algorithms for Affect Recognition in Faces. In: Proceedings of the 2022 ACM Conference on Fairness, Accountability, and Transparency (FAccT '22). Association for Computing Machinery, New York, NY, USA, 973–987. https://doi.org/10.1145/3531146.3533159.

[14] Mehrabi N., Morstatter F., Saxena N., Lerman K., Galstyan A. A Survey on Bias and Fairness in Machine Learning. ACM Comput. Surv. 2022; 54 (6), Article 115. https://doi.org/10.1145/3457607.

[15] Chen R. J., Wang J. J., Williamson D. F. K. et al. Algorithmic fairness in artificial intelligence for medicine and healthcare. Nat. Biomed. Eng 2023; 7:719–742. https://doi.org/10.1038/s41551-023-01056-8.

[16] Strotherm. J., Ashraf I., Hammer B. Fairness-enhancing classification methods for non-binary sensitive features – How to fairly detect leakages in water distribution systems. PeerJ Comput. Sci. 2024; 10: e2317.

[17] Bell A., Bynum L., Drushchak N., Zakharchenko N., Rosenblatt L., Stoyanovich J. The Possibility of Fairness: Revisiting the Impossibility Theorem in Practice. In: Proceedings of the 2023 ACM Conference on Fairness, Accountability, and Transparency (FAccT '23). Association for Computing Machinery, New York, NY, USA, 400–422. https://doi.org/10.1145/3593013.3594007.

[18] Holzinger A. Explainable AI and Multi-Modal Causability in Medicine. i-com 2020; 19(3): 171–179. https://doi.org/10.1515/icom-2020-0024.

[19] Ribeiro M. T., Singh S., Guestrin C. "Why Should I Trust You?": Explaining the Predictions of Any Classifier. In: Proceedings of the 22nd ACM SIGKDD International Conference on Knowledge Discovery and Data Mining (KDD '16) 2016. Association for Computing Machinery, New York, NY, USA, 1135–1144. https://doi.org/10.1145/2939672.2939778.

[20] Carey S., Pang A., de Kamps M. Fairness in AI for healthcare. Future Healthcare Journal, 2024; 11(3). https://doi.org/10.1016/j.fhj.2024.100177.

[21] Mittermaier M., Raza M. M., Kvedar C. Bias in AI-based models for medical applications: challenges and mitigation strategies. npj Digit. Med. 2023; 6(113). https://doi.org/10.1038/s41746-023-00858-z.

[22] Pineda-Moncusí M., Allery F., Delmestri A. et al. Ethnicity data resource in population-wide health records: completeness, coverage and granularity of diversity. Sci Data 2024; 11(221). https://doi.org/10.1038/s41597-024-02958-1.

[23] Agarwal S. Trade-Offs between Fairness and Privacy in Machine Learning. In: IJCAI 2021 Workshop on AI for Social Good.

[24] Delmestri A., Prieto-Alhambra D. Curator – A data curation tool for clinical real-world evidence. Informatics in Medicine Unlocked 2023;40: 101291, ISSN 2352–9148. https://doi.org/10.1016/j.imu.2023.101291

[25] de Zegher I., Norak K., Steiger D. et al. Artificial intelligence based data curation: enabling a patient-centric European health data space. Frontiers in Medicine 2024; 11. https://doi.org/10.3389/fmed.2024.1365501.

[26] Kummert J., Schulz A., Feldhans R., Mabigt M., Stemmler M., Kohler C., Abel D., Rossaint R., Hammer B. Generating Cardiovascular Data to Improve Training of Assistive Heart Devices. In: SSCI 2023: 1292–1297.

[27] Zafar M. B., Valera I., Rogriguez M. G., Gummadi K. P. Fairness constraints: mechanisms for fair classification. In: Artificial Intelligence and Statistics 2017; 962–970 (PMLR, 2017).

[28] Zemel R., Wu Y., Swersky K., Pitassi T., Dwork C. Learning fair representations. In: Int. Conf. Machine Learning 2013; 325–333 (PMLR, 2013).

[29] Valbuena V. S. M., Seelye S., Sjoding M. W. et al. Racial bias and reproducibility in pulse oximetry among medical and surgical inpatients in general care in the veterans health administration 2013–19: multicenter, retrospective cohort study. BMJ 2022; 378, Article e069775. https://doi.org/10.1136/bmj-2021-069775.

[30] Chugg C., Cortes-Gomez S., Wilder B., Ramdas A. Auditing fairness by betting. In: Proceedings of the 37th International Conference on Neural Information Processing Systems (NIPS '23). Curran Associates Inc., Red Hook, NY, USA, Article 266, 6070–6091.

[31] Cherian J. J., Candès E. J.; Statistical Inference for Fairness Auditing, JMLR 2024; 25(149):1–49.

[32] Weerts H., Dudík M., Edgar R., Jalali A., Lutz R., Madaio M. Fairlearn: Assessing and Improving Fairness of AI Systems, JMLR 2023; 24(257):1–8.

[33] Bellamy R. K. E. et al. AI Fairness 360: An extensible toolkit for detecting and mitigating algorithmic bias. IBM Journal of Research and Development, 2019; 63(4/5):4:1–4:15. https://doi.org/10.1147/JRD.2019.2942287.

[34] Kirillov A., Mintun E., Ravi N., Mao H., Rolland C., Gustafson L., Xiao T., Whitehead S., Berg A. C., W-YLo, Dollár P., Girshick R. Segment Anything, arXiv 2023, https://arxiv.org/abs/2304.02643.

[35] Devlin J., Chang M.-W., Lee K., Toutanova K. BERT: Pre-training of Deep Bidirectional Transformers for Language Understanding. In: Proceedings of the 2019 Conference of the North American Chapter of the Association for Computational Linguistics: Human Language Technologies, Volume 1 (Long and Short Papers), pages 4171–4186, Minneapolis, Minnesota. Association for Computational Linguistics.

[36] Schröder S., Schulz A., Hammer B. The SAME score: Improved cosine based measure for semantic bias. In: IJCNN 2024: 1–8.

[37] Internò C., Olhofer M., Jin Y., Hammer B. Federated Loss Exploration for Improved Convergence on Non-IID Data. In: International Joint Conference on Neural Networks (IJCNN), 1–8, 2024.

[38] Schwalbe G., Finzel B. A comprehensive taxonomy for explainable artificial intelligence: a systematic survey of surveys on methods and concepts. Data Min Knowl Disc 2024; 38:3043–3101. https://doi.org/10.1007/s10618-022-00867-8.

[39] Rohlfing K. J. et al. Explanation as a social practice: Toward a conceptual framework for the social design of AI systems, IEEE Transactions on Cognitive and Developmental Systems 2020; 13 (3):717–728.

Karsten Seidl, Hendrik Wöhrle

15 AI and edge / embedded devices for healthcare

15.1 Introduction

Artificial Intelligence (AI) and especially *Machine Learning* (ML) have gained a significant impact on healthcare in many ways [1–3]. In recent years, machine learning algorithms of a specific nature have garnered significant attention, namely *Edge AI* and *Tiny ML*. Edge AI is an acronym derived from the edge computing paradigm, which means that data is (at least partially) processed at the location where it is collected (i.e., close to the sensor), also referred to as the "edge of a network". This contrasts with the conventional cloud computing paradigm, wherein data is transferred to cloud systems for processing. The range of devices utilized for edge computing can vary depending on the specific application. These devices can include edge data centers and servers, compact edge devices with computing capabilities comparable to a smartphone, and small-scale devices such as microcontrollers or *application-specific integrated circuits* (ASICs). Notably, the latter category of computing devices is characterized by resource constraints, including memory and storage sizes that are highly limited (e.g., in the range of several hundred kilobytes) and significantly reduced computing capabilities. This is where Tiny ML comes into play. Tiny ML refers to the deployment of machine learning (ML) models on these highly resource-constrained edge devices. Since AI today is mostly characterized using ML algorithms, most Edge AI systems depend on Tiny ML.

In the last couple of years, Edge AI and Tiny ML became essential for various fields of application, e.g., the *Internet of Things* (IoT), robotics, autonomous driving, but also for healthcare. In many healthcare devices, physiological data must be processed embedded in the healthcare device. The fields of application in healthcare range from ubiquitously used simple wearable devices, such running watches with analysis of pulse and maximum oxygen uptake (VO2Max), to implantable devices such as retina- or neuro-implants, see, e.g. [4].

This chapter provides an overview of the underlying technology of Edge AI/Tiny ML algorithms and technologies as well as current applications.

15.1.1 A brief introduction to Edge AI and Tiny ML

The terms *Edge AI*, *Tiny ML* and *Embedded AI* are used almost interchangeably nowadays, but is important to recognize that they have, in fact, slightly different meanings. Edge AI is related to *edge computing* , which is a distributed computing paradigm that performs computations close to the source where data is generated, the "edge of the network", and is commonly used as the counterpart of cloud computing, where computing is performed almost exclusively at one or more centralized datacenters that are seen as an abstract, opaque entity, referred to as "the cloud".

Edge computing obeys some key characteristics that are fundamentally different from cloud computing:

(1) Less communication overhead: The computing resources are located close to the source of the data. Hence, there is no or only a minimum of data that is transferred via a network. This reduces the required bandwidth of a network or eliminates the need for a network connection altogether. This can improve energy efficiency, as it reduces the amount of energy required for communication.

(2) Better timing: Due to the proximity, the time overhead to transfer data to a distant cloud computing infrastructure and retrieve the results of performed computations is minimal. Hence, it is possible to achieve a lower latency for responses. Furthermore, the response time is more deterministic, which can fulfill real-time constraints.

(3) Better reliability, safety, and security: Since edge computing is not (or less) dependent on a network connection, connectivity issues usually do not affect the functionality of an edge computing device, resulting in higher reliability. This can directly increase the safety of such a device. Furthermore, transferring data makes it possible for an attacker to intercept or alter data or results. Accordingly, edge computingcan enhance privacy and security.

Edge computing is not necessarily a replacement for cloud computing. Instead, both approaches can be used in combination. In such a scenario, edge computing handles immediate, local processing needs, while cloud computing is used for large-scale data storage and complex computations. This results in a continuum of different computing resources, which is known as the "edge-cloud-continuum".

The definition of the edge-cloud-continuum is not a sharp one. On one hand, edge computing can be conducted on edge servers, which are powerful machines that collect, aggregate, and analyze data from a large number of smaller computing devices and are on the scale of powerful machines that can fill several server racks. On the other hand, edge computing can refer to the computing performed on tiny devices, such as microcontrollers or *application-specific integrated circuits* (ASICs).

The term "micro-edge" refers to computing resources that are even closer to the data source than traditional edge devices. These are small-scale, localized computing units that perform real-time data processing and analytics at the site of data generation. Micro-edge devices are typically used in environments where immediate data processing is crucial, such as in industrial automation, smart cities, or autonomous vehicles. "Extreme edge" pushes this concept even further, referring to computing capabilities embedded directly within the sensors or actuators themselves. This level of integration allows for ultra-low latency and minimal data transfer, making it ideal for applications that require instantaneous decision-making and high levels of autonomy. Hence,

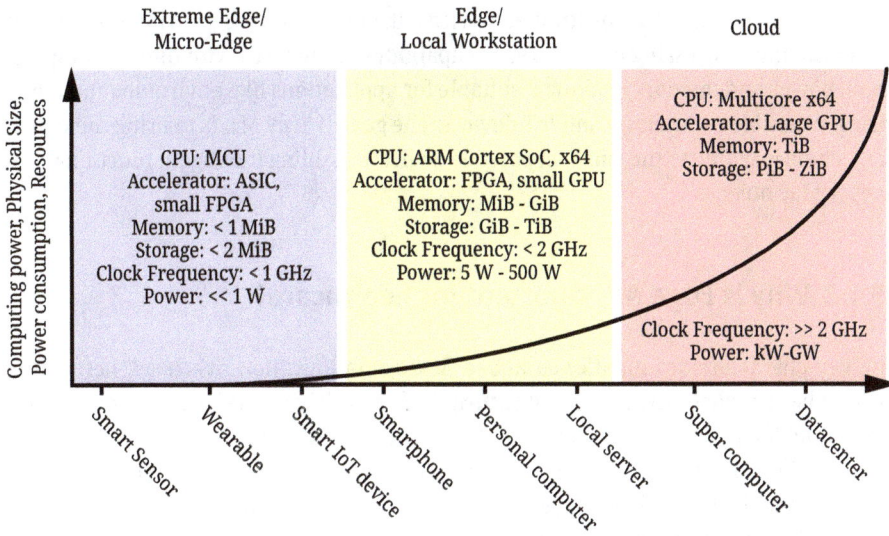

Fig. 15.1: Characteristics of different computing devices in Extreme Edge, Edge and Cloud environments. Adapted from [5].

micro-edge and extreme edge computing are usually performed on "Embedded Systems". An Embedded System is a specialized computing system that performs dedicated functions or tasks within a larger mechanical or electrical system. These systems are typically designed for efficiency, reliability, and real-time operation. Embedded systems can be found in a wide range of applications, from household appliances and automotive control systems to industrial machines and medical devices. Embedded Systems usually consist of a microcontroller or a *"System on Chip"* (SoC), along with software tailored to the specific task. In the last couple of years, the classical microcontrollers and SoCs are increasingly often accompanied by specialized hardware accelerators that are specifically designed to accelerate machine learning-based applications, see Section 15.2.2 for details.

The landscape of different computing devices, i.e., extreme-edge/micro-edge, edge/local workstation and cloud, with its available computer power is shown in Fig. 15.1.

Embedded AI refers to the integration of artificial intelligence (AI) algorithms and models into embedded systems. This enables devices to perform intelligent tasks such as pattern recognition, decision-making, and predictive analytics directly on the device, without relying on cloud-based resources. Embedded AI is crucial for applications where real-time processing, low latency, and data privacy are essential, such as in healthcare devices, autonomous vehicles, and smart home systems. Tiny ML (Tiny Machine Learning) is a subset of embedded AI that focuses on deploying machine learning models on ultra-low-power, resource-constrained devices like microcontrollers. Tiny ML enables advanced data processing and inference capabilities on devices with limited computational power and memory, making it suitable for applications like environmental monitoring, wearable technology, and IoT devices. The goal of Tiny ML is to bring the power of machine learning to the smallest possible devices, enabling intelligent functionalities in everyday objects.

15.1.2 Why is Edge AI important for healthcare?

The key characteristics mentioned above (less communication overhead, better timing and better reliability, safety and security) have decisive benefits for higher performance and lower costs in the context of healthcare applications.

Edge AI processes data locally on devices (e.g., wearable devices, patient monitors, imaging machines), enabling real-time analysis without relying on cloud connectivity. Fast detection of anomalies (like arrhythmias or strokes) can trigger instant alerts, which is vital in life-threatening situations. Edge AI minimizes latency, making it suitable for applications like robotic surgery, real-time imaging analysis, medical implants with closed-loop control or continuous vital sign monitoring. Wearables and at-home medical devices powered by Edge AI can continuously monitor patient vital signs and behaviors. This enables early detection of health issues, better chronic disease management, and tailored interventions without frequent clinic visits.

Sensitive patient data stays thereby on the device or within the hospital's secure infrastructure. It reduces the risk of data breaches associated with transmitting data to the cloud. Many healthcare settings (rural clinics, ambulances, battlefield hospitals) lack constant internet access. Edge AI allows systems to function independently of cloud infrastructure, ensuring uninterrupted care.

Medical devices generate massive amounts of data (e.g., MRI scans, ECGs, neural data). Processing data locally avoids the need to send all of it over networks, reducing bandwidth costs and cloud storage fees. Edge AI supports the massive scaling of interconnected medical devices, which ensures that even with thousands of sensors and endpoints, the system remains responsive and efficient.

15.2 Foundations of Edge AI for medical applications

The integration of Edge AI into medical applications is underpinned by several foundational principles, including energy efficiency, algorithmic design, and technological advancements. These elements are critical in ensuring that Edge AI systems can operate effectively within the constraints and requirements specific to the medical field.

15.2.1 Machine learning workflow for Edge AI

The machine learning workflow for Edge AI in medical applications involves several key stages:

Data Acquisition: The first step is the acquisition of the data itself using dedicated sensors, which convert different kinds of physical measurable properties of the sensed entity to, e.g., an analog voltage and the conversion of the voltage to a time- and value discrete digital representation using an *analog-to-digital converter* (ADC). Since Edge AI is located, by definition, in close vicinity to the sensor, the data acquisition is especially important in the Edge AI workflow. This step can already contain specific precondition-ing and preprocessing procedures, e.g., analogue filtering before analog-to-digital con-version to avoid problems related to the sampling process (e.g., filtering out frequency components above half the sampling frequency according to the sampling theorem), reduce noise or amplify signals. Usually, this is needed to obtain clean data, which is essential for the subsequent machine learning steps. The filtering is performed on the analog data using analog filters and amplifiers, typically summarized as the *analog front-end* (AFE). Various sensors are used for data acquisition in medical applications. See the works by Cong [6], Ha et al. [7] and Pething & Smith [8] for general consider-ations on biomedical data acquisition. Specific examples are:

> **Example 1** – Signal conditioning for noninvasive sensing of *electrocardiogram* (ECG) data: ECG data can be affected by several different types of noise (e.g., baseline drift due to patient movement or respira-tion, powerline noise at 50/60 Hz, high frequency noise due to muscle activity, etc.). To obtain clean ECG signals, this noise should be removed, and the signals need to be amplified to meet the input range of the ADC [9].
>
> **Example 2** – Analog signal conditioning for *electroencephalography* (EEG) data: The processing of EEG signals is particularly challenging due to the following typically low amplitude (typically 10–100 μV); they are vulnerable to noise; and they are susceptible to artefacts. Prior to ADC, these signals must undergo a series of critical analogue signal processing and conditioning steps, to ensure the preservation of signal integrity [10]. In active electrodes, the EEG signal is digitized in the electrode itself; each electrode con-tains a separate AFE for signal processing and amplification [11].
>
> **Example 3** – Analogue filtering in neuro-implants: Different types of neuronal activity can be acquired by electrodes in neuro-implants. To detect *action potentials* (APs, spikes) from single or a small number of neurons, it is essential to filter out low-frequency local field potentials (LFPs), which are caused by the synchronous activity of large populations of neurons before ADC [12].

Preprocessing: This step focuses on the transformation and preparation of raw medi-cal data into a suitable format for machine learning models. Techniques such as data normalization, data augmentation, and feature extraction are employed to enhance the quality and relevance of the input data. This can involve filtering the data using digital filters and transformations, such as transforming the data from the time domain to the frequency domain. With the progress in *deep learning* (DL), the feature engineering became a part of the neural networks that are used for classification, e.g., in *deep neural networks* (DNNs) for image or time series processing, the first part of the network are often convolutional layers that are used for feature extraction. In contrast to classical approaches, the filter coefficients that are used for the convolutions are no longer hand-engineered by experts but learned from the training data during training [13]. Examples in the medical field are:

Example 1 cont'd – Many different methods are used for feature extraction of ECG data [14] to convert the data to different domains (e.g., frequency domain, time–frequency domain, decomposition, sparse domain or remain in time domain). Another EEG-specific famous example is the detection of the QRS-complex (three distinct peaks in the ECG) via the Pan-Tompkins algorithm [15] or Hilbert transform [16] and subsequently to identify properties of the QRS-shape.

Example 2 cont'd – Spatial filtering for EEG data: For use in *Brain Computer Interfaces* (BCIs), for example by detecting *event-related potentials* (ERPs), multi-channel EEG data is often processed vial spatial filters such as axDAWN [17].

Example 3 cont'd – Spike sorting in neuro-implants refers to the process of identifying and classifying APs recorded from extracellular electrodes into groups that correspond to individual neurons. It is an essential step in the feature extraction process for decoding the actual meaningful information and to perform data compression. It is typically located in an ASIC inside the implant [12,18].

Classification, Regression: The core of the workflow involves the processing of the processed data using machine learning models by making predictions. The prediction can either be a categorical output (e.g., "healthy" or "ill") or a real-valued output. In the former case, the process of mapping inputs to category is called classification, the latter case is called regression. The utilized ML models can range from traditional algorithms like *support vector machines* (SVMs) to *deep neural networks* (DNNs), tailored to address specific medical diagnostic or predictive tasks. For instance, in DNNs, the last layers are *fully connected* (FC) neural network layers [13].

Example 1 cont'd – Different types of classifiers have been used for ECG classification, e.g., 1D Convolutional DNNs such as the *fully connected neural network* FCNN [19].

Example 2 cont'd – Various different classifiers have been used for EEG classification, ranging from SVMs [20] to DNNs in EEGNet [22].

Example 3 cont'd –Many different types of deep learning have been used for neural decoding of neuro-implant data [22,23].

Postprocessing: Following model inference, postprocessing techniques are applied to interpret and refine the output. This may include thresholding, result aggregation, and visualization, ensuring the outcomes are actionable and comprehensible for medical professionals.

A significant challenge in this workflow is the limited availability of labeled medical data, which is essential for supervised learning approaches. This scarcity necessitates the exploration of data augmentation, transfer learning, and semi-supervised learning techniques to enhance model performance.

15.2.2 Hardware considerations

Selecting appropriate hardware is crucial for the deployment of Edge AI in medical applications. There exists a wide range of technologies that have different advantages and disadvantages. Evaluation criteria include to select the most suitable technology for a medical application include:

– **Computational Performance**: The device must support fast processing to meet the real-time characteristics of medical diagnostics or to use computationally intensive methods such as DNNs in a device. Computational performance is related to latency, which is the time required to produce an output after data is acquired, and throughput, which is the amount of work or data processed within a given time. Latency and throughput are usually inversely related. However, there are systems where this is not the case, e.g. a deeply pipelined system can have high throughput and high latency at the same time.

– **Low Power Consumption** is often of high importance, particularly for portable or implantable medical devices where battery life is a limiting factor or where generated heat can cause tissue damage (e.g., in neuro-implants). Often computational performance is related to power consumption as a measure of efficiency, usually measured by *total operations per second per watt* (TOPS/W).

– **Flexibility**: The capability to adapt to a variety of tasks and algorithms is advantageous, particularly to encompass a broad spectrum of medical applications and environments. Moreover, the capacity to interface with different sensors and to even convert analog signals is important.

– **Ease of Development**: In the context of biomedical engineering, budget, time and engineers are often scarce resources. Consequently, it is often advantageous to minimize the development complexity of biomedical systems, ensuring that they do not exceed the necessary level. It is acknowledged that considerable variations in development complexity exist between different hardware technologies. This aspect must be considered during the development phase of any medical technology system.

– **Programmability**: The various hardware technologies differ significantly in terms of their flexibility, i.e., the extent to which their functionality can be altered post-assembly. Some technologies are relying on a given program that can be executed and modified at runtime, while other systems are based on a hardwired function. This characteristic of a system is denoted by the term programmability.

Several technologies are pertinent to Edge AI hardware, which differ largely in the properties described above. Fig. 15.2 presents a qualitative comparison of the various options available for constructing Edge-AI systems.

Microprocessors: The majority of classical computing systems are constructed around a *microprocessor* (µP) or *Central Processing Unit* (CPU). A significant number of medical systems also utilize this approach, in which specific AI algorithms are deployed as software components and are executed by the CPU. The approach is advantageous in that it is simple to develop, with widely used programming languages and tools available for the purpose. Since these programming languages are Turing complete (and the main difference between a CPU and a Turing machine is the limited memory), nearly all types of applications and algorithms can be implemented for a CPU and changed by updating the software. Hence, CPU-based systems are easy to develop and have a high programmability. However, the generic nature of CPUs also poses significant disadvantages, particularly regarding power consumption and computational efficiency. In many cases, it is more advantageous to specialize in a specific domain of applications to achieve optimal performance. Furthermore, CPUs themselves generally do not incorporate the necessary interfaces to facilitate connectivity with sensors, a crucial component in medical systems. Consequently, the necessity arises for additional hardware to be incorporated.

Microcontrollers (µC) can be defined as small microprocessors that are accompanied by different additional interfaces that allow them to connect to other devices, such as sensors or actuators. Some microcontrollers also have dedicated *Analog-Digital-Converters* (DACs) that allow them to convert analog voltages that represent physiological signals to a digital representation. Since µCs are usually used for embedded systems, they are usually much more restricted regarding the available computing power, memory and storage, but are optimized regarding energy efficiency. Similar to µPs, µCs are highly programmable, i.e., their functionality is fully specified by the executed software and can be easily adapted. However, developing µC-based systems required knowledge of their internal structure, which results in increased development effort.

Field-Programmable Gate Arrays (FPGAs) offer reconfigurable hardware solutions that balance performance and flexibility, making them suitable for diverse medical applications. FPGAs consist of flexible logic elements (based on look-up-tables and flip-flops), memory blocks and input/output (I/O) ports that can be configured in such a way that they form any digital circuit with a specific functionality, i.e., a filter or dedicated hardware accelerator and nearly arbitrary I/O interfaces. This results in a very high flexibility, high performance due to massive parallelism and nice energy efficiency. However, in contrast to µPs and µCs they are not programmed with typical high-language programming languages but using hardware descriptions languages (e.g., Verilog, VHDL) and require knowledge in digital circuit design to work with, which makes them

Application-Specific Integrated Circuits (ASICs) provide highly optimized, dedicated hardware solutions for specific AI tasks, achieving superior efficiency and speed at the expense of flexibility. Based on advances in CMOS technology, ASICs can now be used to build highly energy-efficient and high-performance systems. However, ASIC design is much more complex than other approaches. Like FPGAs, the development of an ASIC requires digital and often additional analog circuit design knowledge. After production, the functionality of the ASIC is fixed, i.e. it is not possible to reprogram an ASIC.

Another approach is to use **combinations of different computing technologies**, such as combining a CPU with a *graphics processing unit* (GPU) or using a µC with a dedicated hardware accelerator. Many devices, such as the MAX78000 and RISC-V based microcontrollers, integrate dedicated AI accelerators to improve performance while maintaining low power consumption. This approach helps avoid the drawbacks of a single technology. For example, for µPs and µCs, it is possible to offload DNN computations to the GPU or a dedicated DNN accelerator to achieve improved performance and power consumption while retaining the advantages of the CPU. On the other hand, the digital implementation of an accelerator in an FPGA or ASIC can be supported by a CPU to perform software tasks.

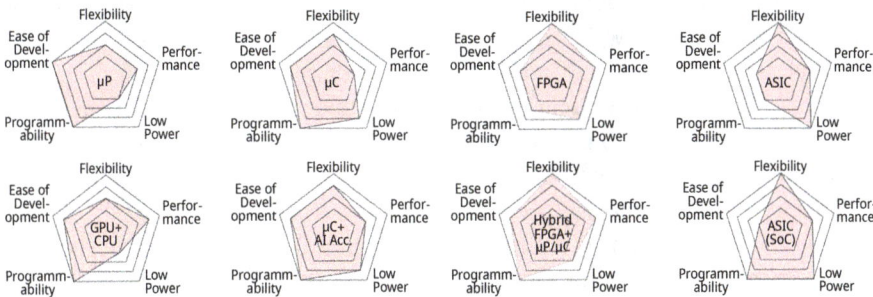

Fig. 15.2: Qualitative comparison of different hardware devices for Edge AI. Graphics provided by the authors (HW).

15.2.3 Software and algorithmic considerations

A crucial part of edge AI systems for healthcare is related to software and the algorithmic foundations. In the case where an algorithm is not directly embedded in the hardware (i.e., in a circuit in an FPGA or ASIC), it must be implemented as a software component. In such cases, the hardware used determines which software can be used and how. In the case of µPs, this process is typically uncomplicated. In such instances, the software is executed by the CPU. This facilitates the utilization of widely adopted software development tools and methodologies. However, when alternative hardware is employed, this process becomes more challenging. For instance, most µP-based systems have operating systems that care about the interaction with I/O-interfaces, memory management and scheduling of tasks; many µCs use no or only special operating systems, e.g. *real time operating systems* (RTOS).

A critical step of Tiny ML involves the optimization of a *deep neural network* (DNN) model to leverage the constrained resources, such as computing capacity and memory, of embedded systems. This approach aims to enhance energy efficiency. In recent years, a range of techniques for this optimization have emerged. The most significant of these techniques are described in the following paragraphs.

Quantization refers to the process of converting a model from floating point to fixed point arithmetic. The utilization of high-resolution floating-point arithmetic (e.g., 32 or even 64 bits) for inference in machine learning (ML) is costly in terms of resources in FPGAs or area in ASICs and is frequently not supported in μCs. However, it is often possible to use integer/fixed-point arithmetic with a small number of bits (e.g., 8 bits) without a major loss in accuracy if a DNN model is quantized carefully. Low-bit-width fixed-point arithmetic reduces the resource/area requirements significantly, which is also beneficial regarding power consumption and computational performance. Different approaches can be used for quantization, e.g., regarding when it is performed: post-training or during training (known as quantization-aware training), what is quantized: activations and/or weights, if single layers, multiple layers or the whole model are quantized and if the quantization is performed uniformly, logarithmic or non-uniformly [24]. Quantization is also frequently applied to transfer DNNs to edge devices in medical applications, e.g., Q-EEGnet [25] for noninvasive BCIs, quantized autoencoders for ASIC-based spike sorting [26].

Pruning: Quantization can result in weights to become zero, effectively eliminating a specific connection in a DNN. Similarly, certain activation functions such as, e.g., *rectified linear unit* (ReLu) can result in output activities to become zero. This means that the DNN can become sparse if many weights and activations are zero. This can also be enforced by using specific methods, such as *pruning*, which intentionally removes weights from DNNs under the assumption that many parameters in DNNs contribute minimally to overall performance. Pruning can, similarly to quantization, be performed during or after training. The sparsity created by pruning can be exploited by skipping the affected operations, which helps to enhance the efficiency and accelerate computations. Furthermore, pruning reduces the model size, which reduces storage requirements [27]. If high compression rates of the DNN are required, pruning can outperform quantization [28].

Knowledge Distillation (KD): This technique refers to the transfer of knowledge from a larger ("teacher") model to a small ("student") model. This process compresses the teacher's capabilities into the more efficient student model that is better suited for execution on an edge device (e.g., by being computationally less expensive) while retaining performance [29]. The student model is designed to learn through the process of imitation, whereby it replicates the outputs of the teacher. In this learning process, "soft targets" (probability distributions) are utilized in place of hard labels. This approach is employed to capture nuanced patterns that might not be adequately addressed by hard labels. KD has been successfully applied for various kinds of biomedical data like ECG [30,31] or EEG [32,33] data.

15.3 Edge AI in healthcare – From concept to approved products

As mentioned above, Edge AI has become increasingly practical thanks to advances in model compression, energy-efficient processors, and specialized accelerators. These innovations allow complex algorithms to run on small, battery-powered medical devices, enabling real-time analysis and response at the point of care. Importantly, this is not just a research trend: several **FDA- and EU-cleared products** already demonstrate how Edge AI can be safely and effectively integrated into medical workflows.

Wearable Cardiac Monitoring: One of the most prominent examples is the **AliveCor KardiaMobile** series, cleared by the FDA and CE-marked in the EU. These pocket-sized ECG devices use on-device algorithms to detect atrial fibrillation and other rhythm abnormalities within seconds of recording. The AI runs locally, ensuring that preliminary results are available instantly – even without an internet connection. Similarly, the **Apple Watch ECG app**, FDA-cleared for detecting irregular rhythms, processes raw electrical signals directly on the watch's integrated neural processing hardware. This local inference minimizes latency and enhances user privacy while offering clinically validated screening capabilities [34].

Seizure and Neurological Event Detection: The **Empatica EmbracePlus** (FDA-cleared as a seizure monitoring device) uses multi-sensor data – such as electrodermal activity and accelerometry – to detect patterns consistent with generalized tonic-clonic seizures. While some functions are cloud-based, key detection algorithms operate on-device to ensure alerts can be issued even if network connectivity is lost. This capability can be critical for patients in remote areas or during emergencies where immediate notification is essential.

Imaging and Point-of-Care Diagnostics: Edge AI is also transforming medical imaging. The **Butterfly iQ+** portable ultrasound system, CE-marked and FDA-cleared, integrates AI models into its companion mobile app to assist with anatomical guidance, measurement suggestions, and image optimization. By running inference locally on the smartphone or tablet – often leveraging built-in neural engines – clinicians can receive guidance in real time without having to upload sensitive patient images to the cloud. Similar AI-driven assistance is beginning to appear in other point-of-care imaging devices, such as handheld fundus cameras for diabetic retinopathy screening.

Surgical Robotics and Intraoperative Assistance: In the operating room, Edge AI is enabling advanced robotic assistance. The **Asensus Surgical Senhance** system, FDA-cleared, incorporates its *Intelligent Surgical Unit* – a real-time computer vision platform that provides automated camera control, image enhancement, and measurement tools. Processing occurs within the surgical console itself, avoiding delays that could result from cloud dependence. Likewise, the **Moon Surgical Maestro** platform, with FDA clearance for its AI-powered *ScoPilot* feature, uses local processing to track laparoscopic instruments and maintain a stable view during minimally invasive surgery.

Implantable Devices: Due to the high demands on the necessary bandwidth of the recorded data, data security, and real-time capabilities, especially in closed-loop applications, intensive research is being conducted in the field of edge AI for medical implants. Details, especially regarding the potential in neuroimplants, e.g., for brain-computer interfaces with an end-to-end pipeline [12], deep brain stimulation, and cochlear implants, are explored in depth in chapter 17 [4].

15.4 Ethical considerations of Edge AI vs. cloud computing

As artificial intelligence becomes increasingly embedded in medical products, the decision between running AI on edge devices or in the cloud brings distinct ethical consequences. Edge AI processes data locally on devices such as wearable devices, patient monitors and medical implants, offering users greater control over their personal information. By avoiding centralized storage, it reduces exposure to large-scale data breaches and misuse. Yet the very decentralization that protects **privacy** also makes it harder to enforce consistent security and data protection standards across countless devices.

Security itself is a double-edged issue. Edge devices often operate with limited computing resources and receive irregular updates, leaving them more vulnerable to attacks. Cloud infrastructure, by contrast, is generally better protected and maintained, but it concentrates risk in a single location where a breach can affect millions. This tension extends to transparency and accountability: while cloud systems can log and audit every decision, edge systems often operate in isolation, making it difficult to trace harmful or biased outcomes or to determine whether the developer, the manufacturer, or the user should bear responsibility.

Fairness is also at stake. Cloud-based AI models can be updated frequently, improving accuracy and reducing bias. Edge AI models, once deployed, may go months or years without updates, potentially perpetuating outdated or discriminatory decision-making. Yet despite these concerns, edge computing offers important benefits. It allows for autonomy in regions with poor connectivity, supports data sovereignty in jurisdictions with strict privacy laws, and can lower energy consumption by reducing the need for constant data transmission to large data centers.

The ethical landscape of Edge AI is therefore complex. It promises improvements in privacy, autonomy, and sustainability, but these come with significant challenges in security, fairness, transparency, and accountability. Navigating these trade-offs will be crucial to ensuring that medical AI systems serve the public good while respecting both individual rights and societal values.

15.5 Summary and future directions for Edge AI in healthcare

Edge AI, i.e. running machine learning models directly on medical devices and local gateway, will reshape healthcare by making diagnostics faster, more private, and more continuous. Over the next years we'll see much smaller, energy-efficient models deployed on wearables, bedside monitors, and point-of-care scanners, enabling real-time analysis of vital signs, ECGs, imaging slices, and biosensor streams without a cloud round-trip. That lowers latency for critical alerts and preserves patient privacy by keeping raw data local.

Model **compression techniques** (quantization, pruning, distillation) and dedicated neuromorphic and **accelerator hardware** will let sophisticated models run on constrained devices while extending battery life. Edge AI will pair with federated and split learning to let institutions collaboratively improve models without sharing raw health records, addressing both data scarcity and regulatory concerns. **Hybrid architectures**, where the edge performs initial triage and the cloud handles heavier analytics or longitudinal aggregation, will balance immediacy with global learning.

Clinically useful Edge AI will require stronger **explainability, standardized validation pipelines**, and **regulatory frameworks** that account for on-device updates. More prospective trials evaluating safety, fairness, and robustness to real-world variability are expected. Finally, tighter integration with **telemedicine platforms** and **electronic health records** will let edge insights trigger workflows, automate documentation, and support personalized interventions. Together, these advances promise more timely, private, and equitable care – if technical progress is matched by careful validation and governance.

References

[1] Yu K. H., Beam A. L., Kohane I. S. Artificial intelligence in healthcare. Nat Biomed Eng 2018; 2(10):719–31. https://doi.org/10.1038/s41551-018-0305-z.

[2] Davenport T., Kalakota R. The Potential for Artificial Intelligence in Healthcare. Future Healthcare Journal 2019;6(2):94–8.

[3] Alowais S. A. et al. "Revolutionizing Healthcare: The Role of Artificial Intelligence in Clinical Practice". BMC Medical Education 2023;23(1):689.

[4] Rosahl S.K., Stieglitz T. Impact of Artificial Intelligence on Neural Implants. In: Manzeschke A and Wittenberg T. (eds.). Ethical Perspectives on Artificial Intelligence in Biomedical Engineering, Chapter 17, DeGruyter, 2025.

[5] Rajapakse V., Karunanayake I., Ahmed N. Intelligence at the Extreme Edge: A Survey on Reformable TinyML. ACM Comput Surv 2023;55(13). https://doi.org/10.1145/3583683.

[6] Cong P. Circuit Design Considerations for Implantable Devices. River Publishers, 2018.

[7] Ha S. et al. Integrated Circuits and Electrode Interfaces for Noninvasive Physiological Monitoring. IEEE Trans Biomed Eng 2014;61(5):1522–37.

[8]   Pethig R. R., Smith S. Introductory bioelectronics: For engineers and physical scientists. John Wiley & Sons, 2012.

[9]   Morales D. P., García A., Castillo E., Carvajal M. A., Banqueri J., Palma A. J. Flexible ECG acquisition system based on analog and digital reconfigurable devices. Sensors and Actuators A: Physical 2011;165(2):261–70. https://doi.org/10.1016/j.sna.2010.10.008.

[10] Teplan T. Fundamentals of EEG Measurement. Meas Sci Rev 2022;2(2):1–11.

[11] Xu J., Mitra S., Van Hoof C., Yazicioglu R. F., Makinwa K. A. Active Electrodes for Wearable EEG Acquisition: Review and Electronics Design Methodology. IEEE Rev Biomed Eng 2017;10:187–98.

[12] Erbslöh A. et al. Technical Survey of End-to-End Signal Processing in BCIs Using Invasive MEAs. J Neural Eng 2024;21(5):051003.

[13] Goodfellow I., Bengio Y., Courville A., Deep Learning. MIT Press, 2016.

[14] Singh A. K., Krishnan S. ECG signal feature extraction trends in methods and applications," BioMed Eng OnLine 2023;22(1):22.

[15] Pan J., Tompkins W. J. A real-time QRS detection algorithm," IEEE Trans Biomed Eng1985;3:230–6.

[16] Benitez D., Gaydecki P., Zaidi A., Fitzpatrick A. The Use of the Hilbert Transform in ECG Signal Analysis," Computers in Biology and Medicine 2001;31(5): 399–406.

[17] Wöhrle H., Krell M. M., Straube S., Kim S. K., Kirchner E. A., Kirchner F. An adaptive spatial filter for user-independent single trial detection of event-related potentials. IEEE Trans Biomed Eng, 2015.

[18] Zhang T., Azghadi M. R., Lammie C., Amirsoleimani A., Genov R. Spike sorting algorithms and their efficient hardware implementation: a comprehensive survey. J Neural Eng 2023;20(2):021001.

[19] Wöhrle H. et al. Multi-Objective Surrogate-Model-Based Neural Architecture and Physical Design Co-Optimization of Energy Efficient Neural Network Hardware Accelerators. IEEE Trans Circ and Sys I: Regular Papers 2022;70(1):40–53.

[20] Kaper M., Meinicke P., Grossekathoefer U., Lingner T., Ritter H. BCI Competition 2003-Data Set IIb: Support Vector Machines for the P300 Speller Paradigm. IEEE Trans Biomed Eng 2004;51(6):1073–6.

[21] Lawhern V. J., Solon A. J., Waytowich N. R., Gordon S. M., Hung C. P., Lance B. J. "EEGNet: a compact convolutional neural network for EEG-based brain–computer interfaces," J Neural Eng 2018;15(5):056013.

[22] Glaser J. I., Benjamin A. S., Chowdhury R. H., Perich M. G., Miller L. E., Kording K. P. Machine Learning for Neural Decoding. eneuro 2020;7(4).

[23] Livezey J. A., Glaser J. I. Deep Learning Approaches for Neural Decoding Across Architectures and Recording Modalities. Briefings in Bioinf 2021;22(2):1577–91.

[24] Rokh B., Azarpeyvand A., Khanteymoori A. A comprehensive survey on model quantization for deep neural networks in image classification. ACM Trans Intelli Sys and Tech, 2023;14(6):1–50.

[25] Schneider T., Wang X., Hersche M., Cavigelli L., Benini L. Q-EEGNet: An energy-efficient 8-bit quantized parallel EEGNet implementation for edge motor-imagery brain-machine interfaces. IEEE Int Conf Smart Comp (SMARTCOMP) 2020, pp 284–9.

[26] Seong C., Lee W., Jeon D. "A multi-channel spike sorting processor with accurate clustering algorithm using convolutional autoencoder," IEEE Transactions on Biomedical Circuits and Sys 2021;15(6):1441–53. https://doi.org/10.1109/TBCAS.2021.3134660.

[27] Cheng H., Zhang M., Shi J. Q. A Survey on Deep Neural Network Pruning: Taxonomy, Comparison, Analysis, and Recommendations. IEEE Trans Pattern Anal Mach Intell 2024;46(12):10558–78. https://doi.org/10.1109/TPAMI.2024.3447085.

[28] Kuzmin A., Nagel M., Van Baalen M., Behboodi A., Blankevoort T. Pruning vs Quantization: Which is Better? Adv Neural Inf Proc Sys 2023;36:62414–27.

[29] Gou J., Yu B., Maybank S. J., Tao D. "Knowledge Distillation: A Survey," Int J Comp Vision 2021;129(6):1789–1819.

[30] Sepahvand M., Abdali-Mohammadi F., A Novel Method for Reducing Arrhythmia Classification from 12-Lead Ecg Signals to Single-Lead ECG with Minimal Loss of Accuracy Through Teacher-Student Knowledge Distillation, Information Sciences 2022;593:64–77.

[31] Wei X. et al. Differentiated Knowledge Distillation: Patient-Specific Single-Sample Personalization for Electrocardiogram Diagnostic Models. Eng Appl Artif Intell 2024;136:108880.

[32] Zhang S., Tang C., Guan C. Visual-to-Eeg Cross-Modal Knowledge Distillation for Continuous Emotion Recognition. Pattern Recognition 2022;130:108833.

[33] Liang H., Liu Y., Wang H., Jia Z., Center B. Teacher assistant-based knowledge distillation extracting multi-level features on single channel sleep EEG. IJCAI, 2023;3948–56.

[34] Putra K. T. "A review on the application of 4in wearable personal health monitoring: A cloud-edge artificial intelligence approach," IEEE Access 2024;12:21437–52.

Steffen K. Rosahl, Thomas Stieglitz

16 Impact of artificial intelligence on neural implants

16.1 Definition of neural implants

Implanting medical devices inside the human body can replace missing biological structures, support damaged biological structures, modulate function of physiological systems or enhance existing biological structures and physiological systems, respectively. A "neural implant" is an implant that interacts with neurons. Since it needs electrical power for interaction, it is classified as "active implantable medical device" (AIMD) and covered by the medical device regulation in the EU (MDR, 745/20167EU). Because of their potential to interfere with cognition, emotions and the psyche, neural implants connected to the brain ("brain-machine-interfaces", "brain-computer interfaces" [1]) continue to raise both hope and ethical concerns.

As of today, the most successful active implants are cardiac pacemakers. Interestingly, the hearts own neural pacemaker cells in conjunction with peripheral glia cells closely resemble anatomical brain architecture [2]. However, when neural implants are discussed, we usually talk about direct connections to nerves and to the brain. Among those, cochlear implants (CI) are the most frequently employed devices. More than one million CIs have been implanted worldwide. They have changed the treatment of profound hearing loss bordering on deafness that cannot be adequately treated with other hearing aids. CI use electricity to stimulate the spiral ganglion cells of the auditory nerve to restore sensorineural hearing loss, bypassing the damaged hearing apparatus. A prerequisite is the presence of the cochlear nerve, a cranial nerve connecting to the brainstem with relatively preserved anatomy. If this is not the case, similar implants placed at specific sites of the hearing pathway in the brainstem can partially restore hearing function [3].

The most relevant and successful direct brain implant is a pacemaker for neural cells that regulate movement and behavior related to Parkinson's disease (PD). The method has been termed "deep-brain stimulation" (DBS) [4] because targets are not on the surface of the brain. As of 2023, around 244.000 DBS systems have been implanted worldwide [5]. While first developed to treat movement-related symptoms like tremor and akinesia, DBS was soon found to influence emotion and personality in patients, too, which in turn widened the medical indications for these implants and led to the discovery of other anatomical targets in the brain. FDA-approved stimulation targets are the globus pallidus internus (GPi) located in the basal ganglia on either side of the thalamus, the subthalamic nucleus (STN) situated in the basal ganglia above the substantia nigra for akinetic-rigid PD, and the anterior limb of the internal capsule for medically resistant obsessive-compulsive disorder (OCD). Symptoms are generally improved by 50–75%, often with significant medication reduction [6].

Another FDA-improved target is the ventral intermedius nucleus (VIM) in the thalamus itself which has become the target of choice for controlling dominant Parkinson's disease. Crosstalk of electrical stimulation to other structures can cause problems with speech and swallowing, weakness, loss of fine motor control and cramping in the face or hand as most often side effects. Hence, patients may choose to switch between pre-set stimulation programs to strike a balance between symptom control and adverse effects.

The emerging of other, investigational deeper located brain stimulation targets shows that mankind indeed sets out to interfere with neurophysiological processes that today are only partially understood. The anterior nucleus of the thalamus and the hippocampus which is involved in memory storage are investigational DBS targets for medically refractory epilepsy. The medial thalamus – a relay site for limbic, sensory and motor signals to the cerebral cortex and a brain center that regulates consciousness, sleep and alertness also has potential in the DBS treatment of medically resistant obsessive-compulsive disorder. Other targets include the pedunculopontine nucleus (PPN) that is thought to help control posture and gait [7], the posterior hypothalamus (PHypTh) which is involved in regulation of blood pressure, pupillary dilation and shivering or body heat conservation as an experimental DBS target for medically refractory chronic cluster headache [8], and several targets for the treatment of medically refractory depression [9].

Neural implants that have received most of the popular attention are those that are implanted in the brain to record electrical signals that would directly generate motor output to extremities [10] or speech [11]. The function of these invasive brain-computer interfaces or iBCI [1] (Fig. 16.1) are particularly impressive because implanted subjects would be incapable of normal movements or speech due to neuropathological conditions like spinal cord injury, motor neuron disease or a brainstem stroke [6]. However, all of these applications are still on the level of clinical studies and are not yet approved as medical devices for broad use.

Research studies also focus on neural implants connected to peripheral nerves to deliver sensory feedback after amputation of limbs [13–18], partial restoration of movement after spinal cord injury and stroke [19,20]. Further applications in clinical practice with approved medical devices include spinal cord stimulation to modulate chronic pain [21,22] and incontinence [23–26] as well as stimulation of the vagus nerve at the level of the neck to modulate severity and occurrence of epileptic seizures [27,28]. In general, the field is expanding and emerging with respect to companies and applications. Nevertheless, some companies have been closed due to economic but also due to performance and lately also due to regulatory reasons even though they had approved devices on the market. The most prominent examples of neural implants which are no longer available in the market are implantable phrenic nerve stimulators to stimulate breathing (MedImplant Corp.), drop foot stimulators (ActiGait Corp.), hand stimulation

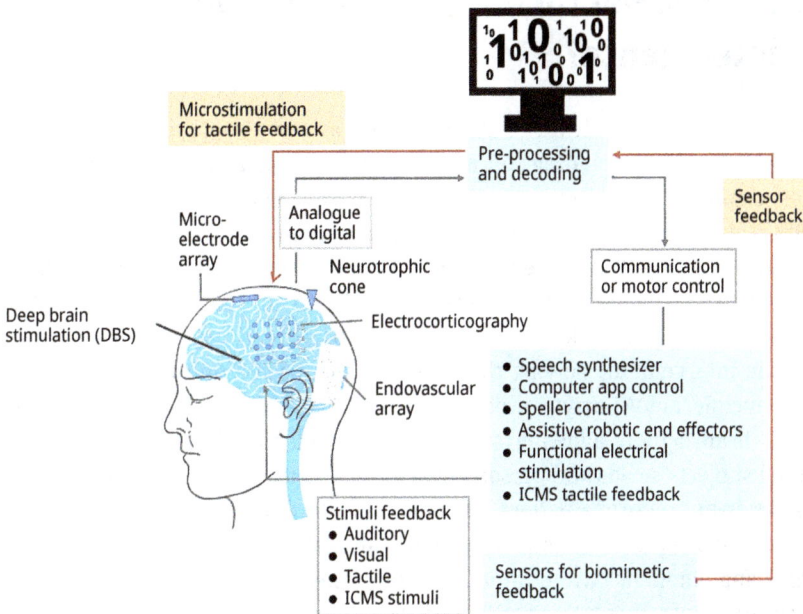

Fig. 16.1: Overview of important features of current iBCI systems. Electrodes (epicortical or intracortical probes, needles, cones, endovascular arrays etc.) either collect neural signals (passive BCI, pBCI) or stimulate brain areas (active BCI, aBCI). In pBCIs, analogue neural signals are digitized and send via cables or wirelessly to a computer for pre-processing and decoding to either drive a computer application (such as an AI-driven signal to speech converter) or control an external device such as a prosthetic arm. ABCIs can alleviate disorders like Parkinson's by stimulation of structures located in more depth (DBS) or deliver intracortical microstimulation (ICMS), e.g. to simulate the sense of touch. Modified after [12]. (© with permission of Nature-Springer.)

implants for spinal cord injured subjects (Freehand System, Neurocontrol Corp.), or vision prostheses (Retina Implant, Second Sight Corp.). Stimulation of autonomic nerves has been investigated under the terms of "electroceuticals" [29–33] and "bioelectronics medicine" [34] and promised treatments with electrical stimulation as alternative to pharmaceutical paradigms, e.g., to treat hypertension, COPD, rheumatic arthritis and autoimmune diseases [35]. First results from research studies are promising [36] but translation into clinical practice will need ample of time and money. Some approaches rely on already established technologies with known materials and manufacturing steps might be relatively fast on the market but are limited in miniaturization and complexity. Other approaches take advantage of latest technologies with high potential in miniaturization and channel count but need a plethora of mandatory accredited tests to pass all regulatory requirements to become a medical device.

16.2 How do neural implants profit from artificial intelligence?

Recent developments in software technology, such as new signal processing techniques and machine learning, including approaches from artificial intelligence (AI), are among the most significant contributions to the rapid advancement of neural implants [37]. AI support has the potential to revolutionize communication and improve quality of life for individuals with impaired neuronal functions, even in generalized afflictions of the brain like Alzheimer's disease. AI-powered Brain Machine Interfaces (BMIs) can effectively identify and track the progression of Alzheimer's, leading to more effective therapeutic intervention, slowing the course of the disease and improving outcome [38]. In principle, any AI-driven prosthetic device would be able to detect and monitor changes in brain activity, allowing to tailor treatment plans and medication regimens to individual subjects' needs and personalized approaches to therapy can optimize medical resources and improve patient outcomes [39]. In devastating degenerative brain disorders, AI-powered brain implants could potentially allow patients to convey their "thoughts and emotions" without the need for spoken language, thus improving their quality of life, given that adequate signals are known and can be recorded and interpreted.

AI can be used to improve noise reduction and signal processing techniques, including the automatized interpretation of electrical signals in the brain [37,40,41]. Safety as well as reliability questions need new testing paradigms for verification and validation and regulations which assess outcome. Logical reasoning may need to be paired with explainable AI [90] to deal with these issues. Different concepts are currently under evaluation and in discussion for medical devices [42]. Liability is quite often the driving factor in these discussions.

In general, implant development in the future might be guided by the question if new technologies like AI-based implementation can be considered an actual improvement for users compared to the current gold standard. Since the amount of available neural data is still quite sparse, development and application of AI algorithms have to address the question how to learn the desired tasks from such sparse data and how many data may at least be needed to come to robust and reliable performance without the hazard of "halluzinating" data. "Sparse data" or "Small data" approaches need to be developed, as e.g., transfer learning approaches, in which pre-trained networks are able to perform well with relatively small additional data sets from the target application to prevent life-threatening risks in neural implants.

16.3 Examples of AI improvement of neural implants

We have selected three examples to show the implementation of AI in neural implants: (1) AI-speech-BCI, (2) aDBS, and (3) AI-CI. Because of its most intriguing implications in ethics, data protection, and ownership, the speech implant results will be outlined more in detail.

16.3.1 AI-driven speech-Brain Computer Interface (AI-speech-BCI)

The ability to speak can be lost in a variety of diseases including amyotrophic lateral sclerosis (ALS) and stroke. Intracortical speech neuroprostheses with electrode arrays implanted into the left precentral gyrus, a cortical region responsible for coordinating motor activities related to speech, can restore speech partially by detecting electrical field potentials from the cortex evoked by the patient's voluntary intention to speak [42–44]. Using a speech-to-text brain-implant in the sensorimotor brain area responsible for moving the muscles in the mouth and face that produce speech, a woman suffering from ALS was able to reach a rate of 62 words per minute decoded by an AI algorithm after four months of training twice a week [44]. In comparison the speed of conversational English is about 160 words per minute [45].

An even higher rate (with a median of 78 words/min) was reached by another research group in a stroke patient using surface electrodes, but at a rather low median word error rate of 25% [42]. However, in this study the AI-decoded text was converted back into speech that was delivered by an avatar.

A recent milestone study made use of open-source large language models (LLMs) to translate the sequence of words and phonemes initially predicted from the neural activity into the most likely English sentence. One ALS patient reached a level of performance suitable to restore naturalistic communication after brief training of 30 min for 50-word and 1.4 hours for 125,000 words vocabulary, respectively [46]. This is currently probably the most significant example for AI-driven neural implants up to date and therefore deserves a more detailed exploration. in this chapter: Without any acoustic input, on the first day of system-use, the patient with this neuroprosthesis achieved an accuracy of 99.6% with the 50-word vocabulary and on the second day, after 1,5 hours of training, he achieved 90.2% accuracy using a 125,000-word vocabulary. Further training resulted in 97.5% accuracy for self-paced conversations for over 248 cumulative hours over 8.4 months. The implant in this study [46] consisted of four microelectrode arrays (each 3.2 × 3.2 mm², 64 electrodes with an area of 50 µm² in an 8 × 8 grid; NeuroPort Array, Blackrock Neurotech, Salt Lake City, Utah, USA) inserted 1.5 mm deep into the left precentral gyrus with a pneumatic insertion tool. The target was an anatomical structure of the cortex that was identified in the Human Connectome Project [48] as implicated in phonologic representation (Brodmann area 55b24). Two percutaneous connectors attached to the skull were connected to a computer by detachable HDMI cable (Fig. 16.2). Acquired electrical brain signals are were sent to a series of commercially available computers running publicly available software for real-time signal processing and decoding. First, the subject was asked to attempt to say words presented on a computer screen after a visual/audio cue ("copy task" of the study). In a second task ("self-paced conversation mode" of the study), the subject attempted to say whatever he wanted (although the computer outputs were limited to a 125,000-word dictionary) in an unstructured conversational setting [46]. As he spoke, the cortical activity was recorded and decoded, and the predicted words were presented on the screen in real time. Completed sentences were read aloud by a computer program or send to the subject's personal computer. Sampled phonemes and words used for decoder training accumulated over the course of the study [46].

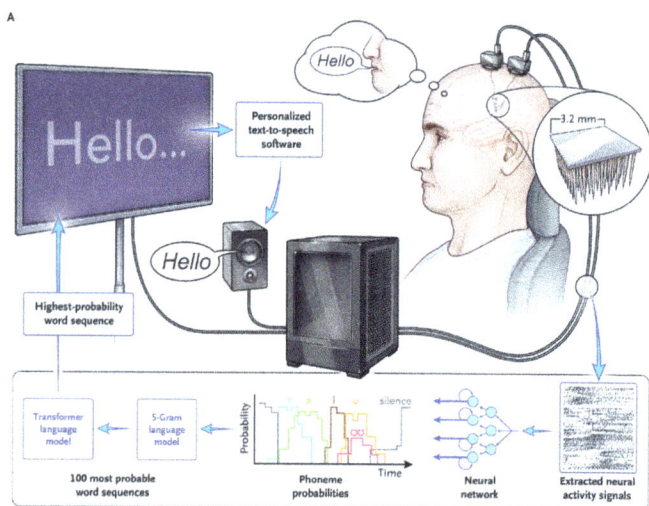

Fig. 16.2: Brain-to-text' speech neuroprosthesis. Cortical neural activity is decoded by machine learning techniques into phonemes every 80 ms. Imagined words are recorded from language areas of the brain, are transferred to text on a screen and are transferred to spoken words over a loudspeaker [46]. (© with permission of the Massachusetts Medical Society (USA).)

To put these results into perspective and match them to our initial statement that the improvement over the previous gold standard for the patient's benefit should be the decisive criterion for any AI-driven implant (see section 16.2), we will should look at pre- and post-implant performance here. When speaking to expert listeners/interpreters, the severely dysarthric patient under investigation has communicated at 6.8 correct words per minute without the implant. On comparison, the typing speed using a gyroscopic head mouse has been measured at a median of 6.3 correct words per minute.

In the "'Copy Task'" the patient's self-paced speaking rate is reported to be 31.6 words per minute, with 97.3% correctly identified attempted words (error rate of 2.7%). In relationship, the state-of-the-art for English automated speech recognition (e.g., smartphone dictation) has a word error rate of about 5% and able-bodied speakers have a 1–2% word error rate [47].

16.3.2 Adaptive Deep Brain Stimulation (aDBS)

As a technology to alleviate the symptoms of PD, essential tremor, dystonia and other disorders, DBS has been around for clinical use since the beginning of the century. Recently, an AI approach has been employed to individualize this implant-based treatment ("adaptive deep brain stimulation", aDBS) [49].

In this application, the AI helps to monitor changes in a patient's brain activity in real time and to react to these changes by adapting the strategy of electrical brain stimulation accordingly. AI-driven DBS can reduce motor symptoms like tremor and akinesia by up to 50% today [49]. It has also been successful in insomnia, a symptom that is notoriously hard to treat in Parkinson patients. In a clinical trial involving four Parkinson's patients, aDBS could identify brain activity associated with different sleep states and accurately predict when a patient would wake up [50].

Apart from employing AI, this new line of clinical research includes recording of patterns of brain activity not only in the subthalamic anatomical structures where the stimulating electrodes are located and stimulation may mute the useful signals, but also in cortical areas. At the motor cortex, signals used to monitor electrical brain activity are not directly influenced by the DBS stimulation [51].

Different medication and stimulation levels render the electrical signals dynamic. One of the challenges for these "closed-loop" control systems is to analyze exactly how external and internal variables can change the signals, and feed this information into algorithms to control DBS in an environment outside the lab. The AI-based data analysis pipeline then turns this into personalized algorithms to record, analyze, detect, and respond to the unique brain activity associated with each patient's symptom state. The individual response of the device is to deliver targeted electrical stimulation to the anatomical treatment that have been identified to be responsible for movement disorders during the day and sleep problems at night. Thus, an aDBS system in Parkinson's treatment via "closed-loop" technology may self-regulate electrical stimulation in response to real-time brain activity [52].

In comparison with constant DBS (cDBS) systems, closed-loop brain implants are capable to deliver individualized treatment in much more an immediate, round-the-clock fashion. The technology can be further rolled-out in other neurological conditions, such as dystonia, depression and obsessive-compulsive disorder. Just as in these disorders, AI can be combined with brain implants to anticipate and detect epileptic seizure [53].

Closed-loop systems that deliver individualized treatment for epilepsy patients are clearly on the horizon [54].

16.3.3 AI-driven Cochlear Implant (AI-CI)

AI technology is currently being used to improve the listening experience of CI-users by developing personalized, context-aware noise suppression and speech enhancement in CI speech processors and in fitting procedures [40,55–61]. AI methods are developed to optimize the speech signal, perform auditory scene analysis, and combine binaural signals to enhance speech understanding in noise and to follow target voices in complex scenes, which will impact sound quality and perception. The implant's stimulation parameters stay in the safe range during modifications and stimulation series are based on better speech extraction algorithms.

16.3.4 Scenarios of further AI-driven neural implants

Many more approaches exist to implement artificial intelligence in neural implants besides these three examples. One further example relates to AI-driven visual neural implants to restore visual function in blind individuals by generating artificial visual perceptions [62]. These implants may be AI-enhanced for task-oriented image pre-processing, and automatic scene selection for recognizing the context the user is in as well as selecting the correct settings to convert the camera footage to phosphene vision that contains the most important visual information in that context [59,62]. Even though AI has shown tremendous potential in discovering patterns and signals out of noisy data, performance always depends on the input and the training data. The better the signals are, for example due to low noise electrodes with stable transfer properties, the better the performance of any algorithm. Therefore, further hardware development should also not be disregarded, especially in the context of longevity and reliability.

In a more visionary view, direct cerebral interfaces could open a host of new diagnostic and treatment avenues, e.g., in neurodegenerative diseases like Alzheimer's. This would probably come along with dramatic regulatory, ethical and clinical trial hurdles, even if enhancement of healthy individuals with transhumanistic intentions can be halted at this point [64,66,67].

16.4 Stratification of ethical implications in AI-driven neurotechnology

The field of "neuro-ethics" could mostly be discussed in a realm that was demarcated by medical ethics as addressed by generally accepted documents like the Declaration of Helsinki in 1964 and by the Belmont Report in 1978. Respect of autonomy and informed consent, guaranteed beneficence, non-maleficence with minimization of risks and side effects, responsibility, cognitive liberty, privacy and data-security, distributive justice including accessibility to neuro-technologies [68,69]. Enhancement was contrasted to therapy and mostly rejected or ignored [37,70].

With digitalization and the employment of machine learning algorithms – including deep neural network – neural implants expand these existing concerns and introduce new ones, including those regarding agency and identity, mental privacy, augmentation, accuracy, transparency and biases [40,41,71–73]. Not only are the boundaries dissolving between technology and biological life, but there exist new possibilities with the rise of AI-driven technology, envisioning the emergence of "technical life" [75]. These new possibilities come with uncertainties regarding AI-driven neural implants, which open possibilities of unauthorized access and alteration to confidential neural data by individuals or organizations (hackers, corporations or government agencies), tracking or even manipulating an individual's mental experience [74].

Today, most researchers agree that these issues need to be addressed with a new set of instruments, both in ethics and in regulation arguably to be embedded in broader societal, cultural and governance approaches [67]. Furthermore, we may even need new conceptual or normative foundations to deal with the concept of "identity", as constituted by our embodied self-narratives in the face of information derived from implantable predictive BCIs [76,77].

Since changes in legal regulations will take time and often are not universally accepted, the development of "neuro-rights" has been proposed to introduce a kind of "soft law" or guidelines and directive that may be adhered to voluntarily by developers and medics and users [78,79]. There exists also a call for mechanisms for improved user control since a well-functioning device that increases independence may simultaneously harm users' autonomy [59].

In 2017, "The Morningside Group", an international group of neuroscientists, neurotechnologists, clinicians, ethicists and machine-intelligence engineers –concluded that existing ethics guidelines would be insufficient for the realm of neurotechnology and artificial intelligence. In a workshop hosted by biological scientist Rafael Yuste at Columbia University in New York City, the group identified four areas of concern: (1) privacy and consent, (2) agency and identity, (3) augmentation, and (4) bias [74].

However, when compared to the existing "neuro-ethics" (based on the Declaration of Helsinki, the Belmont Report, and additionally the "Asilomar artificial intelligence statement of cautionary principles" from 2017) centering around autonomy, non-maleficence, beneficence and justice [65], with respect to AI, the Morningside Group's addition mainly concerns the issues of unauthorized extraction, manipulation and (mis-)use of neural data and (AI) bias.

16.4.1 Privacy and consent

With respect to privacy and consent, citizens should have the ability and right to keep their "neural data" (i.e., data extracted directly from the brain as a biological substrate) private by opting out of sharing being the default choice. Furthermore, consent procedure should clearly specify who will use the data, for what purposes and for how long.

Even with this approach, neural data from many willing sharers, combined with big non-neural data could be used to draw "good enough" conclusions about individuals who choose not to share. This, clearly, is an issue that has significantly more importance with the advent of AI in neurotechnology. Therefore, Yuste et al. [79] demand that the possibility of people giving up their neural data or having neural activity written directly into their brains for financial reward should be limited and restricted. Centralized processing of personal neural data should be alleviated by employing computational techniques, such as differential privacy or "federated learning", "blockchain", "smart contracts" to allow for control over data without having to employ authorities, and open-source technology to promote transparency [79].

16.4.2 Agency and identity

The claim, that the threat of neurotechnology to agency (our ability to choose our actions) and individual identity (our bodily and mental integrity) requires a separate chapter in international conventions on basic human rights ("neuro-rights") and calls for an associated United Nations working group, is quite high-aimed. AI raises high-risk concerns in many other human affairs, too, and legislation is beginning to address these concerns in a more general and systematic way (e.g., AI act of the European Union).

The people's right to be educated about the possible cognitive and emotional effects of neuro-technologies would also be true for other technology and there is probably no actual need for separate international declarations on "neuro-rights". However, the advent of AI in neural implants certainly intensifies the debate about agency and identity for implantees. When "auto-complete" or "auto-correct" functions powered by AI in brain implants designed to restore speech take over, the identity of a person can be challenged [80]. When an artificial arm steered via an iBCI hurts another human being, issues of agency and even free will need to be clarified, not only in the context of liability. Still, while these issues become more eminent with AI and its potential misinterpretation of neural data, they are not exactly new.

16.4.3 Augmentation

The term "augmentation" is used synonymous to the well-established term "enhancement". Consequently, the group of Yuste et al. [79] does not add no new concepts in this area of concern. The coercive drive to adopt enhancing neurotechnologies, such as those that allow people to radically expand their endurance or sensory or mental capacities, and its implication for normative values, equitable access, possible forms of discrimination, and even military misuse have long been under discussion before [63]. The demand for in-depth and open debate as well as for guidelines to set limits to or even outright ban certain augmenting neurotechnologies legally is also not novel or original.

16.4.4 Bias

The most important concern raised by the Morningside Group is bias. Yuste et al. [79] wrote: "When scientific or technological decisions are based on a narrow set of systemic, structural or social concepts and norms, the resulting technology can privilege certain groups and harm others." If "scientific and technologic decisions" is replaced with the term "AI decisions", a discussion is entered that is raging on in many other matters of human society today.

Although it's hard to pinpoint where the "bias" has crept into AI models today, according to Data Robot's [81] state of AI bias report, technology leaders are concerned about its consequences, and mostly with respect to the loss of customer trust (56%), followed by compromised brand reputation (50%), increased regulatory scrutiny (43%), and loss of employee trust (42%) (Fig. 16.3) [82]. More than one in three organizations surveyed had experienced challenges or direct business impact due to an occurrence of AI bias in their algorithms, with 77 % of organizations having test in place to discover bias [82].

CONCERNS AROUND AI BIAS:

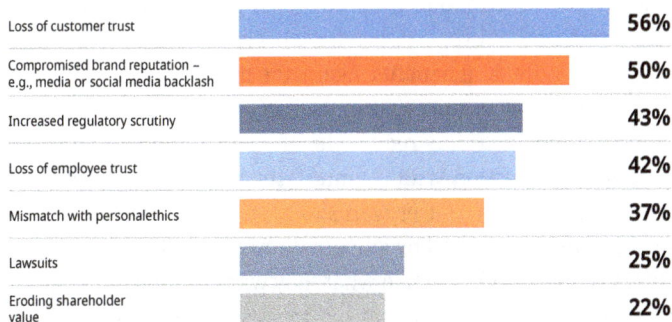

Loss of customer trust	56%
Compromised brand reputation – e.g., media or social media backlash	50%
Increased regulatory scrutiny	43%
Loss of employee trust	42%
Mismatch with personalethics	37%
Lawsuits	25%
Eroding shareholder value	22%

Fig. 16.3: Concerns around AI bias [81–83].

Significant focus and investment already exist across the industry in removing AI bias. Challenges in eliminating this problem include understanding the reasons for a specific AI decision, understanding the patterns between input values and AI decisions, developing trustworthy algorithms, and determining what data is used to train AI. These challenges expand onto the global stage, heightening existing concerns over the digital divide.

One example of AI bias [83] which was discussed in this context [79] reports on algorithms used by US law-enforcement agencies which wrongly predicted that black defendants are more likely to reoffend than white defendants with a similar criminal record. There is concern that such biases could become embedded in neural devices. Hence, the authors advocate that counter measures and the need for societally well-balanced datasets to combat bias become the norm for machine learning in neuro-technology, without going into more detail here. They refer to the IEEE Standards Association which created a global ethics initiative with the aim of embedding ethics into the design of processes for all AI and autonomous systems [84]. The program has established free access to sociotechnical standards in AI Ethics and Governance that provide guidance and considerations towards 'trustworthy AI' including standards for Data Privacy Process and Transparency of Autonomous Systems [85].

Recently ethical challenges have been pointed out by the convergence of neural implants with AI from the perspective of developers [59]. With its technological insight, this group has focused on already existing AI-driven neural implants: a cochlear implant, a visual neural implant, and a motor intention decoding speech-brain-computer-interface (see examples above). They conducted semi-structured focus groups with developers and subsequently clustered their priorities into three topics: design aspects, challenges in clinical trials, and impact on users and society. Their investigations points to accuracy and reliability as crucial to implant design for users' safety, authenticity, and mental privacy. They also warn that balancing these needs with AI benefits such as efficiency and complex data interpretation can be challenging. For clinical trials, apart from accuracy, developers characterized effectiveness of AI-driven neural implants as essential. Both criteria are related to validation, user privacy, and long-term outcomes.

Van Stuijvenberg et al. [59] also see fundamental impact of this kind of neurotechnology on users and society, stating that broader societal concerns such as privacy and equity need to be balanced with individual benefits. Again, the need for user-control of the implant is demanded, but it is also argued that user-control over the devices may interfere with predictive algorithms and thus reduce the efficiency of an implant. An AI-CI, for instance, would ideally function without interference of the user, with an AI-based scene selector to predict what the user wants to hear, and in which context. Such automatism, however, would be affected by any erroneous function of predictive algorithms. Allowing users to choose and switch to what they want to listen to, as hearing people can also do would install a sense of control in users. As in any technology with a human interface, the solution will probably be a compromise of both layers.

For the AI-speech-BCI, similarly arguments arise. The implants output may lead to the expression of sentences that have different meanings and are not specifically what the user intended to say. Also, with visual neuro-implants, essential visual information may be missed by the system's algorithm. Therefore, developers are hinted, that preferences regarding user-control are likely to vary between users.

Closely linked to ethical issues is the assessment of technology risk assessment [86]. However, it would go beyond the scope of this chapter to delve into this field. Conventional procedures for risk assessment in medical technology are probably not complex enough to evaluate scenarios and arrive at a societal consensus [75,77,86].

16.5 Governance and regulation

Governance and regulation have become cross-cutting themes in the social sciences. Classical definitions of governance prioritize the role of the state, its institutions of authority and its use of legal rules while contemporary opinion reveals a world in which both states and non-state actors create networks of governance to address problems of market failure, distributive justice and global public goods [87]. Regulation has also become more broadly theorized, as "responsive regulation", "smart regulation", as well as new concepts to capture the changing dynamics like meta-regulation, co-regulation, and transnational regulation have been introduced. The European Union's arrangements of shared or collaborative sovereignty require implementation in national regulatory models within the normative framework of governance reflected in attributes like transparency, legitimacy, accountability and authority [87].

The convergence of AI and neural implants presents unique complexities not only in data privacy, personal agency, and AI bias, but also within the current intellectual property (IP) law framework [88]. When a company that provides an AI-powered neural implant solution declares bankruptcy, does the user, whose life quality has been considerably enhanced by the implant, retain the product? Or can the firm, the holder of the IP rights, retrieve it? Moreover, the classical definition of an inventor as a "natural person" becomes insufficient. Can an AI be classified as an "inventor" when it contributes significantly to the creation of a neural device? Disclosure requirements may be impossible to fulfil as AI innovations are often the result of black box operations by the machine. Patents, copyright, and trademarks may not be sufficient anymore to protect AI-related inventions. As a consequence, there is considerable pressure on policymakers, research organizations, scientific communities, as well as companies to develop robust ethical frameworks and regulations.

The EU has rushed forward to develop regulation and on Dec 23, 2023 adopted an AI Act entered into force 1 August, 2024 that comes with a clear timeline for implementation starting with Chapters I and II (February 2025) and ending with Article 6(1) and the corresponding obligations effective from 2 August 2027. The EU AI Act is binding in its entirety and directly applicable in all Member States [89,94].

While neural implants are not specifically mentioned, Article 50 (Chapter IV) regulates transparency obligations for providers and deployers of "certain AI systems", a term that is not specifically defined. It can be speculated that medical products will be categorized under this term [90]. Considering the societal and individual issues in AI-driven neural that we have discussed, these implants would be considered "high-risk applications" according to annex III of the regulation. For research studies, Article 60 may be relevant which states that "testing of high-risk AI systems in real world conditions shall be without prejudice to any ethical review that is required by Union or national law" when certain conditions are met. This almost certainly would apply only to real-world laboratories and not to clinical trials. Member states currently strive to allocate or even create the appropriate agencies to fulfil requirements of Article 70 of the AI Act: "Each Member State shall establish or designate as national competent authorities at least one notifying authority and at least one market surveillance authority for the purposes of this Regulation". Recommendations for operators of high-risk AI systems in Germany have already been published, too [91].

In a work about aligning explainable artificial intelligence and implants, Sofrano et al. (2024) propose a methodology to ensure compliance with EU regulations [92]. The authors provide a practical framework analyses the compliance of XAI methods with EU regulations for smart biomedical devices and provide a practical framework that helps meeting the explainability requirements of the GDPR, AIA, and MDR for specific methods.

16.6 Conclusions

The interest in neural implants and especially in brain-machine-interface application has grown significantly in the last years. More and more start-up companies have been founded and work towards medical device approval with the support of venture capital of private persons, strategic investments of medical device as well as pharmaceutical companies. AI catalyzes the "gold rush mood" in the field. Investments in the multi-billion range and growth rates in the two-digit percent range are predicted by market analysis agencies. Quite some asymmetries can be observed in the enthusiasm of the technology-push side and societal perceptions of opportunities and concerns. AI already significantly improves signal analysis, feature extraction and decision making in the context of nerve signals in neural implants. More and more scenarios and applications will increase the performance of neural implants by these techniques. Ethical, legal and regulatory questions have been risen and both, soft and hard law is under development. Cross-sectional and transdisciplinary research as well as inclusion of patients as stakeholders in development and dissemination processes needs to be continued and strengthened to jointly promote technological progress and safeguard personal identity for the benefit of patients who deserve best possible medical devices.

Societal norms and guidelines on what should and should not be done need to be developed on a broad societal basis and in consensus independent of the particular technology to be used in such a device but with the knowledge of opportunities and risks of the technologies involved.

References

[1]   Hofmann U. G., Stieglitz T. Why some BCI should still be called BMI. Nat Commun. 2024;15(1):6207.

[2]   Bychkov R., Juhaszova M., Calvo-Rubio Barrera M., Donald L. A. H., Coletta C., Shumaker C. et al. The Heart's Pacemaker Mimics Brain Cytoarchitecture and Function: Novel Interstitial Cells Expose Complexity of the SAN. JACC Clin Electrophysiol. 2022;8(10):1191–215.

[3]   Lim H. H., Lenarz T. Auditory midbrain implant: research and development towards a second clinical trial. Hear Res. 2015; 322:212–23.

[4]   Schwalb J. M., Hamani C. The history and future of deep brain stimulation. Neurotherapeutics. 2008;5(1):3–13.

[5]   Sandoval-Pistorius S. S., Hacker M. L., Waters A. C., Wang J., Provenza N. R., de Hemptinne C. et al. Advances in Deep Brain Stimulation: From Mechanisms to Applications. J Neurosci. 2023;43(45):7575–86.

[6]   Hitti F. L., Ramayya A. G., McShane B. J., Yang A. I., Vaughan K. A., Baltuch G. H. Long-term outcomes following deep brain stimulation for Parkinson's disease. J Neurosurg. 2019 Jan 18;132(1):205–210.

[7]   French IT, Muthusamy K. A. A Review of the Pedunculopontine Nucleus in Parkinson's Disease. Front Aging Neurosci. 2018; 10:99.

[8]   Pant A., Farrokhi F., Krause K., Marsans M., Roberts J. Ten-Year Durability of Hypothalamic Deep Brain Stimulation in Treatment of Chronic Cluster Headaches: A Case Report and Literature Review. Cureus. 2023;15(10): e47338.

[9]   Schlaepfer T. E, Lieb K. Deep brain stimulation for treatment of refractory depression. The Lancet. 2005: 366(9495): 1420–1422.

[10] Levett J. J., Elkaim L. M., Niazi F., Weber M. H., Iorio-Morin C., Bonizzato M. et al. Invasive Brain Computer Interface for Motor Restoration in Spinal Cord Injury: A Systematic Review. Neuromodulation. 2024;27(4):597–603.

[11] 5. Berezutskaya J., Freudenburg Z. V., Vansteensel M. J., Aarnoutse E. J., Ramsey N. F., van Gerven M. A. J. Direct speech reconstruction from sensorimotor brain activity with optimized deep learning models. J Neural Eng. 2023;20(5).

[12] Patrick-Krueger K. M., Burkhart I. & Contreras-Vidal J. L. The state of clinical trials of implantable brain–computer interfaces. Nat Rev Bioeng 3, 50–67 (2025).

[13] Chandrasekaran S., Nanivadekar A. C., McKernan G., Helm E. R., Boninger M. L., Collinger J. L. et al. Sensory restoration by epidural stimulation of the lateral spinal cord in upper-limb amputees. Elife. 2020;9: e54349.

[14] Gonzalez M., Bismuth A., Lee C., Chestek C. A., Gates D. H. Artificial referred sensation in upper and lower limb prosthesis users: a systematic review. J Neural Eng. 2022; 19(5):10.1088/1741–2552/ac8c38.

[15] Ortiz-Catalan M., Mastinu E., Sassu P., Aszmann O., Branemark R. Self-Contained Neuromusculoskeletal Arm Prostheses. N Engl J Med. 2020;382(18):1732–8.

[16] Ortiz-Catalan M., Zbinden J., Millenaar J., D'Accolti D., Controzzi M., Clemente F. et al. A highly integrated bionic hand with neural control and feedback for use in daily life. Sci Robot. 2023;8(83): eadf7360.

[17] Page D. M., George J. A., Wendelken S. M., Davis T. S., Kluger D. T., Hutchinson D. T. et al. Discriminability of multiple cutaneous and proprioceptive hand percepts evoked by intraneural stimulation with Utah slanted electrode arrays in human amputees. J Neuroeng Rehabil. 2021;18(1):12.

[18] Strauss I., Valle G., Artoni F., D'Anna E., Granata G., Di Iorio R. et al. Characterization of multi-channel intraneural stimulation in transradial amputees. Sci Rep. 2019;9(1):19258.

[19] Powell M. P., Verma N., Sorensen E., Carranza E., Boos A., Fields D. P. et al. Epidural stimulation of the cervical spinal cord for post-stroke upper-limb paresis. Nat Med. 2023;29(3):689–99.

[20] Serruya M. D., Napoli A., Satterthwaite N., Kardine J., McCoy J., Grampurohit N. et al. Neuromotor prosthetic to treat stroke-related paresis: N-of-1 trial. Commun Med (Lond). 2022; 2:37.

[21] Ali R., Schwalb J. M. History and Future of Spinal Cord Stimulation. Neurosurgery. 2024;94(1):20–8.

[22] Ho J. S., Poon C., North R., Grubb W., Lempka S., Bikson M. A Visual and Narrative Timeline Review of Spinal Cord Stimulation Technology and US Food and Drug Administration Milestones. Neuromodulation. 2024:1020–5.

[23] Duelund-Jakobsen J., Buntzen S., Lundby L., Laurberg S., Sorensen M., Rydningen M. One-stage implant in sacral neuromodulation for faecal incontinence – short-term outcome from a prospective study. Colorectal Dis. 2024;26(5):968–73.

[24] Hendrickson W. K., Zhang C., Hokanson J. A., Nygaard I. E., Presson A. P. Predicting success using response after lead implantation with sacral neuromodulation for urgency incontinence. Neurourol Urodyn. 2024;43(8):1776–83.

[25] Jezernik S., Craggs M., Grill W. M., Creasey G., Rijkhoff N. J. Electrical stimulation for the treatment of bladder dysfunction: current status and future possibilities. Neurol Res. 2002;24(5):413–30.

[26] Van Kerrebroeck P. E. V., van den Hombergh U. The history of neuromodulation for lower urinary tract dysfunction: An overview. Continence. 2024:101328.

[27] Bagic A. I., Verner R., Afra P., Benbadis S., Group AS. ASCEND: A randomized controlled trial of titration strategies for vagus nerve stimulation in drug-resistant epilepsy. Epilepsy Behav. 2023; 145:109333.

[28] Rosenberg A., Wang R., Petchpradub M., Beaudreault C., Sacknovitz A., Cozzi F. M. et al. Responsive neurostimulation in pediatric epilepsy: a systematic review and individual patient meta-analysis supplemented by a single institution case series in 105 aggregated patients. Childs Nerv Syst. 2024.

[29] Balasubramanian S., Weston D. A., Levin M., Davidian D. C. C. Electroceuticals: emerging applications beyond the nervous system and excitable tissues. Trends Pharmacol Sci. 2024;45(5):391–4.

[30] Famm K., Litt B., Tracey K. J., Boyden E. S., Slaoui M. Drug discovery: a jump-start for electroceuticals. Nature. 2013;496(7444):159–61.

[31] Long Y., Li J., Yang F., Wang J., Wang X. Wearable and Implantable Electroceuticals for Therapeutic Electrostimulations. Adv Sci (Weinh). 2021;8(8):2004023.

[32] Magisetty R., Park S. M. New Era of Electroceuticals: Clinically Driven Smart Implantable Electronic Devices Moving towards Precision Therapy. Micromachines (Basel). 2022;13(2).

[33] Majid A. Electroceuticals: Advances in Electrostimulation Therapies. Cham: Springer, 2017.

[34] Koutsouras D. A., Malliaras G. G., Langereis G. The rise of bioelectronic medicine. Bioelectron Med. 2024;10(1):19.

[35] Horn C. C., Ardell J. L., Fisher L. E. Electroceutical Targeting of the Autonomic Nervous System. Physiology (Bethesda). 2019;34(2):150–62.

[36] Xi H., Li X., Zhang Z., Cui X., Zhu B., Jing X., Gao X. Continuous peripheral electrical nerve stimulation improves cardiac function via autonomic nerve regulation in MI rats. Heart Rhythm. 2024 Oct;21(10):2010–2019.

[37] Valeriani D., Santoro F., Ienca M. The present and future of neural interfaces. Front Neurorobot. 2022; 16:953968.

[38] Rowe T. W., Katzourou I. K., Stevenson-Hoare J. O., Bracher-Smith M. R., Ivanov D. K., Escott-Price V. Machine learning for the life-time risk prediction of Alzheimer's disease: a systematic review. Brain Commun. 2021;3(4): fcab246.

[39] Malcangi M. AI-Based Methods and Technologies to Develop Wearable Devices for Prosthetics and Predictions of Degenerative Diseases. Methods Mol Biol. 2021; 2190:337–54.

[40] Crowson M. G., Lin V., Chen J. M., Chan T. C. Y. Machine Learning and Cochlear Implantation-A Structured Review of Opportunities and Challenges. Otol Neurotol. 2020;41(1): e36-e45.

[41] Zhang X., Ma Z., Zheng H., Li T., Chen K., Wang X. et al. The combination of brain-computer interfaces and artificial intelligence: applications and challenges. Ann Transl Med. 2020;8(11):712.

[42] Metzger S. L., Littlejohn K. T., Silva A. B., Moses D. A., Seaton M. P., Wang R. et al. A high-performance neuroprosthesis for speech decoding and avatar control. Nature. 2023;620(7976):1037–46.

[43] Moses D. A., Metzger S. L., Liu J. R., Anumanchipalli G. K., Makin J. G., Sun P. F. et al. Neuroprosthesis for Decoding Speech in a Paralyzed Person with Anarthria. N Engl J Med. 2021;385(3):217–27.

[44] Willett F. R., Kunz E. M., Fan C., Avansino D. T., Wilson G. H., Choi E. Y. et al. A high-performance speech neuroprosthesis. Nature. 2023;620(7976):1031–6.

[45] Yang J., Libermann M., Cieri C. (eds.). Towards an integrated understanding of speaking rate in conversation. 9th Intl Conf on Spoken Language Processing; 2006; Pittsburgh, PA: Curran Associates, Inc.

[46] Card N. S., Wairagkar M., Iacobacci C., Hou X., Singer-Clark T., Willett F. R. et al. An Accurate and Rapidly Calibrating Speech Neuroprosthesis. N Engl J Med. 2024;391(7):609–18.

[47] Thomson D. R., Besner D., Smilek D. In pursuit of off-task thought: mind wandering-performance trade-offs while reading aloud and color naming. Front Psychol. 2013; 4:360.

[48] Human Connectome Project (Accessed January 21, 2025, at https://www.humanconnectome.org/).

[49] Oehrn C. R., Cernera S., Hammer L. H., Shcherbakova M., Yao J., Hahn A. et al. Chronic adaptive deep brain stimulation versus conventional stimulation in Parkinson's disease: a blinded randomized feasibility trial. Nat Med. 2024.

[50] Anjum M. F., Smyth C., Zuzuarregui R., Dijk D. J., Starr P. A., Denison T. et al. Multi-night cortico-basal recordings reveal mechanisms of NREM slow-wave suppression and spontaneous awakenings in Parkinson's disease. Nat Commun. 2024;15(1):1793.

[51] Hollunder B., Ostrem J. L., Sahin I. A., Rajamani N., Oxenford S., Butenko K. et al. Mapping dysfunctional circuits in the frontal cortex using deep brain stimulation. Nat Neurosci. 2024(3):573–586.

[52] Krauss J. K., Lipsman N., Aziz T., Boutet A., Brown P., Chang J. W. et al. Technology of deep brain stimulation: current status and future directions. Nat Rev Neurol. 2021 Feb;17(2):75–87.

[53] Singh A., Velagala V. R., Kumar T., Dutta R. R., Sontakke T. The Application of Deep Learning to Electroencephalograms, Magnetic Resonance Imaging, and Implants for the Detection of Epileptic Seizures: A Narrative Review. Cureus. 2023;15(7): e42460.

[54] Ferrero J. J., Hassan A. R., Yu Z., Zhao Z., Ma L., Wu C., Shao S., Kawano T., Engel J., Doyle W., Devinsky O., Khodagholy D., Gelinas J. N. Closed-loop electrical stimulation to prevent focal epilepsy progression and long-term memory impairment. bioRxiv [Preprint]. 2024.

[55] Aliyeva A., Sari E., Alaskarov E., Nasirov R. Enhancing Postoperative Cochlear Implant Care With ChatGPT-4: A Study on Artificial Intelligence (AI)-Assisted Patient Education and Support. Cureus. 2024;16(2): e53897.

[56] Goehring T., Monaghan J. Helping People Hear Better with "Smart" Hearing Devices. Front Young Minds. 2022; 10:703643.

[57] Olze H., Uecker F. C., Haussler S. M., Knopke S., Szczepek A. J., Grabel S. Hearing Implants in the Era of Digitization. Laryngorhinootologie. 2019;98(S 01): S82–S128.

[58] Rapoport N., Pavelchek C., Michelson A. P., Shew M. A. Artificial Intelligence in Otology and Neurotology. Otolaryngol Clin North Am. 2024;57(5):791–802.

[59] van Stuijvenberg O. C., Broekman M. L. D., Wolff S. E. C., Bredenoord A. L., Jongsma K.R. Developer perspectives on the ethics of AI-driven neural implants: a qualitative study. Sci Rep. 2024;14(1):7880.

[60] Waltzman SB, Kelsall DC. The Use of Artificial Intelligence to Program Cochlear Implants. Otol Neurotol. 2020;41(4):452–7.

[61] Wathour J., Govaerts P. J., Lacroix E., Naima D. Effect of a CI Programming Fitting Tool with Artificial Intelligence in Experienced Cochlear Implant Patients. Otol Neurotol. 2023;44(3):209–15.

[62] Lozano A., Suárez J. S., Soto-Sánchez C., Garrigós J., Martínez-Alvarez J. J., Ferrández J. M., Fernández E. Neurolight: A Deep Learning Neural Interface for Cortical Visual Prostheses. Int J Neural Syst. 2020 (9):2050045.

[63] Aliyeva A. Transhumanism: Integrating Cochlear Implants With Artificial Intelligence and the Brain-Machine Interface. Cureus. 2023;15(12): e50378.

[64] Lee J. Cochlear Implantation, Enhancements, Transhumanism and Posthumanism: Some Human Questions. Sci Eng Ethics. 2016;22(1):67–92.

[65] Merkel R., Boer G., Fegert J., Hartmann D., Galert T., Nuttin B. et al. Intervening in the Brain: Changing Psyche and Society. Berlin – Heidelberg – New York: Springer; 2007 2007.

[66] Rosahl S. K. Neuroprosthetics and neuroenhancement: Can we draw a line. Virtual Mentor – American Medical Association Journal of Ethics. 2007;9(2):132–9.

[67] Stieglitz T., Coenen C. Neurotech-Ethics: Suggestions for the Way Forward. 10th International IEEE/EMBS Conference on Neural Engineering (NER); 2012; Italy.

[68] Bioethics NCo. Novel neurotechnologies: intervening in the brain. London2013.

[69] Beauchamp T. L., Childress J. F. Principles of Biomedical Ethics. 7 ed. New York: Oxford University Press; 2013.

[70] Garden H., Winickoff D. Issues in Neurotechnology Governance. OECD Science, Technology and Industry Working Papers. Paris: OECD; 2018.

[71] Burwell S., Sample M., Racine E. Ethical aspects of brain computer interfaces: a scoping review. BMC Med Ethics. 2017;18(1):60.

[72] Roelfsema P. R., Denys D., Klink P. C. Mind Reading and Writing: The Future of Neurotechnology. Trends Cogn Sci. 2018;22(7):598–610.

[73] van Velthoven E. A. M., van Stuijvenberg O. C., Haselager D. R. E., Broekman M., Chen X., Roelfsema P. et al. Ethical implications of visual neuroprostheses-a systematic review. J Neural Eng. 2022;19(2).

[74] Yuste R., Goering S., Arcas B. A. Y., Bi G., Carmena J. M., Carter A. et al. Four ethical priorities for neurotechnologies and AI. Nature. 2017;551(7679):159–63.

[75] Grünwald A. Living Technology: Philosophy and Ethics at the Crossroads Between Life and Technology. Singapore: Jenny Stanford Publishing Pte. Ltd.; 2021.

[76] Postan E. Narrative Devices: Neurotechnologies, Information, and Self-Constitution. Neuroethics. 2021;14(2):231–51.

[77] Grünwald A. Technology assessment for health and care. In: Grünwald A. (ed.). Handbook of Technology Assessment. Cheltenham: Edward Elgar Publishing Ltd.; 2024.

[78] Goering S., Klein E., Specker Sullivan L., Wexler A., Aguera Y. A. B, Bi G. et al. Recommendations for Responsible Development and Application of Neurotechnologies. Neuroethics. 2021;14(3):365–86.

[79] Yuste R. Advocating for neurodata privacy and neurotechnology regulation. Nat Protoc. 2023;18(10):2869–75.

[80] Freudenburg Z., Berezutskaya J., Herbert C. Editorial: The ethics of speech ownership in the context of neural control of augmented assistive communication. Front Hum Neurosci. 2024; 18:1468938.

[81] Data Robot (Accessed January 22, 2025, at https://www.datarobot.com/wp-content/uploads/2022/01/DataRobot-Report-State-of-AI-Bias_V5.pdf).

[82] AI Bias 101: How to Mitigate It in 2025 (Accessed January 22, 2025, at https://www.ometrics.com/blog/how-to-prevent-ai-bias/#:~:text=DataRobot%20surveyed%20technology%20leaders%20in,%2C%20and%20real%2Dlife%20examples).

[83] Machine Bias (Accessed January 22, 2025, at go.nature.com/29aznyw).

[84] IEEE Global Initiative 2.0 on Ethics of Autonomous and Intelligent Systems (Accessed January 22, 2025, at https://standards.ieee.org/industry-connections/activities/ieee-global-initiative/).

[85] IEEE Standards Initiative: Free Access to AI Ethics and Governanve Standards (Accessed January 22, 2025, at https://standards.ieee.org/news/get-program-ai-ethics/).

[86] Grünwald A. Technology assessment in practice and theory. Oxford: Routledge; 2018.

[87] European University Institute: Governance and Regulation (Accessed January 22, 2025, at https://www.eui.eu/en/public/research/topics?id=governance-and-regulation).

[88] AI and microelectronics: Navigating the policy maze in the era of neural implants (Accessed January 22, 2025, at https://accesspartnership.com/ai-and-microelectronics-navigating-the-policy-maze-in-the-era-of-neural-implants/).

[89] EU AI Act (Accessed January 22, 2025, at https://artificialintelligenceact.eu/the-act/ and https://ai-act-law.eu/).

[90] Johner Institut: Was der AI Act für Medizinprodukte- und IVD-Hersteller bedeutet (Accessed January 22, 2025, at https://www.johner-institut.de/blog/iec-62304-medizinische-software/ai-act-eu-ki-verord-nung/).

[91] Wybitul T. Welche Pflichten haben Betreiber von Hochrisiko-KI-Systemen nach der EU-KI-Verordnung? Überblick, Handlungsempfehlungen und Checklist. Betriebs-Berater. 2024:2179–83.

[92] Sovrano F., Lognoul M., Vilone G.. Aligning XAI with EU Regulations for Smart Biomedical Devices: A Methodology for Compliance Analysis. 2024. In: Frontiers in Artificial Intelligence and Applications [Internet]. 27th European Conference on artificial intelligence (ECAI 2024), Santiago de Compostela ECAI 2024; [826–33]. Available from: https://arxiv.org/pdf/2408.15121.

[93] Hammer B. Fairness in AI – how to design 'unbiased' algorithms?. In: Manzeschke A. and Wittenberg T. (eds.). Ethical Perspectives on Artifical Intelligence in Biomedical Engineering, Chapter 14, DeGruyter, 2025.

[94] Gassner U. M. Regulation of Artificial Intelligence in Medical Technologies. In: Manzeschke A. and Wittenberg T. (eds.). Ethical Perspectives on Artifical Intelligence in Biomedical Engineering, Chapter 26, DeGruyter, 2025.

Jannis Hagenah, Maria Henke, Massimo Kubon, Thomas Wittenberg

17 AI-supported robots in healthcare

17.1 Introduction and motivation

For more than two decades, various types of robots have been supporting and relieving clinical healthcare professionals in their diverse and often strenuous activities. Surgeons, physicians, nurses, laboratory technicians as well as patients benefit equally from this technological development. In surgery, tele-mainpulated robots have become widely established for precision procedures such as prostatectomies [1] or are used for robot-supported medical imaging [2]. Mobile autonomous platforms [3] take over the transportation of food, laundry, medication and empty beds over long distances in healthcare facilities such as hospitals, outpatient clinics and retirement and nursing homes. Within the field of sports and exercise medicine, robotic systems support the rehabilitation process by motivating, guiding and accompanying patients during exercises [4]. Within laboratory medicine, autonomous robots increase the throughput, efficiency and accuracy of processes, particularly in the handling and processing of tissue and cell samples [5]. Finally, so-called social robots are specially designed to interact with people and provide emotional support in retirement and nursing homes, to reduce loneliness and promote social interactions [6]. These examples illustrate, that robotic systems of various characteristics and manifold applications are already established across the wide field of healthcare.

Nevertheless, the integration of Artificial Intelligence (AI) in form of deep neural networks and large language models into healthcare has in the past ten years been transforming the medical landscape. Many AI-based applications are purely *virtual*, such as e.g. image-based diagnostics in radiology [7] and digital pathology [8] or making prognostic predictions in hospital wards [9]. However, as the human body exists in a physical world, many diagnostic and therapeutic procedures require physical interaction with the human body. Diagnostic palpation, ultrasound imaging, interventional endoscopy, obtaining biopsies or tumor resection are just a few examples of interventions necessitating direct contact with a patient's body. In these cases, robots can serve as *embodiments* of AI-based systems [10], enabling them to interact with the physical world and equally facilitating complex medical procedures at or within the patient's bodies. These physical interactions are multifaceted, involving not only the patient's physique, but also medical tools and devices, the clinical staff, as well as also other robots or machinery. As a result, robotic systems are essential for bringing AI to healthcare in the physical world, hence bridging the gap between *virtual intelligence* and *real-world applications*.

However, embodiments of AI in the form of robots also raises new and unique ethical considerations, which extend beyond the technical challenges of developing and implementing these systems. Therefore, this chapter will delve into the ethics of

AI-driven robots across a wide range of healthcare applications, exploring the complex moral and societal implications of integrating these intelligent systems into medical practice.

17.2 Applications of robots in healthcare

The applications of robots in healthcare are vast and new fields are opened regularly. While many hospitals already rely on robots to automize transports, logistics or laboratory examinations, there is little to no interaction with humans in these scenarios. Given this chapter's focus on the influence of embodied AI in the physical and mental interaction with humans, this section focuses on applications with a degree of invasiveness and potential harmfulness. Thus, the following paragraphs evolve around robot applications in surgery (Sec. 17.2.1), rehabilitation and prosthetics (Sec. 17.2.2) and social robotics (Sec. 17.2.3)

17.2.1 Robot-assisted surgery

Surgery is one of the most tactile and haptic fields of medicine, where the success of a procedure highly depends on manual precision and exact movement of the surgical instruments with respect to the patient's body. However, human limitations, such as fatigue, tremor, or muscle pain, can compromise even the most skilled surgeon's performance. In contrast, robots can hold their positions and move surgical instruments with precision for hours, hence making surgery a promising application field for robotic technology. Despite the potential benefits, surgery is an extremely high-risk field, where even minor errors can have severe consequences. Furthermore, the decision-making processes involved in surgery, such as determining where to cut, place incisions, and sew, are complex and highly dependent on individual patient characteristics. As a result – rather than replacing them – the current approach of integrating robotics in surgery is to support human surgeons by providing precise and reliable assistance that enhances their cognitive abilities, while still leveraging their expertise and judgment to make critical decisions.

17.2.1.1 Telematic surgical robots

The beginnings of surgical robotics date back to the 1980s with the ZEUS and AESOP systems [11], but it wasn't until the introduction of the da Vinci Surgical System in the late 1990s that the field began to gain momentum. The da Vinci system, developed by Intuitive Surgical, revolutionized the field of robotic-assisted surgery (RAS) with its innovative design and precise instrumentation. Through strong patent strategies, Intuitive Surgical was able to establish a dominant position in the market, limiting competition and maintaining a virtual monopoly on RAS systems for over two decades. However, with the expiration of key patents, the market is now experiencing a resurgence of innovation, with new players and systems emerging to challenge the status quo. Modern RAS systems, such as the HUGO RAS system from Medtronic [12] (see Fig. 17.1)., the DistalMotion Dexter system [13], and the CMR system from Cambridge Medical Robotics, are being developed with advanced features, improved ergonomics, and enhanced capabilities, offering surgeons and hospitals a range of options and potentially disrupting the market dominance of the da Vinci system [14].

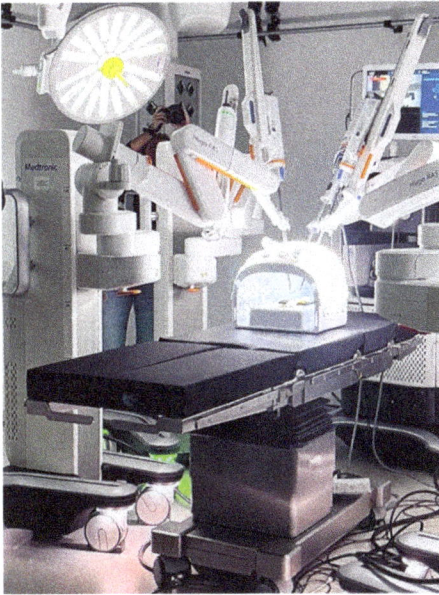

Fig. 17.1: An example from for a telematic surgical robot with one robotic arm holding the stereo endoscope and two further arms guiding two laparoscope instruments into an abdominal phantom.

The current generation of robotic surgery systems, including the da Vinci and its newer competitors, are all based on the concept of tele-manipulation [15]. In this approach, the surgeon sits at a console and manipulates input devices, which are sophisticated controllers that track the surgeon's hand and finger movements. These movements are then precisely replicated by the robotic arms at the operation table and inside the patient, allowing the surgeon to perform delicate procedures with enhanced dexterity and precision. The robot essentially acts as a telematic extension of the surgeon's

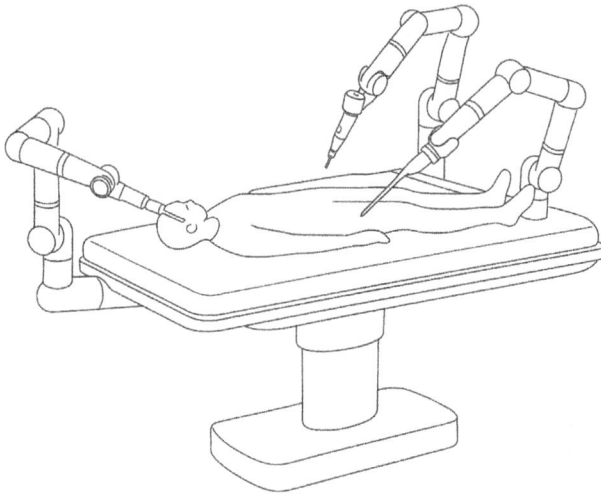

Fig. 17.2: Novel approach for surgical robotics, where the robotic arms are directly integrated in the operation table. (Figure redrawn from [17]).

hands, faithfully following the movements of the input devices, with no autonomy to make surgical decisions. This means that the surgeon always remains fully in control of the procedure, with the robot serving as a highly advanced precision tool to extend their capabilities. Notably, these systems are specifically designed for minimally invasive surgery, where small incisions and natural orifices are used to access the surgical site, reducing tissue trauma and promoting faster recovery times. The robotic arms are typically equipped with specialized instruments, such as a laparoscopic stereo camera, forceps and scissors, which are inserted through tiny ports or incisions, allowing the surgeon to perform complex procedures with minimal disruption to the surrounding tissue. Interestingly, from a technical standpoint, these systems can be classified more accurately as tele-manipulators rather than robots, as they do not possess any degree of autonomy or independent decision-making capability. However, within the field of medical robotics, the term 'robot' has become deeply ingrained and is still widely used to describe these systems, reflecting the significant impact they have had on the practice of surgery. The term 'robot' also implicates the possibilities, which these systems *could* have, if the telematic control is enhanced or even exchanged by artificial intelligence.

An important trend in surgical robotics is the shift from robots as individual devices towards a stronger integration and combination of robotic arms and other medical products. One example is the development project OTTAVA, recently announced by Johnson & Johnson [16], where the robotic arms are directly integrated into an operation table (see Fig. 17.2). This resolves two core problems of previous systems: (a) the large footprint of the robot carts in the OR, as well as (b) the collision avoidance, since the arms always know its relative position towards the patient and to each other. However, the product blurs the line between surgical robots and operating tables, paving the way for a novel age, where robots are no extra devices to be added to existing setups. Thus, robots become increasingly an integral part of core components to promote seamless integration of hardware in the OR.

17.2.1.2 Assistive robots

Beyond the realm of telemanipulation systems, a diverse range of assistive robots is emerging to support surgeons in various aspects of the surgical workflow. Examples of such systems include the SoloAssist System (AktorMed, Germany) [18], which provides automatic laparoscopic camera positioning and tracking, and the RoboticScope system [19], which enables precise navigation of surgical microscopes. Additionally, systems like the MAKO [20] system offer drilling guidance and navigation, which can be particularly useful in orthopedic and neurosurgical procedures. Equally, using the Guidoo system [21], for example, a robot is precisely placing and orienting a biopsy needle under CT-guidance at a patient's body, hence relieving the surgeon with planning. These assistive robots have the potential to improve surgical outcomes, reduce complications, and enhance the overall efficiency of the surgicalteam, making them a valuable addition to the conventional operating room.

17.2.1.3 Autonomy of surgical robots

The current level *of autonomy* in surgical robotic systems is relatively low, with most systems functioning as tele-manipulators that enhance the surgeon's capabilities rather than operating independently. Even when robots are programmed to perform specific steps, currently human supervisors must always be present to supervise the task and actively agree to the planned procedures. However, Artificial Intelligence (AI) is increasingly being applied to support surgeons in a range of subtasks, such as reducing the tremor of the surgeon's hand, augmenting visual data with detected information, or providing real-time (haptic) feedback. Moreover, surgical robotic systems are strongly benefiting from AI-driven tools that have evolved around the robot itself, including intelligent navigation, image segmentation, and detection of anatomical landmarks to visualize for the user. Additionally, Natural Language Processing (NLP) is being used to enable voice commands and speech interfaces, further enhancing the surgeon's experience. However, it is important to note that most AI systems are currently designed for cloud usage by individual manufacturers, which raises two significant concerns. Firstly, interoperability becomes a challenge, making it difficult to connect devices and visualize navigation of robotic systems from different manufacturers. Secondly, data protection and IT security become particularly challenging, especially in international contexts, such as when a European hospital uses a robotic system manufactured in the US, highlighting the need for standardized solutions and robust security protocols to ensure the safe and effective integration of AI in surgical robotics.

17.2.1.4 Benefits of surgical robots

While the benefits of surgical robotics for patients are still a subject of ongoing debate and research, with some studies suggesting a significant reduction in complication rates for certain procedures [22], and others showing no difference compared to conventional surgery [23], the advantages for surgeons are more clear-cut. From an ergonomic perspective, surgical robotics offers several benefits, including reduced fatigue, improved posture, and enhanced comfort during long and complex procedures [24]. The use of robotic systems can also help to reduce the physical demands of surgery, such as the need to maintain a static position or perform repetitive motions, which can lead to musculoskeletal disorders and other occupational health issues. Additionally, high-definition or 3D-visualization as well as precise instrumentation provided by robotic systems can help to reduce eye strain, cognitive load and improve the overall surgical experience for the surgeon. However, the translation of these benefits into improved patient outcomes is still an area of active research, and more studies are needed to fully understand the impact of surgical robotics on patient care and recovery.

As we look to the future of surgical robotics, the field is poised for significant growth and transformation. Despite the regulatory hurdles that must be overcome, numerous novel systems are currently in development and pushing towards market approval, promising to further refine and expand the capabilities of surgical robotics. As the field continues to evolve, we can expect to see a more nuanced landscape emerge, with highly specific surgical robotic systems tailored to meet the unique needs of various specialties and procedures. Moreover, the future of surgical robotics will undoubtedly be marked by increasing levels of autonomy, enabling robots to perform more complex tasks and procedures with greater precision and accuracy. This trend is driven in part by the pressing need to address the demographic change and staff shortage that is affecting the surgical profession, where automatization will soon become necessary to simply maintain current levels of healthcare availability, let alone improve them. By automating routine and repetitive procedures, experts will be freed to focus on the most challenging and complex cases, where their expertise is truly essential. Furthermore, there is a vast middle ground between tele-manipulation and fully autonomous surgery, where specific steps can potentially be performed autonomously [25]. Specific sequences such as sewing or intelligent guidance can be provided with AI-support to support less experienced surgeons, enhancing their skills and confidence. As the field of surgical robotics continues to advance, it can be expected to see a more seamless integration of human and machine capabilities, leading to improved patient outcomes, enhanced surgical training, and a more sustainable and effective healthcare system.

17.2.2 Robots for prevention, therapy, rehabilitation and sports

17.2.2.1 General aspects and definitions

Sports and Exercise Medicine (SEM) most commonly involves the medical fields of orthopedics, internal medicine and neurology. Hollmann (1925–2021, sport medic and physician at University Cologne) defined SEM as a theoretical and practical part of medicine investigating the influence of exercise, training and sports and the lag thereof to healthy and unhealthy humans [26]. Today, the field of SEM addresses three main fundamental focus fields such as (a) *prevention*, (b) *therapy and rehabilitation*, and (c) *sports* activity. Each field represents a clear purpose and goal to the human organism, which shall be reached when performing its activities.

The terms *rehabilitation* and *therapy* are hardly distinguishable and are hence regarded together. Therapy refers to specific or singular treatment steps designed to address physical, cognitive or mental health issues. In the context of rehabilitation, therapy can be categorized into several types. However, rehabilitation is a comprehensive process aimed to restore patient abilities after injury or illness. It may also be restoring due to a post-traumatic medical intervention (e.g. surgery). It comprises various coordinated therapeutic aspects to address physical, cognitive, and emotional impairments, facilitating a return of the patient to independent living. Thus, several and different therapeutic tasks may be directly involved in a comprehensive rehabilitation program taking up to at least weeks or months of treatment time.

The term *sports* is mainly defined from various forms of physical or mental training activity that are organized, competitive, and aim to improve physical fitness and mental well-being beyond the state of a healthy person. It is assumed that the activity and purpose arise out of a certain motivation driving to continuously increase overall performance to achieve a sportive and competitive goal.

In SEM, *prevention* involves strategies to avoid injuries and medical conditions related to physical or mental activity, and it requires a multidisciplinary approach to maintain health and performance. SEM has been proven to effectively prevent affluent diseases like diabetes, cardiovascular issues, and joint disorders. Jadon et al. [27] provided an overview how to systematically address primordial, primary and secondary prevention. From SEM perspective prevention is a proactive, often self-driven effort to protect health. Despite its cost-saving potential, prevention remains underutilized in healthcare. Future interest will likely focus on how AI and robotics can enhance these strategies.

17.2.2.2 Relationship of SEM to medicine and robotics

Fig. 17.3 provides a conceptual framework linking the three primary focus areas of SEM – prevention, therapy/rehabilitation, sports – to traditional medical disciplines, namely *orthopedics, internal medicine*, and *neurology*. The matrix highlights the intersections where combined robotic and artificial intelligence (AI) technologies – specifically strength, motion, physical, performance, endurance – can contribute to improved outcomes.

Within orthopedics, SEM goals primarily address the restoration or enhancement of strength and motion. These areas are well-suited to robotic applications, for example through exoskeletons for gait training [28] or collaborative robots (so-called *cobots*) supporting repetitive movement training [29]. Rehabilitation robotics aim to restore joint range of motion and muscular function, which is foundational to orthopedic sports recovery and prevention of injury recurrence.

Internal medicine aspects within SEM focus on physical performance and endurance. These domains can benefit from robotically enhanced exercise devices and AI-driven adaptive training platforms. Examples include smart fitness equipment that uses AI to optimize workload and progression [30], or robotic ergometers with real-time biofeedback for cardiovascular conditioning. By combining sensor data and machine learning models, internal medicine approaches can be personalized to match each athlete's or patient's metabolic and cardiovascular profile.

In the field of neurology, SEM targets mental performance and coordination are mostly promising for AI-based approaches. Neurocognitive training platforms using AI, as well as VR-based rehabilitation supported by machine learning algorithms, show potential to improve executive function and motor coordination post-injury [31]. These systems are designed to adaptively challenge patients to enhance neuroplasticity and regain complex movement patterns vital for both prevention and sports performance.

Overall, it is shown that robotics is especially applicable to motor function, strength, and endurance-oriented SEM tasks, while AI technologies are particularly relevant to cognitive and coordination-based challenges. For the future, it is expected that both technologies will interact even more and merge to AI-Robotic-Systems.

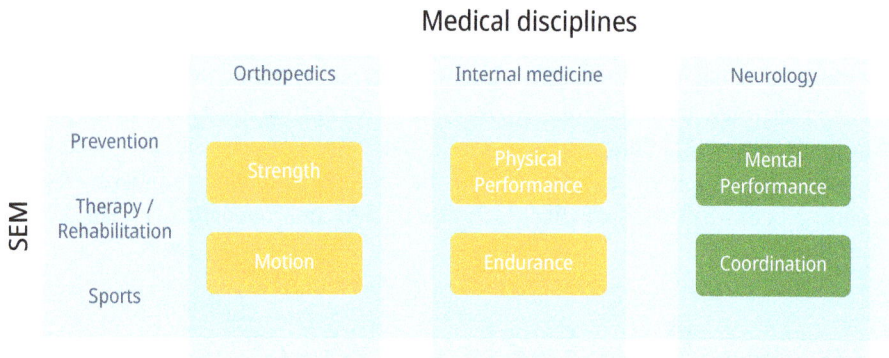

Fig. 17.3: Conceptual matrix linking Sport & Exercise Medicine (SEM) focus areas with traditional medical disciplines, highlighting potential application domains for robotic (yellow/orange) and AI-based (green) technologies.

The integration of robotic systems into medical sport and rehabilitation engineering arises from a dual imperative: first, to compensate for the growing shortage of qualified therapeutic personnel, and second, to enable patients to participate more autonomously in their recovery. Physical rehabilitation robots augment therapeutic capacity, reduce physical load on clinicians, and provide consistent, high-frequency, controlled, data-driven training. Additionally, robotics empower patients through interactive interfaces, biofeedback, and AI-driven adaptation. This user-centric approach is especially critical in outpatient and home care settings, where therapy intensity often suffers due to logistical constraints.

17.2.2.3 Rehabilitation

Rehabilitation robotics focuses on restoring motor function and cognitive engagement through mechanically assisted training programs. The diversity of devices – ranging from wearable exoskeletons via exo-suits to cobots – supports therapy across neurorehabilitation, orthopedic recovery, and geriatric care. For example, robotic gait trainers like the Lokomat [32] allow for repetitive, precision-controlled walking exercises which are crucial in neurological rehabilitation post-stroke or spinal cord injury. As recovery becomes more personalized, systems like the ReStore Exo-Suit by ReWalk [33] provide dynamic, user-dependent assistance in real time, motivating users to self-initiate movement.

These systems provide key advantages: they increase training intensity and precision, collect real-time biomechanical data, and reduce the therapist's physical workload. Modern robotic systems often operate in adaptive assistance modes, using real-time sensor data and AI-based algorithms to tailor interventions based on patient performance. Clinical studies have shown that robotic therapy can lead to improved outcomes in post-stroke recovery, Parkinson's disease, and spinal cord injury rehabilitation [34,35].

Exoskeletons are special wearable devices designed to support or replicate limb movement. Active exoskeletons, such as EksoNR [36] and ReWalk [33], incorporate powered joints controlled by sensors and microprocessors. They are used extensively in spinal cord injury and stroke rehabilitation to support upright walking and correct gait deficiencies. Passive systems, like the HANK exoskeleton, provide unpowered mechanical support for stability and posture correction. Supportive or 'overtaking' exoskeletons enable patients with minimal residual function to participate in task-specific training with robotic compensation. Studies have shown that robotic-based gait training using exoskeletons can significantly improve walking ability and reduce spasticity in neurological patients [28].

Unlike rigid-frame exoskeletons, exo-suits are made of soft materials and focus on assisting motion via tensile forces or muscle compression. They are lightweight, minimally restrictive, and particularly effective for elderly or frail patients. One prominent example is the ReStore Exo-Suit (ReWalk Robotics), which provides hip and ankle assistance during gait and has been shown to improve walking speed and endurance in stroke survivors [37]. These devices often incorporate various sensors to adapt assistance dynamically to the user's gait phase.

In addition to facilitating physical movement, cobots are increasingly employed as interactive therapeutic assistants. These systems can guide patients through cognitive-motor training routines, monitor adherence, and provide motivational feedback. An example is the REX Bionics platform, which allows upright rehabilitation without crutches or walkers. The robot independently balances and moves, enabling therapists to interact with the patient on cognitive or emotional levels during exercises. Other systems integrate game-based interfaces or virtual environments to enhance engagement – especially valuable in pediatric and neuropsychological treatments [38]. Equally, the ROBERT system assists in performing repetitive motor exercises, stretching routines, or passive mobilization. These devices can be programmed to deliver consistent therapy sessions, ensuring reproducibility and reducing therapist workload. Their compliant joints and safety features make them suitable for direct physical contact with patients, even in unsupervised settings. Clinical integration has shown positive effects on shoulder and upper-limb recovery after orthopedic surgery or stroke [27].

17.2.2.4 Prosthetics and sports

The development of prosthetic technology has advanced rapidly with the integration of robotics and smart materials. Passive prosthetics, such as carbon fiber blades used in competitive athletics (e.g., Össur's Flex-Foot Cheetah), rely on mechanical properties and design geometry to mimic spring-like behavior. While effective for experienced users, these require significant adaptation and residual limb strength. Active prosthetics, in contrast, include embedded motors and microcontrollers to deliver powered movement. Systems such as the Genium X3 and the Empower ankle (both by Ottobock Medical) use onboard sensors and AI algorithms to adapt to terrain, user gait, and activity type. These devices offer enhanced stability, smoother transitions, and improved energy efficiency, which is particularly valuable in demanding sport environments. Customization and further improvement of the human/machine interface is a key consideration: while off-the-shelf solutions are readily available, high-performance users typically require tailored socket designs, sensor calibration, and biomechanical fitting. AI-enabled diagnostic tools are now being used to optimize prosthetic alignment and motion pattern analysis [39]. In addition, the interface with direct neuronal connections is in development [40].

Smart training robots are revolutionizing both professional and amateur sports, as they provide dynamic resistance training, motion correction, and injury prevention insights. Examples include Tonal and Vitruvian Trainer+, which use adaptive digital weights and AI-powered feedback to adjust intensity in real time based on muscle engagement and fatigue. Ball sports are integrating robots like the Slinger Bag (tennis) and the RoboCoach system (table tennis) to simulate real opponents. These allow players to train continuously without human partners while receiving quantitative data on speed, angle, and timing. Martial arts disciplines employ robotic dummies and force-feedback targets. Products such as the StrikeTec [41] sensor suite and the BotBoxer use motion tracking and AI to simulate sparring sessions while analyzing technique and power output. Board sports like skateboarding or snowboarding are also exploring robotic balance platforms and dynamic slope simulators for skill transfer and core strengthening.

17.2.2.5 Prevention

In the context of SEM, prevention focuses on avoiding injuries and health deterioration before they occur. Robotics combined with AI are increasingly central to this proactive strategy, particularly in monitoring biomechanical risks, improving neuromuscular coordination, and tailoring exercise programs based on real-time data. Neuro-coordinators are robotic systems or wearables that support the central nervous system in optimizing balance, coordination, and reaction time. Systems like the BalanceTutor (MediTouch) [42] integrate perturbation-based treadmill training with VR feedback to reduce fall risk and improve dynamic stability in elderly or neurologically compromised populations. The LUNA coordinator by SensoPro [43] is based on flexible tapes and a complex joint / rocker platform forcing the trainee to be in balance. Software and AI algorithms are augmenting such systems, adjusting the level of challenge based on patient performance, encouraging neuroplastic adaptation and provide real-time feedback to the trainee without external supervision.

Muscle stimulators, including electrical muscle stimulation (EMS) and functional electrical stimulation (FES) allow for precise timing and spatial targeting of muscle groups. The Mollii Suit by Ottobock [44] is a notable wearable that integrates electrical stimulation to relax spastic muscles and enhance movement control in individuals with cerebral palsy, multiple sclerosis, or stroke. AI is employed to personalize stimulation patterns and track muscle response.

17.2.2.6 General aspects and future perspectives

Robotic systems in SEM serve a dual function: they alleviate strain on human caregivers while providing individualized, adaptive care to patients. The integration of AI into such systems enables dynamic adjustment of training parameters, remote monitoring, and predictive health modeling, effectively broadening the reach and impact of therapeutic interventions. At the same time, robotic systems are either directly connected to the human motion apparatus or they augment/substitute care labor wherever needed.

Future trends point toward fully autonomous systems that not only deliver therapy, but also assess psychological state, detect motivational drop-offs, and adjust stimulation modes accordingly. Brain-computer interfaces (BCIs), soft robotic materials, and digital twin simulations are being actively explored to close the gap between machine support and natural recovery processes. Equally important is the ethical and regulatory framework in which these systems operate. Ensuring equitable access, safeguarding user data, and validating therapeutic claims will be key to broader clinical and consumer adoption. Moreover, the distinction between medical treatment and personal enhancement is expected to receive increasing attention in the future. [45–47] Standardization of protocols and interoperability between platforms will facilitate integration into existing medical infrastructures. Ultimately, robotic rehabilitation and training systems have the potential to shift the paradigm of health care from reactive treatment to proactive and personalized prevention – creating not only longer lifespans but also healthier ones.

17.2.3 Social robots

In contrast to the surgical (Section 17.2.1) or rehabilitation robots (Section 17.2.2), which are mainly high-precision tools to support surgeons or relieve rehabilitation experts in demarcated environments, the relative novel field of 'social robotics' describes anthropomorphic or zoomorphic machines specifically designed to interact with humans in a socially meaningful way [48]. In this context 'anthropomorphic' means, that – for reasons of acceptance – robots partially resemble human appearance (having a head, a torso, arms and legs) and mimic human behavior (using speech, movements, gestures and mimics). Equally, 'zoomorphic' refers to social robots having an animal-like appearance.

17.2.3.1 Human-robot-interaction strategies

The implemented *human-robot-interaction* (HRI) strategies for such social robots are usually based on an a combination of different technologies and techniques to mimic the social behaviors of humans, where key schemes of social robots for HRI are (a) verbal communication using natural language processing (NLP), (b) non-verbal communication, (c) emotional intelligence as well as (d) physical interaction possibilities.

NLP is used to let the robot understand and generate human language, hence allowing it to hold meaningful conversations, answer questions and provide information in such a way that it feels natural to the interacting humans [49]. Most current NLP approaches are based on *Large Language Models* (LLMs), which provide social robots with versatile conversational skills, depending on the training of the LLMs and the specific applications.

Non-verbal communication possibilities [50] of social robots include the use of hand and arm gestures (including handshakes), the generation of facial expressions (such as smiling or nodding), as well as the use of body language (turning or bending forward) to convey emotions and intentions. The intention of non-verbal communication strategies is to support NLP by showing non-verbal empathy towards the conversational partner.

The counterpart of non-verbal communication is emotional intelligence, which is achieved by different types of contactless (mainly optical) sensors mounted on or integrated in social robots, whose multimodal data is analyzed in real time to detect and respond to human emotions. Typical examples of such sensors are the analysis of facial expressions [51], the tone of the voice [52] or vital signs [53,54] (such as the pulse or respiratory rate) to assess how the human counterpart is feeling and adjusting the communication behavior of the social robot accordingly [55].

Finally, some social robots can also perform some type of physical actions such as shaking hands, hugging, or handing over objects [56]. Nevertheless, as these physical interaction possibilities may not harm humans, such interaction strategies are quite limited.

All these possibilities for HRI are nowadays based on some type of artificial intelligence, ranging from machine-learning to deep-learning approaches and partially even making used of foundation models [57]. Using *adaptive* or *active learning* strategies [58], social robots also able to adapt their behavior to the humans they are interacting with and are even able to remember previous conversations and unique characteristics of the humans [59]. In this sense, social robots could be reagreed as *social intelligent agents* (SIAs) with an embodiment [60]. In Fig. 17.4, some currently available social robots are depicted.

17.2.3.1 Examples for social robots in healthcare

Social robots are increasingly being integrated into various healthcare settings to provide emotional support and assistance to patients, particularly the elderly and children. By utilizing advanced technologies such as NLP and emotion recognition, these robotics systems enhance patient care and bridge the gap between technology and meaningful human interaction.

One prominent example of social robotics in healthcare is their use as companions for elderly patients, particularly those with dementia or living in long-term care facilities. Robots such as *PARO* [61], a zoomorphic baby seal, or *Pepper* [62] and *Navel* [59,63] – two humanoid robots, are designed to offer emotional support and reduce feelings of loneliness. The humanoid robots use (local or cloud-based) versions of NLP to trigger and engage in conversations with the elderly and respond appropriately to free-text speech. They also exhibit non-verbal behaviors like eye blinking and subtle body movements such as gesturing and head movements that try to mimic human empathy. Equipped with various sensors that detect facial expressions, voice tone, or even vital signs, these humanoid robots are able to adjust their communication based on the emotional state of the user. Based on face recognition technologies and local storage, the *Navel* robot even has the possibility to remember the names of and the dialogues with of the interacting users and can hence continue previous communication and interaction threads. Physical interaction is currently usually gentle and limited – PARO, for instance, responds to touch and can be cuddled, providing a calming effect similar to that of a therapy animal.

Another application of social robots is in pediatric care, where social robots like *NAO* [64], *Pepper* [65] or *Robear* [66] are used to support children undergoing medical procedures. These robots are designed to alleviate anxiety and fear, especially during tasks like blood draws or vaccinations. They interact with children through friendly dialogue, storytelling, or simple games powered by NLP. Their expressive body language, such as waving, dancing, or making eye contact, helps capture the child's attention and create a playful atmosphere. Nao and Peeper robots can – at least partially – also interpret emotional cues using facial expression or voice analysis and adjust their behavior accordingly – speaking in a softer tone or using reassuring language when a child appears anxious. Physical interaction is minimal but meaningful, such as offering a high-five or mimicking comforting gestures. The *Robear*, robot made of plastic and metal with a cute polar-bear-cub face, is able to provide patient-transfer functions for people who cannot get out of bed unaided. The robot can lift (young) patients in and out of bed, placing them into a wheelchair or assisting them if they are unsteady on their feet. This provides relief for carers who often have strained backs from lifting patients on a regular basis.

A further example is the *Care-O-Bot* [67], a robot designed to assist caregivers and patients in clinical and domestic settings. While not strictly humanoid, the Care-O-Bot has an approachable design with some anthropomorphic features and social interaction capabilities. It can engage in conversations using NLP, provide reminders for medication, guide patients to different locations, and – using an integrated robotic arm and vision sensors – is able to support daily tasks like fetching objects. The robot uses a combination of verbal and non-verbal communication, such as turning toward the user, changing its tone of voice, and displaying status through colored lights or gestures. Care-O-Bot's emotional intelligence is facilitated by multimodal sensors that allow it to interpret human behavior and respond appropriately, for example by slowing down movements or repeating instructions if a user / patient appears confused. Though its physical interaction capabilities are limited, it can safely hand over objects, open doors, or operate buttons. The Care-O-Bot 4 exemplifies how socially interactive service robots can bridge the gap between assistive technology and meaningful human engagement in healthcare environments.

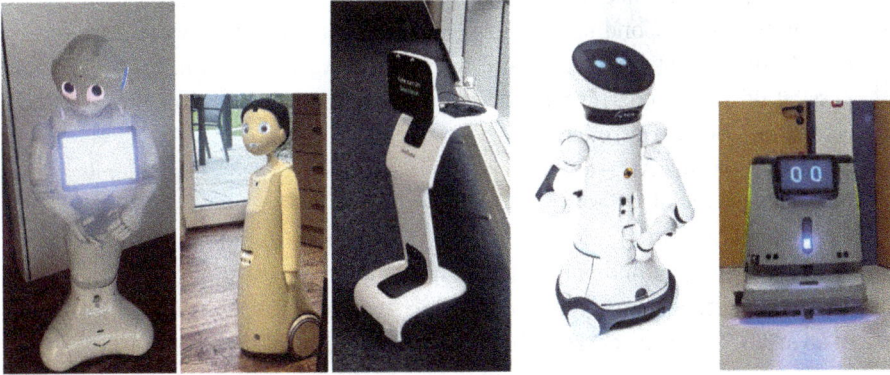

Fig. 17.4: Examples for different types of social robots: (a) Pepper, (b) Navel, (c) Temi, (d) Care-O-Bot; (e) Pudu cleaning robot.

17.3 Discussion

17.3.1 Dimensions of healthcare robotics

In order to classify and discuss robots in healthcare with respect to AI and ethics, in this work three dimensions are used, namely the *degree of autonomy* (D1), *degree of invasiveness* (D2) and AI based on *intelligence and general abilities* (D3).

To define the *degree of autonomy* (D1) for the robotic systems we adapted the *levels of autonomy in surgical robotics* (LASR) classification scheme for system automation and robotic autonomy [68]. LSAR is a six-level scale, related the degrees 0 = "no autonomy", 1 = "robot assistance", 3 = "task autonomy", 4 = "conditional autonomy", 4= "high autonomy" and 5 = "full autonomy". Even though the LSAR scale was originally defined for surgical robots only, we tried adapting it all other robot systems as well.

Equally we describe the *levels of invasiveness* (D2) of a robot with respect to the patients or users in a similar way. Hence, we defined the following six grades: 0 = "complete outside and away from the patient", 1 = "in the proximity of the patient", 2 = "touching the body of the patient", 3 = "having full contact to the patient's body outside", 4 = "partially in the patient's body ", and 5 = "fully inside the patient's body".

To describe the degree of *intelligence and general ability* (D3) provided by AI (running on the robots) the following scaling between 0 and 5 was employed, inspired by the work of Morris at al. [69]:

- 0 = "No intelligent functions, only fixed rules, and no ability to learn".
- 1 = "Simple AI", responding to simple inputs but without the ability to learn.
- 2 = "Weak AI" – aka ANI (Artificial Narrow Intelligence) – with limited learning possibilities, able to perform specialized tasks (as e.g. voice control, image classification) and can learn from data.
- 3 = "Context-aware AI" – aka General Purpose AI, GPAI – with limited understanding and some possibilities to react adaptively.
- 4 = "General AI" (AGI), which as human-like cognitive abilities and can solve any task flexibly and autonomously. This currently does not exist.
- 5 = "Artificial super intelligence (ASI), which as able to surpass human intelligence in all areas. This is purely hypothetical.

Table 17.1 provides our rating of some robots within healthcare with respect to these dimensions, while Fig. 17.5 provides a graphical visualization of these dimensions.

It can be observed that laboratory and transport (or logistic) robotics (autonomy 5/3, invasiveness 0) operate *without* any patient contact as completely non-invasive systems and employ simple (AI=1) to weak learning methods (AI=2). Scrub nurse robots and social robots (Section 17.2.3) (autonomy 4/3, invasiveness 1) are minimally invasive and make use of context-aware AI (AI=3), such as NLP, emotion recognition or context awareness to adaptively intervene in supportive procedures and patient communication. Robot-assisted surgery (Section 17.2.1) (autonomy 1, invasiveness 5) as well as radiation therapy robots – discussed in Chapter 18 in this book [70] – (autonomy 2, invasiveness 4) are highly invasive but human-controlled applications that use weak AI (AI=2) to support precise execution without making decisions independently. Rehabilitation aids such as exoskeletons (1,3,2), rehab cobots (3,2,1), and exo-prostheses (2,4,1) (Section 17.2.2) are in the medium invasiveness range and use simple or weak AI to augment and predict user-driven movements. Overall, we conclude that the more invasive and riskier a medical application becomes, the lower the autonomy and AI level and the greater the human control systems. Robotic systems with higher AI levels, on the other hand, tend to take on supportive, non-invasive roles. Nevertheless, as indicated in Fig. 17.5 on the right side in pink, even though social robotics may have very low level of physical invasiveness, it could also be argued, that employing chat-bots, nonverbal communication schemes in combination with emotional intelligence, social robots have a high level of *psychological invasiveness*.

Tab. 17.1: Rating of some healthcare robots with respect to the three dimensions "autonomy", "invasiveness" and "AI" (based on intelligence and general abilities)

	Autonomy	Invasiveness	AI
Laboratory Robotics	5	0	2
Transport Robotics	3	0	1
Scrub Nurse Robot	4	1	3
Robot-Assisted Surgery	1	5	2
Radiation Therapy	2	4	2
Exoskeletons	1	3	2
Rehab Cobot	3	2	1
Exo-Prothesis	2	4	1
Social Robots	3	1	3

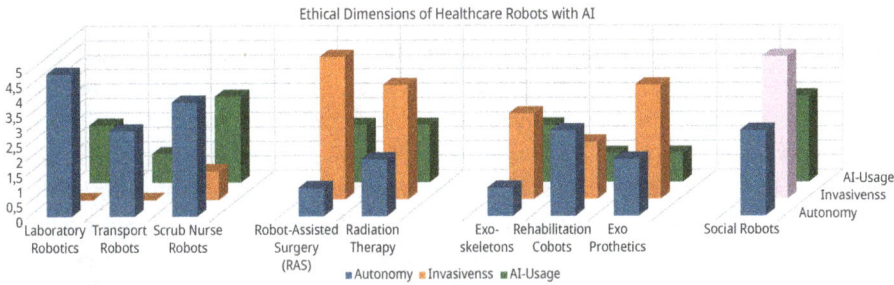

Fig. 17.5: Different types of healthcare robots with respect to the three dimensions autonomy (D1), invasiveness (D2) and AI based on intelligence and general abilities (D3)

17.3.2 Healthcare robotics and limitations of AI

The integration of different types of Artificial Intelligence (AI) into the currently available medical robots – ranging from telematic systems for surgical interventions via rehabilitation robotics to social robots, but also including robots for transportation, laboratory and logistics – poses a unique challenge in terms of execution speed, as intelligent robots with a close proximity near or in the patient require fast and reliable processing (of all the acquired sensor data) and response (with respect to the patient or user) to operate effectively and smoothly within their specific environments. In contrast to many other medical applications, such as pre-operative planning, prognostic prediction, or lab result interpretation, where computation time is not a critical factor, robots demand rapid response times. Social robots, for instance, need to react fast to interact fluently with patients, while surgical robots require real-time processing to ensure precise and safe operations, guided by the surgeons. As a result, relying on cloud computation with long transfer times is often not feasible. Thus, instead, *embedded AI* and *Edge AI* – discussed in chapter 15 in this book [71] –, which involve processing data locally on the robot or on nearby devices, respectively, are becoming increasingly important. This approach, however, limits the capacities of AI algorithms, as they must be optimized to run on less powerful hardware. Also, if the employed cloud service is outside the vicinity of the hospital or elderly home, data and privacy protection measures must be implemented, as – especially for social robots – sensible data such as emotions or speech is stored and transferred back and forth. Furthermore, for mobile robots, the limited energy supply due to battery lifetime adds an additional constraint, requiring AI models to be not only fast but also energy-efficient, which can further restrict their complexity and capabilities.

17.3.3 Paradigm shifts in the ethical perspective

The continuous integration of novel medical robots into the healthcare is driving paradigm shifts on two scales. On one hand, their increased existence and availability is changing the way users (surgeons, physical therapists, nurses, staff, patients, relatives, visitors, …) interact with and perceive medical robots, redefining their role in the medical profession. On the other hand, it is also shifting social attitudes and expectations regarding the use of autonomous medical robots, prompting a re-evaluation of their potential benefits and risks. These dual paradigm shifts will be explored in the following sections, which will delve into the changing perspectives of users and the evolving societal acceptance of medical robots.

17.3.3.1 Shifting perspectives of the user

The integration of Artificial Intelligence (AI) as essential component in all types of medical robots is sparking a profound paradigm shift in the way users perceive and interact with these systems. As AI-powered robots evolve from mere precision power tools (e.g., in the appearance of a high-tech telematic surgery system) towards intelligent assistants (as e.g. in form of intelligent prothesis directly worn on or under the skin), and eventually to social interaction partners with emotional possibilities (in the form of humanoid social robots as embodied social interacting agents), the boundaries between human and machine are becoming increasingly blurred. This transformation is currently advancing, shifting and redefining the role of the robot from a simple object to an *artificial colleague*, with which humans can build bonds and trust. As a result, medical procedures are being revolutionized, with the robot's ability to provide emotional support and empathy becoming an integral aspect of the treatment process.

While this vision may seem like a distant future, recent advances in affective computing and open-end machine learning are bringing it closer to reality.

Moreover, this paradigm shift may hold the key to addressing a fundamental challenge in AI-powered healthcare: the fact that all *learning systems* are prone to making mistakes. Unlike traditional devices, which rely on certificates and standardized tests to ensure safety, AI systems require a different approach to error mitigation. Interestingly, society has developed various safety mechanisms to catch human errors, such as four-eye principles, expertise-based hierarchies, and multi-expert discussions, which may become equally relevant for detecting and correcting mistakes made by intelligent machines. By embracing this new paradigm, we may uncover innovative solutions to the challenges posed by AI in healthcare and ultimately create a more harmonious and effective collaboration between humans and machines.

17.3.3.2 Shifting perspectives of society

As medical robots become increasingly integrated into the healthcare system, societal perspectives on their role and acceptance are undergoing a significant shift. While some individuals may feel a sense of fear or loss of control when confronted with the idea of being treated by a robot or interacting with a robot as embodied social interactive agent, others will recognize the potential benefits of higher treatment accuracy and precision as well as social interaction. The question of whether one can imagine being treated by a robot is met with ambiguous responses, reflecting the complex and multifaceted nature of this issue. Interestingly, patients are actively seeking out robotic surgery options, such as surgical tele-manipulators, despite the lack of comprehensive studies on their clinical outcome advantages. However, the prospect of semi-autonomous or autonomous robots taking on more significant roles in healthcare remains a fearful scenario for many. Also, people who have already been interacting with any type of social or service robots confirm that their use has a positive impact on their acceptance and everyday life for nursing staff and residents alike. Concerns and fears, especially among older caregivers, can significantly be reduced by getting acquainted with a new system through direct application and daily usage.

Currently, ethical discussions focus on the importance of human decision-makers, such as surgeons, physicians, physio therapeutist or nurses, being supported by any robotic assistance system. Nevertheless, this paradigm may shift in the future, driven by two key factors. Firstly, if research in the future demonstrates that AI-enhanced robots are possibly superior to humans in performing certain tasks (as small as these may be) [72], it may probably become *unethical* to continue relying on human operators alone for those steps. Secondly, the pressing issues of demographic change with an overaged population, high shortages in clinical experts of all types, and an increasing demand for healthcare services are exerting significant pressure on healthcare systems, straining their capacity to provide quality care [73]. In this context, AI-enhanced medical robots may offer a crucial solution, hence enable the stepwise automatization of certain procedures and therefore freeing up strongly needed human resources to address the growing needs of the healthcare sector. By leveraging the potential of medical robots of all types and variations, we may be able to create a more stable and sustainable healthcare system, one that can meet the challenges of the future while maintaining the highest standards of care and compassion. This shifting perspective may ultimately change the ethical considerations and discussions surrounding autonomous medical robots, prompting a reevaluation of the role of human autonomy and machine decision-making in healthcare.

Acknowledgements

The contribution of TW was partially supported by the Bavarian Research Foundation under the project 'FORSocialRobots' AZ-1594-23.

References

[1] Brassetti A., Ragusa A., Tedesco F., Prata F., Cacciatore L., Iannuzzi A., Bove A. M., Anceschi U., Proietti F., D'Annunzio S. et al. Robotic Surgery in Urology: History from PROBOT® to HUGOTM. Sensors. 2023; 23(16):7104. https://doi.org/10.3390/s23167104.

[2] Salcudean S. E., Moradi H., Black D. G. and Navab N., Robot-Assisted Medical Imaging: A Review, in Proceedings of the IEEE, vol. 110, no. 7, pp. 951–967, July 2022. https://doi.org/10.1109/JPROC.2022.3162840.

[3] Marmaglio P., Consolati D., Amici C., Tiboni M. Autonomous Vehicles for Healthcare Applications: A Review on Mobile Robotic Systems and Drones in Hospital and Clinical Environments. Electronics. 2023; 12(23):4791. https://doi.org/10.3390/electronics12234791.

[4] Mohebbi A. Human-Robot Interaction in Rehabilitation and Assistance: a Review. *Curr Robot Rep* **1**, 131–144 (2020). https://doi.org/10.1007/s43154-020-00015-4.

[5] Wheeler M. J. Overview on robotics in the laboratory. *Annals of Clinical Biochemistry.* 2007;44(3):209–218. https://doi.org/10.1258/000456307780480873.

[6] Breazeal C., Dautenhahn K., Kanda T. (2016). Social Robotics. In: Siciliano, B., Khatib, O. (eds.). Springer Handbook of Robotics. Springer Handbooks. Springer, Cham. https://doi.org/10.1007/978-3-319-32552-1_7.

[7] Hosny A., Parmar C., Quackenbush J. et al. Artificial intelligence in radiology. *Nat Rev Cancer* **18**, 500–510 (2018). https://doi.org/10.1038/s41568-018-0016-5.

[8] Rodriguez J. P. M., Rodriguez R., Silva V. W. K., Kitamura F. C., Corradi G. C. A., de Marchi A. C. B., Rieder R., 2022. Artificial intelligence as a tool for diagnosis in digital pathology whole slide images: A systematic review. Journal of Pathology Informatics 13, 100138. https://doi.org/10.1016/j.jpi.2022.100138.

[9] Carrasco-Ribelles L. A., Llanes-Jurado J., Gallego-Moll C., Cabrera-Bean M., Monteagudo-Zaragoza M., Violán C., Zabaleta-del-Olmo E., Prediction models using artificial intelligence and longitudinal data from electronic health records: a systematic methodological review, *Journal of the American Medical Informatics Association*, 30 (12) 2023, 2072–2082. https://doi.org/10.1093/jamia/ocad168.

[10] Lee D. (2025). Design Consideration of Autonomous Robots Based on Embodied Intelligence. *Clinical Research and Clinical Trials*, *12*(3).

[11] Pugin F., Bucher P., Morel P. (2011). History of robotic surgery: from AESOP® and ZEUS® to da Vinci®. Journal of visceral surgery, 148(5), pp. e3–e8.

[12] Cacciatore L., Costantini M., Tedesco F., Prata F., Machiella F., Iannuzzi A. et al. (2023). Robotic medtronic Hugo™ RAS system is now reality: introduction to a new simulation platform for training residents. *Sensors*, *23*(17), 7348.

[13] Conrad P. V., Mehdorn A. S., Alkatout I., Becker T., Beckmann J. H., Pochhammer J. (2024). The combination of laparoscopic and robotic surgery: first experience with the dexter robotic System™ in visceral surgery. *Life*, *14*(7), 874.

[14] Picozzi P., Nocco U., Labate C., Gambini I., Puleo G., Silvi F., Pezzillo A., Mantione R., Cimolin V. (2024) Advances in Robotic Surgery: A Review of New Surgical Platforms. Electronics 13(23):4675. https://doi.org/10.3390/electronics13234675.

[15] Guthart G. S, Salisbury J. K. (2000) The Intuitive TM/ telesurgery system: overview and application. In: Proceedings 2000 ICRA. Millennium Conference. IEEE International Conference on Robotics and Automation. Symposia Proceedings (Cat. No. 00CH37065). IEEE, pp. 618–621.

[16] Mayor N., Coppola A. S., Challacombe B. (2022). Past, present and future of surgical robotics. *Trends in Urology & Men's Health*, *13*(1), 7–10.

[17] De Fonzo J. F., Hassan A. T., Moll F. H., Mintz D. S., Schummers D. M., Maeder P. H., O'Rourke A. F. Systems and methods for concomitant medical procedures (US Patent Publication No. 2020/0085516 A1). US Patent and Trademark Office.

[18] Morgan A. A., Abdi J., Syed M. A. Q., Kohen G. E., Barlow P., Vizcaychipi M. P. (2022) Robots in Healthcare: a Scoping Review. Curr Robot Rep 3(4):271–280. https://doi.org/10.1007/s43154-022-00095-4.

[19] Piloni M., Bailo M., Gagliardi F., Mortini P., 2021. Resection of intracranial tumors with a robotic-assisted digital microscope: a preliminary experience with robotic scope. World Neurosurgery, 152, pp. e205–e211.

[20] Roche M. 2021. The MAKO robotic-arm knee arthroplasty system. Archives of orthopaedic and trauma surgery, 141(12), pp. 2043–2047.

[21] Lautenschlaeger P., Rathmann N., Rothfuss A., Kuhne M., Stork S., Noll M., Hetjens S., Schoenberg S.O., Stallkamp J., Diehl S. Learning Needle Placement in Soft Tissue with Robot-Assisted Navigation. In Vivo. 2023 Mar–Apr;37(2):702–708. https://doi.org/10.21873/invivo.13131. PMID: 36881085; PMCID: PMC10026658.

[22] Ricciardi R., Seshadri-Kreaden U., Yankovsky A., Dahl D., Auchincloss H., Patel N. M., Hebert A. E., Wright V. 2025. The COMPARE Study: comparing perioperative outcomes of oncologic minimally invasive laparoscopic, Da Vinci robotic, and open procedures: a systematic review and meta-analysis of the evidence. Annals of Surgery, 281(5), pp. 748–763.

[23] Chabot S., Calleja-Agius J., Horeman T., (2024). A comparison of clinical outcomes of robot-assisted and conventional laparoscopic surgery. Surgical Techniques Development, 13(1), pp. 22–57.

[24] Wee I. J. Y., Kuo L. J., Ngu J. C. Y., (2020). A systematic review of the true benefit of robotic surgery: Ergonomics. The international journal of medical robotics and computer assisted surgery, 16(4), p.e2113.

[25] Ostrander B. T., Massillon D., Meller L., Chiu Z. Y., Yip M., Orosco R. K., (2024). The current state of autonomous suturing: a systematic review. Surgical Endoscopy, 38(5), pp. 2383–2397.

[26] Hollmann W. Sports medicine: Fundamental aspects. In: Sport science in Germany: An interdisciplinary anthology. Berlin, Heidelberg: Springer Berlin Heidelberg, 1992. 105–118.

[27] Jadon G. R., Muthukrishnan J., Datta K. Sports and exercise medicine: Beyond injury management. Med J Armed Forces India. 2025 Jan-Feb;81(1):1–6. https://doi.org/10.1016/j.mjafi.2024.03.007. Epub 2024 May 13. PMID: 39872191; PMCID: PMC11762633.

[28] Esquenazi A., Talaty M., Packel A., Saulino M. (2017). The ReWalk powered exoskeleton to restore ambulatory function to individuals with thoracic-level motor-complete spinal cord injury. American Journal of Physical Medicine & Rehabilitation, 91(11), 911–921.

[29] Moucheboeuf G., Griffier R., Gasq D., Glize B., Bouyer L., Dehail P., Cassoudesalle H. Effects of robotic gait training after stroke: A meta-analysis. Ann Phys Rehabil Med. 2020 Nov;63(6):518–534. https://doi.org/10.1016/j.rehab.2020.02.008. Epub 2020 Mar 27. PMID: 32229177.

[30] Naughton M., Salmon P. M., Compton H. R., McLean S. Challenges and opportunities of artificial intelligence implementation within sports science and sports medicine teams. Front Sports Act Living. 2024 May 20;6:1332427. https://doi.org/10.3389/fspor.2024.1332427. PMID: 38832311; PMCID: PMC11144926.

[31] Zhang J., Jiang X., Xu Q., Cai E., Ding H. Effect of Virtual Reality-Based Training on Upper Limb Dysfunction during Post-Stroke Rehabilitation: A Meta-Analysis Combined with Meta-Regression. J Integr Neurosci. 2024 Dec 27;23(12):225. https://doi.org/10.31083/j.jin2312225. PMID: 39735963.

[32] Baronchelli F., Zucchella C., Serrao M., Intiso D., Bartolo M. (2021). The effect of robotic assisted gait training with Lokomat® on balance control after stroke: systematic review and meta-analysis. Frontiers in neurology, 12, 661815.

[33] Kóra S., Bíró A., Prontvai N., Androsics M., Drotár I., Prukner P. et al. (2024). Investigation of the effectiveness of the robotic restore soft exoskeleton in the development of early mobilization, walking, and coordination of stroke patients: a randomized clinical trial. Robotics, 13(3), 44.

[34] Wu J., Cheng H., Zhang J., Yang S., Cai S. Robot-Assisted Therapy for Upper Extremity Motor Impairment After Stroke: A Systematic Review and Meta-Analysis, Physical Therapy, Volume 101, Issue 4, April 2021, pzab010. https://doi.org/10.1093/ptj/pzab010.

[35] Louie D. R., Eng J. J. (2016). Powered robotic exoskeletons in post-stroke rehabilitation of gait: a scoping review. Journal of neuroengineering and rehabilitation, 13(1), 53.

[36] Patricio J. J. E., Sharifi M., Thu S. S. (2025). Mechatronics Development and Control of a Lower Limb Exoskeleton With High-Torque Assistance. Journal of Medical Devices, 19(3), 031002.

[37] Awad L. N., Bae J., Kudzia P., Long A., Hendron K., Holt K. G., Walsh C.J. (2020). A soft robotic exosuit improves walking in patients after stroke. Science Translational Medicine, 9(400), eaai9084.

[38] Clark W. E., Sivan M., O'Connor R. J. Evaluating the use of robotic and virtual reality rehabilitation technologies to improve function in stroke survivors: A narrative review. J Rehabil Assist Technol Eng. 2019 Nov 13;6:2055668319863557. https://doi.org/10.1177/2055668319863557. PMID: 31763052; PMCID: PMC6854750

[39] Altamimi Z.I. et al. (2025). IOT and AI Integration for Smart Prosthetic Limb Systems. In: Liu W., Wang Q., Feng J., Zhang W. (eds.). Procs 4th Int Conf Frontiers of Electronics, Information & Computation Technologies.

[40] Song H., Hsieh T. H., Yeon S. H. et al. Continuous neural control of a bionic limb restores biomimetic gait after amputation. Nat Med 30, 2010–2019 (2024).

[41] Omcirk D., Vetrovsky T., Padecky J., Malecek J., Tufano J. J. (2023). Validity of commercially available punch trackers. The Journal of Strength & Conditioning Research, 37(11), 2273–2281.

[42] Shan M., Li C., Sun J., Xie H., Qi Y., Niu W., Zhang M. (2025). The trunk segmental motion complexity and balance performance in challenging seated perturbation among individuals with spinal cord injury. Journal of NeuroEngineering and Rehabilitation, 22(1), 4.

[43] Hegi H., Kredel R. (2025). A Simple Model for Estimating the Kinematics of Tape-like Unstable Bases from Angular Measurements near Anchor Points. Sensors (Basel, Switzerland), 25(5), 1632.

[44] Palmcrantz S., Pennati G. V., Bergling H., Borg J. (2020). Feasibility and potential effects of using the electro-dress Mollii on spasticity and functioning in chronic stroke. Journal of neuroengineering and rehabilitation, 17(1), 109.

[45] Jaynes T. L. The legal ambiguity of advanced assistive bionic prosthetics: Where to define the limits of 'enhanced persons' in medical treatment. Clinical Ethics, 2021, 16. Jg., Nr. 3, S. 171–182.

[46] Compagna D., Şahinol M. Enhancement technologies and the politics of life. NanoEthics, 2022, 16. Jg., Nr. 1, S. 15–20.

[47] Firdhous M. F. M., Pirapaharan A. Cyborg Technology in Bio Engineering: Enabling Technologies, Implications, Applications and Future Trends. Journal of Human Centered Technology, 2025, 4. Jg., Nr. 1, S. 56–67.

[48] Henschel A., Laban G. Cross ES. What Makes a Robot Social? A Review of Social Robots from Science Fiction to a Home or Hospital Near You. Curr Robot Rep 2, 9–19 (2021). https://doi.org/10.1007/s43154-020-00035-0.

[49] Graterol W., Diaz-Amado J., Cardinale Y., Dongo I., Lopes-Silva E., Santos-Libarino C. Emotion Detection for Social Robots Based on NLP Transformers and an Emotion Ontology. *Sensors*. 2021; 21(4):1322. https://doi.org/10.3390/s21041322.

[50] Lee, Y. K., Jung, Y., Kang, G., & Hahn, S. (2023). Developing social robots with empathetic non-verbal cues using large language models. arXiv preprint arXiv:2308.16529.

[51] Rawal N., Stock-Homburg R. M. (2022). Facial emotion expressions in human–robot interaction: A survey. *International Journal of Social Robotics*, 14(7), 1583–1604.

[52] Gasteiger N., Lim J., Hellou M., MacDonald B. A., Ahn H. S. (2024). A scoping review of the literature on prosodic elements related to emotional speech in human-robot interaction. International Journal of Social Robotics, 16(4), 659–670.

[53] Klein S., Eixelberger T., Werling A., Kraus M., Shen S., André E., Folwerk J., Lang-Richter N., Wittenberg T. Robot-based Optical Assessment of Vital Signs in Healthcare with a Social Interface – Components, Workflows and Interfaces. Accepted to CURAC 2025, Heidelberg,

[54] Mireles C., Sanchez M., Cruz-Ortiz D., Salgado I., Chairez I. (2023). Home-care nursing controlled mobile robot with vital signal monitoring. Medical & Biological Engineering & Computing, 61(2), 399–420.

[55] Wittenberg T., Ernst A., Hauenstein T., Merz N., Sassen S., André E. et al.: A Concept of Emotion-Driven Human-Robot-Interaction for Nursing Care Scenarios, Procs' 2024 2nd International Conference on Integrated Systems in Medical Technologies (ISMT) https://doi.org/10.1109/ISMT62540.2024.10986197.

[56] Paterson M. (2023). Social robots and the futures of affective touch. The Senses and Society, 18(2), 110–125.

[57] Lai Y., Yuan S., Zhang B., Kiefer B., Li P., & Zell A. (2025). FAM-HRI: Foundation-Model Assisted Multi-Modal Human-Robot Interaction Combining Gaze and Speech. arXiv preprint arXiv:2503.16492.

[58] Maroto-Gómez M., Marqués-Villaroya S., Castillo J. C., Castro-González Á., & Malfaz M. (2023). Active learning based on computer vision and human–robot interaction for the user profiling and behavior personalization of an autonomous social robot. Engineering Applications of Artificial Intelligence, 117, 105631.

[59] Toussaint C., Schwarz P. T., & Petermann M. (2023, April). Navel-a social robot with verbal and non-verbal communication skills. In Extended Abstracts of the 2023 CHI Conference on Human Factors in Computing Systems (pp. 1–4).

[60] Gebhard P., Schneeberger T. Socially Interactive Agents as Interface to Health Technology. In: Manzeschke A. and Wittenberg T. (eds.). Ethical Perspectives on Artificial Intelligence in Biomedical Engineering, Chapter 20, DeGruyter, 2025.

[61] Inoue K., Wada K., Ito Y. Effective application of Paro: Seal type robots for disabled people in according to ideas of occupational therapists. In International Conference on Computers for Handicapped Persons (pp. 1321–1324). Berlin, Heidelberg: Springer Berlin Heidelberg. 2008.

[62] Pandey A. K., Gelin R., A Mass-Produced Sociable Humanoid Robot: Pepper: The First Machine of Its Kind, in IEEE Robotics & Automation Magazine 25(3) pp. 40–48, 2018.

[63] Moroz D., Baumgärtner K., & Schoch J. "Navel is like a friend."-Acceptance of a social robot in long-term care. ISG2026 Abstract Submission System, 23(2), 2025.

[64] Robaczewski A., Bouchard J., Bouchard K., Gaboury S. Socially Assistive Robots: The Specific Case of the NAO. Int J of Soc Robotics 13, 795–831. 2021.

[65] Goes N., Seßner J., Dziobek I., Steffan J., Struck M., Franke J., Kirst S., Naumann S., Lang, Wittenberg T. (2021): Evaluation of an algorithm for optical pulse de-tec-tion in chil-dren for application to the Pepper robot. Current Directions in Biomedical Engineering 7(2), pp. 484–487. https://www.degruyter.com/document/doi/10.1515/cdbme-2021-2123/html.

[66] Çetin I., (2024). The robot nurses. New Generation Technologies and Sustainability in Health: Current Studies; The International Society for Research in Education and Science: Konya, Turkey, 1.

[67] Graf B., Reiser U., Hägele M., Mauz K., Klein P. Robotic home assistant Care-O-bot® 3 – product vision and innovation platform, 2009 IEEE Workshop on Advanced Robotics and its Social Impacts, Tokyo, Japan, 2009, pp. 139–144. https://doi.org/10.1109/ARSO.2009.5587059.

[68] Lee A., Baker T. S., Bederson J. B., Rapoport B. I. Levels of autonomy in FDA-cleared surgical robots: a systematic review. NPJ Digit Med. 2024 Apr 26;7(1):103. https://doi.org/10.1038/s41746-024-01102-y. PMID: 38671232; PMCID: PMC11053143.

[69] Morris M. R., Sohl-Dickstein J., Fiedel N., Warkentin T., Dafoe A., Faust A., Farabet C., Legg S., 2024. Position: levels of AGI for operationalizing progress on the path to AGI, in: Proceedings of the 41st International Conference on Machine Learning, ICML'24. JMLR.org, Vienna, Austria.

[70] Pott P. P. Artificial Intelligence and Image-guided Interventions. In: Manzeschke A. and Wittenberg T. (eds.). Ethical Perspectives on Artificial Intelligence in Biomedical Engineering, Chapter 18, DeGruyter, 2025.

[71] Seidl K., Wöhrle H. AI and Edge / Embedded Devices for Healthcare. In: Manzeschke A. and Wittenberg T. (eds.). Ethical Perspectives on Artificial Intelligence in Biomedical Engineering, Chapter 15, DeGruyter, 2025.

[72] Kim J. W., Chen J. T., Hansen P., Shi L. X., Goldenberg A., Schmidgall S., Scheikl P. M., Deguet A., White B.M., Tsai D. R., Cha R., Jopling J., Finn C., Krieger A. SRT-H: A Hierarchical Framework for Autonomous Surgery via Language Conditioned Imitation Learning. https://doi.org/10.48550/arXiv.2505.10251.

[73] Sharkey N., Sharkey A. The eldercare factory. Gerontology. 2012;58(3):282–8. https://doi.org/10.1159/000329483. Epub 2011 Sep 24. PMID: 21952502.

Peter P. Pott

18 Artificial intelligence and image-guided interventions

18.1 Introduction

Robots are being used in interventional medical settings since the late 1990ies [1,2]. First commercially available systems were for instance ROBODOC [3], NEUROMATE [4], CYBERKNIFE [5], and also DaVinci [6]. Many other robotic systems under investigation then have reached advanced state of development or even early state of use but were not successful – neither surgically nor commercially. These rather large systems were in most cases based on bulky industrial robotic arms and promised better fit for prostheses, simplified Navigation during neurosurgery, more precision in radiation therapy, and better surgical outcome, and more ergonomic work conditions for surgeons.

The *Robotics Industries Association* (RIA) defines a robot as an "automatically controlled, reprogrammable multipurpose manipulator, programmable in three or more axes, which can be either fixed in place or mobile for use in industrial automation applications." [7] while ISO's definition states that a robot is "programmed actuated mechanism with a degree of autonomy to perform locomotion, manipulation or positioning" [8]. Both standards look at robots from a rather behavioral view point.

Looking at medical robots from this industrial point of view, it becomes clear, that the term "robot" is not met in all details in medical robots. Industrial robots are usually used for repetitive tasks such as handling items, pick & place procedures, welding, or manipulating objects in general. Industrial robots are universal systems that can manipulate or navigate different types of end- effectors that make them adaptable to certain jobs in a very specialized way – but the robot itself doesn't change. Apart from some mobile robots for logistic applications, which find their way through structured or unstructured environments, industrial robots do not make decisions. Rather, they are pre-programmed for certain tasks and might be adopted to little changes in their environment in a very limited way, e.g. by compensating for part tolerances. Industrial robots traditionally operate in their own environment – well protected from human intervention – and in rigid coordinate frames. However, in surgery and radiology, there are no repetitive tasks or items to be manipulated, but rather surgical tools and instruments as well as imaging devices (ultrasound-handpiece, X-ray sources, endoscopes, …) must be positioned with sufficient precision (in the sub-millimeter range) and orientated within the patient's coordinate system. Interventional robots work directly on, at or even in the human, hence being the absolute opposite compared to industrial applications. Consequently, interventional robots can be regarded as machines, that either

- realize a pre-defined trajectory with its end- effectors (milling out a cavity in bone, for example),
- hold a static pose in the patients coordinate frame (e.g. keeping a drill sleeve or an endoscope in place) and possibly compensating the patients' motions such as heartbeat or breathing, or
- replicate input movements from a master console such as tele-robots or tele-manipulators.

To achieve the desired medical outcomes, the major advantages of robotic systems are exploited. Robots are

- powerful and strong,
- fatigue-proof and always patient,
- can work under harsh environmental conditions, and are
- precise – but yet dumb.

In addition, robots can operate under stressful working conditions anytime of the day without the need for rest. In the following sections some applications for interventional robots are summed up with a focus on existing and future AI-based functions.

18.2 Applications

Looking at the advantages of robots described above, the major fields of use of interventional robots can be identified. These will be explained in the following.

18.2.1 Powerful and strong

Medical technology can be characterized by many scales, as the human being has very fine anatomical structures in the (sub-)micron range on the one hand, but can also exert large forces on the other hand, and furthermore has a considerable mass. This means that, on one side, very small and precise movements have to be carried out and, but on the other side, very large loads sometimes have to be moved. In many therapeutic situations robots can be useful to maneuver (imaging) devices or even patients in space. Typical healthcare-applications and scenarios are:

Milling cavities in bone for artificial joints on hip, knee, and shoulder. In this very early medical robot application, the robot performs a pre-programmed three-dimensional milling trajectory in the bone to precisely realize an implant bed for cement-free implantation of the metal stem or surface of a joint-replacing implant [9].

Replicating movements in tele-surgical settings. The robot sits next to the patient while the surgeon uses a console to define the desired robot movements in real-time. The distance between both ends can be between a few meters in the same room and up to a few thousand kilometers [10]. Still, the latency in data transmission must be kept as low as possible to allow for speedy procedures and safe operation [11].

Moving X-ray systems for intraoperative imaging. Here, a robot is used to navigate the well-known fluoroscopic C-arm with relation to the patient, the OR furniture (OR table, instrument tables, appliances), additional OR equipment and within other boundary conditions to achieve the desired imaging volume. While in standard C-arms, the radiation source and target are fixed to each other, in twin robot-based CT -systems, source and detector are only coupled by the line of projection, but are able to move independently from each other [12].

Aligning radiation sources such as X-ray, gamma, or electron beams for irradiating tumors while sparing healthy tissue. To do so, the beam is moved to different positions around the patient so that the lethal dose accumulates only in the region where all beams intersect. A precise dose-planning can thus be realized in the OR. Additionally, the personnel can control this intervention from a safe distance or outside the room [13].

Moving patients during radiation therapy. For instance, in neutron radiation therapy the radiation source is too large or too heavy to be moved. In this case, it appears easier to align the patient in relation to a beam fixed in space. This is achieved by mounting a patient bed to the robot and immobilize the patient by e.g. vacuum drapes. During the application of the radiation therapy, it must be made sure that the robot itself is "hardened" to withstand the radiation.

Moving limbs during physiotherapy or for other rehabilitation approaches. As the repetitive movement of limbs is exhaustive for the therapist but very purposeful for the patient, robots can take over the repetitive part while the actual movement trajectories are defined by the therapist or the patient [14].

Navigating magnets for capsule endoscopy [15] or magnetic particle therapy [16]. To provide a defined magnetic field gradient over the patient with relation to e.g. inner organs, large permanent magnets or coils need to be positioned and moved against the patient. Robotic devices can be built in a way to allow this without additional input by the personnel.

Directing High Intensity Focused Ultrasound (HIFU) sources [17] for cancer therapy in CT scanners or MRI devices. The active treatment volume of a HIFU source must be aligned in the patient coordinate frame to properly treat the tissue under imaging control. This can be achieved by dedicated kinematics that fit in the small gantry of scanners. This also spares the surgeon from additional radiation in the case of CT-based interventional radiology [18].

Positioning needles or drill sleeves for interventions during CT, MRI, or X-ray-controlled imaging. Small and slender robot kinematics allow the use of needle-based interventions in the confined space between the patient and the bore of tomographs. By doing so, interventions become faster because the patient does not have to be moved in and out the scanner for each needle. With conventional articulated arm robots drill sleeves or needles can be place in the patient or orientated correctly to be then manually inserted by a surgeon. Advanced trajectory planning based on real-time acquired X-ray imaging data allows to spare other anatomical structures and to precisely reach the desired region in the body [19].

18.2.2 Fatigue proof and always patient

Robots are designed in a way that allows continuous application under full load and with the specified precision, which can be well in the sub-millimeter range. This applies to any trajectory: from continuous motion with constant velocity along a pre-defined path, to exactly holding still in the world coordinate frame or the patient coordinate frame. Consequently, robots supporting surgical interventions can, e.g., be deployed to position needles for biopsy or drill sleeves for neurosurgical interventions in the patient's coordinate frame according to pre-operative planning or intra-operative decision-making. The same is valid for the navigation of endoscopes in minimally invasive laparoscopic surgery. Here, the robot moves the endoscope or holds it steady, according to inputs by the surgeon or following the trajectory of his or her instruments. This function is not limited to static tasks but can be used for dynamic stabilization to compensate for heartbeat or breathing movement [20]. In addition, preset trajectories of the endoscope tip can be recalled. Finally, the lasting strength and perseverance of robots allows the development of massage robots.

As machines, robots do not get tired, un-concentrated, or innerved by long-lasting, repetitive, or boring tasks. During collaboration with humans, robots thus will not contradict and do not tend to rage. This fact makes them predestined for tele-surgical interventions – which need a reliable and broad data connection with very low latency – or repetitive tasks such as hair transplantation and deployment for probe-handling in a medical lab.

One emerging field of robots in the medical environment is the robotic scrub nurse. Here, the robot is assisting the surgeon in a way comparable to the human [21,22]. It can hand over surgical instruments and materials, take it back and organize the process in the surgical theater. To achieve this, the robot not only must be safe in its movements but it must also be able to identify up to 150 different surgical instruments or items in the tray, grasp and pass objects to a human physician and take them back without a risk of injury. Moreover, it must be able to understand the progress of the intervention and predict the next instrument to be used.

18.2.3 Harsh environmental conditions

As robots are not prone to injury or negative aspects of radiation, they can be deployed under harsh conditions. This includes radiation therapy and X-ray based interventions as most prominent cases, but is also valid for situations with many human interactions.

Robots can be deployed under such harsh conditions. This explains why early medical robotic systems are used for radiation therapy. Here, a radiation source (gamma, electron beam, X-ray, neutron...) must be positioned within the patient's coordinate frame – or vice versa: In the case of very large appliances such as neutron sources, the patient is positioned against the beam. In both cases the radiation dose delivered to the personnel must be kept to a minimum. It is thus straight forward that the radiation source is mounted to the robot and the patient is more or less rigidly fixed to the robot's base coordinate system. Based on pre-operatively acquired CT or MRI images, an adequate dose and related trajectory planning can be performed. Doing so, delicate structures like nerves, the urinary tract, blood vessels, or whole organs can be spared from high doses while tumors are precisely radiated from a set of different angles. The robot then moves the beam to pre-defined positions and orientation and delivers the desired dose. Patient ego movements from heartbeat and breathing can be compensated for by deploying e.g. a stereo X-ray system that tracks tantalum fiducials implanted in the tumor [23] or by using optical stereo or time-of flight (ToF) camera systems tracking the surface of the patient [24]. Consequently, the robot 'breathes' together with the patient.

In the future, AI-based image analysis and patient-individual anatomical models derived from a generic 'first guess' and extrapolated from a set of easy-to-measure parameters of a patient could be used to predict organ movement from camera images of the patient only, hence sparing the additional X-ray dose and the implantation of fiducials. This can be further enhanced by patient-specific models (also referred as 'anatomical twins' [43]), which account for anatomic peculiarities of a patient.

18.2.4 Precise – yet dumb

While all (industrial as well as surgical) robots are still less precise than tooling machines milling metals with sub-micron precision in production facilities, surgical robots can be used for milling cavities in bones for e.g. the implantation of hip or knee joints [9], pedicle screw placement [25], or cochlea implants [26,27] with a considerable and sufficient precision. Such systems can also be used for bone repositioning or drilling in pedicles. In these cases, the robot follows pre-operatively defined trajectories that take into account the implants' geometry, the bone's structure, and the required orientation of the implant. The traditional way of mechanically digitizing the bones' surfaces during the opening phase of the intervention or even using pre-operatively implanted fiducials can in the future be replaced by optical recognition of surfaces where AI-based approaches will be used to determine the transformation between the pre-operatively known patient coordinate frame from imaging and the intraoperatively defined real patient coordinate frame. This registration process is crucial to achieve the desired precision at the desired location in the bone.

Also in tele-surgical applications, the robots' precision and tremor-free movements are useful when it comes to delicate tasks in soft-tissue surgery. Here, the patient's coordinate frame is not easy to define due to missing bony landmarks. Because the human operator defines the robot's trajectory in real-time the challenge with this coordinate frame is of less importance. Still, it would be advantageous to know the exact location of the robot's end effectors in the patient's coordinate frame and supply the surgeon with additional anatomical information. To allow this, AI algorithms will be used to interpret the situation and merge further data into an augmented reality (AR) image in future applications [28]. In addition, the definition of 'no-go-areas' can be helpful to avoid unintended cutting of structures or other injuries – even outside the surgeon's field of view.

18.3 AI comes into play

As described briefly in the previous sections, Artificial Intelligence in medical robotics has several aspects. These include the automatic analysis of image data such as MRI, CT, US, endoscopy or optical camera images, the continuous monitoring and analysis of vital parameters and physiological values such as ECG, EMG, or EEG during an intervention, the control of movements (e.g. path planning, motion prediction/compensation, or system identification for control theory), and finally the decision-making in diagnosis or therapy.

18.3.1 Example 1: Radiation Therapy

Radiation therapy utilizes ionizing radiation to treat malignant and, in some cases, benign conditions. The primary goal of radiation therapy is to deliver precise doses of radiation to cancerous tissues in order to induce irreparable damage to their DNA, thereby inhibiting cell division and promoting cell death. This approach exploits the fact that cancer cells are typically more sensitive to DNA damage and have a diminished capacity for repair compared to normal, healthy cells. Radiation can be administered either externally or internally via radioactive sources placed inside or near the tumor (brachytherapy).

Depending on the cancer type, location, and stage, radiation therapy is often integrated into a multimodal treatment plan, used in conjunction with surgery, chemotherapy, or immunotherapy. It can serve curative, palliative, or adjuvant purposes – either aiming to eradicate the disease, relieve symptoms, or reduce the risk of recurrence after surgical removal of a tumor. Advanced imaging technologies and treatment planning systems allow for highly targeted radiation delivery, minimizing exposure to surrounding healthy tissue and reducing side effects.

Ionizing radiation used in external radiation therapy primarily comes from the following sources:

X-rays – (photon radiation) are generated by linear accelerators (linac), which accelerate electrons on very high energies (e.g. CyberKnife up to 6 MeV). The electrons then hit a target and lead to X-ray radiation. X-rays are the most commonly used form of external beam radiation therapy. They can penetrate deep into the body and are suitable for treating a wide range of tumors.

Gamma Rays – Emitted by radioactive isotopes (e.g. cobalt-60), gamma rays are used in both external therapies and internal therapies such as brachytherapy .

Electron Beams – Also produced by linear accelerators are used for treating superficial tumors, as they deposit most of their energy near the surface of the body and do not penetrate deeply.

Proton Beams – allow for highly targeted treatment, delivering maximum energy at a specific depth (the Bragg peak), which minimizes damage to surrounding tissue.

Neutron Beams – deliver high biological effectiveness and also greater risk to normal tissue and are used in specialized settings for radioresistant tumors.

Heavy Ions (e.g., Carbon Ions) – offer enhanced precision and biological effectiveness, but are available in only a few advanced centers worldwide.

These different radiation sources vary in their physical properties and biological effects, allowing clinicians to tailor treatment to the specific characteristics of the tumor and the patient. By continuously changing the direction, the rays or particles are concentrated in the target region, while healthy tissue can be spared.

For internal radiation therapy (brachytherapy) different isotopes are placed in or near the tumor. As with external radiation, a precise dose planning must be achieved to prevent healthy tissue from excessive irradiation. E.g., in prostate cancer, Iodine-125, Palladium-103, Cesium-131 are used in low-dose radiation settings, while Iridium-192 is used for high-dose treatment. Half-life rates vary from 9.7 days (Caesium) to 74 days (Iridium).

Medical robots in radiation therapy are currently incorporating various AI-based functions to improve precision, efficiency, and patient outcomes [29]. Some key AI applications within radiation therapy include:

Treatment Planning – AI assists in automating and optimizing radiation therapy plans by analyzing pre-operatively obtained medical images (CT, MRI, PET, US etc.) to accurately locate, identify, segment, and characterize tumorous lesions and surrounding organs.

Motion Tracking and Adaptation – To ensure accuracy and reduce radiation loss, AI-powered robots can track the patient's voluntary and unvoluntary movements (such as breathing and even heartbeat) and adjust the radiation beams and trajectories accordingly.

Dose Optimization – AI algorithms help determine the most effective radiation dose distribution, by balancing tumor control with reduced side effects.

Workflow Automation – AI streamlines administrative and operational processes in the OR, hence reducing the time needed for treatment planning and execution.

Examples where AI-based control modules are already included and implemented for adaptive therapy and real-time adjustments are systems like Varian's *Ethos* (Varian Medical Systems, Inc, Palo Alto, CA, USA) [30], *CyberKnife* (Accuray Corp. Madison, WI, USA) [5]. Radiotherapy solutions by Elekta AB (Stockholm, SE) already implement integrated AI for adaptive therapy and real-time adjustments [31].

Elekta *Gammaknife* [32] and Varan *Ethos* [30] are AI-driven adaptive radiation therapy systems designed to personalize treatment for cancer patients in real time. Nevertheless, they are gantry-based devices – not real robots. They integrate artificial intelligence, intraoperative imaging, and automation to improve the accuracy and efficiency of radiation therapy. Consequently, the AI-aspect does not concern the device as such, but the whole treatment process. The *Ethos* system allows for daily adaptation of treatment plans based on a patient's anatomy at the time of treatment. It's AI algorithm automatically analyses and adjusts the radiation dose based on daily CT images [33]. Before each treatment session, the system uses a cone-beam CT to capture the patient's actual anatomy and the specific location, orientation and size of the lesion to be treated. The AI-based planning supports the surgeon in comparing these current images with the original treatment plan and suggests to make necessary adjustments. AI is also used to optimize the dose distribution to minimize exposure to healthy tissue. By optimizing the systems' movements using an AI-approach in general, the actual treatment time per session is strongly reduced, hence leading to more comfort for the patient and the chance of more treatments per time for the user. Finally, the whole workflow is streamlined, reducing manual intervention and increasing efficiency for medical staff.

In contrast, the *CyberKnife* (Accuray Corp, Madison, WI, USA) [5] moves a radiation source around the patient to deliver radiation with highest intensity in the tumor only. The duration of the radiation sessions can be longer but their number can be reduced. Again, the initial treatment definition, the actual trajectory based on intra-operative online X-ray images, the session dose planning, and the treatment workflow are supported by AI-based procedures [29]. For continuous tracking of the tumor during breathing, *CyberKnife* uses Recursive Least Squares (RLS) adaptive filtering and is able to learn from previously obtained motion patterns to adjust beam positioning without stopping treatment. In addition, Kalman filtering is deployed to estimate a tumor's future position based on historical motion data. To recognize and segment tumors from X-ray images, *CyberKnife's* imaging system applies Deep Convolutional Neural Networks (DCNNs) [34]. AI is also able to detect markers or anatomical features (such as bones) to track tumors that are difficult to see on X-rays (e.g., soft tissue tumors). This is crucial for marker-less tumor tracking, like in lung cancer treatment [35]. While the dose distribution and radiation scattering estimation is performed using Monte Carlo Simulations, the derivation of the optimal angles of the beam is based on a Reinforcement Learning approach based on individual patient anatomy and is able to obtain the best approach to maximize tumor coverage and minimize side effects [35]. Finally, Natural Language Processing (NLP) for Clinical Decision Support (CDS, suggesting treatment modifications) is used and the system helps to automate routine tasks like contouring tumors and generating treatment plans [36].

18.3.2 Example 2: Robotic Scrub Nurse

The operating theater is a highly complex, functional workplace characterized by increasing differentiation and specialization of tasks, where the growing mental and physical strain on staff is a major problem [37]. Combined with a shortage of skilled personnel [38], there is a need to reduce the workload of medical staff. Automated and robotic systems offer potential for relief. One of the most highly stressed roles in the operating theater is that of the surgical technician (scrub nurse). The scrub nurse is responsible for the organized and orderly workflow in the operating theater. Fast and proactive instrumentation is crucial to the success of the operation. Scrub nurses therefore have knowledge of anatomy and the procedure involved in the operation. This results in a fast and smooth workflow, which is particularly important in critical phases of the operation. To ensure that this is not interrupted, error-free communication between the surgeon and the scrub nurse is important. Much of the communication is non-verbal. Non-verbal communication includes body posture, gestures, mood, tone of voice and facial expressions. In the past, attempts have been made to implement robotic systems for handling surgical instruments in the operating theater. Worldwide, a number of research projects investigate robotic scrub nurses. The majority of these approaches were not pursued further, presumably because their implementation in existing surgical workflows had not been investigated. Still, several interesting approaches exist. Outstanding examples are the device developed at Leibniz Universität Hannover, DE [39] using both, electromagnetic and granular jamming grippers [40], the eye-tracking-based device under development at Imperial College London [41], or the multi-finger gripper robot SASHA-OR developed at TU München, DE [42]. These systems provide deep insight into workflows and especially communication, gripping technology, gesture-based control, and AI-based object recognition.

At the moment, no robotic scrub nurse system reaches an advanced stage of development. The current challenges are:

User interaction and acceptance– robotic scrub nurse systems must be able to communicate in both directions. This means they need to understand not only the situation and the process, but also predict the users' needs. Only then these systems will provide an advantage and be accepted by the personnel.

Safety and regulatory approvals – Medical robots must pass strict safety standards. This not only applies to the robots' movements but also to gripper technologies, trajectory planning, biocompatibility, and hygiene.

AI perception limitations – Recognizing and correctly handling a variety of up to 150 different tools and objects in dynamic surgical environments is challenging, thus safe algorithms and multimodal or redundant sensors must be deployed.

Integration issues – Robotic scrub nurse systems need to work smoothly with existing surgical teams and workflows. Thus, they must be integrated in the surgical workflow, communication, and procedures in a meaningful and advantageous way.

Cost – the deployment of robotic scrub nurse systems must come with less financial effort than human scrub nurses. This can be realized by using off-the-shelf hardware, universal end-effectors, and simple reprocessing methods.

To achieve the above-mentioned goals and meet the resulting requirements of cost, integration, perception, and safety AI technology is needed to:

Recognize the environment – by integrating sensor data from optical cameras (white light, IR, depth), radar/lidar etc. as well as background information on the procedure as such, the particular patient, future robotic scrub nurse systems will be able to recognize their environment and particular situation, devices, and instruments.

Prediction of the surgeons' needs – the background information together with online learning will make it possible to adopt to the surgeons' particular needs in every situation and surgical phase.

Communication – humans are able to communicate not only straight-forward verbally but also by inflection, hand gestures, gaze, and even eyebrows or body language. Consequently, speech-, tone-, gesture-, and situational recognition must be implemented on scrub nurse robots.

Path planning – the robot's movements in the OR must be in conjunction with the personnel but under the restriction of collision avoidance. The same applies to boundary conditions like OR furniture, devices and other objects.

18.4 Ethics and interventional robots

When interventional medical robots are involved in decision-making processes, particularly those affecting patient outcomes, ethics become especially multifaceted. One of the central questions is: Where and when do robots make decisions – before or after human clinicians do? In practice, medical AI and robotic systems often operate in decision-support roles, offering recommendations based on vast data analysis. However, as autonomy increases, robots may act within pre-defined parameters, such as adjusting a surgical path in real time to avoid a vessel. This raises the crucial issue of delegated authority: who decides that the robot can decide? Typically, it is human designers, clinicians, or institutions that set the scope of the robot's autonomy – implicitly or explicitly programming its decision space. Hence, the way these decisions are made has to be defined during the development of the robot.

In case the robot makes the decision, which is then confirmed by the human surgeon, he or she could tend to blindly follow the AI after a number of good experiences. Vice versa, if AI algorithms confirm the human surgeon's decision, the algorithm could learn behaviors that differ from the initial programming. Both cases or situations must be considered when programming AI for interventional applications.

Responsibility, then, becomes a shared and diffused concept. Engineers create the system, clinicians deploy it, hospitals approve its use, and regulators certify its safety. But when something goes wrong the question of blame is far from straightforward. It would be often unclear whether fault lies in the algorithm's design, the data it was trained on, the clinical context, or the oversight mechanisms. Moreover, risk itself becomes a different entity in robotic intervention. When humans take risks, we assume intention, judgment, and accountability. Robots, however, do not possess intentions – they execute programmed responses or learned patterns. The ethical weight of risk, therefore, shifts from the agent taking the action to the system that permits or constrains that action. In this way, robotic risk is always human risk, displaced but not diminished. This displacement complicates traditional notions of consent, trust, and moral responsibility, requiring new ethical frameworks that acknowledge distributed agency without diluting accountability.

18.5 Conclusion

Artificial intelligence is increasingly integrated into medical robotics, ORs, and planning procedures. Supporting tasks are ranging from surgical assistance to rehabilitation and planning. While the level of AI involvement varies across applications, its presence generally enhances accuracy, adaptability, and decision-making. Current systems often combine human control with AI-driven functions, reflecting a trend toward collaboration rather than full autonomy. As both robotics and AI evolve, their intersection is likely to expand the scope and effectiveness of medical interventions, while continuing to require careful oversight and ethical consideration.

References

[1]   Preising B., Hsia T. C., and Mittelstadt B. "A literature review: robots in medicine," IEEE engineering in medicine and biology magazine : the quarterly magazine of the Engineering in Medicine & Biology Society, vol. 10, no. 2, pp. 13–22, 1991. https://doi.org/10.1109/51.82001.

[2]   Pott P. P., Scharf H.-P., and Schwarz M. L. R. "Today's state of the art in surgical robotics," Computer aided surgery : official journal of the International Society for Computer Aided Surgery, vol. 10, no. 2, pp. 101–132, 2005. https://doi.org/10.3109/10929080500228753.

[3]   Taylor R. H. et al., "An image-directed robotic system for precise orthopaedic surgery," IEEE Trans. Robot. Automat., vol. 10, no. 3, pp. 261–275, 1994. https://doi.org/10.1109/70.294202.

[4]   Lavallee S., Troccaz J., Gaborit L., Cinquin P., Benabid A. L. and Hoffmann D. "Image guided operating robot: a clinical application in stereotactic neurosurgery," in Proceedings 1992 IEEE International Conference on Robotics and Automation, Nice, France, May. 1992, pp. 618–624.

[5]   Chang S. D., Main W., Martin D. P., Gibbs I. C., and Heilbrun M. P. "An Analysis of the Accuracy of the CyberKnife: A Robotic Frameless Stereotactic Radiosurgical System," Neurosurgery, vol. 52, no. 1, 2003. [Online]. Available: https://journals.lww.com/neurosurgery/fulltext/2003/01000/an_analy-sis_of_the_accuracy_of_the_cyberknife__a.18.aspx.

[6]   Cadeddu J. A., Stoianovici D., and Kavoussi L. R. "Robotics in urologic surgery," Urology, vol. 49, no. 4, pp. 501–507, 1997. https://doi.org/10.1016/s0090-4295(96)00561-4.

[7]   Industrial Robots and Robot Systems – Safety Requirements, ANSI/RIA R15.06–2012, Robotic Industries Association.

[8]   Robotik und Robotikgeräte – Wörterbuch, ISO 8373:2012, International Standard Organisation.

[9]   Suarez-Ahedo C. et al. "Revolutionizing orthopedics: a comprehensive review of robot-assisted surgery, clinical outcomes, and the future of patient care," Journal of robotic surgery, vol. 17, no. 6, pp. 2575–2581, 2023. https://doi.org/10.1007/s11701-023-01697-6.

[10]   Marescaux J. et al. "Transatlantic robot-assisted telesurgery," Nature, vol. 413, no. 6854, pp. 379–380, 2001. https://doi.org/0.1038/35096636.

[11]   Zidane I. F., Khattab Y., Rezeka S., and El-Habrouk M. "Robotics in laparoscopic surgery – A review," Robotica, vol. 41, no. 1, pp. 126–173, 2023. https://doi.org/10.1017/S0263574722001175.

[12]   Kunz A. S. et al., "Twin Robotic Gantry-Free Cone-Beam CT in Acute Elbow Trauma," Radiology, vol. 306, no. 3, e221200, 2023. https://doi.org/10.1148/radiol.221200.

[13]   Lanza C. et al. "Robotics in Interventional Radiology: Review of Current and Future Applications," Technology in Cancer Research & Treatment, vol. 22, 15330338231152084, 2023. https://doi.org/10.1177/15330338231152084.

[14]   Banyai A. D., and Brişan C. "Robotics in Physical Rehabilitation: Systematic Review," Healthcare (Basel, Switzerland), vol. 12, no. 17, 2024. https://doi.org/10.3390/healthcare12171720.

[15]   Khattab Y., and Pott P. P. "Active/Robotic Capsule Endoscopy – A Review," Alexandria Engineering Journa, submitted.

[16]   Kraan A., and Del Guerra A. "Technological Developments and Future Perspectives in Particle Therapy: A Topical Review," IEEE Transactions on Radiation and Plasma Medical Sciences, vol. 8, no. 5, pp. 453–481, 2024. https://doi.org/10.1109/TRPMS.2024.3372189.

[17]   Mihcin S., and Melzer A. "Principles of focused ultrasound," Minimally invasive therapy & allied technologies : MITAT : official journal of the Society for Minimally Invasive Therapy, vol. 27, no. 1, pp. 41–50, 2018. https://doi.org/10.1080/13645706.2017.1414063.

[18]   Gunderman A., Montayre R., Ranjan A., and Chen Y. "Review of Robot-Assisted HIFU Therapy," Sensors (Basel, Switzerland), vol. 23, no. 7, 2023. https://doi.org/10.3390/s23073707.

[19]   Matsui Y. et al., "Robotic systems in interventional oncology: a narrative review of the current status," International journal of clinical oncology, vol. 29, no. 2, pp. 81–88, 2024. https://doi.org/10.1007/s10147-023-02344-8.

[20]   Ozhasoglu C. et al., "Synchrony – Cyberknife Respiratory Compensation Technology," Medical Dosimetry, vol. 33, no. 2, pp. 117–123, 2008. https://doi.org/10.1016/j.meddos.2008.02.004.

[21]   Wagner L. et al., "Robotic scrub nurse to anticipate surgical instruments based on real-time laparoscopic video analysis," Communications medicine, vol. 4, no. 1, p. 156, 2024. https://doi.org/10.1038/s43856-024-00581-0.

[22] Bernhard L. et al. "Mobile service robots for the operating room wing: balancing cost and performance by optimizing robotic fleet size and composition," International journal of computer assisted radiology and surgery, vol. 18, no. 2, pp. 195–204, 2023. https://doi.org/10.1007/s11548-022-02735-8.

[23] Kothary N. et al. "Safety and efficacy of percutaneous fiducial marker implantation for image-guided radiation therapy," Journal of vascular and interventional radiology : JVIR, vol. 20, no. 2, pp. 235–239, 2009. https://doi.org/10.1016/j.jvir.2008.09.026.

[24] Placht S., Stancanello J., Schaller C., Balda M., and Angelopoulou E. "Fast time-of-flight camera based surface registration for radiotherapy patient positioning," Medical Physics, vol. 39, no. 1, pp. 4–17, 2012. https://doi.org/10.1118/1.3664006.

[25] Shoham M., Burman M., Zehavi E., Joskowicz L., Batkilin E., and Kunicher Y. "Bone-mounted miniature robot for surgical procedures: concept and clinical applications," IEEE Trans. Robot. Automat., vol. 19, no. 5, pp. 893–901, 2003. https://doi.org/10.1109/tra.2003.817075.

[26] Panara K., Shahal D., Mittal R., and Eshraghi A. A. "Robotics for Cochlear Implantation Surgery: Challenges and Opportunities," Otology & neurotology : official publication of the American Otological Society, American Neurotology Society [and] European Academy of Otology and Neurotology, vol. 42, no. 7, e825-e835, 2021. https://doi.org/10.1097/MAO.0000000000003165.

[27] Caversaccio M. et al., "Robotic middle ear access for cochlear implantation: First in man," PloS one, vol. 14, no. 8, e0220543, 2019. https://doi.org/10.1371/journal.pone.0220543.

[28] Fu J. et al. "Recent Advancements in Augmented Reality for Robotic Applications: A Survey," Actuators, vol. 12, no. 8, p. 323, 2023. https://doi.org/10.3390/act12080323.

[29] Panda D. K., Das S. R., and Kumar S. "Artificial Intelligence (AI)-Driven Adaptive Motion Management in Helical and Robotic Radiotherapy: Innovations, Challenges, and Future Directions," Cureus, vol. 17, no. 4, 2025. https://doi.org/10.7759/cureus.81702.

[30] Yoon S. W. et al. "Initial Evaluation of a Novel Cone-Beam CT-Based Semi-Automated Online Adaptive Radiotherapy System for Head and Neck Cancer Treatment – A Timing and Automation Quality Study," Cureus, vol. 12, no. 8, e9660, 2020. https://doi.org/10.7759/cureus.9660.

[31] Barten D. L. et al., "Towards artificial intelligence-based automated treatment planning in clinical practice: A prospective study of the first clinical experiences in high-dose-rate prostate brachytherapy," Brachytherapy, vol. 22, no. 2, pp. 279–289, 2023. https://doi.org/10.1016/j.brachy.2022.11.013.

[32] Narayanasamy G., Saenz D., Cruz W., Ha C. S., Papanikolaou N., and Stathakis S. "Commissioning an Elekta Versa HD linear accelerator," Journal of applied clinical medical physics, vol. 17, no. 1, pp. 179–191, 2016. https://doi.org/10.1120/jacmp.v17i1.5799.

[33] Pokharel S., Pacheco A., and Tanner S. "Assessment of efficacy in automated plan generation for Varian Ethos intelligent optimization engine," Journal of applied clinical medical physics, vol. 23, no. 4, e13539, 2022. https://doi.org/10.1002/acm2.13539.

[34] Miao Y. et al. "Three-dimensional dose prediction based on deep convolutional neural networks for brain cancer in CyberKnife: accurate beam modelling of homogeneous tissue," BJR Open, vol. 6, no. 1, tzae023, 2024. https://doi.org/10.1093/bjro/tzae023.

[35] Miao Y. et al. "Dose prediction of CyberKnife Monte Carlo plan for lung cancer patients based on deep learning: robust learning of variable beam configurations," Radiat Oncol, vol. 19, no. 1, p. 170, 2024. https://doi.org/10.1186/s13014-024-02531-5.

[36] Ahmed U., Iqbal K., Aoun M., and Khan G. Natural Language Processing for Clinical Decision Support Systems: A Review of Recent Advances in Healthcare, 2023. [Online]. Available: https://www.researchgate.net/profile/muhammad_aoun2/publication/373097248_natural_language_processing_for_clinical_decision_support_systems_a_review_of_recent_advances_in_healthcare.

[37] Berentzen J., and Lennartz S. "Arbeitsplatz Operationsabteilung: Physische Belastungen für OP-Personal – Möglichkeiten der Gesundheitsförderung und Prävention," OP-JOURNAL, vol. 26, no. 01, pp. 48–53, 2010. https://doi.org/10.1055/s-0030-1265094.

[38] Marć M., Bartosiewicz A., Burzyńska J., Chmiel Z., and Januszewicz P. "A nursing shortage – a prospect of global and local policies," International nursing review, vol. 66, no. 1, pp. 9–16, 2019. https://doi.org/10.1111/inr.12473.

[39] Badilla-Solórzano J., Ihler S., and Seel T. "HybGrip: a synergistic hybrid gripper for enhanced robotic surgical instrument grasping," Int J CARS, vol. 19, no. 12, pp. 2363–2370, 2024. https://doi.org/10.1007/s11548-024-03245-5.

[40] Friedrich J., Hotz J., Worbs L., Weiland S., and Pott P. P. "https://www.degruyter-brill.com/document/doi/10.1515/cdbme-2023-1044/xml," (in 9), Current Directions in Biomedical Engineering, no. 1, pp. 174–177, 1044. [Online]. Available: https://www.degruyter.com/document/doi/10.1515/cdbme-2023-1044/html.

[41] Ezzat A., Kogkas A., Holt J., Thakkar R., Darzi A., and Mylonas G. "An eye-tracking based robotic scrub nurse: proof of concept," Surg Endosc, vol. 35, no. 9, pp. 5381–5391, 2021. https://doi.org/10.1007/s00464-021-08569-w.

[42] Wagner L. et al. "Versatile end effector for laparoscopic robotic scrub nurse," Int J CARS, vol. 18, no. 9, pp. 1589–1600, 2023. https://doi.org/10.1007/s11548-023-02892-4.

[43] Wesarg S., Kohlhammer J. "Digital Twins and AI in Health". In: Manzeschke A. and Wittenberg T. (eds.). Ethical Perspectives on Artifical Intelligence in Biomedical Engineering, Chapter 19, DeGruyter, 2025.

Stefan Wesarg, Jörn Kohlhammer

19 Digital twins and AI in health

19.1 Digital twins in the health sector

The digitization in the health sector and the representation and access to medical data is a very timely and much discussed topic in Germany and beyond. Even if we set aside the legal discussions about accessibility to patient data and the EU's general data protection regulation (GDPR), there are many challenges in aligning the representation of medical data across institutions and the secure and authorized access to patient data. The interest in this highly sensitive medical data is driven by the promise of machine learning and data analytics, namely that in all this data there are insights and knowledge that can bring benefits to patients through better diagnosis and more personalized treatments and drugs. This chapter wants to shed some light on medical digital twins as an emerging form of medical data representation, and the benefits and pitfalls of using AI on and with these digital twins. We will start with an introduction of medical digital twins (MDTs), before we look at cohort studies and current applications of MDTs. The following sections will then focus on AI methods that are applied to MDTs and how medical decision making can benefit from this. Finally, we will cover ethical considerations in this area.

19.1.1 Medical digital twins and shadows

Medical digital twins (MDTs) denote a comprehensive model of a patient's history and health status. Ideally, they are based on anatomical, physiological, diagnosis- and treatment-related information from multiple sources. While often incomplete, an MDT may also provide derived information about the patient based on known relations between the medical data. A medical digital twin also comprises information that is among the most critical and sensitive data according to the EU GDPR (General Data Protection Regulation), motivating a dedicated approach to secure such MDTs. Nevertheless, it is essential to be able to transparently share the data contained in MDTs in a fine-grained way to give medical experts in different institutions access to specific parts of the data.

The essential concept of a *digital twin* (DT) was first described by Grieves for manufacturing organizations [1]. In his concept, he described a *physical object* (PO), such as a manufacturing machine, and a corresponding instance of a digital model/process (i.e., the DT) that mirrors the state of the PO using a bidirectional connection between them. The connection between the two entities should allow data to flow from the PO to the DT and vice versa. Data from the PO updates the DT's state model of the PO while data from the DT can adjust the PO's settings. However, the DT can be regarded more than a remote control as it may process data from additional sources, e.g., data from environmental sensors, to find and propagate settings that may further improve the PO's performance. In the works by van der Horn and Mahadevan [2] and Jones at al. [3], an overview of recent background and details on DTs in general can be found. Of course, DTs are not limited to manufacturing but have also been discussed for other fields like agricultural production [4], medicine [5–7], or smart cities [8]. In this chapter, we will focus on MDTs.

An MDT can be described by observations of and measurements taken from a certain patient [9]. By processing a patient's data, an analytical model can be built for the MDT that can provide a comprehensive view of the patient [10] which may support health professionals in achieving timely diagnoses, possibly simulate different diagnostic scenarios, and to develop personalized treatment plans [11].

If we view an MDT as a holistic medical data model of a specific patient, then only a part of it will typically be required by a certain health professional. That part, e.g, medical data on the patient's heart condition, can be regarded as state data which can be processed on its own, e.g., by a heart MDT. Such a "factored out" MDT can be seen as a separate DT instance (DTI) that may have connections to other DTIs, e.g., a lung MDT. Following that, a *digital twin aggregate* – comprised of various specific DTIs – "allow[s] for a larger and more complete dataset regarding the operation of a type of physical object" [12]. Similarly, Haße et al. [13] denote a *sub-model* of a digital twin when it comes to sharing parts of it. Shared digital twins are of particular interest in the medical field because they can facilitate more effective collaboration among health professionals [7].

A digital twin can be considered as a numerical model of a physical process or an object. In case of *digital twins of patients*, it becomes obvious that a comprehensive modelling of all physiological processes going on in such a complex organism seems infeasible. Therefore, a medical digital twin always focuses on a subset of relevant aspects. This can be organ-driven (e.g., a digital twin of the heart), focused on a specific disease and the related therapy process (e.g., a digital twin of chronic inflammatory bowel diseases), or more generally on a patient journey covering patients' pathways through treatment and the healthcare system.

An MDT – no matter what it specifically represents – acts as a data repository and therefore requires well-defined data structures, allowing a systematic aggregation of medical and health-related data. An MDT may contain information such as attributes from an electronic health record (e.g. age, gender, social background, ...), additional attributes that are relevant for medical research, collected sensor data over time (e.g., temperature, heart and breathing rates, or ECGs), laboratory data, as well as self-reported patient diary entries – just to give a few examples. For storing and accessing those data entries, the data needs to be managed accordingly.

When considering specific use-cases of an MDT, a subset of the comprehensive MDT needs to be created. That means a specific subset of data structures is used for representing the case-related data, like relevant lab parameters, image-derived biomarkers, medication information, and many more. In addition, that data needs to be made accessible to the involved physicians, patients, medical nurses as well as other relevant stakeholders. Another important aspect is the integration of specific analysis capabilities that work on the data contained in the medical patient twin. As an example, a shadow focusing on a cardiology-related use case might integrate algorithms for detecting abnormalities in ECG data.

19.1.2 Definition and analysis of MDT cohorts

In a medical context, *cohorts* are groups of subjects that share certain characteristics. Taking our definition of MDTs into account, we may state that cohorts are a set of MDTs that share certain attribute values. Each attribute is linked to a specific measure on the patient or is deterministically derived from other attributes. In clinical settings, such measures are stored in an electronic health record system, typically part of the clinical information system. For example, we can store all relevant data of patients with a kidney disease that are treated in a clinic in MDTs. The MDTs can then be separated into cohorts based on the attribute *comorbidity*, forming three cohorts: "diabetes", "blood pressure", "none/unknown". The diabetes cohort can be further divided into sub-cohorts, e.g. into several age groups or based on their dialysis treatment. For medical treatment (and prevention), the goal of such a division of cohorts is to yield treatment or risk groups. This division is then also called *stratification*. The resulting risk groups form the basis for medical guidelines and cohort-specific treatment and prevention plans. For example, the guidelines for preventive measures in prostate cancer look different for patients older than 70 years of age and a family history of prostate cancer, than for men younger than 50 years.

Another basis of medical guidelines are cohort studies. Cohort studies are longitudinal studies in which cohorts are analyzed over a certain period of time. Such cohort studies can be retrospective or prospective. In retrospective studies, cohorts are formed based on specific characteristics of patients to analyze the development of a patient journey in order to find risk factors in the past that have led to the current status. Prospective studies, on the other hand, follow up on each patient in the cohort over a certain period of time to find commonalities or differences in disease progression, often *with* or *without* a specific treatment, but also dependent on certain patient behavior. Both types of cohort studies ultimately look for cause-and-effect relations and have to rely on highly robust processes to enable statistically significant findings. Cohort studies and their analysis are certainly expensive, complex, and time-consuming.

Our focus here is the beneficial use of MDTs for cohort studies and analysis, and the possibilities that come with it with respect to hypothesis creation and visualization. MDTs are the basis for more IT-enabled and more structured data-driven processes not only for core method during cohort studies, but also for the prior steps of hypothesis generation, study planning, and cohort definition. For example, one highly time-consuming step of cohort studies is the recruitment of patients. With MDTs, the search for suitable patients is facilitated by filter functions or a facetted search, where previously several databases or data collections – and, in the worst case, records on paper – had to be searched and patient records had to be combined to determine each patient's suitability.

One often encountered goal is the division of the cohort that contains all available MDTs into several sub-cohorts, under the side condition to have sub-cohorts (or clusters) for which all MDTs are as similar as possible to all other MDTs in the same cohort, but as dissimilar as possible to MDTs in other cohorts. To achieve this side condition quality measures for clustering approaches can be applied. A prerequisite for any clustering method (or similarity calculations) to work is a metric M that denotes the distance D (A,B) between entities A and B in a d-dimensional space, where d is the number of attributes in the MDT, or its shadow of interest [14]. By applying adequate metrics allowing the determination of a similarity value D between two entities A and B (e.g. by using the Euclidean distance between each of $d = 10$ numerical attributes for two MDTs), we receive an overall distance D (or similarity) between these two d-dimensional entities. Nevertheless, this approach becomes more complicated if we also include categorical attributes [16], or if we analyze the similarity of univariate or multivariate time series with different possibilities depending on the analysis goal [15,18]. We refer the reader to the above references for more in-depth information on these similarity measures. If we look at the challenges of data analytics in healthcare as put forward by Shneiderman et al. [17], MDTs and analytical interfaces can support several tasks. Within this contribution we want to focus on two tasks in particular: (1) characterizing and understanding similarity D as an underlying goal of searching for patterns in large patient databases; and (2) detecting potentially relevant data within the cohorts for prognosis.

To emphasize these two tasks and the benefits of MDTs we will look at an example from the field of nephrology. A clinical research center has collected and combined data about their patients with chronic kidney disease (CKD). Patients with this disease are typically grouped into 6 stages, from CKD stage 0, which is a pre-stage of CKD, to CKD stage 5 for patients with severe symptoms and dialysis. The medical guidelines suggest different treatment plans for each stage, also dependent on underlying co-morbidities. The research center is now interested in further understanding the similarity (or remaining differences) of the patients in each CKD stage to potentially further divide cohorts for a more targeted treatment (Task 1 above). They are also interested in finding attributes that predicts a transition to another CKD stage (Task 2).

Fig. 19.1 shows a screenshot of a system that uses MDTs and visualizes patient data to support these two tasks. All MDTs and their attributes can be accessed through a list and a search interface on the left side. At the center, we see a similarity scatterplot, in which each MDT (or patient) is a dot. The scatterplot is the result of a dimensionality reduction (from d attributes to 2 dimensions), in which MDTs close to each other are very similar, and MDTs far away from each other are dissimilar.[1] The definition of similarity can be adjusted on the right side, where medical experts can see all patient attributes and adjust the importance of each attribute for similarity of CKD patients.

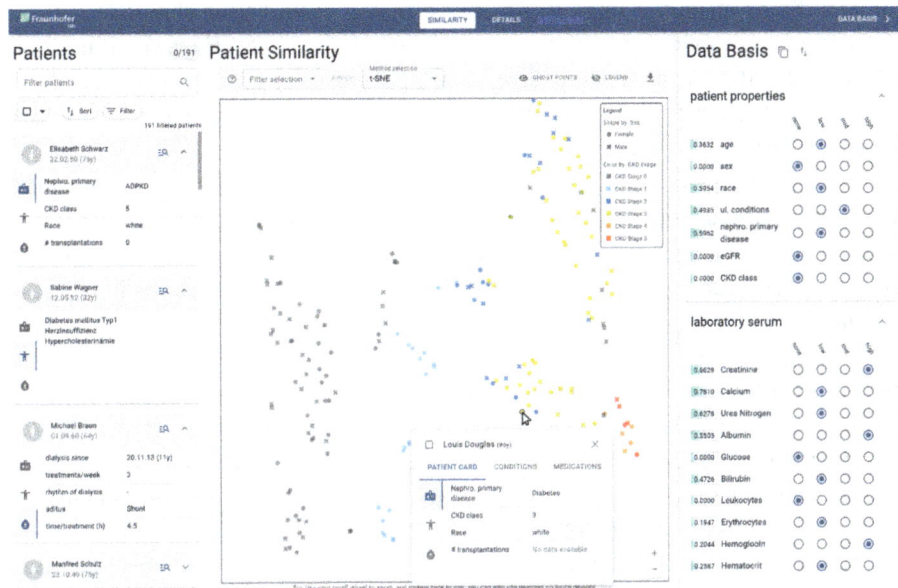

Fig. 19.1: A screenshot of RenalViz [19], a system to analyze similarities and cohorts of patients (and their MDTs) with chronic kidney disease (CKD). The central scatterplot shows all MDTs, with each point representing one MDT. The distance between the points (MDTs) shows the similarity of MDTs. Medical experts can browse the list of MDTs on the left side to find a particular patient. They can also click on a dot in the center to access the patient record. Users can influence the similarity metric by ranking attributes in the MDTs on the right side. (© Fraunhofer IGD).

19.2 Current applications of medical digital twins

Having MDTs of individuals on the one hand and information about larger cohorts of certain aspects of similar patients on the other, allows the application of this concept to real world clinical problems. The ultimate goal within healthcare would be to use MDTs in the context of personalized medicine as a *comprehensive digital copy* of a patient

---

1 The x- and y-axis in such a scatterplot that results from, e.g., a principal component analysis, do not have any meaning per se. Similar to puzzle pieces that are grouped on a tabletop to ease later assembly, the purpose of such a display is to group similar items and look for insights within or between groups.

where many simulations can be run in highest detail, these simulations could, e.g., be a virtual surgical intervention applied to the MDT to know what the outcome will be, before the real intervention is performed. Depending on the available data, such a virtual surgical intervention can consider the tissue reaction on the cellular level, flow simulations, or metabolic impacts. Another example could be the simulation of the effect of a drug application across all scales of the human body. However, it must be understood and considered that to date, an MDT is only a *partial representation* of the real patient. Thus, current applications of MDT technology are limited to only a subset of medical tasks.

Considering the above stated example, one current application is the simulation of surgical procedures in a virtual model of the patient. As an example, within cardiac surgery, the planning of mitral valve replacements combines an anatomical model of the heart (e.g. obtained from volumetric CT or MRI data) with physically based flow simulation and the valve replacement's geometry and material for finding the individually best fitting one [20]. As a second example, in orthopedic surgery, personalized bone models (e.g. obtained from CT data) are used to simulate the shear stress (based on the CT data combined with physical knowledge) that different implants or screws will exercise on the remaining bone [21]. Thus, the best fitting implants and screws as well as the implantation angles can be chosen before real surgical intervention. This simulation not only improves preoperative planning but also reduces the risk of complications.

MDTs can also be used for monitoring real-time data or for analyzing retrospective health information. Based thereon, solutions for disease prevention can be realized. Such tools are for instance those for the prevention of severe cardiac events by analyzing cardiac function data like heart rate, heart rate variability and ECG information [22]. Combining and linking all these parameters into one model is a very simple MDT but allows for an alert if the analysis predicts an imminent malfunction. Also, prevention strategies can be explored and established using MDTs. By analyzing individual factors, the risk for female patients to develop breast cancer can be prognosed. The parameter set of an individual is projected on 2D using dimensionality reduction. Afterwards, the similarity with the parameter sets of other patients – called MDTs [23] – can be computed. If the considered individual turns out to be in the high-risk group, appropriate measures can be taken.

One application of MDTs in rehabilitation is related to bio-mechanical virtual patient models. Based on capturing and analyzing patients' data, movement patterns can be assessed, and therapists can make informed decisions about the effectiveness of treatment plans [24]. Again, the individual biomechanics focused MDT is compared to a cohort of MDTs of similar patients. Another example is the simulation of various therapy scenarios to identify the most effective interventions. This helps in optimizing rehabilitation strategies and improving patient outcomes [25]. Finally, MDTs are useful in customizing rehabilitation devices such as prosthetics and others to meet the specific needs of patients. This allows for real-time adjustments based on the individual's performance and requirements [26].

Not only with the Covid-19 pandemic, epidemiology modeling has emerged. The spread of infectious diseases within populations by integrating real-time data on infection rates, demographics, and environmental factors can be simulated using MDTs helping public health officials predict outbreaks and implement timely interventions. Further, researchers can assess the impact of various public health interventions, such as vaccination campaigns or social distancing measures, on disease transmission [27].

Patients as well as care providers benefit from applying MDT technology for chronic disease management. Virtual replicas of patients with chronic diseases (such as, e.g., inflammatory bowel disease) allow to develop personalized treatment plans based on individual health data and responses to therapy. The following section discusses such an example in more detail. Furthermore, by integrating wearable devices and health data, MDTs enable real-time monitoring of chronically ill patients' metrics. This continuous feedback loop allows for timely adjustments to treatment and lifestyle recommendations, thus improving disease management [28].

In personalized medicine MDTs can optimize drug therapy and improve clinical outcomes through a better understanding of genetic influences on drug response. Virtual representations of patients, incorporating genetic, phenotypic, and environmental data can predict individual drug responses to specific medications helping to tailor pharmacotherapy based on genetic profiles [29]. To identify adverse effects and to optimize drug combinations before clinical application as well as determining optimal dosing regimens can be crucial. MDTs can be employed to simulate potential drug interactions in patients with specific genetic backgrounds or to minimize the risk of toxicity and to maximize therapeutic efficacy [30,31].

The response to drugs or other therapeutic measures play an important role in clinical trials. Here, the MDT cohorts discussed above can simulate patient populations based on specific inclusion and exclusion criteria, helping researchers identify suitable candidates for clinical trials [32]. In addition, various trial designs, including different treatment arms and dosage regimens can be simulated to evaluate potential outcomes and refine trial protocols prior to implementation [33]. Further areas of application for MDTs include predictive analytics to forecast trial outcomes based on individual patient characteristics and treatment responses, as well as generative AI [34].

For education, MDTs are used to create realistic simulations of patients for medical training [35]. This enables surgeons to develop and train their skills before performing on actual patients. By providing real-time feedback during training exercises, it allows learners to adjust their techniques based on performance analytics [36].

19.3 AI approaches for digital twins

The definition and representation of medical data in the form of medical digital twins (see Section 19.1) addresses an essential topic for any AI approach: data readiness. AI approaches require an adequate data basis for them to work. For instance, most learning models require a sufficiently large and representative training data set, a validation data set, and a test data set. A common situation in research environments is a combination of small sets (small n) of medical data with a large number of dimensions (large d), in the worst cases with many interpretable attribute values and even missing values. Such a situation does not support the identification of statistically significant conclusions, let alone the application of AI methods. After all, these methods typically require a large number of data sets (large n) and work best with a small and well-defined set of attributes (small d).

The prerequisite for data-driven approaches is a well-defined data set, as complete and unbiased as possible. The clear definition of MDTs (and, e.g., morbidity- or organ-specific shadows) build the syntactical basis for such data sets (with adequate value of d) and solves the problem of the correct interpretation of attribute values. The acquisition of a sufficient number of data sets (adequate value of n) is a challenge in the healthcare sector for various reasons, that range from the sensitive nature and restrictive distribution of medical data to the fact, that a single clinic usually does not treat enough patients for a certain illness. Many of the current initiatives in Germany, like the Netzwerk Universitätsmedizin (NUM) [37] or the Nationale Forschungsdateninfrastruktur (NFDI; i.e.: National Research Data Infrastructure) [38], have the goal, among others, to interconnect medical institutions and enlarge the data basis for medical research in Germany. Ensuring a common structure for medical data and combining data sets across clinics in a secure, ethical and legal way is an immense challenge.

While we certainly cannot solve this problem of data availability addressed in this subsection, we will look at areas in which AI methods are successfully used on medical twin data to support decision making. We will also take a closer look at the Fraunhofer lighthouse project MED²ICIN which shows the steps required to form MDTs from a disparate set of clinic-internal and external sources. Finally, we consider the possibilities of virtual cohorts and synthetic data sets to enlarge the data basis (enlarge n) for certain scenarios.

19.3.1 The role of AI and DTs in decision support

The possibilities to combine AI and MDTs are multi-fold. First, AI is one tool that is used to build MDTs of individuals. For instance, machine learning (ML) helps to derive biomarkers from medical image data (e.g., the volume of a tumor mass) that can then be added as additional descriptors to the data representing an MDT. Second, AI-based learning is performed on MDTs of numerous patients. This helps to identify and define patient cohorts (see Section 19.2), which in turn allows to learn from specific sub-cohorts using AI how a certain treatment affects patients with specific disease characteristics or what the expected disease progression is – a third application of AI to MDTs. Thus, if clinical decisions need to be taken, nowadays physician can rely more and more on MDTs that are built with or employed trough AI technology.

For about the last ten years, ML has been one important aspect of applying AI to the medical sector. Such approaches allow to process large amounts of data from various sources and thereby contribute to patient profiling. In the context of electronic health records, AI automates the analysis of both structured as well as unstructured data such as anamnesis information, laboratory results, and data from medical imaging. Data on nutrition, exercise and sleep patterns as well as environmental factors are collected and analyzed to create a holistic view of the patient and thereby enriching the MDT.

By integrating relevant data from different sources AI can be used for computing individual risk profiles. In addition, relevant features that influence the risk of a disease can be derived by building models that weigh these factors. Employing supervised learning, models can be trained on historical data to recognize patterns associated with specific treatment outcomes. These models can then be applied to a new patient and his or her individual MDT. Also, unknown patterns in data can be discovered without requiring prior labels. This so-called 'unsupervised learning' can help identify unexpected relationships between treatment approaches and outcomes. Thus, physicians can test various therapeutic approaches before making a final decision relying on AI models that predict the impact of each decision on the patient.

Once, individual risk profiles have been computed and the decision for a specific treatment has been taken, it is important to monitor whether it delivers the expected outcome. For that, the data obtained through monitoring the therapy process needs to be analyzed in real-time. Here, AI helps to reliably detect changes in a patient's health status. Additionally, AI can automatically suggest therapy adjustments based on the latest health data, if necessary. To make the AI-driven therapy suggestions understandable to the human user and thereby acceptable, visualization plays an important role. This is one important aspect of explainable AI – Mienye et al. [39] have recently published an overview article on that topic. Usually, those visualizations need to be highly user specific. And that is why, the generation of well-adapted visualizations, e.g. for displaying real-time data analysis results or interactive dashboards is still in the hand of the humans, and AI is playing only a significant role 'under the hood' – creating and aggregating data that is visualized in the next step.

19.3.2 MED²ICIN

When diagnosing and treating chronic conditions such as multiple sclerosis, cancer or neurodegenerative diseases the decision for a specific therapy path is of uttermost importance. Not only, that the patient greatly benefits from getting the optimal treatment, taking that decision is often extremely complex and related to significant costs. The data that is recorded and stored is often unstructured and not always available to the professionals treating the patient. Thus, processing, aggregation and visualization

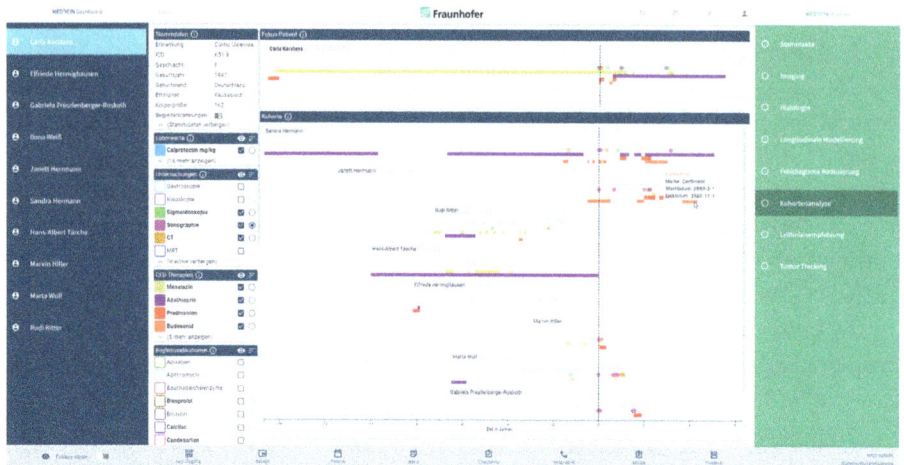

Fig. 19.2: A screenshot of the cohort module of the MED²ICIN dashboard. It consists of three vertical parts. In the view on the left, the list of patients is shown. The view on the right allows selecting one of the available modules. The largest view in the center shows the selected module that is populated with data of the selected patient. In the shown cohort module, the time graphs of medication and lab values for the selected patient is displayed (upper row). Below, similar patients together with their individual medication and lab values are shown. This allows for a comparison within a patient sub-cohort. (© Fraunhofer).

of patient data as well as direct access to the latest study data or clinical guidelines is not possible during visits in daily clinical practice.

In the Fraunhofer lighthouse project MED²ICIN, a holistic digital patient model was created – an MDT that combines all of a patient's various medical data, see Fig. 19.2. It not only collates this with parameters from population studies and data on specific clinical parameters but also takes into consideration clinical guidelines and health economic aspects. This MDT has specifically been implemented and evaluated in the context of chronic *inflammatory bowel disease* (IBD) – integrating around 170 parameters into the patient model.

With this MDT, clinicians don't just have the potential to significantly improve the care provided to individual patients but also to optimize public health spending. One key aspect of MED²ICIN is to help to effectively manage continually rising costs and thereby ensure patients receive the best possible care. By drawing on a data pool of similar cases and analyzing that data, the developed decision support systems which is based on an IBD-specific MDT goes far beyond existing digitalization projects such as electronic patient records or hospital information systems (HIS).

The clinical decision support system is designed as a modular dashboard where data is processed and visualized. For processing and analyzing the data, AI tools, as discussed above, are used. For instance, diagnosis reports from earlier visits are analyzed by the help of AI. However, the clinical decision itself is not made by an AI but by the human expert. The aim of the MED²ICIN dashboard is to enable the clinician to better understand the individual patient based on the presented data. Thus, data visualization has been of key importance when developing the system. Among the several integrated modules, the cohort analysis proved to be very helpful in evaluating the developed prototype. Putting an individual in the context of a cohort of similar patients, makes it easier to decide for a specific medication. For IBD, it is extremely important to start the treatment of that life-long chronic disease with the correct medication. To make a better treatment decision, it helps to compare the current patient with similar ones and to see which medications these patients have received and what treatment outcomes were achieved with them. In initial tests of the prototype gastroenterologists reported 23 % cost savings as well as 35 % time savings when relying on the MED²ICIN dashboard.

19.3.3 Virtual cohorts

Our original definition of MDTs (see Section 19.1) assumes that all available digital information is linked to data in the real world, either observed or measured for the patient represented by this MDT. For certain well-defined scenarios, it can be beneficial to extend this definition to MDTs that represent a so-called virtual patient, i.e. an MDT with attribute values that are created through a model. Majeed and Hwang [40] provide an excellent overview of the current developments, benefits, and drawbacks of using synthetic data, all topics that can be only briefly mentioned here. The benefits of virtual patients are manifold, because of the much lower curation costs, sensitivity, and legal requirements. In addition, virtual patients who have realistic data but essentially do not exist are more readily available and more flexible.

Synthetic data is typically created from real datasets that cover the typical variability in relation to a specific. Giving an adequate statistical or deep learning model, this variability and analytical knowledge can be preserved in the synthetic dataset [40] (this type of synthetic data is also called partial synthetic). Fully synthetic datasets are created without reference to real data and are more rarely used in sensitive contexts. Creating a realistic virtual cohort of synthetic MDTs is certainly a challenge. Not only do all attributes in each MDT have to form a coherent and realistic representation of a patient, but the entirety of all MDTs has to mirror the characteristics of real patient cohorts in all relevant aspects. The relevance of each attribute and their interdependencies for this realism is the central question. The risk of creating a virtual cohort that leaves out important attributes or ignores crucial relations between certain attributes has to be minimized. The risk is also reduced by focusing very specifically on a particular illness that is deeply understood by medical experts who support and monitor the creation and use of the virtual cohort.

In certain scenarios, for instance, the development of tools that need a sufficient number of MDTs during the user-centered development of their interfaces, a verification of epidemiological realism is of less importance. An AI tool that is (partly) trained with virtual cohorts to give advice to physicians during diagnosis or treatment is certainly on the other extreme end of the spectrum. We want to emphasize that virtual cohorts and synthetic data can only substitute real medical data in specific scenarios. For the use of virtual cohorts in diagnosis and treatment, statistics experts, epidemiologists, and medical experts for the morbidity at hand are necessary to analyze and verify the realistic distribution of attributes. We also refer the reader to the list of drawbacks when using synthetic data in the article by Majeed and Hwang [40].

In summary, the use of synthetic MDTs can support the development of technologies that require larger data sets than typically available during each of the development phases. However, synthetic data cannot completely replace real patient data and still requires access to a certain set of medical data. The decision to reasonably use synthetic data has to be made for each particular use case, which is especially important for decision support during diagnosis and treatment.

19.4 Ethical considerations

In the previous section, we discussed the use of MDTs and the application of AI methods on medical data mostly from a technical point of view. There is, however, the clear need to evaluate MDT approaches and AI technologies from an ethical point of view. First of all, medical data is probably the most sensitive personal data. Some companies have prejudices against certain mental illnesses, to just name one example, and patients naturally would like to control who has access to their data. At the same time, preventing the wider use of medical data is not in the public interest either (see Section 19.4.1). Doctors have always learned from the patients they treated, and today's technologies can support more targeted treatments with potential benefits for all. Section 19.4.2 will look at the ethical concerns about increasingly accurate predictions of future illnesses for currently healthy patients. At the end, we will look at efforts to build trust and comprehensibility into AI approaches (see Section 19.4.3).

19.4.1 Digital self-determination vs public interest

The applications of MDTs can be distinguished into four different groups. First, patients should be able to easily grant access to all data related to a specific disease for which they are treated. Second, it should also be possible to grant this access in the context of a treatment process across multiple treatment facilities. In research use cases, it is also necessary to gain access to data to build patient cohorts that, thirdly, are based on certain patient characteristics or, fourth, on organ-specific features. All use cases should be supported by easy and usable ways to grant access to specific data attributes and to use the MDTs on the medical side.

Information security is paramount for MDTs as a compromised MDT may have direct or indirect consequences for patients that go beyond impairing their health. In its foresight report for 2030, ENISA [41] expects the "exploitation of e-health (and genetic) data" to be among the top threats by 2030 and states that such sensitive data "may be exploited or used by criminals to target individuals or by governments to control populations, e.g., using diseases as a reason for discriminating against individuals". In addition, a compromised MDT may draw wrong conclusions about a patient's current state of health. Stated by Jiang et al. [42], general attack principles (e.g., eavesdropping, integrity violations) and defense mechanisms (e.g., encryption, digital signatures) for industrial cyber-physical systems are discussed that also apply to MDTs. Many defense mechanisms work well within an organization, like role-based access control [43]. However, when data leaves an organization's control, as with a shared MDT, an equal or similar level of control over the data can no longer be guaranteed. Data encryption is always an option for protecting shared data, but it is not a panacea, as implementing cryptography-based access control across organizations can be complex [44].

19.4.2 Simulated outcomes for individual digital twins

One of the key benefits of MDTs is the ability to simulate the outcome of a certain therapy or a disease progression. However, this implies that several problems and challenges need to be faced, and solutions have to be developed. The accuracy of simulations depends heavily on the quality of the underlying data. Incomplete, inaccurate, or outdated datasets can lead to unreliable predictions. Furthermore, non-accessible data and lack of standardization across healthcare systems can hinder the availability of high-quality data. The human physiology is intricate, with numerous variables influencing health outcomes. Therefore, creating models that accurately capture these complexities is a significant challenge. An over-simplification might lead to less reliable outcomes. Also, achieving a sufficient level of personalization is challenging due to the vast variability among individuals, which may not be fully represented in existing datasets. Assuming that good models can be built, before deploying MDTs in clinical settings, rigorous validation is essential to ensure that they produce accurate and reliable results. Finally, the regulatory landscape for MDTs is often unclear, with many countries lacking specific guidelines governing their use in clinical practice. The use of patient-specific data raises significant ethical and privacy concerns [45]. Patients need to trust that all their activities are compliant with data protection laws, such as the GDPR, while utilizing MDTs presents a complex challenge, as organizations must balance innovation with the need to protect patient privacy.

But what about the outcome of these simulations? Shall every patient be confronted with the predictions that can be derived from the use of MDTs? The right not to know is rooted in the principle of patient autonomy, which enables individuals to make informed decisions about their healthcare. Patients should have the option to refuse to receive information about their health status, potential risks, or treatment outcomes. MDTs can generate sensitive insights that may be distressing for patients. It is of crucial importance to find a balance between providing necessary information for informed decision-making and respecting patients' wishes to remain unaware of certain aspects of their health. This helps patients to avoid anxiety and distress associated with confronting difficult health realities. Therefore, informed consent should include not only the right to receive information, but also the right to refuse it. If patients exercise their right not to know, this may have an impact on the quality of care they receive. This will certainly create tension between respecting patient autonomy and ensuring optimal care. All this leads to the conclusion that comprehensive regulations are needed to protect this right and to promote the responsible use of MDTs in order to safeguard the interests of patients.

19.4.3 Trustworthy Artificial Intelligence

While AI techniques have come under scrutiny in many areas, the sensitive nature of medical data and the high stakes of medical decisions have raised increased concerns about the trustworthiness, fairness, interpretability, and accountability of AI-driven systems. This certainly goes in line with several guidelines that have been published, for instance, by the EU's high-level expert group on artificial intelligence [46], the prominent EU's Artificial Intelligence act [47], or in the US by the standards committee of IEEE on Ethically Aligned Design [48].

Discussing and addressing concerns regarding AI systems is an inherently multidisciplinary problem and requires research activities across disciplines. In order to foster trust in AI, it is important to strongly involve the human interactively in such a system – a topic that has been pursued by visualization research for many years. In a recent paper from a Dagstuhl seminar [49] published on this topic, the following claims were made, especially with respect to the human-machine interface and visualization:

– Trust is not a technical problem. Organizational, sociological, and psychological factors affect trust, but are often not taken into account when building AI-based systems. Neglecting these issues can hinder trusting even otherwise trustworthy AI-based systems.
– Trust is dynamic. A regular evaluation is necessary to take a changing world and human perception of it into account. Another dynamic is the situation and context of the use of AI, which calls for the support of deciding if, when, and to what extent to trust a specific system [49].
– While visualization cannot address all aspects of trust it is crucial for the human agency in AI and especially adequate to bridge humans, data, and algorithms. After all, we need more multidisciplinary research for a better understanding of AI-based technologies.

These claims emphasize that approaches to trustworthy AI must carefully consider and adapt to people's evolving needs and non-technical factors that influence trust.

19.5 Conclusion

MDTs offer extensive opportunities for improving medical processes and patient care. In the field of personalized medicine, MDTs allow for the simulation of individual patient scenarios to optimize treatments. Virtual patient models can help predict treatment outcomes and support clinical decision-making. Regarding larger patient groups, they can be created for entire cohorts to conduct epidemiological studies and identify patterns in the spread of diseases. Thereby, AI plays a crucial role in the creation and enhancement of digital twins. It can autonomously analyze large data sets to create precise models and to continuously update them. ML helps to integrate new medical insights and improve the twins.

Employing MDTs for real-world healthcare solutions, rises ethical questions that need to be considered. Data protection and privacy must be ensured to protect personal health data. Patients must be fully informed and provide consent before their data is used. Furthermore, it must be ensured that AI models do not deliver biased results and are fair. Data security is also a vital aspect. It is important to use encryption and secure networks to protect sensitive health data. Regular security audits and system updates are necessary to close security gaps and ensure the integrity of the data.

In the coming years, MDTs will gain increased significance. Advances in AI technology and data analytics will enable the creation of even more accurate and comprehensive patient simulations and allowing for real-time adjustments to individual treatment plans. Additionally, MDTs might play a central role in prevention by identifying risks early and suggesting appropriate measures. The integration of MDTs into telemedicine services could also significantly enhance the accessibility and efficiency of medical care.

However, one should not overestimate the potential of MDTs. They rather represent an evolution than a revolution for healthcare. We will not carry a complete copy of ourselves with us. But, relevant aspects of our individual anatomy, our metabolism or our genetic footprint will be part of our individual digital shadows. Having access to this well-structured information will lead to an improved care – where all stakeholders will benefit from.

Acknowledgements

The underlying research of this chapter is funded by ATHENE, the national research center for applied cybersecurity. ATHENE is a research center of the Fraunhofer-Gesellschaft with the participation of the Fraunhofer Institutes SIT and IGD as well as the TU Darmstadt, Goethe University Frankfurt am Main and Darmstadt University of Applied Sciences. The research center is funded by the Federal Ministry of Education and Research (BMBF) and the Hessian Ministry of Science and Art (HMWK) and is located in Darmstadt, Germany. We especially thank our collaborators in the ATHENE project *MeDiTwin*: Salmah Ahmad, Bianca Bartelt, Matthias Enzmann and Ruben Wolf.

References

[1] Grieves M. W. Product lifecycle management: the new paradigm for enterprises. Int. J. Product Development. 2005; 2(1,2).

[2] VanDerHorn E., Mahadevan S. Digital Twin: Generalization, characterization and implementation. Decision Support Systems. 2021; 145.

[3] Jones D., Snider C., Nassehi A., Yon J., Hicks B. Characterising the Digital Twin: A systematic literature review. CIRP Journal of Manufacturing Science and Technology. 2020; 29: 36–52.

[4] Verdouw C., Tekinerdogan B., Beulens A., Wolfert S. Digital twins in smart farming. Agricultural Systems. 2021; 189.

[5] Björnsson B., Borrebaeck C., Elander N., Gasslander T., Gawel D. R., Gustafsson M. et al. Digital twins to personalize medicine. Genome Medicine. 2020; 12(4).

[6] Coorey G., Figtree G. A., Fletcher D. F., Snelson V. J., Vernon S. T., Winlaw D. et al. The health digital twin to tackle cardiovascular disease – a review of an emerging interdisciplinary field. npj Digital Medicine. 2022; 5(126).

[7] Vallée A. Digital twin for healthcare systems. Frontiers in Digital Health. 2023 Sep.; 5.

[8] Bujari A., Calvio A., Foschini L., Sabbioni A., Corradi A. IPPODAMO: a Digital Twin Support for Smart Cities Facility Management. In GoodIT '21: ACM International Conference on Information Technology for Social Good.; 2021. pp. 49–54.

[9] Erol T., Mendi A. F., Doğan D. The Digital Twin Revolution in Healthcare. In Proc. of 4th International Symposium on Multidisciplinary Studies and Innovative Technologies (ISMSIT). Istanbul: IEEE; 2020. pp. 1–7.

[10] Haleem A., Javaid M., Singh R. P., Suman R. Exploring the revolution in healthcare systems through the applications of digital twin technology. Biomedical Technology. 2023; 4: 28–38.

[11] Farsi M., Daneshkhah A., Hosseinian-Far A., Jahankhani H. (eds). Digital Twin Technologies and Smart Cities: Springer Cham; 2020.

[12] Human C., Basson A. H., Kruger K. A Design Framework for a System of Digital Twins and Services. Computers in Industry. 2023; 144.

[13] Haße H., van der Valk H., Möller F., Otto B. Design Principles for Shared Digital Twins in Distributed Systems. Bus Inf Syst Eng. 2022; 64(6): 751–772.

[14] Becker F., Bibow P., Dalibor M., Gannouni A., Hahn V., Hopmann C. et al. A Conceptual Model for Digital Shadows in Industry and its Application. In Ghose A., Horkoff J., Silva Souza V. E., Parsons J., Evermann J. Conceptual Modeling, ER 2021.: Springer; 2021. pp. 271–281.

[15] Bernard J., Hutter M., Reinemuth H., Pfeifer H., Bors C. and Kohlhammer J. (2019), Visual-Interactive Preprocessing of Multivariate Time Series Data. Computer Graphics Forum, 38: 401–412. https://doi.org/10.1111/cgf.13698.

[16] Ahmad S., Sessler D. and Kohlhammer J., "Towards a Comprehensive Cohort Visualization of Patients with Inflammatory Bowel Disease," 2021 IEEE Workshop on Visual Analytics in Healthcare (VAHC), New Orleans, LA, USA, 2021, pp. 25–29. https://doi.org/10.1109/VAHC53616.2021.00009.

[17] Shneiderman B., Plaisant C., and Hesse B. W. "Improving Healthcare with Interactive Visualization," Computer, vol. 46, no. 5, 2013, pp. 58–66.

[18] Bernard J., Sessler D., May T., Schlomm T., Pehrke D. and Kohlhammer J. "A Visual-Interactive System for Prostate Cancer Cohort Analysis," in IEEE Computer Graphics and Applications, vol. 35, no. 3, pp. 44–55, May–June 2015. https://doi.org/10.1109/MCG.2015.49.

[19] Höhn M., Schwindt-Drews S., Hahn S., Patyna S., Büttner S., Kohlhammer J., "RenalViz: Visual analysis of cohorts with chronic kidney disease", Computers & Graphics, Volume 125, 2024: 104–120. https://doi.org/10.1016/j.cag.2024.104120.

[20] Viola F., Del Corso G., De Paulis R. et al. GPU accelerated digital twins of the human heart open new routes for cardiovascular research. Sci Rep 13, 8230 (2023). https://doi.org/10.1038/s41598-023-34098-8.

[21] Aubert K., Germaneau A., Rochette M., Ye W., Severyns M., Billot M., Rigoard P., Vendeuvre T. Development of Digital Twins to Optimize Trauma Surgery and Postoperative Management. A Case Study Focusing on Tibial Plateau Fracture. Frontiers in Bioengineering and Biotechnology, 9 (2021). https://doi.org/10.3389/fbioe.2021.722275.

[22] Gu, F., Meyer, A.J., Ježek, F. et al. Identification of digital twins to guide interpretable AI for diagnosis and prognosis in heart failure. npj Digit. Med. 8, 110 (2025). https://doi.org/10.1038/s41746-025-01501-9.

[23] Chang H.-C., Gitau A. M., Kothapalli S., Welch D. R., Sardiu M. E., McCoy M. D. Understanding the need for digital twins' data in patient advocacy and forecasting oncology. Frontiers in Artificial Intelligence, 6 (2023). https://doi.org/10.3389/frai.2023.1260361.

[24] Lauer-Schmaltz M., Cash P., Hansen J., Das N. (2024). Human Digital Twins in Rehabilitation: A Case Study on Exoskeleton and Serious-Game-Based Stroke Rehabilitation Using the ETHICA Methodology. IEEE Access. PP. 1–1. https://doi.org/10.1109/ACCESS.2024.3508029.

[25] Chen Y., Wang W., Diao J., Wang D., Jian Z., Wang Y., Jiang Z. 2023. Digital-Twin-Based Patient Evaluation during Stroke Rehabilitation. In Proceedings of the ACM/IEEE 14th International Conference on Cyber-Physical Systems (with CPS-IoT Week 2023) (ICCPS '23). Association for Computing Machinery, New York, NY, USA, 22–33. https://doi.org/10.1145/3576841.3585923.

[26] Cellupica A., Cirelli M., Saggio G., Gruppioni E., Valentini P. P. An Interactive Digital-Twin Model for Virtual Reality Environments to Train in the Use of a Sensorized Upper-Limb Prosthesis. Algorithms 2024, 17, 35. https://doi.org/10.3390/a17010035.

[27] Ettilla M. A systematic review of Digital Twins in efficient pandemic management with challenges and emerging trends, Decision Analytics Journal, Volume 12, 2024, 100502. https://doi.org/10.1016/j.dajour.2024.100502.

[28] Mosquera-Lopez C., Jacobs P. G. Digital twins and artificial intelligence in metabolic disease research, Trends in Endocrinology & Metabolism, Volume 35, Issue 6, 2024, pp 549–557. https://doi.org/10.1016/j.tem.2024.04.019.

[29] Fischer R.-P., Volpert A., Antonino P., Ahrens T. D. Digital patient twins for personalized therapeutics and pharmaceutical manufacturing, Frontiers in Digital Health, 5 (2024). https://doi.org/10.3389/fdgth.2023.1302338.

[30] Bahrami F., Rossi R. M., De Nys K. et al. An individualized digital twin of a patient for transdermal fentanyl therapy for chronic pain management. Drug Deliv. and Transl. Res. 13, 2272–2285 (2023). https://doi.org/10.1007/s13346-023-01305-y.

[31] Laubenbacher R., Niarakis A., Helikar T., An G., Shapiro B., Malik-Sheriff R. S., Sego T. J., Knapp A., Macklin P., Glazier J. A. Building digital twins of the human immune system: toward a roadmap. NPJ Digit Med. 2022 May 20;5(1):64. https://doi.org/10.1038/s41746-022-00610-z.

[32] Chandra S., Prakash P. K. S., Samanta S. et al. ClinicalGAN: powering patient monitoring in clinical trials with patient digital twins. Sci Rep 14, 12236 (2024). https://doi.org/10.1038/s41598-024-62567-1.

[33] Susilo M. E., Li C.-C., Gadkar K., Hernandez G., Huw L.-Y., Jin J.Y., Yin S., Wei M. C., Ramanujan S., Hosseini I. Systems-based digital twins to help characterize clinical dose–response and propose

predictive biomarkers in a Phase I study of bispecific antibody, mosunetuzumab, NHL (2023) Clinical and Translational Science, 16 (7), pp. 1134–1148. https://doi.org/10.1111/cts.13501.

[34] Bordukova M., Makarov N., Rodriguez-Esteban R., Schmich F., Menden M. P. Generative artificial intelligence empowers digital twins in drug discovery and clinical trials. Expert Opin Drug Discov. 2024 Jan-Jun;19(1):33–42. https://doi.org/10.1080/17460441.2023.2273839.

[35] Li X., Loscalzo J., Mahmud A. K. M. F. et al. Digital twins as global learning health and disease models for preventive and personalized medicine. Genome Med 17, 11 (2025). https://doi.org/10.1186/s13073-025-01435-7.

[36] Asciak L., Kyeremeh J., Luo X. et al. Digital twin assisted surgery, concept, opportunities, and challenges. npj Digit. Med. 8, 32 (2025). https://doi.org/10.1038/s41746-024-01413-0.

[37] Netzwerk Universitätsmedizin (NUM). (Accessed March 24, 2025, at https://www.netzwerk-universitaetsmedizin.de/).

[38] Verein Nationale Forschungsdateninfrastruktur (NFDI). (Accessed March 24, 2025, at https://www.nfdi.de/).

[39] Mienye I. D., Obaido G., Jere N., Mienye E., Aruleba K., Emmanuel I. D., Ogbuokiri B. A survey of explainable artificial intelligence in healthcare: Concepts, applications, and challenges, Informatics in Medicine Unlocked, Volume 51, 2024, 101587. https://doi.org/10.1016/j.imu.2024.101587.

[40] Majeed A., Hwang S. O., "Synthetic Data: A New Frontier for Democratizing Artificial Intelligence and Data Access" in Computer, vol. 58, no. 02, pp. 106–114, Feb. 2025. https://doi.org/10.1109/MC.2024.3515412.

[41] European Union Agency for Cybersecurity (ENISA). Identifying Emerging Cyber Security Threats and Challenges for 2030; 2023.

[42] Jiang Y., Wu S. M. R., Liu M., Luo H., Kaynak O. Monitoring and Defense of Industrial Cyber-Physical Systems Under Typical Attacks: From a Systems and Control Perspective. IEEE Transactions On Industrial Cyber-Physical Systems. 2023:1.

[43] National Institute of Standards and Technology (NIST). American National Standard for Information Technology – Role Based Access Control, INCITS 359–2012. 2012 May.

[44] Zhang L., Kan H., Huang H. Patient-Centered Cross-Enterprise Document Sharing and Dynamic Consent Framework using Consortium Blockchain and Ciphertext-Policy Attribute-Based Encryption. In CF '22: Proceedings of the 19th ACM International Conference on Computing Frontiers.; 2022. pp. 58–66.

[45] European Health Data Space – EHDS (Accessed March 21, 2025, at https://health.ec.europa.eu/ehealth-digital-health-and-care/my-rights-over-my-health-data_en).

[46] High-level expert group on artificial intelligence. (Accessed March 14, 2025, at https://digital-strategy.ec.europa.eu/en/policies/expert-group-ai).

[47] EU Artificial Intelligence Act. Up-to-date developments and analyses of the EU AI Act (Accessed March 14, 2025, at https://artificialintelligenceact.eu/).

[48] Ethically Aligned Design – A Vision for Prioritizing Human Well-being with Autonomous and Intelligent Systems. The IEEE Global Initiative on Ethics of Autonomous and Intelligent Systems (Accessed March 14, 2025, at https://standards.ieee.org/wp-content/uploads/import/documents/other/ead_v2.pdf).

[49] Beauxis-Aussalet E. et al., "The Role of Interactive Visualization in Fostering Trust in AI," in IEEE Computer Graphics and Applications, vol. 41, no. 6, pp. 7–12, 1 Nov.-Dec. 2021. https://doi.org/10.1109/MCG.2021.3107875.

Patrick Gebhard, Tanja Schneeberger

20 Socially interactive agents as interface to health technology

20.1 Introduction

Modern societies are facing pressing needs in mental health, psychological well-being, and physical rehabilitation. Rising levels of stress, anxiety, and mental disorders, along with increasing social isolation, make it clear that there is an urgent demand for accessible therapy and support. The same is true in logopedics, where many individuals – ranging from children with developmental language disorders to stroke survivors – struggle to access consistent and effective treatment due to a lack of specialists. In the fitness and rehabilitation sectors, people often require expert guidance to maintain physical health, recover from injuries, or manage chronic conditions. In general, the demand for healthcare professionals and caregivers is at a critical level. Despite this urgent need, there is a significant shortage of caregivers across various healthcare settings, including hospitals, nursing and rehabilitation facilities, and assisted living communities, which limits the availability of timely and personalized care [1].

This deficiency of medical experts and caregivers has far-reaching consequences, affecting individuals of all ages who are requiring physical or mental care. Moreover, the shortage places additional strain on the existing healthcare workforce, impacting their ability to provide optimal care and maintain their own well-being [2,3]. Therefore, healthcare represents a significant opportunity for AI driven solutions in general and empathic *human-machine-interaction* (HMI) in particular.

AI-driven advances in *socially interactive technologies* have led to innovations such as chatbots, digital assistants and robotic social companions that are increasingly assisting people in various health-related contexts. These technologies have significant potential to bridge gaps in psychotherapy, psychology, speech therapy and fitness by providing scalable, interactive and personalized support. Today, AI-powered virtual mental companions and chatbots can provide psychological counselling and emotional support, while intelligent speech therapy applications can support language and communication development. In fitness and rehabilitation, AI-powered virtual trainers can provide personalized exercise plans and real-time feedback (cf. [4,5]). By complementing human professionals, socially interactive technologies could play a crucial role in meeting the growing demand for expert guidance and support in these vital areas.

This contribution explores how *Socially Interactive Agents* (SIAs) can be used as an artificially empathic interface to health technology. After a brief historical description, the social and behavioral aspects of SIAs are explained. The potential of using SIAs as patient interfaces in medicine and biomedical engineering is then explored, particularly in the context of biosignal processing, rehabilitation technology, and artificial intelligence and data analysis. Several research projects are presented in which SIAs are used in the role of assistants but also as triggers to measure certain medical or psychological aspects, mimicking human experts and their procedures. The chapter concludes with a discussion of the ethical implications of how SIA technology can support and respect human values, followed by a general conclusion and future perspectives.

20.2 Socially interactive agents as interface to health technology

Socially Interactive Agents (SIAs) are *virtual agents* or *physically embodied artificial agents* (robots) that interact autonomously with people and each other in a socially intelligent manner using multi-modal behaviors (verbal, paraverbal, and nonverbal) known from human-human interaction. From a technological perspective, they extend conventional user interfaces by incorporating human-like social communication abilities. Because they exhibit such abilities, people tend to attribute roles and responsibilities to them. This characteristic can be leveraged for their employment as companions, coaches, or assistants to human experts.

The initial goal of applying SIAs in the field of HMI was to enable human users to interact with machines via natural communication channels, e.g., speech, vision, gestures and facial expressions [6]. By equipping the HMI-interface with a "body" that interacts multi-modally and hence adding humanoid aspects, such agents are able to communicate with users verbally (e.g., by speech), para-verbally (e.g., pitch, volume, tempo and pauses in speech, emphasis and pronunciation) and non-verbally (e.g., by human-like-gestures or mimics) [7] (Fig. 20.1). This technical development incorporates human-like cues into the computer interfaces, and with these new social dimensions enter a new level of HMI [8]. The transfer from communication styles that are known from human face-to-face interactions to the interaction with machines results in a more human-like interface that is intuitive to understand and to interact with. In recent years, the use of *SIAs* has been extended beyond the improvement of HMI [9].

Technology-wise, SIAs intensively make use of modern AI tools and methods, such as automatic speech recognition, recognition of emotional cues in face and voice, text-to-speech systems [9], and large language models (LLMs), or even learned listening behavior for psychotherapy experts [10]. The noticeable differences between SIAs and LLM-based chatbots are that the interaction with SIAs considers the reciprocal real-time exchange of both – verbal and non-verbal – information featuring complex social tasks such as attention guiding [11], (dis)functional turn-taking behavior [12,13], and even social co-regulation abilities [14].

As a use case for SIA research and application, the health context has received attention for more than two decades. One of the first approaches of such agents – as

Fig. 20.1: SIA Lydia (Source: DFKI, used under CC BY-ND license).

surrogate for a clinical expert – is *Laura* of the Fit Track system [15]. Laura embodies the role of an exercise advisor who interacts with patients daily for one month to motivate them to exercise more. Laura was equipped with practical *patient-provider communication skills* (e.g., empathy, social dialogue, nonverbal immediacy behaviors) to establish and maintain good working relationships over multiple interactions. A study has demonstrated that the incorporation of such relational communication behaviors significantly enhances the working alliance and the users' propensity to persist in engaging with the system [15]. These findings suggest that such technology that is able to socially interact with patients and other recipients of health services, particularly those involved in dialogue or sustained, repeated interactions (e.g., psychologists, psychiatrists, physiologists, and logopedics), could benefit from the intentional design of emotional and relational communication strategies.

One of the first frameworks for a psychotherapeutic application of SIAs is *SimSensei* Kiosk [16]. In this, the SIA *Ellie* conducts semi-structured interviews that are intended to create interactional situations favorable to the automatic assessment of distress indicators, defined as verbal and nonverbal behaviors correlated with depression, anxiety or post-traumatic stress disorder (PTSD). The goal is to create clinical decision support tools that complement existing self-assessment questionnaires by giving healthcare providers objective measurements of the user's verbal and nonverbal behaviors that are correlated with psychological distress.

Lucas et al. [17] showed how the employment of SIAs in healthcare can help patients share honest information. Patients often do not share everything with their healthcare providers because they fear being judged [18,19]. To deal with this, the researchers compared two types of interviewers in a health screening setting. Study participants interacted with the employed SIA, believing it was either human- or automation-operated. The findings revealed that those believing they interacted with an automation system shared more information and were seen as more willing to share information.

Overall, the use of SIAs in healthcare appears to present new, unique opportunities and potential.

20.2.1 Social behavior towards socially interactive agents

Reeves and Nass' *"media equation"* [20] suggests that people tend to treat computers, media, and technology as if they were real people or social entities, applying the same social rules and behaviors to interactions with machines as they would with humans.

Nass and Steuer [21] conducted empirical studies in that context. They found several examples of social behavior towards computers: A computer is getting evaluated better, if it is praised by another computer than by itself [21]. People would rather help a computer that has helped them before, than a computer that has *not* helped them before [22]. Also, gender stereotypes are transferred to computers by finding that a computer with a female voice apparently *"knows"* more about love and relationships than a computer with a male voice [22].

To trigger social reactions in the user, the technology, which the user interacts with, needs to elicit certain social cues. The cues – or stimuli – considered especially effective in evoking a human association have been grouped into three categories: (1) speech as output modality, (2) interactivity (i.e., responses based on previous interactions), and (3) the filling of roles traditionally filled by humans [22]. Therefore, it is not surprising that using a human-like SIA as an interface results in an even more pronounced social behavior towards computers [8].

Numerous studies yield social effects, demonstrating that humans' reactions towards SIAs are remarkably *similar* to those towards human interlocutors. To provide an overview of this research area, several results from the authors (with a background in psychology as well as computer science) will be presented, examining social reactions towards such agents.

20.2.2 Behavioral reactions towards socially interactive agents

SIAs can evoke communication behavior in humans that is equivalent to that expected in a face-to-face conversation. This includes human-like communication strategies, cooperative behavior [23], polite behavior [24], and rapport building [25].

In a field study, Kopp et al. [23] used the SIA *Max* as a guide in a public museum. The human-shaped 2D agent, projected at human size on a canvas, engaged in natural face-to-face speech and gesture-based communication with visitors, providing them with information about the museum or exhibition, and engaging in natural small talk conversations. The analysis of conversations showed that museum visitors accepted the agent as a conversation partner. The visitors showed human-like communication strategies (e.g., greetings) and behaved cooperatively towards the agent. Moreover, visitors asked many personal questions (e.g., background, preferences)and tried to flirt with the agent. The authors concluded that the visitors' engagement indicates the attribution of "sociality" towards the agent [23]. Using the same virtual agent, Hoffmann et al. examined how participants evaluated the agents after a 10-minute conversation [24]. The evaluation was either done by (a) being questioned by the agent itself, (b) being questioned by a paper-and-pencil questionnaire in the same room facing the agent, and (c) being questioned by means of a paper-and-pencil questionnaire in another room. When the agent was interactively asking participants how they would evaluate it, participants gave a better evaluation, which the authors describe as "more polite" behavior. Hence, the participants seemed to have difficulty giving negative feedback face-to-face to the assessed.

Gratch et al. [25] found evidence that a SIA might engender feelings of rapport – or connectedness – in human speakers. They compared a human to an agent designed to elicit rapport within a dyadic narrative task. The 2D rapport agent, displayed in a computer monitor and equipped with a microphone and stereo camera as sensors, provided non-verbal auditory feedback associated with rapportful interactions. Those included backchanneling behavior (e.g., nods), postural mirroring, and mimicry of certain head gestures (e.g., gaze shifts and head nods). Their study results indicate that the rapport agent was as good as human listeners in creating rapport. However this result could not be replicated in a recent study from 2018 [8].

Krämer et al. [26] let participants do small talk for eight minutes with the SIA *Max* (see above) displayed on a computer monitor. The agent either did not smile, showed occasional smiles, or displayed frequent smiles. The study results showed that though the smiling behavior of the agent has *not* been perceived consciously, it influenced the participant's smiling behavior. When the agent was smiling, the duration of the participants' smiling was longer. Also, smiling behavior did not affect the evaluation of the agent. The authors concluded that participants' behavioral reactions were rather unconscious and automatic [26]. Though smiling has been analyzed within the mimicry paradigm [27,28], the authors stress that this reciprocation might not be defined as mimicry as other mechanisms can come into play, as e.g., politeness rules or usage as a communication facilitator. However, smiling behavior has a special function in interpersonal interactions. Expressing emotions, a smile can represent a major component of a facial display that might be associated with and caused by feelings of happiness or joy [29]. Moreover, which might be even more crucial, it regulates the relationship between interaction partners. Smiling has strong and robust associations with social motivation and is an important means of communication [30]. Therefore, it seems that participants experienced small talk with a SIA as a typical social situation.

Overall, it can be summarized that numerous studies find evidence of a *similar* human communication behavior towards both, SIAs and humans. Therefore, it could be assumed and expected that in future studies with SIAs as interactants, researchers will also observe communication behavior and patterns that are similar to human-human interactions.

Affective Reactions Towards Socially Interactive Agents. SIAs activate not only human-like *conversational behavior* in human interaction partners (see previous section, but also similar *affective responses* like in human-human interaction.

Comparing a text interface with a *conversational interface* depicting a face, Sproull et al. [31] found evidence that a more human-like social interactive agent (SIA) can affect the affective state and behavior of a human interaction partner. For example, in an interaction with a computer career counseling service, participants attributed *personality* to the conversational SIA differently than to the pure text display. Moreover, they reported *higher* arousal and presented themselves more positively when interacting with the conversational interface.

Deladisma et al. [32] observed medical students conducting a professional interview with a SIA in the role of a patient with pain. To trigger empathic responses, the virtual patient expressed its fear and asked for help. Though less than with a standardized human patient, the students showed nonverbal communication behaviors (such head nod and body lean) and responded in an empathic way towards the virtual patient. These empathic responses indicate that the students appreciate the agent's emotional situation, which supports the assumption that there is a creation of a common understanding of the illness.

The presence of a SIA also seems to have effects on the users' trust [33,34]. In two experiments, it was studied whether *explainable artificial intelligence* (XAI) visualizations profited from an enrichment with virtual agents [59]. The results of the earlier study showed that integrating a human-like virtual agent that explains complex facts led to increased trust in an autonomous intelligent system [33]. In the latter study, the authors found evidence that the more human-like explainable artificial intelligence interactions appeared, the more the users tended to trust the classification model whose predictions were explained [34].

One reason for the high trust of humans in SIAs might be that they are experienced as supportive and safe interaction partners. For example, Lucas et al. [35] studied the potential of SIAs in the role of interviewers. In their study, participants were led to believe that a SIA conducting a semi-structured health screening was controlled by either a human or by automation. Their results showed that the employed agent evoked lower fear of self-disclosure and lower impression management. Moreover, participants interacting with a SIA displayed negative emotions more intensely and were rated by observers as more willing to disclose themselves [17]. In a follow-up study, it was shown that service members – after a year-long deployment in Afghanistan – reported more openly to a SIA (presented as a virtual human on a 2D screen with speech interaction) about posttraumatic stress disorder symptoms compared to a questionnaire [35]. In both studies, the SIAs were designed to build rapport. *Human-human* rapport is a subjective experience of attunement between interactants that is strongly connected to *nonverbal behavior* [36]. Its various positive influences on the interpersonal process have driven researchers to recreate this interpersonal state within *human-agent interactions*, especially by creating agents that show appropriate backchanneling behavior (see above) [22,31–32].

Within a similar use-case of *disclosing stigmatized information*, Bickmore et al. [37] developed and validated a virtual agent designed to automate the administration of a substance-use screening instrument. In two studies, they found that the agent led to *more disclosure* compared to a human interviewer and to more satisfaction compared to a text-based tool. The qualitative data revealed that the agents' superiority lay in their perceived non-judgmental way of conducting the screening [37]. The finding replicates the results of a former study that revealed the preference to disclose negative, personally sensitive information to a virtual agent is mainly driven by their lack of judgment, criticism, as well as verbal or nonverbal reactions [38].

Krämer et al. [8] examined whether interactions with a virtual agent are experienced as *socially rewarding* and can meet social needs like human-human interactions. In their experiment, a SIA that asked the participants five questions with increasing intimacy either displayed socially responsive nonverbal behavior (e.g., head nods, smiling and posture shifts) or not. Their results showed an effect of individual differences in the need to belong (= the desire for interpersonal attachments as a fundamental human motivation) [39]. For participants with a high need to belong, the interaction with a virtual agent lowered their intention to engage in social contact, but only for the agent that displayed socially responsive behavior.

It seems that conversations with SIAs are not only socially rewarding but also socio-emotionally supporting [40]. Study results showed that after talking about two negative emotions, ("anger" and "worry"), and getting emotional and cognitive support, participants felt better – the target emotion was reduced, and the affect was generally improved. This has led to the conclusion that talking to a virtual human can be a valuable form of support at times of distress.

The research on interactions between humans and SIAs has shown that SIAs are perceived as social entities. They can not only activate human-like conversational behavior in human interaction partners, but also yield affective responses that would be expected in human-human interactions. Studies in the context of disclosing relevant information in healthcare indicate that SIAs can help to overcome a critical barrier, as they guarantee anonymity while also building rapport. As they also seem to give socio-emotional support, they could be applied to gather sensitive mental health information of patients.

20.3 Applications of socially interactive agents in health care

This section starts with some selected projects in which virtually embodied SIAs are employed for *psychological support* and assistance. Further presented applications are focused on support in other medical domains, such as biofeedback trainers. Moreover, an overview of some physically embodied SIA applications is given.

SIAs have a long history of being used as interfaces to health technology. Still disembodied, as far back as 1966, the first chatbot – ELIZA – was developed to simulate the behavior of a Rogerian psychotherapist [41]. Almost half a century later, more sophisticated systems that function as therapeutic assistance were developed and studied. Moreover, they are also employed for other medical or psychological procedures.

The *SimSensei* Kiosk [16] is an implemented virtual human interviewer designed to create an engaging face-to-face interaction where the user feels comfortable talking and sharing information. The virtual human *Ellie* conducts semi-structured interviews that are intended to create interactional situations favorable to the automatic assessment of distress indicators, defined as verbal and nonverbal behaviors correlated with depression, anxiety, or post- traumatic stress disorder.

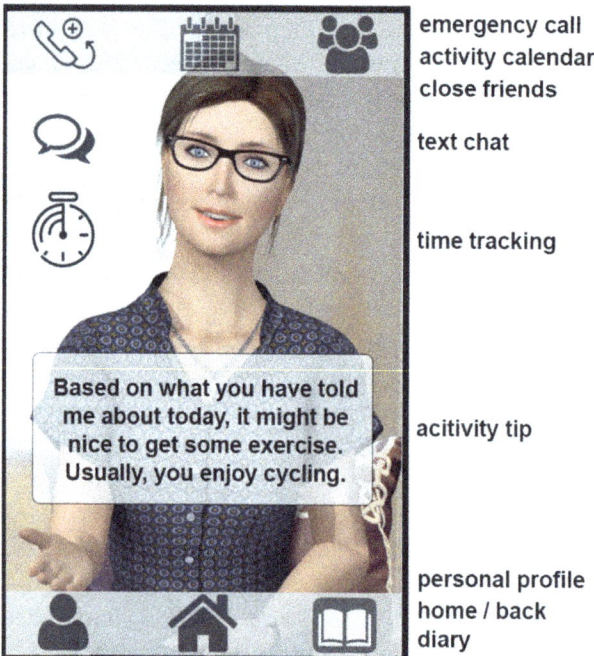

Fig. 20.2: SIA *EmmA*, providing pro-active structural support for the reintegration process of burn-out patients [42] (Source: DFKI, used under CC BY-ND license).

Gebhard et al. [42] presented *EmmA*, a SIA in the role of a vocational reintegration assistant for burn-out outpatient treatment. Complementing the current state-of-the-art of burnout outpatient treatment, *EmmA* is an always present assistant offering relevant services identified by patients and therapist experts supporting daily and weekly tasks, psychoeducation, and stimulating actions (Fig. 20.2). For communicating empathically, *EmmA* employs a real-time social signal interpretation together with a computational simulation of emotion regulation. *EmmA*'s behavior is dynamically adapted to the current social-emotional situation as well as the situational selection of verbal support strategies, which are defined by experts. Both emulate important strategies of therapists.

Schneeberger et al. [43] presented a virtual stress management training using biofeedback derived from the cardiovascular response of the *heart rate variability* – measured with an electrocardiogram (ECG) local differential triode with the Plux wireless biosignal toolkit – with a SIA as biofeedback trainer (Fig. 20.3). Their evaluation included both, a subject-matter expert interview and an experiment with 71 participants. In the experiment, they compared the novel SIA-based stress management training to a conventional stress management training using stress diaries. The results indicated that the SIA-based biofeedback training significantly decreased the self-assessed stress levels immediately after the training, as well as in a socially stressful task. Moreover, a significant correlation between stress level and the assessment of one's performance in a socially stressful task was found. Participants that received the SIA-based training assessed their performance higher than participants getting stress diaries. Taken this together, the authors evaluated using a SIA as a biofeedback trainer as a valid method for learning techniques on how to cope with stressful situations.

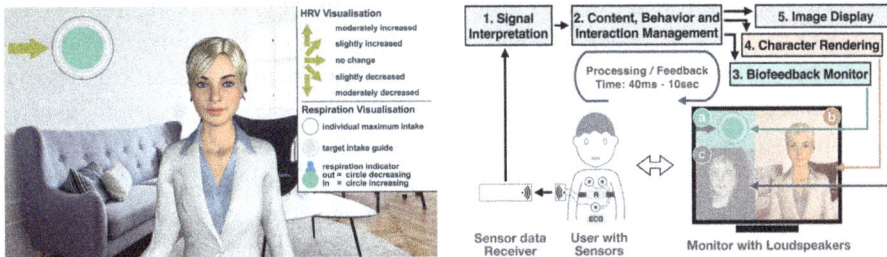

Fig. 20.3: Biofeedback Training: SIA Gloria as trainer (left), technological set-up and architecture (right) [43] (Source: DFKI, used under CC BY-ND license).

Bickmore [44] recently presented an overview of health-related applications of SIAs for overweight and obesity interventions, chronic disease management (e.g., diabetes, hypertension, atrial fibrillation), and substance abuse screening and interventions. He points out the positive factors for patients and health experts: cost savings, 24×7 availability, and location independence. Moreover, patients experience SIAs as being patient, trustworthy, and non-judgmental.

Physically embodied SIAs, also known as *social robots* or *care robots*, as a new development, are currently mostly employed in elder care, but also in childcare, support for individuals with disabilities, hospital settings, rehabilitation, walking assistance, and various other healthcare contexts. For elder care in the context of speech-based tasks, they enhance individual independence, simplify daily routines, reduce reliance on human caregivers, and facilitate communication with family through remote telematic connections [45]. Such robots are designed to monitor and assist older adults both mentally and physically. Examples of their tasks are: emotional support, reminders, motivation, and – if the robots are mobile and/or have arms to interact – delivering items, and assisting with dining [46]. The most popular social robots currently available are PARO (AIST, Japan) followed by Pepper (SoftBank Robotics, Japan) and NAO (SoftBank Robotics, Japan) [47].

PARO[1] is a baby harp seal robot that can move and make sounds in addition to responding to stimuli. PARO has five kinds of sensors: tactile, light, audition, temperature, and posture sensors, with which it can perceive people and its environment. It was initially designed as a pet therapy for older people with dementia, where it still has its most applications. However, there are studies examining it with participants for pain and stress relief [48].

Pepper[2] was introduced in 2014 as the first programmable social humanoid robot that can recognize faces and basic human emotions and interact with people through conversation and his touch screen. Pepper has so far been applied in several areas in healthcare. Efstratiou et al. [49] as well as Lang et al. [50] examined how Pepper can help children with autism to acquire daily life skills and self-reliance. Blindheim et al. [51] used Pepper to promote activity in long-term care facilities and qualitatively examined the experiences of residents and care staff. Staff and residents reported enjoying their interactions with Pepper, highlighting opportunities for new types of activities and actions that differed from the daily routine. Carros et al. [52] placed a Pepper for a three month long-term study in a nursing home to gain empirical insights into the way the robot was used. They showed that the care workers used the robot regularly, on average more than one hour a day, mostly in one-to-one interactions with residents. Overall, they have found an enhancement of care quality due to the robot.

NAO[3] is a biped small humanoid robot (58 cm height) that can move and adapt to the environment. It has two cameras, seven tactile sensors, four directional microphones and speakers to interact with humans and the environment. Vocal recognition and dialogue are available in 20 different languages. In their review, Robaczewski et al.

---

1 http://www.parorobots.com/
2 https://corporate-internal-prod.aldebaran.com/en/pepper
3 https://corporate-internal-prod.aldebaran.com/en/nao

[53] gathered research that has been done using NAO to see how it can be used and what could be its potential as a socially assistive robot. They found several application domains and positive effects for NAO including psychological and physical therapy assistance. For example, NAO is assessed as a great model for the participants to imitate physical exercises, despite some physical limitations of the robot, which limit the movements it can do. For patients with mild cognitive impairment and dementia, the NAO robot demonstrates promising potential as both a cognitive rehabilitation tool and a supportive companion. Its interactive capabilities and programmed interventions can help stimulate mental engagement and provide social interaction for individuals struggling with cognitive decline.

Another robot used for care applications is Navel, a mobile social robot that supports nonverbal interaction in addition to verbal communication [54]. It's hardware-software system enables human-robot interactions that emulate natural human-to-human communication, ensuring intuitive usability across diverse user populations. Social signal perception is facilitated by multiple computer vision algorithms operating in near real-time on an embedded NVIDIA edge device, optimizing low-latency processing while preserving data privacy. Social signal representation is achieved through an innovative integration of displays and fiber-optic plates, enabling the rendering of expressive three-dimensional eyes capable of realistic eye contact. A streamlined high-performance software architecture supports agile, context-sensitive behavioral generation. The robot's abstracted humanoid design mitigates Uncanny Valley effects.

20.4 Ethical considerations

Employing SIAs for medical applications necessitates careful attention to ethical considerations, particularly in autonomy, privacy, cultural sensitivity, and the responsible use of data. As SIAs become more central to care delivery, their design and implementation must align with core human values, ensuring respect, empathy, and fairness in their interactions.

Empathy is one critical component of ethical care, serving as a universal motivator for action and a medium for meaningful communication. Scholars such as Mary Jeanne Larrabee [55] and Nel Noddings [56] highlight the importance of care ethics, emphasizing the relational nature of compassion and empathy. SIAs, as artificially empathic agents, must navigate the delicate balance between providing support and respecting individual autonomy. Therefore, the process of designing SIAs should include mechanisms that maintain user autonomy by separating the programmed goals of the agent from the wants and needs of the individuals it serves. This separation is critical to fostering trust and ensuring that the agent does not impose its functionality in a way that undermines the dignity or decision-making capacity of the user.

Cultural, familial, ethnical and societal values are deeply connected to empathy and care. As Slote [57] argues, values such as compassion and racial favoritism are not innate but culturally shaped. When designing SIAs, developers must account for these contextual factors to ensure that the agents align with the values and expectations of the communities they serve. The risk of introducing foreign or incompatible values through technology underscores the need for culturally adaptive systems. Incorporating cultural sensitivity into SIA design requires interdisciplinary collaboration. Frameworks such as Spiekermann's value-based IT design provide valuable insights, advocating for the integration of values like health, safety, privacy, trust, dignity, and respect [58]. By tailoring SIAs to the unique cultural contexts of their users, designers can avoid ethical pitfalls and foster greater acceptance and efficacy in diverse settings.

Also, SIAs' reliance on sensitive health and behavioral data raises significant concerns about privacy and security. Ensuring robust data protection measures is paramount, as health data breaches or misuse can have far-reaching implications for individuals and communities. Transparent data storage, management, and sharing policies, such as those provided by the SEMLA[4] research framework, are essential to building trust in these systems. Moreover, the potential for SIAs to influence user behavior through empathy-driven interactions necessitates vigilance against manipulation or exploitation. Ethical guidelines must address how SIAs collect and use data to ensure their actions remain supportive rather than coercive or invasive.

20.5 Conclusion and future work

Integrating Socially Interactive Agents (SIAs) in a virtual or physical form as interfaces for healthcare technology represents a transformative approach to addressing critical gaps. By their embodiment of knowledgeable experts and combining social and empathic strategies with advanced medical sensor technology, SIAs offer innovative solutions that enhance patient and care personnel experiences. Their application in diverse domains, e.g., from stress management and therapeutic interventions to elder care and rehabilitation, has demonstrated their ability to reduce caregiver shortages, improve patient compliance, and foster meaningful interactions. Furthermore, the deployment of physical and virtual SIAs underscores their versatility in supporting a range of healthcare needs while maintaining cost efficiency and scalability.

Despite these advancements, significant opportunities remain for future exploration. Enhancing the cultural adaptability of SIAs to align with diverse values and expectations is a pressing need, as empathy and trust are deeply rooted in cultural contexts. Further research is required to ensure data security and ethical considerations, par-

---

4 https://semla.dfki.de/

ticularly regarding privacy and autonomy in patient-agent interactions. Additionally, advancing the social-emotional abilities of SIAs to more fitting non-verbal behavior that supports trust and acceptance.

Future work could also focus on longitudinal studies to evaluate the sustained impact of SIAs on health outcomes and user satisfaction. Exploring their integration with emerging technologies, such as wearable devices and real-time biosignal processing, holds promise for creating more responsive and proactive care models. Collaboration across interdisciplinary fields will be essential in designing SIAs that not only meet the functional requirements of healthcare but also respect the dignity and individuality of users.

In conclusion, SIAs have immense potential to redefine healthcare delivery. With continuous development, they are poised to play a pivotal role in fostering a more compassionate, inclusive, and efficient healthcare ecosystem.

References

[1] Chew C. M. "Caregiver Shortage Reaches Critical Stage," *Provider*, vol. 43, no. 5, pp. 14–16, 18, 21–22, 24, 27–28, May 2017.

[2] Poghosyan L., Clarke S. P., Finlayson M., and Aiken L. H. "Nurse burnout and quality of care: cross-national investigation in six countries," *Res Nurs Health*, vol. 33, no. 4, pp. 288–298, Aug. 2010. https://doi.org/10.1002/nur.20383.

[3] Hall L. H., Johnson J., Watt I., Tsipa A., and O'Connor D. B. "Healthcare Staff Wellbeing, Burnout, and Patient Safety: A Systematic Review," *PLoS ONE*, vol. 11, no. 7, p. e0159015, Jul. 2016. https://doi.org/10.1371/journal.pone.0159015.

[4] Thiam P. et al. "Multi-Modal Pain Intensity Recognition Based on the SenseEmotion Database," in *IEEE Transactions on Affective Computing*, vol. 12, no. 3, pp. 743–760, 1 July-Sept. 2021. https://doi.org/10.1109/TAFFC.2019.2892090.

[5] Arora R., Prajod P., Nicora M. L., Panzeri D., Tauro G., Vertechy R., Malosio M., André E. and Gebhard P. (2024) Socially interactive agents for robotic neurorehabilitation training: conceptualization and proof-of-concept study. *Frontiers in Artificial Intelligence* 7:1441955. https://doi.org/10.3389/frai.2024.1441955

[6] Cassell J., Sullivan J., Churchill E., and Prevost S., *Embodied conversational agents*. MIT press, 2000.

[7] Pelachaud C. "Studies on gesture expressivity for a virtual agent," *Speech Communication*, vol. 51, no. 7, pp. 630–639, 2009.

[8] Krämer N. C., Lucas G., Schmitt L., and Gratch J. "Social snacking with a virtual agent – On the interrelation of need to belong and effects of social responsiveness when interacting with artificial entities," *International Journal of Human-Computer Studies*, vol. 109, pp. 112–121, Jan. 2018. https://doi.org/10.1016/j.ijhcs.2017.09.001.

[9] Lugrin B. "Introduction to Socially Interactive Agents," in *The Handbook on Socially Interactive Agents*, 1st ed., Lugrin B., Pelachaud C., and Traum D. (eds.). New York, NY, USA: ACM, 2021, pp. 1–20. https://doi.org/10.1145/3477322.3477324.

[10] Don D. S. W., Müller P., Nunnari F., André E., and Gebhard P. "ReNeLiB: Real-time Neural Listening Behavior Generation for Socially Interactive Agents," in *Proceedings of the. 25th International Conference on Multimodal Interaction*, Paris, France, 2023, pp. 507–516. https://doi.org/10.1145/3577190.3614133.

[11] Mehlmann G., Häring M., Janowski K., Baur T., Gebhard P., and André E. "Exploring a Model of Gaze for Grounding in Multimodal HRI," in *Proceedings of the 16th International Conference on Multimodal Interaction*, Istanbul, Turkey, 2014, pp. 247–254. https://doi.org/10.1145/2663204.2663275.

[12] Gebhard P., Schneeberger T., Mehlmann G., Baur T., and André E. "Designing the Impression of Social Agents' Real-time Interruption Handling," in *Proceedings 19th ACM International Conference on Intelligent Virtual Agents*, Paris, France, 2019, pp. 19–21. https://doi.org/10.1145/3308532.3329435.

[13] Cafaro A., Glas N., and Pelachaud C. "The Effects of Interrupting Behavior on Interpersonal Attitude and Engagement in Dyadic Interactions," in *Proceedings of the International Conference on Autonomous Agents and Multiagent Systems*, 2016, pp. 911–920.

[14] Schneeberger T., Gebhard P., and Tsovaltzi D. ExHAIL: "Explicit and Implicit Emotion Regulation Training with a Social Agent", *Proceedings of the International Society of the Learning Sciences*, 2018

[15] Bickmore T. W., Caruso L., Clough-Gorr K., and Heeren T. "'It's just like you talk to a friend' relational agents for older adults," *Interacting with Computers*, vol. 17, no. 6, pp. 711–735, 2005.

[16] DeVault D. et al. "SimSensei Kiosk: A Virtual Human Interviewer for Healthcare Decision Support," in *Proceedings of the 2014 International Conference on Autonomous Agents and Multi-agent Systems*, 2014, pp. 1061–1068.

[17] Lucas G. M., Gratch J., King A., and Morency L.-P. "It's only a computer: Virtual humans increase willingness to disclose," *Computers in Human Behavior*, vol. 37, pp. 94–100, 2014.

[18] Farber B. A. "Patient self-disclosure: A review of the research," *Journal of Clinical Psychology*, vol. 59, no. 5, pp. 589–600, May 2003. https://doi.org/10.1002/jclp.10161.

[19] Kang S. and Gratch J. "Virtual humans elicit socially anxious interactants' verbal self-disclosure," *Computer Animation & Virtual*, vol. 21, no. 3–4, pp. 473–482, May 2010. https://doi.org/10.1002/cav.345.

[20] Reeves B. and C. I. Nass, *The media equation: How people treat computers, television, and new media like real people and places.* Cambridge university press, 1996.

[21] Nass C. and Steuer J. "Voices, Boxes, and Sources of Messages: Computers and Social Actors," *Human Communication Research*, vol. 19, no. 4, pp. 504–527, Mar. 2006. https://doi.org/10.1111/j.1468-2958.1993.tb00311.x.

[22] Nass C. and Moon Y. "Machines and mindlessness: Social responses to computers," *Journal of Social Issues*, vol. 56, no. 1, pp. 81–103, 2000.

[23] Kopp S., Gesellensetter L., Krämer N. C., and Wachsmuth I. "A conversational agent as museum guide–design and evaluation of a real-world application," in *International Workshop on Intelligent Virtual Agents*, Springer, 2005, pp. 329–343.

[24] Hoffmann L., Krämer N. C., Lam-Chi A., and Kopp S. "Media equation revisited: do users show polite reactions towards an embodied agent?," in *International Workshop on Intelligent Virtual Agents*, Springer, 2009, pp. 159–165.

[25] Gratch J., Wang N., Gerten J., Fast E., and Duffy R. "Creating rapport with virtual agents" in *International Workshop on Intelligent Virtual Agents*, Springer, 2007, pp. 125–138.

[26] Krämer N., Kopp S., Becker-Asano C., and Sommer N. "Smile and the world will smile with you – The effects of a virtual agent's smile on users' evaluation and behavior," *International Journal of Human-Computer Studies*, vol. 71, no. 3, pp. 335–349, Mar. 2013. https://doi.org/10.1016/j.ijhcs.2012.09.006.

[27] Chartrand T. L. and Bargh J. A. "The chameleon effect: the perception–behavior link and social interaction.," *Journal of Personality and Social Psychology*, vol. 76, no. 6, p. 893, 1999.

[28] Chartrand T. L., Maddux W. W., and Lakin J. L. "Beyond the perception-behavior link: The ubiquitous utility and motivational moderators of nonconscious mimicry," *The new unconscious*, pp. 334–361, 2005.

[29] Ekman P. and Friesen W. V. "Constants across cultures in the face and emotion.," *Journal of Personality and Social Psychology*, vol. 17, no. 2, p. 124, 1971.

[30] Kraut R. E. and Johnston R. E. "Social and emotional messages of smiling: an ethological approach.," *Journal of Personality and Social Psychology*, vol. 37, no. 9, p. 1539, 1979.

[31] Sproull L., Subramani M., Kiesler S., Walker J. H., and Waters K. "When the interface is a face," *Human-Computer Interaction*, vol. 11, no. 2, pp. 97–124, 1996.

[32] Deladisma A. M. et al. "Do medical students respond empathetically to a virtual patient?," *The American Journal of Surgery*, vol. 193, pp. 756–760, 2007.

[33] Weitz K., Schiller D., Schlagowski R., Huber T., and E. André. "'Do you trust me?' Increasing user-trust by integrating virtual agents in explainable AI interaction design," in *Proceedings of the 19th ACM International Conference on Intelligent Virtual Agents*, 2019, pp. 7–9.

[34] Weitz K., Schiller D., Schlagowski R., Huber T., and André E. "'Let me explain!': exploring the potential of virtual agents in explainable AI interaction design," *Journal of Multimodal User Interfaces*, vol. 15, no. 2, pp. 87–98, Jun. 2021. https://doi.org/10.1007/s12193-020-00332-0.

[35] Lucas G. M. et al. "Reporting mental health symptoms: breaking down barriers to care with virtual human interviewers," *Frontiers in Robotics and AI*, vol. 4, p. 51, 2017.

[36] Tickle-Degnen L. and Rosenthal R. "The Nature of Rapport and Its Nonverbal Correlates," *Psychological Inquiry*, vol. 1, no. 4, pp. 285–293, Oct. 1990. https://doi.org/10.1207/s15327965pli0104_1.

[37] Bickmore T., Rubin A. and Simon S. "Substance Use Screening using Virtual Agents: Towards Automated Screening, Brief Intervention, and Referral to Treatment (SBIRT)," in *Proceedings of the 20th ACM International Conference on Intelligent Virtual Agents*, Virtual Event Scotland UK: ACM, Oct. 2020, pp. 1–7. https://doi.org/10.1145/3383652.3423869.

[38] Pickard M. D., Roster C. A. and Chen Y. "Revealing sensitive information in personal interviews: Is self-disclosure easier with humans or avatars and under what conditions?," *Computers in Human Behavior*, vol. 65, pp. 23–30, Dec. 2016. https://doi.org/10.1016/j.chb.2016.08.004.

[39] Baumeister R. F. and Leary M. R. "The Need to Belong: Desire for Interpersonal Attachments as a Fundamental Human Motivation," in *Interpersonal Development*, Zukauskiene R. (ed.). Routledge, 1995, pp. 57–89.

[40] Pauw L. S., Sauter D. A., Van Kleef G. A., Lucas G. M., Gratch J. and Fischer A. H. "The avatar will see you now: Support from a virtual human provides socio-emotional benefits," *Computers in Human Behavior*, vol. 136, p. 107368, Nov. 2022. https://doi.org/10.1016/j.chb.2022.107368.

[41] Weizenbaum J. "ELIZA – a computer program for the study of natural language communication between man and machine," *Commun. ACM*, vol. 9, no. 1, pp. 36–45, Jan. 1966. https://doi.org/10.1145/365153.365168.

[42] Gebhard P., Schneeberger T., Dietz M., André E. and N. ul Bajwa H. "Designing a Mobile Social and Vocational Reintegration Assistant for Burn-out Outpatient Treatment," in *Proceedings of the 19th ACM International Conference on Intelligent Virtual Agents*, Paris France: ACM, Jul. 2019, pp. 13–15. https://doi.org/10.1145/3308532.3329460.

[43] Schneeberger T., Sauerwein N., Anglet M. S. and Gebhard P. "Stress Management Training using Biofeedback guided by Social Agents," in *Proceedings of the 26th International Conference on Intelligent User Interfaces*, College Station TX USA: ACM, Apr. 2021, pp. 564–574. https://doi.org/10.1145/3397481.3450683.

[44] Bickmore T. "Health-Related Applications of Socially Interactive Agents," in *The Handbook on Socially Interactive Agents*, 1st ed., Lugrin B., Pelachaud C. and Traum D. (eds.). New York, NY, USA: ACM, 2022, pp. 403–436. https://doi.org/10.1145/3563659.3563672.

[45] Søraa R. A., Tøndel G., Kharas M. W. and Serrano J. A. "What do Older Adults Want from Social Robots? A Qualitative Research Approach to Human-Robot Interaction (HRI) Studies," *Int J of Soc Robotics*, vol. 15, no. 3, pp. 411–424, Mar. 2023. https://doi.org/10.1007/s12369-022-00914-w.

[46] Kyrarini M. et al. "A Survey of Robots in Healthcare," *Technologies*, vol. 9, no. 1, p. 8, Jan. 2021. https://doi.org/10.3390/technologies9010008.

[47] Morgan A. A., Abdi J., Syed M. A. Q., Kohen G. E., Barlow P. and Vizcaychipi M. P. "Robots in Healthcare: a Scoping Review," *Curr Robot Rep*, vol. 3, no. 4, pp. 271–280, Oct. 2022. https://doi.org/10.1007/s43154-022-00095-4.

[48] Geva N., Hermoni N. and Levy-Tzedek S. "Interaction Matters: The Effect of Touching the Social Robot PARO on Pain and Stress is Stronger When Turned ON vs. OFF," *Front. Robot. AI*, vol. 9, p. 926185, Jul. 2022. https://doi.org/10.3389/frobt.2022.926185.

[49] Efstratiou R. et al. "Teaching Daily Life Skills in Autism Spectrum Disorder (ASD) Interventions Using the Social Robot Pepper," in *Robotics in Education*, vol. 1316, Lepuschitz W., Merdan M., Koppensteiner G., Balogh R., and Obdržálek D. (eds.). in Advances in Intelligent Systems and Computing, vol. 1316., Cham: Springer International Publishing, 2021, pp. 86–97. https://doi.org/10.1007/978-3-030-67411-3_8.

[50] Lang N., Goes N., Struck M., Wittenberg T., Seßner J., Franke J., Dziobek I., Kirst S. and Naumann S. "Evaluation of an algorithm for optical pulse detection in children for application to the Pepper robot," *Current Directions in Biomedical Engineering*, 7(2), 484–487, 2021. https://doi.org/10.1515/cdbme-2021-2123.

[51] Blindheim K., Solberg M., Hameed I. A. and Alnes R. E. "Promoting activity in long-term care facilities with the social robot Pepper: a pilot study," *Informatics for Health and Social Care*, vol. 48, no. 2, pp. 181–195, Apr. 2023. https://doi.org/10.1080/17538157.2022.2086465.

[52] Carros F. et al. "Care Workers Making Use of Robots: Results of a Three-Month Study on Human-Robot Interaction within a Care Home," in *CHI Conference on Human Factors in Computing Systems*, New Orleans LA USA: ACM, Apr. 2022, pp. 1–15. https://doi.org/10.1145/3491102.3517435.

[53] Robaczewski, A., Bouchard, J., Bouchard, K. & Gaboury, S. (2021). Socially assistive robots: The specific case of the NAO. *International Journal of Social Robotics, 13*(4), 795–831. https://doi.org/10.1007/s12369-020-00664-7.

[54] Toussaint C., Schwarz P. T. and Petermann M. "Navel – A Social Robot with Verbal and Nonverbal Communication Skills," in *Extended Abstracts of the 2023 CHI Conference on Human Factors in Computing Systems (CHI EA '23)*, Hamburg, Germany, 2023, Art. no. 463. https://doi.org/10.1145/3544549.3583898.

[55] Larrabee M. J. and Larrabee M. J. *An Ethic of Care: Feminist and Interdisciplinary Perspectives*. in Thinking Gender. s.l: Taylor and Francis, 2016.

[56] Noddings N. *Caring: A Relational Approach to Ethics and Moral Education.*, 2nd ed. University of California Press, 2013. Accessed: Jan. 27, 2025. [Online]. Available: http://www.jstor.org/stable/10.1525/j.ctt7zw1nb.

[57] Slote M. A. *The ethics of care and empathy*. London: Routledge, 2008.

[58] Spiekermann S. *Digitale Ethik: ein Wertesystem für das 21. Jahrhundert*. München: Droemer, 2019.

[59] Fonck S. and Stollenwerk A. "Explainable Artificial Intelligence in Biomedical Engineering" In: Manzeschke A. and Wittenberg T. (eds.). Ethical Perspectives on Artificial Intelligence in Biomedical Engineering, Chapter 13, DeGruyter, 2025.

Galia Assadi, Arne Manzeschke, Nadine Lang-Richter,
Thomas Wittenberg

21 Emotion recognition in healthcare

21.1 Emotions and technology – opposition or analogy?

Before developments in the field of automated emotion recognition and representation, the relationship between emotions and technology was considered almost oppositional. While emotionality, understood as the ability to recognize and demonstrate emotions, was clearly considered a purely human (and in some cases animal) characteristic, technology was seen as a representative of rationality and objectivity – the exact opposite of emotion. Technology functions precisely because it has no emotions [1]. However, this relationship has been questioned at least since the beginnings of *affective computing*, a term coined by Rosalind Picard in the 1990s [2]. It refers to the development of technical systems that claim the potential to both, recognize *and* simulate human emotions, thereby enabling socially appropriate emotional interactions between people and technical systems [3]. This technology has gained considerable importance in recent years due to advances in machine learning and multimodal data collection methods. Affective computing nowadays has a wide range of applications in areas such as social robotics, education, the automotive industry, neuromarketing, customer service as well as healthcare.

In order to understand and, based on this, to ethically evaluate which desirable and undesirable effects are associated with the (further) development and social spread of affective computing (and the closely related fields of *affective sensing* [4] and *affective robotics* [5]) in the field of healthcare, and how desirable effects can be promoted, it is necessary to reflect on both, the understanding of emotions and the functioning of affective computing. This shows that the technologization (perception and production) of emotions is the result of (1) specific presuppositions yielding a selection process, since (2) a selection is made from a variety of emotion theories or models from the fields of philosophy, psychology and sociology, (3) only technically identifiable human expressions can be used to identify emotions, and (4) only certain emotions can be represented from a technical perspective.

In order to be able to explicitly reflect on these (mostly) unreflected presuppositions and the following implicit selection processes, and thus arrive at a reflected ethical decision, the following Section 21.2 provides a brief overview of various emotion theories of different disciplinary origins. Following this, in Section 21.3 the technical principles and methods in the field of affective sensing and affective computing are explained. Building on this foundation, a structured model for the ethical analysis of emotions in the context of human-technology is presented (Section 21.4), which can be used as an orientation tool in the service of independent ethical judgment.

21.2 Understanding human emotions

Emotions are complex phenomena that encompass physiological, psychological and social dimensions. They play a crucial role in the human (self-)experience and influence interactive behavior, decision-making and social relations. Over time, various theories have been developed in philosophy, sociology and psychology to explain and categorize emotions. Some of the most important theories will be briefly presented in an overview.

21.2.1 Psychological theories of emotions

The *James-Lange theory* (1884/85), named after psychologists William James and Carl Lange, posits that emotions arise in response to physiological alteration in the body. According to this theory, people first experience a physical response to a stimulus (e.g., heart palpitations when afraid) and then interpret this response as an emotion (e.g., "fear"). This perspective places emphasis on physical experience as the basis of emotional states [6].

In contrast to the James-Lange theory, the *Cannon-Bard theory* (~ 1925) argues that emotions and physiological responses occur simultaneously and independently of each other. Cannon and Bard [7] claim that an emotional stimulus triggers both the emotional experience and the physiological changes in the body. This theory highlights the role of the brain, within which the control center for emotional responses is located.

Schachter's and Singer's two-factor theory (1962) [8] understands emotions as consisting of two components: physiological arousal and the cognitive interpretation of this arousal. This theory emphasizes that people place their physiological reactions in an emotional context, which determines the specific emotion.

Paul Ekman sees emotions and facial expressions as a universal human characteristic. He identifies seven basic emotions: "joy", "sadness", "fear", "surprise", "disgust", "contempt" and "anger". Ekman [9] argues that certain emotions have similar expressions around the world, suggesting a biological basis for emotions.

Richard Lazarus, a prominent representative of the cognitive school of theory, emphasizes the role of cognitive appraisals in the emergence of emotions. He argues that emotions are the result of evaluations that people make about events and their significance for their own well-being. These evaluations determine how a person responds to a particular stimulus, which elicits the emotion [10].

As shown above, the study of emotions is a dynamic field in which different psychological theories illuminate different aspects of the emotional experience. These differences can be explained by reflecting on the construction of the theories as e.g. Luc Ciompi does [11]:

> "How is it possible that the scientists involved have such difficulty arriving at a clear definition of a phenomenon that, despite all its diversity, is also typically holistic, a phenomenon that not only is familiar to everyone from personal experience and intuitively understood as something unified even by laypeople, but whose essential core, one might think, is also quite obvious? [...] The central problem, however, in my opinion, lies in the fact that a fundamental difference between affective and cognitive phenomena, as it will be elaborated below, is nowhere grasped with sufficient clarity. For this reason, the boundary between the two phenomena can be arbitrarily redrawn again and again; the inevitable consequence is a constant mixing and confusion of affective and cognitive phenomena." (translated by G. Assadi)

However, emotions have not only been the focus of scientific attention since the beginnings of psychology, as philosophy also offers valuable insights into emotions and their significance for human existence, which are presented in an overview below.

21.2.2 Philosophical perspectives on emotions

While psychology examines emotions particularly as *physical* phenomena, the philosophical perspective focuses primarily on the nature and composition of emotions and furthermore their meaning in a moral and social context. The question of the nature of emotions, their origins, their role in human practice and their relationship to other cognitive processes such as thinking and willing has a long tradition in Western philosophy [12,13].

For Plato, emotions (especially "passion") are often the result of a conflict between reason and the lower, animal parts of the soul. Emotions such as "anger" or "desire" are seen as disruptive to reason, which should represent the highest goal of man. Thus, in this view, emotions are mostly negative and must be controlled to promote the welfare of the individual and society [14].

Aristotle offers a more nuanced view in his *Nicomachean Ethics* [15] (Aristotle, 350 BC). He sees emotions not only as failures of reason, but as central components of human ethics. For Aristotle, the right balance between emotion and reason is necessary to lead a virtuous life. The importance of emotions lies in their ability to motivate people to fulfill their moral and social obligations.

In his work *Passions of the Soul* [16], René Descartes (1596–1650) describes emotions as physical reactions to external events that are experienced by the soul as "passions". In Descartes' view, emotions are not the product of an irrational part of the soul, but a fundamental component of human existence that interacts with reason and the body. In Descartes' theory, emotions have two functions: (1) a motivating function that supports reason by influencing human behavior, but (2) emotions simultaneously represent a source of danger when they overwhelm reason, which is why passions should be controlled through the use of reason.

Immanuel Kant (1724–1804) emphasized the importance of the categorical impera-tive and saw emotions as potentially problematic for the moral agent. Nevertheless, he also recognized that emotions play an important role in aesthetic judgment and human experience [17].

Modern philosophical theories about emotions focus on the cognitive and social aspects of emotions. For example, Martha Nussbaum [18] sees emotions as complex reactions based on evaluations of (external and internal) events. She does not under-stand emotions as just physical reactions to external stimuli but argues that they can only be understood as phenomena linked to our internal beliefs and evaluations of the world. In her theory, emotions fulfill a central function with regard to moral perception, as they encourage us to think about ethical questions and evaluate our actions towards others.

The philosophical argument of Hermann Schmitz [19] boils down to the fact that, as early as Plato, the subjective introjection of atmospheres and moods as moving powers had been relocated to the inner side of the subject, while what we today call "emotions" were initially perceived as external forces. Accordingly, the soul becomes the place of emotions. Following Schmitz there evolved two opposing types of human self-under-standing: (1) the human being under the spell of gripping powers (feelings or gods, today we should add atmospheres and moods [20,21]) in bodily-affective involvement, (2) the human being as a person who can assert himself against the gripping power and even manipulate feelings [22]. Especially with regard to the understanding of human emotions in the age of artificial intelligence (AI), Schmitz's position offers interesting impulses for reflection. Schmitz's concept of *atmospheres* allows us to transcend the idea of emotions as a purely subjective state and thus the sharp separation between the subject's inner world and the surrounding external world. Against the backdrop of affective computing, affective sensing and affective robotics (see Section 21.1), the notion of "atmospheres" that address us humans from the outside proves to be much more appropriate to AI technology than the *introjective perspective*. However, these external factors are not gods or powers, but corporations and states [23,24].

One could venture the thesis that the *psychologization of humans* is now followed by the *psychologization of machines* [25]. This involves the machine not only learning and being able to recognize human emotions (the process of *digital perception*), but that *machine learning* (ML, including AI) as such is not just a computational process, but is accompanied by evaluations that could exhibit something like *machine emotions* as an internal state of machine self-reflection. Furthermore, based on such intrinsic *emotional state* of the machine, the machine itself could be able to exhibit and display some empathic reaction, e.g., by employing *social interactive agents* (SIAs) [26] or even in form of social robots as affective computers with an embodiment [27].

In addition, *the social dimension* of emotions is becoming increasingly important. Emotions are not just individual phenomena but are deeply rooted in the social. Robert Solomon [28] and Ronald de Sousa [29] argue that emotions are primarily social phenomena that structure our relationships and our understanding of the world. Emotions serve as a means of communication with which we express our values and needs.

Without digging too deep in, a basic distinction about the nature of emotions is important for further considerations. On the one hand so-called *physicalists* can be found (who might call themselves 'realists') to whom an emotion is a mental representation based on physical conditions which can be reconstructed in neurophysiology or neuropsychology. On the other hand, phenomenologists claim that emotion is an intentional content of consciousness that can only be captured in transcendental philosophy [30]. We assume that the technology of emotion recognition (see Section 21.3) as it is practiced today builds on the preliminary theoretical decisions of the first position – which are worthy of discussion.

21.3 Affective computing – technologization of emotions

Emotion recognition through novel AI approaches includes various technologies that aim to detect an individual's emotional states using various data such as facial expressions, pupillometry, speech and voice patterns, as well as physiological responses (as e.g. ECG, EEG, EDA). The main technical methods of emotion recognition include the camera-based analysis of facial activities (Section 21.3.1), the analysis of voice and speech parameters (Section 21.3.2), or the measurement and extraction of adequate parameters from vital signs (Section 21.3.3):

21.3.1 Recognition of facial activities

The image-based recognition of facial activities and emotional states from video and image-streams, such as "happiness", "sadness", "anger", or "surprise", is based on various complementary and hierarchical methods from the field of image processing, image analysis (for adequate feature extraction) and machine learning (for classification and discrimination), including deep neural networks (DNNs). The main steps for facial activity analysis consist of (1) the detection of one or more faces in the camera's field of view [31], (2) the subdivision or segmentation of the detected *face-objects* into their individual *facial components* (e.g., "mouth", "eyes", "nose", "eyebrows", "chin") [32], (3) the identification of *unique facial* landmarks (or prominent points of interest) of these facial components (corners of the eyes, corners and edges of the mouth, nostrils, ends of the eyebrows,....) and, based on these facial landmarks (4) the recognition of the so-called *action units* (AUs) [33], which relate to the temporal displacement of these landmarks in relation to the underlying facial musculature. The expression and combination of different AUs can then be used in a further step to (5) draw conclusions about the actual emotions of the person using machine and deep learning approaches. Overall, these named analysis steps are based on the so-called "Facial Activity Coding System" (FACS), originally suggested by Ekman & Friesen [34].

This approach, based on the subtle observable movements of landmarks in the face (as e.g. "inner brow raiser" = action unit #1, "nose wrinkler" = AU #9, or "lip pucker" = AU #18), enables certified experts (so-called FACS-coders) to systematically analyze and code human facial expressions with regard to emotional information based on the movements of 46 visually observable different landmarks. For instance, as depicted in Fig. 21.1, AU #12 ("Lip corner puller") combined with AU #6 ("Cheek raiser") yields a "smile". There furthermore exist additional codes for head and eye movements as for the gross behavior of the observed persons.

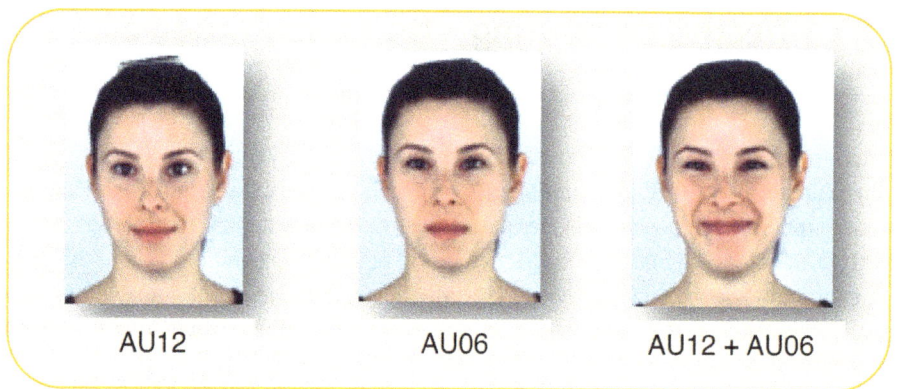

AU12	AU06	AU12 + AU06

Fig. 21.1: Action unit AU #12 ("Lip corner puller") combined with AU #6 ("Cheek raiser") yields a "smile". Source: Fraunhofer IIS.

However, as the associated coding process is time-consuming, as well as error prone, in the past decades, the FACS approach has been implemented as part of various (semi- or fully automated) software approaches in order to reduce the workload of FACS coders and to speed up and simplify the process of analyzing and transcribing. These automated approaches are now as robust as human coding while saving time. The approaches to contactless detect, characterize and identify basic human emotions based on the action units are nowadays used and investigated in various health-scenarios, including social robots or pain-assessment [35].

One example of this approach is the Fraunhofer IIS' SHORE technology [36,37], which is an image-based assessment of basic emotions such as "happy", "sad", "angry", "neutral" or "surprised", see Fig. 21.2. In addition, this approach can also be used to determine the "valence" of an emotion, hence the extent to which an emotion can be regarded as "positive" or "negative".

Fig. 21.2: Subjects whose basic emotions ("angry", "happy", "sad", "surprised") as well as age and gender are automatically detected using a machine learning approach. Source: Fraunhofer IIS.

21.3.2 Speech and voice analysis

Voice and speech-based emotion recognition is an area that enables machines to recognize specific elements of what constitutes human emotions in the aggregate based on vocal cues. Initially rooted in psychology, it has matured into a robust interdisciplinary domain combining signal processing, machine and deep learning, and multimodal fusion techniques [38]. Prosodic features like pitch quantization and spectral cues are increasingly integrated to capture nuanced emotional expressions.

Additionally, emotion recognition is currently being enhanced by incorporating speaker-specific modeling and contextual embeddings from large language models (LLMs). Current state-of-the-art systems leverage large-scale pretrained audio models often combined with textual and prosodic features, to enhance emotion classification accuracy. One current trend is the use of *Graph Attention Networks* (GATs) to improve robustness in naturalistic speech environments. These models excel in handling spontaneous, real-world audio where emotional cues are subtle and context-dependent. Future challenges of voice- and speech-based emotion recognition, are the recognition of inner and group emotions, as well as sarcasm [39].

21.3.3 Vital data for emotion assessment

Besides the assessment of emotions via the acquisition and analysis of facial expressions (based on image and video data, see Section 21.3.1) and speech (via microphones, see Section 21.3.2), also other vital signs and related measurements can be used to acquire information about a person's emotional states. These technical possibilities include measurements such as MRI (magnetic resonance imaging), ECG (electrocardiogram), EEG (electroencephalography), EDA (electrodermal activity), the heartrate variability (HRV) derived from the pulse rate, the breathing rate or even pupillometry. While MRI and EEG directly derive the reaction and activation of brain activities in response to – internal and external – emotional stimuli, other vital data are less obvious to connect to emotion assessment. However, based on the assumption that vital signs and emotions are connected or at least co-dependent, emotions (if strong enough) can trigger an activity of the central nervous system. As such, for example, the breathing rate and heart rate and derived from that the heart rate variability (HRV) are considered as an indicator of raised emotions [39]. Similarly, a raised EDA, promoting itself for example through enhanced sweat production especially in the palms, is considered as reaction to emotions like "fear" or "anger" [40]. Pupillometry, captured with specialized infra-red camera systems, is known to be related to emotional reactions. Sudden changes of the pupils' size, eye blinks and specific gaze patterns can be linked to the activation of the central nervous system when emotions like "happiness" or "fear" are present [41]. In contrast to audio information, which can be acquired contactless and quite sponta-neous, the assessment of optical data (video, image, pupillometry) needs line-of-sight, the acquisition of vital data usually requires some cable-bound (ECG, EMG, EEG) or device-dependent (MRI, wearables) technologies as well as multi-model (optical, acous-tical, mechanical, electrical, …) affects, stimuli or paradigms to trigger and induce emo-tions such as "pain", "happiness", or "sadness".

21.3.4 Data fusion

Due to the fact that the presentation of (external) emotions can be strongly influenced by various situational or socially conditions as, e.g., the need to smile instead of showing anger because the person is in a situation where smiling is mandatory, it makes sense to combine different sensor and data sources to capture and detect emotions. Therefore, advanced technologies in *data fusion* are used to combine for example facial expres-sions, speech and voice patterns, vital signals and more [42]. When using technologies like early, late or intermediate fusion or even generative technologies like foundation models, it is important to have in depth knowledge of not only the fusion technologies but also the vital signals themselves to avoid wrong causalities and connections.

    With the integrated use of artificial intelligence based on LLMs into emotion detec-tion systems, the use of AI-models for facial-based emotion recognition have recently been restricted or even prohibited in certain areas such as public surveillance or education by the EU-AI Act.

21.4 Applications of emotion assessment in healthcare

The rapid development of new types of technical sensors in combination with new powerful methods (such as deep neural networks, DNNs) within the field of AI in recent years has revolutionized numerous fields of applications in the healthcare domain, including emotion recognition, pain detection, or the assessment of cognitive load. The following paragraphs provide a brief overview of the range of current applications.

21.4.1 Emotion assessment for mental care

In mental healthcare, emotion detection and recognition systems can be used as diagnostic tools as they offer real-time insights into patients' emotional states and are able to monitor patients' emotional responses. These systems use AI to interpret facial expressions, voice tone, and behavioral cues, enabling early identification of emotional distress and detection of mental illnesses such as depression, anxiety disorders and autism, which can lead to faster and more precise treatment. For example, tools like *TheraSense* [43] integrate deep learning with teleconsultation platforms, enhancing remote therapy by providing clinicians with live emotional feedback. Such systems of *emotional AI* are also able to support continuous monitoring, keeping track of mood fluctuations and effectiveness of treatment.

21.4.2 Pain assessment

The regular (daily or even hourly) recording, assessment and documentation of pain is an essential task for nursing staff in the field of geriatric and intensive care, as well as for dementia patients. Numerical rating scales (NRS) are generally used for this assessment, which are completed both by nursing staff (external assessment) and by the patient (self-assessment) at rest or under stress. However, both approaches (self-assessment and external assessment) are highly subjective, contradictory and also highly dependent on many other external factors.

AI-assisted scoring and documentation systems can potentially be used to provide the best possible support for available nursing staff in times of acute nursing staff shortages. As "pain" can be considered as one specific expression of a set of emotions, automatic detection systems for the assessment of "pain" can potentially be applied for this task using image-based recognition and the description of pain on the basis of AUs (see Fig. 21.1). E.g., within the DFG-funded project "PainFaceReader" explainable and comprehensible approaches to image-based recognition and description of pain have been investigated and evaluated on several data collections [44–49].

21.4.3 Social robotics

Recent research shows that the use of *social robots* such as Pepper [50], Temi [51] or the Navel Robot [52] offer great advantages in communication with residents of retirement and nursing homes, as these mobile robotic systems simultaneously support social participation through telepresence and intellectual stimulation.

These social robots integrate various optical and acoustical sensors for contactless acquisition, processing and analysis of emotions as well as vital data, such as heart rate and respiratory rate or even temperature. For example, the Navel robot provides social signals by using AI-based natural language processing (NLP) for fluent communication with elderly residents. The navel robot also makes use of optical and acoustical clues to identify possible changes in emotion of the interacting humans, using this information to react adequately based on such observations.

In addition, such social robots have the potential to interact more easily with autistic children and people with dementia, whose ability for interpersonal interaction can be limited. Considering current technical systems of automated emotion recognition (see Section 21.3) and their anthropological and ethical aspects, one notices by looking at the different theories of emotions used (see Section 21.2) that the most prominent ones (using images, videos, voices, speech) are all based on Ekman's theory of emotions. The choice of this theoretical basis represents the (often forgotten) result of a selection process that does not follow an exclusively scientific logic. Instead, this selection can be understood as the result of a transfer of technical logic and possibilities to the field of human existence, which follows the motto emotion in the context of human-technology is what can technically be "observed as" or "related to" as emotions.

However, the consequences or even "fate" of Ekman's emotion theory, which has been widely criticized since its publication, also illustrates the social character of technology, the development and use of which is often driven not only by technical but also by non-technical motives, as Crawford explains [23]. She points out that the development of Ekman's theory has originally been due, among other things, to financial support from the military and secret services, who had an eminent interest in a technology that allows access to the otherwise hidden inner side of the human subject. The motive of directly extracting hidden emotions while bypassing subjective self-disclosure still plays a central role in emotion recognition today, which is why special attention is required from an ethical point of view, especially with regard to its use with vulnerable groups. Nevertheless, specifically this notion has led to the investigation and application of alternative technical measurement, such as EEG, or EMG, ECG or HRV (see Section 21.3.3.)

What can on the one hand be assessed as a mere *functional* requirement turns out to be questioned and possibly criticized on closer inspection due to the often forgotten parameter selection processes and motive layers. This necessity is also exacerbated by the reception and expectations towards technical systems that are perceived as objective, neutral and exclusively observing reality. However, if the underlying emotion model can be understood as the result of an interest-driven selection process in which relevant aspects of human emotionality are not taken into account, then it is not a mere recognition process but also a formation operation. Hence, besides trying to capture, analyze and interpret emotions from technical devices including sensors and AI, also structured self-assessment, e.g., person-reported outcome measures (PROMs) remain similar wise important and supplement any technical measurements.

If one realizes that individual insight into one's own emotional life is not always determined by great accuracy and that one's own emotional state often corresponds to an ensign in the wind, – as Montaigne [53] said – then it has some plausibility that in such moments people fall back on the seemingly technically objective evaluation of an emotion recognition. This has significant effects on the human relationship to self and the world and is therefore of high ethical sensitivity, especially since influence on the emotional level is more difficult to identify than on verbal, rational levels.

21.5 Ethical challenges of automated emotion recognition

In order to identify ethical implications of the automated recognition, processing and representation of emotions using sensors and AI, *intuitive moral judgments* can serve as a starting point, which often express themselves in or cause emotions. However, in order to fully comply with the ethical obligation to assume responsibly, which applies particularly to vulnerable target groups such as the addressed mental ill (see Section 21.4), a methodically guided approach is necessary.

Especially with regard to the identification and evaluation of ethical issues in the health care system, reference is often made to the *balancing model* developed by Tom Beauchamps and James Childress [54]. This model identifies four medium-range ethical principles (*beneficence, non-maleficence, respect for autonomy, justice*) and thus creates an evaluation framework that represents common morality on the one hand and combines insights from different philosophical theories on the other. Originally not explicitly developed for the evaluation of human-machine relationships, it can be applied for the ethical evaluation of emotion-sensitive technical systems [55]. When constructing their ethical model, Beauchamps & Childress explicitly pursued the objective that it should be both, theory-based *and* understandable for lay people, which almost necessarily involves a reductionism due to connectivity. However, if one is looking for a suitable methodological framework that takes into account the specifics of the development and use of technical systems in the field of affective computing, the question arises as to whether the reduced scheme of principle ethics is sufficient to provide a complete overview of ethically relevant aspects. In the authors' opinion, this is only partially the case, since although important questions such as autonomy (and thus the risk of manipulation [56]) or justice can be asked, central aspects such as the machine-based model of emotion are not taken into account, as are contextual factors that are central both to understanding emotions [57] and to ethical evaluation. However, because systems in the field of affective computing access a level of the human that people are often not fully aware of [58] and on which people may therefore be easier to influence, special care must be taken in the development and use of these systems.

To this end, an orientation tool is presented below that allows an analysis and assessment of the situations in which emotions are technically detected and displayed and thus helps to include some ethical insights in the development and implementation process in a constructive manner (for detailed explanation see [59]).

21.6 MTEmotions: Model for the analysis of emotional Human-Machine-Interaction

Since the human-technology relationships enabled by the use of affective computing or affective robotics are relatively new, it is crucial not to jump too quickly from an abstract representation of the socio-technical setting to an ethical evaluation, as otherwise there is a risk of misinterpretation and misjudgment. Therefore, in order to conduct a well-founded ethical evaluation, it is important to first attempt to describe and analyze what occurs between humans and technology in as much detail and concrete a manner as possible. Only on the basis of this thorough scrutiny can ethical implications be meaningfully identified and responsibly evaluated. Therefore it is necessary to focus not only on the technical or the human side, but to analyze the complete situation (as well as the context) between concrete humans and concrete technical systems. In order to discuss the opportunities and risks of automated emotion recognition in an ethically meaningful way, it is crucial to adopt an understanding of emotions that does not reduce them to physical states but rather conceives them as effects of social interaction between specific people and specific technical systems. This makes it possible to identify and shape what biologically reductive concepts often neglect: social conditions that are just as crucial to the emergence, perception, and regulation of emotions as psychological factors. On this basis, the problems inherent in abstract, decontextualized ethical judgments can be addressed, as these often lack sufficient practical guidance and are therefore not compatible with existing systems.

The theoretical foundation of the proposed model is formed by phenomenological theories of emotions, such as those advocated by Waldenfels [60]:

> "The crucial idea here [in compassion], however one elaborates it in detail, is that feelings are not – as one says in the modern tradition – mere states attributed to the individual, such as: someone is sad, i.e., they are in a state that can be measured as needed, e.g., via blood pressure or hormone secretions. The radical revision of this conception, as proposed by all phenomenological authors, consists in the fact that feelings are conceived as the way of relating to things, and in this, others are involved from the outset. Joy is not a state in which I find myself or which I bring about, but a state of being with others in the world. Thus, feelings evade the temptation of mere subjectification." (translated by G. Assadi)

A phenomenological understanding of emotions abolishes the strict (and often theory-constitutive) separation between a private, subjective *inner space* of emotion and an emotion-triggering *outer world*. This transcends the substantializing and fixating approach of emotion theories that operate with the clear distinction between inside and outside and instead emphasizes their constitutive relatedness. Emotion can therefore only be understood as a *relational phenomenon* that can never be understood in isolation, but only in connection with other elements. This allows individualizing perspectives on emotions as individual states to be reconstructed as the results of processes of differentiation, and the context necessary for understanding emotions [57] to be reintegrated into the analysis.

We pursue a system-based approach for understanding and evaluating. Thus, emotion is perceived as one out of a bunch of a socio-technological setting. To assess the role and meaning of emotion in this setting, the dimension *emotion* (D1) has to be set in relation to other dimensions, being: *actor* (D2), *actant* (D3), *context* (D4), and *interaction* (D5). Combining these five dimensions is necessary for the analysis and the ethical evaluation since only on the basis of an understanding of these dimensions it is possible to make a well-founded judgment as to whether and, if so, under what circumstances the development or use of a technical system for AI-based interpretation is ethically legitimate or illegitimate. The dimensions are illustrated in Fig. 21.3 using exemplary questions, the answers to which allow both a concrete system and fundamental considerations to be made based on the concrete case.

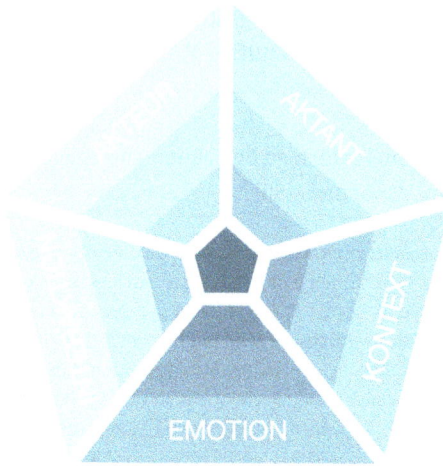

Fig. 21.3: Model MTEmotion.

D1: Emotions: Which emotions can and should AI-based recognition systems in health-care specifically be able to detect? How can this reaction of internally perceived emotional states to internal or external triggers be adequately measured and interpreted by the means of various (contactless or contact-related) sensors and post-hoc AI-analysis of the acquired sensory data? What does that mean for the application in healthcare? Which emotions can be recognized and distinguished by a certain system?

D2: Actant (non-human actor): What role is attributed to the technical systems or devices (smartphones, robots, tablets, machines ...) in these and why? Are these attributions based on real technical options or on human visions? What goals are associated on the human side with these attributions and the expectations associated with them? What do these attributions say about people?

D3: Actor: What role is attributed to the interacting humans in emotion-based, social communication contexts and why? What adaptation performance is implicitly expected and with what consequences can these be carried out?

D4: Interaction: What type of possible action should humans and technology carry out during the process of automated recognition? What type of interactions (stimuli, paradigms, affects) can be applied by humans or technological systems? How are the human and technical scope of affects limited? How are transgressions (e.g. aggressive behavior towards the technical system for providing stimuli and capturing emotional reactions) dealt with? What relationship should be established between people and technical systems?

D5: Context: In which possible healthcare contexts (see Section 21.4) should which technical system be used and why? Which contextual factors do we need to know in order to understand emotions correctly? What predictable effects will be connected with the use of the system?

In order to illustrate the functionality of the model using a concrete example, the social robot Navel [52] designed for the social intervention in elderly homes can be examined for its ethical implications in a healthcare setting. While the model by Beauchamps & Childress focuses ethical attention on questions of autonomy, beneficience, non-maleficience, and justice, the proposed MTEmotion model (see Fig. 21.3) can identify more far-reaching implications. With regard to the dimension of emotion (**D1**), for example, the question arises as to the underlying emotion concepts (which classes of emotions can be assessed by which types of sensor) as well as the question of the data basis with which the AI -based measuring system (**D1**) was trained to recognize these emotions. This system must be examined for questions of discrimination power and possible biases [61], which are relevant both with regard to technical functionality and ethical evaluation. Which emotions can the robot recognize? And how does the robot (as the actant **D2**) offer or present *affects* (or stimuli) to the interacting users or patients (**D3**) with an interaction scheme (**D4**), e.g., by the modulation of the voice, moving the head towards the user, changes in facial expressions, to capture in response emotions of the users? Which social rules [62] are used here? Should the robot imitate an interpersonal communication situation or should it point out its robotic status during the interaction and thus the difference between interpersonal relationships and human-technology relations? Reflection on the healthcare context (**D5**) is important, both in terms of understanding the observed/ measured human emotions and in terms of the objective associated with the use of the robot, as e.g. as social companion in an elderly home.

The question of whether a social robot (such as Navel) acts as a supplement to existing interpersonal relationships or as a replacement or surrogate for them also determines the ethical assessment. In addition, questions can be asked about the understanding of affect and measured emotions, and thus, questions about the roles that human users (patients, residents, relatives, nursing or clinical staff) and AI-based emotion recognition technology play. Hence, it is of eminent importance how the human who applies or uses the system is understood and technically modeled. If the human is understood primarily as autonomous, rational being, the central focus is on avoiding manipulation and the sovereignty of the user, which must be preserved. However, if humans are understood primarily as emotional beings, the encounter with a technical system to capture emotions must be used differently and new questions arise. How can and should a social robot such as, e.g., Navel deal with human emotions? Should it validate them and constantly look for a way to satisfy emotional needs? Or should it offer impulses for change through confrontational and resistant behavior? An analysis using the proposed MTEmotions model therefore broadens the horizon of reflection, contributes to a thorough understanding of the situation and helps in deciding on the meaningfulness of the intervention by making alternative courses of action conceivable.

In summary, we can argue that although emotion recognition by AI might offer potential benefits, the used technologies also relate to a number of ethical challenges.

– **Privacy**: One of the biggest ethical concerns is the collection and analysis of non-emotional data (sounds, voices, images, videos, vital data) *without* the explicit consent of the people concerned. Emotion recognition technologies often require the collection, curation and analysis of large-scale personalized multi-modal data that provide very intimate insights into an individual's emotional state. The question of privacy and informed consent is increasingly discussed in research [63]. Furthermore, videos and images of facial activity depicting emotions cannot hardly be anonymized, hence the written consent of the data-providers (or their relatives) must always be obtained to build an adequate AI-model for, e.g., pain assessment.

– **Bias and discrimination**: AI algorithms that recognize emotions in healthcare scenarios are susceptible to distortions (bias) that can result from faulty training data sets. For example, if training data is not representative of all population groups with respect to age, gender, or ethnical background, this could lead to emotional states being misinterpreted in certain social or cultural contexts. This could particularly disadvantage minorities and marginalized groups [64].

– **Trust and manipulation**: AI-based emotion recognition systems could be used in ways that undermine users' trust in the technology. For example, commercial settings could attempt to manipulate users by targeting emotional responses. The possibility of emotional exploitation through advertising and political campaigns is also an important ethical point of discussion [65].

– **Autonomy and decision-making**: Computer-based emotion recognition systems could be used to influence the behavior of individuals without their knowledge or consent. This poses a challenge to personal autonomy, as decisions based on emotion recognition could potentially be controlled or manipulated by third parties [66].

If we think about more than just the ethical implications of specific human-technology relationships in the field of affective computing, but also, starting from concrete use cases within healthcare scenarios, the question of the (potential threat) to human sovereignty posed by the use of these systems comes also into mind. This raises the question of whether technical access to the landscape of emotions (which is often only rudimentarily mapped individually and collectively) not only restricts human autonomy, as can be formulated following Beauchamps & Childress, but also raises more fundamental questions about the possibility of sovereign living in the face of affective computing technologies. Considering Freud's famous dictum that the ego is no longer master in its own house [67], an aspect emerges that fundamentally distinguishes human emotionality, emotional reactions, and emotional dynamics from human rationality, rational reflection, and rational decision-making. While rational processes are constitutively linked to consciousness, emotional processes often occur unconsciously and can, at best, be reconstructed ex post. This raises questions about the controllability of emotional expression [55] and thus about the conditions of possibility for human sovereignty. Affective computing thus not only confronts humans with the limits of their self-knowledge but also targets a dimension of the (partially) uncontrollable. Furthermore, the emotional is not only one's own, but also that which is constituted in exposure to the other. What if moods, emotions, and atmospheres are no longer divine or natural events, but rather are intended by other humans to nudge the person in a certain direction? But how could the person 'immunize' or defend themselves against them?

In order to clarify these questions, it will not be sufficient to evaluate specific systems and, if necessary, to optimize them in this regard, as this requires a societal debate about the legitimacy and responsibility of using these systems, which, on the one hand, exceeds the responsibility of individual developers, but on the other hand, must also be led proactively by them in order to avoid dilemmas such as those described by Collingridge [68].

The contribution of GA and AM was partially supported by the Federal Ministry of Research, Technology and Space under the project 'OrDiLe' FKZ: 16SV8626.

The contribution of NLR and TW was partially supported by the Bavarian Research Foundation under the project 'FORSocialRobots' AZ-1594–23.

References

[1] Manzeschke A., Assadi G., Karsch W. Viehöver W. Funktionale Emotion und emontionale Funktionalität – Über die neue Rolle von Emotionen und Emotionalität in der Mensch-Technik-Interaktion. In Manzeschke A., Karsch F. (eds.). Roboter, Computer und Hybride. Was ereignet sich zwischen Menschen und Maschinen? Baden-Baden: Nomos, 2016, 109–129.

[2] Picard R. Affective Computing. Cambridge: MIT Press, 1997.

[3] Bellon J., Eyssel F., Gransche B., Nähr-Wagener S., Wullenkord R. (eds.). Theory and Practice of Sociosensitive and Socioactive Systems. Wiesbaden: Springer VS, 2022.

[4] Kanjo E., Al-Husain L., Chamberlain A. Emotions in context: examining pervasive affective sensing systems, applications, and analyses. Pers Ubiquit Comput 19, 2015: 1197–1212. https://doi.org/10.1007/s00779-015-0842-3.

[5] Spitale M., Gunes H. "Affective Robotics For Wellbeing: A Scoping Review" 2022 10th International Conference on Affective Computing and Intelligent Interaction Workshops and Demos (ACIIW), Nara, Japan, 2022: 1–8. https://doi.org/10.1109/ACIIW57231.2022.10085995.

[6] James W. What is an Emotion? Mind Volume IX 1884; 34: 188–205.

[7] Cannon W. B. The James-Lange theory of emotions: A critical examination and an alternative theory. The American Journal of Psychology; 39, 1927: 106–124.

[8] Schachter S., Singer J. Cognitive, social, and physiological determinants of emotional state. Psychological Review, 69(5), 1962: 379–399.

[9] Ekman P. Are there basic emotions? Psychological Review, 99(3), 1992: 550–553.

[10] Lazarus R. S. Emotion and Adaptation. Oxford: Oxford University Press, 1991.

[11] Ciompi L. Die emotionalen Grundlagen des Denkens. Entwurf einer fraktalen Affektlogik. 2. Aufl. Göttingen: Vandenhoeck & Ruprecht 1999: 65f.

[12] Perler D. Transformationen der Gefühle. Philosophische Emotionstheorien 1270–1670. Frankfurt am Main: S. Fischer, 2011.

[13] Burton R. Anatomy of Melancholy. What it is, with all the kindes, causes, symptomes, prognostickes & several cures of it. Oxford: Printed by Lichfield J for Cripp H 1621, 6th ed., 1651.

[14] Plato. The Republic. transl. by B Jowett. https://www.guten-berg.org/cache/epub/1497/pg1497-images.html.

[15] Aristotle. Nicomachean Ethics, transl. by J A Smith, https://www.gutenberg.org/cache/epub/8438/pg8438-images.html.

[16] Descartes R. Passions of the Soul, transl. by J Bennett, https://www.earlymoderntexts.com/assets/pdfs/descartes1649.pdf.

[17] Kant I. Anthropology from a Pragmatic Point of View. Carbondale: Southern Illinois University Press, 1978.

[18] Nussbaum M. Political Emotions. Why Love Matters for Justice. Cambridge: Harvard University Press, 2013.

[19] Schmitz H. Der unerschöpfliche Gegenstand. Grundzüge der Philosophie. Bouvier Verlag: Bonn, 2007.

[20] Schmitz H. *Der Gefühlsraum*. System der Philosophie, Bd. III/2. Bonn: Bouvier, 1969.

[21] Schmitz H. Atmosphären. Freiburg/München: Karl Alber, 2016.

[22] Schmitz H. Der Weg der europäischen Philosophie. Eine Gewissenserforschung. Bd. 1: Antike Philosophie. Freiburg/München: Karl Alber, 2007.

[23] Crawford K. Atlas of AI: Power, Politics, and the Planetary Costs of Artificial Intelligence. New Haven: Yale University Press, 2022.

[24] Zuboff S. The Age of Surveillance Capitalism: The Fight for a Human Future at the New Frontier of Power. New York: Public Affairs 2020.

[25] Liggieri K., Tamborini M., Del Fabbro O. Technikphilosophie. Neue Perspektiven für das 21. Jahrhundert. Darmstadt: Wissenschaftliche Buchgesellschaft, 2023.

[26] Gebhart P., Schneeberger T. Socially Interactive Agents as Interface to Health Technology. In: Manzeschke A. and Wittenberg T. (eds.). Ethical Perspectives on Artificial Intelligence in Biomedical Engineering, Berlin/Boston: DeGruyter, 2025.

[27] Hagenah J., Henke M., Kubon M., Wittenberg T. AI-supported robots in healthcare. In: Manzeschke A. and Wittenberg T. (eds.). Ethical Perspectives on Artificial Intelligence in Biomedical Engineering, Berlin/Boston: DeGruyter, 2025.

[28] Solomon R. Emotions, Thought, and the Body. Oxford: Oxford University Press, 2003.

[29] de Sousa R. The Rationality of Emotion. Cambridge: MIT Press, 2007.

[30] Meixner U. Die Aktualität Husserls für die moderne Philosophie des Geistes. In: Seele, Denken, Bewusstsein. Zur Geschichte der Philosophie des Geistes, Meixner U., Newen A. (eds.). Berlin / New York: de Gruyter, 2003:308–88.

[31] Guo G., Zhang N. A survey on deep learning based face recognition [online]. Computer Vision and Image Understanding, 2019, 189, 102805. ISSN 1077–3142. https://doi.org/10.1016/j.cviu.2019.102805.

[32] Juhong A., Pintavurooj C. Face recognition based on facial landmark detection. 10th Biomedical Engineering International Conference (BMEiCON), 2017, 1–4.

[33] Jacob G. M., Stenger B. Facial Action Unit Detection With Transformers. In: Proceedings of the IEEE/CVF Conference on Computer Vision and Pattern Recognition (CVPR), 2021: 7680–7689.

[34] Ekman P., Friesen W. F. Facial action coding system. Environmental Psychology & Nonverbal Behavior, 1978.

[35] Hassan T., Seuß D., Wollenberg J., Weitz K., Kunz M., Lautenbacher S., Garbas J.-U., Schmid U. Automatic Detection of Pain from Facial Expressions: A Survey. IEEE Trans Pattern Anal Mach Intell 43, 2021: 1815–1831. https://doi.org/10.1109/TPAMI.2019.2958341.

[36] Ruf T., Ernst A., Küblbeck C. Face Detection with the Sophisticated High-speed Object Recognition Engine (SHORE), in: Heuberger, A., Elst, G., Hanke, R. (eds.). Microelectronic Systems: Circuits, Systems and Applications. Berlin/Heidelberg: Springer, 2011: 243–252. https://doi.org/10.1007/978-3-642-23071-4_23Seuss.

[37] Hassan T., Dieckmann A., Unfried M., Scherer K. R. R., Mortillaro M., Garbas J. U. Automatic Estimation of Action Unit Intensities and Inference of Emotional Appraisals. IEEE Transactions on Affective Computing 2021: 1–1. https://doi.org/10.1109/TAFFC.2021.3077590.

[38] Schuller, B. W., 2018. Speech emotion recognition: two decades in a nutshell, benchmarks, and ongoing trends. Commun. ACM 61, 90–99. https://doi.org/10.1145/3129340.

[39] Lane R. D., McRae K., Reiman E. M., Chen K., Ahern G. L., Thayer J. F. Neural correlates of heart rate variability during emotion. Neuroimage, 44(1), 2009: 213–222.

[40] Caruelle D., Gustafsson A., Shams P., Lervik-Olsen L. The use of electrodermal activity (EDA) measurement to understand consumer emotions–A literature review and a call for action. Journal of Business Research, 104, 2019: 146–160.

[41] Allaert J., Sanchez-Lopez A., De Raedt R., Baeken C., Vanderhasselt M. A. Inverse effects of tDCS over the left versus right DLPC on emotional processing: A pupillometry study. PloS one, 14(6), 2019: e0218327.

[42] Singh A., Wittenberg T., Salman, M.M., Holzer N., Göb S., Pahl P., Götz T., Sawant S. Bio-Signal Based Multimodal Fusion with Bilinear Model for Emotion Recognition, *2023 IEEE International Conference on Bioinformatics and Biomedicine (BIBM)*, Istanbul, Turkiye, 2023, pp. 4834–4839. https://doi.org/10.1109/BIBM58861.2023.10385273.

[43] Hadjar H., Vu B., Hemmje M. TheraSense: Deep Learning for Facial Emotion Analysis in Mental Health Teleconsultation. *Electronics* 2025, *14*, 422. https://doi.org/10.3390/electronics14030422.

[44] Hassan T., Seuß D., Wollenberg J., Weitz K., Kunz M., Lautenbacher S., Garbas J. U., Schmid U. Automatic Detection of Pain from Facial Expressions: A Survey. IEEE Trans. Pattern Anal. Mach. Intell. 43(6), 2021: 1815–1831.

[45] Kunz M., Seuß D., Hassan T., Garbas J. U., Siebers M., Schmid U., Schöberl M., Lautenbacher S. Problems of video-based pain detection in patients with dementia: a road map to an interdisciplinary solution. BMC Geriatr 17, 33,2017. https://doi.org/10.1186/s12877-017-0427-2.

[46] Seuß D. Exploiting domain-specific knowledge for classifier learning – AU-based facial expression analysis and emotion recognition. PhD Thesis, Univ. Bamberg, 2021.

[47] Weitz K., Hassan T., Schmid U., Garbas J. U. Deep-learned faces of pain and emotions: Elucidating the differences of facial expressions with the help of explainable AI methods. tm – Technisches Messen, vol. 86, no. 7–8, 2019: 404–412. https://doi.org/10.1515/teme-2019-0024.

[48] Rieger I., Finzel B., Seuß D., Wittenberg T., Schmid U. Make Pain Estimation Transparent: A Roadmap to Fuse Bayesian Deep Learning and Inductive Logic Programming. Proc's 41st Ann. Int. Conf. IEEE Engineering in Medicine & Biology Society (EMBC, 23.-27. Juli 2019, Berlin).

[49] Seuß D., Dieckmann A., Hassan T., Garbas J. U., Ellgring J. H., Mortillaro M. Emotion Expression from Different Angles: A Video Database for Facial Expressions of Actors Shot by a Camera Array, 8th Int. Conf. on Affective Computing & Intelligent Interaction (ACII), 2019: 35–41. https://doi.org/10.1109/ACII.2019.8925458.

[50] Goes N., Seßner J., Dziobek I., Steffan J., Struck M., Franke J., Kirst S., Naumann S., Lang N., Wittenberg T. Evaluation of an algorithm for optical pulse detection in children for application to the Pepper robot. Current Directions in Biomedical Engineering 7(2), 2021: 484–487.

[51] Weigand C., Flemming D., Borutta P., Hofmann F., Wieland G., Zweyer G., Hayir E., Seuß D., Wittenberg T. A concept and technical requirements for the Temi platform supporting care and nursing. Current Directions Biomedical Engineering 8(2), 2022: 241–244. |10.1515/cdbme-2022–1062.

[52] Toussaint C., Schwarz P.T., Petermann M. Navel – a social robot with verbal and nonverbal communication skills, in: Extended Abstracts of the 2023 CHI Conference on Human Factors in Computing Systems, Chi Ea 2023. Association for Computing Machinery, New York, NY, USA).

[53] Montaigne M. de. Essais. Villey P, Saulnier V. – online edition by P. Desan, University of Chicago, https://artflsrv03.uchicago.edu/philologic4/montessaisvilley/navigate/1/4/2/; p. 337.

[54] Beauchamp T. L., Childress J. F. Principles of Biomedical Ethics. Seventh Edition. New York/London: Oxford University Press, 2013.

[55] Weber-Guskar E. Gefühle der Zukunft. Wie wir mit emotionaler KI unser Leben verändern. Berlin: Ullstein, 2024.

[56] Hickel S. Gefahren für die Autonomie durch gesundheitsbezogenes Self-Tracking. In: EthMed 2025; 37: 7–29.

[57] Feldman Barret L., Adolphs R., Marsella S., Martinez A. M., Pollack S. (2019). *Emotional Expressions Reconsidered. Challenges to Inferring Emotion from Human Facial Movements*. Psychological Science in the Public Interest 2019; 20.1: 1–68.

[58] Roth G., Strüber N. (2023). Emotion, Motivation, Personality and Their Neurobiological Foundations. In: Roth G., Heinz A., Walter H. (eds.). Psychoneuroscience. Springer: Berlin/ Heidelberg. 2023: 143–174.

[59] Manzeschke A., Assadi G.. Künstliche Emotion – Zum ethischen Umgang mit Gefühlen zwischen Mensch und Technik. *Ethik Med 2023*; 35: 201–219. https://doi.org/10.1007/s00481-023-00766-6.

[60] Waldenfels B. Das leibliche Selbst. Frankfurt am Main: Suhrkamp 2000, 79.

[61] Pahl J., Rieger I., Möller A., Wittenberg T., Schmid U. Female, white, 27? Bias Evaluation on Data and Algorithms for Affect Recognition in Faces. Procs' 2022 ACM Conference on Fairness, Accountability, and Transparency ACM FAccT 2022: 973–987. https://doi.org/10.1145/3531146.3533159.

[62] Krämer N., Manzeschke A. Social Reactions to socially interactive agents and their ethical implications. In Lugrin B., Pelachaud C., Traum D. (eds.). The Handbook on Social Interactive Agents. 20 Years of Research on Embodied Conversational Agents, Intelligent Virtual Agents, and Social Robotics, Vol. 1: Methods, Behavior, Cognition. New York: ACM Books 2021, 77–103.

[63] Khare S. K., Blanes-Vidal V., Nadimi E. S., Acharya U. R. Emotion recognition and artificial intelligence: A systematic review (2014–2023) and research recommendations, Information Fusion 2024; 102:102019. https://doi.org/10.1016/j.inffus.2023.102019.

[64] Crawford K., Paglen T. Excavating AI: the politics of images in machine learning training sets. AI & Soc 2021; 36: 1105–1116. https://doi.org/10.1007/s00146-021-01162-8.

[65] Pade R. Moral und künstliche Intelligenz im Marketing. Beiträge zur empirischen Marketing- und Vertriebsforschung. Springer Gabler: Wiesbaden 2024.

[66] Wessel D. KI & Ethik. In: Heine M., Dhungel A., Schrille T., Wessel D. (eds.). Künstliche Intelligenz in öffentlichen Verwaltungen: Grundlagen, Chancen, Herausforderungen und Einsatzszenarien. Wiesbaden: Springer Gabler, 2023, 167–189.

[67] Freud S. Eine Schwierigkeit der Psychoanalyse. In: Imago. Zeitschrift für Anwendung der Psychoanalyse auf die Geisteswissenschaften, 1917; Band V: 1–7.

[68] Collingridge D. The Social Control of Technology. London: Pinter, 1982.

Julia Kämmer, Daniel Flemming
22 AI and nursing

22.1 Digitalization in nursing

As the largest professional group in healthcare, the nursing profession faces several significant challenges. These challenges are arising from demographic changes and the resulting increase in the number of people requiring care [1–3]. This also applies to the shortage of skilled nursing staff, which remains significant, even though to a lesser degree in hospitals [4,5]. For nursing care, the necessary structural transformation in hospital care will be accompanied by a further transfer of services to the purview of the long-term care insurance funds and an increased complexity in hospital treatment [6]. Furthermore, in the context of expanding academic training [7] in nursing, the mix of competencies and qualifications will be a central point of discussion in the future [8,9]. Improving the working conditions for nursing staff will be a pivotal factor in countering the intensification of work in the context of a simultaneous shortage of skilled labor while maintaining the required staffing ratios and skills mix [10]. In this context, digitalization is a potential means of enhancing the organization and administration of core nursing processes [11].

The current focus of research and development in the intersection between nursing care and technology is on the area of electronic documentation/patient records, the associated sensors, and wearables for monitoring vital signs in the context of medical records [11]. The government's recent funding for the digitalization of hospitals in last years and the obligation to connect nursing facilities to the digital infrastructure for healthcare (telematics infrastructure) are contributing to an increase in the number of installations of digital nursing documentation systems [12]. The extant literature suggests that digital documentation may contribute to enhanced patient safety and quality of care [13]. Other domains in which digitalization in nursing makes a difference include digital technologies supporting duty and route planning [12,14]. Empirical evidence indicates that digital routing and duty planning tools in outpatient care can positively impact patient satisfaction, the quality of care and nursing, and the stress level of nurses [15].

22.2 AI as a "new" resource in nursing care

Artificial Intelligence (AI) in nursing can be regraded as a "new" resource within the domain of digital care technologies [16]. The following paragraphs investigate the extent to which AI can transform outpatient care, and the potential benefits and constraints associated with this transformation.

As part of a qualitative survey, the "Learning Systems" platform [17] discussed the use of AI with the input of healthcare professionals. The primary expectation regarding using AI is that it can alleviate mental and physical strain by assuming responsibility for routine tasks. As described by Montemayor et al. [18], the objective is to utilize the time gained through AI for patient-centered or more complex care activities. Consequently, patients and nurses may benefit from an optimized quality of care [17]. Furthermore, the usage of AI frequently results in alterations to the work processes of nurses. In this regard, the acceptance and willingness of nursing professionals to use technology must be a crucial factor in ensuring its practical use. The most tremendous potential of AI in care, therefore, lies in its capacity to support administrative and routine care activities and care coordination. This creates the potential for additional time resources for patient-centered care [19,20].

The scope for the application of AI in nursing is currently constrained. This is because nursing remains primarily an activity-based profession. Moreover, evidence indicates that negative effects are also possible. Wosny et al. [21] point to a potential increase in workload, safety risks, and challenges in ensuring the quality of information. Evaluation studies or evidence-based assessments of the potential consequences of using AI in care make early assessment and appropriate countermeasures difficult [22].

Additionally, Wolf-Ostermann and Rothgang have observed that the current focus of research in this field is primarily on the development of various AI methods, with less attention directed toward the practical applications of AI in nursing practice [11]. It is, therefore, essential that AI will be integrated into nursing in a structured and systematic manner in order to counteract any potentially harmful experiences and, at the same time, promote positive aspects such as the creation of time capacities. In this context, AI can be regarded as a potential solution to relieve nurses' workload, as Budde et al. described [17]. Moreover, ethical considerations must be addressed, including the potential for dehumanization in care and concerns related to data protection and security [23,24]. There is a concern that decision-making authority in care matters may be transferred to AI, which could impair independent nursing care. Researchers advocate for implementing fair and responsible AI in healthcare to address these ethical concerns [25–28]. Developing an ethical framework for the utilization of AI in care is also essential.

The application of artificial Intelligence (AI) in nursing has the potential to release time for patient-centered tasks by assuming responsibility for routine activities. However, this requires structured integration, acceptance by the nursing staff and consideration of ethical considerations, including data protection, decision-making autonomy and potential workload.

22.3 Use of AI in nursing care

Implementing AI into work processes and the infrastructure of care facilities is challenging [17]. Exemplary use case scenarios were developed to illustrate the potential of AI in care. The hospital setting was selected for illustration purposes, as research in this area appears to be most advanced [19]. Selected scenarios are presented below as examples.

22.3.1 Predictive AI (fall prediction)

Example: A patient with dementia is hospitalized for inpatient treatment due to a general decline in health. He/she wants to return home to his/her familiar surroundings as quickly as possible. Despite his/her ability to get out of bed without assistance, walking without socks and looking for his/her shoes leads to a fall. Due to the considerable workload caused by another patient in another room who also required care, the nurse in charge noticed the fall approximately an hour later. Because of the fall, the patient with dementia suffered a knee injury.

Consequently, more extended hospitalization is required, despite the patient's discomfort, and will presumably attempt to escape again. In such scenarios, implementing AI-supported fall prediction can prove beneficial as a preventative measure. For example, an AI system such as that offered by the company cogvis Software und Consulting GmbH [29] or the Lindera mobility analysis app [30], could be a potential solution. Such AI-based systems can prevent the fall event or at least mitigate its effects. This is because the implementation of real-time alerts allows for a notable reduction in the response time of nurses. By collecting AI data, preventative measures can be taken for falls. This could have allowed the dementia patient to be cared for earlier, faster and, ideally, even prevented a fall. There is evidence in the literature that predicting falls has the potential to improve the quality of care and reduce the burden on nursing professionals [19,31].

The functionality of AI systems for fall detection is generally based on autonomous alerting, i.e., a check by a specialist does not usually take place in this context. As a result, false alarms cannot be completely ruled out, which leads to an interruption in care during ongoing processes. Consequently, technology may become a new burden rather than a source of relief [32]. Moreover, Ma et al. call for the implementation of an anonymous image recognition for fall detection to protect the privacy of patients [33].

Performing predictive analyses can assist in optimizing nursing staff preparation, ensure more targeted nursing care, and reduce the healthcare system's burden [34] and has the potential to provide time resources and improve patient safety [35,36]. However, potential video and audio recordings must be carefully examined and evaluated before implementation to minimize risks and ensure effectiveness and safety. Other examples of applications of predictive AI in the care sector include the use of image analysis for pressure wounds [37], the prediction of specific care interventions for cancer [38], and the detection of behavioral disorders [39].

22.3.2 Decision support (care planning)

Example: A new AI-based care planning tool is to be used in a hospital. The nurses hope this will make the care process more efficient and support them in deciding suitable care measures. The nursing professionals can access the AI via a user interface that is integrated into the hospital information system (HIS). The system is designed to continuously collect data from various sources, including patient records, vital signs, laboratory results, and previous treatment histories. The information, which is analyzed in real-time, is employed by AI to generate recommendations for individually tailored care planning.

An exemplary use case could look like this: A 65-year-old patient is admitted as an inpatient following a surgical procedure to repair a hip fracture. The AI analyzes the patient's medical and nursing history and anamnesis, as well as current vital signs and postoperative risks, and uses this as the basis for developing a care plan that is tailored to the patient. This plan includes nursing diagnosis and nursing interventions. Furthermore, it draws on evidence-based guidelines, expert nursing standards, and facility-specific instructions. Such assessments include regular pain assessments, specific mobilization plans, monitoring of fluid balance, and protocols for preventing postoperative infections. The suggestions are reviewed by nursing professionals, who can make any necessary modifications.

The Fraunhofer Institute for Industrial Mathematics ITWM is currently investigating this hypothesis in a real-world setting. The project "Care-integrated artificial intelligence in the professional care process" ("ViKI pro") aims to facilitate care planning in the context of long-term inpatient care through the utilization of AI. The project does not only use artificial Intelligence but also employs systems that facilitate the integration of existing care expertise. In the next step, the knowledge gained will be utilized to derive care measures that real nurse experts can evaluate and consider or reject [40]. Consequently, the final decision-making authority regarding the care plan and the measures to be implemented resides with the nursing professionals. Topol posits that AI should be regarded as a tool to support clinical decision-making rather than a substitute for human expertise [41]. Stefan Selke [72] proposes an alternative approach that sees AI as an instrument, assistant or partner, depending on the context. Viewing AI purely as an instrument runs the risk of oversimplifying the complexity of AI applications. It is essential that critical thinking and interpersonal skills are strengthened in this context.

In addition to AI-generated recommendations for individualized care planning (e.g. [38]), clinical decision support has also been demonstrated to be a practical approach in the context of triage in emergency departments or intensive care units [42,43] in direct care. Moreover, there are further possibilities for clinical management in the context of structured personnel requirement planning [44]. Such clinical decision support can be based on either classical decision systems or large language models.

22.3.3 Image analysis and augmented reality (wound care)

In hospitals as well as elderly homes, wound care is an essential part of daily nursing activities. Wounds are visually inspected, photographed, treated, and documented by nurses. Subsequently, the wound healing process can be evaluated by physicians and nurses based on the documentation of progress, and new measures can be initiated if necessary. The application of AI-controlled image analyses could optimize these processes by automating wound observation, providing more consistent data, and supporting personalized treatment plans.

To assess chronic wounds in particular, a nurse may utilize a camera or augmented reality (AR) glasses to record the wound and subsequently analyze the data through the application of Artificial Intelligence (AI). Parameters such as wound size, depth, and signs of inflammation are subjected to analysis. Based on this information, the AI can suggest evidence-based nursing diagnoses and interventions for wound care to support clinical decision-making. If AR glasses are used, such as the Clausthal University of Technology's Care Glasses 2.0 [45], the AI can guide the patient through the wound care workflow using instructions displayed on the glasses. At the subsequent assessment, the glasses can automatically record and assess the status of the wound healing process. In the event of any adverse developments, the nursing professionals are informed via the AR glasses.

The AI assuming responsibility for wound documentation promises to reduce the burden of previous documentation if observations are automatically transferred to the appropriate documentation. Furthermore, AI-supported wound care has the potential to reduce complications by enabling the early recognition of warning signals, which can then be addressed through the initiation of targeted, individualized care [47]. For accurate image analysis, AI requires good data quality to generate an accurate analysis. It is recommended that a final assessment of the AI-supported wound analysis conducted by the nurse should remain an integral part of the wound care process. Nevertheless, considering the increasing utilization of international nursing professionals and the organization of nursing skills and grade mix, this can also serve as a foundation for ensuring high-quality care. For example, due to the shortage of qualified nurses, less qualified assistants could provide evidence-based and guided wound care.

22.3.4 Generative AI (voice assistance, reporting)

Voice assistance

Another starting point for potential relieve of nurses is the documentation of nursing actions or treatment processes. This is particularly true as nurses, like all professionals in healthcare, prefer verbal communication to written documentation, which can take place directly alongside the action [47]. As documentation frequently occurs at the end of the shift rather than at the end of the task, documentation tools that record real-time information can enhance information transfer assurance [48]. For capturing information in real-time in this way, contactless interaction with the information is also required in numerous applications [49]. This may be necessary, for example, when both hands are required for the task or when an aseptic procedure is necessary [50].

For illustration, the following application example will demonstrate the practical use: A nurse works on a postoperative monitoring unit in a hospital. She has to deal with new patients daily, as patients typically remain in the monitoring unit for only a brief period following surgery until they are transferred to another unit for continued care until discharged. She must continuously monitor vital signs, ensure that analgesics are administered, and document the patient's condition hourly. For example, the "voize" voice assistant [49] was recently implemented for this purpose, with the intention of alleviating the nurse's daily workload. While examining the patient, the nurse inputs the current information directly into the digital patient file with the assistance of the AI-supported voice assistant. The AI then structures and corrects the spoken text to automatically merge routine data into the documentation. The nurse then seeks to ascertain the scheduled time for the next analgesic administration and asks the voice assistant: "When is the next administration of analgesics for Mrs. Müller in room 820?". Based on the previously transmitted information regarding the last administered medication dose, the AI can identify the subsequent dose and provide an accurate response based on the patient's data. If a patient's vital signs exceed pre-established threshold values, the AI recognizes this and notifies the nurse by voice message or text message. The AI can automatically remind the nurse of upcoming routine tasks such as changing dressings or checking medication. Upon the nurse's request, the voice assistant also collects relevant data for the transfer of care and fills it automatically, thus eliminating the need for the nurse to manually input the last remaining gaps

The "voize" example mentioned here offers care documentation via a smartphone and can be integrated into numerous existing systems [49]. Initial surveys have shown that the "voize" voice app has the potential to achieve subjective time savings for nurses and may assist in reducing their workload [52].

Nevertheless, further research is required to adequately evaluate the AI-based voice assistance scenario in terms of acceptance, safety, and cost-effectiveness [53,54]. Introducing voice assistance will also transform nursing work processes [12]. Existing processes must be restructured to effectively integrate AI. One possibility for integration is the combination of voice assistance with a robotic system or a mobile platform, enabling the simultaneous recording and documentation of vital parameters from sensors on the patient [55]. More evidence is still needed to inform the design of processes for adapting to this new technology. Initial findings on AI-based voice assistance show relatively positive outcomes regarding efficiency, user-friendliness, and satisfaction, suggesting the potential for enhancement in nursing care [54].

Reporting

Example: A patient with significant care needs is hospitalized for inpatient treatment and is subsequently discharged to their home environment. Further care is provided by informal caregivers, such as family members. In addition to the doctor's letter, a structured nurse transfer form is typically provided as a transfer document upon discharge. The expansion of the telematics infrastructure makes it possible to store these transfer documents (i.e., hospital discharge letters and PIO Überleitungsbogen, a standardized high-structured nursing discharge summary) in the EHR for all patients or the targeted transmission of these documents using KIM messages, i.e. a secure e-mail format.

Previous transfer documents in nursing, such as the PIO Überleitungsbogen [56], mainly address the intraprofessional exchange of nursing-relevant information at the end of a nursing treatment episode. The content is primarily structured information derived from the professional knowledge corpus of professional nursing, e.g., elements of nursing terminology.

In order to develop an understanding of the nursing care situation for all those involved in the care process – including those outside the nursing profession – it is essential to enable a nursing narrative about the person with care needs as a nursing condensate. It is not the intention that a continuous nursing text in the form of a nursing discharge letter should replace the structured information but rather enable the information; instead, it should facilitate the preparation of information in a format that is appropriate for the target group and adapted to informal carers, care assistants or other professions and their respective use of language. Creating a nursing letter can be accomplished using Artificial Intelligence, eliminating the necessity for additional manual documentation. Initially, only a care documentation system, such as apenio®, is used as a data source. The (structured) information documented is then summarized by a large language model-based system into the most critical information and formulated as continuous text. This generation can be fully automated or, if necessary, further customized with AI support.

22.4 Needs for (further) development

The following section analyzes the current development needs for the meaningful use of AI in nursing care. Three central needs have been identified. Firstly, the development of trust in AI in care is discussed. Secondly, the development of expertise and participatory and interdisciplinary research is described. Thirdly, further open fields of research on AI in nursing care are identified.

22.4.1 Trust in AI

In the discourse surrounding the use of AI in nursing care, the need for responsible and trustworthy AI is frequently highlighted [26–28,57]. In this context, researchers have stated that the human component must not be replaced by AI [23]. It is imperative to recognize that the prospective contribution of AI in the care sector should not be conceptualized as a replacement but rather as a supplement to preserve or even promote interpersonal contact. This chapter showed what the future use of AI could look like so that it can be used as a responsible tool to relieve the burden on professional nurses and what aspects need to be considered. In this context, De Raeve et al. and Ronquillo et al. emphasize the crucial role of nurses' trust in AI [25,27]. Accepting AI in the nursing sector will only be possible if nurses, as end users, can build sufficient trust in AI. Implementing and using explainable AI methods (xAI) is becoming increasingly important [57]. According to Hammer [73], bias in AI healthcare models can be reduced through responsible data use, fair model development, and understandable algorithms, with audits and explainable AI (xAI) ensuring transparency and fairness. Simon Fonck and André Stollenwerk see potential in "Explainable Artifical Intelligence (xAI)" to make AI explainable in the healthcare sector [74]. A joint discussion with the user groups and all relevant stakeholders is necessary to determine how trust can be built and strengthened and to identify the values the nursing care sector wishes to represent. One overriding aspect seems to be the inclusion and preservation of interpersonal connections.

22.4.2 Development of competences

In education and training, there is a need to develop essential digital competencies in the domain of AI [17,58–60]. Mir et al. consider it possible to optimize teaching in medical training, for example, using virtual query systems, medical distance learning, or recording instructional videos [61]. The integration of ChatGPT into nursing training is also conceivable [62].

O'Connor et al. (2023) and Buchanan et al. (2020) emphasize the need to integrate AI into curricula and develop new pedagogical concepts to adequately teach AI [36,20]. In this context, confidence building in AI is also relevant.

22.4.3 Participation & interdisciplinarity

In specialist literature, the issue of building trust in Artificial Intelligence represents a pivotal concern within the context of digital transformation. In this discourse, the approach of continuous co-design and participation is a crucial factor [17,25]. Nurses have the potential to exert considerable influence on the implementation of AI. By including end users in the process, it can be ensured that AI fulfills contextual requirements and can be integrated into the workflow by nurse professionals [63]. To integrate practical needs into technological development from the outset and to do justice to the complex care context, all stakeholders must be involved at an early stage of the process [19,64]. Liebe and Esdar point out that current approaches, such as human-centered artificial Intelligence [65], refer to three axioms [66]:

- "... to find the right problem and then fulfill it with a suitable solution ...",
- "... to look at the entire system from the micro to the macro level ..."
- "... early and continuous involvement of the intended users ..."

The design process can follow the double diamond model [67], first in a metaphorical problem space and then in a similar solution space [66]. Von Gerich et al. consider the development of a guideline that would ensure participatory and interdisciplinary research [59].

> The practical implementation of AI in healthcare relies on three key factors: firstly, the establishment of trust through the utilization of explainable methods; secondly, the development of digital skills through targeted training programs; and thirdly, the early and interdisciplinary involvement of care staff, with a particular focus on the maintenance of ethical standards and the preservation of interpersonal relationships.

22.4.4 Further fields of research

In their review from 2024, researchers Kilpatrick et al. pointed out that research in the field of AI in nursing care has so far been insufficiently considered [68]. This is also reflected in the need for further research.

At this time, it is impossible to identify any specific effects that AI will have on day-to-day care. AI tools in nursing are being introduced, and it will take some time before they can be tested and evaluated in practical applications. The current research agenda is still primarily focused on the early development phases, trials, and implementation of AI in nursing. For example, researchers are also investigating the involvement of nurses in these processes or which applications appear to be helpful in practice [59].

Schultz et al. identify current research needs regarding the acceptance of AI and patient safety [69]. Shang, on the other hand, identifies conceptual and theoretical issues [70]. These topics include, for example, the development of concepts for building digital competencies and promoting trust. In addition, randomized controlled studies in real settings are necessary to enable implementation in the everyday work of nurses [35,71].

In conclusion, an increasing number of research projects are currently focusing on AI in nursing. This indicates that the topic is also increasingly establishing itself as a subject of interest.

22.5 Future work

Artificial Intelligence (AI) can potentially improve and relieve the burden of care in the future, particularly in specific use cases [35]. It is necessary to focus more scientific attention on the aforementioned fields of research in the coming years. In this manner, the benefits of AI for care and possible risks for practice can be identified and addressed in a preventative manner. Systematic evaluation and monitoring of research projects with AI in nursing are essential [22]. For this purpose, end users must be involved in all research steps through high participation. It is advisable to have an interdisciplinary research team to link the technology with practice and generate application-related solutions that are only brought together later. Also trustworthy AI, in addition to participatory and interdisciplinary research approaches, can support the empowerment of carers as the primary decision-makers and interpersonal authorities in the utilization of AI.

It is also necessary for policymakers to support the implementation and ongoing costs associated with AI, for example, by providing financial resources [11]. The implementation of digitalization strategies must be examined with good care due to the interaction with vulnerable people. Ongoing evaluation and assessment and the inclusion of current evidence are essential in this context.

References

[1] Demografischer Wandel in Deutschland, Heft 1, Bevölkerungs- und Haushaltsentwicklung im Bund und in den Ländern, Ausgabe 2011. Statistische Ämter des Bundes und der Länder. Statistisches Bundesamt, Wiesbaden. (Accessed November 23, 2024, at https://www.destatis.de/DE/Themen/Querschnitt/Demografischer-Wandel/Publikationen/Downloads/bevoelkerungs-haushaltsentwicklung-5871101119004.pdf?__blob=publicationFile).

[2] Fuchs D. J., Busch M., Lange C., Scheidt-Nave C. Prevalence and patterns of morbidity among adults in Germany. Bundesgesundheitsbl. 2012;55(4):576–86.

[3] Demografischer Wandel in Deutschland, Heft 2, Auswirkungen auf Krankenhausbehandlungen und Pflegebedürftige im Bund und in den Ländern, Ausgabe 2010. Statistische Ämter des Bundes und der Länder. Statistisches Bundesamt, Wiesbaden. (Accessed October 31, 2024, at https://www.destatis.de/DE/Themen/Querschnitt/Demografischer-Wandel/Publikationen/Downloads/krankenhausbehandlung-pflegebeduerftige-5871102109004.pdf?__blob=publicationFile).

[4] Wasem J., Blase N.. Personalentwicklung im Krankenhaus seit 2000. In: Klauber J., Wasem J., Beivers A., Mostert C. (eds.). Krankenhaus-Report 2023, Schwerpunkt: Personal. Berlin, Heidelberg: Springer, 2023:3–18. https://doi.org/10.1007/978-3-662-66881-8_1.

[5] Pflegekräftevorausberechnung. Statistisches Bundesamt, 2024. (Accessed October 09, 2024, at https://www.destatis.de/DE/Themen/Gesellschaft-Umwelt/Bevoelkerung/Bevoelkerungsvorausberechnung/pflegekraeftevorausberechnung.html).

[6] Geissler A., Krause F., Leber W. D. Neugestaltung der deutschen Krankenhauslandschaft. In: Klauber J., Wasem J., Beivers A., Mostert C., Scheller-Kreinsen D. (eds.). Krankenhaus-Report 2024: Strukturreform. Berlin, Heidelberg: Springer, 2024:81–105. https://doi.org/10.1007/978-3-662-68792-5_5

[7] Meng M., Peters M., Dauer B., Hofrath C., Dorin L., Hackel M. Pflegemonitoring: Hochschule – Erste Analysen des BIBB-Pflegepanels. Pflege & Gesellschaft o.J.; 27(1):5–18.

[8] Die erweiterte pflegerische Versorgungspraxis. Weidner F, Schubert C. Deutsches Institut für angewandte Pflegewissenschaften e.V. (eds.). (Accessed October 09, 2024, at https://www.bosch-stiftung.de/de/publikation/die-erweiterte-pflegerische-versorgungspraxis).

[9] Entwurf eines Gesetzes zur Stärkung der Pflegekompetenz. Bundesministerium für Gesundheit, 2024. (Accessed October 9, 2024, at https://www.bundesgesundheitsministerium.de/fileadmin/Dateien/3_Downloads/Gesetze_und_Verordnungen/GuV/P/240903_RefE_Pflegekompetenzgesetz.pdf).

[10] Oswald J., Neumeyer H., Visarius M. Rahmenbedingungen und Herausforderungen im Personalmanagement. In: Klauber J., Wasem J., Beivers A., Mostert C. (eds.). Krankenhaus-Report 2023, Schwerpunkt: Personal. Berlin, Heidelberg: Springer, 2023:85–106. https://doi.org/10.1007/978-3-662-66881-8_6.

[11] Wolf-Ostermann K., Rothgang H. Digitale Technologien in der Pflege – Was können sie leisten? [Digital technologies in nursing-what can they achieve?]. Bundesgesundheitsblatt Gesundheitsforschung Gesundheitsschutz. 2024;67(3):324–331. https://doi.org/10.1007/s00102-024-03843-3.

[12] DAA-Stiftung Bildung und Beruf (ed.). Die Digitalisierung der Pflege in Deutschland. Status quo, digitale Transformation und Auswirkungen auf Arbeit, Beschäftigte und Qualifizierung. Follow-up Studie. Stuttgart: DAA-Stiftung Bildung und Beruf, 2022.

[13] Wayhuni E. A., Nursalam N., Dewi Y. S., Arifin H., Benjamin L. S. Electronic nursing documentation for patient safety, quality of nursing care, and documentation: a systematic review. J Pak Med Assoc. 2024;74(9):1669–1677. https://doi.org/10.47391/JPMA.9996.

[14] Bayerisches Forschungszentrum Pflege Digital (BZPD) (eds.). Potenziale und Anwendungsszenarien künstlicher Intelligenz in häuslichen Pflegearrangements im Kontext einer alternden Gesellschaft. Kempten: BZPD Working Paper, 02/2022.

[15] IGES Institut GmbH. Digitalisierung in der ambulanten Pflege – Chancen und Hemmnisse. Kurzfassung. Berlin: IGES, 2017.

[16] Younis H. A., Eisa T. A. E., Nasser M., Sahib T. M., Noor A. A., Alyasiri O. M., Salisu S., Hayder I. M., Younis H. A. A Systematic Review and Meta-Analysis of Artificial Intelligence Tools in Medicine and Healthcare: Applications, Considerations, Limitations, Motivation and Challenges. Diagnostics (Basel) 2024;14(1):109. https://doi.org/10.3390/diagnostics14010109.

[17] Budde K., Hiltawsky K., Eskofier B., Heismann B., Kirchner E., Klevesath M., Lang M., Loskill H., Neumuth T, Schapranow M.-P., Schmidt-Rumposch A., Susec B., Welskop-Deffaa E. M., Wolf-Ostermann K. KI für Gesundheitsfachkräfte – Chancen und Herausforderungen von medizinischen und pflegerischen KI-Anwendungen. Whitepaper aus der Plattform Lernende Systeme. München: Lernende Systeme – Die Plattform für Künstliche Intelligenz, 2023.

[18] Montemayor C., Halpern J., Fairweather A. In principle obstacles for empathic AI: why we can't replace human empathy in healthcare. AI Soc. 2022;37(4):1353–1359. https//doi.org/10.1007/s00146-021-01230-z.

[19] Seibert K., Domhoff D., Bruch D., Schulte-Althoff M., Fürstenau D., Biessmann F., Wolf-Ostermann K. Application Scenarios for Artificial Intelligence in Nursing Care: Rapid Review. J Med Internet Res. 2021;23(11):e26522. https://doi.org/10.2196/26522.

[20] Buchanan C., Howitt M. L., Wilson R., Booth R. G., Risling T., Bamford M. Predicted Influences of Artificial Intelligence on the Domains of Nursing: Scoping Review. JMIR Nurs. 2020;3(1):e23939. https://doi.org/10.2196/23939.

[21] Wosny M., Strasser L. M., Hastings J. Experience of Health Care Professionals Using Digital Tools in the Hospital: Qualitative Systematic Review. JMIR Hum Factors 2023:10:e50357. https://doi.org/10.2196/50357

[22] OECD. Empowering the health workforce: Strategies to make the most of the digital revolution. Paris: OECD Publishing; 2021.

[23] Deutscher Ethikrat (eds.). Mensch und Maschine – Herausforderungen durch Künstliche Intelligenz. Stellungnahme. Kurzfassung. Berlin: Deutscher Ethikrat, 2023.

[24] Mohanasundari S. K., Kalpana M., Madhusudhan U., Vasanthkumar K., B R, Singh R., Vashishtha N., Bhatia V. Can Artificial Intelligence Replace the Unique Nursing Role? Cureus 2023;15(12):e51150. https://doi.org/10.7759/cureus.51150.

[25] De Raeve P., Davidson P. M., Shaffer F. A., Pol E., Pandey A. K., Adams E. Leveraging the trust of nurses to advance a digital agenda in Europe: a critical review of health policy literature. Open Res Eur. 2021;1:26. https://doi.org/10.12688/openreseurope.13231.2.

[26] Cary M.P. Jr., Bessias S., McCall J., Pencina M. J., Grady S. D., Lytle K., Economou-Zavlanos N. J. Empowering nurses to champion Health equity & BE FAIR: Bias elimination for fair and responsible AI in healthcare. J Nurs Scholarsh. 2024. https://doi.org/10.1111/jnu.13007.

[27] Ronquillo C. E., Booth R. G., Adzo Vittor W., Mendoza I., Wood N., Gomes van Berlo O., Chan R., Recsky C. Mapping Trust in Nurses with Dimensions of Trustworthy Artificial Intelligence: A Scoping Review. Stud Health Technol Inform. 2024;315:717–718. https://doi.org/10.3233/SHTI240295.

[28] Nashwan A. J., Gharib S., Alhadidi M., El-Ashry A. M., Alamgir A., Al-Hassan M., Khedr M. A., Dawood S., Abufarsakh B. Harnessing Artificial Intelligence: Strategies for Mental Health Nurses in Optimising Psychiatric Patient Care. Issues Ment Health Nurs. 2023;44(10):1020–1034. https://doi.org/10.1080/01612840.2023.2263579.

[29] Die Zukunft der Pflege: cogvis Software und Consulting GmbH (Accessed March 31, 2025, at https://cogvis.ai/).

[30] Sturzprävention für die professionelle Pflege: LINDERA GmbH (Accessed March 31, 2025, at https://lindera.de/de-de/sturzpraevention-professionelle-pflege).

[31] O'Connor S., Gasteiger N., Stanmore E., Wong D. C., Lee J. J. Artificial Intelligence for falls management in older adult care: A scoping review of nurses' role. J Nurs Manag. 2022;30(8):3787–3801. https://doi.org/10.1111/jonm.13853.

[32] Considine J., Berry D., Mullen M., Chisango E., Mart M. W., Michell P., Darzins P., Boyd L. Nurses' experiences of using falls alarms in subacute care: A qualitative study. PLoS One 2023;18(6):e0287537. https://doi.org/10.1371/journal.pone.0287537.

[33] Ma C., Shimada A., Uchiyama H., Nagahara H., Taniguchi R. Fall detection using optical level anonymous image sensing system. Optics & Laser Technology 2019;110:44–61. https://doi.org/10.1016/j.optlastec.2018.07.013.

[34] González-Castro A., Leirós-Rodríguez R., Prada-García C., Benítez-Andrades J. A. The Applications of Artificial Intelligence for Assessing Fall Risk: Systematic Review. J Med Internet Res. 2024:26:e54934. https://doi.org/10.2196/54934.

[35] Ng Z. Q. P., Ling L. Y. J., Chew H. S. J., Lau Y. The role of artificial Intelligence in enhancing clinical nursing care: A scoping review. J Nurs Manag. 2022;30(8):3654–3674. https://doi.org/10.1111/jonm.13425.

[36] O'Connor S., Vercell A., Wong D., Yorke J., Fallatah F. A., Cave L., Anny Chen L. Y. The application and use of artificial Intelligence in cancer nursing: A systematic review. Eur J Oncol Nurs. 2024;68:102510. https://doi.org/10.1016/j.ejon.2024.102510.

[37] Jiang M., Ma Y., Guo S., Jin L., Lv L., Han L., An N. Using Machine LearningnTechnologies in Pressure Injury Management: Systematic Review. JMIR Med Inform. 2021;9(3):e25704. https://doi.org/10.2196/25704.

[38] Brydges G., Uppal A., Gottumukkala V. Application of Machine Learning in Predicting Perioperative Outcomes in Patients with Cancer: A Narrative Review for Clinicians. Curr Oncol. 2024;31(5):2727–2747. https://doi.org/10.3390/curroncol31050207.

[39] Fernandes S., von Gunten A., Verloo H. Using AI-Based Technologies to Help Nurses Detect Behavioural Disorders: Narrative Literature Review. JMIR Nurs. 2024;7:e54496. https://doi.org/10.2196/54496.

[40] Artifical Intelligence in the Care Process. Project ViKI pro: AI-based Organization, Design and Evaluation in Long-term Care: Fraunhofer Institute for Industrial Mathematics ITWM, 2024. (Accessed October 11, 2024, at https://www.itwm.fraunhofer.de/en/departments/optimization/life-sciences/ai-long-term-care.html).

[41] Topol E. J. High-performance medicine: the convergence of human and artificial Intelligence. Nat Med. 2019;25(1):44–56. https://doi.org/10.1093/cki/sfad168.

[42] Picard C., Kleib M., Norris C., O'Rourke H. M., Montgomery C., Douma M. The Use and Structure of Emergency Nurses' Triage Narrative Data: Scoping Review. JMIR Nurs. 2023;6:e41331. https://doi.org/10.2196/41331.

[43] Riboli-Sasco E., El-Osta A., Alaa A., Webber I., Karki M., El Asmar M. L., Purohit K., Painter A., Hayhoe B. Triage and Diagnostic Accuracy of Online Symptom Checkers: Systematic Review. J Med Internet Res. 2023;25:e43803. https://doi.org/10.2196/43803.

[44] Barbieri C., Neri L., Stuard S., Mari F., Martín-Guerrero J. D. From electronic health records to clinical management systems: how the digital transformation can support healthcare services. Clin Kidney J. 2023;16(11):1878–1884. https://doi.org/10.1093/ckj/sfad168.

[45] Janßen M., Prilla M. Investigating the Use of Head Mounted Devices for Remote Cooperation and Guidance during the Treatment of Wounds. Proceedings of the ACM on Human-Computer Interaction, 2022;6(3):1–27. https://doi.org/10.1145/3492822.

[46] Chen M. Y., Cao M. Q., Xu T. Y. Progress in the application of artificial Intelligence in skin wound assessment and prediction of healing time. Am J Transl Res. 2024; 16(7):2765–2776. https://doi.org/10.62347/MYHE3488.

[47] Collins S. A., Bakken S., Vawdrey D. K., Coiera E., Currie L. M. Clinician preferences for verbal communication compared to EHR documentation in the ICU. Appl Clin Inform. 2011;2(2):190–201. https://doi.org/10.4338/ACI-2011-02-RA-0011.

[48] Collins S. A., Bakken S., Vawdrey D. K., Coiera E., Currie L. M. Discuss now, document later: CIS/CPOE perceived to be a 'shift behind' in the ICU. Stud Health Technol Inform. 2010;160(Pt 1):178–182.

[49] Afkari H., Eivazi S., Bednarik R., Mäkelä S. The potentials for hands-free interaction in micro-neurosurgery. Proceedings of the 8th Nordic Conference on Human-Computer Interaction: Fun, Fast, Foundational. Helsinki, 2014:401–410.

[50] Mewes A., Hensen B., Wacker F., Hansen C. Touchless interaction with software in interventional radiology and surgery: a systematic literature review. Int J Comput Assist Radiol Surg. 2017;12(2):291–305. https://doi.org/10.1007/s11548-016-1480-6.

[51] Pflegedokumentation einfach einsprechen: voize GmbH, 2022 (Accessed October 10, 2024, at https://wwwvoize.de/).

[52] Breuer-Stengel E., Güttler C., Heidl C., Konrad R., Kühhorn R., Bauer C. Werkstattbericht voize Neugestaltung des Pflegedokumentationsprozesses via Spracheingaben – am Beispiel der Applikation voize. Nürnberg: Pflegepraxiszentrum Nürnberg, 2023.

[53] Tudor Car L., Dhinagaran D. A., Kyaw B. M., Kowatsch T., Joty S., Theng Y. L., Atun R. Conversational Agents in Health Care: Scoping Review and Conceptual Analysis J Med Internet Res 2020;22(8):e17158. https://doi.org/10.2196/17158.

[54] Milne-Ives M., de Cock C., Lim E., Shehadeh M. H., de Pennington N., Mole G., Normando E., Meinert E. The Effectiveness of Artificial Intelligence Conversational Agents in Health Care: Systematic Review J Med Internet Res 2020;22(10):e20346. https://doi.org/10.2196/20346.

[55] Weigand C., Flemming D., Zweyer G., Borutta P., Hofmann F., Wieland G., Hayir E., Seuß D., Wittenberg T. A concept and technical requirements for the Temi platform supporting care and nursing. Current Directions in Biomedical Engineering 2022;8(2): 241–244. https://doi.org/10.1515/cdbme-2022-1062.

[56] PIO-Festlegung: Überleitungsbogen. Kassenärztliche Bundesvereinigung, 2022. (Accessed November 19, 2024, at https://www.kbv.de/temp/Anlage_1_PIO-Festlegung.pdf).

[57] Hannemann N., Kutza J. O., Kücking F., Przysucha M., Hübner U. H., Babitsch B. Die Wahrnehmung der Vertrauenswürdigkeit eines KI-Systems zur Wundklassifizierung aus der Perspektive von Gesundheitsfachkräften. Gesundheit – gemeinsam. Kooperationstagung der Deutschen Gesellschaft für Medizinische Informatik, Biometrie und Epidemiologie (GMDS), Deutschen Gesellschaft für Sozialmedizin und Prävention (DGSMP), Deutschen Gesellschaft für Epidemiologie (DGEpi), Deutschen Gesellschaft für Medizinische Soziologie (DGMS) und der Deutschen Gesellschaft für Public Health (DGPH). Dresden: 2024. https://doi.org/10.3205/24GMDS379.

[58] Tischendorf T., Hasseler M., Schaal T., Ruppert S. N., Marchwacka M., Heitmann-Möller A., Schaffrin S. Developing digital competencies of nursing professionals in continuing education and training – a scoping review. Front Med (Lausanne) 2024;13:11:1358398. https://doi.org/10.3389/fmed.2024.1358398.

[59] von Gerich H., Moen H., Block L. J., Chu C. H., DeForest H., Hobensack M., Michalowski M., Mitchell J., Nibber R., Olalia M. A., Pruinelli L., Ronquillo C. E., Topaz M., Peltonen L. M. Artificial Intelligence -based technologies in nursing: A scoping literature review of the evidence. Int J Nurs Stud. 2022;127:104153. https://doi.org/10.1016/j.ijnurstu.2021.104153.

[60] Mannevaara P., Kinnunen U. M., Egbert N., Hübner U., Vieira-Marques P., Sousa P., Saranto K. Discovering the importance of health informatics education competencies in healthcare practice. A focus group interview. Int J Med Inform. 2024;187:105463. https://doi.org/10.1016/j.ijmedinf.2024.105463.

[61] Mir M. M., Mir G. M., Raina N. T., Mir S. M., Mir S. M., Miskeen E., Alharthi M. H., Alamri M.M.S. Application of Artificial Intelligence in Medical Education: Current Scenario and Future Perspectives. J Adv Med Educ Prof. 2023;11(3):133–140. https://doi.org/10.30476/JAMP.2023.98655.1803.

[62] Liu J., Liu F., Fang J., Liu S. The application of Chat Generative Pre-trained Transformer in nursing education. Nurs Outlook 2023;71(6):102064. https://doi.org/10.1016/j.outlook.2023.102064.

[63] Sodeau A., Fox A. Influence of nurses in the implementation of artificial Intelligence in health care: a scoping review. Aust Health Rev. 2022;46(6):736–741. https://doi.org/10.1071/AH22164.

[64] Zhou Y., Li Z., Li Y. Interdisciplinary collaboration between nursing and engineering in health care: A scoping review. Int J Nurs Stud. 2021;117:103900. https://doi.org/10.1016/j.ijnurstu.2021.103900.

[65] Thieme A., Hanratty M., Lyons M., Palacios J., Marques R. F., Morrison C., Doherty G. Designing Human-centered AI for Mental Health: Developing Clinically Relevant Applications for Online CBT Treatment. ACM Trans. Comput.-Hum. Interact. 2023;30(2), 27:1–50. https://doi.org/10.1145/3564752.

[66] Liebe J. D., Esdar M. Human Centered Design – Ein effektives Mittel gegen "Wickedness" und "Pilotitis" komplexer Digitalisierungsprojekte? In: Henke V., Hülsken G., Schneider H., Varghese J. (eds.). Health Data Management: Schlüsselfaktor für erfolgreiche Krankenhäuser. Wiesbaden: Springer Fachmedien, 2024:675–688. https://doi.org/10.1007/978-3-658-43236-2_57.

[67] Melles M., Albayrak A., Goossens R. Innovating health care: Key characteristics of human-centred design. International Journal for Quality in Health Care 2021;33(1): 37–44. https://doi.org/10.1093/intqhc/mzaa127.

[68] Kilpatrick K., Savard I., Audet L. A., Costanzo G., Khan M., Atallah R., Jabbour M., Zhou W., Wheeler K., Ladd E., Gray D. C., Henderson C., Spies L. A., McGrath H., Rogers M. A global perspective of advanced

practice nursing research: A review of systematic reviews. PLoS One. 2024;19(7):e0305008. https://doi.org/10.1371/journal.pone.0305008.

[69] Schultz M. A., Walden R. L., Cato K., Coviak C. P., Cruz C., D'Agostino F., Douthit B. J., Forbes T., Gao G., Lee M. A., Lekan D., Wieben A., Jeffery A. D. Data Science Methods for Nursing-Relevant Patient Outcomes and Clinical Processes: The 2019 Literature Year in Review. Comput Inform Nurs. 2021;39(11):654–667. https://doi.org/10.1097/CIN.0000000000000705.

[70] Shang Z. A Concept Analysis on the Use of Artificial Intelligence in Nursing. Cureus 2021; 13(5):e14857. https://doi.org/10.7759/cureus.14857.

[71] Krick T., Zerth J., Klawunn R. Einführung und Orientierung. In: Krick T., Zerth J., Rothgang H., Klawunn R, Walzer S, Kley T. (eds.). Pflegeinnovationen in der Praxis. Erfahrungen und Empfehlungen aus dem "Cluster Zukunft der Pflege". Berlin: Springer Gabler, 2023:1–16.

[72] Selke S. AI between tool and super-ego – Role pluralism as a prerequisite for ethical reflections

[73] Hammer B. Fairness in AI – how to design 'unbiased' algorithms? In: Manzeschke A. and Wittenberg T. (eds.). Ethical Perspectives on Artifical Intelligence in Biomedical Engineering, Chapter 14, DeGruyter, 2025.

[74] Fonck S., Stollenwerk A. Explainable Artificial Intelligence in Biomedical Engineering In: Manzeschke A. and Wittenberg T. (eds.). Ethical Perspectives on Artifical Intelligence in Biomedical Engineering, Chapter 13, DeGruyter, 2025.

Stefan T. Kamin, Martina Simon, Stephanie Schmitt-Rüth

23 Acceptance of AI by physicians: The role of AI autonomy and explainability

23.1 Introduction

The integration of Artificial Intelligence (AI) in healthcare has demonstrated significant potential for enhancing diagnostic accuracy, improving patient outcomes, and optimizing operational efficiency [1–3]. However, empirical evidence suggests considerable heterogeneity in physicians' acceptance of AI technologies, ranging from enthusiasm to anxiety and fear [4–6]. Several barriers to AI implementation have been identified, including insufficient technical familiarity [7], inadequate training in AI-based systems [8,9], and uncertainty regarding AI tool utilization [10]. Critical factors influencing AI acceptance include data privacy considerations, system trust dynamics, effects on physician-patient interactions, and perceived threats to clinical autonomy [11–13]. Although existing research provides valuable insights into general attitudes toward AI in healthcare, significant knowledge gaps persist regarding the specific technological characteristics that influence healthcare professionals' acceptance. Another limitation of the current evidence is its reliance on self-reported questionnaire data without concrete AI scenarios, which potentially compromises ecological validity. To address these methodological constraints, this study examined the relationship between physician acceptance of specific AI applications and two critical system attributes: AI autonomy and explainability. Both are recognized as key factors influencing AI acceptance [14]; however, there is a lack of experimental designs that systematically investigate their interactions within a medical context. We address this gap by explicitly testing how explainability depends on the level of autonomy in an AI system and how this interplay affects physicians' acceptance of AI-driven decision-making.

23.2 What is AI acceptance?

AI acceptance in healthcare represents healthcare professionals' behavioral intentions and attitudinal disposition toward incorporating artificial intelligence systems into clinical practice workflows [15]. This construct is derived from the Technology Acceptance Model (TAM) [16], which theorizes that technology adoption is predominantly determined by two fundamental cognitive assessments: perceived usefulness and ease of use. In the healthcare AI context, perceived usefulness encompasses clinicians' evaluations of an AI system's potential to enhance clinical performance metrics, optimize patient outcomes, and improve operational efficiency. Perceived ease of use reflects clinicians' anticipated effort requirements for system implementation and workflow integration.

Methodologically, acceptance has typically been operationalized as a dependent variable, enabling systematic investigation of its determinants through empirical analysis. This approach facilitates the identification of critical adoption factors and implementation barriers, which helps inform evidence-based strategies for system design optimization and organizational change management that align with healthcare providers' operational requirements and professional objectives.

23.3 Factors affecting AI acceptance

Recent studies have identified several critical aspects affecting AI acceptance in healthcare, revealing a complex interplay of technological, psychological, and ethical factors. For example, the level of trust in AI systems has emerged as a critical determinant for their acceptance [17,18], and is particularly relevant in healthcare contexts [19], reflecting the high-stakes nature of medical decision-making processes [2]. This is also reflected in concerns that AI might depersonalize patient care or erode the human elements of medical practice, which are crucial for effective treatment and patient satisfaction [20]. Furthermore, the perceived threat to professional autonomy reflects concerns regarding the changing roles of healthcare providers in the AI-augmented medical landscape [13,21]. These aspects resonate with the EU AI Act and the proposed regulatory framework for AI, which emphasizes the importance of transparency, accountability, and human oversight in AI systems. Consequently, *explainability* and *autonomy* have emerged as key factors that influence the acceptance of AI technologies in healthcare.

Explainability refers to how well humans understand the decisions of an AI system and is crucial for building trust in medical environments. Explainable AI (XAI) [49] techniques aim to address this issue by providing clear and relevant explanations of AI decisions, thereby increasing transparency. Evidence suggests that, under the right conditions, explainability can foster trust. In a recent systematic review of clinicians' trust in AI [22], half of the included studies found that providing explanations significantly increased trust in AI recommendations, especially when the explanations were concise and clinically relevant. Other studies on the use of Large Language Models (LLMs) in healthcare settings have found that professionals are more likely to trust AI when they have a better understanding of the systems [23].

Autonomy relates to the level of independence of AI in decision-making, ranging from fully autonomous to human-in-the-loop systems. There is a broad consensus that AI should act as a supportive tool or partner for clinicians rather than as a replacement [24]. AI systems are more widely accepted when they support diagnosis or offer recommendations while allowing humans to make the final decisions rather than functioning entirely on their own. This is supported by studies with patients [25,26] and physicians

[24], indicating a strong preference for AI systems that allow human oversight and intervention.

While explainability and autonomy reflect the technological characteristics of specific AI systems, there are also interindividual and psychological factors that shape attitudes towards AI. For example, fear and anxiety are often discussed as individual barriers in the literature, with findings showing that AI-related anxiety levels correlate with more negative attitudes and lower usage intention among healthcare practitioners [20]. Furthermore, qualitative evidence from patients suggested that emotional needs influence acceptance [27]. Patients with a strong preference for human interaction in care or those who experience discomfort relying on technology are more likely to resist AI-based care. These emotional responses operate within broader attitudinal frameworks that encompass several psychological components. Several instruments have been developed to assess these attitudes. One example is the *Attitude Toward Artificial Intelligence* (ATAI) scale [28], a brief measure that captures cognitive and affective evaluative orientations toward AI use. Empirical evidence supports the predictive validity of such attitudinal measures, with studies revealing significant associations between ATAI scores and outcomes such as AI literacy among medical students [29] and trust in ChatGPT [30].

Finally, the specific application context significantly influences AI acceptance patterns. For example, AI in diagnostic processes may be more prevalent in radiology than in other medical fields, which might account for the varying degrees of AI acceptance among healthcare professionals [31]. Another example pertains to perceived safety, where systems that perform simple tasks show greater acceptance than AI-driven systems that manage complex tasks, such as surgical robots [31]. Consequently, studies should control for the practical context of AI deployment, which shapes physicians' attitudes and adoption behavior.

23.4 The current research

This study extends previous work on AI acceptance in healthcare by investigating physicians' acceptance of specific AI applications, focusing on the influence of AI autonomy and explainability. Although the existing literature has explored these factors independently, their combined effects and potential interactions remain to be studied. This study employed a multifaceted approach to examine how AI autonomy (human vs. AI decision-making), explainability (brief vs. detailed explanations), and application type (ECG analysis, insulin pump management, and assistance in colonoscopy) collectively affect physicians' acceptance of AI technologies in healthcare, while controlling for potential confounding variables such as age, gender, job stress, and general attitudes towards AI (ATAI) that may impact acceptance.

23.5 Methods

23.5.1 Participants and recruitment

The sample consisted of 121 physicians recruited through multiple channels in Northern Bavaria, Germany. Recruitment was primarily conducted through hospitals, professional medical associations, physician networks, personal contacts, press releases, and social media. The participating physicians had a mean age of 54 years (SD = 12), and the majority were male (63%, n = 76). Through random assignment, 53% (n = 64) of the participants were allocated to the human decision-making condition and 47% (n = 57) to the AI decision-making condition. Regarding explainability, 45% (n = 54) of the participants received detailed explanations, whereas 55% (n = 67) received brief explanations. The distribution of AI applications was relatively balanced, with 40% (n = 48) evaluating ECG analysis, 28% (n = 34) insulin pump management, and 32% (n = 39) colonoscopy assistance. Tab. 23.1 provides a detailed description of the sample.

Tab. 23.1: Descriptive Statistics for Study Variables (N = 121)

Variable	M	SD	Range	n (%)
TAM composite score	3.07	0.64	1–4	—
Age	53.98	12.20	27–79	—
ATAI	7.04	2.00	1–10	—
Job Stress	2.35	0.68	1–4	—
Gender (male)	—	—	—	76 (62.8)
AI Autonomy (AI condition)	—	—	—	57 (47.1)
AI Explainability (low condition)	—	—	—	67 (55.4)
ECG condition	—	—	—	48 (39.7)
Insulin pump condition				34 (28.1)
Colonoscopy condition	—	—	—	39 (32.2)

Note: M = Mean; SD = Standard Deviation

23.5.2 Design

The study employed a 2×2×3 between-subjects factorial design to investigate the effects of AI explainability (high vs. low), AI autonomy (high vs. low), and the medical application domain (ECG analysis vs. insulin pump management vs. colonoscopy assistance) on physicians' acceptance of AI systems in healthcare. The participants were randomly assigned to one of the 12 experimental conditions. To control for potential confounding effects, age, gender, job stress, and general attitudes towards AI (ATAI) were included as covariates in the analysis.

23.5.3 Experimental manipulations

AI explainability was manipulated by varying the amount of information provided about the AI system's decision-making process. In the high-explainability condition, participants received detailed information about how the AI system processed data and reached conclusions, including references to the underlying clinical database and comparisons with similar cases. In the low explainability condition, participants received only basic information about the AI system's output without additional explanatory details.

AI autonomy was manipulated by varying the degree of human oversight. In the high-autonomy condition, the AI system operated independently, making and implementing decisions *without* requiring human confirmation or intervention. In the low-autonomy condition, the system made suggestions but required explicit physician approval before any decisions could be implemented, thereby maintaining human control over the final medical decisions.

Medical applications were selected through a systematic process by Simon et al. [32], which involved expert interviews and validation. This framework enables the strategic selection of AI technologies based on medical disciplines, healthcare processes, technological foundations, and target groups. The selected applications were categorized into diagnostic, therapeutic, and preventive AI systems.

a) *ECG analysis* falls within the domain of digital cardiology and leverages machine learning and big data analytics to optimize algorithms for signal processing and prediction. The primary objective of this application is to enhance diagnostic accuracy as *a diagnostic support* through improved pattern recognition in biosignals. AI can assist in the early detection of arrhythmias and ischemic events, thereby supporting medical decision-making and potentially preventing life-threatening conditions.

b) *Insulin pump* control represents *a therapeutic AI system* that actively intervenes in treatment processes. This application relies on real-time data processing and control systems to facilitate the optimization of adaptive therapy. Its primary goal is the automated adjustment of insulin dosage based on continuously monitored sensor data.

c) *Colonoscopy* assistance is an *AI application in preventive medicine* that enables the automated analysis of endoscopic images to detect polyps or abnormalities in the intestinal tract. Its primary objective is the early detection of carcinomas through AI-driven pattern recognition in the video recordings.

These applications were chosen based on their relevance to current technological developments in healthcare and their representation of different levels of medical complexity and risk, where the AI system to control the insulin level reflects a higher risk to the patients than the diagnostic support systems do. The experimental manipulations were validated through manipulation checks that assessed the participants' comprehension of their assigned condition.

23.5.4 Procedure and questionnaire

The study was conducted using an online questionnaire. Each participant first viewed an introductory video on AI in healthcare. Subsequently, participants viewed an animated video presentation of their randomly assigned experimental conditions (see Fig. 23.1). Technical implementation was performed using the SoSci Survey platform, which enabled the automated randomization of conditions and stimulus presentation.

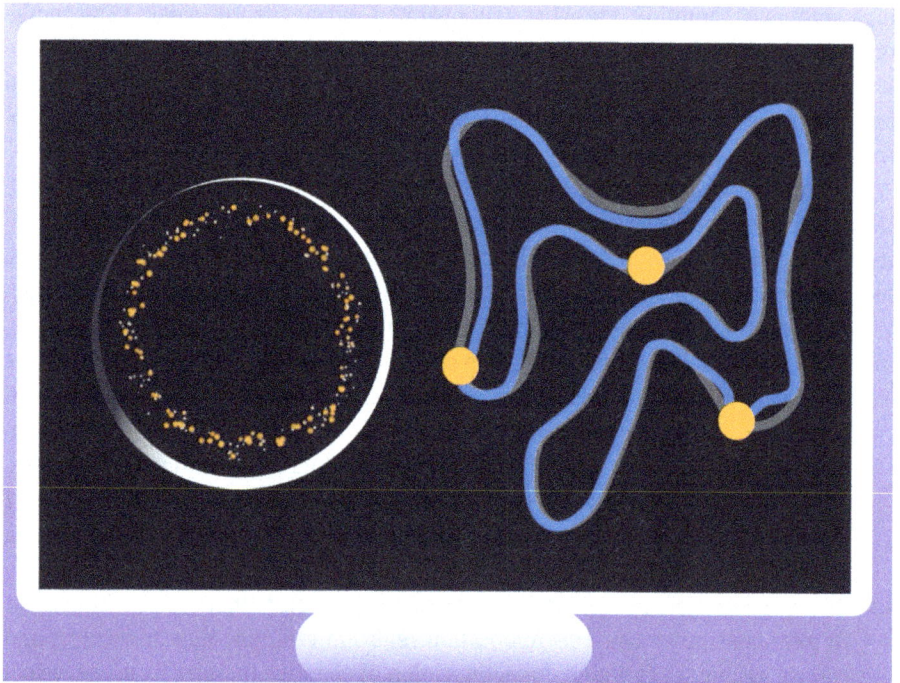

Fig. 23.1: Screenshot from the video about AI in colonoscopy (Source: Fraunhofer IIS).

23.5.5 Measures

23.5.5.1 Technology acceptance

The acceptance of the presented AI system was measured using a modified version of the Technology Acceptance Model [16]. The scale consists of nine items assessing perceived usefulness (e.g., "I find this AI application useful"), perceived ease of use (e.g., "I believe this AI application would be easy to use"), and behavioral intention to use (e.g., "I can imagine using this AI application"). Items were rated on a 4-point scale from 1 ("does not apply at all") to 4 ("fully applies"). The scale showed good internal consistency across all experimental conditions ($\alpha = .89$).

23.5.5.2 Attitudes Toward AI (ATAI)

General attitudes toward artificial intelligence were assessed using the ATAI scale [28]. The scale consists of 5 items measuring acceptance and fear of AI as two negatively associated attitudinal domains (e.g., "I trust artificial intelligence," "Artificial intelligence will destroy humanity") rated on an 11-point scale from 0 ("strong rejection") to 10 ("strong agreement"). For analytical purposes, the fear dimension items were reverse-coded, and the mean of all items was calculated to represent a general attitudinal factor, with higher scores indicating more positive attitudes toward AI. The scale showed good internal consistency ($\alpha = .80$).

23.5.5.3 Job stress

Occupational stress was assessed using a single item from the Marburger Bund Monitor Survey asking, "How do you rate your workload?" with the following four response options: 1 ("I do not experience any stress at work"), 2 ("the stress is manageable"), 3 ("I am frequently overloaded"), and 4 ("I constantly exceed my limits").

23.5.5.4 Sociodemographic variables

Demographic information, including age and gender (0 = female, 1 = male), was collected.

23.6 Results

We conducted our analysis in two steps: first, we examined the main effects, and then we tested for interaction effects between AI autonomy and explainability. The analyses employed linear regression models (see Tab. 23.2), where unstandardized coefficients (*b*) indicate the estimated change in technology acceptance per unit increase in the predictor variable, while holding all other variables constant. Standard errors (*SE*) quantify estimation precision, whereas *p*-values denote statistical significance levels. The *t*-statistic represents the coefficient divided by its standard error and is used in significance testing.

23.6.1 Main effects model

Tab. 23.2 shows the initial main effects model, which explains 31.1% of the variance in technology acceptance. *Explainability* showed a significant main effect (b = -0.20, SE = 0.09, p = .031), with lower acceptance when minimal information about the AI system was provided compared with detailed explanations. AI *autonomy* did not show a significant main effect (b = -0.10, SE = 0.08, p = .226), suggesting no overall difference in acceptance between human and AI decision-making conditions. Among the control variables, *general attitudes* toward AI (ATAI) showed a strong positive association with acceptance (b = 0.17, SE = 0.02, p < .001). *Gender* had a significant effect (b = -0.21, SE = 0.10, p = .034), with male physicians showing lower acceptance than female physicians. Higher levels of job stress were associated with lower acceptance (b = -0.16, SE = 0.08, p = .045). Age did not significantly predict acceptance (b = 0.003, SE = 0.004, p = .420). There was a marginally non-significant effect for ECG applications compared with insulin pump management (b = -0.20, SE = 0.12, p = .086), while colonoscopy applications did not differ significantly from the reference category (b = -0.14, SE = 0.12, p = .237).

23.6.2 Interaction effects model

Adding the interaction between AI autonomy and explainability significantly improved the model fit (ΔR^2 = .014, p = .047). The interaction term was significant (b = 0.37, SE = 0.18, p = .047), indicating that the effect of AI autonomy varied depending on the level of explainability (see Fig. 23.2). Simple slope analysis revealed that AI autonomy had a significant negative effect on acceptance when detailed information about the AI system was provided (b = -0.31, SE = 0.13, p = .018). However, when minimal information was provided, there was no significant difference between human and AI decision-making (b = 0.06, SE = 0.12, p = .605). Estimated marginal means showed that acceptance was highest when humans made decisions and detailed explanations were provided

($M\mu$ = 3.32, SE = 0.09), while all other conditions showed similar, lower levels of acceptance ($M\mu$s = 2.94–3.01, SEs = 0.09–0.11). The pattern of results for the control variables remained largely consistent with the main effects model.

Tab. 23.2: Regression models predicting TAM composite score (N = 121)

Variable	Main Effects Model			Interaction Effects Model		
	b (SE)	t	p	b (SE)	t	p
Age	0.003 (0.004)	0.810	.420	0.003 (0.004)	0.738	.462
Gender	-0.211 (0.098)	-2.141	.034	-0.245 (0.101)	-2.419	.017
ATAI	0.166 (0.023)	7.286	< .001	0.164 (0.023)	7.007	< .001
Job Stress	-0.164 (0.081)	-2.024	.045	-0.167 (0.080)	-2.097	.038
AI Autonomy (low)	-0.103 (0.085)	-1.218	.226	-0.308 (0.128)	-2.398	.018
AI Explainability (low)	-0.201 (0.092)	-2.187	.031	-0.380 (0.123)	-3.091	.003
ECG application	-0.201 (0.116)	-1.730	.086	-0.187 (0.112)	-1.667	.098
Colonoscopy application	-0.142 (0.120)	-1.189	.237	-0.132 (0.117)	-1.129	.261
Autonomy × Explainability	-	-	-	0.371 (0.185)	2.010	.047

Note. b = unstandardized regression coefficient; SE = standard error; t = t-test statistic. $p < .05*$, $p < .01**$, $p < .001***$.

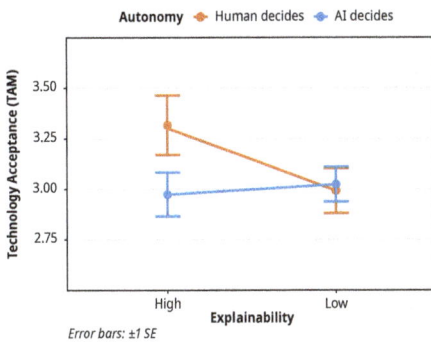

Fig. 23.2: Interaction effect (Source: Fraunhofer IIS).

23.7 Discussion

This study investigated how AI autonomy and explainability influence physicians' acceptance of AI systems in healthcare settings. Our findings reveal a complex interplay between these factors, which has important implications for both theory and practice.

23.7.1 Theoretical implications

Our results revealed a significant main effect of explainability on physicians' acceptance of AI systems. When minimal information about the AI system was provided compared to detailed explanations, physicians showed lower acceptance rates. This finding aligns with previous research suggesting that healthcare professionals value transparency in AI systems [22,24,33], which can enhance trust and facilitate system use. This supports the growing emphasis on Explainable AI (XAI) in healthcare applications [34], where clinicians must comprehend system decisions to maintain their professional judgment.

Contrary to explainability, we did not find a main effect of AI autonomy, contradicting research suggesting that clinicians are less likely to cede control to autonomous AI systems [24]. This finding may be attributed to methodological differences; existing studies often rely on self-reported attitudes across heterogeneous clinical settings, whereas we used specific clinical vignettes with experimental variable manipulation. Additionally, our sample showed considerable age heterogeneity, which may indicate significant variations in clinical expertise and decision-making authority. This is relevant because the literature indicates that perceived threats to autonomy are associated with aspects of professional identity formation and career stage [35]. For example, senior physicians are typically more concerned about potential overreliance on AI-based decision-support systems; in contrast, junior physicians are more likely to perceive such systems as autonomy-enhancing tools [35].

The significant interaction revealed that the effect of AI autonomy varied depending on the level of explainability and vice versa. Specifically, when detailed explanations were provided, physicians showed significantly lower acceptance of autonomous AI systems than human-controlled systems. However, when minimal information was provided, there was no significant difference between the human and AI decision-making conditions. This pattern suggests that physicians' concerns about autonomous AI emerge primarily when they are presented with detailed information, which corresponds with research on algorithm aversion [36,37]. We can conclude that explainability makes the limitations and potential risks of AI more salient when systems operate autonomously. However, when minimal information is provided, physicians may rely on heuristics or general trust, which could explain the lack of difference in acceptance between human-controlled and AI-driven systems under such conditions.

These findings also contribute to the growing body of literature on XAI in healthcare [34]. That is, there is currently no clear consensus on what constitutes a suitable explanation or how to evaluate its quality [38]. Our study adds empirical evidence to this ongoing discussion by demonstrating that the effectiveness of explanations can vary depending on the level of system autonomy, thus challenging the assumption that maximum transparency is always beneficial for user acceptance.

Regarding the control variables, general attitudes toward AI showed a strong positive association with acceptance and explained a substantial portion of the variance. This highlights the importance of considering individual attitudes and predispositions towards AI when planning implementation strategies. Consequently, future research should explore the interplay between ATAI scores and stable personality traits. Sindermann et al. [39] demonstrated significant associations between personality traits and AI attitudes in German and Chinese samples. Investigating how these factors influence healthcare professionals' AI acceptance may help tailor AI training programs and user interfaces based on individuals' ATAI scores and relevant personality traits, which could enhance AI integration in clinical practice. Gender differences were significant, with male physicians showing lower acceptance than female physicians. While classic literature on technology acceptance research has discussed gender-related differences [40], explicit evidence on gender-based patterns in healthcare AI remains limited, suggesting the need for further exploration of these findings. Job stress negatively influenced acceptance, indicating that workplace pressure may function as a barrier to acceptance in healthcare settings. This finding is supported by Lambert et al. [31], who identified time constraints and workload as significant barriers to AI acceptance. An interesting finding is the non-significance of age in predicting AI acceptance, despite the relatively older sample. This result challenges the common stereotype that older adults are less accepting of new technology. The absence of an age effect suggests that chronological age alone may not be a reliable predictor of AI-acceptance among healthcare professionals. This finding aligns with aging research, highlighting that age is not a causal variable in technology acceptance or use [41,42]. Instead, age-related differences result from other factors that correlate with age, such as cognitive abilities, experience, and attitudes [43–45]. In the context of our study, professional expertise and exposure to technological advancements in healthcare may be more important than age in shaping the acceptance of AI.

23.7.2 Practical implications

Our findings have implications for the development and implementation of AI systems in healthcare. The results provide empirical evidence for tailoring explainability strategies according to the level of AI autonomy, addressing individual differences in AI acceptance, and considering organizational factors during implementation.

The interaction between autonomy and explainability was the most relevant finding of this study. When detailed explanations were provided, physicians showed lower acceptance of autonomous AI systems than human-controlled systems. This suggests that a one-size-fits-all approach to explainability is suboptimal. For highly autonomous AI systems, designers should carefully calibrate the level of technical details provided, as excessive explanations may trigger resistance among physicians. Conversely, in AI systems where physicians retain decision-making control, explanations can enhance trust and support clinical judgment. In these scenarios, implementation strategies should focus on providing interpretable visual representations of AI decision-making processes and clearly delineating the supportive role of the technology.

The effect of general attitudes toward AI indicates that targeted training and change management strategies are essential. Organizations implementing AI should assess healthcare professionals' attitudes and develop differentiated approaches for users with varying predispositions. This may include exposure-based interventions for those with negative attitudes and advanced skill development for those with positive orientations. Moreover, change management efforts should address varying expectations and concerns across different medical professions, ensuring early user involvement and participation in AI development to align the technology design with end-user needs. Practical approaches, such as socio-ethical acceptance workshops [46] and usability testing, can be effective in identifying potential barriers and refining system implementation.

The gender effect found in our study, with male physicians showing lower acceptance than female physicians, suggests that implementation strategies may need to consider these demographic factors in the future. While further research is needed to fully understand these differences, we argue that varying concerns and priorities across different user groups should be considered.

The significant negative effect of job stress on AI acceptance emphasizes the importance of considering a broader organizational context when implementing new systems. Healthcare organizations should address workplace stressors before or concurrently with AI introduction, as high stress levels may exacerbate resistance to new technologies. Implementation strategies should prioritize minimizing the additional cognitive workload when designing AI interfaces for high-stress clinical environments. This may include streamlined interfaces, customizable notification settings, and integration with existing electronic health record systems to reduce friction. These recommendations align with change management literature, emphasizing the importance of creating a receptive context for technological innovation [47].

23.7.3 Limitations and future research

The experimental design prioritized internal validity through controlled manipulations of AI autonomy and explainability, which necessarily entailed certain trade-offs in ecological validity. Specifically, the study examined physicians' reported behavioral intentions toward hypothetical AI systems rather than observing their actual adoption behaviors in clinical settings. This approach, while allowing for precise experimental control, may not fully capture the complexity of the technology acceptance processes that unfold over time in authentic healthcare environments. Field experiments in clinical settings with functioning AI systems would complement our controlled experimental approach, potentially revealing implementation barriers that are not evident in hypothetical scenarios. Such research should incorporate objective usage metrics alongside self-reported intentions to provide a more comprehensive assessment of the determinants of AI acceptance in healthcare contexts. Another limitation is the geographical homogeneity of the sample, which constrains the generalizability of the findings to broader international contexts. Given that technology acceptance may be influenced by cultural factors, regulatory environments, and country-specific health-care systems, the observed patterns may reflect region-specific dynamics rather than universal psychological processes governing AI acceptance. A significant limitation emerges from the temporal gap between the study's conceptualization in 2019 and the rapidly evolving technological landscape. This discrepancy is particularly evident in AI-assisted colonoscopy, which transitioned from a hypothetical application in the study design to commercially available technology during manuscript preparation. This technological evolution potentially affects the ecological validity of our findings, as perceptions of hypothetical systems may differ from attitudes toward operational tech-nology. Another issue pertains to the operationalization of explainability as a binary variable, which may not capture the construct's multidimensional nature [48]. Further-more, we did not account for the costs associated with the explanation modes, such as the additional time physicians must allocate to process detailed AI rationales. This time investment represents a barrier to implementation, as increased workload and effort expectancy issues can hinder adoption [31].

23.7.4 Conclusion

Our findings highlight the complexity of the factors influencing AI acceptance in healthcare and suggest that a one-size-fits-all approach to system explainability may be suboptimal. As healthcare organizations continue to implement AI systems, careful consideration must be given to how system characteristics interact with and influence acceptance among medical professionals. This study provides a foundation for more nuanced approaches to AI implementation in healthcare settings, emphasizing the need to balance transparency with other factors affecting user acceptance.

Acknowledgement

This work was funded by the Innovation Fund of the Joint Federal Committee in Ger-many as part of the project "KI-BA Artificial Intelligence in Healthcare – Conditions of Acceptance by Insured Persons and Physicians" (01VSF 20016). The authors declare no conflicts of interest. Informed consent was obtained from all individuals included in this study.

References

[1]   Kumar Y., Koul A., Singla R., Ijaz M. F. Artificial intelligence in disease diagnosis: a systematic literature review, synthesizing framework and future research agenda. J Ambient Intell Humaniz Comput. 2023 Jul;14(7):8459–86.

[2]   Alowais S. A., Alghamdi S. S., Alsuhebany N., Alqahtani T., Alshaya A. I., Almohareb S. N. et al. Revolutionizing healthcare: the role of artificial intelligence in clinical practice. BMC Med Educ. 2023 Sep 22;23(1):689.

[3]   Secinaro S., Calandra D., Secinaro A., Muthurangu V., Biancone P. The role of artificial intelligence in healthcare: a structured literature review. **BMC Med Inform Decis Mak. 2021 Apr 10;21(1):125.**

[4]   European Society of Radiology (ESR). Impact of artificial intelligence on radiology: a EuroAIM survey among members of the European Society of Radiology. Insights Imaging. 2019 Dec;10(1):105.

[5]   Pakdemirli E. Perception of Artificial Intelligence (AI) among radiologists. Acta Radiol Open. 2019 Sep;8(9):2058460119878662.

[6]   Wagner G., Raymond L., Paré G.. Understanding Prospective Physicians' Intention to Use Artificial Intelligence in Their Future Medical Practice: Configurational Analysis. JMIR Med Educ. 2023 Mar 22;9:e45631.

[7]   Oh S., Kim J. H., Choi S. W., Lee H. J., Hong J., Kwon S. H. Physician Confidence in Artificial Intelligence: An Online Mobile Survey J Med Internet Res 2019;21(3):e12422.

[8]   Briganti G., Le Moine O. Artificial Intelligence in Medicine: Today and Tomorrow. Front Med (Lausanne). 2020 Feb 5;7:27. https://doi.org/10.3389/fmed.2020.00027. PMID: 32118012; PMCID: PMC7012990.

[9]   Waymel Q., Badr S., Demondion X., Cotten A., Jacques T. Impact of the rise of artificial intelligence in radiology: What do radiologists think? Diagn Interv Imaging. 2019 Jun;100(6):327–336. https://doi.org/10.1016/j.diii.2019.03.015. Epub 2019 May 6. PMID: 31072803.

[10] Kimiafar K., Sarbaz M., Tabatabaei S. M., Ghaddaripouri K., Mousavi A. S., Raei Mehneh M. et al. Artificial Intelligence Literacy Among Healthcare Professionals and Students: A Systematic Review. Front Health Inform. 2023 Nov 11;12:168.

[11] Al Kuwaiti A., Nazer K., Al-Reedy A., Al-Shehri S., Al-Muhanna A., Subbarayalu A. V. et al. A Review of the Role of Artificial Intelligence in Healthcare. J Pers Med. 2023 Jun 5;13(6):951.

[12] Lekadir K., Feragen A., Fofanah A. J., Frangi A. F., Buyx A., Emelie A. et al. FUTURE-AI: International consensus guideline for trustworthy and deployable artificial intelligence in healthcare [Internet]. arXiv; 2023 [cited 2024 Aug 30]. Available from: https://arxiv.org/abs/2309.12325

[13] Van Cauwenberge D., Van Biesen W., Decruyenaere J., Leune T., Sterckx S. "Many roads lead to Rome and the Artificial Intelligence only shows me one road": an interview study on physician attitudes regarding the implementation of computerised clinical decision support systems. BMC Med Ethics. 2022 Dec;23(1):50.

[14] Hauptman A. I., Schelble B. G., Duan W., Flathmann C., McNeese N. J. Understanding the influence of AI autonomy on AI explainability levels in human-AI teams using a mixed methods approach. Cogn Technol Work. 2024 Sep;26(3):435–55.

[15] Kelly S., Kaye S. A., Oviedo-Trespalacios O. What factors contribute to the acceptance of artificial intelligence? A systematic review. Telemat Inform. 2023 Feb;77:101925.

[16] Davis F. D. Perceived usefulness, perceived ease of use, and user acceptance of technology. MIS Q. 1989;13:319–40.

[17] Bach T. A., Khan A., Hallock H., Beltrão G., Sousa S. A Systematic Literature Review of User Trust in AI-Enabled Systems: An HCI Perspective. Int J Human–Computer Interact. 2024 Mar 3;40(5):1251–66.

[18] Leschanowsky A., Rech S., Popp B., Bäckström T. Evaluating privacy, security, and trust perceptions in conversational AI: A systematic review. Comput Hum Behav. 2024 Oct;159:108344.

[19] Tucci V., Saary J., Doyle T. E. Factors influencing trust in medical artificial intelligence for healthcare professionals: a narrative review. J Med Artif Intell. 2022 Mar;5:4–4.

[20] Dingel J., Kleine A. K., Cecil J., Sigl A. L., Lermer E., Gaube S. Predictors of Health Care Practitioners' Intention to Use AI-Enabled Clinical Decision Support Systems: Meta-Analysis Based on the Unified Theory of Acceptance and Use of Technology. J Med Internet Res. 2024 Aug 5;26:e57224.

[21] Ahuja A. S. The impact of artificial intelligence in medicine on the future role of the physician. PeerJ. 2019 Oct 4;7:e7702.

[22] Rosenbacke R., Melhus Å., McKee M., Stuckler D. How Explainable Artificial Intelligence Can Increase or Decrease Clinicians' Trust in AI Applications in Health Care: Systematic Review. JMIR AI. 2024 Oct 30;3:e53207.

[23] Cherrez-Ojeda I., Gallardo-Bastidas J. C., Robles-Velasco K., Osorio M. F., Velez Leon E. M., Leon Velastegui M. et al. Understanding Health Care Students' Perceptions, Beliefs, and Attitudes Toward AI-Powered Language Models: Cross-Sectional Study. JMIR Med Educ. 2024 Aug 13;10:e51757.

[24] Chen M., Zhang B., Cai Z., Seery S., Gonzalez M. J., Ali N. M., Ren R., Qiao Y., Xue P., Jiang Y. Acceptance of clinical artificial intelligence among physicians and medical students: A systematic review with cross-sectional survey. Front Med (Lausanne). 2022 Aug 31;9:990604. https://doi.org/10.3389/fmed.2022.990604. PMID: 36117979; PMCID: PMC9472134.

[25] Lennartz S., Dratsch T., Zopfs D., Persigehl T., Maintz D., Große Hokamp N. et al. Use and Control of Artificial Intelligence in Patients Across the Medical Workflow: Single-Center Questionnaire Study of Patient Perspectives. J Med Internet Res. 2021 Feb 17;23(2):e24221.

[26] Riedl R., Hogeterp S. A., Reuter M. Do patients prefer a human doctor, artificial intelligence, or a blend, and is this preference dependent on medical discipline? Empirical evidence and implications for medical practice. Front Psychol. 2024 Aug 12;15:1422177.

[27] Sobaih A. E. E., Chaibi A., Brini R. Abdelghani Ibrahim TM. Unlocking patient resistance to AI in healthcare: a psychological exploration. Eur J Investig Health Psychol Educ [Internet]. 2025;15(1). Available from: https://www.mdpi.com/2254-9625/15/1/6.

[28] Sindermann C., Sha P., Zhou M. et al. Assessing the Attitude Towards Artificial Intelligence: Introduction of a Short Measure in German, Chinese, and English Language. Künstl Intell 35, 109–118 (2021). https://doi.org/10.1007/s13218-020-00689-0.

[29] Laupichler M. C., Aster A., Meyerheim M., Raupach T., Mergen M. Medical students' AI literacy and attitudes towards AI: a cross-sectional two-center study using pre-validated assessment instruments. BMC Med Educ. 2024 Apr 10;24(1):401.

[30] Montag C., Ali R.. Can We Assess Attitudes Toward AI with Single Items? Associations with Existing Attitudes Toward AI Measures and Trust in ChatGPT. J Technol Behav Sci [Internet]. 2025 Feb 11 [cited 2025 Mar 16]; Available from: https://link.springer.com/10.1007/s41347-025-00481-7

[31] Lambert S. I., Madi M., Sopka S., Lenes A., Stange H., Buszello C. P. et al. An integrative review on the acceptance of artificial intelligence among healthcare professionals in hospitals. Npj Digit Med. 2023 Jun 10;6(1):111.

[32] Simon M., Kamin S., Hamper A., Wittenberg T., Schmitt-Rüth S. Strategizing AI in Healthcare: A Multidimensional Blueprint for Transformative Decision-Making in Clinical Settings. Curr Dir Biomed Eng. 2024 Dec 1;10(4):595–9.

[33] Ahmed M. I., Spooner B., Isherwood J., Lane M., Orrock E., Dennison A. A Systematic Review of the Barriers to the Implementation of Artificial Intelligence in Healthcare. Cureus [Internet]. 2023 Oct 4 [cited 2025 Mar 14]; Available from: https://www.cureus.com/articles/170025-a-systematic-review-of-the-barriers-to-the-implementation-of-artificial-intelligence-in-healthcare.

[34] Tjoa E., Guan C. A Survey on Explainable Artificial Intelligence (XAI): Toward Medical XAI. IEEE Trans Neural Netw Learn Syst. 2021 Nov;32(11):4793–813.

[35] Ackerhans S., Huynh T., Kaiser C., Schultz C. Exploring the role of professional identity in the implementation of clinical decision support systems – a narrative review. Implement Sci. 2024 Feb 12;19(1):11.

[36] Burton J. W., Stein M., Jensen T. B. A systematic review of algorithm aversion in augmented decision making. J Behav Decis Mak. 2020 Apr;33(2):220–39.

[37] Dietvorst B. J., Simmons J. P., Massey C. Algorithm aversion: People erroneously avoid algorithms after seeing them err. J Exp Psychol Gen. 2015;144(1):114–26.

[38] Markus A. F., Kors J. A., Rijnbeek P. R. The role of explainability in creating trustworthy artificial intelligence for health care: A comprehensive survey of the terminology, design choices, and evaluation strategies. J Biomed Inform. 2021 Jan;113:103655.

[39] Sindermann C., Yang H., Elhai J. D., Yang S., Quan L., Li M. et al. Acceptance and Fear of Artificial Intelligence: associations with personality in a German and a Chinese sample. Discov Psychol. 2022 Dec;2(1):8.

[40] Venkatesh V., Morris M. G. Why Don't Men Ever Stop to Ask for Directions? Gender, Social Influence, and Their Role in Technology Acceptance and Usage Behavior. MIS Q. 2000 Mar;24(1):115.

[41] Rogers W. A., Fisk A. D. Toward a psychological science of advanced technology design for older adults. J Gerontol B Psychol Sci Soc Sci. 2010;65(6):645–53.

[42] Kamin S. T., Lang F. R., Beyer A. Subjective Technology Adaptivity Predicts Technology Use in Old Age. Gerontology. 2017;63:385–92.

[43] Kamin S. T., Lang F. R. Internet Use and Cognitive Functioning in Late Adulthood: Longitudinal Findings from the Survey of Health, Ageing and Retirement in Europe (SHARE). J Gerontol B Psychol Sci Soc Sci. 2020;75(3):534–9.

[44] Kamin S. T., Lang F. R. Cognitive Functions Buffer Age Differences in Technology Ownership. Gerontology. 2016;62(2):238–46.

[45] Seifert A., Kamin S. T., Lang F. R. Technology Adaptivity Mediates the Effect of Technology Biography on Internet Use Variability. Innov Aging. 2020;4(2).

[46] Schmitt-Rüth S., Simon M. Sozio-ethische Betrachtungen in Technikentwicklungsprojekten – Zeitverschwendung oder Erfolgsfaktor für Nutzerakzeptanz? HMD Prax Wirtsch. 2020 Jun;57(3):541–57.

[47] Greenhalgh T., Robert G., Macfarlane F., Bate P., Kyriakidou O. Diffusion of Innovations in Service Organizations: Systematic Review and Recommendations. Milbank Q. 2004 Dec;82(4):581–629.

[48] Ridley M. Human-centered explainable artificial intelligence: An Annual Review of Information Science and Technology (ARIST) paper. J Assoc Inf Sci Technol. 2024;76(1):98–120.

[49] Dössel O., Loewe A. Uncertainties, errors, explainability and responsibility for AI in medicine. In: Manzeschke A. and Wittenberg T. (eds.). Ethical Perspectives on Artifical Intelligence in Biomedical Engineering, DeGruyter, 2025.

Ana Álvarez-Mena, Birgit Habenstein

24 Artificial intelligence shaping a new era in molecular medicine

24.1 How AI is changing science and medicine

Currently, artificial intelligence (AI) is transforming the way machines think, learn, and solve problems – similar to humans. By processing vast amounts of data, AI systems can adapt, improve, and make decisions autonomously, offering solutions to complex challenges across various fields, from healthcare to engineering.

In contrast to traditional programming, where data analysis is developed in a sequential manner, machine learning (ML), a leading AI tool, focuses on developing algorithms that enable computers to learn from data through multi-layered evaluation. By applying advanced statistical methods, ML identifies patterns in data and adjusts its models over time based on the information it processes. These self-adaptive systems continuously enhance their analytical precision, uncovering intricate patterns and improving performance as it integrates new data and gains experience.

Building on the principles of ML, deep learning (DL) represents a more advanced subset that employs deep artificial neural networks for the efficient processing and understanding of large-scale data [1]. By mimicking and simulating structures and functions of the human brain, deep learning algorithms excel in recognizing patterns and solving complex problems, particularly in areas such as visual classification and fast recognition. Convolutional neural networks (CNN), also known as deep neural networks (DNN), is a specific DL architecture that uses a hierarchical structure of interconnected layers, following mathematical models to automatically learn spatial hierarchies from data, including the ability to learn unsupervised from the data without explicit labeling. By efficiently handling complex data sets, CNNs excel to provide valuable insights across virtually all areas of study, ranging from genomics to medical imaging.

AI is also reshaping the landscape of molecular medicine, unlocking new potential for overcoming the most challenging biological problems [2]. Molecular medicine focuses on the role of genes, proteins, and other molecules in health and disease, offering insights into how diseases arise and how they can be treated or prevented. With its ability to process vast datasets, identify patterns, and predict outcomes with a very high precision, AI is accelerating advancements in diverse areas such as drug discovery, diagnostics, and personalized treatments, effectively bridging molecular research and clinical applications. Alongside these advancements, critical questions arise regarding data integrity and security, unconscious bias, algorithm transparency, and equitable access to these technologies.

In this review, we explore how AI is reshaping molecular medicine by focusing on selected key applications, the technologies behind these innovations, and the associated ethical and practical challenges.

24.2 The role of AI in discovering new drugs

Drug discovery, the process of identifying new therapeutic compounds, has traditionally relied on time-consuming methods like trial-and-error experimentation and large-scale screening [3]. Developing a new drug from the initial research phase to market typically takes more than a decade, with financial investments often exceeding several billions of euros. Despite these efforts, only around 14% of drug candidates gained approval between 2000 and 2015 [4], and for example, nearly 97% of cancer drugs fail during clinical trials [5], underscoring the challenges of bringing effective therapies to patients.

Recent advancements have prompted greater interest in the implementation of AI techniques for enhancing various stages of the drug discovery pipeline, including novel molecule design and optimization, structure-based drug discovery, and preclinical and clinical development processes [6]. AI has significantly transformed this landscape by accelerating and optimizing tasks such as compound screening and drug-target interaction predictions, thereby reducing development timelines and costs, while enabling researchers to focus on the most promising drug candidates [7].

Target identification, one of the first and most critical steps in drug discovery, involves finding specific biomolecules, such as proteins or genes, that play a central role in the disease process, and these targets serve as the foundation for developing drugs that can modulate their activity by either inhibiting or enhancing their function. Here, AI, including ML and DL, are having a significant impact by processing large-scale omics data, including gene expression patterns, protein interaction pathways, and molecular data from genomics and proteomics, to identify new disease targets that were once considered difficult to discern [8]. ML and DL methods have been used to classify proteins as drug targets or non-targets for breast, pancreatic and ovarian cancers, based on features such as protein interactions, gene expression, DNA copy number, and mutation occurrences [9]. The primary method for identifying disease-target connections is through literature, with text mining and natural language processing (NLP) used to extract target-disease pairs. Deep learning-based systems [10], such as the tool PKDE4J (Public Knowledge Discovery Tool) [11], help link drugs, genes, and targets identified in published studies. Drug-target interactions can be predicted by analyzing descriptor similarities to known ligands, with tools like SPiDER (SOM-based Prediction of Drug Equivalence Relationships) utilizing neural network-inspired mapping techniques to identify these relationships efficiently [12].

24.2.1 Compound screening

Compound screening has been dramatically improved by AI, enabling researchers to evaluate millions of compounds virtually in a fraction of the time required by traditional methods. AI-driven platforms analyze large datasets of chemical structures, physicochemical properties and molecular interactions, enabling the models to identify and prioritize compounds that are most likely to be therapeutically effective [13]. Important factors such as solubility, partition coefficient, degree of ionization, and intrinsic permeability significantly influence drug-target interactions and are key in drug design [14]. This approach has shortened screening times from months to just days, minimizing the number of compounds requiring physical testing. Such advancements have been particularly impactful in addressing complex diseases such as prostate cancer [15], where AI-driven drug discovery, has already improved precision in treatment options.

24.2.2 Target structure prediction

Solving or predicting how potential drug candidates interact with their molecular targets is an unavoidable step in the drug discovery pipeline. Focusing on a protein target, determining the atomic structure of the protein is essential, as its three-dimensional fold dictates its biological activity. Protein structures are traditionally determined using techniques such as nuclear magnetic resonance, X-ray diffraction, or cryo-electron microscopy – processes that are naturally lengthy and expensive. AI-based tools such as AlphaFold [16] and RoseTTAFold [17] have revolutionized protein structure prediction, making this process faster, more accurate, and accessible.

AlphaFold has made it possible to predict the structures of proteins for almost the entire human proteome [18], predicting protein structures with unprecedent quality, achieving in some cases atomic-level accuracy (around 1.5 Å), a significant improvement compared to earlier methods. The high level of precision is supported by the predicted Local Distance Difference Test (pLDDT) value, which measures the confidence in different regions of the predicted structure, helping researchers focus on regions of high accuracy and improving drug discovery and therapeutic design.

Building on its earlier success, AlphaFold3 [19] has recently been released, with its code now publicly available. This version incorporates a so-called diffusion network that iteratively refines protein structures to improve prediction accuracy. The refinement of the algorithm not only enhances the results of protein structure prediction, but also strengthens the ability to model interactions between proteins and organic moieties, such as DNA, RNA, and ligands. While being a powerful tool, AlphaFold3 still has limitations and may struggle with certain proteins, especially those with disordered regions, large proteins, or multi-chain complexes. Furthermore, the model typically predicts a single, static structure and does not account for protein conformational flexibility, a key feature for many proteins. Although AlphaFold3 has improved in predicting membrane proteins, it still faces challenges in modeling transmembrane regions and lipid interactions, and it does not account for post-translational modifications, such as phosphorylation and glycosylation, which influence protein function.

In parallel to Alphafold, RoseTTAFold [17] has been developed specializing in protein-protein interactions and complex formation. It complements other protein structure prediction, methods by using DL techniques to reveal key findings about molecular interactions that are more complex than those involving single proteins alone. RoseTTAFold of the Baker laboratory [17] and AlphaFold, developed by Google DeepMind [16], are rapidly becoming an essential tool in both protein analysis, design and drug discovery. In recognition of this groundbreaking work, Demis Hassabis, John Jumper and David Baker were awarded the 2024 Nobel Prize in Chemistry [21].

The groundbreaking impact of AlphaFold is exemplified by its accurate structural predictions of PINK1 [22], a protein linked to early-onset Parkinson's disease, where mutations impair mitochondrial clearance and lead to neuronal degeneration. AlphaFold was used to model the effects of specific mutations on the formation of PINK1 dimers, confirming how these mutations contribute to Parkinson's disease pathogenesis and potentially guiding the development of mutation-specific therapeutic strategies. Furthermore, AlphaFold has advanced malaria research by helping to decipher the structure of the Pfs48/45 protein [23] (see Fig. 24.1.A), essential for the development of Plasmodium falciparum in the mosquito midgut. While it remained tedious to obtain detailed structural information on this protein using X-ray crystallography and cryo-electron microscopy, the integration of AlphaFold's predictions with the experimental data allowed to visualize the structure in detail. This milestone allowed for identifying which parts of the protein are of interest as malaria vaccine immunogen, transitioning their work from basic research to clinical development. Beyond Parkinson's and malaria, AlphaFold has enhanced our understanding of antibiotic resistance in bacteria [24], identified risk factors for osteoporosis before its onset [25] (Fig. 24.1.B), and revealed the effects of protein mutations associated with cancer and autism [26] (Fig. 24.1.C).

While AlphaFold has revolutionized protein structure prediction, it does not fully address the impact of specific mutations, especially missense mutations. AlphaMissense [27], developed by DeepMind and based on an AlphaFold-derived system, fills this gap by focusing on the potential consequences of these mutations on protein function.

24.2.3 Predicting drug-target interactions

To predict drug-target interactions precisely, molecular dynamics simulations and docking methods are the key technologies. These simulations assess the orientation, stability, and behavior of compounds in their binding environment, offering insights into their main atomic interaction sites. Among the most widely used open-source platforms for these tasks are AutoDock [28], a software tool for protein-ligand docking and virtual screening, and GROMACS [29], which simulates the molecular dynamics of proteins, lipids, and other molecules. When integrated with AI techniques, these analyses further enhance the design of more effective drug candidates, optimizing them before experimental testing. A notable example is PCMol [30], an AI tool that enhances drug discovery by using detailed protein structures (Fig. 24.2.A). This model employs protein embeddings derived from AlphaFold2, predicting molecular interactions across multiple protein targets, especially valuable for proteins with limited known drug interaction data. PCMol generates diverse, novel compounds that resemble known active drugs and exhibit comparable docking scores, highlighting its potential for multitarget drug design and demonstrating how AI can optimize drug discovery (Fig. 24.2.B).

24.2.4 Correlation identification and drug repurposing

Beyond discovering novel drug candidates, AI plays a transformative role in analyzing large-scale biomedical datasets to identify correlations between therapeutic agents and diseases. This significantly contributes to drug repurposing" – the process of finding new therapeutic uses for existing drugs – and provides an efficient strategy to address urgent medical needs by circumventing lengthy drug development and approval processes, as seen with COVID-19 [31], bone-related diseases [32], and parasitic infections [33,34]. Avenues to exploit the full potential of efficient drug repurposing are reinforced by collaborative European consortia such as RePo4EU [35], REMEDi4ALL [36] and RePo-SUDOE [37], funded to integrate molecular characterization, bioinformatics, and drug repurposing strategies, fostering interdisciplinary cooperation to identify therapeutic targets and repurpose existing drugs.

24.3 AI enhances individualized healthcare approaches

Personalized medicine focuses on creating treatments tailored to an individual's unique traits, such as genetics, lifestyle, and environment. As an integral part of molecular medicine, it combines advanced molecular and genetic analyses to develop precise diagnostics and therapies. By integrating multi-omics data, medical history, and environmental factors, personalized medicine can accurately characterize health and diseases states. AI and big data are transforming this field, particularly in cancer diagnosis and monitoring, identifying at risk-populations, classifying genetic variations, and predicting ancestry, making healthcare more precise, predictive, and patient-centered [38].

24.3.1 AI-guided treatments

One of the most extensively studied effects of personalized molecular medicine on healthcare today is the use of genotype-guided treatments. A study has recently demonstrated that tumor genomic profiling can help develop personalized treatment plans for patients with, e.g., breast or lung cancer by identifying rare cancer variants [39]. Pharmacogenomics, the study of how genetic variations influence drug metabolism, is essential to personalized medicine, and AI facilitates the analysis of genetic data to enhance understanding of how these profiles impact drug responses. This integration is revolutionizing pharmacogenomics, particularly in optimizing drug dosages and predicting adverse reactions. By integrating genetic, medical, and real-time health data, AI algorithms enable more precise drug dosing tailored to individual patients, particularly in oncology, where chemotherapy regimens are adjusted based on tumor genetic profiles. For example, the deep learning framework DIPK (Deep neural network Integrating Prior Knowledge) integrates gene interactions, expression profiles, and molecular topologies to improve drug response prediction in cancer cell lines at single-cell level (Fig. 24.3), addressing challenges caused by tumor heterogeneity and individual diversity [40]. DIPK effectively predicted better responses to paclitaxel in patients with a complete response to chemotherapy compared to those with residual disease, demonstrating its potential to guide personalized treatment decisions41. Similarly, the PERCEPTION (PERsonalized Single-Cell Expression-Based Planning for Treatments In ONcology) pipeline [41], developed for precision oncology, utilizes single-cell transcriptomic data from large-scale drug screens to predict treatment responses for individual cancer patients. It outperforms existing models by predicting responses to targeted therapies in both cell cultures and clinical trials, including for multiple myeloma and breast cancer, while also tracking resistance development in lung cancer patients treated with tyrosine kinase inhibitors.

24.3.2 AI-based disease prediction

In addition to optimizing treatments, AI is increasingly being utilized for disease prediction, offering the potential to anticipate the development and progression of several disorders. This is achieved by analyzing integrated multi-omics and clinical data, identifying early disease markers, and detecting high-risk groups, thereby enhancing preventive healthcare strategies. For example, the AI model named Clinical Histopathology Imaging Evaluation Foundation (CHIEF) reads digital tumor slides, accurately detects cancer cells, identifies molecular profiles of tumors, and predicts patient cancer survival [42]. The model identifies image patterns related to cancer aggressiveness and therapeutic responses, offering insights into the potential benefits of experimental treatments, while outperforming existing AI models with an accuracy rate of nearly

94% for detecting cancer across multiple types. These models enhance risk assessments, offering more precise predictions than traditional methods.

As AI continues to evolve, it is not only transforming the way we understand complex diseases on the molecular level but also revolutionizing personalized medicine by enabling more accurate diagnoses, refined risk assessments, and tailored treatments. By integrating multi-omics data, clinical records, and advanced ML models, AI is unlocking new possibilities for predicting disease progression and therapeutic responses, thus opening the door to more precise, effective, and patient-centered healthcare strategies across oncology, cardiology, neurology, autoimmune disorders, and rare diseases. These advancements promise to further enhance treatment outcomes and initiate a new era of preventive medicine, where interventions are personalized based on the unique genetic and molecular profiles of each individual.

24.4 Challenges and ethical considerations

Despite the promising potential of AI in molecular medicine, integrating AI technologies into clinical and research environments presents several challenges. These include data-related issues, such as the need for high-quality and diverse datasets, as well as concerns around the transparency, responsibility, adequacy and fairness of AI models. Ethical considerations, for example, data privacy, bias, and the impact of AI-driven decisions on patient care, must also be addressed to ensure equitable and responsible use. Ensuring the robustness of AI models through rigorous validation and diverse, representative datasets is critical to avoid exacerbating existing health disparities. Moreover, establishing clear accountability frameworks for AI-driven decisions, particularly in critical healthcare contexts, is essential for maintaining patient trust and preventing harmful applications.

High-quality and diverse datasets are fundamental to the success of AI in healthcare. Poor-quality data, such as incomplete or mislabeled records can compromise model performance and lead to inaccurate outcomes. Furthermore, data diversity ensures AI systems are inclusive and effective across different populations. Achieving both quality and diversity in datasets requires collaborative efforts among global institutions, with initiatives like the All of Us [43] from the National Institutes of Health and the UK Biobank [44] aiming to create comprehensive, high-quality datasets to support AI in personalized medicine while adhering to strict data protection and privacy regulations.

Transparency in AI is essential for building trust in healthcare. AI models must be able to explain their decisions in a way that clinicians and patients can understand, especially when these decisions impact treatment options with significant consequences. However, many models, such as DNNs, are complex "black boxes" that are difficult to interpret. To overcome this challenge, the scientific field of explainable AI

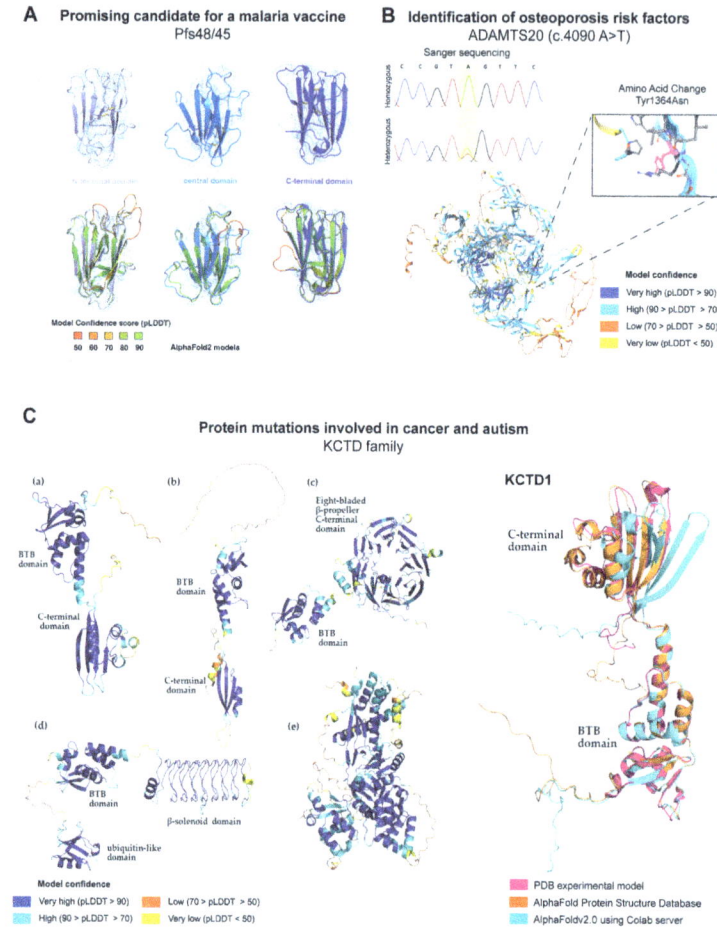

Fig. 24.1: Examples of AlphaFold impact on disease-related protein studies. A) Comparison of the N-terminal, central, and C-terminal domains of Pfs48/45 determined by X-ray crystallography and predicted by AlphaFold2 models [24]. Top: Structures for each domain resolved by X-ray diffraction in complex with the antibody Fab fragment 10D8. Botton: Overlay of the experimental structures with AlphaFold2 predictions for each domain, using a color gradient (green for high, red for low). Adapted from Ko et al. [24] (CC BY 4.0 license). B) Study of the rare missense variant ADAMTS20, associated with osteoporosis [26]. Sanger sequencing revealed a heterozygous c.4090A>T change, causing a Tyr 1364 to Asn substitution. Its impact on protein structure was analyzed using the model provided by the AlphaFold Protein Structure Database, with the color pattern based on the pLDDT confidence value. Modified from Cilia et al. [26] (CC BY 4.0 license) C) On the left: Human KCTD protein structures predicted by AlphaFold (a: KCTD1, b: KCTD5, c: KCTD3, d: KCTD9, e: KCTD19) share common features and significant conformational variability [27]. All models display a conserved BTB domain with a β-sheet and five helices, along with additional folded regions and low-confidence unstructured fragments are also observed. The coloring of the predicted models reflects the confidence values provided by AlphaFold. On the right: Structural alignment of human KCTD1 models performed using the BTB domain as a reference. The AlphaFold Protein Structure Database model is shown in orange, the ColabFold server prediction in cyan, and the experimental structure in pink. Source: Esposito et al. [27] (CC BY 4.0 license).

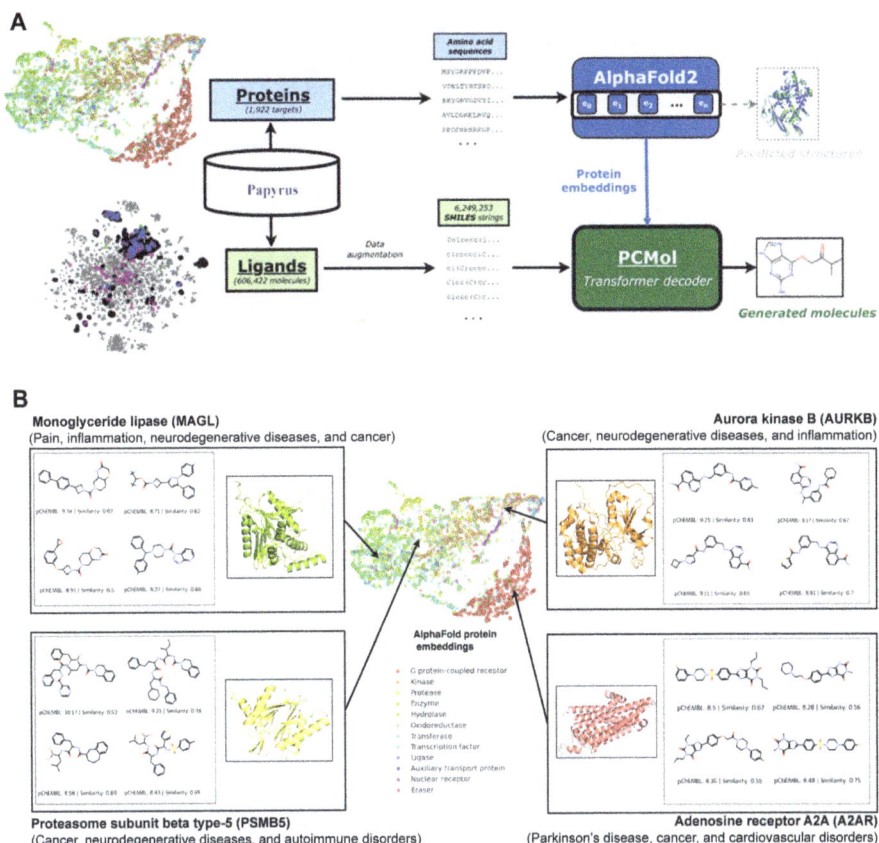

Fig. 24.2: Integrating AlphaFold with de novo drug development using protein structure data in multitarget molecular generative models [31]. A) PCMol utilizes protein embeddings from AlphaFold, derived from the amino acid sequence of a target protein. These embeddings are used as input into a transformed model, which generates SMILES (Simplified Molecular Input Line Entry System) strings (chemical structures) for various targets. The transformer processes both protein and chemical structure data simultaneously, enabling it to create new chemical structures tailored to the protein targets. B) Four clinically relevant protein targets were chosen to demonstrate the potential of PCMol. For each target, random forest QSAR (Quantitative Structure-Activity Relationship) models were trained using ChEMBL-reported ligands. PCMol generated 100 candidates per target, ranked by the QSAR algorithm. The Tanimoto similarity score of the closest molecule in the training set is shown next to each generated molecule. The top four ligands for each target are: (i) urea- and carbamate-based inhibitors for MAGL, (ii) quinazoline motifs for AURKB, (iii) peptide-like molecules with boronic acid groups for PSMB5, and (iv) xanthine derivatives for A2AR. Adapted from Bernatavicius et al. [31] (CC-BY 4.0 license).

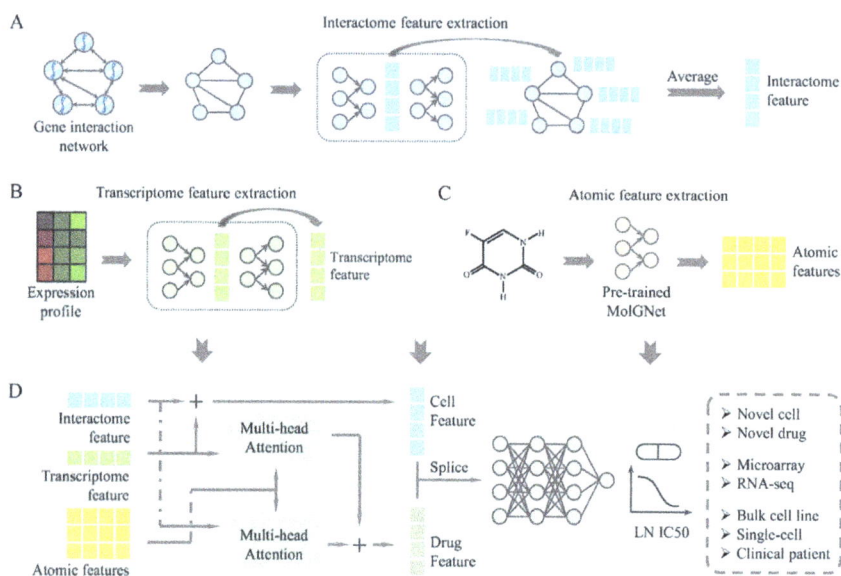

Fig. 24.3: Computational structure of DIPK tool for cancer drug response prediction [41]. A) To effectively capture key cell features, DIPK employs a method called BIONIC (Biological Network Integration using Convolutions) [49], which integrates various gene interaction networks. This process generates a single, detailed vector that represents the gene interactions within a given cell line. The gene interaction network is then encoded using a graph auto-encoder to extract gene features that reflect these interactions. The most highly expressed gene features are averaged to form a comprehensive representation of the interactome specific to the given cell line. B) A denoising auto-encoder is used to compress the gene expression data of the cell line into a lower-dimensional vector, simplifying the data while retaining the essential information. By combining gene interaction analysis with gene expression data, DIPK offers a more accurate and complete view of the cell profile. C) To analyze the drug compound, DIPK uses a pre-trained molecular graph neural network (MolGNet) [50], which converts the molecular graph into continuous atomic vectors. This approach helps capture important patterns in the molecular structure, providing clear and useful representation. D) Finally, the interactome, transcriptome and atomic features are integrated using a multi-head attention mechanism, creating a complete drug profile that is then processed with the cell data to predict drug response. Figure adapted from Li et al. [41] (CC BY 4.0 license).

[45] is advancing techniques to clarify how AI models make and recommendations, helping to ensure that decisions are understandable and trustworthy for healthcare professionals.

As AI technologies become increasingly integral to healthcare, ensuring their responsible use is crucial for patient safety and ethical standards. AI models must be developed, tested, and used with clear guidelines that define the roles and responsibilities of developers, healthcare providers, and institutions. This includes ensuring that AI models are reliable, free from biases, and aligned with ethical medical practices. The

European Union's AI Act [46] and General Data Protection Regulation (GDPR) [47] work together to ensure fairness, transparency, and security in AI systems, with the AI Act regulating AI applications and the GDPR safeguarding personal data and individual rights.

Through ongoing advancements and global collaboration, AI could the field of molecular medicine molecular medicine; setting the stage for a future where personalized and highly effective treatments are available, leading to revolutionary discoveries and enhancing the precision of therapeutic interventions.

References

[1]   LeCun Y., Bengio Y., Hinton G. Deep learning. Nature. 2015;521(7553):436–444. https://doi. org/10.1038/nature14539.

[2]   Emmert-Streib F. Grand Challenges for Artificial Intelligence in Molecular Medicine. Front Mol Med. 2021;1:734659. https://doi.org/10.3389/fmmed.2021.734659.

[3]   Wess G., Urmann M., Sickenberger B. Medicinal Chemistry: Challenges and Opportunities. Angew Chem Int Ed. 2001;40(18):3341–3350. https://doi.org/10.1002/1521-3773(20010917)40:18<3341:: AID-ANIE3341>3.0.CO;2-D.

[4]   Wong C. H., Siah K. W., Lo A. W. Estimation of clinical trial success rates and related parameters. Bio-statistics. 2019;20(2):273–286. https://doi.org/10.1093/biostatistics/kxx069.

[5]   Lin A., Giuliano C. J., Palladino A. et al. Off-target toxicity is a common mechanism of action of cancer drugs undergoing clinical trials. Sci Transl Med. 2019;11(509):eaaw8412. https://doi.org/10.1126/sci-translmed.aaw8412.

[6]   Qureshi R., Irfan M., Gondal T. M. et al. AI in drug discovery and its clinical relevance. Heliyon. 2023;9(7):e17575. https://doi.org/10.1016/j.heliyon.2023.e17575.

[7]   Blanco-González A., Cabezón A., Seco-González A. et al. The Role of AI in Drug Discovery: Challenges, Opportunities, and Strategies. Pharmaceuticals. 2023;16(6):891. https://doi.org/10.3390/ph16060891.

[8]   Shaker B., Ahmad S., Lee J., Jung C., Na D. In silico methods and tools for drug discovery. Comput Biol Med. 2021;137:104851. https://doi.org/10.1016/j.compbiomed.2021.104851.

[9]   Jeon J., Nim S., Teyra J. et al. A systematic approach to identify novel cancer drug targets using machine learning, inhibitor design and high-throughput screening. Genome Med. 2014;6(7):57. https://doi.org/10.1186/s13073-014-0057-7.

[10] Alam T., Schmeier S. Deep Learning in Biomedical Text Mining: Contributions and Challenges. In: Househ M., Borycki E., Kushniruk A. (eds.). Multiple Perspectives on Artificial Intelligence in Health-care. Lecture Notes in Bioengineering. Springer International Publishing; 2021:169–184. https://doi. org/10.1007/978-3-030-67303-1_14.

[11] Song M., Kim M., Kang K., Kim Y. H., Jeon S. Application of Public Knowledge Discovery Tool (PKDE4J) to Represent Biomedical Scientific Knowledge. Front Res Metr Anal. 2018;3:7. https://doi.org/10.3389/ frma.2018.00007.

[12] Reker D., Rodrigues T., Schneider P., Schneider G. Identifying the macromolecular targets of de novo-designed chemical entities through self-organizing map consensus. Proc Natl Acad Sci U S A. 2014;111(11):4067–4072. https://doi.org/10.1073/pnas.1320001111.

[13] Sarkar C., Das B., Rawat V. S. et al. Artificial Intelligence and Machine Learning Technology Driven Modern Drug Discovery and Development. IJMS. 2023;24(3):2026. https://doi.org/10.3390/ ijms24032026.

[14] Zang Q., Mansouri K., Williams A. J. et al. In Silico Prediction of Physicochemical Properties of Environmental Chemicals Using Molecular Fingerprints and Machine Learning. J Chem Inf Model. 2017;57(1):36–49. https://doi.org/10.1021/acs.jcim.6b00625.

[15] Lloyd L. AI for drug discovery. Nat Rev Urol. 2024;21(9):517–517. https://doi.org/10.1038/s41585-024-00931-6

[16] Jumper J., Evans R., Pritzel A. et al. Highly accurate protein structure prediction with AlphaFold. Nature. 2021;596(7873):583–589. https://doi.org/10.1038/s41586-021-03819-2.

[17] Baek M., DiMaio F., Anishchenko I. et al. Accurate prediction of protein structures and interactions using a three-track neural network. Science. 2021;373(6557):871–876. https://doi.org/10.1126/science.abj8754.

[18] Tunyasuvunakool K., Adler J., Wu Z. et al. Highly accurate protein structure prediction for the human proteome. Nature. 2021;596(7873):590–596. https://doi.org/10.1038/s41586-021-03828-1.

[19] Abramson J., Adler J., Dunger J. et al. Accurate structure prediction of biomolecular interactions with AlphaFold 3. Nature. 2024;630(8016):493–500. https://doi.org/10.1038/s41586-024-07487-w.

[20] Open-Access Code AlphaFold3. Google DeepMind, 2024 (Accessed January 20, 2025, at https://github.com/google-deepmind/alphafold3).

[21] The Nobel Prize in Chemistry 2024. Nobel Foundation Outreach, 2024 (Accessed January 20, 2025, at https://www.nobelprize.org/prizes/chemistry/2024/press-release/).

[22] Gan Z. Y., Callegari S., Cobbold S. A. et al. Activation mechanism of PINK1. Nature. 2022;602(7896):328–335. https://doi.org/10.1038/s41586-021-04340-2.

[23] Ko K. T., Lennartz F., Mekhaiel D. et al. Structure of the malaria vaccine candidate Pfs48/45 and its recognition by transmission blocking antibodies. Nat Commun. 2022;13(1):5603. https://doi.org/10.1038/s41467-022-33379-6.

[24] Malekian N., Agrawal A. A., Berendonk T. U., Al-Fatlawi A., Schroeder M. A genome-wide scan of wastewater E. coli for genes under positive selection: focusing on mechanisms of antibiotic resistance. Sci Rep. 2022;12(1):8037. https://doi.org/10.1038/s41598-022-11432-0.

[25] Cilia C., Friggieri D., Vassallo J., Xuereb-Anastasi A., Formosa M. M. Whole Genome Sequencing Unravels New Genetic Determinants of Early-Onset Familial Osteoporosis and Low BMD in Malta. Genes. 2022;13(2):204. https://doi.org/10.3390/genes13020204.

[26] Esposito L., Balasco N., Smaldone G., Berisio R., Ruggiero A., Vitagliano L. AlphaFold-Predicted Structures of KCTD Proteins Unravel Previously Undetected Relationships among the Members of the Family. Biomolecules. 2021;11(12):1862. https://doi.org/10.3390/biom11121862.

[27] Cheng J., Novati G., Pan J. et al. Accurate proteome-wide missense variant effect prediction with AlphaMissense. Science. 2023;381(6664):eadg7492. https://doi.org/10.1126/science.adg7492.

[28] AutoDock site, 2014 (Accessed January 20, 2025, at https://autodock.scripps.edu).

[29] Abraham M., Alekseenko A., Basov V. et al. GROMACS 2024.4 Source code. Published online October 31, 2024. https://doi.org/10.5281/ZENODO.14016590.

[30] Bernatavicius A., Šícho M., Janssen A. P. A., Hassen A. K., Preuss M., Van Westen G. J. P. AlphaFold Meets De Novo Drug Design: Leveraging Structural Protein Information in Multitarget Molecular Generative Models. J Chem Inf Model. 2024;64(21):8113–8122. https://doi.org/10.1021/acs.jcim.4c00309.

[31] Chakravarty K., Antontsev V. G., Khotimchenko M. et al. Accelerated Repurposing and Drug Development of Pulmonary Hypertension Therapies for COVID-19 Treatment Using an AI-Integrated Biosimulation Platform. Molecules. 2021;26(7):1912. https://doi.org/10.3390/molecules26071912.

[32] Yadalam P. K., Anegundi R. V., Ramadoss R., Shrivastava D., Almufarrij R. A. S., Srivastava K. C. AI-based 3D-QSAR model of FDA-approved repurposed drugs for inhibiting sclerostin. THC. 2024;32(5):3007–3019. https://doi.org/10.3233/THC-231358.

[33] Bezerra-Souza A., Fernandez-Garcia R., Rodrigues G. F. et al. Repurposing Butenafine as An Oral Nanomedicine for Visceral Leishmaniasis. Pharmaceutics. 2019;11(7):353. https://doi.org/10.3390/pharmaceutics11070353.

[34] Mshani I. H., Jackson F. M., Mwanga R. Y. et al. Screening of malaria infections in human blood samples with varying parasite densities and anaemic conditions using AI-Powered mid-infrared spectroscopy. Malar J. 2024;23(1):188. https://doi.org/10.1186/s12936-024-05011-z.

[35] RePo4EU – The Euro-Global Platform for Mechanism-based Drug Repurposing (Accessed January 20, 2025, at https://repo4.eu).

[36] REMEDi4ALL – Repurposing of Medicines For All (Accessed January 20, 2025, at https://www.eurordis.org/projects/remedi4all/).

[37] RePo-SUDOE – Drug Repurposing for Effective and Accelerated Drug Development in the SUDOE Space (Accessed January 20, 2025, at https://interreg-sudoe.eu/en/proyecto-interreg/repo-sudoe/)

[38] Johnson K. B., Wei W. Q., Weeraratne D. et al. Precision Medicine, AI, and the Future of Personalized Health Care. Clin Transl Sci. 2021;14(1):86–93. https://doi.org/10.1111/cts.12884.

[39] Hartmaier R. J., Albacker L. A., Chmielecki J. et al. High-Throughput Genomic Profiling of Adult Solid Tumors Reveals Novel Insights into Cancer Pathogenesis. Cancer Res. 2017;77(9):2464–2475. https://doi.org/10.1158/0008-5472.CAN-16-2479.

[40] Li P., Jiang Z., Liu T., Liu X., Qiao H., Yao X. Improving drug response prediction via integrating gene relationships with deep learning. Briefings in Bioinformatics. 2024;25(3):bbae153. https://doi.org/10.1093/bib/bbae153.

[41] Sinha S., Vegesna R., Mukherjee S. et al. PERCEPTION predicts patient response and resistance to treatment using single-cell transcriptomics of their tumors. Nat Cancer. 2024;5(6):938–952. https://doi.org/10.1038/s43018-024-00756-7.

[42] Wang X., Zhao J., Marostica E. et al. A pathology foundation model for cancer diagnosis and prognosis prediction. Nature. 2024;634(8035):970–978. https://doi.org/10.1038/s41586-024-07894-z.

[43] All of Us Research Program from the National Institutes of Health (Accessed January 20, 2025, at https://allofus.nih.gov).

[44] UK Biobank (Accessed January 20, 2025, at https://www.ukbiobank.ac.uk/enable-your-research/about-our-data).

[45] Ali S., Abuhmed T., El-Sappagh S. et al. Explainable Artificial Intelligence (XAI): What we know and what is left to attain Trustworthy Artificial Intelligence. Information Fusion. 2023;99:101805. https://doi.org/10.1016/j.inffus.2023.101805.

[46] AI Act – Regulation (EU) 2024/1689 laying down harmonised rules on artificial intelligence, 2024. (Accessed January 20, 2025, at https://digital-strategy.ec.europa.eu/en/policies/regulatory-framework-ai).

[47] The General Data Protection Regulation (GDPR) in the EU, 2016 (Accessed January 20, 2025, at https://commission.europa.eu/law/law-topic/data-protection/data-protection-eu_en).

[48] Forster D. T., Li S. C., Yashiroda Y. et al. BIONIC: biological network integration using convolutions. Nat Methods. 2022;19(10):1250–1261. https://doi.org/10.1038/s41592-022-01616-x.

[49] Li P., Wang J., Qiao Y. et al. An effective self-supervised framework for learning expressive molecular global representations to drug discovery. Briefings in Bioinformatics. 2021;22(6):bbab109. https://doi.org/10.1093/bib/bbab109.

Ulrich M. Gassner

25 Regulation of artificial intelligence in MedTech

25.1 Introduction

The entire life cycle of far the most of medical technology products, including mainly market access, is comprehensively regulated in the European Union in the Medical Device Regulation (MDR) [1] and the In Vitro Diagnostic Medical Devices Regulation (IVDR) [2] to ensure a high level of health protection for patients and users whilst guaranteeing the smooth functioning of the internal market and supporting innovation. Both regulations are as technology neutral as, for example, the General Data Protection Regulation (GDPR) [3] and therefore do not contain any provisions on the integration of artificial intelligence (AI) into medical devices. This changed when the Artificial Intelligence Act (AIA) [4] entered into force on 1 August 2024 and will be fully applicable 2 years later on 2 August 2026, with some exceptions: prohibitions and AI literacy obligations entered into application from 2 February 2025, the governance rules and the obligations for GPAI models became applicable on 2 August 2025 and the rules for high-risk AI systems – embedded into regulated products – have an extended transition period until 2 August 2027. The AIA is the world's first comprehensive cross-sector regulation for AI and will have a profound impact on the future of medical devices. Some of the related basic legal issues will be discussed in this paper.

25.2 Ethical foundations of the AIA

The European Commission's proposal of an AIA in 2021 [5] was based on the preparatory work of the High-Level Expert Group on Artificial Intelligence (AI HLEG) that was appointed to provide advice on its artificial intelligence strategy. They published Ethics Guidelines for Trustworthy AI [6] and an Assessment List for Trustworthy Artificial Intelligence (ALTAI) [7]. Both the guidelines and the checklist are based on seven key requirements that AI systems (AISs) should fulfil to be trustworthy: (1) human agency and oversight; (2) technical robustness and safety; (3) privacy and data governance; (4) transparency; (5) diversity, non-discrimination and fairness; (6) environmental and societal well-being; and (7) accountability.

   The AI HLEG does not address AI in healthcare specifically. This has motivated the development of a consensus guideline for trustworthy and deployable AI in healthcare medicine by a network of European Commission funded research projects together with international inter-disciplinary experts. Entitled FUTURE-AI, this guideline highlights six principles: (1) fairness; (2) universality; (3) traceability; (4) usability; (5)

robustness; and (6) explainability [8]. A set of 28 best practices were defined, addressing technical, clinical, legal and socio-ethical dimensions. The recommendations cover the entire lifecycle of medical AI, from design, development and validation to regulation, deployment, and monitoring. Researchers are encouraged to take them into account in proof-of-concept stages to facilitate future translation towards clinical practice of medical AI. However, these recommendations are neither factually nor legally binding.

25.3 Basic features of the AIA

The fundamental principles and objectives of the AIA are set out in its recitals. These include: (1) ensuring AI systems' safety and respect for fundamental rights and EU values; (2) promoting AI innovation and uptake within the EU; (3) ensuring legal certainty to facilitate investment and innovation in AI; (4) facilitating the development of a single market for lawful, safe and trustworthy AI applications and prevent market fragmentation; and (5) addressing risks associated with specific uses of AI.

The last-mentioned basic feature means that the AIA, broadly speaking, adopts a functional 'risk-based' approach, which tailors the degree of regulatory intervention depending on the function of an AIS or the risk level of a general-purpose AI models (GPAIM). 'AIS' is defined as "a machine-based system that is designed to operate with varying levels of autonomy and that may exhibit adaptiveness after deployment, and that, for explicit or implicit objectives, infers, from the input it receives, how to generate outputs such as predictions, content, recommendations, or decisions that can influence physical or virtual environments" (Art. 3(1) of the AIA). 'GPAIM' is defined as "an AI model, including where such an AI model is trained with a large amount of data using self-supervision at scale, that displays significant generality and is capable of competently performing a wide range of distinct tasks regardless of the way the model is placed on the market and that can be integrated into a variety of downstream systems or applications, except AI models that are used for research, development or prototyping activities before they are placed on the market" (Art. 3(63) of the AIA).

The higher the risks, the higher the regulatory requirements for the AIS. AISs that pose unacceptable risks to health, safety and fundamental rights are banned altogether (Art. 5 of the AIA). These include, i.a., AI used for cognitive behavioral manipulation and social scoring. At the next level are the 'high-risk' AISs (HRAISs) which are considered to pose significant potential risks to health, safety and fundamental rights. They face the highest degree of regulation under the AIA (Art. 6–49 of the AIA) (see Section 25.5.2 below). As regards AISs that are considered as being 'limited risk' users should be aware that they are interacting with a machine. Therefore, the AIA introduces specific transparency requirements for this kind of AI applications (Art. 50 of the AIA) (see also Section 25.5.3.2 below). The lowest category refers to AI tools with minimal risk which are subject to the existing legislation without additional legal obligations. Rather, the EU legislator encourages drawing up codes of conduct, as well as voluntary application of requirements for HRAISs or other requirements (Art. 69 of the AIA).

In addition, the AIA considers systemic risks which could arise from GPAIMs if they are very capable or widely used. Systemic risk GPAIMs are subject to greater regulatory obligations while the obligations on non-systemic risk GPAIMs focus on transparency and technical documentation requirements (Art. 51–59 of the AIA).

With respect to the goal of promoting AI innovation it is of pivotal importance that AISs and AIMs specifically developed and put into service for the sole purpose of scientific research and development are excluded from the scope of the AIA (Article 2(6) of the AIA). As regards product-oriented research, testing and development activity regarding AISs and AIMs, the provisions of the AIA should also not apply prior to those systems and models being put into service or placed on the market (Art. 2(8)(1) of the AIA).

Finally, it should be noted that the AIA has an extraterritorial reach. It applies to providers placing AISs and GPAIs on the market or putting them into service AISs or placing on the market in the EU, users in the EU, and also to providers and deployers established in third countries if the output produced by the system is used in the EU (Art. 2 of the AIA).

25.4 Basic features of MDR and IVDR in comparison to the AIA

The objectives of MDR and IVDR are to achieve a high level of protection of health for patients and users and to ensure the smooth functioning of the internal market for medical device products whilst supporting innovation. To fulfil these objectives, the medical device regulations establish a conformity assessment framework designed to ensure the quality, safety, and performance of devices marketed within the EU and EEA. Like the AIA, they strive to strike a balance between the need to protect people from the potential harms of the regulated products and the legal objective of fostering innovation and trade. Both legal frameworks are based on a risk-based approach. Consequently, risk classification is the pivotal tool to ensure the principle of proportionality with regard to both manufacturers and patients [9].

A medical device regulated under the MDR is assigned to one of four risk classes: class I, class IIa, class IIb, or class III. The IVDR also divides IVDs into four different risk classes (class A, B, C, and D). The classification is based on the intended purpose and the resulting risk profile. The classification scheme refers to the vulnerability of the human body and considers the potential risks associated with the technical design and manufacture of the devices. Some classification rules are related to specific product categories, e.g. Rule 11 of Annex VIII of the MDR refers to software. Only class I and A products can gain market access through self-declaration of conformity; all other classes rely on

368 — 25 Regulation of artificial intelligence in MedTech

the involvement of a Notified Body in the conformity assessment procedure. The higher the risk class, the higher the expenditure for the conformity assessment.

Unlike the AIA, MDR and IVDR expressly declare software to be the subject of regulation if the definitional requirements for a medical device or an IVD are met. Accordingly, a Medical Device Software (MDSW) is to be assumed if the software is intended by the manufacturer to be used, alone or in combination, for one or more of specific medical purposes including diagnosis, prevention, monitoring, prediction, prognosis, treatment or alleviation of disease (Art. 2(1)(1) of the MDR, Art. 2 (1) of the IVDR). Intended purpose or intended use within the meaning of this definition means the use for which a device is intended according to the data supplied by the manufacturer on the label, in the instructions for use or in promotional or sales materials or statements and as specified by the manufacturer in the clinical or performance evaluation (Art. 2(12) of the MDR, Art. 2 (12) of the IVDR). Thus, in principle, it is up to the manufacturer to decide on the intended purpose of its software. An exception applies in cases where the intended purpose specified by the manufacturer is not scientifically tenable. After all, a manufacturer should not be able to circumvent the qualification as a medical device by formulating an intended purpose that is obviously scientifically incompatible with the mode of function of the device. Moreover, software can only qualify as an MDSW if its intended purpose is not too generic. Rather, it must be intended for specific medical purposes directed at individual patients. Examples of software which are not considered as being for the benefit of individual patients are those which are intended only to aggregate population data, provide generic diagnostic or treatment pathways, scientific literature, medical atlases, models and templates as well as software intended only for epidemiological studies or registers. MDSW may be independent, by having its own intended medical purpose. If the software drives or influences a (hardware) medical device and has a medical purpose, then it is qualified as an MDSW. Further, software may be qualified as MDSW regardless of its location (e.g. operating in the cloud, on a computer, on a mobile phone, or as an additional functionality on a hardware medical device). MDSW can be intended to be used by healthcare professionals or laypersons (e.g. patients or other users). Finally, a software may only be considered an MDSW if it performs an action on data, or performs an action beyond storage, archival, communication, simple search, and lossless compression [10].

25.5 Interplay between the AIA and the MDR/IVDR

25.5.1 General applicability

According to the categorial risk-related differentiation between AISs (Art. 3(1) of the AIA) and GPAIMs (Art. 3(63) of the AIA) two types of MDSW algorithms may be distinguished which can fall under the AIA.

Almost all AISs used for medical purposes (Medical Device Artificial Intelligence, MDAI [11], or so-called 'intelligent medical devices') are classified as HRAISs (Art. 6 (1) of the AIA) (see Section 25.5.2 below). The key characteristics of AISs include that they are designed to operate with varying levels of autonomy (1) and that they are capable to infer, which refers to the process of obtaining outputs from inputs or data (2), which can influence physical and virtual environments (3) (Recital 12 of the AIA). Yet, under the AI Act, adaptiveness is a soft and optional feature of AIS – one that "may" (Art. 3(1) of the AIA) or "could" (Recital 12) be exhibited, rather than a core component of every AIS. So, e.g., an algorithm intended to calculate the risk of a given clinical condition from a series of health parameters (i.e. inferential model) that is developed and validated based on a large set of scientific publications but is itself a static predetermined model could be qualified as an AIS if it were viewed as designed with "some degree" of autonomy [12].

The second type of MDSW algorithms may correspond to GPAIMs. Probably the most prominent example for GPAIMs are large language models (LLMs) such as OpenAI's GPT-5 which powers ChatGPT or Anthropic's Claude 3 Opus that can also analyze images. They have shown great potential within medical settings, e.g. with respect to clinical decision support (CDS) [13]. Therefore, one may first ask whether a qualification as MDSW could be taken into consideration. However, GPAIMs are conceptualized by their key functional characteristics, in particular their generality and their capability to competently perform a wide range of distinct tasks (Recital 97 of the AIA). If serving a general purpose is a defining requirement, it follows that they do not meet the criteria for being qualified as MDSW [14]. This equally applies to medically tuned large language models (LLMs), such as Google Research's Med-PaLM 2, as well as to general-purpose AI systems (GPAISs). A GPAIS is defined as an AIS which is based on a GPAIM and which has the capability to serve a variety of purposes, both for direct use as well as for integration in other AISs (Art. 3(66) of the AIA). GPAIMs require the addition of further components, such as application programming interfaces (APIs) or graphical user interfaces (GUIs) to become GPAISs (Recital 97 of the AIA). Thus, ChatGPT or Google's MedLM is to be considered a GPAIS.

Admittedly, this categorization is not suited to alter the conclusion that, in the absence of a specific medical purpose defined by the provider, the application of the medical device regulations is excluded. Nonetheless, the undifferentiated argument by some authors that LLM-based chatbots fall outside the scope of medical device legislation [15] is far from compelling. That is because a medical purpose may be determined at the application level as pursuant to Recital 85 of the AIA a GPAIS may be used directly, or it may be integrated into other AISs. It follows that a GPAIS – depending on the respective use – may be regarded an ordinary AIS, at least in terms of risk classification, and therefore is to be categorized as a high-risk AI system (HRAI) if the prerequisites of Art. 6(1) of the AIA are met.

25.5.2 High-risk AI systems (HRAIs)

25.5.2.1 Prerequisites

To minimize potential restrictions on international trade, the classification as an HRAI is limited to those AISs that have a significant harmful impact on the health, safety and fundamental rights of persons in the Union (Recital 46 of the AIA). There is only one way for a medical device to qualify as an HRAIS. The AIS must be subject to a conformity assessment by a notified body under the medical device regulations and is either:
- intended to be used as a safety component, or
- itself a product, e.g. a so-called stand-alone software
(Art. 6(1)(a) in connection with Annex I of the AIA).

As MDR and IVDR do not require conformity assessment procedures for medical devices in risk classes I and A, they are not subject to these provisions. However, according to Annex VIII Rule 11 of the MDR, the vast majority of MDAI is classified at least class IIa. In practice, the far more significant use case for the requirement of the conformity assessment procedure the so -called hospital exemption which entails products that are only manufactured and used within healthcare institutions, provided that the requirements of Art. 5(5) of the MDR/IVDR are fulfilled.

A safety component within the meaning of Art. 6(1)(a) of the AIA can be part of both the stand-alone software and a physical product and means a component of a product or of an AIS which fulfils a safety function for that product or AIs, or the failure or malfunctioning of which endangers the health and safety of persons or property (Art. 3(14) of the AIA). Regarding the second part of the definition and taking into account Recital 47 of the AIA, it could be argued that virtually any AI component in a MDSW can jeopardize the safety of patients and therefore constitutes a safety component. However, if n AI component only ensures general product functionality, it should not be considered a safety component within the meaning of Art. 6(1)(a) of the AIA. Otherwise, all software in a medical device would have to be treated as a safety component, as its failure would always have consequences that could endanger patients. This appears normatively flawed, among other reasons, because in that case the first alternative – of a specific safety function – would become meaningless, and the second alternative would encompass all risks arising from the operation of products or systems that do not serve specific personal safety purposes like medical devices do, but rather serve other purposes, as is the case with critical infrastructure (cf. Recital 55).

According to Art. 6(2) of the AIA, the AISs listed in Annex III of the AI Regulation, e.g. AISs intended to be used for emotion recognition, are also considered high risk because 'they pose a high risk of harm to the health and safety or the fundamental rights of persons' in light of their intended purpose (Recital 52(1) of the AI Regulation). If, for example, an AI-based emotion recognition system for the diagnosis and/or treatment of mental illnesses is integrated into a medical device, it does not fall under Art. 6(1)(a) of the AIA but is nevertheless to be classified as an HRAIS pursuant to Art. 6(2) of the AIA. If an AIS, e.g. an emergency healthcare patient triage system, is classified as high-risk under Art. 6(2) and Annex III of the AIA and at the same time qualifies a (part of a) medical device under MDR or IVDR Art. 6(1)(a) in connection with Annex I of the AIA prevail. In other words, Annex III use cases are only relevant for AIS that are not high-risk pursuant to Annex I of the AIA and the less stringent rules for them are not applicable to HRAISs.

25.5.2.2 Requirements

HRAISs must comply with an array of mandatory requirements to ensure they are safe, ethical, and aligned with fundamental rights before they can be placed on the market or put into service. Pursuant to Art. 8 ff. of the AIA, the key requirements for HRAISs include:

HRAISs under Annex I must comply with an array of mandatory requirements to ensure they are safe, ethical, and aligned with fundamental rights before they can be placed on the market or put into service. Pursuant to Art. 8 ff. of the AIA, the key requirements for them include:

Risk Management (Art. 9 of the AIA)
Comprehensive risk management systems must be established, implemented, documented, maintained, and regularly updated. These systems should identify and analyze foreseeable risks associated with the AI, mitigating or eliminating such risks wherever possible. Where risks cannot be completely reduced, suitable control measures must be applied.

Data and Data Governance (Art. 10 of the AIA)
HRAISs relying on data to train models must utilize training, validation, and testing datasets that comply with stringent data governance and management standards. These datasets must be relevant, representative, free of errors, and complete, while also reflecting the specific geographical, behavioral, or functional characteristics pertinent to the context in which the AIS is intended to operate.

Technical Documentation (Art. 11 of the AIA)
Prior to being placed on the market or deployed, HRAISs must be accompanied by a comprehensive technical documentation, incorporating at minimum the details specified in Annex IV of the AIA. This documentation must provide a detailed account of the system's components and development processes and must be kept up-to-date to ensure accuracy and relevance.

Record Keeping (Art. 12 of the AIA)
HRAISs must incorporate logging capabilities to ensure traceability of their functionality throughout their lifecycle. The level of traceability should be proportionate to the system's intended purpose and operational scope.

Transparency and User Information (Art. 13 of the AIA)
The operation of high-risk HRAISs must be sufficiently transparent to enable users to understand and appropriately interpret the system's outputs. These systems must also be accompanied by clear and detailed user instructions, outlining known and foreseeable risks to health, safety, or fundamental rights, as well as human oversight measures and the expected lifetime of the AIS. The information provided must be concise, complete, accurate, and readily accessible to users in a comprehensible format.

Human Oversight (Art. 14 of the AIA)
HRAISs must be designed to allow effective oversight by natural persons, aimed at preventing or minimizing risks to health, safety, or fundamental rights. Providers should identify and, where feasible, integrate oversight mechanisms into the system. Oversight personnel must possess a thorough understanding of the system's capabilities and limitations, enabling them to monitor its operations for anomalies, malfunctions, or unexpected behavior. Additionally, they must have the ability to intervene and, if necessary, halt the system's operation.

Accuracy, Robustness, and Cybersecurity (Art. 15 of the AIA)
HRAISs must be designed to achieve an appropriate level of accuracy for their intended purpose, with declared accuracy metrics included in the user instructions. Furthermore, these systems must exhibit robustness and resilience, capable of withstanding errors, malfunctions, or inconsistencies and must be resilient to third parties intending to exploit system vulnerabilities.

25.5.3 Obligations of providers

25.5.3.1 Providers of high-risk AI systems (HRAIs)

Providers of HRAISs must ensure that they are compliant with the requirements set out above. Further they are obligated, inter alia, to have a quality management system (QMS) in place, to keep technical documents at the disposal of the national competent authorities, to keep the logs automatically generated by their HRAISs when under their control, to ensure that the HRAIs undergoes the relevant conformity assessment procedure, to draw up an EU declaration of conformity, and to affix the CE marking to the HRAISs (Art. 16 ff. of the AIA).

As both AIA and MDR/IVR are New Legislative Framework legislation there are many commonalities between the two frameworks. So, e.g., the roles of provider (Art. 3(3) of the AIA) and manufacturer (Art. 2(30) of the MDR, Art. 2(23) of the IVDR) are equivalent in that they are the principal operator responsible for the compliance of the MDAI with the applicable regulations. It follows, that manufacturers of MDAI that qualify as HRAISs are used to this kind of requirements and procedures. However, despite some overlapping, the requirements of the AIA are often higher and more far-reaching. So, e.g., both regulations highlight the importance of quality management to ensure the safety and effectiveness of medical devices. But QMS defined under the AIA is rather broader as it requires "a strategy for regulatory compliance" (Art. 17(3)(a) of the AIA). Nevertheless, manufacturers are explicitly entitled to include the elements of the QMS provided for in the AIA as part of the existing MDR/IVDR QMS (Recital 81 of the AIA).

25.5.3.2 All providers of AI systems (AISs)

Health literacy

All providers of AISs must ensure a sufficient level of AI literacy of their staff and other persons dealing with the operation and use of AISs (Art. 4 of the AIA). The concept of AI literacy relies on the definition of the term given in Art. 3(56) of the AIA, according to which 'AI literacy' means skills, knowledge and understanding that allow providers, deployers and affected persons, taking into account their respective rights and obligations in the context of the AIA, to make an informed deployment of AI systems, as well as to gain awareness about the opportunities and risks of AI and possible harm it can cause. This means that manufacturers of MDAI must equip their staff with the right skills, knowledge and understanding of the AISs provided or deployed. This concerns primarily anyone in the company directly dealing with an MDAI and reinforces the provisions of transparency (Art. 13 of the AIA) and human oversight (Art. 14 of the AIA). In parallel (Art. 4 of the AIA) indirectly enhances the safeguarding of individuals by ensuring the proper application of the AIA's requirements.

Transparency

Transparency obligations apply under the AIA in some situations where the EU legislator considered it important to flag that content was AI generated, or a user was interacting with an AIS. According to Recital 27 of the AIA transparency means that AI systems are developed and used in a way that allows appropriate traceability and explainability, while making humans aware that they communicate or interact with an AI system, as well as duly informing deployers of the capabilities and limitations of that AI system and affected persons about their rights". In line with this description, separate transparency requirements are stipulated for HRAISs under Art. 13 of the AIA. Notably, the obligation to comply with these rules falls on the providers of HRAISs, in order to ensure transparency towards stakeholders, including deployers of MDAI such as physicians. In this respect, the manufacturers of MDAI are required to design and develop their MDSW in a way that ensures sufficient transparency for deployers to reasonably understand the system's functioning and output accordingly and to provide 'instructions for use' to deployers along with MDAI, which must give clear and complete information on the characteristics, functioning and other key features of the respective MDAI deployers. The information must be provided in a clear and distinguishable manner at the latest time of the first interaction or exposure (Art. 50 AIA). Where personal data is processed, the GDPR transparency requirements apply in addition to these obligations.

25.6 Analysis

25.6.1 Frictions of sectoral integration

The intersection of horizontal legislation, as realized in the AIA, and sector-specific legislation, such as the MDR and IVDR, gives rise to challenges regarding the design and implementation of legal requirements. Although the Artificial Intelligence Board (AIB) and the Medical Device Coordination Group (MDCG) – both advisory bodies comprising representatives from each EU Member State – published Frequently Asked Questions (FAQs) in June 2025 to clarify the intersection of the AIA, MDR, and IVDR [11], this has not resolved all existing frictions.

First, with respect to the interplay between the AIA and the medical device regulations there is some uncertainty about the precise content of definitions, boundaries, and requirements that is specifically relevant for practical implementation. For example, in light of the research exemption under Art. 2(8)(1) of the AIA, it remains unclear whether, or at what stage of clinical research, testing, or development activities, MDAI becomes subject to the full regulatory requirements of both the MDR and the AI Act. This is a key issue in the translation and technology transfer of AI innovation into clinical application for patients.

Second, there are substantial frictions of sectoral integration. One of them concerns the requirement for human oversight (Art. 14 of the AIA) which helps ensuring that an AIS does not undermine human autonomy or causes other adverse effects. Oversight may be achieved through governance mechanisms such as a human-in-the-loop (HITL), human-on-the-loop (HOTL), or human-in-command (HIC) approach and is key for preventing or minimizing risks to health and safety caused by MDAI. However, under circumstances, there may be a conflict with the objectives of MDR and IVDR to achieve a high level of protection of health for patients, as profound empirical evidence suggests that human interventions decrease accuracy [16]. This trade-off is particularly noticeable in cases where MDAI perform better than a physician at the given task (e.g., error rates are lower). Namely, the design-related requirement that the MDAI shall enable the individuals performing the task of oversight to correctly interpret the HRAISs output (Art. 14(3)(c) of the AIA) carries the risk that physicians may draw incorrect conclusions from the output, thereby worsening its quality. False positive or false negative corrections could then result in a damage to health due to omitted or unnecessary therapeutic treatments. Thus, the most preferable solution at deployer level would be to kick those physicians out of the loop [17]. In addition, the software design should not allow human intervention in critical parts of the surgical operation of a highly autonomous surgical MDAI whereby leaving the patient at risk [11:17].

Whereas many frictions of sectoral integration may be mitigated by means of the principle of proportionality, enshrined, e.g., in Art. 14 (3) of the AIA [18], or by appropriate construction of the law, this approach proves significantly less effective when dealing with systemic divergences between general and sector-specific requirements. MDR and IVDR on the one hand and the AIA on the other hand pursue complementary but not congruent objectives: While MDR and IVDR focus primarily on the safety and effectiveness of medical devices, the AIA is aimed at further minimizing the risks of AISs, particularly regarding discrimination, lack of transparency and IT security [19:32]. A particularly notable example in that respect pertains to the domain of risk management. Under the AIA, all risks must be mitigated to the greatest extent technically feasible (Art. 9(5a) of the AIA). In contrast, the medical device regulations mandate a different approach: risks to patients must be counterbalanced by benefits, thereby establishing a positive benefit-risk ratio (Annex I, Chapter I of the MDR/IVDR). This divergence arises from the fundamental regulatory assumption that medical devices inherently carry critical risks that cannot be fully eliminated. Residual risks of this kind are deemed acceptable by the MDR/IVDR in light of the significant benefits such devices offer to patients.

25.6.2 Caught in the safety paradox trap?

A legislative paradox is characterized by the fact that the objectives that the legislator wanted to achieve lead to adverse effects through the implementation of the respective legal act. MDR and IVDR are prominent examples of this paradox. According to the European Parliament, significant challenges have been encountered in implementing the MDR and the IVDR in recent years, resulting in shortages of medical devices, thus restricting patient access to innovative and life-saving therapeutic and diagnostic technologies [20]. Instead of providing for a higher level of protection of health for patients compared to the previous legal situation the opposite was achieved. Well-established medical devices disappeared from the market and new innovative products were not developed and placed on the market due to the enormous certification expenditure. Given the AIA's one-size-fits-all approach, which fails to account for the specific regulatory logic of medical device legislation – particularly the necessity of a benefit-risk ratio – there is a compelling argument that the legislator has failed to learn this important lesson.

Consequently, there is a tangible risk that, considering the ambiguous and conflicting relationship between the AIA and the MDR/IVDR, the Union legislator has once again fallen into the safety paradox. In doing so, it may have undermined one of the four foundational principles of medical ethics – namely, patient beneficence – [21] which has traditionally guided the regulation and use of medical devices.

25.7 Result and outlook

The joint application of the MDR/IVDR and the AIA presents a unique opportunity to build trust in MDAI while simultaneously improving patient safety. Yet, the integration of AI into medical devices leads to double regulation and delimitation difficulties between both legal frameworks. The frictions in sectoral integration can only partly be addressed through sub-legislative measures. Admittedly, the FAQs on the intersection of the AIA and the MDR/IVDR issued by AIB and MDCG are a valuable tool in the absence of legal solutions, such as priority or exemption clauses. In addition, especially with respect to the conformity assessment procedure, the questionnaire "Artificial Intelligence (AI) in medical devices" jointly published by the German Notified Bodies Alliance for Medical Devices and Team NB – The European Association of Medical Devices Notified Bodies in November 2024 [22] plays a pivotal role in the current absence of AIMD specific standards and specifications. However, the specific requirements of AIA have not yet been considered there and will be part of a comprehensive revision which is to follow. There is not too much time left for this as enforcement of Art. 6 of the AIA (and the corresponding obligations regarding AIMD) starts from 2 August 2027.

References

[1]   Regulation (EU) 2017/745 of the European Parliament and of the Council of 5 April 2017 on medical devices, amending Directive 2001/83/EC, Regulation (EC) No 178/2002 and Regulation (EC) No 1223/2009 and repealing Council Directives 90/385/EEC and 93/42/EEC (OJ L 117, 13.5.2017, p. 1), lastly amended by Regulation (EU) 2024/1860 of the European Parliament and of the Council of 13 June 2024 amending Regulations (EU) 2017/745 and (EU) 2017/746 as regards a gradual roll-out of Eudamed, the obligation to inform in case of interruption or discontinuation of supply, and transitional provisions for certain in vitro diagnostic medical devices (OJ L, 2024/1860, 9.7.2024).
[2]   Regulation (EU) 2017/746 of the European Parliament and of the Council of 5 April 2017 on *in vitro* diagnostic medical devices and repealing Directive 98/79/EC and Commission Decision 2010/227/EU

(OJ L 117, 13.5.2017, p. 176), lastly amended by Regulation (EU) 2024/1860 of the European Parliament and of the Council of 13 June 2024 amending Regulations (EU) 2017/745 and (EU) 2017/746 as regards a gradual roll-out of Eudamed, the obligation to inform in case of interruption or discontinuation of supply, and transitional provisions for certain in vitro diagnostic medical devices (OJ L, 2024/1860, 9.7.2024).

[3] Regulation (EU) 2016/679 of the European Parliament and of the Council of 27 April 2016 on the protection of natural persons with regard to the processing of personal data and on the free movement of such data, and repealing Directive 95/46/EC (General Data Protection Regulation) (OJ L 119, 4.5.2016, p. 1).

[4] Regulation (EU) 2024/1689 of the European Parliament and of the Council of 13 June 2024 laying down harmonised rules on artificial intelligence and amending Regulations (EC) No 300/2008, (EU) No 167/2013, (EU) No 168/2013, (EU) 2018/858, (EU) 2018/1139 and (EU) 2019/2144 and Directives 2014/90/EU, (EU) 2016/797 and (EU) 2020/1828 (Artificial Intelligence Act) (OJ L, 2024/1689, 12.7.2024).

[5] European Commission. Proposal for a Regulation of the European Parliament and of the Council laying down harmonised rules on artificial intelligence (Artificial Intelligence Act) and amending certain Union legislative acts. 21.4.2021. COM(2021) 206 final.

[6] European Commission, Directorate-General for Communications Networks, Content and Technology. Ethics guidelines for trustworthy AI. Publications Office. 2019. (Accessed August 11, 2025, at https://data.europa.eu/doi/10.2759/346720).

[7] European Commission, Directorate-General for Communications Networks, Content and Technology. The Assessment List for Trustworthy Artificial Intelligence (ALTAI) for self assessment. Publications Office. 2020. (Accessed August 11, 2025, at https://data.europa.eu/doi/10.2759/00236).

[8] Lekadir K., Frangi A. F., Porras A. R., Glocker B., Cintas C., Langlotz C. P. et al. FUTURE-AI: international consensus guideline for trustworthy and deployable artificial intelligence in healthcare. BMJ 2025; 388 :e081554. (Accessed August 11, 2025, at https://doi:10.1136/bmj-2024-081554).

[9] Hauglid M. K., Mahler T. Doctor Chatbot: The EU's Regulatory Prescription for Generative Medical AI. Oslo Law Review, 2023;10:1–23 (Accessed August 11, 2025, at https://do.org/10.18261/olr.10.1.1).

[10] Medical Device Coordination Group (MDCG). MDCG 2019–11, Guidance on Qualification and Classification of Software in Regulation (EU) 2017/745 – MDR and Regulation (EU) 2017/746 – IVDR. October 2019. (Accessed August 11, 2025, at https://health.ec.europa.eu/system/files/2020-09/md_mdcg_2019_11_guidance_qualification_classification_software_en_0.pdf).

[11] The term was coined in the guidance document AIB 2025–1/MDCG 2025–6, Interplay between the Medical Devices Regulation (MDR) & In vitro Diagnostic Medical Devices Regulation (IVDR) and the Artificial Intelligence Act (AIA). June 2025. (Accessed August 11, 2025, at https://health.ec.europa.eu/document/download/b78a17d7-e3cd-4943-851d-e02a2f22bbb4_en?filename=mdcg_2025-6_en.pdf).

[12] Lacalle H. AI Medical Device Software under EU MDR & IVDR. 30.8.2024. (Accessed August 11, 2025, at https://decomplix.com/ai-medical-device-software-eu-mdr-ivdr/#).

[13] See e.g. Filali Ansary R., Lechien J. R. Clinical decision support using large language models in otolaryngology: a systematic review. Eur Arch Otorhinolaryngol, 2025 Jun 6. (Accessed August 11, 2025, at https://doi.org/10.1007/s00405-025-09504-8).

[14] See with respect to ChatGPT Hauglid M. K., Mahler T. Doctor Chatbot: The EU's Regulatory Prescription for Generative Medical AI. Oslo Law Review, 2023;10:1–23. (Accessed August 11, 2025, at https://doi.org/10.18261/olr.10.1.1).

[15] Sele D., Chugunova M. Putting a human in the loop: Increasing uptake, but decreasing accuracy of automated decisionmaking. PLoS ONE, 2024;19,2:e0298037. (Accessed August 11, 2025, at https://doi.org/10.1371/journal.pone.0298037).

[16] Freyer O., Wiest I. C., Kather J. N., Gilbert S. A future role for health applications of large language models depends on regulators enforcing safety standards. Lancet Digit Health, 2024; 6:e662–e672 (Accessed August 11, 2025, at https://www.thelancet.com/journals/landig/article/PIIS2589-7500(24)00124-9/fulltext).

[17] Muyskens K., MaY., Menikoff J. et al. When can we Kick (Some) Humans "Out of the Loop"? An Examination of the use of AI in Medical Imaging for Lumbar Spinal Stenosis, ABR 2024 (Accessed August 11, 2025, at https://doi.org/10.1007/s41649-024-00290-9).

[18] Enqvist L. 'Human oversight' in the EU artificial intelligenceact: what, when and by whom? Law, Innovation and Technology 2023;15:2, 508–535 (Accessed August 11, 2025, at https://https://doi.org/10.1080).

[19] Hacker P. The AI Act between Digital and Sectoral Regulations. Bertelsmann Stiftung. Gütersloh. December 2024 (Accessed August 11, 2025, at https://www.bertelsmann-stiftung.de/fileadmin/files/user_upload/The_AI_Act_between_Digital_and_Sectoral_Regulations__2024_en.pdf).

[20] European Parliament resolution of 23 October 2024 on the urgent need to revise the Medical Devices Regulation (2024/2849(RSP)) (Accessed August 11, 2025, at https://www.europarl.europa.eu/doceo/document/TA-10-2024-0028_EN.html).

[21] Beauchamp T. L., Childress J. F. Principles of Biomedical Ethics. 8th ed. Oxford University Press; 2019.

[22] Joint Team-NB/IG-NB. Questionnaire on Artificial Intelligence (AI) in Medical Devices, adopted 14.1.2024 (Accessed August 11, 2025, at https://www.team-nb.org/wp-content/uploads/2024/11/Team-NB-PositionPaper-AI-in-MD-Questionnaire-V1-20241125.pdf).

Christian Djeffal

26 From the AI Act to responsible innovation: The potential of legal design research

26.1 Can we integrate innovation and responsibility through law?

This article examines how legal frameworks can effectively integrate innovation and responsibility in artificial intelligence regulation, with a particular focus on the European Union's AI Act and its implementation in digital health technologies. The study analyzes how legal design methodologies can bridge the gap between regulatory requirements and practical governance frameworks. Through the development and testing of two novel approaches – the Constitutional Realization Framework (CRF) and Shared Legal Assessment – the research demonstrates how legal design can transform regulatory compliance from a constraint into an enabler of responsible innovation. The article argues that while the EU AI Act provides comprehensive regulation, its effectiveness depends largely on practical implementation approaches. The findings reveal that structured legal design methodologies enable meaningful stakeholder participation and facilitate the integration of diverse perspectives in AI governance while maintaining regulatory compliance. The research emphasizes the need for continued development of legal design approaches and stronger interdisciplinary collaboration to address emerging challenges in AI regulation, particularly in the digital health sector. This study contributes to the growing body of literature on AI governance by providing practical frameworks for implementing regulatory requirements in ways that advance both technological progress and societal wellbeing.

The intersection of technological innovation's promises and perils represents one of the most critical challenges of our era, particularly evident in the domain of digital health. [1–3] The potential benefits of digital health technologies are substantial and far-reaching: advancing disease treatment, enabling personalized medicine, supporting healthcare professionals in complex decision-making processes, optimizing healthcare system efficiency, and driving economic growth. It is therefore unsurprising that digital health has emerged as a primary sector where artificial intelligence (AI) applications promise transformative benefits.

However, this technological advancement presents significant risks. Technical errors, systemic malfunctions, and algorithmic biases can have severe consequences in healthcare contexts, with disadvantaged populations often bearing a disproportionate burden of these risks. This creates a fundamental challenge: how can we foster innovation while ensuring responsible development and deployment?

The European Commission recognized this challenge in its 2019 White Paper on Artificial Intelligence, stating:

> "Artificial Intelligence is developing fast. It will change our lives by improving healthcare (e.g., making diagnosis more precise, enabling better prevention of diseases), [...] and in many other ways that we can only begin to imagine. At the same time, Artificial Intelligence (AI) entails a number of potential risks, such as opaque decision-making, gender-based or other kinds of discrimination, intrusion in our private lives or being used for criminal purposes." [4]

In response to this dual nature of AI technology, the European Commission, like other regulatory bodies, adopted "a regulatory and investment-oriented approach with the twin objective of promoting the uptake of AI and addressing the risks associated with certain uses of this new technology" [4]. This approach culminated in the EU AI Act, which came into force on August 1, 2024, representing a landmark attempt to balance innovation promotion with risk mitigation.

There are many critical voices concerning the AI Act [5–10]. However, merely analyzing the AI Act's statutory provisions would be insufficient for understanding its potential to integrate innovation and responsibility. The Act deliberately maintains flexibility to accommodate the dynamic nature of technological innovation. Therefore, the critical analysis must extend beyond the literal interpretation of legal text to examine implementation methodologies. The focus should shift from static rule content to dynamic application mechanisms that translate legal requirements into practical governance frameworks.

Contemporary legal practice's approach to these challenges should not be accepted as definitive. Instead, there is a pressing need to explore how legal frameworks can be more effectively applied to technological innovation processes. This chapter posits that significant potential exists in repositioning legal practice within development and innovation processes to address the tension between technological advancement and responsible governance.

This repositioning requires conceptualizing law not merely as an external constraint but as an integral resource within the innovation process. From a legal perspective, this necessitates developing new tools and methodologies to shape AI development processes that optimize both innovation and responsibility outcomes. Legal design thinking emerges as a crucial framework in this context, offering structured approaches to integrate legal considerations throughout the technology development lifecycle.

26.2 Legal design research and the AI Act

Legal design offers significant value in contemporary legal research, particularly in the context of technological regulation and implementation. While traditional legal methodologies often present law application as a purely deductive process, practitioners frequently encounter scenarios requiring substantial discretionary judgment, especially when dealing with emerging technologies and their regulation.

The intersection of legal design and technology regulation has become increasingly relevant, particularly in the context of the European Union's AI Act. Legal design methodology provides practitioners with structured approaches when establishing new regulatory processes and engaging in technology development projects. This approach has evolved from a theoretical framework to a practical methodology that bridges the gap between legal requirements and technological implementation.

Legal design, while variously defined, consistently emphasizes the application of design methodologies to legal challenges [11–13]. This evolution parallels the broader expansion of design thinking beyond traditional product development. In the context of technology regulation, legal design offers several key advantages: it enables proactive problem-solving, focuses on future-oriented solutions rather than reactive remedies, and provides a systematic framework for testing regulatory approaches. This is particularly valuable when addressing novel challenges posed by artificial intelligence and other emerging technologies.

The methodology emphasizes collaborative innovation, requiring legal practitioners and scholars to work closely with technical experts, policymakers, and other stakeholders in a participatory process. This multi-stakeholder approach is especially crucial when dealing with complex technological regulations like the AI Act, where technical understanding must align with legal requirements and practical implementation.

While early applications of legal design primarily focused on visualizing legal information to enhance comprehension, [14] the field has expanded significantly. Contemporary legal design encompasses a comprehensive range of methods and objectives, particularly relevant to technology regulation [15]. It now addresses complex challenges such as algorithmic transparency, AI risk assessment frameworks, and compliance mechanisms for automated decision-making systems.

In practical application, a legal design challenge typically involves an interdisciplinarity team employing various methodologies to address specific regulatory challenges. The process begins with problem identification through qualitative research methods, including stakeholder interviews and systematic observations. Teams then utilize ideation techniques and conduct user testing to develop and refine solutions. This approach is particularly valuable in operationalizing complex regulatory frameworks like the AI Act, where theoretical legal requirements must be translated into practical implementation strategies.

In the following, the article will present two key questions of law of compliance with the AI Act and will show practical answers that have been developed within the project RechTech, which has been funded by the Federal Ministry of Education and Research.

26.2.1 Realizing legal principles

As a law, the AI Act departs from a command and control style of regulation and resorts to regulatory techniques that allow for discretion in complying with the AI Act. One challenge that comes with the AI Act is to apply methods that allow to determine the exact scope of the provisions in a way that balances innovation and responsibility effectively.

26.2.1.1 Law-by-design obligations

In analyzing the material requirements of the European Union's AI Act, it becomes evident that many of the substantive obligations beginning with Article 9 transcend simple checkbox compliance approaches. A prime example is Article 13(1), which states:

"High-risk AI systems shall be designed and developed in such a way as to ensure that their operation is sufficiently transparent to enable deployers to interpret a system's output and use it appropriately. An appropriate type and degree of transparency shall be ensured with a view to achieving compliance with the relevant obligations of the provider and deployer set out in Section 3."

The implementation of transparency measures under Article 13(1) is intentionally non-prescriptive. Rather than mandating specific technical solutions, it establishes a principle-based obligation ensuring deployers can effectively utilize the system. Even harmonized standards, while offering a presumption of compliance, remain voluntary. This approach exemplifies what should be properly characterized as law-by-design obligations.

Law-by-design obligations represent a sophisticated regulatory paradigm in European digital technology regulation, requiring the incorporation of legal principles into technological design processes. [16]

While these obligations originated in privacy, data protection, and IT security domains, they have evolved significantly, now encompassing over 45 distinct design objectives within European legislation [16–17].

The distinctive feature of law-by-design obligations lies in their principle-based nature rather than their prescription of specific technical requirements or mandatory processes. This approach provides necessary flexibility in translating legal principles into technological implementations. Such obligations manifest either explicitly, as exemplified by Article 25 of the GDPR, or implicitly, requiring careful legal interpretation to determine their scope [18]. Furthermore, they operate through both positive mechanisms – implementing protective principles – and negative mechanisms – focusing on risk mitigation.

Article 9 of the AI Act exemplifies a negative law-by-design obligation, mandating continuous risk assessment and mitigation processes. This creates an iterative cycle of evaluation and adaptation, necessitating effective collaboration between risk assessment experts and technical developers to implement necessary modifications to AI systems for risk mitigation purposes.

While the flexibility inherent in law-by-design obligations offers advantages, it also presents challenges through its inherent indeterminacy. Investment in addressing these open-ended requirements becomes worthwhile only when the provided freedom is utilized to develop tailored solutions for specific AI systems. Although the legislation does not prescribe specific implementation methodologies, the adoption of standardized or adapted law-by-design methods can provide valuable frameworks for compliance.

26.2.1.2 Constitutional Realization Framework (CRF)

The Constitutional Realization Framework (CRF) serves as a crucial bridge between legal principles and their technological implementation, particularly relevant in the context of the European Union's AI Act and its comprehensive regulatory approach. This framework enables stakeholders to align their domain expertise with AI development opportunities, proving especially valuable when legal principles must be translated into technological solutions without an established implementation precedent [19]. It empowers them to participate in AI innovation practice, but also to make their voice known when it comes to questions of risk governance.

The framework's significance is particularly evident in scenarios where organizations must implement concepts such as transparency by design – a key requirement under the EU AI Act's transparency obligations for high-risk AI systems. It generates meaningful ideas on new ways to think, design and use existing technologies. It, thereby, facilitates meaningful participation from stakeholders who, while lacking technical expertise, possess valuable domain knowledge.

The CRF establishes a structured co-creation methodology that integrates risk assessment protocols and innovation techniques. This approach has proven effective in realizing fundamental legal principles, including human rights protection, democratic values, and rule of law considerations, as well as specific legal-by-design requirements such as privacy by design, transparency by design, and inclusion by design (cf. Fig. 26.1).

The methodology has been extensively tested in the context of AI governance, particularly focusing on technologies that fall within the scope of the AI Act. Workshop sessions begin with an overview of operational AI applications, followed by a three-phase process:
1. Technology Impact Assessment: Interdisciplinary groups evaluate an existing application against potential risks and benefits in an open technology assessment.
2. Innovation Phase: Participants employ the SCAMPER Method to generate novel solutions to use technology in other ways or other settings.
3. Socio-Technical Design: Teams develop comprehensive implementation strategies that consider risks and opportunities of the new idea

This structured approach enables stakeholders to contribute meaningfully to AI governance discussions while also tapping into their creative potential to harness AI for their purposes. Participants naturally gravitate toward technological affordances relevant to their expertise, facilitating the development of solutions that address both practical needs and regulatory requirements.

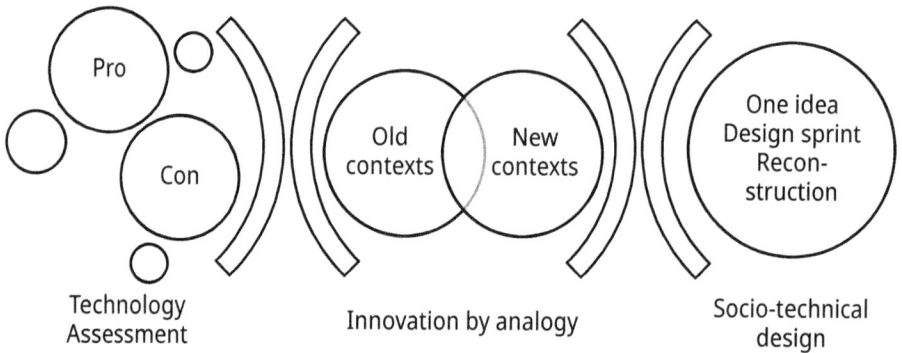

Fig. 26.1: Structure of CRF.

A notable application emerged in the domain of text simplification, where workshops revealed significant potential for AI-driven language processing to enhance accessibility. This finding led to further research and knowledge transfer, demonstrating the framework's effectiveness in identifying and addressing specific regulatory challenges.

26.2.2 Knowledge governance

Knowledge governance represents a cornerstone of the AI Act's regulatory framework, manifesting through multiple interconnected obligations and mechanisms. The Act establishes a comprehensive system for managing, sharing, and utilizing knowledge throughout the AI development and deployment lifecycle. This emphasis on knowledge governance materializes in several critical dimensions: mandatory documentation requirements, transparency obligations, and information-sharing protocols between stakeholders. To operationalize these requirements effectively, organizations must implement sophisticated legal design approaches that focus on information architecture and knowledge management. These approaches should not merely satisfy compliance requirements but should create actionable, accessible, and meaningful information flows that advance both regulatory objectives and practical implementation. By integrating structured knowledge governance frameworks with human-centered legal design principles, organizations can develop more effective mechanisms for knowledge capture, dissemination, and utilization across the regulatory pipeline. This article examines the core elements of knowledge governance within the AI Act's framework and introduces a novel methodological approach that enhances this governance structure through technology-aware design principles. This methodology specifically addresses the challenges of translating regulatory requirements into actionable technical specifications while maintaining the integrity of knowledge flows between legal and technical domains.

26.2.2.1 The AI Act's regulation of knowledge

The AI Act establishes comprehensive documentation requirements as a fundamental aspect of knowledge governance. According to Article 11 and Article 12, providers must maintain detailed technical documentation throughout a system's lifecycle and implement automatic recording capabilities (logs) that ensure traceability of system operations. This documentation serves as a critical knowledge repository, demonstrating compliance and providing authorities with necessary oversight information.

Transparency and knowledge transfer between providers and deployers form another crucial element of the governance framework. Article 13 mandates that high-risk AI systems must be designed with sufficient transparency to enable deployers to interpret and appropriately use system outputs. Providers must furnish deployers with comprehensive instructions containing detailed information about system capabilities, limitations, and operational requirements, ensuring effective knowledge transfer between these key stakeholders.

The Act also establishes a bidirectional feedback mechanism between providers and deployers. As outlined in Article 26(5), deployers have an obligation to monitor system operation and inform providers of any risks or serious incidents encountered during system use. This creates a continuous learning loop that enhances system safety and performance through shared operational knowledge and experience.

Finally, the Act addresses knowledge sharing with affected individuals through Article 86, which establishes a right to explanation for persons subject to AI-based decisions. This provision ensures that deployers must provide clear and meaningful explanations about the role of AI systems in decision-making processes, extending knowledge governance to end-users affected by these systems. Article 60 establishes a structured approach to knowledge generation through real-world testing under certain circumstances.

This multi-layered approach to knowledge governance creates an interconnected ecosystem where information flows between providers, deployers, and affected individuals, ensuring transparency, accountability, and continuous improvement of AI systems throughout their lifecycle.

26.2.2.2 Shared legal assessment

Our shared legal assessment was initiated in the context of the RechTech project and developed and refined by two groups of researchers[1] in order to allow for knowledge production that precedes real word testing and allows to obtain knowledge in the early phases of risk assessment.

The Shared Legal Assessment workshop is carefully structured to facilitate meaningful dialogue between innovators and stakeholders in healthcare technology development. The preparation phase involves several essential components that set the foundation for productive engagement.

Before the workshop, project teams must prepare an initial mapping of their technology's benefits and potential risks. This preliminary assessment serves as a crucial starting point for discussions and helps frame the subsequent stakeholder interactions. Teams are also required to develop an early prototype or demonstration of their technology that can be presented to stakeholders during the workshop.

The workshop itself follows a well-defined structure that begins with project teams presenting their early prototypes to stakeholders. This presentation phase allows for immediate feedback and opens channels for constructive dialogue about the technology's practical implications. Following the initial presentation, participants engage in scenario work that takes place in breakout groups for approximately 45 minutes. During this session, stakeholders collaborate to develop and analyze realistic scenarios of how the technology might be used in real-world situations.

The final phase of the workshop involves a reconstruction period during which stakeholders and project teams come together to discuss relevant aspects requiring further consideration. This phase is particularly valuable as it helps identify potential gaps in the development process and areas needing additional attention. Throughout the workshop, there is a strong focus on constructive exchange between all participants, with particular emphasis on technology assessment, early feedback regarding risks and benefits, and integrating legal knowledge, especially concerning duties of care in liability law.

This structured approach ensures that both technical and legal considerations are thoroughly addressed while maintaining a collaborative and productive environment for all participants. The workshop format effectively bridges the gap between theoretical assessment and practical implementation, allowing for meaningful integration of stakeholder perspectives into the development process at a very early stage.

---

1 First by a design thinking team of Chithra Madsuran, Verena Müller, Carlotta Schichor, and Dr. Desantila Hysa coached by Prof. Dr. Christian Djeffal. Then by a research team of Philipp Mehl and Verena Müller led by Prof. Dr. Christian Djeffal.

26.3 Conclusions

The integration of innovation and responsibility through legal frameworks represents a critical challenge in the era of artificial intelligence, particularly in the context of digital health technologies. This article has examined how the EU AI Act, while providing a comprehensive regulatory framework, deliberately maintains flexibility in its implementation to accommodate the dynamic nature of technological innovation. The analysis demonstrates that the Act's effectiveness in balancing innovation promotion with risk mitigation will largely depend on the practical approaches adopted in its implementation. Our examination of legal design methodologies reveals promising pathways for translating regulatory requirements into practical governance frameworks. The Constitutional Realization Framework (CRF) and Shared Legal Assessment approach exemplify how legal design can bridge the gap between abstract legal principles and concrete technological implementations. These methodologies enable meaningful stakeholder participation and facilitate the integration of diverse perspectives in AI governance, while maintaining compliance with regulatory requirements. The success of these approaches in areas such as text simplification and knowledge governance demonstrates their practical utility in addressing complex regulatory challenges.

The research underscores the importance of moving beyond traditional legal interpretations toward more proactive and creative implementation strategies. Legal design emerges as a particularly valuable approach, offering structured methodologies that enable responsible innovation while ensuring value-aligned development of AI technologies. By incorporating multiple stakeholder perspectives and facilitating creative legal solutions, legal design helps transform regulatory compliance from a constraint into an enabler of responsible innovation.

Looking forward, there is a clear need to strengthen legal design research, particularly in the digital health sector. As the complexity of AI technologies continues to grow, the integration of ethical, legal, and social aspects into health technologies becomes increasingly critical. Future research should focus on developing and refining legal design methodologies that can effectively address emerging challenges while promoting responsible innovation. This will require sustained investment in interdisciplinary collaboration and the continued evolution of practical frameworks for implementing regulatory requirements in ways that advance both technological progress and societal wellbeing.

References

[1] Gianni R., Pearson J., Reber B. (eds.). Responsible Research and Innovation: From Concepts and Practices. Milton: Routledge; 2018. (Routledge Studies in Innovation, Organizations and Technology Ser.).
[2] Low S., Buck H. J. The practice of responsible research and innovation in "climate engineering". WIREs Clim Change 2020; 11.

[3] Stilgoe J. Monitoring the evolution and benefits of responsible Research and Innovation. Luxembourg: European Union; 2018. Policy brief.

[4] European Commission. White Paper on Artificial Intelligence: a European approach to excellence and trust. Brussels; 2020 COM/2020/65 final.

[5] Li Z. Why the European AI Act transparency obligation is insufficient. Nat Mach Intell 2023; 5:559–60.

[6] There are holes in Europe's AI Act – and researchers can help to fill them. Editorial. Nature 2024; 625:216.

[7] Prainsack B., Forgó N. New AI regulation in the EU seeks to reduce risk without assessing public benefit. Nat Med 2024 30:1235–7.

[8] Hutson M. Rules to keep AI in check: nations carve different paths for tech regulation. Nature 2023; 620:260–3.

[9] Gibney E. What the EU's tough AI law means for research and ChatGPT. Nature 2024; 626:938–9.

[10] Fleming N. Proposed EU data laws leave researchers out in the cold. Nature Index 2023.

[11] Doherty M. The relationship between legal design cultures: tension and resolution. In: Corrales M., Haapio H., Hagan M., Doherty M. (eds.). Legal design: Integrating business, design and legal thinking with technology. Cheltenham, UK, Northampton, MA, USA: Edward Elgar Publishing; 2021. p. 32–53.

[12] Kohlmeier A., Krawietz L. Legal Design. In: Ebers M. (eds.). Stichwort Kommentar Legal Tech. Baden-Baden: Nomos; 2023.

[13] Le Gall A. Legal design beyond design thinking: processes and effects of the four spaces of design practices for the legal field. In: Ducato R., Strowel A. (eds.). Legal design perspectives: Theoretical and practical insights from the field. Milan: Ledizioni; 2021. p. 27–69.

[14] Berger-Walliser G., Barton T. D., Haapio H. From Visualization to Legal Design: A Collaborative and Creative Process. American Business Law journal 2017; 54:347–92.

[15] Hagan M. UserCentered Legal Design: Making the Law More Accessible, Usable, and Engaging; 2015 [cited 2021 Mar 22]. Available from: URL: Making the Law More Accessible, Usable, and Engaging.

[16] Djeffal C. Law by Design Obligations: The Future of Regulating Digital Technologies in Europe? SSRN Electronic Journal 2024:1–37.

[17] Djeffal C. The Normative Potential of the European Rule on Automated Decisions: A New Reading for Art. 22 GDPR. ZaöRV 2020; 81:847–79.

[18] Bygrave L. A. Security by Design: Aspirations and Realities in a Regulatory Context. OLR 2022; 8:126–77.

[19] Verwaltungsakademie Berlin. Gute Künstliche Intelligenz (KI) in der öffentlichen Verwaltung gestalten; 2018. Available from: URL: https://www.berlin.de/vak/aktuelles/aktuelles-2018/artikel.708143.php.

Thomas Wittenberg, Christian Münzenmayer, Matthias Struck

27 Business models for artificial intelligence in healthcare

27.1 Introduction and objectives

Commonly *medical technology* is defined as the research and business area dedicated to the prevention, diagnosis, treatment and monitoring of diseases using technologies consisting of devices and/or software and processes. Thus, within this broad field a multitude of different application areas are addressed as well as a plethora of biomedical devices is used and services are offered. Such *medical devices* can range from very simple instruments (such as thermometers), over mobile and body-worn vital sensors to highly complex imaging systems such as single photon emission computed tomography (SPECT) as well as tele-manipulators and partially automated surgical robots. Examples for services are, e.g., maintenance and/or support, calibration, regular updates of software components, or integrated leasing and maintenance offerings for complex devices.

In addition to that, the advent of artificial intelligence (AI) is opening another dimension of complexity and opportunity at the same time. Advances in AI not only have the potential to revolutionize medical technology, but are already doing so by significantly improving efficiency, precision and personalization in healthcare.

Furthermore, the integration and use of AI within the healthcare systems will also have significant impact and will change processes of care delivery, distribution of cost and revenues.

After briefly introducing the idea of business models and providing some prominent AI-based applications in healthcare, this contribution links these two topics and shows how, among other things, AI methods could be used to innovate existing business models in the medical device and software industry and solve some of the numerous challenges in healthcare in the future.

27.2 Introduction to business models

The term *business model* has developed as early as the mid-1950s, but only became established at the end of the 1990s with the advent of the internet and e-commerce. Nevertheless, up to now there does not exist a standard definition of this term. Generally, a company's business model is often equated with its strategy, but the business model is much more the interface between the corporate strategy on the one hand and its business processes on the other. A *business model* describes the basic architecture of a company and, according to Gassman's well-known *St. Gallen Business Model Navigator* [1,2], can be defined by the following four dimensions:

D_1: WHO are the target *customers*?

D_2: WHAT is sold to the customers? This can also be regarded as the *value proposition*;

D_3: HOW is the service or the product provided or produced? This aspect is related to the *value chain*;

D_4: HOW do you generate VALUE with the business? This relates to the *revenue mechanics*.

Therefore, a business model can be regarded as a conceptual framework that outlines a company's strategy for generating revenue. It details the value proposition the company offers to different customer segments (here, the firm's structure), and its network of partners and resources used to create, market, and deliver this value. Additionally, it also encompasses the relationships and capital needed to ensure profitable and sustainable revenue streams. In essence, a business model describes how a company operates and earns money [3].

In the healthcare sector we are considering here, the dimension of the *value propositions* (D_2) relates to all products, goods, services, licenses, etc., which a company or vendor in the healthcare sector offers to its customers. The addressed customer segments (D_1) may include a variety of stakeholders, ranging from hospitals, physicians, registered doctors, pharmacies, up to patients and their relatives. The traditional value chains (D_3) have in the past been mostly related to pipeline businesses (see Section 27.2.1), while – since the establishment of the internet –, so-called platform economies (see Section 27.3.1) have appeared. Finally, there exist many different possibilities revenue mechanics (D_4), which will be detailed throughout this contribution.

In the following sections we will provide examples of traditional as well as novel business models with respect to different *value chains* as well as to the related revenue mechanics revenue mechanics, based on various stages of digitalization, including the availability and use of artificial intelligence (AI) as essential part of these business models.

27.2.1 Pipeline business models

The most simplest business models are known as pipeline businesses (see Fig. 27.1). In these models the producers or providers of goods or services (Fig. 27.1 on the left) deliver them to users and customers (Fig. 27.1 on the right) through a series (or pipeline) of successive steps, such as manufacturing, marketing and sales, delivery, and maintenance. These traditional pipeline businesses usually compete based on quality, cost, and market reach. They aim to capture parts of the value chain by leveraging economies of scale, unique intellectual property, specialized resources, geographic presence, and brand. Traditionally, mergers and acquisitions (M&A) are used to grow and diversify these businesses [3].

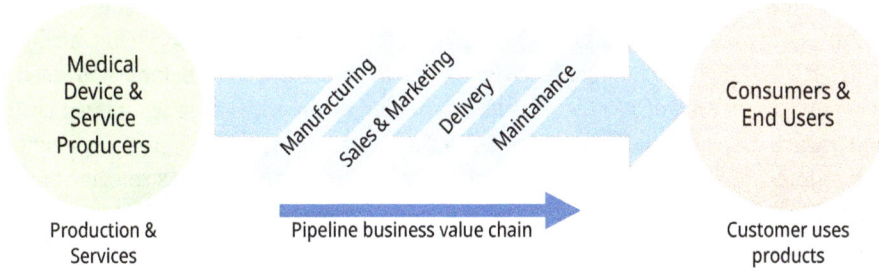

Fig. 27.1: Principle of traditional *pipeline business models* (inspired by [16], created by TW) that deliver goods or services through a linear pipeline of successive steps that may or may not include other partners.

Hence, let us have a look at some examples of companies, whose traditional (pipeline) business models were once quite good, but who were *not able* to make the transformation into these new eras. What do the German companies *AEG* and *Grundig* (consumer electronics), *Triumph* (cars and motor bikes), *Agfa* (consumer and medical photography, video and film equipment), *Quelle* (mail order company) or *Schlecker* (retail drugstore) have in common? These are all once highly successful German companies that were known for decades for their high-quality products, services and processes. Nevertheless, today these companies either no longer exist, or have sunk into insignificance, or continue to operate as small niche businesses under foreign ownership. Some of these former traditional company names are probably no longer known to the younger readers.

Most of these traditional pipeline business models have come to age, especially with the advent of e-commerce (since approximately 2000), *m(obile)-commerce* (since approximately 2010) and artificial intelligence (AI) (since approximately 2020) [4]. What has gone wrong? These companies have rested on their laurels for far too long and simply failed to adapt their business models to the uprising e-commerce and m-commerce markets as well as the competitive conditions related to these new markets. In contrast, some well-known examples of *innovative new business* models *outside* the healthcare market include the cab service company *Uber* (connecting riders with drivers), the streaming service *Netflix* (providing streaming services by licensing content), or the booking and rental portal *AirBnB* (facilitating short-term rentals by connecting hosts with guests). None of these companies own any cars, films or apartments themselves, but bring together the supply and the demand for these services on individual online broker platforms (see Section 27.3.1).

27.2.2 Power-by-the-hour and Total Care

Another business model, *power-by-the-hour* was originally introduced in 1962 by the British aircraft turbine manufacturer *Rolls-Royce*: instead of selling turbines outright to airlines, they are leased based on usage [5]. Under this model, Rolls-Royce retained ownership of the turbines but was responsible for their maintenance and servicing. Airlines paid a fee based on the number of flight hours, which created a predictable and steady revenue stream for *Rolls-Royce*. This also benefited airlines by reducing upfront costs and ensuring operational reliability. Hence the companies maximized their efficiency and minimized downtime through advanced service and maintenance strategies. Some years later, Rolls Royce extended the thought of power-by-the-hour and advanced it to the *Total Care* model, defining a new era of life cycle business models [6,7] for large machinery. Vendors of expensive medical imaging equipment, such as computed tomography (CT), magnetic resonance imaging (MRI), ultrasound (US) or endoscopy systems have already adopted that kind of business models [8].

Through the advancement and availability of the new technological developments of e-commerce and m-commerce possibilities the power-by-the-hour business models have in the past decades progressed towards the novel pay-per-use business models (see Section 27.3.2).

27.2.3 Razor-and-Blade

One further example for a typical classic business model is the *razor-and-blade* model [9]. This was supposedly invented by K.C. Gilette and then adopted and applied by many other companies: the basic products (razor, printer, coffee-machines, cameras, ...) are offered and sold either very cheaply or even provided free of charge. The essential but consumable by-products, which are necessary for the use of the basic product, are sold at a high price and generate the main revenue. Examples are the razor blades from Gillette, printer ink-cartridges from Hewlett-Packard, Nespresso coffee-capsules from Nestlé, or instant films from Polaroid.

These razor-and-blade models have already been established in the past decades in the healthcare sector. The most prominent examples for such business models were X-Ray systems (the *razor*), where the acquired images were captured on expensive analogue film material (the consumables), which was sold (together with developer chemicals) by huge companies such as AGFA or Eastman Kodak [10]. Nevertheless, when X-ray machines become digital, these companies had huge difficulties keeping up with their business models.

Other examples for razor-and-blade business models are high-end imaging devices such as endoscopy or X-ray-systems which are supplemented with different types of single-use instruments as, e.g., catheters, needles, biopsy-forceps, grippers, snares or loops. While the imaging systems themselves can usually be cleaned, reprocessed or sterilized, the consumable instruments must usually be disposed, as reprocessing is either not possible or economic. To this end, the currently most prominent example for the *razor-and-blade* model is the DaVinci telematic surgical robot [11], whose average sales price is about 1.5 million €, while the revenue from consumables (e.g., surgical instruments) comes to about, 800 € per procedure and the service contract revenue range from 100,000 € to 200,000 € per system, per year [12].

Leveraging the potential of e- and m-commerce (Section 27.3), these razor-and-blade models have evolved significantly, with most consumables now being sold through online stores or platform broker models (Section 27.3.1).

27.2.4 Disposables

Even without a 'razor' (or a similar 'anchor' device), a new market of *disposables* has been established in the healthcare sector. Instead of having a tangible *anchor* device, clinical regulations stating that contaminated equipment must either be adequately reprocessed or sterilized, or must be incinerated, have fostered the research, development and production of different disposable items and devices. These devices relate to clinical (surgical) equipment as well as those covering basic hospital hygiene requirements. Typical examples for such disposables (or single use equipment) are syringes, needles, scalpella, biopsy-forceps, wrappers, covers, gowns and masks, and even include wireless capsule endoscopes (WCEs) [13].

An increased sale and amplified application and need of different types of single-use equipment (from gloves to endoscopes, from masks to surgical instruments) has further been driven by the Covid 19 pandemia, as especially contaminated equipment, such as e.g. bronchoscopes [14] or plastic gloves are very hard or even impossible to reprocess or sterilize. Hence, the healthcare and the supply industries have invested immensely in these single-use technologies, using the increased possibility of contamination or cross-contamination as leverage for new products. The distribution of almost all disposables can nowadays be realized, e.g., via web-shops or platform models (s. Section 27.3.1).

27.2.5 New business models in healthcare

To not only secure and expand competitive advantages in today's fast-moving age of digitalization, but also to keep pace with the often much more agile companies from China and from the United States' Silicon Valley, modern companies in the healthcare sector must continuously question themselves and develop and establish new and innovative value proposition (D_2) as well as new types of value chains (D_3) as well as innovative ideas of mechanics or revenue (D_4). In combination, a change or progression of these dimensions leads to advanced and agile new business models. More specifically, according to the St. Gallen Business Model Navigator [1], a business model can be described as *innovative*, if it has a significant impact on at least two of the four dimensions (D1–D4) introduced above. Furthermore, the results of empirical studies (e.g. by the Boston Consulting Group [15]) show that innovations in business models are also associated with significantly greater potential for success than pure product and service innovations. AI enables businesses to analyze customer preferences, predict commercial trends, and offer personalized services, transforming models into subscription or pay-per-use structures. Technologies like cloud computing and blockchain support platform-based models, connecting customers and partners to create value through networks and marketplaces.

27.3 Business models in the era of e-commerce and m-commerce

As introduced above, traditional business models within the medical device industry have primarily been based on the sale (or rental) of devices, instruments, and software (mainly using the pipeline model), possibly together with disposable single-use accessories (razor-and-blade), or long-term maintenance contracts (power-by-the-hour) for generally high-quality products and associated services.

Nevertheless, based on digitalization of all types of data (images, vital signs, speech, text, processes) combined with possibilities of the (high-speed) internet, the possibilities of e- and m-commerce and the rapid development of artificial intelligence [4], completely new business models have been emerging ever since.

With respect to changing the value chain (D3), especially platform economies (Section 27.3.1) have been a complete new approach to connect producers and service providers with end users. Addressing the revenue mechanics (D4), pay-per-use (Section 27.3.2), freemium (Section 27.3.3), subscription models (Section 27.3.4), pay-per-outcome (Section 27.3.5) or reimbursement models (Section 27.3.6) have had a great impact.

27.3.1 Platform economies

Platform business models [16] are digital infrastructures facilitating the creation and exchange of values between various players in the healthcare system, and can thus be considered as new form of value chains. As depicted in Fig. 27.2, the producers and providers of medical equipment or healthcare services (Fig. 27.2 on the left) and the users or customers, such as doctors and healthcare providers as well as patients or relatives (depicted on the right in Fig. 27.2) are connected by third-party hosted digital broker platforms in between. The broker's roles are the organization of the offering, marketing and sales of the vendor's goods and services towards the customers, and likewise collecting and providing valuable information about the customers buying behavior and interests back to the vendors. The most prominent and well known broker platforms with related business models are for example *eBay*^TM and *Amazon*^TM, whereas Amazon is already offering a large palette of medical products to the end-customers.

Furthermore, these platform economies and the related platform business models have actually extended and shifted their offers from e-commerce to m-commerce, which are nowadays provided by apps on handheld mobile devices (smartphones, tablets, smart-watches) to the end-users fingertips.

Such *healthcare platforms* can either be used to provide different healthcare services offered by community, public or emergency healthcare centers [3], or – in the form of web-shops – offering goods and devices needed for professionals as well as patients.

Using already available broker platforms (as, e.g. *Talkspace* [17], *Teladoc Health* [18], *DoctoLib* [19]), patients can book online medical consultations (OMCs) [20] or online therapies with licensed physicians or therapists via video calls. Similarwise, also mental health support, or chronic condition management is offered and can be booked. Thus, these broker platforms exemplify how the platform economy can enhance healthcare delivery by improving accessibility, convenience, and personalization. Various companies in the healthcare sector have already moved parts of their value proposition (D_2) in these directions, e.g., offering expensive medical imaging systems (CT, MRI, US, endoscopes) through broker services (D_3) between radiologists and patients, or providing remote on-demand (AI-based) diagnostic software services (Section 27.4.2).

For the payments of these healthcare services, various reimbursement models are known, ranging from pay-per-use models (Section 27.3.2) to freemium (Section 27.3.3), or subscription models (Section 27.3.4) where the costs (D_4) are covered either by the patients themselves, by employers or also by insurances (Section 27.3.6).

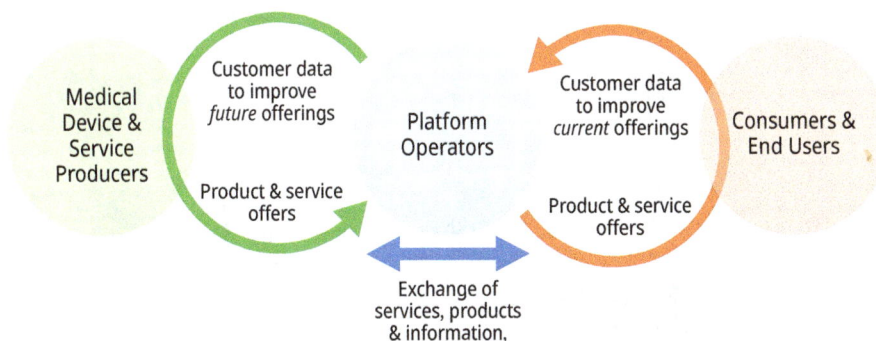

Fig. 27.2: Principle of *platform businesses* (inspired by [16], created by TW), see text for further explanations.

27.3.2 Pay-per-Use

The *pay-per-use* (PpU) business model is a broader approach of the above introduced power-by-the-hour approach (Section 27.2.2), which additionally encompasses various models where customers pay based on their usage of a product or service. This can include anything from cloud computing services, where users pay for the amount of data they store or process, to equipment sharing or leasing services, where users pay for the time they use a device.

In the past decades pay-per-use business models have been introduced also to the field of medical technology, especially for expensive large-scale imaging equipment (CT, MRI, US, Endoscopes). Instead of selling these devices directly to hospitals, clinics or ambulances, various manufacturers have already implemented either as pay-by-use [21,22] or *radiology-as-a-service* (RaaS) models [23]. Within these service and business models, health care providers are not required anymore to purchase expensive imaging equipment at front. Instead, they can partner with vendors of high-end imaging equipment, who provide them with the necessary high-end-equipment and related services, and with payments made either on a pay-per-use or on a periodic basis, see Fig. 27.3.

Within this business model, hospitals and clinics are paying per scan or per imaging procedure (*Imaging-as-a-Service*, IaaS), while the manufacturers remain the ownership of the imaging device and provide full maintenance, upgrades, and support. This allows the healthcare providers to provide cutting-edge imaging technology to the patients without a significant capital investment, while enabling the manufacturers to build long-term customer relationships and optimize device performance through real-time monitoring and predictive maintenance.

The concept of real-time self-monitoring of the medical equipment can furthermore be supported by novel *Internet-of-Things* (IoT) technologies, which combine various low-energy sensors (as e.g., RFIDs) placed inside the imaging equipment (CT, MRI, US, or endoscopy systems) to measure or read the internal state of the device (hours used, worn-out bowden, LED usage, image quality) and send this data directly to the

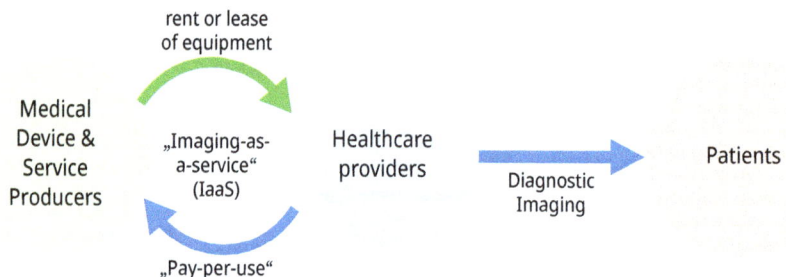

Fig. 27.3: Principle of *pay-per-use* for high-end medical imaging devices exemplified by *Imaging-as-a-Service*, see text for further explanations.

vendor. This collected sensor information can then either be used for predictive maintenance or to count how often or how long the device has been used [24].

Both business models – the original power-by-the-hour as well as pay-per-use – have shifted the focus from device ownership to device usage, aligning costs more closely with actual consumption and often providing more flexibility and cost efficiency for customers. This shift is particularly relevant in today's economy, where digital transformation and the rise of the sharing economy are driving new ways of thinking about consumption and ownership.

27.3.3 Freemium models

One modern counterpart to the razor-and-blade models (see Section 27.2.3) in the digital era are *freemium* models, also known as *try-before-you-buy* models. For example, for a piece of software or a specific online service, users obtain basic features at no cost and can then access richer functionalities for subscription fees. Most freemium offers are coupled to some online economy platform or also social networks. Prominent examples for freemium platform models are e.g. the social business platforms *LinkedIn*™ and *XING*™, the podcast and music streaming service *Spotify*™ or the online storage portal *Dropbox*™. The basic features of all these offers are free, but additional features (network analytics for *LinkedIn*™, unlimited advertising-free music streaming from *Spotify*™, endless storage possibilities from *Dropbox*™) can be booked or bought in addition.

Within the healthcare sector, many freemium offers are related to some type of *online medical consultations* (OMCs) (Section 27.3.1) [25], which have emerging from e-health services based on electronic healthcare platforms (Section 27.3.1). Nevertheless, also offline software is available for many different applications, as e.g. medical analysis services. Two examples for freemium business models for image analytics are the *OsiriX* [26] DICOM viewers or the *MIKAIA* platform [27] for digital pathology. *OsiriX* [28] offers a free version called *OsiriX Lite* (see Fig. 27.4 top), providing basic functionalities for viewing DICOM images, but is *not* certified as a medical product. For more advanced features and capabilities, professional users can opt for the paid version, *OsiriX MD*, which is certified for medical use and includes additional tools and support. Similar, *MIKAIA Lite* [29] (Fig. 27.4 bottom) provides possibilities to interact, view and annotate digital whole slide images captured from different scanners, while the extended version of MIKAIA allows creating individual AI-powered analysis methods in the field of digital pathology.

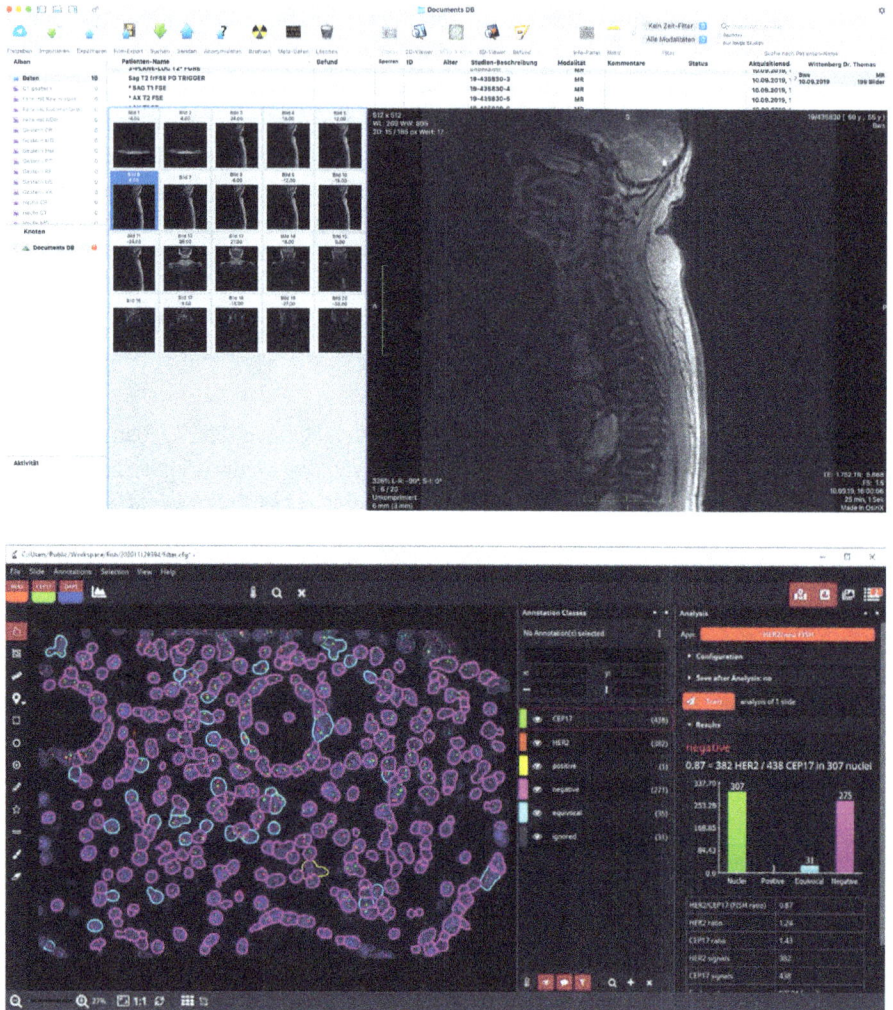

Fig. 27.4: Examples for a *freemium* image analysis software. Top: *OsiriX Lite*; bottom: *MIKAIA Lite*.

27.3.4 Subscription models

Another business model is related to *subscription-based* healthcare services. Instead of charging a one-time fee for software or for a device, companies offer software licenses (as e.g. Microsoft's Office or SAP Salescloud) through *subscription plans*. These plans not only cover the cost of the software license itself, but also include ongoing access to extended individual services such as, e.g., cloud-based health data analytics, the integration and usage of specialized data visualization apps, secure cloud storage options and backups, regular updates, or even telemedicine consultations.

For example, using devices such as smartwatches and wearables that are able track vital health metrics, the related providers offer to accumulate and store the acquired data in a cloud, and provide various telehealth services based on the data. Prominent examples are *Apple*[TM], *FitBit*[TM] or *Garmin*[TM], offering a subscription services such as Apple Fitness+ [30], Fitbit Premium, or Garmin Coach [31]. Such subscription models ensure continuous revenue for the companies while providing users and patients personalized health reports, health monitoring features or guided programs for fitness, nutrition, and sleep. Subscribers also get access to additional features like stress management tools and wellness reports [31].

Likewise, providers such as GE Healthcare, Philips, Nexus AG, or Agfa HealthCare of documentation and terminology software for the structured documentation of medical images and clinical findings offer their customers (hospitals, clinics) a – yearly or quarterly – subscription of their software, which can easily be bundled with a package of additional services such as regular software patches and updates, apps for analytics or remote control and repair services [32].

27.3.5 Outcome-based payment models (OBPM)

The *Outcome-Based Payment Model* (OBPM) in modern medicine is a *results-oriented reimbursement models* in which the payment of the healthcare providers (D_4) is linked to actual treatment *outcomes* rather than simply paying for services rendered or procedures performed. This business model is applied in areas where technology, such as e.g. wearable devices, plays a key role in health monitoring and improving health.

Some examples are as follows: For patients with chronic conditions like hypertension (high blood pressure) or diabetes, wearable devices, as e.g. smart watches, provide an opportunity to better control their blood pressure. This continuous monitoring of vital signs most likely results in fewer hospital stays or emergency room visits. Consequently, the healthcare provider or device manufacturer may charge a fee, based on these improved health outcomes. This could be a *success-based fee* that is only charged if the patient demonstrates measurable health improvements. Devices that monitor overall vital signs including lifestyle can also be integrated into OBPMs. This applies especially to patients and users who want to improve their physical activity, diet, sleep habits, or stress levels. If the users achieve their fitness goals, such as weight loss, improved stamina, or stress reduction, the provider could tie the payment to the success of these goals. Hence, a success-based fee could be charged depending on the measurable improvement in the user's physical condition. Another example of OBPMs is telemedicine. In this sector, healthcare providers (e.g., physicians, psychologists or therapists) may charge not just for the number of online-sessions, but for the health outcomes achieved, such as improving mental health or successfully managing a chronic condition.

By focusing on measurable outcomes, such as recovery rates or patient satisfaction, OBPMs help healthcare providers to tailor their services and interventions to the most effective strategies for maintaining health of their customers. This could potentially lead to better, more personalized healthcare services. Secondly, with objective measurements, healthcare systems can assess the cost-effectiveness of treatments and services. This means that resources can be allocated where they have the greatest impact, hence optimizing the use of funds. Thirdly, OBPMs provide additional data on the performance of healthcare providers and institutions. This can enhance trust among patients and the public while encouraging institutions to maintain high standards of care.

Nevertheless, there exist challenges implementing OBPMs, such as the difficulty collecting accurate, comprehensive data across a variety of different settings and integrating it into a unified system, as the healthcare system rely on various disparate platforms and formats that complicate the measurement of the envisioned outcomes. Also, healthcare professionals may be resistant to shifting from traditional models of care to a more performance-driven system. Collecting and analyzing patient data for performance measurement raises also concerns about data privacy and ethical issues (see Section 27.5). Therefore it is crucial to ensure that OBPMs respect patient confidentiality and do not lead to the misuse of sensitive information.

27.3.6 Value-Based Health Care (VBHC)

Finally, one of the most fundamental influence on OBPMs is obvious in the highly regulated reimbursement systems that are the dominant determinant for possible revenue streams. Thus, the so-called *Value-Based Health Care* (VBHC) approach to reimbursement shall be referred to here as well because it is based on a similar idea, however primarily considering reimbursement for healthcare providers instead of MedTech companies. The basic concept of putting so-called *Value* at the core of healthcare systems has been introduced by M. Porter, an US economics professor, who defines value as the quotient between quality of medical outcome to treatment costs [33]. Thus, it is also obvious that the definition of outcome is of central importance to such reimbursement systems and significant efforts to find common standards have been invested by the International Consortium for *Health Outcomes Measurement* (ICOM) [34].

Various institutions have started implemented VBHC and a lot of material is available on the topic of VBHC which is well beyond the scope of this article. An overview of the state of the art in VBHC in Swiss and Germany has been published by Deerberg-Wittram et al. [35] and an overview of various case-studies in Europe and implementation guidelines for VBHC can be found in the treatise by Katz et al. [36].

The transition to VBHC represents a fundamental shift in the way healthcare systems operate, prioritizing patient outcomes and efficiency over service volume. By integrating evidence-based outcome measurement, interdisciplinary collaboration, and cost-effective care models, VBHC offers a pathway to sustainable and high-quality healthcare. However, its successful implementation requires continuous research, standardized evaluation methods, and the alignment of incentives across all stakeholders. As healthcare systems evolve, the principles of VBHC will remain essential in ensuring that medical advancements translate into tangible benefits for patients and society as a whole.

27.3.7 Reimbursement models

As has shown in the previous sections, driven by innovative technological advancements such as e-commerce and m-commerce, the healthcare sector has witnessed transformative changes for the value chain delivery, as well as for the revenue mechanics. Nevertheless, also regulatory shifts, and the growing demand for more patient-centered services have fostered the development of new types of revenues. Specifically in Germany, two key elements in this evolution are DiGAs (Digitale Gesundheitsanwendungen – Digital Health Applications) and DiPAs (Digitale Pflegeanwendungen – Digital Nursing Applications), both of which are currently reshaping the landscape of healthcare delivery in Germany [37] and are blueprints for other European Countries such as Austria, Belgium or Sweden. These digital solutions are not only revolutionizing patient care but are also creating new, business models in the healthcare sector.

DiGAs are software applications intended to support the diagnosis, treatment, or management of medical conditions, and are often used in the form of specialized apps for smartphones or other digital devices. The use of these applications are part of the German Digital Healthcare Act (Digitales Versorgungsgesetz, DVG), which was introduced in 2019 to encourage the use of digital tools within the healthcare system. The goal of DiGAs is to provide patients with accessible, real-time, and personalized health management solutions at the point of care, hence improving clinical outcomes, reducing administrative burdens, and optimizing the use of healthcare resources. Up to now (2025) 57 different DiGAs have been accepted by the German Federal Institute for Drugs and Medical Devices (Bundesinstitut für Arzneimittel und Medizinprodukte, BfArM) [38]. Examples of DiGAs include, e.g., mental health apps (such as *deprexis* [39], *edupression* [40], *elona therapy* [41], *HelloBetter* [42]) providing therapeutic exercises or mood tracking, or chronic disease management tools, such as diabetes management apps that monitor glucose levels and provide personalized recommendations.

DiPAs, on the other hand, focus on the care sector, providing digital solutions that assist caregivers in managing elderly or disabled patients. These applications aim to streamline caregiving processes, improve efficiency, and enhance the quality of care provided to patients. DiPAs includes tools for care documentation, medication management, and even remote monitoring of patient's health status (D_2). Examples of DiPAs include apps for caregivers to track medication administration or vital signs, or *telecare services* that allow family members or healthcare professionals to remotely monitor (D_3) the well-being of elderly or chronically ill individuals [38].

Both, DiGAs and DiPAs, are recognized as part of a broader effort to integrate digital health tools into the mainstream healthcare systems, with regulatory frameworks designed to ensure safety, privacy, and efficacy. DiGAs and DiPAs can be prescribed by certified healthcare providers and are reimbursed by statutory health insurances. Once a DiGA or DiPAs is included and listed in the directory of the German Federal Institute for Drugs and Medical Devices, these applications can be prescribed by doctors, physio- or psychotherapists. However, the process for getting DiGAs or DiPAs finally reimbursed (D_4) involves several steps, including clinical evaluation, application for inclusion in the respective directory, and price negotiations. It may be added that there has been a lot of public debate on the complexity and bureaucracy for the registration process of DiGAs with the BfArM on the one hand and on the medical benefits and treatment effectiveness from the payers and insurance companies on the other hand. Thus, strategic advice and consulting is sought after by tech companies aiming for putting their own DiGAs and DiPAs on the market effectively.

Even though for DiGAs and DiPAs the main revenue mechanics (D_4) are related to the reimbursement from the insurance companies, they can also – depending on the negotiations – be related and coupled to subscription-based, pay-per-use, freemium or even outcome-based models to access digital health services or care applications.

For example, a DiGA that supports the management of chronic diseases such as diabetes could, e.g., either be priced based on whether it helps patients maintain a healthy blood glucose level, hence reducing the risk of complications. Insurance companies might reimburse for these tools if they are proven to improve patient outcomes, such as fewer hospitalizations or better disease management. In this context, outcome-based models might create strong incentives for developers to focus on the effectiveness and efficiency of their applications, as the revenue is tied to tangible improvements in health and care.

27.4 Business models and artificial intelligence

27.4.1 Application of AI in healthcare

AI is increasingly being applied across all sectors of the healthcare spectrum, ranging from diagnosis to personalized medicine, and from prevention to intervention. AI applications are used to enhance efficiency, improve diagnostic accuracy, and elevate treatment quality. The main advantage of AI in healthcare lies in its ability to analyze vast amounts of data quickly and identify patterns that may be difficult for humans to detect. AI methods are able to assess or search large-scale multimodal medical data collections (images, vital data, texts, gene databases) for similarities and patterns, or abnormalities and outliers in a very short time and thus provide fast and precise suggestions for diagnostics. In addition, the analysis of genetic information and comparison with other patient data allows the creation of individualized treatment plans. Personalized treatment increases its effectiveness while at the same time reducing side effects. However, AI can not only raise patient care to a new level of quality, but also significantly increase operational efficiency in clinics and practices [43]. For example, AI methods optimize the management of patient allocation, scheduling and the allocation of resources [44]. An examples for hospital optimization already in use is, for instance, the *arkangel.ai* [45] system.

While many new business models have in the past been created based on the new technical possibilities of e-commerce and m-commerce, the availability of AI offers and opens up new possibilities to either extend existing business models but also to create new ones.

27.4.2 Improving the value chain using AI

Examples of AI integrated directly integrated into the value chain (D_3) are AI-based *extensions* which allow the *prediction* and *suggestion* of products, devices or services (D_1), which the customers (D2) want or need, based on the plethora of patterns of available customer data and buying behavior. Typical examples for such automatic AI-generated offers (customers *"who bought this syringe also bought those needles"*, or *"these scalpella are often bundled with those band-aids"*) are already integrated and provided in many online portals, such as *Amazon healthcare* or similar ones, who serve as a broker-interfaces (D_3) for different small and medium vendors. Even though approaches to generate and provide customized product suggestions to the end-user have been around for two decades, using AI-based *prognostic* methods for personalized suggestions and product advertising has given the game an additional twist. In these cases AI methods are used to as a leverage to motivate the customers to buy more or additional value proposition (D_2), hence increasing the revenue mechanics (D_4).

27.4.3 Software-as-a-Service (SaaS) or AI as a service

Software-as-a-Service (SaaS) [46,47] or *AI-as a service* business models use a different approach and offer already trained AI algorithms as the value proposition (D_2) itself for a fee. Usually SaaS offers are organized via a broker platform (Section 27.3.1) or hosted by companies themselves. The main idea of SaaS is that the customers usually have no own resources to train or run an extensive AI model for a certain purpose (because of missing data, or missing computational hardware, or both). In this case the customers have to bring their query data to the AI and get the AI-based results on return. Depending the complexity of the AI-model, the frontend interface of such a SaaS can either be an app on a (powerful) mobile device (and possibly an NPU on board) or needs a secure update of the data to the providers AI-server.

Depending on the companies individual provision model, the reimbursement of the AI-powered SaaS-service can either be provided by one of the above introduced charging models (pay-per-use, subscription, …) and paid from the end users (patients, physicians, hospitals) using the service, or can also be provided by third parties by reimbursement (DiGA).

One prominent example of AI-based SaaS in healthcare is *Zebra Medical Vision*, leveraging AI to enhance radiology services [48]. A cloud service is used to enable healthcare professionals to upload (anonymized) medical images, analyze them with support of artificial intelligence and machine learning methods, and receive diagnostic findings [49] and AI-generated diagnostic reports.

27.4.4 Data-as-a-Service (DaaS)

The quality of AI-based methods is on one hand related to the AI-model itself, but is on the other hand always dependent on the quality and amount of healthcare data which the AI approaches have been trained on. Only large-scale data collections – in this case the novel value positions (D_2) – which have been curated and annotated [50,51] by specialists can lead to outstanding results for diagnostic and therapeutic AI-based procedures. Hence, adequate data-as-a-service (DaaS) platforms can provide centralized hosting and management of various healthcare data collections, making it easier for organizations to access and utilize large-scale curated data from multiple sources [52]. Furthermore, by centralizing data, DaaS-platforms facilitate better collaboration among healthcare providers, researchers, and other stakeholders. Such data treasures are correspondingly sought-after, as not every company or research institute – the potential *customers* (D_1) of the data, – can create and maintain its own databases or data collections as part of clinical studies. It therefore makes sense to establish adequate business models that grant customers access to curated medical and clinical data sets by selling or renting them. This data can then be used to train or validate new AI-based solutions.

An example of a DaaS business model emerges from wearables [53] such as sensor-enhanced watches, rings, textiles, which are able to collect critical health data as, e.g., heart and breathing rate, blood pressure, SpO2- and glucose levels, or gait and sleep patterns, and store this data in the cloud. Possible revenue mechanics (D_4) for such data are, e.g. subscription models, where healthcare providers, insurers, or users may pay fees to access the collected data, or companies *licensing* aggregated and anonymized health data to research institutions or pharmaceutical companies, for R&D purposes. Interesting value chains (D_3) for DaaS could be companies like *Fitbit, Apple*, and *Garmin* who produce and sell novel wearables (see Section 27.3.4) and aggregate, analyze and display the collected data to their users (for a fee); or insurers who can leverage wearable data to assess risk, personalize insurance plans, and incentivize healthy behaviors among policyholders. The value proposition (D_2) to the user is not just the device itself, but the continuous insights and storage to essential vital signs it provides.

In that context we have to mention dataspaces established on the basis of national and international legislation and public initiatives such as the so-called *European Health Data Space (EHDS)* [54] that has been agreed on in spring 2024 by the European parliament and Council. The EHDS shall facilitate the exchange of health data for the delivery of healthcare (primary use) across the EU complying with European data protection standards, especially the GDPR. Secondly, the EHDS shall provide a trustworthy system to access electronic health records for secondary use, such as research, innovation, regulatory and policy-making activities. While still in its infancy the EHDS will certainly have an important impact on the availability of health data for research and development in the years and decades to come. However, at the time of this writing it is to early to engage in predictions about how the EHDS may influence commercial models of data re-use and brokerage.

27.4.5 AI-based ChatBots

Based on *large-language models* (LLMs) for AI-based human-machine-interaction, so-called *chatbots* or *conversational AI* systems have in the past become new players in the healthcare domain. Chatbots can be regarded as automated programs that simulate human conversation and replicate user behavior in chat communications, typically through text-based interfaces. Early versions of chatbots make use of predefined rule-based workflows or scripts to respond to user queries and complete basic tasks. While they were able to improve efficiency by handling routine interactions, they often lacked the possibility to understand context or adapt to complex conversations. Modern conversational AI systems make extended use of LLMs, natural language processing (NLP), as well as machine learning (ML) to create dynamic, context-aware interactions. Thus, as chatbots can interpret intent, recognize context, and adapt responses in real-time. As they are able to mimic conversations between individuals, they provide a platform for effective and seemingly 'intelligent' interactions with users [55]. Health Chatbots are therefore AI programs that can conduct conversations within restricted intellectual limits via textual (or auditory) methods regarding healthcare issues [56].

Within the healthcare sector, Chatbots emulate the roles of clinical experts – physicians, pharmacists, nurses, radiologists, oncologists –, offering services similar to those provided by these professionals. For instance, *Florence* [57] can remind patients to take their medication, track the user's health, and locate the nearest doctor's office and pharmacy, if needed [58]. *Babylon Health* [59] is a London-based digital healthcare company offering online consultations with doctors [60]. It allows users to report symptoms of their illnesses and asks dedicated questions, checks the collected information against a database of diseases, and offers appropriate courses of action. By this the chatbot supports telehealth services and can be particularly useful in managing chronic conditions. *Ada Health* is a Germany-based company offering a similar chatbot helping users assess their symptoms and providing guidance on the next steps. It uses AI to deliver personalized health assessments [61]. These are only some prominent examples as there exists many more chatbots in the worldwide healthcare systems.

The new value position (D_2) of chatbots relates to the interactive communication and information about someone's physical or mental health state. The addressed customers (D_1) can either be patients or the relatives as well as the healthcare experts, looking for advice and guidance about a clinical problem. The value chains (D_3) for chatbots are mainly provided by e- or m-commerce platforms, the past been mostly related to pipeline business (see Section 27.2.1), while – since the establishment of the internet – so-called platform economies (see Section 27.3.1) have appeared. Finally, there exist many different possibilities of revenue mechanics (D_4), as e.g. subscription models, pay-per-use or freemium models. Alternative business models are also coupled with chatbots, as e.g. *Advertising and Partnerships*, where chatbots generate revenue through partnerships with insurance providers or pharmaceutical companies by displaying targeted advertisements. Another business model can be *Data Monetization* where aggregated and anonymized user and interaction data collected by the chatbots can be valuable for research and analytics.

27.5 Ethical considerations

The use and application of AI in medical technology and related services has the potential to fundamentally change the industry and the healthcare sector. New business models and innovative applications offer both challenges and great opportunities. As technology continues to develop and AI becomes more widely accepted in the healthcare sector, it is highly likely that business models will continue to evolve and innovate. By combining the new possibilities of e-commerce and AI, companies that can adapt to the changing developments and offer new innovative solutions will also be able to achieve sustainable success in this dynamic market. Companies that fail to do so will quickly disappear from the scene. With the availability of AI systems, not only the AI services themselves – such as diagnostics, predication, or prevention – offer new lines of value propositions, but also the data needed to fuel and train the various AI-systems can be regarded as its own *product* (e.g. by DaaS, or Data Monetization).

Nevertheless, DaaS or similar data-related business models present several ethical considerations that need to be carefully addressed to ensure that patients' rights, autonomy, and well-being are protected, including informed consent, safeguarding personal health information, ensuring data is used in ways aligning with patients' best interests, preventing discriminatory outcomes, and maintaining transparency in how patient data is collected, shared, and monetized.

27.5.1 Patient-related considerations

Specifically, such ethical considerations concern the data privacy and security of the patient data needed to train any AI system, which is highly sensitive, and any breach may have severe consequences for individuals. Ethical considerations also imply implementing robust *security measures, encryption,* and *access controls* to protect sensitive patient data from unauthorized access and cyber threats. Also, all patients must be fully be informed beforehand about how their data will be used, stored, and shared. Hence, obtaining informed consent is crucial to respect patient autonomy. Also clarifying in advance who owns the data and who has control over it is essential. All patients should aways have the right to access or withdraw their provided medical data from any data pool, request corrections, and decide who can use their data and for what purposes [62]. Mühlhoff (2024) [63] discusses ethical and legal challenges posed by the secondary use of AI models, particularly models trained on proprietary data. Specifically it is pointed out, once a model is trained, it could be repurposed in ways that circumvent the original data protection agreements, hence creating significant risks. These risks arise as AI-models may indirectly reveal or exploit data they were trained on, even without direct access to it. Therefore, development of adequately regulatory frameworks are needed to ensure responsible AI use.

27.5.2 Company related considerations

Healthcare providers and companies offering AI-based services must be transparent about their data practices, which includes clear communicating to customers and the public about their individual data usage policies, purposes of data collection, and any third parties involved. For reliable healthcare outcomes, defining and maintaining high standards of data accuracy and quality (*data curation*) is crucial. To this end, ethical considerations involve regular data validation and updates to prevent errors that could negatively impact patient care. Finally, when applying AI and machine learning approaches on healthcare data, it is essential to ensure that these technologies are used ethically. This includes avoiding biases in algorithms, ensuring transparency in decision-making processes, and regularly auditing the developed AI systems and services for fairness and accuracy [64].

27.6 Summary

The integration of artificial intelligence (AI) is currently revolutionizing medical technology by enhancing efficiency, precision, and personalization in healthcare. AI's impact extends to care delivery processes, cost distribution, and revenue models. In this contribution we have tried explore how AI can innovate business models in the medical device and software industry. In healthcare, business models address products, services, and licenses offered to various stakeholders, including hospitals, physicians, and patients. Traditional value chains have evolved from pipeline business to platform economies with the advent of the internet. Digitalization and AI have led to new business models, including platform economies, pay-per-use, freemium, subscription, outcome-based payment, and reimbursement models. AI-based business models include Software-as-a-Service (SaaS), AI-as-a-Service, or Data-as-a-Service (DaaS), leveraging large-scale data collections for innovative solutions.

References

[1] Gassmann O., Frankenberger K., Csik M. (2014). The business model navigator: 55 models that will revolutionise your business (1st ed.). Upper Saddle River, NJ: FT Press.
[2] Osterwalder A. & Pigneur Y. Business Model Generation: 2011 Campus Verlag GmbH, Frankfurt am Main.
[3] Viswanadham N. Ecosystem model for healthcare platform. Sādhanā 46, 188 (2021). https://doi.org/10.1007/s12046-021-01708-y.
[4] Raji M. A., Olodo H. B., Oke T. T., Addy W. A., Ofodile O. C., Oyewole A. E-commerce and consumer behavior: A review of AI-powered personalization and market trends. GSC Advanced Research and Reviews, 2024, 18(03), 066–077. https://gsconlinepress.com/journals/gscarr/sites/default/files/GSCARR-2024-0090.pdf.
[5] Smith D. J. (2013). Power-by-the-hour: the role of technology in reshaping business strategy at Rolls-Royce. Technology Analysis & Strategic Management, 25(8), 987–1007. https://doi.org/10.1080/09537325.2013.823147.
[6] Erol H., Friedl W. H. Der Rolls-Royce Ansatz für Lebenszykluskostenmodellierung von Triebwerken für den Geschäfts-, Kurz-und Mittelstreckenflugzeugmarkt. Deutsche Gesellschaft für Luft-und Raumfahrt-Lilienthal-Oberth eV, 2012.
[7] Hurdle T. Cost-Effective Intelligent Engine Health Monitoring for Naval Gas Turbines.Proc's of the ASME Turbo Expo 2007: Power for Land, Sea, and Air. Volume 1: Turbo Expo 2007. Montreal, Canada. May 14–17, 2007. pp. 937–945. ASME. https://doi.org/10.1115/GT2007-27507.
[8] Fricks R. B., Trivedi K. S. Automated life cycle processing for complex medical imaging devices, 2017 Annual Reliability and Maintainability Symposium (RAMS), Orlando, FL, USA, 2017, pp. 1–6. https://doi.org/10.1109/RAM.2017.7889693.
[9] Manshreck J. The Business Model. Transformation of the Electric Utility Business Model: From Edison to Musk, Berlin, Boston: De Gruyter, 2022, pp. 18–28. https://doi.org/10.1515/9783110714036-003 r
[10] Alt L. Photographic Equipment and Supplied, 38.6. Manufacturing: A Historiographical and Bibliographical Guide 1 (1990): 367.
[11] Broeders I. A. M. J., Ruurda J. (2001) Robotics revolutionizing surgery: the Intuitive Surgical 'Da Vinci' system, Industrial Robot, (28) 5, pp. 387–392.
[12] Collins S. What Does Intuitive Surgical's Business Model Look Like?. Market Realist. May 30, 2016. https://marketrealist.com/2016/05/intuitive-surgicals-business-model-look-like/.
[13] Ciuti, G., Menciassi, A., Dario, P. 2011. Capsule endoscopy: from current achievements to open challenges. IEEE Rev Biomed Eng 4, 59–72. https://doi.org/10.1109/RBME.2011.2171182.

[14] Barron S. P., Kennedy M. P. Single-Use (Disposable) Flexible Bronchoscopes: The Future of Bronchoscopy?. Adv Ther 37, 4538–4548 (2020). https://doi.org/10.1007/s12325-020-01495-8.

[15] Lindgardt Z., Hendren C. Using Business Model Innovation to Reinvent the Core https://www.bcg.com/publications/2014/growth-innovation-using-business-model-innovation-reinvent-core.

[16] Gisby S., Micca P., Kheyn-Kheyfets B., Chang C., Wagh M. New business models in health care: Building platform-enabled ecosystems. Deloitte Insights. February 24, 2022 https://www2.deloitte.com/content/dam/insights/articles/us165009_chs-health-care-ecosystem/DI_CHS-Health-care-ecosystem.pdf.

[17] Darnell D., Pullmann M. D., Hull T. D., Chen S., Areán P. Predictors of Disengagement and Symptom Improvement Among Adults With Depression Enrolled in Talkspace, a Technology-Mediated Psychotherapy Platform: Naturalistic Observational Study. JMIR Form Res 2022;6(6):e36521.

[18] Numata K., Tanaka T., Matsumoto J. A Case Study of Non-specialist Disease Management Using Teladoc Health Support: A Case Report. Cureus. 2024 May 16;16(5):e60401. https://doi.org/10.7759/cureus.60401. PMID: 38883039; PMCID: PMC11179123.

[19] Höhl R. Beinahe revolutionär: Patienten vereinbaren Arztbesuche online. DNP 17, 49–50 (2016). https://doi.org/10.1007/s15202-016-1446-0.

[20] Jiang H., Mi Z., Xu W. Online Medical Consultation Service-Oriented Recommendations: Systematic Review. J Med Internet Res. 2024 Jul 30;26:e46073. https://doi.org/10.2196/46073. PMID: 38777810; PMCID: PMC11322685.

[21] Kharat A. T., Safvi A., Thind S. S., Singh A. (2012). Cloud computing for radiologists. Indian J Radiology & Imaging, 22(03), 150–154.

[22] Du Y., Greuter M. J., Prokop M. W., de Bock G. H. (2023). Pricing and cost-saving potential for deep-learning computer-aided lung nodule detection software in CT lung cancer screening. Insights into Imaging, 14(1), 208.

[23] Kuppuswamy S. Radiology-as-a-Service: The future of medical imaging, Health & Social Care , January 17, 2020 https://www.openaccessgovernment.org/radiology-future-of-medical-imaging/80962/.

[24] Shazril M., Mashohcr S., Amran M. E., Hafiz M. F., Ali A. M., Naseri MSB. Assessment of IoT-Driven Predictive Maintenance Strategies for Computed Tomography Equipment: A Machine Learning Approach, in IEEE Access (2), pp. 195505–195515, 2024. https://doi.org/10.1109/ACCESS.2024.3518516.

[25] Jinglu Jiang, Ming Yang, Melody Kiang, Ann-Frances Cameron, Exploring the freemium business model for online medical consultation services in China, Information Processing & Management,Volume 58(3),2021, 102515, ISSN 0306–4573.

[26] Rosset A., Spadola L. & Ratib O. OsiriX: An Open-Source Software for Navigating in Multidimensional DICOM Images. J Digit Imaging 17, 205–216 (2004). https://doi.org/10.1007/s10278-004-1014-6.

[27] Benz M., Kuritcyn P., Kletzander R., Bruns V. (2024). Robust and Adaptive AI for Digital Pathology. In: Mutschler C., Münzenmayer C., Uhlmann N., Martin A. (eds.). Unlocking Artificial Intelligence. Springer, Cham. https://doi.org/10.1007/978-3-031-64832-8_12.

[28] https://www.imaios.com/en/imaios-dicom-viewer (last visited on Feb, 2nd, 2025).

[29] https://www.iis.fraunhofer.de/de/ff/sse/health/medical-image-analysis/mikaia.html (last visited on Feb, 2nd, 2025).

[30] Raemont N. Your next Apple Watch or smart ring could have a feature that transforms healthcare. ZDNET 2025 https://www.zdnet.com/article/your-next-apple-watch-or-smart-ring-could-have-a-feature-that-transforms-healthcare/.

[31] Masoumian Hosseini M., Masoumian Hosseini S.T., Qayumi K. et al. Smartwatches in healthcare medicine: assistance and monitoring; a scoping review. BMC Med Inform Decis Mak 23, 248 (2023). https://doi.org/10.1186/s12911-023-02350-w.

[32] https://www.gehealthcare.com/insights/article/optimizing-imaging-operations-in-radiology-with-subscription-software-solutions.

[33] Blackstone E. A., Fuhr J. P. Redefining Health Care: Creating Value-Based Competition on Results. Atl Econ J 35, 491–501 (2007). https://doi.org/10.1007/s11293-007-9091-9.

[34] Porter M. E., Larsson S., Lee T. H. Standardizing Patient Outcomes Measurement. N Engl J Med. 2016 Feb 11;374(6):504–6. https://doi.org/10.1056/NEJMp1511701. PMID: 26863351.

[35] Deerberg-Wittram J., Kirchberger V., Rüter F. (Hrsg.): Das Value-Based Health Care Buch. MWV Medizinisch Wissenschaftliche Verlagsgesellschaft 2023.

[36] Katz G. EIT Health, Implementing Value-Based Health Care in Europe: Handbook for Pioneers. 2020. https://eithealth.eu/wp-content/uploads/2020/05/Implementing-Value-Based-Healthcare-In-Europe_web-4.pdf.

[37] https://www.pflege.de/hilfsmittel/digitale-pflege-gesundheits-apps/.

[38] https://www.gkv-spitzenverband.de/.

[39] Twomey C., O'Reilly G., and Meyer B. Effectiveness of an individually-tailored computerised CBT programme (Deprexis) for depression: a meta-analysis. Psychiatry research 256 (2017): 371–377.

[40] Pezawas L. Evidenzbasierte digitale Depressionstherapie. Psychopraxis. Neuropraxis 27.1 (2024): 35–38.

[41] Atik E., Stricker J., Schückes M., Pittig A Efficacy of a Brief Blended Cognitive Behavioral Therapy Program for the Treatment of Depression and Anxiety in University Students: Uncontrolled Intervention Study JMIR Ment Health 2023;10:e44742. https://doi.org/10.2196/44742.

[42] Müller-Waldeck R., Nohl-Deryk P. HelloBetter ratiopharm chronischer Schmerz. (2022): 20–22.

[43] Topol E. Deep Medicine: How Artificial Intelligence Can Make Healthcare Human Again 2019New York, NY: Basic Books; 2019. ISBN: 9781541644632.

[44] Christensen C. M, Grossman J. H., Hwang J. The Innovator's Prescription: A Disruptive Solution for Health Care. McGraw-Hill, 2009.

[45] Castano-Villegas N., Villa M. C., Monsalve K., Llano I., Velásquez L., & Zea J. (2025). Arkangel AI, OpenEvidence, ChatGPT, Medisearch: are they objectively up to medical standards? A real-life assessment of LLMs in healthcare. medRxiv, 2025-0.

[46] Zaki J., Islam S. M. R., Alghamdi N. S., Abdullah-Al-Wadud M., Kwak K. S. Introducing Cloud-Assisted Micro-Service-Based Software Development Framework for Healthcare Systems, in IEEE Access, vol. 10, pp. 33332–33348, 2022. https://doi.org/10.1109/ACCESS.2022.3161455.

[47] Garbuio, MLin N. (2019). Artificial Intelligence as a Growth Engine for Health Care Start-ups: Emerging Business Models. California Management Review, 61(2), 59–83. https://doi.org/10.1177/0008125618811931.

[48] YounisR., Iqbal M., Munir K., Javed M. A., Haris M., Alahmari S. A Comprehensive Analysis of Cloud Service Models: IaaS, PaaS, and SaaS in the Context of Emerging Technologies and Trend, 2024 International Conference on Electrical, Communication and Computer Engineering (ICECCE), Kuala Lumpur, Malaysia, 2024, pp. 1–6. https://doi.org/10.1109/ICECCE63537.2024.10823401.

[49] Satyanarayanan M. The Role of Cloud Computing in Medical Imaging: A Case Study with Zebra Medical Vision, IEEE Internet Computing, vol. 21, no. 5, pp. 50–57, 2017.

[50] Wittenberg T., Lang T., Eixelberger T., Gruber R. (2024). Acquisition of Semantics for Machine-Learning and Deep-Learning based Applications. In: Mutschler C, Münzenmayer C, Uhlmann N, Martin A. (eds). Unlocking Artificial Intelligence. Springer, Cham. https://doi.org/10.1007/978-3-031-64832-8_8.

[51] Oppelt M. P. Foltyn A., Deuschel J., Lang-Richter N. Holzer N., Eskofier B. M., Yang S. H. ADABase: A Multimodal Dataset for Cognitive Load Estimation. Sensors 2023, 23, 340. https://doi.org/10.3390/s23010340.

[52] Terzo O., Ruiu P., Bucci E., Xhafa F. Data as a Service (DaaS) for Sharing and Processing of Large Data Collections in the Cloud, 2013 Seventh International Conference on Complex, Intelligent, and Software Intensive Systems, Taichung, Taiwan, 2013, pp. 475–480. https://doi.org/10.1109/CISIS.2013.87.

[53] Cedillo P., Valdez W., Cárdenas-Delgado P., Prado-Cabrera D. (2020). A Data as a Service Metamodel for Managing Information of Healthcare and Internet of Things Applications. In: Rodriguez Morales, G.,

Fonseca C, Salgado ER, Pérez-Gosende JP, Orellana Cordero P, Berrezueta M. (eds.). Information and Communication Technologies. TICEC 2020. Communications in Computer and Information Science, vol 1307. Springer, Cham. https://doi.org/10.1007/978-3-030-62833-8_21.

[54] Hendolin M. (2022). Towards the European health data space: from diversity to a common framework. Eurohealth, 27(2), 15–17.

[55] Bhirud N. S., Tataale S., Randive S., Nahar S. A Literature Review on Chatbots in HealthCare Domain. Int. J. Scientific & Technology Research, 2019 (8), 225–231, https://api.semanticscholar.org/CorpusID:203120847.

[56] Wang W. & Siau K. (2018). Trust in health chatbots. Proc's International Conference on Information.

[57] https://florence.chat/.

[58] Gupta J., Singh V., Kumar I. Florence- A Health Care Chatbot, 2021 7th International Conference on Advanced Computing and Communication Systems (ICACCS), Coimbatore, India, 2021, pp. 504–508. https://doi.org/10.1109/ICACCS51430.2021.9442006.

[59] Khadija A., Zahra F. F., Naceur A., 2021. AI-Powered Health Chatbots: Toward a general architecture. Procedia Computer Science 191, 355–360. https://doi.org/10.1016/j.procs.2021.07.048.

[60] Ciesla R. The Book of Chatbots– From ELIZA to ChatGPT. Springer 2024. https://doi.org/10.1007/978-3-031-51004-5.

[61] Jungmann S. M., Klan T., Kuhn S. Jungmann F. Accuracy of a Chatbot (Ada) in the Diagnosis of Mental Disorders: Comparative Case Study With Lay and Expert Users. JMIR Form Res 2019;3(4):e13863doi: 10.2196/13863.

[62] Radic M., Busch-Casler J., Vosen A. et al. Data sovereignty requirements for patient-oriented AI-driven clinical research in Germany. *Ethik Med* **36**, 547–562 (2024). https://doi.org/10.1007/s00481-024-00827-4

[63] Mühlhoff R. Das Risiko der Sekundärnutzung trainierter Modelle als zentrales Problem von Datenschutz und KI-Regulierung im Medizinbereich. In Ruschemeier & Steinrötter (Eds.). Der Einsatz von KI & Robotik in der Medizin. Interdisziplinäre Fragen. pp. 27–52. Datenrecht und neue Technologien 8. Baden-Baden: Nomos, 2024.

[64] Crawford K. *Atlas of AI*: Power, Politics, and the Planetary Costs of Artificial Intelligence, New Haven: Yale University Press, 2021. https://doi.org/10.12987/9780300252392.

Notes on contributors

Prof. Dr. theol. habil. Arne Manzeschke

Since 2015, Arne Manzeschke has been Professor of Ethics and Anthropology at the Lutheran University of Applied Sciences Nuremberg (EVHN), focusing on human-technology interaction, the digitalization of life worlds, and the methodology of integrated research. Numerous national and international research projects and workshops give concrete form to the demand for interdisciplinary and transdisciplinary research and development, which are continuously further developed in scientific contributions on individual aspects, models, and methods. – Since 2020, he has headed the Institute for Nursing Research, Gerontology and Ethics (IPGE) and the Ethics Commission for Nursing and Social Research at EVHN. Since 2015, he has been deputy chairman of the Ethics Commission for Preimplantation Genetic Diagnosis (PGD) in Bavaria, since 2020 spokesman for the Committee on Medical Technology and Society in the German Society for Biomedical Engineering (DGBMT), and president of Societas Ethica (European Research Society for Ethics) from 2018 to 2021.

Email: arne.manzeschke@evhn.de
Homepage: https://mensch-maschine-relationen.de/

Priv.-Doz. Dr. Ing. habil. Thomas Wittenberg

is Chief Scientist and Research Manager for Biomedical Engineering and Artificial Intelligence in the Department for Digital Health and Analytics at the Fraunhofer Institute for Integrated Circuits IIS in Erlangen, as well as Associate Professor (PD) and head of the research group "Visual Healthcare Computing" at the Chair for Visual Computing of the Friedrich-Alexander-University Erlangen-Nuremberg (FAU). He is in the scientific boards of the German Society of Computer & Robot-Assisted Surgery (CURAC) as well as the German Society for Biomedical Engineering (DGBMT) and is co-heading the DGBMT working group for optical imaging & endoscopy. – He studied computer science and biomedical engineering at the Christopher Newport University in Newport News, VA, USA and the FAU, and obtained his PhD and Habilitation at the FAU. Between 2007 and 2011 he was visiting scientist at the NSF Engineering Research Center for Computer-Integrated Surgical Systems and Technology of The Johns-Hopkins University, Baltimore MD, USA. He has been PI in many public funded research projects and is author and co-author of more than 300 publications in journals, books, monographs, and conference papers.

Email: thomas.wittenberg@iis.fraunhofer.de
ORCID: https://orcid.org/0000-0003-0840-8695

Dr. Ana Álvarez-Mena

is a postdoctoral researcher at the French National Centre for Scientific Research (CNRS). Since 2024, she has been at the Institute of Chemistry and Biology of Membranes and Nano-objects (CBMN) in Bordeaux, where she specializes in structural biophysics, using NMR spectroscopy to study the interplay between membrane proteins and lipid membranes, examining both lipid behavior and protein structure at the atomic level. She obtained her Biochemistry degree in 2017 and her PhD in 2023 at the University of Málaga, Spain, with research focused on molecular and cellular microbiology. Recently, she was awarded a Marie Skłodowska-Curie Actions (MSCA) postdoctoral fellowship to continue her research.

Email: a.alvarez-mena@iecb.u-bordeaux.fr

Dr. phil. Galia Assadi

studied social pedagogy and sociology and earned her doctorate in philosophy on the topic of responsibility at LMU Munich. After working in the fields of business ethics and medical ethics, she has spent the last few years researching ethical and anthropological aspects of human-technology interaction and developing tools for the ethically responsible design of digitalization in healthcare. She is currently working at the Evangelische Hochschule Nürnberg as a research assistant and is involved in ethical and anthropological support of projects in the field of human-machine interaction.

Email: galia.assadi@evhn.de

Prof. Dr. Christian Djeffal

is Professor of Law, Innovation and Legal Design at the Technical University of Munich (TUM), focusing on the intersection of law and technology, particularly artificial intelligence. His research encompasses interdisciplinary and transdisciplinary legal approaches like legal design, examining how law can shape and be shaped by emerging technologies, with an emphasis on democracy, human rights, and the rule of law in the digital age. Since 2025, he has served as Director of the Center for Responsible AI Technologies (CReAITech) at TUM. Since 2019, he has been a board member of the National E-Government Competence Center (NEGZ), where he chairs the Committee for Research and Projects. He was previously head of the research area "Global Constitutionalism and the Internet" at the Alexander von Humboldt Institute for Internet and Society from 2016 to 2019. Christian Djeffal received his doctorate in international law from Humboldt University of Berlin with his dissertation "Static and Evolutive Treaty Interpretation: A Functional Reconstruction," which was published by Cambridge University Press in 2016.

Email: christian.djeffal@tum.de
Homepage: www.sts.sot.tum.de/en/sts/people/professors/prof-dr-christian-djeffal

Prof. em. Dr. Olaf Dössel

is Professor at the Institute of Biomedical Engineering at Karlsruhe Institute of Technology (KIT) since 1996, he is retired now since 2023. Before he was head of a research department at Philips Research Laboratories in Hamburg. He is member of several academic societies, among them: the Academy of Science of Berlin-Brandenburg (BBAW), the German Academy of Technical Sciences (acatech), the North Rhine-Westphalian Academy of Sciences, Humanities and the Arts. He was member of the advisory board of the Physikalisch Technische Bundesanstalt (the German Metrology Institute). He is Fellow of the International Union for Physical and Engineering Sciences in Medicine (IUPESM), the International Academy for Medical and Biological Engineering (IAMBE), the European Alliance of Medical and Biological Engineering and Science (EAMBES) and Fellow of Deutsche Gesellschaft für Biomedizinische Technik (DGBMT im VDE). He was Editor in Chief of the Journal Biomedical Engineering / Biomedizinische Technik for many years. And he was member of the board of Computing in Cardiology CinC. His main interests are bioelectric signals, computer modeling of the heart, the inverse problem of Electrocardiography, ECG biosignal processing, and new methods of medical imaging.

Email: olaf.doessel@kit.edu
Homepage: www.ibt.kit.edu/english/doessel.php

Prof. Dr. Daniel Flemming

is a professor of informatics and information technology in nursing and social work at the Catholic University of Applied Sciences in Munich (KSH) and currently teaches and conducts research at KSH on digitalization in healthcare and the use of robotic systems in nursing. – Since 2023, Daniel Flemming has taken on the role of scientific director at atacama blooms GmbH & Co. KG in addition to his professorship, where he is involved in the further development of the nursing knowledge corpus, i.e., the apenio® nursing classification and (evidence-based) regulations, as well as the use of artificial intelligence in nursing. – He represents German nursing informatics in international working groups and is currently a member of the board of HL7 Germany and the expert commission on digitalization in nursing of the German Nursing Council (Deutscher Pflegerat e.V.).

Email: daniel.flemming@ksh-m.de

Simon Fonck

studied computer science at RWTH Aachen University, where he subsequently began a doctoral position at the Embedded Software Lab. Here, he worked on various research projects and teaching assignments. In his research in the field of medical informatics, he focused in particular on the use of AI for intensive care units. His work focused on data analysis, data quality, the development of AI methods, and explainable AI. At the time of this book's publication, Simon is coming to the end of his doctoral studies. He is also a member of the AUTOMED technical committee.

Email: fonck@embedded.rwth-aachen.de

Prof. Dr. iur. Ulrich M. Gassner, Mag. rer. publ., M.Jur. (Oxon.)

is the founder and Executive Director of the Institute of Medical Device Law at the Faculty of Law, University of Augsburg. He also lectures in the postgraduate program "Pharmaceutical Law" at the Faculty of Law, Philipps University Marburg. Since 2023, he has been a partner at the law firm Ratajzak & Partners, where he advises both public and private clients on a wide range of health law matters. Professor Gassner has authored more than 300 publications, including a leading commentary on medical device law and numerous articles on the intersection of the Medical Device Regulation (MDR)/In Vitro Diagnostic Medical Devices Regulation (IVDR) and the Artificial Intelligence Act (AIA). He studied law at the Universities of Tübingen and Oxford, and administrative sciences at the German University of Administrative Sciences in Speyer. He earned both his PhD and Habilitation from the University of Tübingen.

Email: ulrich.gassner@uni-a.de, gassner@rpmed.de

Dr.-Ing. Patrick Gebhard

a DFKI Research Fellow and Principal Researcher in the COS department (Saarbrücken), has been leading the Affective Computing Group there since 2007. His work is centered on developing computational models of affect and social behavior for socially interactive agents. Notably, he created the ALMA model of emotions, moods, and personality, and has made significant contributions to empathy/trust mechanisms in human-AI interaction. Gebhard and his group have created frameworks and tools, such as Visual SceneMaker, which are widely used to build and evaluate socially interactive agents. These tools and computational models of affect have been applied in numerous national and EU projects across healthcare, education, and HRI, where this collaborative approach has been instrumental in enhancing trustworthiness and effectiveness. His overarching research goal is to imbue interactive systems with human-like emotional intelligence through robust user and social-emotion models that also include internal regulative processes.

Email: patrick.gebhard@dfki.de

PD Dr. Bruno Gransche

is a philosopher and futures studies scholar with a focus on emerging human-technology relationships, particularly in the areas of digitalization, AI, socio-active systems, innovation and responsibility, and modal shaping of futures. His academic profile includes philosophy of technology, ethics, and anticipatory thinking, which he teaches at various universities and research internationally. – Gransche has been an Associate Professor (PD) and Principal Investigator at the Institute of Technology Futures ITZ at the University of Karlsruhe KIT since 2020; he worked, studied, and completed his doctorate and habilitation at the universities of Heidelberg, Bologna (IT), Siegen, and Karlsruhe. He is a Fellow at the Fraunhofer Institute for Systems and Innovation Research ISI, where he worked in applied research in Futures Studies and Foresight until 2016. Gransche is involved in numerous academic and socio-political committees and is active as a speaker and consultant. His involvement extends beyond academia into politics and business, for example via his "Transformative Philosophy" consultancy program for decision-makers in industry.

Email: bruno.gransche@kit.edu

Dr. habil. Birgit Habenstein

is a research director at the French National Centre for Scientific Research (CNRS). She leads a scientific team at the Institute of Chemistry and Biology of Membranes and Nano-objects in Bordeaux. After her studies at the University of Berlin and her PhD diploma in 2011 at the University of Lyon, she performed her research at the ETH in Zürich and the MPI in Göttingen. In 2014, she joined the CNRS to start her independent research with a two-year break from 2020–2022, to take over the position as director of the German Society for Biomedical Engineering (DGBMT) in Frankfurt. Her team focuses on advanced experimental biophysics, mainly NMR, supported by computational methods, to understand physicochemical mechanisms in biomolecular processes.

Email: b.habenstein@cbmn.u-bordeaux.fr

Prof. Dr. Jannis Hagenah

is Associate Professor for Digital and Robotic Surgery at the University Medical Center Göttingen, where he is head of the Center for Digital Surgery. Additionally, he is an affiliated researcher at Fraunhofer IMTE on Surgical Data Science. – He has held postdoctoral positions at the University of Oxford and Fraunhofer IMTE and completed his doctoral degree at the University of Lübeck under the supervision of Prof. Floris Ernst. He holds a M.Sc. and B.Sc. in Medical Engineering Sciences, both from University of Lübeck, and serves in the board of the Medical Imaging with Deep Learning (MIDL) society, the German chapter of IEEE Engineering Medicine and Biology (EMBS) as well as the working group Medical Robotics within the German Society for Biomedical Engineering (DGBMT).

Email: jannis.hagenah@med.uni-goettingen.de

Prof. Dr. habil. Barbara Hammer

is a full Professor for Machine Learning at the Research Center for Cognitive Interaction Technologies (CITEC) at Bielefeld University, Germany, focusing on research and innovation of machine learning methods which can reliably work with limited data and under realistic conditions by means of hybrid approaches, physics-informed models, or neuro-symbolic approaches. In doing so, she embraces the multi-faceted requirements posed by a human-centered design, such as explainability, safety, and fairness, and the opportunities offered for relevant applications such as critical infrastructure, engineering challenges, or biomedical data analysis. – She received her PhD in Computer Science in 1999 and her venia legendi in 2003, both from the University of Osnabrück, Germany, where she was head of an independent research group on the topic 'Learning with Neural Methods on Structured Data'. Several research stays led her to Rutgers University, University of Birmingham, Universities of Pisa and Padova, University of Paris, and CAIR Bangalore. She was chair of the IEEE CIS Technical Committee on Data Mining and Big Data Analytics, the IEEE CIS Technical Committee on Neural Networks, and the IEEE CIS Distinguished Lecturer Committee, and member of the IEEE CIS Administrative Committee and the INNS Board. Currently, she is member of the Scientific Directorate Schloss Dagstuhl and deputy spokesperson for the section Computer Science of the German Research Foundation. In 2020, she received an ERC Synergy Grant (Smart Water Futures) as one of four PIs. She has been elected as member of Academia Europaea in 2024.

Email: bhammer@techfak.uni-bielefeld.de
Homepage: https://hammer-lab.techfak.uni-bielefeld.de/

Prof. Dr. Maria Henke

is a Professor for Interactive Mechatronics in Biomedical Engineering at the Technical University of Applied Sciences Mittelhessen in Gießen (THM) since 2024. Previously, she held a postdoctoral position at the University of Lübeck at the Institute for Robotics and Cognitive Systems and worked in the Regulatory Affairs and Quality Management department at Siemens Healthineers headquarters in Erlangen. – She completed a Diploma in Electrical Engineering with a focus on Biomedical Device Technology at Technische Universität Dresden in 2004, with the diploma thesis carried out at the Ruhr University Bochum at the institute of Prof. Helmut Ermert. She then pursued a PhD at Friedrich-Alexander-University Erlangen-Nuremberg (FAU), at the Institute of Medical Physics led by Prof. Willi Kalender. Additionally, she holds a Master's in Vocational Education. – Her research and teaching focus on Medical Robotics and the application of Medical Device Regulations. Since the founding of the committee, she has served as the deputy spokesperson in the Medical Robotics committee of the German Society for Biomedical Engineering (DGBMT).

Email: maria.henke@lse.thm.de
LinkedIn: www.linkedin.com/in/maria-henke-687b718/

Prof. Dr. Tanja Henking, LL.M. (Medical Law)

Since 2015 Tanja Henking has been Professor of Health Law, Medical Law, and Criminal Law at the Technical University of Würzburg-Schweinfurt. Since 2019, she has headed the Institute for Applied Social Sciences (IFAS), which was founded in the same year. – From 2012 to 2015, she was head of the junior research group "Ethics and Law of Modern Medicine" at the Institute for Medical Ethics and History of Medicine at the Ruhr University Bochum. Before that she worked for over seven years at the University of Bremen, where she had also studied law. She started out as a research assistant at the Chair of Criminal Law and Criminal Procedure at the University of Bremen, then became a lecturer and finally a substitute professor for criminal law. In addition to her work at the university, she also has practical experience as a lawyer and specialized lawyer for medical law. – Her research focuses on legal and ethical issues at the beginning and end of life, the use of artificial intelligence in medicine, and patient rights, particularly the rights of patients with mental disorders and the issue of coercive measures. She has published around 100 articles. – Prof. Dr. Henking is member of the Central Ethics Committee at the German Medical Association (ZEKO), member of the "Ethics and Law" commission of the DGPPN, a member of the "Ethics" project group of the DKG, chair of the board of the Mainfranken e.V. outpatient ethics network, and member of the board of the Academy for Ethics in Medicine (AEM).

Email: tanja.henking@thws.de

Julia Kämmer, M.A.

is a research associate at the "Kompetenzzentrum Zukunft Alter" at the Catholic University of Applied Sciences in Munich, where her research focuses on assistive robotics in elderly care from a nursing science perspective. Drawing on her background in intensive care nursing, she leverages both practical and scientific expertise for her research. She applies participatory research methods to ensure that the needs of end users are systematically incorporated into the development of technology, and she collaborates closely with interdisciplinary teams to integrate multiple perspectives and develop comprehensive, user-centered solutions.

Email: julia.kaemmer@ksh-m.de

Dr. Stefan T. Kamin

is Senior Scientist and Deputy Head of the Human Centered Innovation Group at the Fraunhofer Institute for Integrated Circuits IIS. He specializes in aging research and Human-AI interactions across the human lifespan, coordinating the competence pillar HUMAN AI at the ADA Lovelace Center for Analytics, Data, and Applications. His research explores the impact of digital innovations throughout life, focusing on the intersection of digitalization processes and the human factor to understand how digital innovations can enhance health and social participation. Stefan has extensive experience leading user-centered research and development projects, identifying requirements of diverse user groups for digital innovations, and deriving suitable technical solutions. His work is characterized by interdisciplinary collaborations and focuses on individual conditions necessary for the acceptance of digital innovations. He studied Gerontology at the University of Vechta and Friedrich-Alexander-University Erlangen-Nuremberg, where he obtained his PhD in Psychogerontology.

Email: stefan.kamin@iis.fraunhofer.de

Dr. Franziska Klatt

is leading the Teaching Library and Public Relations at the Economics and Management Library at Technische Universität Berlin, where she plays a pivotal role in advancing information literacy. Her work focuses on the integration of AI tools into academic research and education, and she has developed a wide range of workshops, guidelines, and online learning programs for students, researchers, and information professionals. She studied Business Administration and earned her PhD with a dissertation on cultural factors influencing consumer behavior in the adoption of innovations.

Email: franziska.klatt@tu-berlin.de

Prof. Dr.-Ing. Jörn Kohlhammer

is head of the Competence Center for Information Visualization and Visual Analytics and honorary professor at TU Darmstadt. His team develops innovative visualization solutions for several industry sectors, including visual business analytics, medical data analysis of electronic health records, decision support in the public sector, and visualization for cyber-security. Jörn is co-author of more than 60 publications in journals and books, and of monographs and conference papers. He is Associate Editor at the IEEE Transactions of Visualization and Computer Graphics, and regular member of program committees for conferences like IEEE VAST and EuroVis. His research interests include decision-centered information visualization based on semantics, and visual business analytics. Jörn is member of IEEE and the Gesellschaft für Informatik (GI) and represents Fraunhofer in the TDWI. – Jörn Kohlhammer studied computer science with a minor in business administration at the Ludwig-Maximilian University in Munich, Germany. After that he received his diploma in 1999, he worked as a research scientist at the Fraunhofer Center for Research in Computer Graphics (CRCG) in Providence, RI, USA until 2003. In 2004 he joined Fraunhofer IGD in Darmstadt, Germany to finish his PhD on decision-centered visualization in 2005. In 2015, he received an honorary professorship for user-centered visual analytics at TU Darmstadt.

Email: joern.kohlhammer@igd.fraunhofer.de
Homepage: www.igd.fraunhofer.de/de/institut/mitarbeitende/joern-kohlhammer.html

Prof. Dr. Marc Kraft

has been head of the Medical Technology department at the Technical University of Berlin since 2004. He completed his first degree at the Officer Training College for Military Pilots in Bautzen in 1989 and was then deployed as a fighter pilot in Neubrandenburg. He then completed in 1994 a second degree in mechanical engineering, followed by a position as a research assistant at the Technical University of Berlin. After obtaining his doctorate in 1999, he spent five years working in industry as head of development at Vanguard AG, Berlin, and technology project manager at Otto Bock HealthCare GmbH, Duderstadt. – Prof. Kraft is spokesperson for the Technical Committee on Education and Training at the German Society for Biomedical Engineering. At the VDI, he is chairman of the advisory board for the medical technology division and heads or works in various VDI guidelines committees. Prof. Kraft advises various medical technology companies and industry associations and is active as an expert and supervisory board member. He has received various awards and prizes, including the Science Prize of the Officer Academy for Military Pilots in Bautzen, the Erwin Stephan Award of the Technical University of Berlin, and the Prize of the DGBMT and the Klee Family Foundation.

Email: marc.kraft@tu-berlin.de

Prof. Dr.-Ing. Massimo Kubon

is a medical engineer and earned his PhD in Microsystems Engineering in 2012 at the University of Freiburg (IMTEK). His early research interests included biomechanics, organ-on-chip systems, and implantable sensors, which were recognized by the Klee Award (2nd place, DGBMT) and the Science2Start Award (1st place, BioRegioStern, BW). He then worked in the medical industry for more than ten years in various engineering and management roles, where he developed, patented and registered 2D/3D visualization systems for minimal-invasive and robotic-assisted surgery with market leading international OEM customers. Since 2022, MK has held a professorship in Medical Engineering at Hochschule Furtwangen University (HFU). His research and teaching focus is on digital operating room and sports medicine technologies, with a strong emphasis on applied AI for robotic control. Prof. Kubon is an active member of the German Society for Biomedical Engineering (DGBMT) for more than 15 years and, since 2023, deputy founding board member of its "Medical Robotics" working group.

Email: massimo.kubon@hs-furtwangen.de
LinkedIn: www.linkedin.com/in/massimokubon/

Dr. rer. nat. Nadine Lang-Richter

completed her studies of Physics in Erlangen in 2010 and received a PhD in biophysics in 2014 from the biophysics department of the Friedrich-Alexander-University in Erlangen-Nurnberg. – Since 2015 Dr Lang-Richter has been a fellow of the Fraunhofer Institute for Integrated Circuits IIS in Erlangen, working as a chief scientist in the field of biosignal analysis and subject studies. Since 2021, she has been head of the Fraunhofer IIS research group medical data analysis, working on AI based interpretation of multimodal clinical and biophysical data.

Email: nadine.lang-richter@iis.fraunhofer.de

Prof. Dr. theol. Andreas Lob-Hüdepohl

Since 1996, Andreas Lob-Hüdepohl has been Professor of Theological Ethics at the Catholic University of Applied Social Sciences in Berlin, which he headed as president between 1997 and 2009. His research and teaching focus on social work ethics, bioethics, medical ethics, and environmental ethics. He also deals with the rise of right-wing populism and right-wing authoritarianism in mainstream society – especially in the Catholic Church. He has been a member and advisor to various committees and institutions of the Catholic Church in Germany for 30 years. Since 2016, he has been director of the Berlin Institute for Christian Ethics and Politics (ICEP), which provides political ethics consulting as a political ideas agency. – From 2016 to 2024, he was a member of the German Ethics Council, to which he was elected twice by the German Bundestag. There, he was involved in the preparation of numerous statements, including the comprehensive statements "Big data in healthcare," "Interventions in the human germ line," and "Man and machine – challenges posed by artificial intelligence."

Email: andreas.lob-huedepohl@khsb-berlin.de

Priv.-Doz. Dr.-Ing. Axel Loewe

heads the Computational Cardiac Modeling Group at Karlsruhe Institute of Technology with a focus on cardiac electrophysiology and biomechanics. His group is committed to method development and the application of computational models to answer questions of clinical relevance at the intersection of engineering, computer science, and medicine. To develop methods and conduct simulation studies, methods of software engineering, algorithmics, numerics, signal processing, data analysis, and machine learning are used. The synergy between artificial intelligence and mechanistic computer models have become a primary focus of Axel Loewe's research in recent years. He has a track record of fruitful collaboration with leading clinicians to optimize diagnosis and therapy of cardiac diseases.

Email: axel.loewe@kit.edu
Homepage: ibt.kit.edu/english/loewe.php

Prof. Dr. Klaus Mainzer

studied mathematics, physics, and philosophy, doctorate and habilitation, assistant at the University of Münster; Heisenberg scholarship; professor for foundations of exact sciences, dean and prorector of the University of Constance; chair for philosophy of science, dean, director of the Institute of Philosophy and founding director of the Institute of Interdisciplinary Informatics at the University of Augsburg; chair for philosophy of science and technology, director of the Carl von Linde-Academy and founding director of the Munich Center for Technology in Society (MCTS), since 2016 Emeritus of Excellence at the Technical University of Munich; co-founder and senior professor at the Carl Friedrich von Weizsäcker Center of the University of Tübingen; member of Academia Europaea (London), European Academy of Sciences and Arts (Salzburg, since 2020 President, re-election 2025), National Academy of Science and Engineering (acatech) in Berlin/Munich et al. – Main research: Epistemology and foundations of mathematical sciences, complex systems and AI, future of the technological world. Guest professor and international author of numerous books.

Email: mainzer@tum.de

Dr.-Ing. Ute Morgenstern

is a German biomedical engineer who worked in teaching and research at Technische Universität Dresden until her retirement in 2020. She studied Technical Cybernetics and Biomedical Engineering at TH Ilmenau and earned her doctorate on modeling human ventilation mechanics. She served as assistant professor at TU Dresden's Institute of Biomedical Engineering, where she taught biomedical modeling and simulation, pacemaker technology, mechanical ventilation, and medical imaging. She led research groups in some fields of biomedical engineering, mainly in intraoperative optical and hyperspectral imaging in neurosurgery, in cooperation with clinical and industrial partners. She has published widely, supervised numerous theses, and has been active in the German Society for Biomedical Engineering (DGBMT), education initiatives, and expert committees. Together with colleagues, she co-edits the 12-volume textbook series *Biomedizinische Technik*, launched by De Gruyter in 2014 and now being published as open access edition by Berlin Universities Publishing.

Email: ute.morgenstern@tu-dresden.de

Dr. rer. nat. Christian Münzenmayer, MBA

received the M.Sc. degree in computational engineering from the Friedrich-Alexander University Erlangen-Nuremberg, holds a PhD in Computer Science from the University of Koblenz-Landau and an MBA in General Management from FOM University of Applied Sciences. Since 2000, he is with the Fraunhofer Institute for Integrated Circuits IIS, Erlangen where he started as a research associate. Since 2008 he headed the Medical Image Processing group and coordinated all activities in the business field Digital Pathology and Computational Microscopy. In his current position as head of the Digital Health & Analytics department at Fraunhofer IIS he is also part of the management team of the Smart Sensing and Electronics division.

Email: christian.muenzenmayer@iis.fraunhofer.de
Homepage: www.iis.fraunhofer.de/health

Prof. Dr. rer. nat. habil. Peter P. Pott

is full professor and director of the Institute of Medical Device Technology at Stuttgart University in Germany. Before that he was scientific director at the Institute of Electromechanical Design at Technische Universität Darmstadt, Germany, where he finished his habilitation in Mechatronics in 2015. In between these two positions he spent one year at Leica Microsystems (Mannheim, Germany) developing sophisticated confocal microscopes. – He received his Dr. rer. nat. (PhD) in automatic control in 2008 from the University of Mannheim while working as a research assistant at the Laboratory for Biomechanics and Experimental Orthopedics at the University Medical Center in Mannheim, Germany. In 2000 he received his Dipl.-Ing. degree in mechanical engineering from Mannheim University of Applied Sciences. – During the last years he focused on the field of medical robotics for orthopedic, visceral surgery, and rehabilitation. He also has particular interest in robotics, vibration control, and piezoelectric actuation principles. In recent time topics also include biomimetic actuation and Design 4 Circularity.

Email: peter.pott@imt.uni-stuttgart.de
Homepage: www.imt.uni-stuttgart.de

Prof. Dr. Steffen K. Rosahl

became Professor of Neurosurgery at the University of Freiburg, Germany in 2005 and was appointed Chairman of the Department of Neurosurgery at Helios Erfurt in 2006. A neurophysiologist and neurosurgeon by training, he has been associated with several medical and research centers including the Center for Neuroscience at the University of California Davis (1992–1993), the International Neuroscience Institute Hannover (2000–2003), and the University of Freiburg, Germany (2003–2006). – Steffen K. Rosahl is co-chairman of the task force on neural prosthetics in the Initiative for Micromedicine of the German Association of Electrical Engineers (VDE). As faculty member of the European Academy for consequences of scientific and technological advances Bad Neuenahr-Ahrweiler GmbH he has co-authored a volume on "Interventions in the brain – Changing psyche and society". – Since 2020 he is Speaker of the Commission on Digitalization of the German Society of Neurosurgery (DGNC). In 2022, he contributed to TedxHHL "The science of vibes" with a talk on "Changing minds: Plugging electrodes into our brains".

Email: steffen.rosahl@helios-gesundheit.de
ORCID-ID: https://orcid.org/0000-0002-0589-618X

Prof. Dr. rer. pol. Stephanie M. H. Schmitt-Rüth

Since October 2023, Stephanie Schmitt-Rüth has been Professor of Work Environments and Transformation Psychology at the Ostbayerische Technische Hochschule Amberg-Weiden, where she also co-founded the Institute of Psychology & Behavioral Science. Previously, she held long-standing disciplinary leadership responsibilities and project management roles at the Fraunhofer Institute for Integrated Circuits IIS. Her research focuses on integrating the human factor into life and work contexts, with particular emphasis on accompanying people during technology-driven change. A central emphasis lies on human-technology and AI interaction, addressing key themes such as technology acceptance and acceptability as well as socio-ethical principles. She also emphasizes the importance of critical reflection on technology's dual role in both empowering and challenging people, actively employing adaptive strategies and evidence-based coaching to foster psychological safety and a constructive approach to transformation. Her work encourages individuals and organizations to view change as an impetus for personal growth, effective collaboration, and innovative development.

Email: s.schmitt-rueth@oth-aw.de

Prof. Dr.-Ing. Thomas Schmitt

leads the Medical Engineering degree program at the Cooperative State University of Saxony in Bautzen (former Berufsakademie Sachsen) where he has been teaching as a lecturer since 2007. He studied Electrical Engineering at the Dresden University of Technology, where he obtained the diploma and doctorate degrees in Biomedical Engineering. Between 2001 and 2007 he worked as project manager in a Dresden start-up company on autostereoscopic visualization of medical images. – Since 2007 he has been a member of the working group initial and continuing education of the German Society for Biomedical Engineering (DGBMT).

Email: thomas.schmitt@dhsn.de
Homepage: www.dhsn.de/studienangebot/detail/medizintechnik

Dr. Tanja Schneeberger

Since 2015, Tanja Schneeberger has been a researcher with a background in psychology in the Affective Computing Group at the German Research Center for Artificial Intelligence, focusing on human-agent interaction and computational emotion modeling in the fields of health, social training, and mobility. In 2025, she joined the University of Europe for Applied Sciences as a professor for psychology.

Email: tanja.schneeberger@dfki.de

Prof. Dr.-Ing. Karsten Seidl

is Professor for Micro and Nano Systems for Medical Technology at the University of Duisburg-Essen and Head of the Business Unit Health at the Fraunhofer-Institute for Microelectronic Circuits and Systems (IMS) in Duisburg. His research focuses on smart sensor systems for medical implants, wearables, and precision medicine. He received the Dr.-Ing. Degree from the University of Freiburg / IMTEK in the field of neurotechnology. He holds a diploma degree in Electrical Engineering and Information Technology with the focus on Biomedical Engineering from the Ilmenau University of Technology. He was a Research Scholar at the NSF Engineering Center for Computer-Integrated Surgical Systems and Technology at The Johns Hopkins University (Baltimore, USA) in 2004–2005. He was working in the field of molecular diagnostics with Robert Bosch GmbH and Bosch Healthcare (BHCS) GmbH from 2012 to 2018. Karsten Seidl is the chairman of the executive board of the German Society for Biomedical Engineering (DGBMT).

Email: karsten.seidl@ims.fraunhofer.de

PD Dr. phil. Rudolf Seising

Since 2018 Rudolf Seising is with the Research Institute for the History of Technology and Science at the Deutsches Museum. After studies in mathematics, physics, and philosophy at Ruhr University Bochum (RUB) he received his doctorate in philosophy of science in 1996 and completed his habilitation in the history of natural sciences at Ludwig Maximilian University in Munich in 2004. From 1986 to 1988, he was a research assistant at the Faculty of Philosophy, Education, and Journalism at RUB; from 1988 to 1995, he was a research assistant at the Faculty of Computer Science at the University of the Federal Armed Forces (UniBw) in Munich; from 1995 to 2002, he was a university assistant for the history of science at the Faculty of Social Sciences at UniBw Munich; 2002–2003 University Assistant at the University of Vienna and 2003–2008 at the Medical University of Vienna; Substitute Professor for History of Natural Sciences at Friedrich Schiller University Jena in 2008, 2009–2010, 2014–2017 and at LMU Munich for History of Science in 2010; Visiting Researcher (2009–2010) then Adjoint Researcher (2011–2014) at the European Centre for Soft Computing in Mieres (Spain); 2017–2023: Head of the BMBF project "IGGI – Engineering Spirit and Spirit Engineers: A History of Artificial Intelligence in the Federal Republic of Germany"; since 2024 Head of the project "Artificial Vision at Work" in the DFG priority program "Digitization of the Working World."

Email: r.seising@deutsches-museum.de
Homepage: www.deutsches-museum.de/forschung/person/rudolf-seising-2

Prof. Dr. phil. Stefan Selke

teaches "Sociology and Societal Change" at Furtwangen University (HFU). He is also a research professor for "Transformative and Public Science" and founder of the "Public Science Lab." There, innovative methods for forward-looking dialogues between science and society are developed and tested (e.g., Public Vision Assessments). – Selke first studied aerospace engineering and later earned his doctorate in sociology. As a cross-disciplinary scholar and public scientist, he is a regular speaker, author, and media commentator, even outside the realm of science (TV, radio, newspapers, magazines, online). – His current research topics include future technologies, future narratives, and transformative future design in the context of AI and new space exploration. – In 2021, Stefan Selke was awarded the Wolfgang HeilmannPrize by the Integrata Foundation for his concept of the "NeoUniversity" on the topic of "Human Utopia as a Design Framework for the Post-Corona Society."

Email: stefan.selke@hs-furtwangen.de
Homepage: www.public-science-lab.de

Martina Simon, M.Sc.

heads the group "Human Centered Innovation" at the Division Supply Chain Services of the Fraunhofer Institute for Integrated Circuits IIS. She initiates and is responsible for research and consulting projects in the field of human experience, behavior and decision-making, especially regarding digital living environments and transformation. As a qualified psychologist, her focus is on human-technology interaction, technology/AI acceptance research, and the socio-ethical evaluation of user-friendly technical solutions. Prior to her scientific career, she worked for around 18 years in the start-up and SME context, including product, content, and translation management.

Email: martina.simon@iis.fraunhofer.de
Homepage: www.scs.fraunhofer.de/de/ueber-uns/organisation/innovation-and-transformation/human-centered-innovation.html

Prof. Dr. Nicolai Spicher

is Associate Professor at the Department of Health Technology of the Technical University of Denmark (DTU) with a research focus on extracting information from medical time series using signal processing and machine learning methods. He held positions at the University Medical Center Göttingen as well as the Technical University of Braunschweig before and completed his doctoral degree at the University of Duisburg-Essen. He is spokesman of the Committee on Biosignal Processing within the German Society for Biomedical Engineering (DGBMT), vice chair of the IEEE EMBS Germany/Austria/Swiss Chapter, and young professional representative within the IEEE EMBS Administrative Committee.

Email: nicsp@dtu.dk

Univ.-Prof. Dr.-Ing. habil. Thomas Stieglitz

Since 2004, Thomas Stieglitz has been Professor for Biomedical Microtechnology at the Department of Microsystems Engineering (IMTEK) at the University of Freiburg. His research focuses on implantable neural interfaces and neural implants. He is one of the pioneers of neural engineering in Germany with numerous national and European research projects in the field of neurotechnology and bioelectronics medicine. He was awarded IEEE Fellow for his research on flexible micromachined nerve interfaces in applications for retina implants, brain arrays, and peripheral nerve interfaces. – He is co-spokesperson of the BrainLinks-Brain-Tools Center at the University, serves as elected member of the senate and overtook several service positions at the university. He is elected chairperson of the Neurotechnology section and advisory board member of the German Society for Biomedical Engineering (DGBMT im VDE). He is founding and scientific member and scientific advisor of the neurotechnology companies CorTec GmbH and neuroloop GmbH which work on implantable Brain-Computer Interfaces and a neural implant for hypertension treatment, respectively, from 2018 to 2021.

Email: thomas.stieglitz@imtek.uni-freiburg.de
Homepage: www.imtek.de/professuren/bmt
orcid logo
https://orcid.org/0000-0002-7349-4254

Dr.-Ing. André Stollenwerk

heads a group on biomedical engineering and signal processing at the Embedded Software Lab of RWTH Aachen University. The activities range from algorithms for intensive care equipment, enabling new therapies through the interconnectivity of various medical sensors and actuators, to detection and prediction algorithms. To improve the algorithms developed, the research also includes anomaly detection within the data and enrichment, particularly of AI-based methods for explainability. He studied electrical engineering at RWTH Aachen University and obtained his PhD in the department of computer science ibidem. He is an active member of the technical committees AUTOMED and Bio-Signals within the German Society for Biomedical Engineering (DGBMT).

Email: stollenwerk@embedded.rwth-aachen.de

Dr. rer. pol. Christian M. Stracke

developed interdisciplinary expertise in research, education, and management while leading international large-scale projects (budgets over 50 million euros and up to 200+ researchers). As globally recognized expert and innovator and appointed ICDE Chair in OER, he published over 200 scientific publications on his main research fields: Open Education, Artificial Intelligence, Technology-Enhanced Learning, Competence Building, Impact Assessment and Educational Policies. He consults many educational institutions, international ministries, and global organizations including UNESCO, Council of Europe, European Commission and Parliament. Since 2022, he is member of the AI&ED Expert Group appointed by the Council of Europe developing the international laws for AI use in education and AI literacy. He was appointed as ICDE Chair in OER at the Open University of the Netherlands and coordinates currently the cloud strategy and scientific research at the IT and Data Center of the University of Bonn. He co-founded the UNESCO Unitwin Network on Open Education (UNOE). He serves as editor and board member of peer-reviewed indexed journals and as chair of international conferences. He provided more than 100 invited keynotes worldwide and developed global learning standards as elected Chair of international standardization committees (ISO, IEC, CEN). In 2023, Christian established the German Network Ethical Use of AI and the European Network Ethical Use of AI. He is Founder and Director of eLC, the European Institute for Learning, Innovation and Cooperation (since 2004).

Email: stracke@uni-bonn.de
Homepage: opening-up.education/

Matthias Struck, M.Sc.

studied computer science with focus on medical informatics, and he is working at Fraunhofer IIS since 2006. He was involved in various software projects focusing on machine learning and AI in the field of biomedical engineering. In 2011 he became head of the group 'Medical Data Communication and Bio-Signal Processing'. In 2016 he also became deputy head of the department of 'Image Processing and Medical Engineering'. His role was to integrate innovative prototypes in the field of medical technology into the clinical workflow and to define new projects in close cooperation with the medical experts in hospitals. Since 2021, Matthias Struck has been the Head of the Center for Sensor Technology and Digital Medicine at Fraunhofer IIS. Under his leadership, the center develops and clinically validates patient-centered health technologies in close cooperation with university and hospital as well as industrial partners. The goal is to translate research and prototypes into industrially viable applications with meaningful benefit for both patients and healthcare systems.

Email: matthias.struck@iis.fraunhofer.de

Dr.-Ing. Stefan Wesarg

studied Physics at the Technische Universität Berlin, Germany, the Ecole Nationale Supérieure de Physique de Marseille (now Centrale Marseille), France, and the Universität Heidelberg, Germany. During his studies, he specialized in Astrophysics and Medical Physics. He carried out his diploma thesis at the German Cancer Research Center (DKFZ) Heidelberg, Germany, receiving his diploma degree in 2001. – From 2001 to 2007, he was a researcher at the Fraunhofer IGD Darmstadt, Germany, in the Department *Cognitive Computing & Medical Imaging* (deputy head from 2006 to 2007). In 2007 he received his PhD (Dr.-Ing.) in Computer Science from the TU Darmstadt. From 2007 until end of 2011, he held a Post-Doc position at the Interactive Graphics Systems Group (GRIS) at the Technische Universität Darmstadt. Since 2012, Stefan Wesarg is Head of Department *Visual Healthcare Technologies* at Fraunhofer IGD. His group's work is focused on image-based analysis methods in medicine. For over 30 years, the center works in close collaboration with clinical partners and has gathered wide-spread and in-depth domain knowledge. Stefan Wesarg is one of the organizers of the annual MICCAI workshop on *Clinical Image-based Procedures* (CLIP).

Email: stefan.wesarg@igd.fraunhofer.de
Homepage: www.igd.fraunhofer.de/en/industries/healthcare.html

Prof. Dr. Hendrik Wöhrle

has developed interdisciplinary expertise bridging artificial intelligence, embedded systems, and medical electronics through his work at leading research institutions. As Professor of Medical Electronics at the University of Duisburg-Essen (since 2025) and Research Group Leader at Fraunhofer IMS, he leads research making AI more efficient and safer for medical applications including neural implants, intelligent biosignal sensors, and robotics. He published on AI Hardware Architectures, Efficient AI Models for Embedded Systems, Edge AI, and Biomedical Signal Processing. Before joining UDE, he served as Professor at FH Dortmund (2019–2024), receiving the Research Award 2022 on his pioneering for Edge Computing and Embedded AI, and as Senior Researcher at DFKI Robotics Innovation Center Bremen, where he pioneered rehabilitation robotics including EEG-controlled exoskeletons. He holds a Dr.-Ing. from University of Bremen on specialized computer architectures for robotics, and degrees in Electrical Engineering and Bioinformatics. Currently, his research interests are in the development of open-source domain specific computer architectures, EDA toolchains and collaborates extensively with industry partners transferring innovations to medical technology, robotics, and IoT applications. He is a Seniore Member of the IEEE EMBS, RAS and CAS societies and the GI.

Email: hendrik.woehrle@ims.fraunhofer.de
Homepage: www.uni-due.de/ebs/rechnerarchitekturen_en.php

Prof. Dr.-Ing. habil. Sebastian Zaunseder

graduated in electrical engineering at TU Dresden in 2007. From 2007 to 2011, he worked at the Fraunhofer Institute for Photonic Microsystems on wearable sensors and signal processing for medical applications. In 2011, Sebastian finished his PhD and joined the Institute of Biomedical Engineering (IBMT, TU Dresden). At IBMT, he headed a group on medical sensing and signal processing, and he did his habilitation in the field of medical monitoring. From 2019 to 2022 he was professor in the field of medical engineering at FH Dortmund. Since 2022, Sebastian has been Professor of Diagnostic Sensing at University of Augsburg. Sebastian's main research interests are medical sensing and sensor data processing. In such fields, Sebastian has carried out various projects and (co-)authored more than 100 scientific works. He is an active member in standardization committees and scientific societies. Sebastian was spokesman of the committee Biosignals in the German Society for Biomedical Engineering (DGBMT) at VDE from 2018 to 2024. Currently he is member of the boards of the DGBMT and of the German Society for Arterial Stiffness.

Email: sebastian.zaunseder@uni-a.de
ORCID: https://orcid.org/0000-0001-6114-3142

Index

Publications series Health Academy

The following publications have appeared in the Health Academy series to date:
Series editors: Wolfgang Niederlag and Heinz U. Lemke
ISSN: 2199-2959

HA 1: Verbesserung der radiologischen und kardiologischen Bildgebung durch digitale großflächige Flachbild-Detektoren
Editors: W. Niederlag (Dresden), H. U. Lemke (Berlin), 2001

HA 2: Digital Imaging and Image Communication between Hospitals in the Free State of Saxony, Germany (SaxTeleMed Reference Model Program)
Editors: W. Niederlag (Dresden), H. U. Lemke (Berlin), 2001

HA 3: Telemonitoring & Tele Home Care – Methodische Grundlagen, technische Voraussetzungen, organisatorische Konzepte, praktische Erfahrungen, medizintechnische Produkte
Editors: W. Niederlag (Dresden), H. U. Lemke (Berlin), 2002

HA 4: Advances in Medical Imaging (I)
Editors: W. Niederlag (Dresden), H. U. Lemke (Berlin), 2002

HA 5: Telemedizin & Ökonomie – Ökonomische Effekte, Abrechnungsmodalitäten, Geschäftsmodelle
Editors: W. Niederlag (Dresden), H. Burchert (Bielefeld), H. U. Lemke (Berlin), 2003

HA 6: Ethik und Informationstechnik am Beispiel der Telemedizin
Editors: W. Niederlag (Dresden), H. U. Lemke (Berlin), A. Bondolfi (Lausanne/Schweiz), 2003

HA 7: Telekardiologie – Methodische Grundlagen, technische Lösungen, praktische Erfahrungen, integrierte Versorgungskonzepte
Editors: W. Niederlag (Dresden), B. Lüderitz (Bonn), A. Hempel (Dresden), H. U. Lemke (Berlin), 2004

HA 8: Smart Cards in telemedizinischen Netzwerken
Editors: W. Niederlag (Dresden), O. Rienhoff, H. U. Lemke (Berlin), 2004

HA 9: Hochtechnologiemedizin im Spannungsfeld zwischen Ökonomie, Politik, Recht und Ethik
Editors: W. Niederlag (Dresden), H. U. Lemke (Berlin), L. A. Nefiodow (St. Augustin), D. H. W. Grönemeyer (Bochum), 2005

HA 10: Molecular Imaging – Innovationen und Visionen in der medizinischen Bildgebung
Editors: W. Niederlag (Dresden), H. U. Lemke (Berlin), W. Semmler (Heidelberg), C. Bremer (Münster), 2006

HA 11: Rechtliche Aspekte der Telemedizin
Editors: W. Niederlag (Dresden), C. Dierks (Berlin), O. Rienhoff (Göttingen), H. U. Lemke (Berlin), 2006

HA 12: Gesundheitswesen 2025 – Implikationen, Konzepte, Visionen
Editors: W. Niederlag (Dresden), H. U. Lemke (Berlin), E. Nagel (Augsburg, Bayreuth), O. Dössel (Karlsruhe), 2008

HA 13: Modellgestützte Therapie – Technische Möglichkeiten, potenzielle Anwendungen, gesellschaftliche Auswirkungen
Editors: W. Niederlag (Dresden), H. U. Lemke (Berlin), J. Meixensberger (Leipzig), M. Baumann (Dresden), 2008

HA 14: Personalisierte Medizin – sind wir auf dem Weg zu einer individualisierten Gesundheitsversorgung?
Editors: W. Niederlag (Dresden), H. U. Lemke (Berlin), O. Golubnitschaja (Bonn), O. Rienhoff (Göttingen), 2010

HA 15: Personalisierte Medizin & Informationstechnologie – Innovative Konzepte, realisierte Anwendungen, gesellschaftliche Aspekte
Editors: W. Niederlag (Dresden), H. U. Lemke (Berlin, Los Angeles/USA), O. Rienhoff (Göttingen), 2010

HA 16: Der virtuelle Patient – Zukünftige Basis für Diagnose und Therapie?
Editors: W. Niederlag (Dresden), H. U. Lemke (Berlin), H. Lehrach (Berlin), H.-O. Peitgen (Bremen), 2012

HA 17: Der digitale Operationssaal – Methoden, Werkzeuge, Systeme, Applikationen und gesellschaftliche Aspekte
Editors: W. Niederlag (Dresden), H. U. Lemke (Berlin), G. Strauß (Leipzig), H. Feußner (München), 2012

Continuation of the series published by De Gruyter
Series editors: Wolfgang Niederlag and Heinz U. Lemke, since 2025 Arne Manzeschke and Thomas Wittenberg

Band 1: Der virtuelle Patient
Wolfgang Niederlag, Heinz U. Lemke, Hans Lehrach, Heinz-Otto Peitgen (Editors)
2., erweiterte Auflage, Verlag de Gruyter, 2014
Broschur ISBN: 978-3-11-055434-2
Gebunden ISBN: 978-3-11-033429-6
PDF ISBN: 978-3-11-033566-8
EPUB ISBN: 978-3-11-038925-8

Band 2: Der digitale Operationssaal
Wolfgang Niederlag, Heinz U. Lemke, Gero Strauß, Hubertus Feußner (Editors)
2., erweiterte Auflage, Verlag de Gruyter, 2014
Broschur ISBN: 978-3-11-055431-1
Gebunden ISBN: 978-3-11-033430-2
PDF ISBN: 978-3-11-033562-0
EPUB ISBN: 978-3-11-038924-1

Band 3: Ethische Perspektiven auf Biomedizinische Technologie
Arne Manzeschke, Wolfgang Niederlag (Editors)
Verlag de Gruyter, 2020
Gebunden ISBN: 978-3-11-064460-9
PDF ISBN: 978-3-11-064576-7
EPUB ISBN: 978-3-11-064624-5

Band 4: How Metaphors shape Biotechnology – Interdisziplinäre Perspektiven
Stefan Dübel, Stefan Heuser (Editors)
Verlag De Gruyter, 2025
ISBN: 978-3-11-914512-1
PDF ISBN: 978-3-11-221568-5
EPUB ISBN: 978-3-11-221589-0

www.ingramcontent.com/pod-product-compliance
Lightning Source LLC
Chambersburg PA
CBHW081500190326
41458CB00015B/5296